AN INTRODUCTION TO BANKING

PRINCIPLES, STRATEGY AND RISK MANAGEMENT

SECOND EDITION

AN INTRODUCTION TO BANKING

PRINCIPLES, STRATEGY AND RISK MANAGEMENT

SECOND EDITION

··

Moorad Choudhry

*With contributions from Ed Bace, Polina Bardaeva,
Kevin Liddy, Jamie Paris, Soumya Sarkar and Chris Westcott*

WILEY

First Edition published: April 2011

© 2018 John Wiley & Sons, Ltd and Moorad Choudhry

Registered office
John Wiley & Sons Ltd, The Atrium, Southern Gate, Chichester, West Sussex, PO19 8SQ,
United Kingdom

For details of our global editorial offices, for customer services and for information about how to
apply for permission to reuse the copyright material in this book please see our website at
www.wiley.com.

Wiley publishes in a variety of print and electronic formats and by print-on-demand. Some
material included with standard print versions of this book may not be included in e-books or in
print-on-demand. If this book refers to media such as a CD or DVD that is not included in the
version you purchased, you may download this material at http://booksupport.wiley.com. For
more information about Wiley products, visit www.wiley.com.

Designations used by companies to distinguish their products are often claimed as trademarks.
All brand names and product names used in this book are trade names, service marks,
trademarks or registered trademarks of their respective owners. The publisher is not associated
with any product or vendor mentioned in this book.

Library of Congress Cataloging-in-Publication Data is Available:

ISBN 9781119115892 (Paperback)
ISBN 9781119115915 (ePDF)
ISBN 9781119115908 (ePub)

Cover Design: Wiley
Cover Image: © MaLija/Shutterstock

Set in 10/12pt, TrumpMediaevalLTStd by SPi Global, Chennai, India.

Printed and bound by CPI Group (UK) Ltd, Croydon, CR0 4YY

10 9 8 7 6 5 4 3 2 1

For Lindsay
Ultimate Yummy Mummy

CONTENTS

····································

FOREWORD

....

Steen Blaafalk

I know Moorad Choudhry as an experienced professional and very strong personally, and it is with great pleasure that I accept to write a short foreword for the new edition of *An Introduction to Banking*.

A key role for a bank is to transform short-term deposits from businesses and households into long-term loans to businesses and households that want to borrow for investments or consumption. In this way, banks support growth and wealth in society – not only by creating jobs in the banking sector – but also by supporting growth in many sectors of the economy.

An integral part of banking is taking calculated risks. A professionally run bank will reserve enough capital to absorb expected as well as unexpected losses on the lending book to continue its business, even in a recession.

Another risk is maturity transformation – borrowing short and lending long. On the one hand, it is a source of income for the bank. On the other hand, it is a threat to the survival of the bank if it is funding itself too short or through unstable funding sources that disappear when a crisis occurs.

In the years leading up to the 2008 global financial crisis, banks had become significantly less consolidated as the capital rules allowed them to have a very high gearing of the balance sheet. Moreover, many banks had funded themselves very short in the capital markets since liquidity was ample and spreads were very low – building up huge customer funding gaps. At the same time, the banks had competed fearlessly on margins in order to attract new business. A cocktail that would be doomed to go wrong at some point in time.

When the global financial crisis culminated in September 2008 with the collapse of Lehman Brothers, all confidence in and among financial institutions disappeared. This resulted in liquidity drying out very fast, and institutions with a short/unstable funding profile found themselves unable to refinance their debt. Additionally to this, many banks found themselves too thinly capitalised to absorb the loss incurring during this next period.

The global financial crisis spilled over into the real economy since many banks were not able to fund the loan demand of their customers and they did not have the excess capital to grow their balance sheets. The authorities reacted to the situation by demanding significantly higher capital and liquidity ratios, which of course in the situation catalysed the crisis in the real economy.

An Introduction to Banking describes getting the right balance between running a safe bank and optimising the use of capital and liquidity to the benefit of the shareholders of the bank for the long run.

In the first part of the book, Moorad introduces the reader to the basic concepts of running a bank. I can recommend this part of the book to bankers who need a broader insight into the institutional setup and basic terms in banking. Understanding the basics of banking helps you to get the full benefit when it becomes more detailed, dealing with asset and liability management (ALM) as well as capital and liquidity management later in the book.

Asset & Liability Management is the very essence of banking. To be successful as a bank you need to have professional asset and liability management processes, starting from the top management and flowing down to the different business areas of the bank, including proper Funds Transfer Pricing (FTP) for capital and liquidity, to understand and make transparent the drivers for various banking products.

As a Group Chief Financial and Risk Officer, I have had great professional benefit from the description of the role of the Asset & Liability Committee, the risk policy, reporting, and stress testing, as well as the description of the day-to-day management in the risk and treasury departments. It was also rewarding for me to read the final chapters about best practice in capital and funding management and corporate governance, which we should not forget when we enter into the next period of bull markets.

Moorad manages to describe a comprehensive and complex area of banking in a lively and readable language.

I can highly recommend the book as a handy reference work for anyone who is involved in banking strategy, ALM, and liquidity risk management.

Steen Blaafalk
Group Chief Financial and Risk Officer
Saxo Bank A/S
Copenhagen
10 March 2015

PREFACE

Who among the world's population of authors would not love to write a timeless work? Ideally, a timeless work of fiction, but failing that, something factual that remains the undisputed benchmark for its subject. Somewhat paradoxically, I hold that the latter is actually harder to accomplish. Please don't get me wrong, only a very small minority of us (of which I am not one) have it in them to produce *Hamlet*, or *Dune*, or *The Iliad*, or *The Assistant*, or *Crime and Punishment*, or *The Adventures of Sherlock Holmes*, or *The Crab With The Golden Claws*, or *Seven Pillars of Wisdom*, or *Peanuts, Featuring Good Ol' Charlie Brown*, or countless other such immortal works. But once one has produced classic art, it lives forever. There is no need ever to update or modify it.

Practitioner textbooks, on the other hand, are rarely timeless. In almost every field of learning, society develops and adds to its knowledge base, such that a work of non-fiction rapidly becomes out of date. To maintain currency requires constant updates and further editions, which means more work. An author ambitious of producing a literary masterpiece should avoid the factual learning genre.

But there is an apparent paradox when it comes to works of fact concerning banking: in theory, unlike in so many commercial disciplines, the main principles have not changed since the first modern banks came into being in the fifteenth century. Much of what held good for banks in 1808 and 1908 would have remained fine for banks in 2008, if certain senior bank executives had been competent enough to remember them (or even bothered to learn them in the first place).

The traditionally staid and "conservative" field of banking has experienced considerable development and change of late. However, if anything, this "development" has not been all positive. While lauding the introduction of tools and techniques that have enabled borrowers to reduce their risk and assist economic growth worldwide, most of us are now rightly wary of ever-more sophistication and complexity in finance. It really is time for banks, and banking, to revert somewhat to the basics of finance and look to deliver genuine good customer service, and roll back the ever-increasing complexity in the industry. Why? Because such sophistication often ended up doing more harm than good.

Finance is as much art as science anyway. So much of it is expectations based on assumptions, despite what the financial market "quants" would tell you. That this is not known universally is itself worrying, with bankers the world over convinced that the stated gross redemption yield of a bond purchased in the secondary market is actually what they will receive for holding said bond. The valuation of equities, the calculation of default probability, the expected life of a loan, the "risk weighting" of a loan asset, the "expected shortfall" risk exposure of a trading portfolio … these are all so much estimations based on assumptions. Which person in their right mind, trying to do the right thing for everyone, would wish to build sophistication on such a foundation?

In any case, in many countries banks have managed to transform their image from perceived bastions of stability and good social standing into seeming snake-oil selling hucksters of low repute and lower intentions. This is a pity, because without banks performing their vital roles as secure stores of money and maturity transformation specialists, economic and social development would take place at a much slower pace. So while it is almost unarguable to state the importance of banks and the good they do for society, it is also unarguable to state that the work undertaken by banks must reflect sound risk management principles as well as scrupulous ethics and good intentions.

Hence, it becomes necessary to update the first edition of this "introductory" book about banking. The first edition isn't necessarily out of date, at least not all of it anyway – more that it doesn't emphasise the principles of banking as strongly as it should have. And of course it was never going to be timeless … works of fact so rarely are. But this second edition, requiring readers to shell out their hard-earned cash for a second time, is needed so as to emphasise more of the *principles* of banking as well as update some of the technical content.

In any case, any author would do well to remember the words of Sir Arthur Conan Doyle from the preface to *The Sherlock Holmes Stories* (1903):

> "… all forms of literature, however humble, are legitimate if the writer is satisfied that he has done them to the highest of his power. To take an analogy from a kindred art, the composer may range from the oratorio to the comic song and be ashamed of neither, so long as his work in each is as honest as he can make it. It is insincere work, scamped work, work which is consciously imitative, which a man should voluntarily suppress before time saves him the trouble."

So that is the ultimate objective of this revised second edition: not to attempt to achieve timelessness and immortality, which would reflect only a monstrous and insufferable arrogance and egotism on my part, but rather simply to be viewed by readers as a work of honesty that was done to the best of the author's ability and that, if the market allows it, can remain of value on the bookshelf for many years to come. Irrespective of whether this last ambition is achieved, I hope at least that this book has served its purpose for today. And as Ian MacDonald so memorably said in the preface to his last update of the majestic *Revolution In The Head*, no further editions will be forthcoming.

LAYOUT OF THE BOOK

This book is comprised of 17 chapters, grouped in three parts. There is some rhyme and reason in the split: Part I may be considered a primer on the basics, not just of banking, but also the interest-rate markets, customer service, and credit assessment – essentially, the basics of financial markets. Part II looks at the balance sheet in general, and asset–liability management in particular, while Part III covers strategy, regulatory capital, and operational risk.

For newcomers to the market there is a primer on financial market arithmetic in Appendix A at the back of the book.

New material in this second edition includes:

- Case studies on problem solving involving several real-world risk management issues (and solutions) the author has been involved with;
- A chapter on liabilities strategy setting, as part of the balance sheet optimisation process;
- A detailed look at the importance of understanding net interest margin (NIM);
- Best-practice ICAAP and ILAAP process principles;
- Various reasonably important sundries such as strategy and operational risk management.

As ever, the intention is to remain accessible and practical throughout, and to provide information of value to the practitioner in banking – we hope sincerely that this aim has been achieved. Comments on the text are welcome and should be sent to the author care of John Wiley & Sons Ltd, Chichester, England.

PREFACE TO THE FIRST EDITION

· ·

Banking is a long-established and honourable profession. The provision of efficient loan and deposit facilities is an essential ingredient in human development and prosperity. For this reason, it is important that all banks are managed prudently. The art of banking remains unchanged from when banks were first established. At its core are the two principles of asset–liability mismatch and liquidity risk management. The act of undertaking loans and deposits creates the mismatch, because while investors like to lend for as short a term as possible, borrowers prefer to borrow for as long a term as possible. In other words, the act of banking is the process of maturity transformation, whereby banks "lend long" and "fund short". Banks do not "match-fund", because there would never be enough funds available to match a 25-year maturity mortgage with a 25-year fixed deposit. Thus, banking gives rise to liquidity risk, and bankers are therefore required to take steps to ensure that liquidity, the ability to roll over funding of long-dated loans, is continuously available.

We define banking as the provision of loans and deposits; the former produce interest income for the bank, while the latter create interest expense for the bank. On the bank's balance sheet the loan is the asset and the deposit is the liability, and the bank acts as the intermediary between borrowers and lenders. The fact that all banks, irrespective of their size, approach, or strategy, must manage the two basic principles of asset–liability management (ALM) and liquidity management means that they are ultimately identical institutions. They deal within the same markets and with each other. That means that the bankruptcy of any one bank, while serious for its customers and creditors, can have a bigger impact still on the wider economy because of the risk this poses to other banks. It is this systemic risk which posed the danger for the world's economies in 2008, after Lehman Brothers collapsed, and which remains a challenge for financial regulators.

This book introduces the fundamental art of banking, which is ALM and liquidity risk management. It does not describe the different types of banks and their organisational structures that exist around the world. Neither does it describe the wide range of bank products that are available or the great variation in financial markets and instruments that can be observed.

These topics are covered abundantly in existing textbooks. The object of this book is to present bank ALM and liquidity management at an introductory level, something that is not so common in textbooks on finance. These topics deserve to be understood and appreciated by everyone involved in banking, because it was unsound practices in these fields that helped to create the banking crisis in 2008, and made its impact so much worse than it need have been. Proper respect for the art of ALM will mitigate the impact on banks of the next financial crash.

ACKNOWLEDGEMENTS

∙∙∙

Love, thanks, and respect, as always, to the Raynes Park Footy Boys and The Pink Tie Brigade. *A Solid Bond in Your Heart*. Thanks to Juan Carlos Sihuincha for the great photograph!

You know who your friends are when you're "UB40". Very special thanks to Clax, KMan, Farooq Jaffrey, Zhuoshi Liu, Rich Lynn, Michael Nicoll, Stuart Turner, Colin Johnson, Abu Abdi, Mohamoud Dualeh, Mohammed Dualeh, Dan Cunningham, Ali Andani, Konstantin Nikolaev, Nathanael Yishak, Chris Westcott, Jamie Paris, Polina Bardaeva, Graeme Wolvaardt, Shahrukh Feroz Ahmed, Angel Alchin, A. Mehdi, Nik Slater, Milivoje Davidovic, Aleksandar Doric, David Fance, Barry Howard, David Castle, Nick Carpenter, Balamurali Radhakrishnan, Asif Abdul-Razzaq, Rod Pienaar, Richard Pereira, Michael Widowitz, and Zumi Farooq.

At Wiley I'd like to thank Stephen Mullaly, Jeremy Chia, Syd Ganaden, the now departed Thomas Hyrkiel and the mighty Nick Wallwork, plus Emily Paul, Caroline Maria Vincent, and Aida Ferguson.

Thank you. I won't forget it.

Moorad Choudhry
Surrey, England
24 June 2017

ABOUT THE AUTHOR

Professor Moorad Choudhry lectures on the MSc Finance programme at the University of Kent Business School. He was latterly Treasurer, Corporate Banking Division, at the Royal Bank of Scotland, Head of Treasury at Europe Arab Bank, Head of Treasury at KBC Financial Products, and Vice-President in structured finance at JPMorgan Chase Bank. He was a gilt-edged market-maker at ABN Amro Hoare Govett Securities Limited. He began his City career at the London Stock Exchange in 1989.

Moorad is a Fellow of the Chartered Institute for Securities & Investment, a Fellow of The London Institute of Banking & Finance, and a Fellow of the Institute of Directors. He is a member of the Editorial Boards of *Journal of Structured Finance, Qualitative Research in Financial Markets, International Journal of Economics and Finance*, and *American Securitisation*. He was born in Bangladesh and lives in Surrey, England.

I have a problem with psychometric testing: it is to my mind a spurious device used by large corporations to ensure that anyone with a semblance of wit or independent thought doesn't get anywhere near securing a job. If the entire country were subjected to psychometric testing and all those who failed it humanely put down, we'd be left with a rump of deathly, grey-faced middle managers.

—Rod Liddle, *The Sunday Times*, 18 August 2013.

Bank Business and the Markets

Part I of this book introduces the subject of banking, with a look first at the main products, and then proceeds to discuss all the key aspects of a bank business: namely, customer service, credit assessment, trading and hedging techniques, the yield curve, regulatory capital, and the money and capital markets. This part is the "primer" on banking and is essential reading for all practitioners.

We begin with a look at the fundamentals of banking business, products and customer service, and the different elements of bank capital. This is essentially an introduction to the nature of banking. We then consider further elementary finance background, with a look at the basics of financial statements. The contents of this chapter may appear more at home in a textbook on accounting, but an understanding of ratio analysis is vital for the bank practitioner, who is concerned with issues such as return on capital as well as balance sheet sustainability.

This is followed with more detail on credit risk and credit assessment, and the basics of trading and hedging.

Chapter

1

BANK BUSINESS
AND CAPITAL

B anking has a long and honourable history. Today, it encompasses a wide range of activities of varying degrees of complexity. Whatever the precise business undertaken by specific individual banks, the common denominator of all banking activities is that of bringing together those who require funding with those who possess surplus funding, and acting as a transmission mechanism for the processing of payments. That is in essence all that banks do, and while it isn't a complex service provision, it is nevertheless an important one. Societal and economic development worldwide relies on efficient banking service provision.

In this introductory chapter we describe the financial markets, the basic banking business model, and the concept of bank capital. We begin with a look at the business of banking. We then consider the different types of revenue generated by a bank, the concept of the banking book and the trading book, financial statements, and the concept of provisions. We also introduce the different products offered by banks to their customers.

THE BASIC BANK BUSINESS MODEL

The basic bank business model has remained unchanged ever since banks became an integral part of modern society.[1] Of course, as it is more of an art than a science, the model parameters themselves can be set to suit the specific strategy of the individual bank, depending on whether the strategy operates at a higher or lower risk–reward profile. However, the basic model is identical across all banks. In essence, banking involves taking risks, followed by effective management of that risk. This risk can be categorised as follows:

- Managing the bank's capital;
- Managing the liquidity mismatch – a fundamental ingredient of banking is "maturity transformation", the recognition that loans (assets) generally have a longer tenor than deposits (liabilities).

If we wished to summarise the basic ingredients of the historical bank model, we might describe it in the following terms:

- Leverage: A small capital base is levered up into an asset pool that can be 10 to 30 times greater (sometimes even higher);
- The "gap": Essentially, funding short to lend long is a function of the conventional positive-sloping yield curve and is dictated by recognition of the asset–liability mismatch noted above;
- Liquidity: An assumption that a bank will always be able to roll over funding as it falls due;
- Risk management: An understanding of credit or default risk.

---

[1]The oldest bank still operating, Monte Dei Paschi di Siena, was set up in 1472. Berenberg Bank claims it is the oldest bank still operating in its original form: it was formed in 1509.

These fundamentals remain unchanged. The critical issue for bank management, however, is that some of the assumptions behind the application of these fundamentals *have* changed, as demonstrated by the crash of 2007–2008. The changed landscape in the wake of the crisis has resulted in some hitherto "safe" or profitable business lines being viewed as risky. Although favourable conditions for banking may well return in due course, for the foreseeable future the challenge for banks will be to set their strategy only after first arriving at a true and full understanding of economic conditions as they exist today. The first subject for discussion is to consider what a realistic, sustainable return on the capital target level should be and to ensure that it is commensurate with the level of risk aversion desired by the Board. The Board should also consider the bank's capital availability and what amount of business this could realistically support. These two issues need to be addressed before the remainder of the bank's strategy can be considered.

Strategy

The most important function that a bank's Board can undertake is to set the bank's strategy. This is not as obvious as it sounds. It is vital that banks have a coherent, articulated strategy in place that sets the tone for the entire business from the top down.

In the first instance, the Board must take into account the current regulatory environment. This includes the requirements of the Basel III rules. A bank cannot formulate strategy without a clear understanding of the environment in which it operates. Once this is achieved – before proceeding with a formal strategy – the bank needs to determine what markets it wishes to operate in, and establish what products and what class of customer it wants to service. All its individual business lines should be set up to operate within the main strategy, once markets and customers have been identified.

In other words, a bank cannot afford to operate by simply meandering along, noting its peer group market share and Return on Equity (RoE) and making up its strategy as it goes along. This approach, although it would never be admitted, is evidently what many banks do indeed follow – however inadvertently – and results in a senior management and Board that is not fully aware of what the bank's liabilities and risk exposures are.

The first task is to understand one's operating environment. The bank also needs to incorporate a specific target market and product suite as the basis of its strategy. Concurrent with this, the bank must set its RoE target, which drives much of the bank's culture and ethos. It is important to get this part of the process right at the start. Prior to the crash, it was common for banks to seek to increase revenue by adding to their risk exposure. Assets were added to the balance sheet, or higher risk assets were taken on. In the bull market environment of 2001–2007 – allied to low funding costs as a result of low base interest rates – this resulted in ever higher RoE figures, to the point where it was common for even Tier 2 banks to target levels of 22–25% RoE in their business appraisal. This process was of course not tenable in the long run.

The second task – following on immediately from the first – is to set a realistic RoE target and one that is sustainable over the entire business cycle. This cannot be done without educating Board directors as well as shareholders, who must appreciate new, lower RoE targets. Managing expectations will contribute to a more dispassionate review of strategy. Just as importantly, risk-adjusted RoE should also be set at a realistic level and not be allowed to increase. Hence, the Board and shareholders must accept that lower RoE levels will become the standard. This should also be allied to lower leverage levels and higher capital ratios.

Concurrently with the above process, a bank must ask itself where its strengths lie and formulate its strategy around that. In other words, it is important to focus on core competencies. Again, the experience of the crash has served to demonstrate that many banks found themselves with risk exposures that they did not understand. This may simply have been the holding of assets (such as structured finance securities) whose credit exposures, valuation, and secondary market liquidity they did not understand, or embarking on investment strategies such as negative basis trading without being aware of all the measurement parameters of such strategies.[2] To implement a coherent, articulate strategy properly, a bank needs to be aware of exactly what it does have (or does not have) expertise for undertaking, and not operate in products or markets in which it has no genuine knowledge base.

Allied to an understanding of core competence is a review of core and non-core assets. Bank strategy is not a static process or document, but rather a dynamic one. Regular reviews of the balance sheet need to be undertaken to identify any non-core assets, which can then be assessed to determine whether they remain compatible with the strategy. If they are not, then a realistic disposal process would need to be drawn up. In the long run, this is connected with an understanding of where the bank's real strengths lie. Long-term core assets may well differ from core assets, but this needs to be articulated explicitly. The decision on whether an asset is core or non-core, or short-term core or long-term core, is a function of the bank's overall strategy – based on its expertise – and what markets and customers it wishes to service. This will be embedded in

---

[2] Without naming the banks, the author is aware of institutions that purchased ABS and CDO securities under the belief that the senior tranche, rated AAA, would not be downgraded even if there was a default in the underlying asset pool, presumably because the junior note(s) would absorb the losses. Of course, this loss of subordination does erode the initial rating of the senior note – with a consequent markdown in market value. Another institution, according to anecdotal evidence received by email, entered into negative CDS basis trades without any consideration for the funding cost of the trade package. This resulted in losses irrespective of how the basis performed. In this case, it is clear that the trading desk in question entered into a relatively sophisticated trading strategy without being sufficiently aware of the technical and risk implications.

the strategy and the bank's business model. This drives the choice of products and business lines to which the bank feels it can add value.

BANKING BUSINESS

Banking operations encompass a wide range of activities, all of which contribute to the asset and liability profile of a bank. Table 1.1 shows selected banking activities and the type of risk exposure they represent. The terms used in the table, such as "market risk", are explained elsewhere in this book. In another chapter we discuss the elementary aspects of financial analysis – using key financial ratios – that are used to examine the profitability and asset quality of a bank. We also discuss bank regulation and the concept of bank capital.

All readers should be familiar with the way a bank's earnings and performance are reported in its financial statements. A bank's income statement will break down earnings by type, as we have defined in Table 1.1. So we need to be familiar with interest income, trading income, and so on. The other side of an income statement is costs, such as operating expenses and bad loan provisions.

Table 1.1   Selected banking activities and services

Service or function	Revenue generated	Risk
Lending		
– Retail	Interest income, fees	Credit, market
– Commercial	Interest income, fees	Credit, market
– Mortgage	Interest income, fees	Credit, market
– Syndicated	Interest income, fees	Credit, market
Credit cards	Interest income, fees	Credit, operational
Project finance	Interest income, fees	Credit
Trade finance	Interest income, fees	Credit, operational
Cash management		
– Processing	Fees	Operational
– Payments	Fees	Credit, operational
Custodian	Fees	Credit, operational
Private banking	Commission income, interest income, fees	Operational
Asset management	Fees, performance payments	Credit, market, operational
Capital markets		
– Investment banking	Fees	Credit, market
– Corporate finance	Fees	Credit, market
– Equities	Trading income, fees	Credit, market
– Bonds	Trading income, interest income, fees	Credit, market
– Foreign exchange	Trading income, fees	Credit, market
– Derivatives	Trading income, interest income, fees	Credit, market

That the universe of banks encompasses many different varieties of beasts is evident from the way they earn their money. Traditional commercial banking institutions, perhaps typified by a regional bank in the United States (US) or a building society in the United Kingdom (UK), will generate a much greater share of their revenues through net interest income (NII) than trading income, and vice versa for a firm with an investment bank heritage such as Morgan Stanley. In fact, the vast majority of the world's banks do not even run a "trading book", which is a business activity with a specific accounting definition and treatment. Such firms will earn a greater share of their revenues through fees and loan interest income. The breakdown varies widely across regions and banks.

Let us now consider the different types of income streams and costs.

Interest income

Interest income, or NII, is the main source of revenue for the majority of banks worldwide. It can form upwards of 60% of operating income, and for smaller banks and building societies it reaches 80% or more.

NII is generated from lending activity and interest-bearing assets, while "net" return is this interest income minus the cost of funding loans. Funding, which is a cost to the bank, is obtained from a wide variety of sources. For many banks, customer deposits are a key source of funding, as well as one of the cheapest. They are generally short term, though, or available on demand, so must be supplemented by longer term funding. Other sources of funds include senior debt in the form of bonds, securitised bonds, and money market paper.

NII is sensitive to both credit risk and market risk. Market risk, which we look at later, is essentially interest-rate risk for loans and deposits. Interest-rate risk will be driven by the maturity structure of the loan book, as well as the match (or mismatch) between the maturity of loans against the maturity of funding. This is known as the interest-rate gap.

Fees and commissions

Banks generate fee income as a result of providing services to customers. Fee income is very popular with bank senior management because it is less volatile and not susceptible to market risk like trading income or even NII. There is also no credit risk because fees are often paid upfront. There are other benefits as well, such as the opportunity to build up a diversified customer base for this additional range of services, but these are of less concern to a bank's asset-liability management (ALM) desk.

Fee income uses less capital and also carries no market risk, but does carry other risks, such as operational risk.

Trading income

Banks generate trading income through trading activity in financial products such as equities (shares), bonds, and derivative instruments. This includes acting as a dealer or market-maker in these products, as well as taking proprietary positions for speculative purposes. In some cases, running positions in securities (as opposed to derivatives) generate interest income; some banks strip this out of the capital gain made when the security is traded to profit, while others include it as part of overall trading income.

Trading income is perhaps the most volatile income source for a bank. It also generates relatively high market risk, as well as not inconsiderable credit risk. In the era of Basel III, banks will be migrating from the use of Value-at-Risk (VaR) methodology to measure the risk arising from trading activity to the use of the Expected Shortfall (ES) method, which gives a statistical measure of expected losses to the trading portfolio under certain market scenarios. This is dictated by the Fundamental Review of the Trading Book (FRTB) rules implemented under Basel III. A discussion of this topic is outside the scope of this book but further detail can be obtained from the author's book *Moorad Choudhry Anthology*.

Costs

Bank operating costs comprise staff costs and operating costs, such as provision of premises, information technology, and office equipment. Other significant elements of cost are provisions for loan losses, which are charges against the loan revenues of the bank. Provision is based on subjective measurement by management of how much of the loan portfolio can be expected to be repaid by the borrower.

SCOPE OF BANKING ACTIVITIES

The different aspects of banking business vary widely in nature. For our purposes we may group them together as shown in Figure 1.1. Put very simply, "retail" or "commercial" banking covers the more traditional lending and trust activities, while "investment" banking covers trading activity and fee-based income such as stock exchange listing and mergers and acquisitions. The one common objective of all banking activity is return on capital. Depending on the degree of risk it represents, a particular activity will be required to achieve a specified return on the capital it uses. The issue of banking capital is vital to an appreciation of the banking business; entire new business lines (such as securitisation) have been devised in response to the need to make the use of capital more efficient.

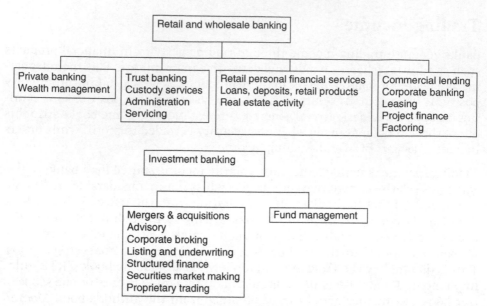

Figure 1.1   Scope of banking activities

As we can see from Figure 1.1, the scope of banking business is wide. Activities range from essentially plain vanilla activity, such as corporate lending, to complex transactions, such as securitisation and hybrid product trading. There is vast literature on all these activities, so we do not need to cover them here. However, it is important to have a grounding in the basic products; subsequent chapters will introduce these.

ALM is the discipline in banking risk management that is concerned with the efficient management of the mismatch between assets (loans) and liabilities (deposits), and with management of the bank's capital. It therefore concerns itself with all banking operations, even if day-to-day contact between the ALM desk (or Treasury desk) and other parts of the bank is infrequent. The ALM desk will be responsible for the Treasury and money market activities of the entire bank. So, if we wish, we could draw a box with ALM in it around the whole of Figure 1.1. This is not to say that the ALM function does all these activities; rather, it is just to make clear that all the various activities represent assets and liabilities for the bank, and one central function is responsible for this side of these activities.

For capital management purposes, a bank's business is organised into a "banking book" and a "trading book". We consider these next; first though, a word on bank capital.

Capital

Bank capital is the equity of the bank. In other words, it is a liability. This is important to remember because frequently in the business media one comes across commentary that banks have to "set aside" capital in order to undertake lending, as if it is some sort of asset. One does not set aside capital; however, depending on the riskiness of the lending, one has to have a minimum of the balance sheet funded by equity liabilities, as opposed to debt liabilities such as deposits or bonds.

Capital is the cushion that absorbs unexpected losses that the bank incurs when loan customers default on their borrowing. By acting as this cushion, it enables the bank to continue operating and thus avoid insolvency or bankruptcy during periods of market correction or economic downturn. When the bank suffers a loss or writes off a loss-making or otherwise economically untenable activity, the capital is used to absorb the loss. This can be done by eating into reserves, freezing dividend payments, or (in more extreme scenarios) a writedown of equity capital. In the capital structure, the rights of capital creditors, including equity holders, are subordinated to senior creditors and deposit holders.

Banks occupy a vital and pivotal position in any economy as the suppliers of credit and financial liquidity, so bank capital is important. As such, banks are heavily regulated by central monetary authorities, and their capital is subject to regulatory rules compiled by the Bank for International Settlements (BIS), based in Basel, Switzerland. For this reason its regulatory capital rules are often called the "Basel rules". Under the original Basel rules (Basel I), a banking institution was required to hold a minimum capital level of 8% against the assets on its book.[3] Total capital is comprised of:

- Equity capital;
- Reserves;
- Retained earnings;
- Preference shares;
- Subordinated debt.

Capital is split into Tier 1 capital and Tier 2 capital. The first four items in the bulleted list comprise Tier 1 capital or "additional tier 1" (AT1) capital, while the remaining item is Tier 2 capital.

The quality of the capital in a bank reflects its mix of Tier 1 and Tier 2 capital. Tier 1 or "core capital" is the highest quality capital, as it is not obliged to be repaid. Tier 2 is considered lower quality capital as it is not necessarily "loss absorbing", although legally it is required to be; it is repayable and also of shorter term than equity capital. Assessing the financial strength and quality of a particular banking institution often requires calculating key capital ratios for the bank and comparing them with market averages and other benchmarks.

Analysts use a number of ratios to assess bank capital strength. Some of the more common ones are shown in Table 1.2.

---

[3]There is more to this than just this simple statement, and we consider it in detail in Chapter 15.

Table 1.2 Bank analysis ratios for capital strength

Ratio	Calculation	Notes
Common equity capital ratio	Tier 1 capital/Risk-weighted assets	A key ratio monitored, in particular, by rating agencies as a measure of high-quality, non-repayable capital, available to absorb losses incurred by the bank
Tier 1 capital ratio	Eligible Tier 1 capital/Risk-weighted assets	Another important ratio monitored by investors and rating agencies. Represents the amount of high-quality, non-repayable capital available to the bank
Total capital ratio	Total capital/Risk-weighted assets	Represents total capital available to the bank
Off-balance-sheet risk to total capital	Off-balance-sheet and continent risk/Total capital	Measure of adequacy of capital against off-balance-sheet risk, including derivatives exposure and committed, undrawn credit lines

Banking and trading books

Banks and financial institutions make a distinction between their activities for capital management purposes, including regulatory capital. Activities are split between the "banking book" and the "trading book". Put simply, the banking book holds the traditional banking activities such as commercial banking, loans, and deposits. This would cover lending to individuals as well as corporates and other banks, and so will interact with investment banking business.[4] The trading book records wholesale market transactions, such as market-making and proprietary trading in bonds and derivatives. Again, speaking simply, the primary difference between the two books is that the overriding principle of the banking book is one of "buy and hold" – that is, a long-term acquisition. Assets may be held on the book for up to 30 years or longer. The trading book is just that, it employs a trading philosophy so that assets may be held for very short terms, less than 1 day in some cases.

---

[4]For a start, there will be a commonality of clients. A corporate client will borrow from a bank and may also retain the bank's underwriting or structured finance departments to arrange a share issue or securitisation on its behalf.

The regulatory capital and accounting treatment of each book differs. The primary difference here is that the trading book employs the "mark-to-market" approach to record profit and loss (P&L), which is the daily "marking" of an asset to its market value. An increase or decrease in the mark on the previous day's mark is recorded as an unrealised profit or loss on the book: on disposal of the asset, the realised profit or loss is the change in the mark at disposal compared with its mark at purchase.

The banking book

Traditional banking activity – such as deposits and loans – is recorded in the banking book. The accounting treatment for the banking book follows the accrual concept, which accrues interest cash flows as they occur. There is no mark to market. The banking book holds assets for which both corporate and retail counterparties as well as banking counterparties are represented. So it is the type of business activity that dictates whether it is placed in the banking book, not the type of counterparty or which department of the bank is conducting it. Assets and liabilities on the banking book generate interest-rate and credit risk exposure for the bank. They also create liquidity and term mismatch ("gap") risks. Liquidity refers to the ease with which an asset can be transformed into cash and to the ease with which funds can be raised in the market. So we see that "liquidity risk" actually refers to two related but separate issues.

All these risks form part of ALM. Interest-rate risk management is a critical part of Treasury policy and ALM, while credit risk policy will be set and dictated by the credit policy of the bank. Gap risk creates an excess or shortage of cash, which must be managed. This is the cash management part of ALM. There is also a mismatch risk associated with fixed rate and floating rate interest liabilities. The central role of financial markets is to enable cash management and interest-rate management to be undertaken efficiently. ALM of the banking book will centre on interest-rate risk management and hedging, as well as liquidity management. Note how there is no "market risk" for the banking book in principle, because there is no marking to market. However, the interest-rate exposure of the book creates an exposure that is subject to market movements in interest rates, so for regulatory purposes the banking book is exposed to market risk.

Trading book

Wholesale market activity, including market-making and proprietary trading, is recorded in the trading book. Assets on the trading book can be expected to have a high turnover, although not necessarily so, and are marked to market daily. Counterparties to this trading activity can include other banks and financial institutions such as hedge funds, corporates, and central banks. Trading book activity generates the same risk exposure as that on the banking book, including market risk, credit risk, and liquidity risk. It also creates a need for cash management. Much trading book activity involves derivative instruments, as opposed to "cash" products. Derivatives include futures, swaps, and options. These can be equity, interest rate, credit, commodity, foreign exchange (FX), weather, and other derivatives. Derivatives are known as "off-balance-sheet" instruments because they are recorded "off" the (cash) balance sheet. Their widespread use and acceptance have greatly improved the efficiency of the process behind risk exposure hedging for banks and other institutions alike.

Off-balance-sheet transactions refer to "contingent liabilities", which are so called because they refer to future exposure contracted now. These are not only derivatives contracts, such as interest-rate swaps or writing an option, but also include guarantees such as a credit line to a third-party customer or a group subsidiary company. These represent a liability for the bank that may be required to be honoured at some future date. In most cases, they do not generate cash inflow or outflow at inception – unlike a cash transaction – but represent future exposure. If a credit line is drawn on, it represents a cash out-flow and that transaction is then recorded on the balance sheet.

BANKING PRODUCTS

We provide a summary description of the main products offered by banks to their customers, grouped into liabilities and assets.

Interest-bearing and non-interest-bearing current account

This is *the* principal banking product and the one that has been a significant factor in global economic development. Sometimes referred to as a money transmission account (MTA) or an "operational deposit", these are also known as cheque accounts or (in the US) "checking accounts". They are the simplest form of short-term deposit or investment instrument. Customer funds may be withdrawn instantly on demand, either by cheque, cash machine ("automated teller machine" or ATM) card, or electronically via telephone or internet mobile app. They may also be set up with regular payments to third parties such as standing orders and direct debits.

Banks generally pay interest on surplus balances, although not always. Cur-rent accounts are a cheap source of funding for banks, as well as a stable one, because their balances, although variable on a monthly basis, are viewed as behaviourally long term.

The current account product defines a bank. Many so-called "challenger banks" or digital mobile app-only banks do not offer such a product, which means that their customers will need to obtain MTA services from another bank.

The other side of the current account, the on-demand instant overdraft facility, is also a very important product.

Demand deposit

Also referred to as a savings account, sight deposit, or call account, these are similar to cheque accounts but are always interest bearing and may not be used for making payments to third parties. The funds are available on demand, but cannot be used for cheques or other similar payments.

Time deposit

Time or term deposits are interest-bearing deposit accounts of fixed maturity and, often, fixed interest rate. They are usually offered with a range of maturities ranging from 1 month to 5 years, with longer dated deposits attracting higher interest. This reflects a positive yield curve, which indicates the funding value to the bank of longer term liabilities. Most time deposits pay a fixed rate of interest, payable on maturity. Accounts of longer than 1-year maturity often capitalise interest on an annual basis.

Fixed term deposits are sometimes called "bonds" or "savings bonds" but are not tradable instruments, so this term is not to be confused with capital market bonds or fixed income securities.

Savings deposit (non-instant access)

A notice account is a savings deposit account that pays a higher rate of interest to a standard demand deposit, provided the customer gives 30, 35, 60, 90, or 180 days' notice before withdrawing funds. Banks also incentivise customers with a higher interest rate when they arrange to pay in a fixed amount each month over a 12- or 24-month period, so-called "monthly saver" accounts. Such deposits are treated as behaviourally stable funds for regulatory purposes.

In some jurisdictions, interest on deposit accounts is paid net of a withholding tax. Some accounts may be set up to pay gross interest, or may be arranged to be tax-free interest-bearing accounts, provided they meet certain stipulated conditions.

Structured deposit

A structured deposit is a deposit whose payoff or return profile is structured to match a specific customer requirement. The structuring results from the use of an embedded derivative in the product, which links the deposit to changes in interest rates, FX rates, stock market indices, or other market rates. There is a wide range of different products available that fall in the class of "structured deposit".

An example is the following: a customer places funds on deposit at a specific interest rate and fixed term. Under the agreement, if the central bank base interest rate remains between 4 and 5%, then return is enhanced by 100bp. If the rate moves below 4% or above 5%, then the deposit forfeits all interest for the remaining term of its life. This is an example of a "collared range accrual" deposit. It's a pretty superfluous product and asks the customer to speculate on interest rates, which makes it more of an investment product than a pure bank deposit.

Personal and corporate loans

The basic customer product of a bank is the retail or corporate customer loan. This may be secured on collateral or unsecured, and may be set with a fixed-rate or variable floating-rate of interest. The loan term is usually fixed, and the repayment may be "bullet", meaning the initial borrowed amount is paid in one go on maturity, or it may be amortising, meaning the borrower pays down a regular portion of the loan during its life.

On-demand overdraft

The basic current account is usually, although not always, able to go "overdrawn" if payments are made through it that are of higher value than its credit balance at the time. Typically, the customer will have arranged such an overdraft in advance, because unarranged overdrafts are charged at a higher interest rate. There is no repayment date on an overdraft, but a bank may withdraw the facility at 30 or 60 days' notice, which would require the overdraft to be repaid in that time. In general, overdraft facilities are renewed on an annual basis.

Liquidity facilities

Liquidity facility is the generic term for a standing loan agreement, against which a borrower can draw down funds at any time up to the maximum value of the line. The borrower pays a fee, called the standing fee, even if the line is not used and then pays the agreed rate of interest on any funds that it does draw.

We distinguish between the following:

- *Back-up facility*: A facility that is not used in the normal course of business. It is generally drawn down if the borrower is experiencing some difficulty in obtaining funding from its usual sources;
- *Revolving credit facility (RCF)*: A commitment from a bank to lend on a revolving basis under prespecified terms. Under an RCF there is usually a regular drawdown and repayment of funds during the life of the facility;
- *Overdaft*: See above;
- *Credit card*: See below.

Liquidity facilities require full regulatory capital backing, as the capital treatment is to assume that they are being used at all times.

Credit card

A credit card is a form of liquidity facility because it references a line of borrowing approved in advance by the bank, which the customer can draw down on at any time and on demand. There is usually a credit limit set when the card is issued to the customer. Credit cards, which are used by both retail and corporate customers, are very useful products because they enable the borrower to purchase goods and services over all communications media, from face to face over the counter to digital and mobile app.

Trade finance: letter of credit

A letter of credit (LoC) is a standard vanilla product available from a commercial bank. It is an instrument that guarantees that a buyer's payment to a seller will be received at the right time and for the specific amount. The buyer is the customer of the bank. If the buyer is unable to make payment on the due date, the bank will cover the full amount of the purchase. The bank therefore takes on the credit risk of the buyer when it writes an LoC on the buyer's behalf. The buyer therefore pays a fee for the LoC that reflects its credit standing.

LoCs are used in domestic and international trade transactions. Cross-border trade transactions involve both parties in issues such as distance, different legal jurisdictions, and lack of any available due diligence on the counterparties. An LoC is a valuable tool that eases the process for the buying and selling parties. The bank also acts on behalf of the buyer (the purchaser of the LoC) because it would only make payment when it knows that the goods have been shipped. For the seller, an LoC substitutes the credit of the buyer for that of the bank, which is an easier risk exposure for the seller to take on.

LoCs represent fee-based income for a bank and are sometimes referred to as "off-balance-sheet" because no actual funded lending is involved.

Commercial letter of credit

A commercial LoC is a contract issued by a bank, known as the issuing bank, on behalf of one of its customers, authorising another bank, known as the advising or confirming bank, to make payment to the beneficiary. The issuing bank makes a commitment to guarantee drawings made under the named credit. The beneficiary is normally the provider of goods and/or services. An advising bank, usually a foreign correspondent bank of the issuing bank, will advise the beneficiary, but otherwise has no other obligation under the LoC.

An LoC is generally negotiable; this means that the issuing bank is obliged to pay the beneficiary but – should the issuing bank so request – any bank nominated by the beneficiary could make the payments. To be negotiable, the LoC features an unconditional promise to pay on demand at a specified time.

Standby letter of credit

A standby LoC is a contract issued by a bank on behalf of a customer to provide assurances of its ability to perform under the terms of a contract between it and the beneficiary. In other words, a standby LoC is more of a guarantee, as both parties to the transaction do not expect the LoC will be drawn on. It essentially provides comfort to the beneficiary, as it enhances the creditworthiness of its customer.

Syndicated loan

To raise debt capital, companies may issue bonds or loans (as well as other debt-like instruments), both of which are associated with a certain seniority or ranking. In a liquidation or winding up, the borrower's remaining assets are distributed according to a priority waterfall: debt obligations with the highest seniority are repaid first; only if assets remain thereafter are obligations with lower seniorities repaid. Further, debt instruments may be secured or unsecured: if certain of the borrower's assets are ring-fenced to serve as collateral for the lenders under a particular obligation only, this obligation is deemed to be "secured". Together, seniority and collateral determine the *priority* of an obligation. As illustrated in Table 1.3, bonds and loans issued by investment-grade companies, as well as bonds issued by sub-investment-grade companies, called "high-yield bonds", are typically senior unsecured. However, loans issued by sub-investment-grade companies are typically senior secured. Often, these are called "leveraged loans" or "syndicated loans". The market often uses both terms interchangeably.

The definition of "leveraged loan" is not universal, however. Various market participants define a leveraged loan to be a loan with a sub-investment-grade rating, while other users view it as one with a certain spread over Libor (say 100bp or more) and sometimes a certain debt/EBITDA ratio of the borrower. S&P, for instance, calls a loan "leveraged" if it is rated sub-investment grade or if it is rated investment grade but pays interest of at least Libor + 125bp. Bloomberg uses a hurdle rate of Libor + 250bp. Essentially, the market refers to leveraged loans and high-yield bonds as "high-yield debt".

Leveraged loans may be arranged either between a borrower and a single lending bank, or, more commonly, between a borrower and a syndicate of

Table 1.3 Typical priorities of corporate bonds and loans of investment grade and sub-investment-grade borrowers

	Investment-grade borrower	Sub-investment-grade borrower
Bonds	Senior unsecured	Senior unsecured (high-yield bonds)
Loans	Senior unsecured	Senior secured (leveraged loans/syndicated secured loans)

Source: Choudhry (2010).

lending banks. In the latter case, one (or more) of the lending banks acts as lead arranger. Before any other lending banks are involved, the lead arranger conducts detailed due diligence on the borrower. Also, the lead arranger and borrower agree on the basic transaction terms, such as the size of the loan, interest rate, fees, loan structure, covenants and type of syndication. These terms are documented in a "loan agreement". Based on the information received in the due diligence process, the lead arranger prepares an information memorandum, also called the "bank book", which is used to market the transaction to other potential lending banks or institutional investors. Together, the lead arranger and the other lenders constitute the primary market. If the transaction is an "underwritten syndication", the lead arranger guarantees the borrower that the entire amount of the loan will be placed at a predefined price. If the loan is undersubscribed at that price, the lead arranger is forced to absorb the difference. If the transaction is a "best efforts syndication", the lead arranger tries to place the loan at the predefined terms but will, if investor demand is insufficient, adjust these terms to achieve full placement.

Leveraged loans are usually secured by particular assets of the borrower. These assets are listed in the loan agreement and may comprise all tangible and intangible assets of the borrower. This means that, in the event of default, lenders can take possession of these assets, liquidate them, and use the proceeds to satisfy their claims in the order of priority stipulated in the loan agreement and the related inter-creditor agreement. This happens before the claims of any unsecured lenders are satisfied.

Leveraged loans commonly mature between 7 and 10 years after issuance. The effective life of leveraged loans, however, tends to be significantly shorter as the borrower is typically allowed to prepay or "call" the loan at any time at no premium or at a limited premium.

CAPITAL MARKETS

A "capital market" is the term used to describe the market for raising and investing long-term finance. The economies of developed countries and a large number of developing countries are based on financial systems that encompass investors and borrowers, markets, and trading arrangements. A market can be one in the traditional sense, such as an exchange where financial instruments are bought and sold on a trading floor, or it may refer to one where participants deal with each other over the telephone or via electronic screens. The basic principles are the same in any type of market. There are two primary users of capital markets: lenders and borrowers. The source of lenders' funds is, to a large extent, the personal sector made up of household savings and those acting as their investment managers, such as life assurance companies and pension funds. The borrowers are made up of the government, local government, and companies (called corporates). There is a basic conflict between the financial objectives of borrowers and lenders, in that those who are investing funds wish to remain liquid, which means having easy access to their investments. They also wish to maximise the return on their investment. A corporate, on the other hand, will wish to generate maximum net profit on its activities, which will require continuous investment in plant, equipment, human resources, and so on. Such investment will therefore need to be as long term as possible. Government borrowing as well is often related to long-term projects such as the construction of schools, hospitals, and roads. So while investors wish to have ready access to their cash and invest short, borrowers desire funding to be as long term as possible. One economist referred to this conflict as the "constitutional weakness" of financial markets (Hicks, 1939), especially as there is no conduit through which to reconcile the needs of lenders and borrowers. To facilitate the efficient operation of financial markets and the price mechanism, intermediaries exist to bring together the needs of lenders and borrowers. A bank is the best example of this. Banks accept deposits from investors, which make up the liability side of their balance sheet, and lend funds to borrowers, which forms the assets on their balance sheet. If a bank builds up a sufficiently large asset and liability base, it will be able to meet the needs of both investors and borrowers, as it can maintain liquidity to meet investors' requirements as well as create long-term assets to meet the needs of borrowers. A bank is exposed to two primary risks in carrying out its operations: that a large number of investors decide to withdraw their funds at the same time (a "run" on the bank) or that a large number of borrowers go bankrupt and default on their loans. The bank in acting as a financial intermediary reduces the risk it is exposed to by spreading and pooling risk across a wide asset and liability base.

Corporate borrowers wishing to finance long-term investment can raise capital in various ways. The main methods are:

- Continued reinvestment of the profits generated by a company's current operations;
- Selling shares in the company, known as equity capital, equity securities, or *equity*, which confers on buyers a share in ownership of the company. Shareholders as owners have the right to vote at general meetings of the company, as well as the right to share in the company's profits by receiving dividends;
- Borrowing money from a bank via a bank loan. This can be a short-term loan such as an overdraft, or a longer term loan over 2, 3, or 5 years or even longer. Bank loans can be at either a fixed or, more usually, variable rate of interest;
- Borrowing money by issuing debt securities in the form of *bills, commercial paper*, and *bonds* that subsequently trade in the debt capital market.

The first method may not generate sufficient funds, especially if a company is seeking to expand by growth or the acquisition of other companies. In any case, a proportion of annual after-tax profits will need to be paid out as dividends to shareholders. Selling further shares is not always popular among existing shareholders as it dilutes the extent of their ownership; moreover, there are a host of other factors to consider, including whether there is any appetite in the market for that company's shares. A bank loan is often inflexible, and the interest rate charged by the bank may be comparatively high for all but the highest quality companies. We say "comparatively" because there is often a cheaper way for corporates to borrow money: by tapping the bond markets. An issue of bonds will fix the rate of interest payable by the company for a long-term period, and the chief characteristic of bonds – that they are *tradable* – makes investors more willing to lend a company funds.

In every capital market the first financing instrument ever developed was the bill and then the bond. Today, in certain developing economies the government short-dated bond market is often the only liquid market in existence. Over time – as financial systems develop and corporate debt and equity markets take shape – the money and bond markets retain their importance due to their flexibility and the ease with which transactions can be undertaken. In advanced financial markets – such as those in place in developed countries today – the introduction of financial engineering techniques has greatly expanded the range of instruments that can be traded. These instruments include instruments used for hedging positions held in bonds and other cash products, as well as meeting the investment and risk management needs of a whole host of market participants. Debt capital markets have been and continue to be important to the economic development of all countries, as they represent the means of *intermediation* for governments and corporates to finance their activities. In fact, it is difficult to imagine long-term capital-intensive projects – such as those undertaken by, say, petroleum, construction, or aerospace companies – taking place without the existence of a debt capital market to allow the raising of vital finance.

FINANCIAL STATEMENTS AND RATIOS

A key information tool for bank analysis is the financial statement, which comprises the balance sheet and the P&L account. Assets on the balance sheet should equal the assets on a bank's ALM report, while receipt of revenue (such as interest and fees income) and payout of costs during a specified period are recorded in the P&L report or income statement.

The balance sheet

The balance sheet is a statement of a company's assets and liabilities as determined by accounting rules. It is a snapshot of a particular point in time, and so

Table 1.4 Components of a bank balance sheet

Assets	Liabilities
Cash	Short-term liabilities
Loans	Deposits
Financial instruments (long)	Financial instruments (short)
Fixed assets	Long-dated debt
Off-balance-sheet (receivables)	Equity

by the time it is produced it is already out of date. However, it is an important information statement. A number of management information ratios are used when analysing the balance sheet; they are considered in the next chapter.

In Chapter 2 we use a hypothetical example to illustrate balance sheets. For a bank, there are usually five parts to a balance sheet, split up in such a way to show separately:

• Lending and deposits, or traditional bank business;
• Trading assets;
• Treasury and inter-bank assets;
• Off-balance-sheet assets;
• Long-term assets, including fixed assets, shares in subsidiary companies, together with equity and Tier 2 capital.

This is illustrated in Table 1.4. The actual balance sheet of a retail or commercial bank will differ significantly from that of an investment bank, due to the relative importance of their various business lines, but the basic layout will be similar.

Profit and loss report

The income statement for a bank is the P&L report, which records all income and losses during a specified period of time. A bank income statement will show revenues that can be accounted for as net interest income, fees and commissions, and trading income. The precise mix of these sources will reflect the type of banking institution and the business lines it operates in. Revenue is offset by operating (non-interest) expenses, loan loss provisions, trading losses, and tax expense.

A more "traditional" commercial bank will have a much higher dependence on interest revenues than an investment bank that engages in large-scale wholesale capital market business. Investment banks have a higher share of revenue comprising trading and fee income. Table 1.5 shows the components of a UK retail bank's income statement.

Table 1.5 Components of bank income statement, typical structure for retail bank

%	Expressed as percentage of
Core operating income	100
Net interest income	64 Core operating income
Commissions and fee income	31 Core operating income
Trading income	8 Core operating income
+Net other operating income	8 Core operating income
−Operating expenses	61 Revenues
Personnel	38 Revenues
Other, depreciation	
−Loan loss provisions	23 Pre-provision net income
=Net operating income	
+Other non-operating income	
=Profit before tax	
−Tax	
=Net income	
−Minority interest	
=Attributable income	

Source: Bank financial statements.

The composition of earnings varies widely among different institutions. Figure 1.2 shows the breakdown for a UK building society and the UK branch of a US investment bank in 2005, as reported in their financial accounts for that year.

Net interest income

The traditional source of revenue for retail banks – NII – remains as such today (see Figure 1.2). NII is driven by lending, interest-earning asset volumes, and the net yield available on these assets after taking into account the cost of funding. While the main focus is on the loan book, the ALM desk will also concentrate on the bank's investment portfolio. The latter will include coupon receipts from money market and bond market assets, as well as dividends received from any equity holdings.

The cost of funding is a key variable in generating overall NII. For a retail bank, the cheapest source of funds is deposits, especially non-interest-bearing deposits such as cheque accounts.[5] Even in an era of high-street competition, the interest payable on short-term liabilities such as instant access deposits is far below the wholesale market interest rate. This is a funding advantage

[5]These are referred to as NIBLs (non-interest-bearing liabilities).

UK building society, core earnings split 2015

Net interest income 83%
Fee income 15%
Trading profit 2%

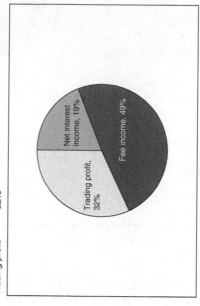

UK subsidiary, North American investment bank, core earnings split 2015

Net interest income 19%
Fee income 49%
Trading profit 32%

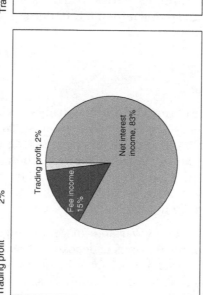

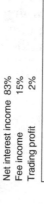

Figure 1.2 Composition of earnings
Source: Bank financial statements.

for retail banks when compared with investment banks, which generally do not have a retail deposit base. Other funding sources include capital markets (senior debt), wholesale markets (the inter-bank money market), securitised markets, and covered bonds. The overall composition of funding significantly affects the net interest margin and, if constrained, can reduce the activities of the bank.

The risk profile of asset classes that generate yields for the bank should lead to a range of net interest margins being reported across the sector, such that a bank with a strong unsecured lending franchise should seek significantly higher yields than one investing in secured mortgage loans; this reflects the different risk profiles of assets. The proportion of non-interest-bearing liabilities will also have a significant impact on the net interest margin of the institution. While a high net interest margin is desirable, it should also be adequate return for the risk incurred in holding the assets.

Bank NII is sensitive to both credit risk and market risk. Interest income is sensitive to changes in interest rates and the maturity profile of the balance sheet. Banks that have assets that mature earlier than their funding liabilities will gain from an environment of rising interest rates. The opposite applies where the asset book has a maturity profile that is longer dated than the liability book. Note that in a declining or low-interest-rate environment, banks may suffer from negative NII irrespective of their asset–liability maturity profile, as it becomes more and more difficult to pass on interest-rate cuts to depositors.

While investment banks are less sensitive to changes in overall NII expectations due to their lower reliance on NII itself, their trading book will also be sensitive to changes in interest rates.

Fee and commission income

Fee revenue is generated from the sale and provision of financial services to customers. The levels of fees and commission are communicated in advance to customers. Fee income known as non-interest income is separate from trading income and is desirable for banks because it represents a stable source of revenue that is not exposed to market risk. It is also attractive because it provides an opportunity for the bank to cross-sell new products and services to existing customers, and provision of these services does not expose the bank to additional credit or market risk. Fee income represents diversification in a bank's revenue base.

Note, though, that although fee-based business may not expose the bank to market risk directly, it does bring with it other risks, and these can include indirect exposure to market risk.[6] In addition, an ability to provide fee-based

---

[6]For example, a strategy pursued by banks in the 1990s was to merge with or acquire insurance companies, creating so-called bancassurance groups. Although much insurance business is fee based, the acquisition of insurance portfolios brought with it added market risk for banks.

financial services may require significant investment in infrastructure and human resources.

Trading income

Trading income arises from the capital gain earned from buying and selling financial instruments. These instruments include both cash and derivative (off-balance-sheet) instruments and can arise from undertaking market-making, which in theory is undertaken to meet client demands and the proprietary business needs of the bank's own trading book. Note that interest income earned while holding assets on the trading book should really be considered NII and not trading income, but sometimes it is not stripped out from overall trading book P&L. There is no uniformity of approach among banks in this regard.

Trading income is the most volatile form of bank revenue. Even a record of consistent profit in trading over a long period is no guarantee against future losses arising out of market corrections or simply making the wrong bet on financial markets. Trading activity was the first type of banking activity whose risk exposure was measured using the VaR methodology, which replaced duration-based risk measures in the 1990s.

Operating expenses

Banking operating costs typically contain human resources costs (remuneration and other personnel-related expenses) together with other operating costs, such as premises and infrastructure costs, depreciation charges, and goodwill.[7] Cost is generally measured as a proportion of revenue. A number of cost–income ratios are used by analysts, some of which are given in Table 1.6.

The RoE measure is probably the most commonly encountered and is usually part of bank strategy, with a target RoE level stated explicitly in management objectives. Note that there is a difference between accounting RoE and market RoE; the latter is calculated as a price return, rather like a standard P&L calculation, taken as the difference between market prices between two dates. During the 1990s, and certainly into 2005, average required RoE was in the order of 15% or higher – with investment banks usually setting a higher target of 20%, 22%, or even higher for certain higher risk business. The RoE target needs to reflect the relative risks of different business activities.

Return on Assets (ROA) is another common measure of performance. It is calculated as follows:

$$\text{Current income (Interest income + Fees)} \times \text{Asset value}$$

---

[7]These are accounting terms common to all corporate entities and are not used just to describe bank operating costs.

Table 1.6 Bank cost–income ratios

Ratio	Calculation	Notes
Pre-tax RoE	Pre-tax income/ Average shareholders' equity	Measures the pre-tax return on equity. A measure above 20% is viewed as above average and strong.
RoE	Attributable net income/Average shareholders' equity	Measures RoE. A measure above 10% is considered strong.
ROA	Net income/Average assets	Measures return on assets. A measure above 1% is considered strong.
Cost–income ratio	Non-interest costs/Total net revenues	Non-interest costs minus non-cash items such as goodwill or depreciation of intangible assets. The cost to produce one unit of net interest and non-interest income. The lower the ratio, the more efficient the bank.
Net interest margin	Net interest income/Average earnings assets	The difference between tax-equivalent yield on earning assets and the rate paid on funds to support those assets, divided by average earning assets.
Loan loss provision	Loan loss provision/Pre-provision, pre-tax income	The proportion of pre-tax income that is being absorbed by loan losses. This is the credit cost of conducting the business.
Non-interest income	Non-interest income/ Net revenues	Non-interest income includes service charges on deposits, trust fees, advisory fees, servicing fees, net trading profits from trading books, and commissions and fees from off-balance-sheet items. Generally, the higher the ratio, the greater the bank's sensitivity to changes in interest rates.

Both financial statement P&L reports and measures such as RoE and ROA are bland calculations of absolute values; that is, they do not make any adjustment for relative risk exposure, so cannot stand too much comparison with equivalent figures from another institution. This is because risk exposure – not to mention the specific type of business activity – will differ from one bank to another. However, there are general approximate values that serve as benchmarks for certain sectors, such as the 15% RoE level we state above. Banks also calculate risk-adjusted ratios.

Provisions

Banks expect a percentage of loan assets, and other assets, to suffer loss or become completely unrecoverable. Provisions are set aside out of reserves to cover for these losses each year; they are a charge against the loan revenues of the bank. The size of the provision taken is a function of what writeoffs may be required against the loan portfolio in the current period and in the future, and the size and adequacy of loan loss reserves currently available. In some jurisdictions there are regulatory requirements that dictate the minimum size of loss provision.

Provisions fund the bank's loan loss reserve, and the reserve will grow in size when the bank provides more for expected credit losses than the actual amount that is written off. If the bank believes subsequently that the size of the reserve built up is in excess of what is currently required, it may write back a percentage of it.

The amount of provisioning will vary with the business cycle. During a boom period in the cycle, corporate and retail default rates are at historically lower levels, and so a bank can afford to lower the level of its provisioning. However, prudent management dictates that senior managers are familiar with their markets and are able to judge when provision levels should increase. In other words, banks should "know their market".

BIBLIOGRAPHY

Choudhry, M. (2007). *Bank Asset and Liability Management*, Singapore: John Wiley & Sons.
Choudhry, M. (2010). *Structured Credit Products*, 2nd edition, Singapore: John Wiley & Sons.
Choudhry, M. (2012). *The Principles of Banking*, Singapore: John Wiley & Sons.
Choudhry, M. (2018). *Moorad Choudhry Anthology*, Singapore: John Wiley & Sons.
Hicks, J.R. (1939). *Value and Capital*, Oxford: Clarendon Press.
Higson, C. (1995). *Business Finance*, Oxford: Blackwell.

Chapter

2

CUSTOMER SERVICES AND MARKETING FOR BANK PRODUCTS

In essence, banking is a commoditised product (or service). Most financial products are of long standing and all of them are nothing more (or less) than a series of cash flows. The more exotic "structured products" are often created to meet a perceived customer need or benefit, rather than the result of customer enquiry. Then again perhaps sometimes, a bit like Steve Jobs, one has to tell the customer what they want.

But banking products are not really like Apple products. To a great extent, most of the main products can be obtained (provided the specific customer is acceptable to the bank in question) from most banks. We summarise the main ones in Table 2.1. Even when a bank thinks it is the first one to introduce a type of product and jealously guards its "proprietary" knowledge, often one finds there is another bank just a few minutes' walk down the road that is offering the same product, just under a different name. So, as we said, banking and financial services are a commoditised product, more akin to a tin of baked beans than the Saturn V rocket (which is another reason this author finds it amusing that bank quantitative analysts are called "rocket scientists" by the business media. They are as much rocket scientists as Sunday league pub footballers are Premiership football players.) And with commoditised products, much of the "unique selling point" for an individual bank comes from superior customer service, the attitude and customer friendliness of its staff, and efficient operations, rather than anything exotic about the product itself.

Note that "products" does not mean "customer interface". Hence, a mobile banking app for use on Apple or Android is not a "product". "Contactless" is not a product, although we would suggest that credit cards are a product because they are a form of instantly available bank loan, distinct from the medium used to draw down the loan. Put another way, one might say a bank that does not offer a credit card product can still offer mobile app service provision to customers, but simply offering a mobile app does not mean a bank can offer a credit card.

By the way, from an accounting perspective, the essential distinction to make is whether the product is "on" or "off" balance sheet (or "cash" or "derivative"). However, off-balance-sheet products, a term still in common use to describe derivative instruments, are ultimately also a package of cash flows. From an asset-liability management (ALM) perspective, the distinction between cash and derivative is something of a red herring, because both types of product give rise to balance sheet risk issues. The ALM practitioner is concerned with cash impact on both sides of the balance sheet, so making a distinction between on- and off-balance-sheet is to miss the point.

In the ALM discipline, cash and its impact on the balance sheet are everything. So it is important to have an intimate understanding of the cash flow behaviour of every product that the bank deals in. This may seem like a statement of the

Table 2.1 Vanilla commercial banking products

Retail products	Corporate banking products	Wholesale banking products
Assets		
Personal loan (unsecured, fixed-rate, or floating-rate)	Corporate loan, unsecured or secured	Money market (CD/CP)
Personal loan (secured, fixed-rate, or floating-rate)	Corporate loan, fixed-rate or floating-rate	Fixed income securities
Personal loan, bullet or amortising	Corporate loan, bullet or amortising	Equity market making
Residential mortgage	Commercial mortgage	Derivatives market making
Credit card	Credit card	
Overdraft	Overdraft	
Foreign exchange (spot)	Liquidity line, revolving credit, etc.	
	Trade finance (letter of credit, trade bill, guarantee, etc.)	
	Invoice discounting, factoring	
	Foreign exchange (spot and forward)	
Liabilities		
Current account	Current account	Structured products (MTNs, etc.)
Deposit account	Deposit account	Structured deposit
Notice and fixed term, fixed-rate deposit accounts	Structured deposit	

obvious, but there is no shortage of senior (and not so senior) bankers who are unfamiliar with the product characteristics of some of the instruments on their balance sheet. When we say "understanding" we mean:

- The product's contractual cash flows, their pattern, and timing;
- The cash flows' sensitivity (if any) to changes in external and/or relevant market parameters such as interest rates, foreign exchange (FX) rates, inflation, credit rating, and so on;
- The cash flows' sensitivity to customer behaviour;
- The cash flows' sensitivity to factors impacting the bank itself.

Without this understanding it is not possible to undertake effective NIM management, let alone effective ALM.

But we'll leave ALM for Part II of this book. Let's look at the customer side of things first.

MARKETING FINANCIAL SERVICES

In order to sell financial services successfully, it is imperative that all bank staff that are in any way customer facing know the firm's products intimately. This means being able to answer detailed questions on specifics from customers with differing needs. Crucially, staff need to know their competitors' products (although this is not commonly understood). Staff need to be able to explain with genuine conviction the benefits that their products offer to the customer at the time. And these benefits should be personalised to the customer.

In this section we consider a wide range of factors relevant to this topic.

Marketing concepts

Marketing a product can be thought of as the process undertaken by a firm to identify, anticipate, and satisfy customer demand profitably. This makes it distinct from the sales process itself, but one can see how the two interact and also have some elements of cross-over in the middle. (Selling a current account or even a credit card may involve less pure marketing, but closing a syndicated loan transaction may well have required an involved marketing process before the lead manager ever mentioned a loan to the customer...).

The distinction from the sales process can be seen from the following considerations:

- Marketing is a management process. It should be something that senior managers undertake in the course of running the operations of the business on a day-to-day basis;
- The marketing process should identify or anticipate customer needs (or create them – see Apple above). This means knowing who one's customers are and understanding their requirements as it affects them personally; it also requires an intelligent proactive approach geared towards "knowing one's customers", both current and future;
- Profitability concerns are a key part of the marketing process: the above must be undertaken in a way that fits in to ensuring business profitability.

In essence, the marketing process should be a customer-focused one, and it is more concerned with knowing the customer base and everything about all one's customers than about actually selling to them. In a commoditised industry such as financial services, one could say it is as important as the balance

sheet risk management side of banking, and equally as important as the shareholder return on capital angle.

Marketing mix

An age-old topic on MBA courses is the concept of the "marketing mix", which
refers to the combination of activities used by a firm to achieve its objectives
by marketing its products effectively to a target group of customers. It has
traditionally been referred to as "the 4 Ps", namely:

- Product;
- Price;
- Promotion;
- Place.

Subsequent to this articulation, which dates from the 1970s, three more Ps
were added, these being People, Processes, and Physical evidence.

The marketing mix is the basic set of tools that marketers possess to carry
out tactical level marketing. All the elements in the marketing mix need to be
brought together and worked together effectively for the marketing campaign
to succeed.

The three additional Ps are particularly relevant to the financial services industry because of the nature of the product – it is intangible. We have noted already
that banking products are commoditised, and genuine differentiation is difficult, if not impossible – one bank's current account or credit card will if not
necessarily "look" at least certainly "act" in an identical manner. They will
do more or less the same thing. So banks need to address the additional 3 Ps
as part of an effort to differentiate themselves.

The "People" part is fairly self-evident, and not unique to the banking industry. It refers to the firm's staff, particularly those that are customer facing or
customer serving in any way. It also covers those who may not necessarily deal
directly with customers but influence the customer service experience, such
as middle and senior management.

"Process" refers to procedures, mechanisms, and activities that lead to an
exchange of value; in other words, the experience of a product or service that
allows a customer to feel that they have received value.

"Physical evidence" is connected with the material part of a service. As there
are no actual physical characteristics of a service, in the banking industry this
strand is concerned with related items, including (but not limited to) marketing collateral (brochures, leaflets, and the like), internet content, mobile app
efficiency and reliability, customer communications (such as bank account
statements), branch layout and design, uniforms, business cards, charity spon-
sorship, and so on.

Constraints in marketing banking services

The characteristics of banking products contribute to a general impression that marketing them is somewhat of a thankless task. This should not surprise anyone with even a limited experience of commerce.

In the first instance, financial services are, frankly, boring. One could not reasonably describe the product class as "exciting". In marketing terms this compares unfavourably with physical products such as automobiles or luxury watches, or with services such as cinema or pop music. The challenge of the bank marketer is to package the product as a means to an end, rather than an end in itself; for example, one isn't selling a 25-year package of amortising cash flows, but rather the ability to live in one's own home.

Secondly, there is a low level of accessibility. While the mathematics behind most financial products is little more than glorified arithmetic (and even the exotic structured stuff doesn't really employ genuinely complex mathematics), in terms of understanding by the general populace, banking services are not straightforward to follow. This is partly because of the way they are explained, as opposed to any real complexity, but attempts to "dumb down" finance also don't always work because they don't necessarily make the products easy to follow. The inaccessibility of financial products also makes them difficult to compare across different providers, which is another reason why banks often try to differentiate themselves using slick and/or entertaining advertising, or getting a well-known personality such as a sports star or movie actor to front their advertising campaigns.

A third factor that makes marketing of banking services problematic is that it can be difficult to gauge the quality of the product, at least at the start. As an extreme example, consider a long-term savings or investment plan. One would only know if it had realised the customer's savings objective (be it retirement, or education fees, and so on) towards the end of the product's life, at which point it's too late to do anything about it or take mitigating action. As a result, customers tend to ascertain product quality based not on the product itself but on the reputation of the bank, what its perceived standing in the business media or community is, and on the recommendation of friends or family. This is a primary reason why the reputation of a bank is a precious commodity that needs to be protected carefully over the long term.

Another factor is what is known as "market clustering". Even within homogeneous groups, customer requirements vary greatly from one customer to another. Banks can only very rarely tailor their services to meet the needs of individual customers (even if they wanted to – the technology constraint is enormous), but one or more products a bank offers may be attractive to a specific group of customers and not able to penetrate the mass market. To get around this, banks need to recognise "market segmentation" and use the information they possess on all their customers to target them and help sell to them, in a similar manner to how the tech giants and social media platforms do.

A final factor is technology and so-called "FinTech". On the customer-facing side, technology has made possible digital and mobile app banking. This makes the branch almost redundant for most (although not all) customer transactions, and the digital interface makes it harder for the bank to "know" its customers in a human sense. From a marketing standpoint, it makes it difficult again to differentiate, because most banks' digital customer offerings are fairly identical.

Advertising banking services

In industries where the product on offer is essentially commoditised, the principal way that competitors seek to differentiate themselves is by advertising. As well as the basic message, which often may not be about the product at all but concentrate instead on some human factor, lifestyle choice, or sense of well-being, the choice of advertising medium is also important. An advert placed in a tabloid newspaper may not generate as much positive "vibe" as one placed in a glossy magazine. Ultimately, the objective with advertising the bank is to build brand awareness and reputation. This is why banks often pay large sums to hire celebrities or sports stars to represent their brand.[1]

The main media that banks use to advertise their services are:

- Television: Generally the most expensive but potentially the largest audience;
- Cinema: Not commonly used but can be effective because the audience is forced to watch;
- Billboards: These are simple but sometimes effective for building brand awareness on the high street, metro, and so on. Among the author's favourites was one for a small regional bank in the EU, which stated simply "Buy a house you can call your own, with a bank you can call your own";
- Press: Often the most commonly used medium due to lower prices, and placing in the business section generally targets an interested audience;
- Radio: Far less commonly used as bank products do not transfer as effectively to it;
- Internet and social media: New banks and smaller banks tend to concentrate on this medium, especially Facebook, Twitter, and LinkedIn, which is often a cheap but effective means to build brand awareness and a positive reputation.

Advertising in itself may not generate any increase in business. Of course, it is important to ensure the adverts are targeted, which means knowing exactly which types of customer one is wishing to attract and pitching to them using the medium they respond to. It is no coincidence that in the UK

---

[1]The author being a big fan of Jessica Ennis (the UK Olympic gold medal-winning heptathlete) could not help but think warm positive things about Santander UK when that bank hired her to front a series of television commercials advertising its products.

the digital-only branchless banks used social media extensively in the period leading up to their launch of business operations.

CUSTOMER SERVICE

Every bank in the world claims to offer "excellent customer service"; certainly, no bank would admit to poor customer service. It is possibly one of the most frequently encountered platitudes in business. That said, it is certainly important to provide genuine good customer service. The concept is one of those that may not be straightforward to define, but one knows when one sees (or receives) it, and it's also apparent when one receives bad customer service. Consider this section to be a primer on the essential elements of acceptable customer service in banking.

Understanding good customer service

In general, any and all customers should expect the following from a bank:

1. The provision of products and services that meet the customer's needs;
2. The provision of the service that customers want, when they want it, and without operational errors;
3. The provision of satisfactory and consistent "aftercare", which is consistent and ongoing backup and response to customer queries.

Incidentally, it is often on (3) that many banks fall down, particularly larger banks with a large number of customers and a mass-market business model.

We noted earlier that banking products are essentially commoditised in nature. This being the case, the primary means to differentiate oneself from peer banks is through a reputation for good service and helpful, welcoming staff. While the product base of a bank is determined at the high or strategy level, even the most junior staff in a branch or call centre are in a position to influence the level of service. It is these employees who deal with customers on a daily basis, and so the way they greet customers, how efficiently and error-free they process transactions and requests, and their face-to-face and telephone manner will influence heavily the public perception of the bank as a good place to take their financial services requirements. These are all ingredients of good customer service.

Service provision is an important part of banking and being a banker, among others for the following reasons:

• Good customer service leads to customer satisfaction, which results in retained customers;
• Generally, it is quicker to deal with a satisfied customer than an unhappy one or one making a complaint, so business volumes should increase as they are processed more efficiently;
• Satisfied customers are a good source of referral business.

Factors that help drive a good customer service experience include:

- Pleasant, helpful, and efficient staff;
- Staff who are interested in customers' needs but also possess the detailed product and process knowledge to be able to answer questions and supply solutions accessibly;
- Receiving the products or service that meet the customer's needs and do not experience operational or process errors during their lifetime;
- Modern, attractive, user-friendly branches that may also include free Wi-Fi, a mini business lounge, and so on.

The factors that may contribute to a negative customer service experience include:

- Staff responding to customer queries with a bureaucratic and/or patronising answer;
- Rude, unhelpful, bored staff;
- Unkempt branches;
- Waiting in a long queue (be it in a branch, on a call centre phone, or on the internet);
- Call centre staff who don't know anything about you;
- Staff trying to sell products that weren't asked for in order to meet sales targets;
- Mistakes in processing requests.

The above are just a small sample of the positive or negative factors that determine whether a customer has a good or bad experience. Readers would most likely be able to add items to both lists from their personal experience. From this list it is easy to see how important the approach and motivation of customer facing staff are in ensuring good service.

All of the issues we list can be addressed by increasing staff, resources, training, and bandwidth. So while addressing customer service costs money, it is unarguably money well spent in the long run. Ultimately, it is all about treating the customer with courtesy or, as the author prefers, treating people the way you would like to be treated by people.[2]

Example 2.1 Importance of customer-facing staff

The transaction experience between a customer and a bank is often the one that takes the shortest time, certainly compared to the timespan of bank loan products, but it is often the most important part of the customer service experience. The interaction between the customer and branch

---

[2]A quote attributed to Richard Branson suggests that customer service isn't something businesses need to worry about: if they treat their staff properly, happy staff will automatically result in good customer service and hence happy customers. There is undoubtedly some truth in this.

or call centre staff is one that must be taken seriously by banks. Poor customer service at the "coal face" can often result in loss of business and poor reputation developing as the customer spreads the word. At the same time, if this experience is a good one, then reputation is enhanced.

It stands to reason then that customer-facing staff should be highly motivated, well trained, and reasonably well paid. This will help deliver a good customer service experience. The reality is that counter and call centre staff are often the least educated, most poorly paid staff in the bank. This does not look like a commitment to customer service excellence.

The private banking arm of a UK bank has a policy that its call centre staff must all be university graduates. This makes them slightly more mature and educated than school leavers. At the same time, all management entry-level staff are required to spend a year working in the call centre before they are eligible for promotion to more senior roles. This makes the staff motivated to deliver good service, as they cannot progress if they receive poor customer feedback.

Follow-up and aftercare

The automobile industry has a saying that the salesperson may be behind an initial sale, but it is the service department that ensures repeat business. This is applicable to banking as well. The initial loan approval, credit card issue, deposit facility, and so on are less likely to be followed by a long-term relationship if there is no follow-up service, or if there are errors in processing, issuing of statements, and so on.

In the first instance, the front office staff should follow up with a general call or email; for example, if a personal finance loan was taken out to purchase a car, the salesperson might enquire if this had been successful, what type of car it was, and if the customer was happy with it. Making this sort of follow-up means that:

- The banker is demonstrating good customer service and a personal touch;
- If there has been a problem, the banker has demonstrated a proactive interest in the customer and moreover is in a position to fix it now;
- There is a higher chance of repeat business with this customer because of the positive impression made, and the customer perceives the banker has having an interest in the customer personally.

Regular, but not intrusive, follow-up calls and efficiency in account settlement and operational processes are the key to good customer service.

Customer complaints

A complaint is any form of grievance that the customer has. In general, if a customer makes a complaint it reflects the fact that one or more aspects of the service or the bank itself has not met with the customer's expectations.

Customers make complaints for all manner of perceived problems or errors, or even slights. It may be a lack of satisfaction with the product, the level of service, the person the customer dealt with or the bank itself. The bank should have a straightforward and easy-to-follow process for dealing with complaints, but the important thing to remember is that a complaint is an opportunity to put things right, and so end in a positive outcome. For this reason, complaints should be viewed in a favourable light. Most unhappy customers don't complain, they simply take their business elsewhere (and this is easy to do with a commoditised product like banking services). So turning an unhappy customer into a happy one is actually another way to work towards retaining business.

Example 2.2   Customer complaint handling

New product launch

A bank has recently launched an integrated current account that combines savings, money transmission services, personal lending, and mortgage facilities into one account. As a result of customers being able effectively to offset their savings against their borrowing, the amount of interest payable on their borrowing is substantially reduced. The effect of this cash balance aggregation is that the interest payable on the mortgage balance is reduced such that the mortgage loan term is reduced. The bank has introduced this product mainly to remain competitive compared to its peers, but also because it is something that delivers a clear benefit to customers. A customer holding such an account will also be a long-term one, meaning that a deep customer relationship develops and so there is more chance of the bank's other products and services being purchased by the customer.

The introduction of this new product has been the subject of a marketing roll-out campaign, and while the account is available to new customers, it has also been offered to some, but not all, existing customers.

Shortly after the promotional campaign has ended, an existing customer who has held both a current account and a mortgage (as well as other products) with the bank for many years walks into the branch where his account is held and complains that this new product, which would have been of obvious benefit, was not offered to him. Moreover, he is angry that he was only made aware of it by a friend of his and not the bank. His friend had been offered (and taken up) the new account and was recommending it to him. As well as his disappointment at not being offered the product, the customer noted that the bank must now owe him a considerable amount of saving on mortgage interest, since that is what he would have received had he moved to this account at inception. His final argument was that as a customer of long standing who had always maintained his accounts in good order, as well as being a purchaser of the bank's other services, he should have been among the first people to have been notified of and offered the new product.

Complaint response

The orthodox response to a customer complaint in any industry should follow the "complaint resolution model", which involves empathy, fact finding, agreeing a solution, and confirming that the customer is now satisfied. The first stage is very important, because a failure to empathise with the customer not only acts as an obstacle to a mutually agreeable outcome, it also risks making the problem worse. In telephone or face-to-face contact, how one looks (or sounds) makes as much impact as what we actually say. So it is important to speak with empathy and state that you understand and accept why the customer is unhappy.

The next stage would be to find out why this customer was overlooked in the promotion campaign. It may have been administrative oversight (the equivalent of a "clerical error") or perhaps a "system error". This is beside the point, however, because the customer doesn't care why the bank made this oversight. So the explanation should occupy only a short time of the conversation; the key part is the solution. As to refunding the excess interest paid on the mortgage compared to what the customer would have paid had the account been offered to him at the start: the answer to this is self-evident, and the reader should not require this book to spell it out. The solution being agreeable to the customer, the immediate steps are straightforward. It is important also to follow up with the customer a few months later to check that all is well.

Customer satisfaction

Any commercial enterprise should always concern itself with ensuring that its customers are "satisfied". Good customer service is essential to long-term viability of a business, and working towards ensuring customer loyalty and retention is as important as winning new customers. Across different industries, including banking, a number of businesses spend a lot of time and effort undertaking slick and glossy marketing to attract new customers, but then have a poor aftercare service such that the customer is left feeling like a number and not a name. This is a trap into which a bank must not fall.

Ascertaining customer satisfaction levels is not straightforward to determine. Satisfaction surveys are a common approach, and certainly worthwhile undertaking, but are sometimes viewed with annoyance by customers and completion levels can be variable. It is important to act on the results of satisfaction surveys, otherwise over time the completion rate for them will fall to a negligible level. Responding directly to a customer who has made comments or recommendations in a survey is also important (provided the customer has ticked the box indicating they are happy to be contacted. But if they have ticked this box, then the bank should contact them.)

Survey design is important as well: one should follow these general guidelines:

- Ensure the survey is quick and easy to complete;
- Ensure it asks the right questions;
- Ensure that the request for feedback is designed to generate responses that are capable of being acted upon.

Finally, a satisfaction survey conducted in the communications media of the customer's choice is also an opportunity to highlight any new services or initiatives.

The two main indicators of customer satisfaction are retention levels and number of complaints. It is true that in the financial services industry, customer apathy is high and often people do not switch provider, not necessarily because they are satisfied with the bank, but because moving is perceived as too much aggravation. That said, customers staying with the bank should still be viewed as something to pursue proactively.

Complaint levels should be monitored regularly and compared to the industry and peer group statistics. A rising number of complaints is a worrying trend; however, banking is a mass volume business and as business grows the absolute number of complaints may increase while its share of the business is steady (or declining). On the other hand, many dissatisfied customers may not complain at all, they may simply leave. So both this and the satisfaction statistics are important metrics for a bank to monitor, investigate, and follow up.

PRODUCT DEVELOPMENT

Banks rarely introduce genuinely brand new, never-been-seen-before products. What people refer to as "new" products are usually variations on a theme, often tailored to meet specific customer requirements or changing market conditions. In any case, it is important always to review the bank's product suite and update it (add to it and remove from it) as the market changes. And introducing a "new" product that another bank brought out 2 years ago is still not necessarily a "bad" thing; the bank's customers may not have been aware of it anyway, and adopting it enables the bank to compete now with its rival.

A bank should review its product suite on a regular basis, and modify it as and when necessary, for the following reasons:

- Customer requirements: This is possibly the most important reason to introduce a new product (or modify an existing one), so as to keep the customer happy, but in practice carries less influence. It is rare for a customer to specify what he or she would like to see in a loan or deposit instrument, and often it is the bank that creates a new or modified product and then trumpets its benefits to the customer. That said, banks have had to respond to changes in society as all other commercial entities have had to: the biggest example is probably the switch to making services available on smartphones via a mobile app, or enabling payment via Apple Pay;
- Technological change: As we noted above, changes in social behaviour and/or technological capability dictate the need to introduce new products, although we should not confuse the actual product (a loan or deposit in whatever form) with a customer interface medium or a payments mechanism;
- Long-run strategy: Being the first to offer a new (and seemingly beneficial) banking product confers first mover advantages to a bank, which may help it to cement a dominant market position. Being the first to offer fixed-rate loans, or a current account that combines with your mortgage, or a premium credit card that combined airport lounge access: anything that is deemed useful and/or prestigious has the potential to deliver long-term benefits to the bank;
- Market and competitor action: This follows from the last point. Once a competitor has introduced a new product, providing it doesn't flop, it is apparent that its peers will need to offer it too, or risk losing customer business.

One can see that if a bank wishes to remain competitive and maintain or grow market share, it will need to review its product suite regularly and make innovations (or, more realistically, modifications) regularly. Of course, bringing in new products is a time-consuming and expensive business, so generally only the larger banks will have a new product development work stream.

PRODUCT PRICING

Pricing is the vital factor in all commercial transactions, although more so in some industries than others. It is a function of a number of interacting factors and getting it right may sometimes require a trial and error process. That said, ultimately the "market" clearing mechanism and supply and demand will have the greatest influence. Price dictates how well a firm will perform in the short and long term, but it is also connected closely to the customer's perception of value and quality. This is especially pertinent in financial services because value for money and quality are difficult to assess directly.

The basic conflict arises because the selling firm will want to set the price as high as possible, whereas the customer will wish it to be as low as possible. If the price is too high, the customer may walk away from the transaction because it is deemed not worth the cost. Then again, if the price is too low, there are two outcomes: (i) the product sells in high volume, but the net profit per unit is insufficient to maintain sustainable performance, or (ii) the customer deems the product to be of insufficient quality and again walks away from the transaction. In banking, however, the "price" is essentially the interest rate, which can never be too low (loan) or too high (deposit) for a customer, so (ii) is less of an issue. Or is it? A common perception among both retail and corporate customers is that if a bank's deposit rate is materially higher than its competitors', then the bank may be signalling that it is in trouble because it is "desperate" for funds. So there are additional subtle nuances to consider.

In all businesses, product pricing brings together the three additional elements of the marketing mix: it influences customer perception of quality, it acts as an incentive to purchase (promotion), and it is possibly the most important factor in persuading the customer to transact online (process). Of course, price and sales volume determine ultimately the firm's income and profit, but unless one is operating in a monopoly or oligopoly, one needs the price to be competitive with the market. Financial service firms have many factors out of their control when pricing, however, which means, apart from the very largest banks, they are more price takers than price makers.

Factors influencing pricing

Setting rates for balance sheet products in banking is on the one hand "complicated" because of the myriad internal and external factors one must take into account, but on the other hand relatively straightforward because for many instruments the market, and one's peer group, have already set the price. As with other industries featuring commoditised products, often a low(er) cost base and efficiency in operations (settlements, customer aftercare, statements, and the like) are what makes a bank long-term viable.

The factors that drive rates and fees in banking include:

- Market rates: The central bank base rate, the sovereign bond yield curve, and (where there is one) the interest-rate swap curve will all be major influences on bank product pricing. Then again, a large bank with excess customer deposits may be able to price beneath these levels;
- Target rate of return: As dictated by orthodox corporate finance theory, each bank will have an estimated "cost of capital" and this cost must be covered after profit has been netted against all operating costs and taxes.

So the set loan rate must in theory at least ensure that the return is higher than the cost of capital;[3]

- Covering costs: On the loan side, products may have a fee element as well as a set interest rate. How do these interplay when calculating overall return and ensuring costs are covered and target return is met? Loans that are repaid early may incur a cost for the bank provider, but the fee payable by the customer for doing so may not cover this cost. It is not straightforward to estimate the cost to the bank of this loan product optionality;
- Quality perception: High net worth or "premium" customers often are willing to pay more for what is to a large extent the same product, but with an element of personal service. The cost of this service drives a perception viewpoint, but needs to be sufficient to cover the bank's costs for service provision;
- Profit generator: The simple approach would be to say, "our target rate of return is 12%, so all loans must be charged at an interest rate that delivers this return net of costs and taxes". Or ideally one would be able to say, "the cost of providing this mortgage is X so we must charge to return X + Y", but the problem is that banking is both sides of the balance sheet, and loans and deposits are closely intertwined. It is difficult to determine the exact cost of providing one specific product. And the cost is not just the funding cost (see next), there are of course factors such as staff and branch networks to take into account;
- Funding cost: Even small relatively simple business model banks will have more than one deposit cost, and the larger the bank, the less straightforward it is to determine what the "funding cost" actually is. Of course, it must be covered when setting loan rates. And the deposit rate: what should that be? The peer group sets this to a large extent, but of course one's requirement for deposits and market presence will also influence this;
- Long-dated tenor: As any FX trader will tell you, it is a "mug's game" attempting to forecast rates and market conditions out to even 12 months, so how do you set the rate for a 25-year loan product such as a mortgage or a 5-year fixed term deposit? The market will be a very different place after 5 years let alone 25 years, so this issue makes fixed-rate pricing problematic. It is also why banks hedge their fixed-rate risk as far as possible. Setting interest rates as "floating" addresses this problem to an extent, and in some countries there are no fixed-rate products available, but fixed-rate is exactly what the customer desires, so banks generally provide them.

---

[3]Estimating the cost of a firm's equity is a great example of theory falling down when it comes into contact with reality. It isn't rocket science, because landing on the Moon or getting into orbit around Jupiter requires extreme precision, whereas corporate finance is all about assumptions and estimations. The true cost of equity is almost impossible to determine; a good proxy is the coupon paid on a Contingent Convertible ("CoCo") bond but only a few banks have issued CoCos. Thankfully for the reader, this topic is outside the scope of this book...

One can see that setting loan and deposit rates is a function of a number of factors, many of which involve uncertainty, which is why the subject can be considered "complicated". But as we noted at the start of this section, observing the market rates around you and knowing one's own cost base generally makes it fairly straightforward to set loan and deposit rates. Being an outlier on prices for either or both of these may cause reputational or customer perception issues.

Example 2.3   Retail mortgage interest rate
The demand for mortgages fluctuates with supply and demand, and also the state of the housing market (and economic conditions generally), and these factors are outside the bank's influence. At the same time, retail mortgage rates are very competitive. If one's peers are offering (for example) 25-year mortgages with the first 5 years fixed at rates between 2.1% and 2.4%, then it will be difficult to generate business if one is offering 3.0% – unless one is willing to lend to lower credit quality borrowers. This is an example of "risk–reward" driving prices.

Price setting process

As we alluded to above, price setting ideally will follow an established process. In the first instance, one will have a pricing objective; this is typically "obtain a rate of return after costs and taxes of X%". On the other hand, a specific business line may be seeking to build market share and price below this required rate. Such a "loss leader" product would be subsidised by other business lines, but is not uncommon with certain products such as syndicated loans or small business deposits.

Objective setting

The objective behind price setting may differ for different business lines and between different banks; what is important is to be able to articulate whatever the objective is so that everyone is aware of it. Specific objectives may be set to:

- Generate profit: This is the most straightforward and easy to understand objective, and is also easy to understand by staff;
- Generate growth: Maximising sales volume, perhaps to increase market share, is a common objective and common "key performance indicator", although in banking it may be an inappropriate one. To meet this objective, product pricing will need to be keenly competitive;
- Increase shareholder value: An orthodox objective in line with corporate finance principles. With this objective the price will be set to help drive share price upward;

- Promote customer satisfaction: it may be that ensuring customer satisfaction is the No. 1 priority for a financial services institution. In this case, price will be set to build a perception of value for money.

Product pricing

It is well to remember that every financial services product is, as we stated at the start of this chapter, simply a series of cash flows. At the same time, most banks are price takers and the external market is the most influential price driver. The general considerations for product pricing are noted below.

- Loans: the four factors used as inputs in an orthodox loan pricing model are:
  - Target rate of return, based on the bank's estimated cost of capital: The cost of capital rate will by definition capture the funding rate of the bank's other (non-equity) funding, so the bank's funding rate will be incorporated in the loan pricing;
  - Customer credit risk, quantified as a "probability of default" and credit rating: In theory, this is implied by the market price of the customer's existing debt; in practice this information is rarely available for all but large corporate borrowers and governments, so banks use a credit scoring model to imply a credit rating, from which a default probability can be implied. The higher the default probability, the higher the loan interest rate will be;
  - Loss-given-default (LGD), also known as recovery rate (RR): This is the amount of the loan value that will be recovered after customer default. It is not possible to know this until some time after default has occurred, so banks use an assumed value based on previous years' experience of this customer or the customer's peer group. The higher the LGD (that is, the lower the RR) the higher the loan rate will be;
  - Collateral: If the loan is provided unsecured ("clean"), it will be priced at a higher rate than if it is secured. This is because if the customer defaults, the bank will have recourse under the law to the security and hence be able to make good its loss. If the loan is overcollateralised, so the security provided is of greater value than the loan amount, the credit risk exposure is effectively nil. Hence, collateralised loans are charged at a significantly lower interest rate;
  - Funds transfer "price" (FTP): There is an additional pricing factor in all but the simplest banks, and that is an internal pricing input that in theory will be seeking to cover the bank's term liquidity premium (TLP). This is the FTP rate supplied by the Treasury department.
- Deposits: Customer deposit rates are strongly influenced by overall market rates. There are also two additional factors to consider:
  - The cost of providing the product and the cost of customer transactions: a current account generally pays no interest because there is the high transaction cost incurred by the bank given the number of frequent withdrawals. On the other hand, a notice period account or a fixed-term

deposit will have a higher interest rate. Some banks offer a higher interest rate on deposits that can only be transacted via the internet or digital mobile app, and not the branch network, as there is a lower associated cost with such accounts;

o The desire for retail and small business funding: the customer funding model is a common one for many banks and so here there is an imperative to pay a high deposit rate to attract customer funds.

• Fixed-rate or floating-rate: in general, customers prefer fixed-rate loans as they reduce uncertainty, but these generate interest-rate risk for the bank lender should market rates rise. This means a higher cost associated with these products because the risk needs to be hedged (see Chapter 12). Hence, the bank would prefer loans to be floating-rate; however, this will be at the expense of customer satisfaction. Only in a market where no bank offered fixed-rate loans could a serious market participant afford not to offer fixed-rate lending.

Pricing is an important factor in sustained success in banking, and it is not a straightforward process to operate because it is driven by so many factors. That said, most banks are more "price takers" than price makers, and so paradoxically, loan and deposit pricing is not something that needs to occupy large amounts of management time. This may sound like a contradiction, and certainly it is important to get pricing right, but the fact remains that unless one is operating a niche or outlier business model, the price range to remain competitive with most customer types is a relatively narrow one.

CONCLUSION

Banking should be about doing good work for and within society. That this has not been so for individual banks at all times in history is evident from the cases of bank failures and excess, not limited to but exemplified by the crash of 2007–2008. But this should not detract from the age-old truth that banking is integral to societal development, so the bank and all its staff from junior to executive should view their work and their goals in this light. And finally, customer satisfaction and employee satisfaction are linked: considering the working environment and team culture are as important as addressing the needs of the customer. Everything works together.

Chapter

3

CREDIT
ASSESSMENT AND
MANAGING CREDIT
RISK

PART 1

In this chapter we introduce the credit risk measurement framework in a banking operation. Credit-risky lending is the core business of a bank and its key to profitability. It is also the biggest driver of a bank's regulatory capital requirement. As credit risk exposure is what banks do, it cannot be avoided, so it must be well managed. Strategy, decision-making, risk–reward optimisation, diversification, and minimisation of loss are not possible without extensive and thorough credit risk management. The bank must use all of its qualitative and quantitative judgement capabilities to best assess credit risk.

This chapter is a long one and focuses on the risk management process and its principles. Regulatory capital requirements, which are driven primarily by credit risk exposure, are considered in Chapter 15.

The business of banking – lending money to and transacting with counterparties who carry default risk – creates credit risk exposure on the bank's balance sheet. This must be managed actively. In many cases, once a loan is originated, it cannot be removed from the balance sheet, so the discipline of credit risk management is essentially one of trying one's hardest to get the loan origination decision right, and avoiding concentration.

The other side of the approach to credit risk management is to sell loans where possible, to remove them from the balance sheet via securitisation, or to use credit derivatives. This topic is covered in detail in Choudhry (2007).

CREDIT PROCESS

Banks generally operate one of two types of approval process: (i) via a credit committee; or (ii) via delegated authority from the credit committee to a business line head. The committee process is designed to ensure that there is proper scrutiny of any transaction that commits the bank's capital. The sponsor bringing the transaction to the committee is the front office business line; the committee will approve or decline based on the risk–reward profile of the transaction.

Procedure (ii) is common for high-volume business, for which the committee process as a consequence of it being time consuming would not be practical. As we note above, there is uncertainty that the "know your risk" principle can be diluted, particularly in a competitive environment where a bank is trying to build volume. Given this uncertainty, "market share" should not be a performance indicator, or target, for a bank's business line. Rather, performance should be measured only via the amount of genuine shareholder value added that the business generates.

Credit limit principles

The point of credit risk limits is to set an upper bound to the loss that can be suffered by a bank at any one time.

The basic principles of credit limit setting are universal for every bank and follow the essential requirements of prudence and concentration. An element of diversification in the loan portfolio is necessary, although at all times the bank should practise the basic principle of "know your risk". In other words, diversity as an end in itself is not recommended good practice; a bank should diversify only into sectors that it thoroughly understands and in which it has some competitive advantage or valuable skill base.

In standard textbooks on finance and banking, we read that it is the capital base that drives the limit-setting process. Essentially, what this is saying in practice is that we take the amount of capital available and allocate it as per credit limit buckets for each of the businesses. Actually, the proper and intellectually robust way to do this is the other way around: the bank should determine its strategy and business model, as well as preparing budgets based on the risk exposure that it considers it has the expertise to manage. This process then drives the level of capital and regulatory capital that the bank should then set up. Once this amount is known and achieved, it can then be allocated to specific business lines as lower level credit limits by geography, industry, product, and so on.

The essential principles governing limit setting include the following:

- All single exposures should be sufficiently contained such that a complete default, running the risk of 0% recovery, can be contained within the existing capital base and does not endanger the bank as a going concern. In other words, after the loss the bank should still be within its regulatory capital limits;
- The loan portfolio should be diversified by industrial sector, geography, and product line, within the knowledge base and expertise of the bank;
- Set minimum internal (and, if desired, external) rating criteria below which the bank will not lend. For example, this may be "investment grade rated only" or "no lending to entities with an internal rating equivalent to BB/Ba2";
- Do not lend to obligors any amount that as a result overextends them and creates a situation in which repayment is put at risk. This requires that the "know your risk" dictum be applied equally to understanding the customer's risks. This should be assessed via an analysis of the borrower's financial indicators, including leverage ratio, debt service coverage ratio, and so on;
- Set limit categories to avoid concentration, and also by borrower rating.

As part of a transaction origination process, reviewers must consider what "ancillary business" can be generated from the same borrower. The bank must set a policy that dictates how much this ancillary business drives the origination process, whether the lending business can be a "loss leader" to an extent or can create sufficient shareholder value added in its own right.

Credit limit setting

The process of setting credit limits is very important to all banks – vanilla commercial banks, in particular – insofar as credit risk exposure generates

the highest losses for such institutions. The process should follow prudent and robust policy and be run according to cycle-proof principles to avoid getting overextended during a bull market, when loan origination standards are relaxed. Credit limits are set for a range of criteria, which are deliberately set as overlapping so as to ensure that all the various different categories of risk exposure are captured.

Macro-level credit limits are set per individual obligor, originated within the business lines but approved by the Executive Credit Committee and secondarily approved by the asset and liability committee (ALCO).[1] When necessary, if the size of a transaction dictates it, further approval may be needed by the Executive Management Committee (ExCo) and the Board itself. The level of capital allocation required for a particular limit application determines how far up the governance structure it needs to go. Formal limits on capital allocation are therefore set at ExCo approval level.

The limit-setting process is designed to produce overlapping limits. Limits will be set in the following categories:

- *Individual obligor* – This is further split into limit by product class, limit globally and limit locally. Sub-limits do not necessarily aggregate to the overall obligor limit: this is to prevent excess exposure in one product class or geographical region. Sub-limits are also set per currency. At all times, the obligor's exposure cannot exceed its overall limit;
- *Geographical region* – This is further split into country limits and individual regions within a country;
- *Industrial sector* – As no individual limit can be breached, any new capital-using transaction must fit into the capacity allowed by all three limit categories.

Limit excess is a serious breach of management governance and must be reported to ALCO (and, if necessary, ExCo) for corrective action. This can be effected by one or more of the following: (i) cease further business with the specific obligor; (ii) transfer some of the exposure, either by secondary market sale, securitisation, or hedging with credit derivatives; (iii) increase the limit; or (iv) transfer some capacity from another part of the business and/or another obligor.

LOAN ORIGINATION PROCESS STANDARDS

The loan origination process differs across banks. The detail of an individual specific process is not of major interest to us. What is important is that

[1]This describes the most common operating model. As we will show in Chapter 8, our recommended operating model for a number of reasons would be to place ALCO as the ultimate oversight authority for credit risk, approving the Credit Committee's policy guidelines.

this origination process adheres to basic principles of prudence, and that these are controlled and managed to ensure they are "through the cycle". That is, a reduction in standards, or a relaxation of standards during a period of economic growth, is something that should require Board approval. Enlarging the balance sheet during a bull market is a risky strategy, because it is during this time that standards are lowered and low-quality and/or underpriced assets are put on the book.

An example of this occurred at the failed UK banks Northern Rock and Bradford & Bingley, which originated large numbers of 100LTV and 125LTV mortgages, as well as more risky buy-to-let mortgages. The failed bank HBOS (in common with many banks at the time) operated a loan origination process for retail and corporate loans that delegated the approval decision to a black box computer model, which rated all applications in a tick box process that assigned a credit score and then approved on that basis. This is understandable for high-volume business models, but sacrifices a large element of "know your customer" in the approval process.

The essential guidelines for a through-the-cycle asset origination standards process include:

- *Know your customer*: For one-off and/or big-ticket transactions this principle is straightforward to apply. It is more difficult for large-volume business, particularly when the bank has adopted a black box system in which approval is granted by a model. (The applicant's details are input to the system and the system generates the approval without any loan officer or credit expert reviewing the application.) This is common practice for retail business such as credit card and mortgage applications, especially for business conducted over the telephone or internet. The danger is that, in a commoditised and competitive market, origination standards are lowered and the bank creates a pool of lower quality assets, the obligors for which it is not familiar with and whose financial strength it cannot be certain of. This was an acute problem for retail mortgage banks in the US, UK, Ireland, and Spain (among others) during 2002–2008, all of whom experienced a housing boom and bust in this period. Business best practice dictates that for all origination business, banks must know their customer base at all times (see below on mortgages). This means that the black box application process must be supplemented with a review by an experienced loan analyst;
- *Loan security*: The collateral acceptable for a loan should at all times be of sufficient liquidity and value. The bank must be able to realise the collateral if the obligor defaults. Genuine liquidity through all market conditions is restricted to sovereign liabilities only, so to cover for the loss of liquidity in other types of collateral, the bank must ensure sufficient margin over and above the loan value;
- *Subprime-lending restrictions*: Assets against which no collateral or insufficient collateral is taken should at all times be subject to restrictions and severe limits because these types of assets are the first to experience default

when the economy experiences a downturn. Mortgages that are not covered by sufficient collateral, such as 100LTV or 125LTV loans where the advance is greater than the value of the security, and other subprime mortgages or higher risk mortgages such as "self-certified" loans, should similarly be subject to restriction.

Excluding the peak of an overheating economy just about to enter a recession, loan defaults typically do not occur at the start or end of a loan's term. Another exception is right at the end of a bull market, when bank loan origination standards have been lowered and asset prices (credit spreads) are at their most undervalued, when banks write much low-quality business. Leaving that aside, the most common time of default is generally between 45 and 55 months after the loan start date. This means that default statistics lag considerably the actual state of the economy. Given historical default rates, which banks use to assist them in setting their credit limits, there is a danger that business continues to be written at lower credit standards at the time when the bank should be reigning in risky business. This is why the basic principles we summarise above should be observed at all times; they should act as a guiding light for a bank's Executive Credit Committee.

QUALITATIVE FACTORS: RETAIL AND NON-RETAIL EXPOSURES

Financial information, metrics, and analysis are central to the extension of credit. Banking is a customer business, however, and ideally decision makers must balance what numbers and models indicate with their own judgements. This approach is not followed by every bank, many of which follow the model-based approach in isolation. Ideally though, qualitative factors, despite being less tangible and harder to quantify, are crucial. There is no substitute for "know your customer".

Non-retail

Traditional banking was very much an "expert system", where bankers allocated credit in their sectors using subjective judgements. A popular framework was the "five Cs" – character, capital, capacity, collateral, and cycle – weighted as deemed appropriate. Without rigorous analytics, credit was sometimes extended to clients sponsored by the relationship banker who shouted loudest. But, again, soft factors are important and two broad areas for consideration are management and business.

Management

Management needs technical and organisational skills to succeed. The team must understand their business, demonstrate adaptability to changing environments, and have the capacity to control risk and act decisively. Do they have the ability to execute their plan? Experience and background checks should be completed to assess past track records of key leaders.

Consistency of message is important and progress in implementing plans can be checked against past annual reports and press releases. The quality and thoroughness of financial reporting are paramount. Face-to-face meetings are highly desirable and an opportunity to ask probing questions. The openness of responses is a good indicator as to whether a good working relationship is possible, through both good and difficult times. Will problems be disclosed promptly, so that they can be worked out with action taken?

Corporate governance must be examined so that the relationships and responsibilities between management and directors are understood. Good corporate governance ensures that proper checks and balances and protections are in place in the interests of investors, lenders, and other stakeholders, and also against unethical and illegal activities. Policies are defined and determined in the company charter and its bylaws, along with corporate rules and regulations. Strong internal controls, authorisation and approval procedures, and the independence of the internal audit department are vital.

Business

As a first step, a lender must understand the basics of its client's business. Beyond knowing the company's business sector, exactly what does it provide, and in so doing, how does it make money? In other words, what is the business model? If a bank cannot meet the company and attain a clear understanding of its business and external operating environment, it does not make sense to extend credit to it.

Success and long-term viability often depend on competitive advantage or franchise value. Is the company innovative, unique, or efficient? Does it benefit from a strong brand? Does it have sufficient market share? How high are the barriers for new entrants to challenge its position?

A bank needs to develop informed views on industry sectors and regions. A company can have a strong financial profile and top market share, but a weak or volatile business environment will reduce its credit quality. The state of the economy in its markets, diversification of buyer base, regulation, labour markets, and the pace and depth of structural change are all key factors.

Retail

For many years, retail credit decisions were made by local bank relationship managers based on qualitative factors. Models used to analyse wholesale loans could not be applied to small, unrated borrowers. Data has been expensive to collect and verify, with the cost amplified given small potential profit. Often, sound retail credit decision frameworks have been developed by smaller banks with dedicated resources, local knowledge, and relationships. Part of the decision should be based only on a borrower's ability to pay, but also on their sense of obligation to pay. Borrowers may have a local business and range of other debts (credit cards, mortgages, loans) to consider.

Strictly subjective retail credit decisions allow for inconsistency, and sometimes bias on the basis of race, religion, national origin, gender, or marital status. Perceptions as to the most favourable types of employment could also lead to less rational decisions.

INTERNAL RATINGS

Ratings act as the basis for bank credit approval, pricing, monitoring, and loan loss provisioning. Whereas external ratings agencies were founded in the nineteenth century (mostly to analyse US railroads), bank internal ratings only took off in the 1990s with Basel I.

Pricing, provisioning, and capital management

The Basel Committee defines a rating as a "summary indicator of the risk inherent in an individual credit". Ratings "typically embody an assessment of the risk of loss due to failure by a given borrower to pay as promised". A rating system is defined as "the conceptual methodology, management processes, and systems that play a role in the assignment of a rating". Ratings have two dimensions: (i) borrower propensity to default; and (ii) transaction characteristics (for example, product, terms, seniority, and collateral).

Under the Basel "Standardised Approach", banks use ratings developed by external rating agencies. The starting point for capital required against assets is 8% of the nominal, against which a risk weighting is applied according to a matrix of ratings and types (sovereign, bank, or corporate). An AAA-rated sovereign asset with a 0% risk weight requires no capital. A $100 million A-rated bank asset with a 20% risk weight requires 1.6% or $1.6 million of capital ($100 million × 8% × 20%).

A bank loan pricing model is based on the capital required and the target return on that capital. The model considers funding, default probability, recovery rate, and taxes as costs against the interest rate charged in calculating a net gain to weigh against the capital required. If loan rates in the marketplace are below the rate needed to meet the target return, the bank needs to decide whether it will accept a lower return to maintain market share or the client relationship.

Since Basel II, banks meeting strict criteria are permitted to use internal ratings to calculate regulatory capital for credit risk. The rationale is that "internal ratings can prove to be more sensitive to the level of risk in a bank's portfolio". Internal ratings may incorporate supplementary customer information, which is usually out of the reach of external credit assessment institutions.

Banks will (have incentives to) further refine internal credit risk management and measurement techniques.

Internal ratings must satisfy the "use test" and serve as the basis of risk, limits, pricing, provisioning, and capital management decisions, and not be simply for regulatory risk capital calculations.

Both Basel I and Basel II were designed to ensure that banks maintain an adequate capital buffer based on an expected loss methodology. The standard credit loss profile, illustrated in Figure 3.1, lies behind the capital calculation.

Figure 3.2 shows how this general credit losses distribution drives the minimum capital level. Expected losses are covered in the loan asset pricing, typically via the target rate of return (given by the cost of capital). Unexpected

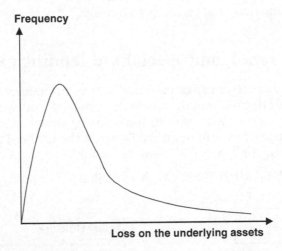

Figure 3.1   Credit loss distribution

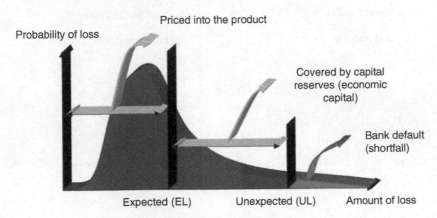

Figure 3.2   Applying credit loss distributions into capital calculation

losses are covered by the capital reserves, shown in Figure 3.2 as economic capital. Of course, regulatory capital rules assign risk weightings based on the type of loan asset counterparty, and these risk weightings drive the regulatory capital minimum. In the Basel II regime, credit ratings are used to determine risk weightings for banks that use the standardised approach.

Where losses exceed the unexpected losses used to derive the capital calculation, the shortfall results in cessation of the bank as a going concern.

In theory (and in practice if one was putting together a bank's capital structure from scratch today), the expected loss profile effectively drives the capital structure. As Figure 3.3 shows, if the UL is 10%, then this is the minimum equity base requirement.

Critics of Basel II believed that while giving banks more responsibility to measure risk creates greater focus and better analysis, it opened up possibilities for opportunistic behaviour and regulatory arbitrage.

Retail, non-retail, and specialised lending exposures

The dominant practice of banks is to use ratings to manage corporate credit risk as described. Ratings remain relatively constant, and are often linked to a schedule of average default probabilities. Rating mobility is a function of a bank's philosophy, which can be either Through-the-Cycle (TtC – more active migration) or Point-in-Time (PIT – less migration).

The quality of the portfolio shifts as the distribution of ratings evolves.

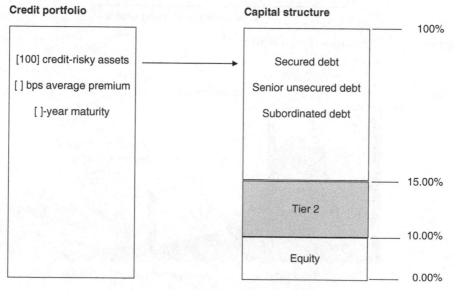

Figure 3.3   Risky asset portfolio and capital structure

Retail exposures are not generally managed using ratings on an individual borrower basis. Exposures are grouped into segments with similar risk characteristics. Often, the distinction between borrower and product is limited or eliminated. Borrower characteristics (for example, population segment, income, credit history) and those of the facility (for example, product type, credit limit, collateral) are blended in formulating segments. To demonstrate homogeneity of risk, genuine segmentation requires all borrowers within a segment to be treated the same.

Retail exposures include loans (for example, personal finance, education loans, auto loans, or leasing), revolving credits (for example, overdrafts, revolving credit plans, or home equity lines), credit cards, residential mortgages, and small business facilities. Typically (and from a BIS regulatory stand point) retail exposures are managed on a product (facility) basis as opposed to an obligor basis.

There are four tests for characterisation as retail exposure:

- Product;
- Credit to individuals;
- Manageable as a pool of exposures;
- Low value.

For retail exposures, delinquent exposures are managed separately.

In specialised lending, both the source of repayment of a loan and prospects for recovery in an event of default are based on the cash flow from a project or property rather than on the ongoing, open-ended operations of the borrower. Assets pledged as collateral serve to mitigate risk and as a secondary source of repayment. Types of specialised lending include project finance, income producing real estate, high volatility commercial real estate, object finance, and commodities finance.

Specialised lending possesses unique loss distribution and risk characteristics. Given the source of repayment, the exposures exhibit greater risk volatility, with both high default rates and high loss rates in times of distress. Banks use different internal risk rating criteria. Historical data is often not as readily available or comparable and relevant to the current special financing exposures being assessed.

A special risk management focus for specialised lending includes financial strength and flexibility, collateral control, project phase, and marketability.

Consistency: internal ratings and external credit rating agencies

As described earlier, the largest rating agencies have been performing analyses and collecting data for well over a century. Rating agencies have large teams and resources, and regular contact with the entities they rate. However, while external ratings are undoubtedly useful, they are no more than opinions, and are not a substitute for analysis and informed decision-making. Banks with borrower relationships may have insights that lead them to assign different ratings from those of the agencies.

Rating agencies serve a wide range of constituencies that use ratings for differing purposes. As such, there are a range of opinions on their process. Some want ratings to be adjusted quickly to give signals of possible deterioration, while others want them to be more stable and uninfluenced by short-term developments. The role of the economic cycle in ratings is often debated.

Rating agencies rely on the accuracy and completeness of information supplied by borrowers, and do not search for or expose fraud. Analysts concluding that available data raises some questions can assign more conservative ratings or fail to assign or withdraw ratings, but users cannot rely on rating agencies for more.

Some are of the opinion that ratings are biased to the upside, given that borrowers pay for their ratings.

COUNTERPARTY RISK PARAMETERS

Counterparty risk parameters for non-defaulted assets

After assigning ratings, banks estimate risk parameters for key exposures including probability of default (PD), loss given default (LGD), and exposure at default (EAD). Exposures are risk weighted by Basel-mandated asset class (corporate, sovereign, bank, retail, and equity) to arrive at total risk weighted assets (RWA) to determine capital requirements.

Probability of default (PD) describes the likelihood of default over a particular time horizon. PD estimates are derived from internal default experience, mapping to external data, and statistical default models. Except for pooled retail exposures, PD for a particular grade must be a long-run average of 1-year default rates. Retail PD estimates must be derived primarily from internal data.

Expected loss given default (ELGD or LGD) is defined as the "economic" loss for non-defaulted assets, accounting for inflows (via sale of supporting collateral, unsecured recoveries, and guarantor payments) and outflows (via additional post-default drawdowns on the credit facility, internal administrative costs, and external legal and valuation fees) measured relative to the exposure at default.

An "economic" loss (unlike an accounting loss) takes into account all relevant factors including material discount effect, and material direct and indirect costs associated with holding and collecting the defaulted facilities.

Methods used to estimate ELGD for credit facilities fall into one of two categories. Subjective methods are primarily driven by expert judgement and used mainly on portfolios with few defaults and/or by banks in the early stage of internal model development. Objective methods largely rely on formal mathematical procedures, and can be further divided into explicit methods (i.e. market LGD approach and workout LGD approach) and implicit methods (i.e. implied market LGD approach). The decision to select one of these objective methods is largely driven by the nature of the portfolio in question, exposure type (loan vs bond), and the availability of data.

Estimates are based on historical recoveries (including collateral) in economic downturn conditions and used in calculating regulatory capital. LGD is economic rather than accounting loss, which includes direct and indirect costs discounted back to the point of default. Interpretations of key parameters differ by bank and are not always comparable. Definitions of downturn vary, with some banks using two consecutive quarters of negative GDP growth, while others emphasise product downturn rather than overall economic conditions. The relative financial condition and capabilities by bank are important, as funding levels affect discount rates, stronger banks negotiate better collateral terms, and more capable and well-staffed teams work through defaults more quickly and efficiently. While PD is largely the same across all types of exposures to a borrower, LGD is likely to vary significantly by product. Banks are expected to be conservative, and auditors and external supervisors must be able to validate the model. Repurchase Value Estimators are used when banks need to take possession of and sell property and goods.

Expected exposure at default (EAD) is the gross exposure upon default. For fixed credit facilities (such as term loans), EAD is simply the amount outstanding (although EADs slightly above 100% are not uncommon given interest accrual). For revolving facilities (such as lines of credit, liquidity facilities, and overdrafts), EAD is the drawn amount plus an estimate of the amount of the remainder of the commitment likely to be drawn at the time of default. These estimates are often referred to as either the Credit Conversion Factor (CCF) or Loan Equivalent.

LGD and EAD for corporate, sovereign, and bank exposures are based on a BIS required period of no shorter than 7 years. Estimates for retail exposures are based on at least 5 years of data unless the bank demonstrates that recent data is a better predictor.

If a supervisor agrees that a bank's total expected loss is less than its provisions, the difference can be included in Tier 2 capital. This can occur in practice as the assumptions used in modelling the provisions required do not necessarily align with those for the capital calculations (for example, a point in time LGD is often used for provisioning, while a downturn LGD is used as a basis for capital calculations).

Counterparty risk parameters for defaulted assets

When exposures default, actual losses can exceed LGD estimates. At this stage, banks need to make a Best Estimate of Expected Losses (BEEL) for each defaulted asset considering the current economic climate, so as to cover the possibility of additional losses. Again, historical data from a full economic cycle should be used as a basis, with losses consistent with any provisions or charge-offs taken.

Impaired assets

Treatment of assets with a reduced likelihood of performing in full was a source of controversy in the financial crisis, as with hindsight it is clear that often problems should have been identified and loss provisions taken earlier. Under the IAS 39 "incurred loss" model, recognition of credit losses was delayed until there was evidence of a trigger event. While designed to limit the ability to build hidden reserves that could be used to boost earnings in future difficult periods, the model enabled earnings management, which postponed losses.

Under IFRS 9, banks are required to recognise expected credit losses at all times and to update the amount of expected credit losses recognised at each reporting date. IFRS 9 broadens the information that banks are required to consider when determining expected credit losses (for example, reasonable and supportable historical, current, and forecast information). To reduce complexity, the same impairment accounting will now be applied to all financial assets.

This forward-looking approach is much more transparent for central banks, regulators, creditors, and shareholders. The model eliminates thresholds and triggers for loss reporting, which should reduce "cliff effects". Disclosure is enhanced, with banks required to explain the basis for their expected credit loss calculations, to explain how they measure expected credit losses, and to explain how they assess changes in credit risk.

DEFAULTS EVENTS AND MEASURES

Even default has no simple definition. While some advocate a quantitative standard for clarity and easy understanding, most regulators believe interpreting default as only non-payment fails to capture clear indicators of loss and recognition of increased expected losses.

The most common objective definition of default is when the borrower is:

- 90 days past due on payment (with allowance made for failure to pay given technical/administrative issues); and/or
- Placed in bankruptcy protection.

Rating agencies use this narrow definition above.

Wider definitions include when the borrower is:

- In default on another obligation; and/or
- In breach of any contractual condition (technical default, for example, breach of covenants, failure to submit audit statements on time).

In practice, banks can only use broader definitions if information is available to them. Sometimes the definition of default is addressed in product documentation, which includes covenant breach and cross-default. Products specifying a broad range of technical defaults mean that default may likely occur well before non-payment. Laws vary by jurisdiction as to the lender's ability to place the borrower in default, so banks may have difficulties in being consistent.

Defaults events and measures: specialised lending

The cash waterfall is the priority of payments by which classes of lenders receive interest and principal. Senior lenders are paid first, followed by junior (also called subordinated or mezzanine) lenders. On loan initiation or bond purchase, senior lenders receive lower returns in exchange for lower credit risk. In a default, equity holders receive what (if anything) remains after assets are distributed to debt holders.

Lenders analyse the size of the company or project assets and collateral relative to debt to assess the value of seniority. If the loan is a general obligation of a large company to finance a small project, seniority may be less important. If repayment is secured only on the asset financed and the cash flow it can generate, a higher priority of payment may be more important.

Loan covenants require borrowers to meet certain conditions over the period of a loan. Breaches of covenants may trigger default, higher pricing, penalties, or termination ("call" or "acceleration") of the loan. Covenants can relate to reporting standards, financial performance, ownership, or business activities.

Common financial covenants include:

- **Debt Service Coverage Ratio (DSCR)** is the ratio of income less expenses to interest and principal payments. DSCR is the main measure to determine whether cash flow is sufficient to service debt. It can be applied to all types of transactions and used as a covenant set at the minimum level acceptable to the lender;
- **Loan Life Coverage Ratio (LLCR)** is the net present value of cash flow available for debt servicing to total debt. LLCR is like DSCR but is a useful standard in project finance as the analysis covers the term of the transaction. LLCR is more difficult to monitor if project cash flows are likely to be inconsistent;
- **Loan to Value Ratio** is central to residential mortgage lending. LTV allows banks to gauge how far prices can fall before loss is incurred should they need to foreclose on the loan and liquidate the property.

Covenants may be waived, and only serve to ensure early alerts and constructive dialogue when conditions become more difficult. However, covenants do cede some control to banks, and management can be forced to take actions not believed by them to be in the best interests of the company.

Defaults events and measures: cross-border lending

Currency convertibility and transfer risk is the loss that can occur if local currency cannot be converted to another currency and/or transferred abroad. The situation can arise when a country is experiencing capital outflows in a time of political and economic crisis. Governments may impose currency controls, or there may be simply no market for the currency. The risk is different from devaluation or appropriation of assets.

Risk assessment must include analysis of economic conditions, political situation, and legal framework. To the extent the country is integrated into the global economy through trade and capital markets activity, currency restrictions would be more likely to be avoided given the severe repercussions.

Risk can be mitigated by the use of cash collateral and letters of credit with banks in other jurisdictions, or increases in interest rates linked to currency disruption.

Impairment vs default

As discussed earlier, definitions of default vary. Impairment can be described generally as when an exposure is judged by management to have deteriorated so there is no longer a reasonable expectation as to the collection of the full amount as scheduled.

Banks can analyse a number of triggers for borrower deterioration to determine whether an asset is impaired:

- Macroeconomic deterioration:
    - National or local economic conditions relevant to the asset class;
    - Unemployment rate;
    - Property prices for mortgages;
    - Industry (or sector).
- Company:
    - Borrower requests for forbearance;
    - Breach of contract or covenants;
    - Credit rating;
    - Debt service capacity;
    - Financial performance;
    - Cash flow;
    - Net worth;
    - Decrease in turnover;
    - Loss of customers or market share;

- o Diversion of cash flows from earning assets to support non-earning assets;
  - o Prospects of the guarantors;
  - o Collateral;
  - o Country risks.
- Mortgage portfolio:
  - o Decrease in rents received;
  - o Absence of refinancing options.
- Retail portfolio:
  - o Early delinquency (for example, one payment in arrears);
  - o Continual high utilisation of facilities;
  - o Steady increase in total debt for the client;
  - o Income less than total debt repayments.

Banks should disclose impairment triggers to supervisors.

Loans generally appear on bank balance sheets as assets using nominal principal values. Once a loan is identified as impaired, the current probability of default and loss given default is applied and discounted to establish the new value. Both the loan and capital (shareholders' equity) are marked down on the balance sheet. Impairment provisions appear on the income statement as an expense. Debate as to the optimal balance accounting for loans is ongoing, with some arguing that constant marking-to-market is needed.

PRODUCT CREDIT RISK MEASUREMENT

Credit risk measurement for standard loans involves the most basic credit risk measures. Some products are undrawn, so exposure is dependent on usage. These contingent liabilities are off-balance-sheet, and Credit Conversion Factors (CCFs) are applied as estimates of risk. The exposure is multiplied by the CCF to assess capital required.

Banks provide liquidity facilities for clients to draw down as needed. Facilities can be committed or uncommitted. Clients issuing commercial paper (CP) (marketable notes maturing in 1 year or less) need backstop liquidity facilities to repay maturing issuance should rollover not be possible. Backstops are a rating agency requirement for the high credit ratings demanded by CP investors.

Under Basel I, the CCF for liquidity facilities under 1 year was 0%. Under Basel II, the CCFs for standard banks providing facilities under 1 year and over 1 year were 20% and 50%, respectively. In reassessing risk and increasing capital requirements under Basel III, the distinction based on term is eliminated and the CCF for all facilities is 50%. Lower CCFs for facilities that could be drawn only in the event of market disruption (not client credit deterioration) have been eliminated.

Any facility that is uncommitted and can be cancelled unconditionally and without notice, and requires the bank to proactively approve new drawdowns, has a CCF of 0%.

Guarantees of financial indebtedness are integral to world trade. These include loan guarantees, letters of credit, and banker's acceptances. Banks must categorise guarantee facilities in three ways: unutilised, utilised, and utilised with payment/obligations owing to the beneficiary. CCFs are generally 0–50%, 50–100%, and 100%, respectively.

BIS rules stated previously that bank exposure to another bank's letter of credit was subject to a "sovereign floor", for example, the risk weighting could not be lower than that of the sovereign. This was prohibitive for importers using local banks to issue letters of credit in countries where the sovereign was unrated and external ratings were used by the other bank. The BIS has now waived the sovereign floor to allow the risk weighting to go below 100%.

The BIS also eased proposals for stricter capital measures for trade finance in certain short-term, self-liquidating, trade-related contingent liability products collateralised by the underlying shipments, allowing the CCF of 20% to apply to the actual remaining maturity rather than a 1-year floor.

Other off-balance-sheet banking products include Revolving Underwriting Facilities, in which a group of underwriters agrees to provide loans or buy notes in the event that a borrower is unable to issue in the capital markets.

CREDIT RISK TERMINOLOGY

The following terms are important in understanding credit risk measurement.

Lending exposure (legal entity)

As a first step, lenders must know exactly to whom they are lending. The legal entity and type (individual, partnership, trust, or corporation) and its powers to conduct business and engage in borrowing must be fully understood. The structure can be simple or highly complex, involving organisational charts and legal shells.

Group entity (obligor)

Banks must analyse exposure to all entities in a legal or economic group when setting limits, and take a view on the group's industry sector to manage concentration. Given support and cross-support arrangements, the performance of non-borrowing entities can either improve or hinder the ability of the borrowing entities to pay. Covenants and default events can be negotiated to apply to the entire group. The bank must be confident that controls are in place so that intragroup loans and transactions are conducted at fair market terms and on an arm's length basis.

On some transactions, co-borrowers are jointly and severally liable, meaning that if one borrower can no longer repay debt, the other is responsible for full payment.

The Basel Committee recognises that banks have complex global businesses across regions and tax regimes, necessitating multiple entities across the group. However, banks' own intragroup support arrangements and dependencies must be fully understood with risks well managed.

Facilities/accounts (transactions): drawdown profile

Credit agreements include the terms of drawing down the amounts of a facility and types of accounts (for example, revolving credit account, term loan account). A schedule of drawdown amounts and dates can be specified, particularly in project finance. Drawdowns are subject to meeting the conditions precedent, which can involve providing these documents:

- Articles of incorporation demonstrating that the company can enter into the transaction;
- Financial statements;
- Project agreements, licences, consents;
- Rating agency confirmations;
- Legal opinions;
- Corporate authorisations or Board approvals for the transaction, which confirm execution by specified individuals.

Often, the provision of collateral is the precedent for another condition.

The timing and likelihood of drawdown are necessary to estimate exposure and risk.

Collateral

Collateral is (an) asset(s) pledged by the borrower to the lender to secure a loan. In the event of default, and where the bank decides not to restructure the transaction (and the counterparty cannot refinance externally), the bank will take possession of the collateral in order to offset their loss exposure. It is essential that the lender "perfect a security interest" in the collateral, so that it can easily take control and sell without dispute should the borrower fail to meet the terms of the loan.

Collateral ranges from cash, securities as well as property, to the asset being financed. The lender is best protected if the collateral is marketable in all economic conditions, characterised by low price volatility and denominated in the same currency. Banks can choose to lend up to a percentage of the value of the asset to protect against a decline in value. This is called taking a "haircut", and the concept behind fixing loan-to-value percentages in the residential mortgage market. Some loans are "overcollateralised", meaning the bank receives collateral worth more than the loan. Collateral value must be monitored regularly, with additional collateral ("margin") required if the value declines.

Taking collateral must not be seen as risk-free lending. Banks must only lend to clients they believe have the ability to repay from their operations. Reputation risk, collateral value volatility, and the process of taking and liquidating collateral must be considered.

Guarantees

Guarantees take many forms and are issued by all types of entities including banks, corporations, and sovereigns, as well as individuals. Banks issue direct guarantees and indirect or counter-guarantees (where non-performance of a second party's guarantee is guaranteed).

Guarantees include:

- A payment guarantee, which assures the seller that the purchase price will be paid on the agreed date if all contractual obligations are met;
- An advance payment guarantee, which assures the buyer that the advanced payment will be reimbursed if the seller does not meet contractual delivery obligations in full;
- A performance bond, which serves as collateral for costs incurred by the buyer due to failure of the seller to provide goods and services promptly and as contractually agreed;
- A bid bond (tender bond), which secures the organiser's expenses in tenders by requiring participants to pay if their bid is accepted but withdrawn;
- A warranty obligations guarantee, which secures any claims by the buyer for defects appearing after delivery;
- A letter of indemnity, which secures the shipping company against any claims if goods are delivered prior to receipt of the original bill of lading;
- A credit security bond, which serves as collateral for loan repayment.

Sovereign guarantees back projects deemed in the public interest, and support development and promotion of infrastructure, new industries, regions, and exports. Many sovereigns have state-owned development and export/import banks.

On-balance-sheet netting

Banks offset client loans against deposits to reduce risk and capital requirements through netting. This is possible when:

- A bank has a well-founded legal basis for concluding that netting is enforceable in each relevant jurisdiction in all conditions, supported by documents such as legal opinions and netting agreements;
- The maturity of the deposit is at least as long as the loan;
- A bank has adequate reporting and monitoring systems in place so it can always identify the relevant assets and liabilities as well as rollovers.

Netting allows a bank to do more business with its clients.

Netting is key to non-balance-sheet activities and businesses including securities clearing, payment systems, and derivatives.

Derivatives and hedging

Derivatives are financial contracts with a value derived from the performance of securities, interest rates, currencies, commodities, indices, credit, and other assets. Derivatives can have set terms (contract size, dates, underlying) and be exchange-traded and highly liquid, or bilateral tailored contracts.

Banks hedge by taking derivative positions designed to perform in a manner opposite to their actual exposures. For example, a bank with a large credit exposure to a corporation can take a position in a credit derivative that would pay out if the corporation defaulted. "Basis risk" is the risk that the derivative does not perform in the direction expected or in the same magnitude as the position being hedged.

The most common types of derivatives are:

- Futures: a commitment to buy or sell at a fixed price at a fixed date in the future;
- Options: the buyer pays a premium for the right to buy (call) or sell (put) at a fixed price within a fixed time period;
- Swaps: parties agree to exchange a fixed payment against a floating payment.

Derivatives do not require the actual purchase and sale of the underlying. Most positions are closed out by buying or selling prior to or at maturity, with the gain or loss exchanged in cash. Derivatives are generally margined throughout the term of the trade.

MODEL DEVELOPMENT

Credit risk management models serve many purposes. While generating outputs mandated by regulation, models must be built to meet the needs of the bank and its business for optimal decision-making. Different measures provide a variety of insights in both normal and stressed conditions, and aid in balancing profitability and business objectives with risk. It is imperative that models are built on sound and reliable data.

Risk estimates (PDs, EADs, and LGDs) for capital purposes may not be the same for pricing or impairment purposes. Point-in-time or through-the-cycle views may differ. For example, one will not necessarily price a 12-month loan on a through-the-cycle credit expectation.

Probability of default

Probability of Default is estimated from a range of sources. The simplest and most widely used throughout the world is rating agency ratings. Banks also use their own historical default databases or purchase those compiled by third parties. For some sectors, decades of default data is available. PD can also be estimated by monitoring bond and credit default prices.

Statistical methods to estimate PDs include:

- Linear regression;
- Discriminant analysis;
- Logit and Probit models;
- Panel models;
- Cox proportional hazards model;
- Neural networks.

Banks must make careful judgements as to how data is used. While default is rare (roughly 2% on average globally), consequences for debt portfolios are severe given small earnings margins and no upside as in equities. While modelling monthly or quarterly data from portfolio segments is common, defaults observed may not be a good indicator for forward-looking analysis if a portfolio is growing or the market is new. The risk of PD being understated is significant.

An important concept in PD is "distance to default". PD increases as the market value of the assets of a company decreases towards the book value of the liabilities. Issues considered are:

- The current asset value;
- The distribution of asset values at time horizon;
- The volatility of the future assets value at time horizon;
- The level of the default point, the book value of the liabilities;
- The expected rate of growth in the asset value over the horizon;
- The length of time horizon.

The default point is sometimes when the two values converge, although companies may continue to trade if the liabilities are longer term and creditors believe in the business.

Models must provide PD in both unstressed and stressed economic scenarios. Higher interest rates, which make debt more costly, can be integral to stress scenarios. "Point-in-time" PDs are estimated for unstressed conditions while "through-the-cycle" PDs estimate the trough. Both are fixed for 1 year, but PIT PDs will be volatile as the economy evolves, while TTC PDs will be more stable. Obligors must be classified as to how they are likely to respond to the economic cycle at both peaks and troughs.

Loss given default

The most common loss given default (LGD) measure is "Gross" (total losses are divided by EAD) because it is simple to calculate and requires the least data. Another LGD measure is "Blanco" (losses divided by the unsecured portion of a credit line), which is important when a bank has significant collateralisation.

As a conservative measure, collateral is "haircut" in the calculation to allow for a fall in value, thereby decreasing LGD. Banks calculate "Downturn" LGD.

LGD can be difficult to calculate as bank recovery rates vary and workouts take different lengths of time, so peer data is not always useful. Formulas have been developed to best achieve comparability. Models "time weight" LGD, meaning historical data is not analysed simply by averaging loss severity of each default, but also considers the time periods in the economic cycle when they are likely to occur.

There are three objective LGD estimation methods:

- Market LGD, which is observed from market prices of defaulted bonds and marketable loans soon after default events. The main benefit is that actual prices can be used. This is the methodology used most by the rating agencies;
- Workout LGD, which is estimated cash flows from the workout process, based on estimated exposure and a discount rate. Users must monitor the timing of payments received and consider the riskiness of any restructured debt;
- Implied Market LGD, which is derived from prices of bonds deemed to be high risk. This is the least developed of the methods, but has the benefit of a large pool of market data.

Given the challenges involved in calibrating LGD models, banks reference external data sources, such as Pan European Credit Data Consortia (PECDC), S&P LossStat, and Paris Club restructure data.

Exposure at default

Exposure at Default is the gross total of extended credit plus estimated additional drawings for 1 year or until maturity. The greatest analytical challenge in setting Credit Conversion Factors (or Loan Equivalents) is estimating additional drawings. Globally, unused commitments are huge and it is logical that a corporation would seek to drawn down in stress scenarios. Examples of products where modelling is needed include committed loan and liquidity facilities and credit cards.

Strong information management systems are vital in assessing EAD, as the bank must ensure that troubled entities draw only under the terms permitted by the facility and up to the limit. Collateral must be monitored, priced, and margined. The bank must deal efficiently and quickly in default situations.

RISK MONITORING AND MODEL VALIDATION

Banks must have a standard and regular process for validation and review of credit risk models. Validation must assess the accuracy and consistency of ratings and risk components in an independent manner, with input from relevant departments. A fundamental role of supervisory authorities is to ensure this process is conducted in a meaningful and thorough manner, with banks making available the inputs and calculations.

Backtesting is an important part of model validation, and includes comparison of model results against actual ratings migration and loss experience by category. Benchmarking of internal estimates against external sources is another useful quantitative review, and can add objectivity. The entire process should make apparent changes in drivers, trends, and correlations. Outcomes can include revision of risk categories and adjustments to data timeframes. Strong risk aggregation capabilities are vital and deficiencies (a problem in the crisis) should be exposed to ensure business grows only as quickly as control infrastructure. Business line leaders must have a basic understanding of the models and ensure their risks are fully incorporated into the bank-wide risk process.

Risk appetite statement

Risk appetite is the quantum of risk a bank is prepared to assume in pursuit of its strategy, and is established, integrated into business plans, and monitored by the Board. The risk appetite statement sets out the risk profile by identifying risks and boundaries. The statement should be actionable and include quantitative measures. High level limit and target measures can be set against earnings at risk, probability of insolvency, and the chance of experiencing an annual loss. Best-practice discipline dictates that the bank's Board sign off on the risk appetite statement. By being a Board-issued document, it ensures that adherence to risk tolerance is taken seriously as a requirement of senior management.

Implementation requires proper policies, procedures, and controls. Regulators will monitor the level of Board involvement, adherence to policies, breach of limits, and policy changes. Crucially, the risk appetite statement must be used to identify excessive risk taking, which can threaten a bank.

TRADING BOOK CREDIT EXPOSURES

Trading book exposures must be managed actively and held for "trading intent" or short-term gain. Positions may be proprietary or arise from market making to serve clients. Capital should be allocated to cover losses from a very short period (10–20 days). Standardised method banks must use set parameters, but advanced banks with approved internal model banks can use their own EAD and Value-at-Risk. In addition to the risk of default of the issuer of the securities, there is a small credit risk in trading, as the counterparty could default before settlement with the position needing to be replaced at a worse price. Most securities trade on a delivery-vs-payment basis (DVP), so there is little or no settlement risk in exchanging securities and cash.

Swaps and exotics exposures

Exchange traded derivatives are margined and guaranteed by exchanges, minimising credit risk. Over-the-Counter (OTC) derivatives are bi-lateral contracts with substantial Counterparty Credit Risk (CCR), which must be carefully measured and managed.

Swap counterparties agree to exchange fixed-rate for floating-rate payments. If one counterparty defaults, the other has a loss if the trade has a mark-to-market gain. Assuming no recovery, the loss is the present value of the net payments remaining (replacement cost). Non-defaulting counterparties with a negative mark-to-market position are not released from the position and will likely make a single cash payment to the receiver. There may also be some transaction cost in replacing the position in the market.

Buyers of options have similar CCR risk.

Potential future exposures and regulatory add-ons

Swaps, foreign exchange and interest rate forwards, options, other derivatives, and securities finance transactions (repo) are subject to fluctuations in value over the life of the contract. Besides replacement value, credit risk measurement must include Potential Future Exposure (PFE), defined as the maximum expected credit exposure. PFE is important because some transactions have longer maturities where losses may emerge over time. Also, positions with large downsides in extreme markets (for example, options sold) are more fully captured.

CCR "add-ons" are determined by multiplying the notional principal amount by Credit Conversion Factors set by type (interest rate, commodities, credit, currency, and equities), features, position, and term.

Netting

Netting agreements allow parties to net the mark-to-market values of their trades so that in the event of default the credit exposure is limited to the net positive value of the total. Netting is generally effected under an International Swap Dealer Association (ISDA) Master Agreement signed between the parties, which specifies methods for calculating a single settlement amount in the termination currency. ISDA has obtained legal opinions from major jurisdictions confirming the enforceability of netting. "The ISDA" also specifies margining arrangements and collateral terms so that CCR in the normal course of business is further reduced with less capital required.

Securities finance transactions have similar netting and are generally executed under the ICMA Global Master Repo Agreement.

Market implied probability of default and survival curves

Bond and credit default swap (CDS) prices can be used to extract the market view on probability of default and guide the pricing of loans and securities.

Default and survival curves

Default curves can be constructed by extracting credit spreads over risk-free (for example, Treasury) rates, using as many securities and maturity pricing observations as possible. Assumptions, requiring carefully thought-out best estimates, must be then made as to:

- Linearity (given infrequent data points);
- Discount rates;
- Recovery rates;
- Role of investor premium in credit spread for:
  - Volatility; and
  - Liquidity.

The process of curve construction is also known as "bootstrapping". Given the investor premiums described above, it must be noted that actual historical default rates are less than those implied by bond and CDS prices.

The default intensity or hazard rate is the default probability for each time period. This is used to construct cumulative probability of default rates and cumulative probability survival rates (the two are inverses) for each time period. Investors generally demand relatively higher increases in credit spreads earlier along the curve for lower rated credits, implying increasing default intensity with time.

Closed form analytical approximations vs Monte Carlo simulation

With the rapid growth and complexity of derivatives markets since the 1980s, credit risk models have advanced in sophistication. Early systems of managing risk were closed form approximations, with limited and static credit categories, default probabilities, recovery rates, term structure, potential future exposure, and netting measures. Little focus was directed to correlation, diversification, and credit migration. With limited historical data and less computing power, more elaborate models were not possible.

Given the complexity, number of dimensions, and uncertainty of the CCR of a bank's derivatives portfolio, Monte Carlo simulations are now the norm. While it is data and IT system intensive, Monte Carlo can incorporate the multiple sources of risk, correlations, and mitigants (including netting). Modelling therefore shifts from the deterministic setting to the probabilistic setting.

Large numbers of joint scenarios are generated based on numerous risk-based factors pertaining to market conditions, defaults, credit migration, correlations, and recovery over the term of the portfolio. This is especially necessary

Example: RWA calculation

CRE = Commercial Real Estate

			Drawn	EAD	RWA	EL	RW %
					CRE		
Curr Acc	Performing						
	Non-performing						
Loans	Performing						
	Non-performing						
Mortgages	Performing						
	Non-performing						
Cards	Performing						
	Non-performing						
RETAIL TOTAL							
Retail	Performing	BIB (business segment)	24	50	27	0	55%
		BBB	18	25	14	0	55%
		BB Dev	352	388	213	5	55%
	Non-performing	BIB	0	0	0	0	46%
		BBB	52	64	8	29	13%
		BB Dev	33	37	12	16	31%
BB Retail Total			478	563	274	52	49%
Corporate CRE	Performing	BIB	3	3	2	0	81%
		BBB	30	30	24	0	81%
		BB Dev	265	268	286	4	107%
	Non-performing	BIB	–	–	–	–	150%
		BBB	–	–	–	–	
		BB Dev	–	–	–	–	
BB Corp CRE Total			297	301	312	4	104%
Corporate Non CRE	Performing	BIB	–	–	–	–	–
		BBB	–	–	–	–	–
		BB Dev	–	–	–	–	–
	Non-performing	BIB	–	–	–	–	–
		BBB	–	–	–	–	–
		BB Dev	–	–	–	–	–
BB Corp Non CRE Total			–	–	–	–	–
Business Banking Total			775	864	587	56	68%

Based on drawn amount plus expectation that the facility usage will increase, up to and beyond limit, as the obligor approaches default. [Historical data and observation of sector in default is used to drive this]

The EAD therefore is invariably above the Drawn amount and up to Facility limit and beyond (includes some "costs")

RW% driven by the credit model

RW% for Retail based on Foundation IRB (uses firm-specific PD and LGD), noting Standardised floor of 72.5%

RW% for CRE uses "Slotting" (set by PRA)

RW% for non-CRE is Standardised (no model needed, uses internal rating, which will be model derived)

Figure 3.4 Summary of a risk-weighted assets calculation for a retail and corporate customer commercial bank

as credit events and in particular defaults are rare, yet have huge impacts. Besides estimating risk, the simulations provide many insights into profit maximisation and hedging.

The exposure at default value (EAD) is based on the specific asset drawn amount plus the expectation that the facility usage will increase, up to and beyond limit, as the obligor approaches default. Historical data and observation of sector in default is used to drive this. The EAD is, therefore, invariably above the drawn amount and up to the facility limit and beyond (includes some "costs" in certain cases.)

The risk weighting percentage (RW%) is driven by the credit model. In this case, the RW% for retail is based on IRB (uses firm-specific PD and LGD), while the RW% for commercial real estate (CRE) has been calculated via the regulatory authority's "slotting" technique (whereby the regulator applies its own risk-weight value because it does not deem the bank's internal model and/or data analytics to be robust enough for this asset class). The RW% for non-CRE is the standardised approach (no model is needed, and it uses internal rating, which will be model derived).

Note that the 150% RW level is used if there are any non-performing assets on the balance sheet.

Figure 3.4 is an illustration of the summary of the RWA calculation using the input parameters described here.

PART 2

Now we examine the credit process of a bank, including how it organises the credit function, and approves, analyses, structures, prices, monitors, and works out credit assets.

Credit risk organisational structures

As made clear in previous chapters, the Board of Directors has overall responsibility for all risks of the bank and sets strategy, policy, and limits. The Board must have a Risk Management subcommittee, which includes the CEO and the heads of the management level Credit, Market, Asset Liability, and Liquidity as well as the Operational Risk Management Committees. The Board subcommittee must take a coordinated and integrated approach to the range of risks. It is vital that its integrity and independence are maintained, with a system in place to report to internal and external auditors, for when and reasons why the full Board does not accept recommendations.

Given the critical importance of credit risk, the Credit Policy Committee (also called the Credit Risk Management Committee) should be chaired by the CEO and include the Chief Risk Officer, Heads of Credit, Credit Risk Management, Treasury, and the Chief Economist. This committee is responsible for implementing Board-level credit strategy and policy as well as the following:

Credit approval:

- Formulating standards for credit proposals:
  - Credit analysis;
  - Ratings;
  - Loan structures, covenants, and collateral.
- Setting credit pricing policy;
- Delegating credit approval authority;
- Monitoring, risk management, and reporting;
- Measuring and monitoring credit risk with precision and consistency across the bank;
- Maintaining credit risk within approved limits;
- Managing the credit portfolio;
- Establishing a review mechanism for loans;
- Setting policy for provisioning;
- Devising a process for loan workout;
- Ensuring compliance with all regulatory requirements.

The Board and Credit Committee policies and strategies must be communicated effectively throughout the bank and permeate to each level and function. Delegation of authority and responsibility with clear reporting lines and accountability are paramount. Credit risk functions must be staffed and resourced sufficiently.

On an operating level, banks need to have separate Banking and Credit Risk Management Departments. The Banking Department (often organised by industry specialisation) manages customer relationships and takes a commercial approach in identifying business opportunities, pitching for deals, and negotiating and closing transactions. The Credit Risk Management Department measures risk and enforces limits and standards, with constant overseeing of the entire portfolio. Subdepartments of the Credit Risk Management Department include Credit Portfolio, Credit Modelling, Monitoring and Collection, Collateral Management, and Restructuring.

While separate, all departments and functions must rely on each other for credit risk management to be effective. Credit Modelling must receive timely and accurate data to provide useful risk measures to the Credit Department and Credit Portfolio for action.

Asset writing strategy consistent with risk appetite statement

Credit scores and credit bureaus

A credit score is a numerical expression of creditworthiness generated by a statistical model using pertinent data. In contrast to commercial lending where extensive analysis is performed on the borrower with judgements being made, high volume/small size transactions generally dictate that retail lending is based on automated scoring without any human intervention. This applies to approval, pricing, terms, monitoring, control, and collections. Credit scores are sometimes also used for Small to Medium Enterprise (SME) lending.

Banks must satisfy supervisors that the data is relevant to exposures, the model has a sound track record in predicting default and is regularly tested and updated, and a system is in place for governing the use of the credit scores.

Credit bureaus (also referred to as consumer reporting or credit reference agencies) collect and aggregate personal and financial information from sources including creditors, lenders, utilities, debt collection agencies, and public records. A particular focus is past borrowing and bill paying habits. Bureaus provide their clients with credit reports for credit risk assessment and scoring, or for other purposes such as offering employment or renting of property.

While formats vary, all credit reports contain the same basic information:

- Identity of the counterparty;
- Trade lines: accounts with date of opening, classification (for example, credit card, auto loan), activity, balances, minimum payments, and payment history;
- Credit enquiries: list of parties accessing reports to evaluate requests for credit;
- Public records: bankruptcy, foreclosure, wage attachment (garnishes/admin orders), lien, lawsuit, and judgements information;
- Collection items: information on overdue payments.

In the past, credit reporting involved only negative information, but now scheduled repayment of debt is used as a positive. Negative items closed out are removed from credit reports over time (there are regulations that govern these time periods, which are often country specific).

The minimum for a report is generally one undisputed account opened for 6 months or more with no indication that one of the holders is deceased.

Credit reports do not contain information on race, religion, national origin, sex and marital status; location of residence; age; income and employment history; interest rates charged on accounts; child support obligations; customer initiated report checks; history of credit counselling; or any information not proven to be predictive of future credit performance. Much of this information is stored at the credit bureaus themselves, and can be used for validating client information required by the local regulations, if required.

Data quality is fundamental to the generation of useful credit scores. Potential sources of mistakes include:

- Lender error in recording payments;
- Incorrect/incomplete data submissions to the bureaus;
- Incorrect recording of identity, transposition of digits;

- Ex-spouse's credit issues linked;
- Identity theft.

Consumers can check their credit reports and notify credit bureaus of any errors. Credit bureaus have a legal duty to respond promptly; however, there is criticism about their efficiency in that a greater burden is placed on the consumer. Credit scores are modelled by both credit bureaus and banks. The most widely used credit scoring system is FICO, pioneered in the US in the 1950s by what was then Fair, Isaac and Company.

Consumers need to know the basics and means to improve their credit scores to meet their financial goals. Steps for consumers to take with the greatest effect are:

- Paying bills on time (setting up payment reminders and automatic payments or debit orders can help);
- Catching up on missed payments;
- Reducing debt (achieved most quickly by paying off highest interest rate debt first);
- Avoiding opening new accounts simply to increase available credit (but not closing accounts likely to be needed);
- Avoid searching extensively for a single loan, as it may appear as an effort to increase borrowing rapidly (by increasing the number of recent bureau enquiries);
- Avoid moving debt around to put off repayment;
- Having some active accounts that reflect on the credit bureaus (this allows an "active credit" score to be generated with positive payment information).

While credit scoring methodologies vary and are not disclosed in detail, overall weighting of factors has been estimated as follows: payment history 35%, debt to credit ratio 30%, average age of accounts 15%, types of credit 10%, and enquiries 10%.

Credit scores constantly change, therefore consumers must be reminded, educated, and be provided with incentives for good personal financial management.

Approvals and cut-offs

Credit scores have a number of benefits:

- Speed: the input of credit bureau data into a model allows for some decisions to be made within minutes;
- Objectivity: they focus on the relevant facts only, with no inappropriate negative (or positive) bias from individual bankers;
- Accuracy: the factors/variables used that are based directly on behavioural information (based on bank internal/bureau data) cannot be gained easily by either the applicant or the sales staff involved with the deal;

- Forward looking: credit issues in the distant past are not necessarily a factor; recent credit behaviour tends to carry more weight in the credit scoring;
- Better differentiation: more risk assessment means better segmentation of borrowers such that interest rates can be charged, terms set, and products offered according to risk;
- Heightened competition: banks are able to assess more loan requests and can therefore attempt to compete for more consumer business.

Lenders will generally not rely on the credit score only. Potential borrowers complete an application where income and employment are generally considered. While larger banks generally use "black box" approaches that allow little autonomy on decision-making for their local managers, smaller banks may often rely on their knowledge of community, customers, businesses, and relationships in approving credit. This makes them, in theory, superior SME lenders compared to the larger banks, although in practice small banks' level of loan losses are generally not markedly superior. There is nevertheless a genuine element of positive customer service perception associated with the ability to apply local knowledge and expertise in the loan origination process.

Some lenders utilise "cut-off scores". Loan applicants with scores below a set level are rejected unless the bank chooses to make an exemption (referred to as overrides). Cut-offs generally are more stringent for home loans than for high interest debt such as credit cards or personal loans.

Limits and risk appetite

As discussed elsewhere, the Board uses the risk appetite statement to set the quantity and type of risk the bank will tolerate within its total capacity to pursue its business objectives. Highest level limits for broad exposure groupings are set after considering the impact of the potential transaction on the regulatory and/or economic capital required to support the credit position. This includes using probabilities of default to estimate expected losses under different scenarios (from normal to recession or to major disruption and with consideration of frequency). These may be expressed in absolute amounts for the riskiest exposures or as a percentage of total exposure. An internal economic capital framework considering correlation, concentration, and large single exposures is integral to setting limits. Risk is then allocated on an operating level across business lines, products, industries, and regions, as well as individual borrowers in the form of further limits.

Limits are incorporated in Pillar II of Basel II as part of the supervisory review process. Limits must not be merely a "rubber stamp" of business requests leading to the approval of further increases when requested only. Forward thinking credit management involves consideration of reasonable exposure levels in anticipation of new business opportunities and the potential medium-term movements of the credit cycle. For instance, when there is an expectation of a downturn in the credit cycle, risk limits may be tightened to alleviate future volatility in the credit outcome (bad debt charge or default rates).

Business lines can work to stay within limits by extending credit only to borrowers with increasingly higher internal ratings (corporates) and credit scores (retail). However, tightening lending standards cannot be relied upon solely to reduce credit risk.

Limits serve varying purposes. In some instances, limits are a firm form of policing against taking on risks not deemed tolerable. In other instances, limits are essentially a form of an early warning system, where credit officers and management are alerted to an increase in risk that merits further discussion and analysis. Sometimes a client is involved in multiple products (including trading) and the bank may not be able to ensure that the total intra-day exposure limits are not breached, in which case limits should be set conservatively low. As credit risk is constantly changing due to portfolio effects and new data, limits need regular adjustment whether nominal exposures change or remain the same.

Credit risk assessment

In extending credit to a corporation, banks will consider attributes such as market share, quality of products and services, innovation, brand, and operating efficiency. However, a company's performance and ability to meet debt obligations are strongly linked to macroeconomic and industry factors.

Key factors include the phase of the economic cycle, interest, inflation, and exchange rates. Sensitivity to these factors varies by industry. While the durable goods, auto, transportation, and informational technology industries tend to perform in line with the economy (cyclical), the household goods, food, and utilities industries are more constant (non-cyclical). Historically, the performance of the financial and homebuilding industries has been highly interest rate sensitive.

Industry characteristics to consider include:

- Size and growth prospects;
- Competition;
- Profit margins;
- Supplier power;
- Buyer power;
- Labour supply and relations;
- Barriers to entry for new entrants;
- Innovation;
- New markets;
- Threat of substitute products;
- Research and development costs;
- Regulatory environment;
- Political risks.

With a broader understanding of the industry, it is then possible to analyse a company's competitive advantages, positioning, and its prospects in the future.

Financial analysis

Corporate financial statements include volumes of data that can be used to perform extensive credit analysis. The most widely used technique is financial ratios, with four main categories:

- Leverage ratios:
  - Indicate the extent of reliance on debt financing;
  - Measure the relative contribution of stockholders and creditors or the extent to which debt is used in the capital structure;
  - Measure the degree of protection of suppliers of long-term funds;
  - Aid in assessing the ability to pay liabilities and raise new additional debt.
- Liquidity ratios:
  - Measure the ability to meet current obligations as they come due;
  - Indicate the ease of turning current assets into cash.
- Profitability ratios:
  - Measure the ability to generate revenues in excess of costs;
  - Measure the ability to earn a return on resources.
- Efficiency ratios:
  - Indicate how well assets are used to generate sales and profits;
  - Measure the ability to control expenses.

It is possible to generate dozens of financial ratios from a company's balance sheet and income statement. However, credit analysts do not rely on ratios as much as in the past or they do not have the same expectation, as in the past, that benchmark ratio levels must be met. Often, one ratio appearing weak is offset by a stronger one, and more sophisticated statistical modelling techniques are available now.

Ratio by industry sector and company size (for example, large corporate, middle market, SME) is used to assess norms and relative strength. Historical ratios are useful in identifying trends. Table 3.1 provides a summary of the formulas and measures for various ratios.

Loan facilities

Once the credit strength of a potential borrower is analysed, a bank can consider the structure and risks of the proposed facility. The bank must understand the purpose, amount, and duration of the borrowing. The loan must be for an activity within a company's business remit or an individual's financial goals. It is acceptable to finance the repayment of existing debts, providing the new loan terms can accommodate the client's needs better and can be serviced.

By understanding a borrower's requirements, the bank can offer the most suitable facilities, which include the following:

- Line of credit:
  - Credit availability is established but approval is needed for each drawdown;

Table 3.1 Formulae and description for the key ratios mentioned above

Ratio	Formula	Measures
Leverage		
Debt to Equity	debt/equity	Owed compared to owned
Interest Coverage	EBIT*/interest expense	Ability to pay interest using cash flow
Liquidity		
Current or Working Capital Ratio	current assets/current liabilities	Liquidity reserves
Quick Ratio or Acid Test	(cash+marketable securities+receivables)/ current liabilities	Ready liquidity (excludes inventory)
Profitability		
Gross Profit Margin	(revenue-cost of goods sold)/revenue	Ability to generate profit
Return on Equity	net income/shareholder equity	Return on shareholder's investment
Return on Assets	net income/average assets	Return on assets used
Efficiency		
Asset Turnover	net sales/average assets	Use of assets to generate sales
Payables Turnover	cost of sales/trade payables	Speed of paying bills
Operating Cycle	average inventory/cost of sales per day	Time between acquisition of inventory and realisation of cash

*EBIT: earnings before interest and taxes

- o Drawings to be repaid in fixed, short periods of time;
- o Attractive to companies with short-term borrowing needs such as seasonable inventory build-up prior to sales.
- Revolving line of credit:
  - o Allows for continuous borrowing up to a limit;
  - o Repayments allow for automatic borrowing back up to the limit;
  - o Credit cards are a popular form of revolving credit;
  - o These are typically subject to a regular (for example, annual) review process.
- Asset based:
  - o Attractive to companies with less free cash flow due to rapid growth or difficult markets that are less able to obtain unsecured credit;
  - o Funds advanced against collateral:
    - Working capital (accounts receivable, inventories);
    - The assets financed;
  - o Factoring is when accounts receivable are sold outright to the bank at a discount that reflects the cost of credit.

- Term loan:
  - Finances longer term assets:
    - Factory and equipment for companies;
    - For individuals, this could include home loans and vehicle finance; as funds are advanced against assets, the bank's assessment of potential losses would be more favourable, resulting in more favourable lending parameters (for example, interest rates) to the customer, compared to, say, personal loans;
  - Ensures funding;
  - Fixed and regular repayment schedule;
    - Bullet: single repayment of principal at maturity;
    - Amortising: principal paid in multiple payments on a schedule (for example, mortgage);
  - Fixed-rate or floating-rate interest;
  - Larger company loans may be syndicated across a number of banks:
    - Sale of the loan position is often possible.

Further detail on this asset classification is given in Chapter 4.

In analysing the risk of a facility, bankers must always ask the question "Just how am I going to be repaid?" The bank must identify the primary source of repayment and consider whether there are secondary sources of repayment. For example, in a revolving line of credit to a company, the bank is looking to the successful conversion of the working capital into cash. Should that fail (decline in sales, receivables not collected), secondary sources could be other cash flow from operations, new business, fees, the sale of other assets, and divestitures.

Figure 3.5 illustrates the nature of outstanding loan balances of different facilities. As the revolver is on demand, usage is unknown and will vary. The bullet payment means principal risk remains for the life of the loan. Amortising loans generally require regular payments combining principal and interest, with the proportion for interest declining as principal is reduced.

Loan balances

For many loans, the bank's exit strategy is important. When a loan to help a company make an acquisition results in high debt levels, the bank needs to believe the merger will be cash generative to reduce leverage in a reasonable timeframe. The bank might also take the view that the company would have access to the bond markets as an alternative funding in the future.

To the extent that a bank's internal rating/scoring, industry, facility, source of repayment, and exit strategy analysis raises questions about the extension of credit, it may still wish to proceed by requiring credit "mitigants".

These include covenants and guarantees (Chapter 4).

Borrowers are assigned a single internal rating/credit score, but risk varies depending on facility type and credit mitigants. Internal ratings assess PD, but

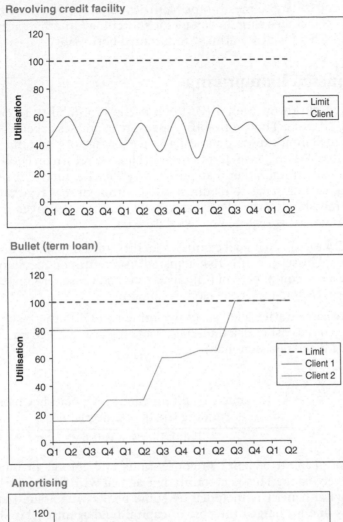

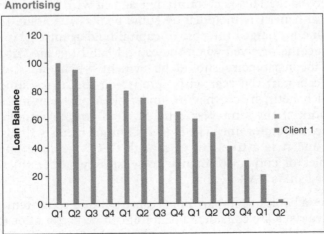

Figure 3.5   Loan principal cash flow profile

guarantees and collateral mean some facilities can have much lower expected losses. Basel II includes a methodology for "notching" internal ratings upward to generate higher "facility ratings" for secured borrowing.

Risk-adjusted loan pricing

Risk-adjusted return on capital (RARoC) is the profitability of capital after considering all costs. This profitability measure expresses expected profit (net of all costs including expected losses) as a percentage of economic capital, or worse case loss. RARoC is preferred to risk-adjusted return on equity (RARoE) as it includes all capital rather than purely core Tier 1 equity. The relationship to economic capital needs to be understood, although it is regulatory capital that ultimately should drive the overall target and strategy, given that the regulatory capital level is required by legislative fiat.

The RARoC (or RARoE) model expresses facility and connection level income net of expected losses (i.e. it is risk adjusted) as a return on regulatory capital. It should be a key component of principal front book asset pricing calculators. By applying a RARoC target the bank is able to:

- Facilitate comparative analysis of investments of differing risk profiles;
- Understand the cost of risk undertaken and reward received for the process;
- Improve MI and decision making.

The formula is given by:

$$RAROC = \frac{[\text{Income} + \text{Capital Benefit} - \text{Operating Costs} - \text{Funding Costs} - \text{Expected Loss}]}{\text{Total Tier 1 Capital}}$$

The element "capital benefit" is contentious and is not an input that is applied at every bank. This is certainly not agreed with by the author of this chapter. Capital benefit is included by some banks who argue that because the business line is charged the cost of capital held against it, it should also benefit from income received when the capital liabilities are "hedged". That this leads to inconsistencies should be evident when one realises that a business line can start the year with "profit" on the books simply because of this capital benefit, before having undertaken any genuine shareholder value-added work of any kind. Nevertheless, it is not uncommon to see this element on the numerator line. The better-managed banks will dispense with this element, and it is a true test of a bank CFO's genuine understanding of the principles of corporate finance to witness whether this element is included in the bank's RARoC analysis.

RARoC enables a bank to compare opportunities more consistently by ensuring that relative risks are considered. Capital can be better allocated to business areas and products, right down to individual loans. RARoC is useful in evaluating ongoing performance as well as deal flow.

Banks set target or "hurdle" RARoCs for the use of capital. Opportunities that do not meet the required RARoC should be rejected or escalated to senior management for additional consideration. Business decisions to proceed can be made because a product is a "loss leader" valued by clients or a new line of business where profitability takes time to develop.

EVA (Economic Value Added) is net profit less the cost of use of economic capital (also known as NIACC – net income after capital charge). The cost is usually calculated as a weighted average cost of the bank's sources of capital. Unlike RARoC, EVA is an absolute measure. EVA is sometimes described as "excess return". This "economic profit" is different from simple accounting profit because it considers implicit costs as well as tangible costs.

A comparison of RARoC and EVA is summarised in Table 3.2.

The basics of loan pricing

A conventional vanilla pricing approach for a corporate bank relationship manager would use these inputs:

1. Set the target margin for the asset (a function of the cost of capital of the bank. Ignoring equity, the cost of which is realistically and notoriously

Table 3.2   Comparison of RARoC vs EVA

RoE: in principle the methodology is:	
$RoE = \dfrac{(Income - Costs)}{Capital}$	– Costs are driven by the transaction – A hurdle RoE % is set to determine the income required – The RoE hurdle can be adjusted as appropriate to market/sector/product – Income required to meet RoE hurdle % less costs drives the price
RoE is return on capital employed, which is usually adjusted for risk purposes as RARoE	
EVA: in principle the methodolgy is:	
$EVA = Income - Costs - Cost\ of\ capital$	– Costs are driven by the transaction – Profit (EVA) is calculated as a % of costs – The EVA can be varied as appropriate to market/sector/product – Total of costs + EVA drives the required price
EVA is the value created (i.e. economic profit) through undertaking the deal	

difficult to ascertain with any real accuracy, the cost of debt capital should drive the minimum expected target rate of return);

2. Factor in margin (spread) for default probability and loss-given-default of the obligor, so in effect its risk weighting, together with any adjustment for size of loan;
3. Factor in margin reduction arising from extent of collateral (so unsecured highest margin, lowest to zero margin for fully collateralised or overcollateralised lending);
4. Factor in term liquidity premium.

Input (4) is the Treasury-applied "term liquidity premium", which is mainly, though not wholly, a function of the tenor of the lending and the liquidity of the asset once originated.

Figure 3.6 shows what the pricing screen might look like.

Credit authorisation process

Beyond risk appetite and measurement, the Credit Policy Committee establishes and monitors the credit authorisation process. This includes:

- Minimum requirements for information and analysis:
  - o Client identity verification (may be a regulatory requirement);
  - o Financial data (for example, payslip for individual, audited financials for SME/corporate);
- Minimum underwriting standards:
  - o Terms;
  - o Documentation (for example, sufficient detail on the contract);
  - o Collateral, covenants, and guarantees.

Asset Pricing Calculator					
Product type	Loan	*Customer*	*ANO & Sons*		
Utilisation	100%				
Interest rate basis	LIBOR	**Asset costs illustration**			
Amount	£1,000,000	Tier 1 capital	£12,640	Cost of capital	£2,100
Term (months)	60	TLP bps	236	TLP	£8,325
PD	0.064%	Expected loss rate	0.06%	Expected loss	£480
LGD	5%	Undrawn liquidity buffer	0.00%	Liquidity buffer	£0
				Total costs	
Recommended pricing		**RM proposed pricing**			
Margin bps	431	Proposed margin bps	325		
Target margin bps	331	Proposed fee	£0		
Minimum margin bps	306	Proposed non-util fee	£0		

Figure 3.6   Corporate lending pricing screen

Larger and more complicated loans are generally approved by credit committees. The client officer sponsors the loan proposal memorandum and is responsible for completeness. The committee scrutinises the proposal to ensure underwriting standards are met and uses their experience and knowledge of similar customers as well as their own facilities to evaluate risk and reward in making a decision. Smaller and less complicated loans are approved through delegation of authority.

Monitoring the credit authorisation process is an important control function and can yield business insights. This includes tracking:

- Processing time and cost per approval;
- Approval rates (rising or falling);
- Acceptance rates (and NTU – not taken up – rates);
- Volume of policy exceptions.

Breaking data down by client, product, and facility can demonstrate where underwriting standards are falling in line with the market.

The Credit Policy Committee should ensure that minutes of Credit Committee Meetings are complete and include the justification for their decisions.

Collateral management

Banking and collateral are synonymous with each other, as evidenced by the numerous references in this and other chapters. Collateral is an excellent risk mitigant and is recognised in the Basel Accord's loss given default methodology. However – and while banks would almost always prefer to receive collateral – credit should only be extended when it is deemed that the borrower is likely to be able to repay without it. The liquidation of collateral can involve legal, market, and reputational risk, as well as time and resources.

The lending bank must have clear legal rights over the collateral, and must be able to liquidate or take possession in a timely manner in the event of default, insolvency, bankruptcy, or defined credit event. This is called "perfecting" an interest in the collateral. Collateral rights vary by jurisdiction, therefore business collateral transactions with multinational corporations will require focused legal advice.

The amounts and types of collateral are negotiated and depend on:

- Client risk;
- Facility risk and maturity;
- Available collateral;
- Volatility of collateral value;
- Liquidity of collateral;
- Legal terms.

Collateral for loans is most commonly real estate (mortgages), equipment, inventory, cash, or securities. The borrower must prove it holds the deed to the collateral, and certify that it is not already pledged to another creditor (unless the bank is willing to take a second charge).

Where possible, banks should use historical data to project liquidation value. Banks consider potential links between borrower default and declines in collateral value. For example, if a company fails because of lack of sales, buyers for equipment for the manufacture of its products may be limited.

Collateral management is often the responsibility of a dedicated department whose responsibilities include:

• Monitoring collateral amounts and value;
• Collecting additional collateral when collateral value declines, as per facility terms (margining);
• Monitoring and limiting collateral concentrations.

In most jurisdictions, a lien refers to a transaction where the bank does not hold the collateral. Banks will ideally hold securities collateral in their own custody department. However, only clear terms in lending documentation ensure the ability to sell the collateral and keep the proceeds in the event of default.

Demand for securities collateral is growing because banks are required increasingly to post collateral for their own financing, derivatives, and clearing businesses. Central bank trades with banks designed to provide liquidity and effect monetary policy are collateralised. Banks seek to rehypothecate (use collateral received for its own collateral pledges) whenever possible.

Credit portfolio monitoring and control

When new loans are booked and the economy, industries, and companies change, the risk and profitability of the overall credit portfolio also change. Credit policy adapts to rebalance the portfolio by adjusting limits, pricing, maturities, and requirements (for example, collateral, guarantees, and covenants) for new business. However, the credit portfolio management team has the tools to control risk and optimise the profitability of the portfolio, which can then complement lending policy and be quicker and more efficient. This is particularly important should concentrations build and credit concerns develop rapidly. Furthermore, portfolio management techniques can reduce risk and maximise the lending capacity for banks to offer competitive market pricing for important clients and products as often as possible.

The effectiveness of credit portfolio management depends on accurate, uniform, aggregated, and timely data.

Strategies include:

• Sell loans;
• Securitise assets (for example, mortgages, loans, trade receivables, credit cards) for sale;

- Hedge using Credit Default Swaps (CDS):
  - ○ Single name;
  - ○ Index;
  - ○ Options on CDS (swaptions).

Selling and securitising loans frees capacity and can improve profitability if returns are low. While basis risk and liquidity are factors, the global credit default swap (CDS) market has grown massively with gross notional CDS amount reported by the Depository Trust Clearing Corporation to have exceeded $25.5 trillion at year end 2010 alone (http://www.isdacdsmarketplace.com/market_statistics). However, it must be noted that the CDS market is not available for the majority of credit risk reference names.

Traditionally, loan profit and loss were attributed to the responsible lending officer from start date through to maturity. Now, many banks credit the lending officer with the EVA or excess return of the loan (spread between expected return and economic capital) at inception, and then transfer the loan and P&L to the credit portfolio team to manage. Regardless, the relationship banker must remain engaged with the loan throughout its duration in working through any issues with the client and keeping management informed.

Banks need to have a periodic, objective, and comprehensive loan review function, which includes audit and is ultimately responsible to the Board. Smaller banks may outsource loan review. Key functions include:

- Identify loans with potential weaknesses;
- Regrade loans and create a watch list;
- Develop a watch list strategy for monitoring and potential action;
- Assess risk trends and underwriting standards in segments of the portfolio;
- Review loan documentation;
- Confirm adherence to credit policy;
- Evaluate data and reporting.

Behavioural scoring is an additional means of assessing credit risk made possible once a credit facility is extended. Banks can observe the patterns of activity and gain insights into how a customer manages their financial affairs. Exceeding credit limits, missed payments, and returned cheques are negative behaviours. Excessive utilisation of overdrafts or numerous credit card advances can be indicators of financial difficulties. Behavioural scores are generated by weighting recent trends, and are used in evaluating renewals or requests for new or larger borrowings.

Vintage analysis is another means of using existing business to better understand risk. Loan underwriting characteristics and standards vary over different periods of time. Similar loans from time periods are grouped together to create vintage pools, which are further segmented by borrower rating. Pools are tracked to assess how performance is linked to changes in the economy, interest rates, and other variables. Vintage analysis is particularly useful for longer term mortgages in forecasting repayment rates, delinquencies, and charge-offs. Newer loans can be compared to earlier vintages at similar points in their lifecycle to test the impact of risk credit policy changes, for instance a decision to cut back on risk.

Workout process

The definition of default is when a borrower fails to meet the conditions of a loan. Default can be a failure to make a payment as scheduled or technical, involving a breach of covenants. Default must be distinguished from the legal terms insolvency (borrower without means to pay) and bankruptcy (borrower under court supervision due to default or insolvency).

Corporations, individuals, banks, and even countries default. Difficult economic conditions, financial mismanagement, poor strategy and investment, excess leverage, and fraud all contribute to default. In almost all instances, it is preferable to work with the borrower to try to maximise value in the future than to become enmeshed in lengthy legal proceedings where lawyers and administrators rank first in order of payments.

Corporate debt restructuring

Banks attempt first to refinance debt, which involves extending the maturity and thus reducing and rescheduling payments. If a realistic assessment of the company's finances and business outlook shows the debt burden is still too great, a debt restructuring is necessary. This will include a distressed situation if the company has defaulted on payments or moved into bankruptcy. Banks have restructuring departments to review businesses and work with the company and other creditors to create a workout plan.

Beyond refinancing, a workout can involve exchanging debt for equity and reduction of debt. Before agreeing to concessions, creditors need to agree that the new business plan will rehabilitate the company and make debt levels serviceable. Parties involved will have different incentives and interests, consequently, agreement is not straightforward.

- Creditors: senior, collateralised creditors have less incentive to keep the company going and continue their exposure relative to junior, unsecured creditors;
- Shareholders: do not want the company wound down with their investment lost;
- Management: do not want the company wound down with their jobs lost.

If parties cannot agree that the company continuing as an ongoing concern is worth more than the assets, the parties should then work towards an orderly liquidation.

Consumer default and debt counselling

Consumer debt problems are often the result of loss of employment, decrease in income (less overtime, for instance), or financial mismanagement/illiteracy. The National Credit Act of 2007 established a debt counselling process for consistent debt restructuring, enforcement, and judgement.

A consumer may apply to a debt counsellor to:

- Provide budget advice and basic information;
- Negotiate with credit providers to:
  - Restructure debt;
  - Lower instalments;
  - Reduce debts to manageable levels.

Provision is made for basic living expenses before setting a new repayment schedule, but the consumer loses access to new credit.

Before applying for court permission to institute repossession, a creditor must first send the customer a written notice of options to repay or seek debt counselling.

All credit providers, credit bureaus, and debt counsellors must register with the NCR.

To be effective, debt counselling must ensure that borrowers (i) pay manageable levels of principal and interest; (ii) incur reasonable debt counselling fees; (iii) are given fair expectations of what can be achieved; and (iv) receive education and help with budgeting to avoid future problems.

CONCLUSIONS

Granting credit and monitoring the resulting default risk is the primary activity of banks. As credit risk is difficult to "hedge" or remove from the balance sheet (for most banks in the world anyway), it is self-evident that the most effective credit risk management policy is to operate a sound loan origination policy. This chapter has described the basic principles of credit risk management, and like most bank risk management issues there is always an element of judgement based on knowledge and experience to apply to ensure good practice. A through-the-cycle approach combined with knowing one's risk, at all times, is probably the most effective ingredient of a viable credit risk management process.

Chapter

4

....

THE MONEY MARKETS

Part of the global debt capital markets, the money markets are a separate market in their own right. Generally, money market securities are defined as debt instruments with an original maturity of less than 1 year.

Money markets exist in every market economy, which is practically every country in the world. They are often the first element of a developing capital market. Money market debt is an important part of global capital markets, and facilitates the smooth running of the banking industry, as well as providing working capital for industrial and commercial corporate institutions. The market provides users with a wide range of opportunities and funding possibilities, and is characterised by the diverse range of products that can be traded within it. Money market instruments allow issuers, including financial organisations and corporates, to raise funds for short-term periods at relatively low interest rates. These issuers include sovereign governments, who issue Treasury bills (T-bills), corporates issuing commercial paper (CP), and banks issuing bills and certificates of deposit (CDs). At the same time, investors are attracted to the market because the instruments are highly liquid and carry relatively low credit risk. The Treasury bill market in any country is that country's lowest risk instrument, and consequently carries the lowest yield of any debt instrument. Indeed, the first market that develops in any country is usually the Treasury bill market. Investors in the money market include banks, local authorities, corporations, money market investment funds and mutual funds, and individuals.

In addition to cash instruments, in certain jurisdictions the money markets also consist of a range of exchange-traded and over-the-counter derivative instruments. These instruments are used mainly to establish future borrowing and lending rates, and to hedge or change existing interest-rate exposure. This activity is carried out by banks, central banks, and corporates. The main derivatives are short-term interest-rate futures, forward rate agreements, and short-dated interest-rate swaps, such as overnight index swaps.

In this chapter we review the cash and derivative instruments traded in the money market, including interest-rate futures and forward rate agreements.

INTRODUCTION

The cash instruments traded in money markets include the following:

- Time deposits;
- Treasury bills;
- Certificates of deposit;
- Commercial paper;
- Banker's acceptances;

- Bills of exchange;
- Repo and stock lending.

Treasury bills are used by sovereign governments to raise short-term funds, while certificates of deposit (CDs) are used by banks to raise finance. The other instruments are used by corporates and occasionally banks. Each instrument represents an obligation on the borrower to repay the amount borrowed on the maturity date, together with interest if this applies. The instruments above fall into one of two main classes of money market securities: those quoted on a yield basis and those quoted on a discount basis. These two terms are discussed below. A repurchase agreement or "repo" is also a money market instrument.

The calculation of interest in the money markets often differs from the calculation of accrued interest in the corresponding bond market. Generally, the day-count convention in the money market is the exact number of days that the instrument is held over the number of days in the year. In the UK sterling market, the year base is 365 days, so the interest calculation for sterling money market instruments is given by (4.1):

$$i = \frac{n}{365} \tag{4.1}$$

However, the majority of currencies, including the US dollar and the euro, calculate interest on a 360-day base. The process by which an interest rate quoted on one basis is converted to one quoted on the other basis is shown at (4.18). Those markets that calculate interest based on a 365-day year are also listed in the last section of this chapter.

Dealers will want to know the interest day base for a currency before dealing in it as foreign exchange (FX) or as money markets. Bloomberg users can use screen DCX to look up the number of days of an interest period. For instance, Figure 4.1 shows screen DCX for the US dollar market, for a loan taken out on 16 November 2005 for spot value on 18 November 2005 for a straight 3-month period. This matures on 21 February 2006; we see from Figure 4.1 that this is a good day. We see also that 20 February 2006 is a USD holiday. The loan period is actually 95 days, and 93 days under the 30/360-day convention (a bond market accrued interest convention). The number of business days is 62.

For the same loan taken out in Singapore dollars, look at Figure 4.2. This shows that 20 February 2006 is not a public holiday for SGD and so the loan runs for the period 18 December 2005 to 20 February 2006.

Settlement of money market instruments can be for value today (generally only when traded before midday), tomorrow, or 2 days forward, which is known as *spot*. The latter is most common.

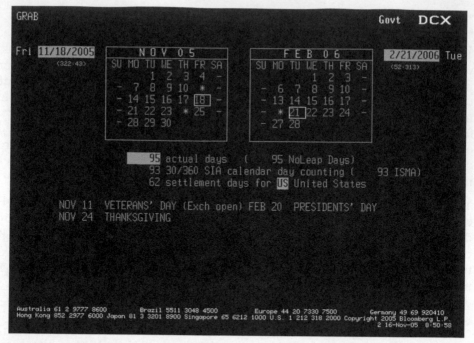

Figure 4.1   Bloomberg screen DCX used for a US dollar market, 3-month loan taken out for value 18 November 2005

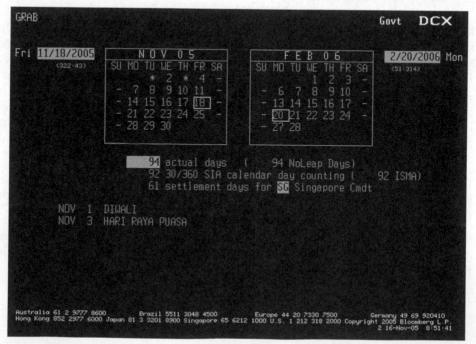

Figure 4.2   Bloomberg screen DCX for a Singapore dollar market, 3-month loan taken out for value 18 November 2005

SECURITIES QUOTED ON A YIELD BASIS

Two of the instruments in the list in the Introduction are yield-based instruments.

Money market deposits

These are fixed interest term deposits of up to 1 year with banks and securities houses. They are also known as *time deposits* or *clean deposits*. They are not negotiable so cannot be liquidated before maturity. The interest rate on the deposit is fixed for the term and related to the London Interbank Offered Rate (LIBOR) of the same term. Interest and capital are paid on maturity.

The effective rate on a money market deposit is the annual equivalent interest rate for an instrument with a maturity of less than 1 year.

LIBOR

A transparent and readily accessible interest-rate benchmark is a key ingredient in maintaining market efficiency. Countries that do not benefit from such a benchmark are markedly less liquid as a result.

Possibly the most well-known interest-rate benchmark is the London Interbank Offered Rate or Libor. It is calculated and published daily by ICE.

Investopedia describes the Libor process thus:

"LIBOR or ICE LIBOR (previously BBA LIBOR) is a benchmark rate that some of the world's leading banks charge each other for short-term loans. It stands for Intercontinental Exchange London Interbank Offered Rate and serves as the first step to calculating interest rates on various loans throughout the world. LIBOR is administered by the ICE Benchmark Administration (IBA), and is based on five currencies: US dollar (USD), Euro (EUR), pound sterling (GBP), Japanese yen (JPY) and Swiss franc (CHF), and serves seven different maturities: overnight, one week, and 1, 2, 3, 6 and 12 months. There are a total of 35 different LIBOR rates each business day. The most commonly quoted rate is the 3-month US dollar rate.

ICE LIBOR was previously known as BBA LIBOR until February 1, 2014, the date on which the ICE Benchmark Administration (IBA) took over the Administration of LIBOR."

Read more: LIBOR Definition | Investopedia http://www.investopedia .com/terms/l/libor.asp#ixzz4KTKJDHkY

Figure 4.3 shows the Libor rates for 13 September 2016, as seen on the Bloomberg service, for USD, GBP, and EUR. We note, for example, that GBP 3-month Libor was 0.38%. Figure 4.4 shows the history for GBP 3-month Libor from September 2011 to September 2016.

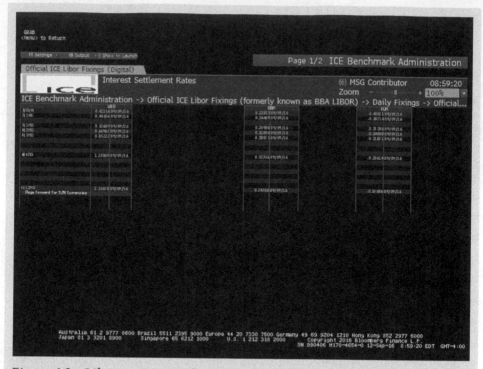

Figure 4.3   Libor screen on Bloomberg, 13 September 2016
© Bloomberg LP. Used with permission.

Figure 4.4   Libor history 2011–2016
© Bloomberg LP. Used with permission.

In developed markets there are of course usually a range of interest-rate indicators. For example, depending on what instrument and market one is concerned with, the sovereign bond interest rates may be worth monitoring, or the overnight-index swap (OIS) rate, and so on. It is important to be aware of rates relevant to the balance sheet risk management of your bank, and to understand how they interact as well as possible. Also important is some knowledge of the predictive power of yield curves and how to analyse and interpret them. For illustration, we show the GBP sovereign, interest-rate swap and overnight index swap (SONIA) yield curves for 13 September 2016 in Figure 4.5.

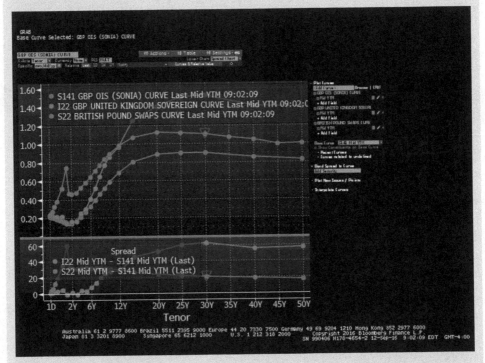

Figure 4.5   Sterling curves, 13 September 2016

Example 4.1

A sum of £250,000 is deposited for 270 days, at the end of which the total proceeds are £261,000. What are the simple and effective rates of return on a 365-day basis?

$$\text{Simple rate of return} = \left(\frac{\text{Total proceeds}}{\text{Initial investment}} - 1 \right) \times \frac{M}{n}$$

$$= \left(\frac{261,000}{250,000} - 1 \right) \times \frac{365}{270} = 5.9481\%$$

$$\text{Effective rate of return} = \left(\frac{\text{Total proceeds}}{\text{Initial investment}}\right)^{M/n} - 1$$

$$= \left(\frac{261,000}{250,000}\right)^{365/270} - 1 = 5.9938\%$$

Certificates of deposit

Certificates of deposit (CDs) are receipts from banks for deposits that have been placed with them. They were first introduced in the sterling market in 1958. The deposits themselves carry a fixed rate of interest related to LIBOR and have a fixed term to maturity, so cannot be withdrawn before maturity. However, the certificates themselves can be traded in a secondary market – that is, they are negotiable. CDs are therefore very similar to negotiable money market deposits, although the yields are usually below the equivalent tenor deposit rates because of the added benefit of liquidity. Most CDs issued are of between 1 and 3 months' maturity, although they do trade in maturities of 1 to 5 years. Interest is paid on maturity except for CDs lasting longer than 1 year, where interest is paid annually or, occasionally, semi-annually.

Banks, merchant banks, and building societies issue CDs to raise funds to finance their business activities. A CD will have a stated interest rate and fixed maturity date, and can be issued in any denomination. On issue a CD is sold for face value, so the settlement proceeds of a CD on issue are always equal to its nominal value. The interest is paid, together with the face amount, on maturity. The interest rate is sometimes called the *coupon*, but unless the CD is held to maturity this will not equal the yield, which is of course the current rate available in the market and varies over time. The largest group of CD investors are banks, money market funds, corporates, and local authority treasurers.

Unlike coupons on bonds, which are paid in rounded amounts, CD coupons are calculated to the exact day.

CD yields

The coupon quoted on a CD is a function of the credit quality of the issuing bank, its expected liquidity level in the market and, of course, the maturity of the CD, as this will be considered relative to the money market yield curve. As CDs are issued by banks as part of their short-term funding and liquidity requirement, issue volumes are driven by the demand for bank loans and the availability of alternative sources of funds for bank customers. The credit quality of the issuing bank is the primary consideration, however. In the sterling market, the lowest yield is paid by "clearer" CDs, which are CDs issued by the clearing banks – such as Lloyds Bank, HSBC, and Barclays plc.

In the US market, "prime" CDs, issued by highly rated domestic banks, trade at a lower yield than non-prime CDs. In both markets, CDs issued by foreign banks – such as French or Japanese banks – will trade at higher yields.

Euro-CDs, which are CDs issued in a different currency from that of the home currency, also trade at higher yields in the US because of reserve and deposit insurance restrictions.

If the current market price of the CD including accrued interest is P and the current quoted yield is r, the yield can be calculated given the price using (4.2):

$$r = \left(\frac{M}{P} \times \left(1 + C \left(\frac{Nim}{B} \right) \right) - 1 \right) \times \left(\frac{B}{N_{sm}} \right) \qquad (4.2)$$

The price can be calculated given the yield using (4.3):

$$P = M \times \left(1 + C \left(\frac{N_{im}}{B} \right) \right) \bigg/ 1 + r \left(\frac{N_{sm}}{B} \right)$$

$$= F \bigg/ \left(1 + r \left(\frac{N_{sm}}{B} \right) \right) \qquad (4.3)$$

where

C = Quoted coupon on the CD;
M = Face value of the CD;
B = Year day basis (365 or 360);
F = Maturity value of the CD;
N_{im} = Number of days between issue and maturity;
N_{sm} = Number of days between settlement and maturity;
N_{is} = Number of days between issue and settlement.

After issue a CD can be traded in the secondary market. The secondary market in CDs in the UK is very liquid, and CDs will trade at the rate prevalent at the time, which will invariably be different from the coupon rate on the CD at issue. When a CD is traded in the secondary market, the settlement proceeds will need to take into account interest that has accrued on the paper and the different rate at which the CD has now been dealt. The formula for calculating the settlement figure is given at (4.4), which applies to the sterling market and its 365 day-count basis:

$$\text{Proceeds} = \frac{M \times \text{Tenor} \times C \times 100 + 36{,}500}{\text{Days remaining} \times r \times 100 + 36{,}500} \qquad (4.4)$$

The settlement figure for a new issue CD is, of course, its face value ...![1]

The *tenor* of a CD is the life of the CD in days, while *days remaining* is the number of days left to maturity from the time of trade.

---

[1] With thanks to Derek "Del Boy" Taylor during the time he was at Tradition for pointing this out after I'd just bought a sizeable chunk of Japanese bank CDs...circa 1994.

The return on holding a CD is given by (4.5):

$$R = \left(\frac{1 + \text{Purchase yield} \times \dfrac{\text{Days from purchase to maturity}}{B}}{1 + \text{Sale yield} \times \dfrac{\text{Days from sale to maturity}}{B}} - 1 \right)$$

$$\times \frac{B}{\text{Days held}} \qquad (4.5)$$

Example 4.2

A 3-month CD is issued on 6 September 1999 and matures on 6 December 1999 (maturity of 91 days). It has a face value of £20,000,000 and a coupon of 5.45%. What are the total maturity proceeds?

$$\text{Proceeds} = 20\,\text{millions} \times \left(1 + 0.0545 \times \frac{91}{365} \right)$$
$$= £20,271,753.42$$

What are the secondary market proceeds on 11 October if the yield for short 60-day paper is 5.60%?

$$P = \frac{20,271,753.42}{\left(1 + 0.056 \times \dfrac{56}{365} \right)} = £20,009,066.64$$

On 18 November the yield on short 3-week paper is 5.215%. What rate of return is earned from holding the CD for the 38 days from 11 October to 18 November?

$$R = \left(\frac{1 + 0.0560 \times \dfrac{56}{365}}{1 + 0.05215 \times \dfrac{38}{365}} - 1 \right) \times \frac{365}{38} = 9.6355\%$$

US dollar market rates

Treasury bills

The Treasury bill (T-bill) market in the US is the most liquid and transparent debt market in the world. Consequently, the bid–offer spread on them is very narrow. The Treasury issues bills at a weekly auction each Monday, made up of 91-day and 182-day bills. Every fourth week the Treasury also issues 52-week bills. As a result there are large numbers of T-bills outstanding at any one time. The interest earned on T-bills is not liable to state and local income taxes. T-bill rates are the lowest in the dollar market (as indeed any bill market is in respective domestic environments) and as such represent the corporate financier's *risk-free* interest rate.

Federal funds

Commercial banks in the US are required to keep reserves on deposit at the Federal Reserve. Banks with reserves in excess of required reserves can lend these funds to other banks, and these inter-bank loans are called *federal funds* or *fed funds* and are usually overnight loans. Through the fed funds market, commercial banks with excess funds are able to lend to banks that are short of reserves, thus facilitating liquidity. The transactions are very large denominations, and are lent at the *fed funds rate*, which can be a relatively volatile interest rate because it fluctuates with market shortages. On average, it trades about 15 basis points or so below the overnight Libor fix. The difference can be gauged by looking at Figures 4.6 and 4.7, which are the graphs for historical USD fed funds and overnight Libor rates, respectively.

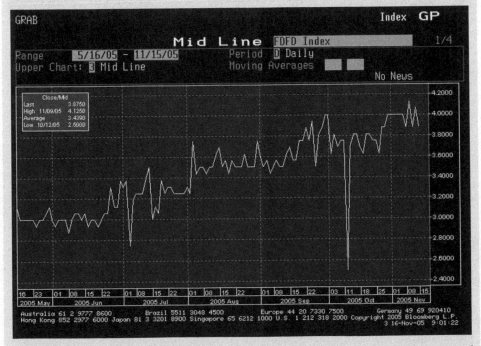

Figure 4.6 Bloomberg screen GP showing fed funds rate for the period May–November 2005

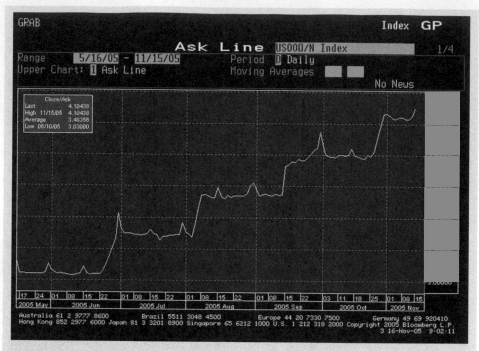

Figure 4.7   Bloomberg screen GP showing USD overnight Libor rates for the period May–November 2005

Prime rate

The *prime interest rate* in the US is often said to represent the rate at which commercial banks lend to their most creditworthy customers. In practice, many loans are made at rates below the prime rate, so the prime rate is not the best rate at which highly rated firms may borrow. Nevertheless, the prime rate is a benchmark indicator of the level of US money market rates, and is often used as a reference rate for floating-rate instruments. As the market for bank loans is highly competitive, all commercial banks quote a single prime rate, and the rate for all banks changes simultaneously.

SECURITIES QUOTED ON A DISCOUNT BASIS

The remaining money market instruments are all quoted on a *discount* basis, and so are known as "discount" instruments. This means that they are issued on a discount to face value, and are redeemed on maturity at face value. Hence, T-bills, bills of exchange, banker's acceptances, and CP are examples of money market securities that are quoted on a discount basis – that is, they are sold on the basis of a discount to par. The difference between the price paid at the time of purchase and the redemption value (par) is the interest earned by the holder of the paper. Explicit interest is not paid on discount instruments, rather interest is reflected implicitly in the difference between the discounted issue price and the par value received at maturity.

Treasury bills

Treasury bills (T-bills) are short-term government "IOUs" of short duration, often 3-month maturity. For example, if a bill is issued on 10 January it will mature on 10 April. Bills of 1-month and 6-month maturity are issued in certain markets, but only rarely by the UK Treasury. On maturity the holder of a T-bill receives the par value of the bill by presenting it to the central bank. In the UK, most such bills are denominated in sterling but issues are also made in euros. In a capital market, T-bill yields are regarded as the *risk-free* yield, as they represent the yield from short-term government debt. In emerging markets, they are often the most liquid instruments available for investors.

A sterling T-bill with £10 million face value issued for 91 days will be redeemed on maturity at £10 million. If the 3-month yield at the time of issue is 5.25%, the price of the bill at issue is:

$$p = \frac{10,000,000}{\left(1 + 0.0525 \times \frac{91}{365}\right)}$$
$$= £9,870,800.69$$

In the UK market, the interest rate on discount instruments is quoted as a *discount rate* rather than a yield. This is the amount of discount expressed as an annualised percentage of the face value, and not as a percentage of the original amount paid. By definition, the discount rate is always lower than the corresponding yield. If the discount rate on a bill is d, then the amount of discount is given by (4.6):

$$d_{value} = M \times d \times \frac{n}{B} \tag{4.6}$$

The price P paid for the bill is the face value minus the discount amount, given by (4.7):

$$P = 100 \times \left(\frac{1 - d \times (N_{sm}/365)}{100}\right) \tag{4.7}$$

If we know the yield on the bill, then we can calculate its price at issue by using the simple present value formula, as shown at (4.8):

$$P = \frac{M}{1 + r\frac{N_{sm}}{365}} \tag{4.8}$$

The discount rate d for T-bills is calculated using (4.9):

$$d = (1 - P) \times \frac{B}{n} \qquad (4.9)$$

The relationship between discount rate and true yield is given by (4.10):

$$\left. \begin{array}{l} d = \dfrac{r}{1 + r \times \dfrac{n}{B}} \\[3em] r = \dfrac{d}{1 - d \times \dfrac{n}{B}} \end{array} \right\} \qquad (4.10)$$

Example 4.3

A 91-day £100 T-bill is issued with a yield of 4.75%. What is its issue price?

$$P = £100 / \left(1 + 0.0475 \left(\frac{91}{365} \right) \right)$$
$$= £98.80$$

A UK T-bill with a remaining maturity of 39 days is quoted at a discount of 4.95%. What is the equivalent yield?

$$r = \frac{0.0495}{1 - 0.0495 \times \dfrac{39}{365}}$$
$$= 4.976\%$$

If a T-bill is traded in the secondary market, the settlement proceeds from the trade are calculated using (4.11):

$$\text{Proceeds} = M = \left(\frac{M \times \text{Days remaining} \times d}{B \times 100} \right) \qquad (4.11)$$

Banker's acceptances

A banker's acceptance is a written promise issued by a borrower to a bank to repay borrowed funds. The lending bank lends funds and in return accepts the banker's acceptance. The acceptance is negotiable and can be sold in the secondary market. The investor who buys the acceptance can collect the loan on the day that repayment is due. If the borrower defaults, the investor has legal recourse to the bank that made the first acceptance. Banker's acceptances are also known as *bills of exchange, bank bills, trade bills*, or *commercial bills*.

Essentially, banker's acceptances are instruments created to facilitate commercial trade transactions. The instrument is called a *banker's acceptance* because a bank accepts the ultimate responsibility to repay the loan to its holder. The use of banker's acceptances to finance commercial transactions is known as *acceptance financing*. The transactions for which acceptances are created include import and export of goods, the storage and shipping of goods between two overseas countries, where neither the importer nor the exporter is based in the home country,[2] and the storage and shipping of goods between two entities based at home. Acceptances are discount instruments and are purchased by banks, local authorities, and money market investment funds.

The rate that a bank charges a customer for issuing a banker's acceptance is a function of the rate at which the bank thinks it will be able to sell it in the secondary market. A commission is added to this rate. For ineligible banker's acceptances (see below), the issuing bank will add an amount to offset the cost of additional reserve requirements.

Eligible banker's acceptance

An accepting bank that chooses to retain a banker's acceptance in its portfolio may be able to use it as collateral for a loan obtained from the central bank during open market operations – for example, the Bank of England in the UK and the Federal Reserve in the US. Not all acceptances are eligible to be used as collateral in this way, as they must meet certain criteria set by the central bank. The main requirement for eligibility is that the acceptance must be within a certain maturity band (a maximum of 6 months in the US and 3 months in the UK), and that it must have been created to finance a self-liquidating commercial transaction. In the US, eligibility is also important because the Federal Reserve imposes a reserve requirement on funds raised via banker's acceptances that are ineligible. Banker's acceptances sold by an accepting bank are potential liabilities for the bank, but the reserve imposes a limit on the amount of eligible banker's acceptances that a bank may issue. Bills eligible for deposit at a central bank enjoy a finer rate than ineligible bills, and also act as a benchmark for prices in the secondary market.

COMMERCIAL PAPER

Commercial paper (CP) is a short-term money market funding instrument issued by corporates. In the UK and US it is a discount instrument. A company's short-term capital and *working* capital requirement is usually sourced directly from banks in the form of bank loans. An alternative short-term funding instrument is CP, which is available to corporates that have a sufficiently strong credit rating. CP is a short-term unsecured promissory note. The issuer of the note promises to pay its holder a specified amount on a specified maturity date. CP normally has a zero coupon and trades at a

---

[2] A banker's acceptance created to finance such a transaction is known as a *third-party acceptance*.

discount to its face value. The discount represents interest to the investor in the period to maturity. CP is typically issued in bearer form, although some issues are in registered form.

Originally, the CP market was restricted to borrowers with high credit ratings, and although lower rated borrowers do now issue CP, sometimes by obtaining credit enhancements or setting up collateral arrangements, issuance in the market is still dominated by highly rated companies. The majority of issues are very short term, from 30 to 90 days in maturity; it is extremely rare to observe paper with a maturity of more than 270 days or 9 months. This is because of regulatory requirements in the US,[3] which state that debt instruments with a maturity of less than 270 days need not be registered. Companies therefore issue CP with a maturity lower than 9 months and so avoid the administration costs associated with registering issues with the SEC.

There are two major markets, the US dollar market with an outstanding amount in 2005 of just under $1 trillion, and the eurocommercial paper market with an outstanding value of $490 billion at the end of 2005.[4] Commercial paper markets are wholesale markets, and transactions are typically very large. In the US, over a third of all CP is purchased by money market unit trusts, known as mutual funds; other investors include pension fund managers, retail or commercial banks, local authorities, and corporate treasurers. A comparison between US CP and eurocommercial paper is given in Table 4.1.

Although there is a secondary market in CP, very little trading activity takes place since investors generally hold CP until maturity. This is to be expected because investors purchase CP that matches their specific maturity requirement. When an investor does wish to sell paper, it can be sold back to the dealer or, where the issuer has placed the paper directly in the market (and not via an investment bank), it can be sold back to the issuer.

Table 4.1 Comparison of US CP and eurocommercial paper

	US CP	**Eurocommercial paper**
Currency	US dollar	Any euro currency
Maturity	1–270 days	2–365 days
Common maturity	30–180 days	30–90 days
Interest	Zero coupon, issued at discount	Fixed coupon
Quotation	On a discount rate basis	On a yield basis
Settlement	T+0; T+1	T+2
Registration	Bearer form	Bearer form
Negotiable	Yes	Yes

[3]This is the Securities Act of 1933. Registration is with the Securities and Exchange Commission.
[4]*Source*: BIS.

Commercial paper programmes

The issuers of CP are often divided into two categories of company: banking and financial institutions, and non-financial companies. The majority of CP issues are by financial companies. Financial companies include not only banks but also the financing arms of corporates – such as British Airways, BP, and Ford Motor Credit. Most of the issuers have strong credit ratings, but lower rated borrowers have tapped the market, often after arranging credit support from a higher rated company, such as a *letter of credit* from a bank, or by arranging collateral for the issue in the form of high-quality assets such as Treasury bonds. CP issued with credit support is known as *credit-supported commercial paper*, while paper backed by assets is known naturally enough as *asset-backed commercial paper*. Paper that is backed by a bank letter of credit is termed *LOC paper*. Although banks charge a fee for issuing letters of credit, borrowers are often happy to arrange for this, since by doing so they are able to tap the CP market. The yield paid on an issue of CP will be lower than that on a commercial bank loan.

Although CP is a short-dated security, typically of 3–6-month maturity, it is issued within a longer term programme, usually for 3–5 years for euro paper; US CP programmes are often open ended. For example, a company might arrange a 5-year CP programme with a limit of $100 million. Once the programme is established, the company can issue CP up to this amount – say, for maturities of 30 or 60 days. The programme is continuous and new CP can be issued at any time, daily if required. The total amount in issue cannot exceed the limit set for the programme. A CP programme can be used by a company to manage its short-term liquidity – that is, its working capital requirements. New paper can be issued whenever a need for cash arises, and for an appropriate maturity.

Issuers often roll over their funding and use funds from a new issue of CP to redeem a maturing issue. There is a risk that an issuer might be unable to roll over the paper where there is a lack of investor interest in the new issue. To provide protection against this risk, issuers often arrange a standby line of credit from a bank, normally for all of the CP programme, to draw against in the event that it cannot place a new issue.

There are two methods by which CP is issued, known as *direct-issued* or *direct paper* and *dealer-issued* or *dealer paper*. Direct paper is sold by the issuing firm directly to investors, and no agent bank or securities house is involved. It is common for financial companies to issue CP directly to their customers, often because they have continuous programmes and constantly roll over their paper. It is therefore cost-effective for them to have their own sales arm and sell their CP direct. The treasury arms of certain non-financial companies also issue direct paper. This includes, for example, British Airways plc corporate treasury, which runs a continuous direct CP programme, used to provide short-term working capital for the company. Dealer paper is paper that is sold using a banking or securities house intermediary. In the US, dealer

CP is effectively dominated by investment banks, as retail (commercial) banks were until recently forbidden from underwriting commercial paper. This restriction has since been removed and now both investment banks and commercial paper underwrite dealer paper.

Commercial paper yields

CP is sold at a discount to its maturity value, and the difference between this maturity value and the purchase price is the interest earned by the investor. The CP day-count base is 360 days in the US and euro markets, and 365 days in the UK. The paper is quoted on a discount yield basis, in the same manner as T-bills. The yield on CP follows that of other money market instruments and is a function of the short-dated yield curve. The yield on CP is higher than the T-bill rate; this is due to the credit risk that the investor is exposed to when holding CP, for tax reasons (in certain jurisdictions interest earned on T-bills is exempt from income tax) and because of the lower level of liquidity available in the CP market. CP also pays a higher yield than CDs due to the lower liquidity of the CP market.

Although CP is a discount instrument and trades as such in the US and UK, euro currency eurocommercial paper trades on a yield basis, similar to a CD. The expressions below illustrate the relationship between true yield and discount rate:

$$P = \frac{M}{1 + r \times \frac{\text{Days}}{\text{Year}}} \qquad (4.12)$$

$$rd = \frac{r}{1 + r \times \frac{\text{Days}}{\text{Year}}} \qquad (4.13)$$

$$r = \frac{rd}{1 - rd \times \frac{\text{Days}}{\text{Year}}} \qquad (4.14)$$

where M is the face value of the instrument, rd is the discount rate, and r the true yield.

Example 4.4

---

1. A 60-day CP note has a nominal value of £100,000. It is issued at a discount of $7\frac{1}{2}\%$ per annum. The discount is calculated as:

$$Dis = \frac{£100,000(0.075 \times 60)}{365}$$

$$= £1,232.88$$

The issue price for the CP is therefore £100,000 − £1,232, or £98,768. The money market yield on this note at the time of issue is:

$$\left(\frac{365 \times 0.075}{365 - (0.075 \times 60)} \right) \times 100\% = 7.594\%$$

Another way to calculate this yield is to measure the capital gain (the discount) as a percentage of the CP's cost, and convert this from a 60-day yield to a 1-year (365-day) yield, as shown below:

$$r = \frac{1,232}{98,768} \times \frac{365}{60} \times 100\%$$

$$= 7.588\%$$

2. ABC plc wishes to issue CP with 90 days to maturity. The investment bank managing the issue advises that the discount rate should be 9.5%. What should the issue price be, and what is the money market yield for investors?

$$Dis = \frac{100(0.095 \times 90)}{365}$$

$$= 2.342$$

The issue price will be 97.658.

The yield to investors will be:

$$\frac{2.342}{97.658} \times \frac{365}{90} \times 100\% = 9.725\%$$

REPO

The term *repo* is used to cover one of two different transactions, the *classic repo* and the *sell/buyback*, and sometimes is spoken of in the same context as a similar instrument, the *stock loan*. A fourth instrument is also economically similar in some respects to a repo, known as the *total return swap*, which is now commonly encountered as part of the market in credit derivatives. However, although these transactions differ in terms of their mechanics, legal documentation, and accounting treatment, the economic effect of each of them is very similar. The structure of any particular market and the motivations of particular counterparties will determine which transaction is entered into; there is also some crossover between markets and participants.

Market participants enter into classic repo because they wish to invest cash, for which the transaction is deemed to be *cash driven*, or because they wish to borrow a certain stock, for which purpose the trade is *stock driven*. A sell/buyback, which is sometimes referred to as a *buy–sell*, is entered into for similar reasons, but the trade itself operates under different mechanics and documentation.[5] A stock loan is just that, a borrowing of stock against a fee. Long-term holders of stock will therefore enter into stock loans simply to enhance their return.

---

[5]We use the term "sell/buyback" in this book. A repo is still a repo whether it is cash driven or stock driven, and one person's stock-driven trade may well be another's cash-driven one.

During the interbank liquidity crisis from September 2008 to well into 2009, when unsecured inter-bank markets dried up, repo was the only funding mechanism still available to many banks.

Definition

A repo agreement is a transaction in which one party sells securities to another, and at the same time and as part of the same transaction, commits to repurchase identical securities on a specified date at a specified price. The seller delivers securities and receives cash from the buyer. The cash is supplied at a predetermined rate – *the repo rate* – which remains constant during the term of the trade. On maturity, the original seller receives back collateral of equivalent type and quality and returns the cash plus repo interest. One party to the repo requires either the cash or the securities and provides *collateral* to the other party, as well as some form of compensation for the temporary use of the desired asset. Although legal title to the securities is transferred, the seller retains both the economic benefits and the market risk of owning them. This means that the "seller" will suffer if the market value of the collateral drops during the term of the repo, as she still retains beneficial ownership of the collateral. The "buyer" in a repo is not affected in P&L account terms if the value of the collateral drops, although there are other concerns for the buyer if this happens.

We have given here the legal definition of repo. However, the purpose of the transaction as we have described above is to borrow or lend cash, which is why we have used inverted commas when referring to sellers and buyers. The "seller" of stock is really interested in borrowing cash, on which she or he will pay interest at a specified interest rate. The "buyer" requires security or collateral against the loan he or she has advanced, and/or the specific security to borrow for a period of time. The first and most important thing to state is that repo is a secured loan of cash, and would be categorised as a money market yield instrument.[6]

THE CLASSIC REPO

The *classic repo* is the instrument encountered in the US, UK, and other markets. In a classic repo, one party will enter into a contract to sell securities, simultaneously agreeing to purchase them back at a specified future date and price. The securities can be bonds or equities but can also be money market instruments, such as T-bills. The buyer of the securities is handing over cash,

---

[6]That is, a money market instrument quoted on a yield instrument, similar to a bank deposit or a CD. The other class of money market products are discount instruments such as T-bills or CP.

which on the termination of the trade will be returned to him, and on which he will receive interest.

The seller in a classic repo is selling or offering stock, and therefore receiving cash, whereas the buyer is buying or bidding for stock, and consequently paying cash. So, if the 1-week repo interest rate is quoted by a market-making bank as "512–514", this means that the market-maker will bid for stock – that is, lend the cash – at 5.50% and offers stock or pays interest on cash at 5.25%.

Illustration of classic repo

There will be two parties to a repo trade, let us say Bank A (the seller of securities) and Bank B (the buyer of securities). On the trade date the two banks enter into an agreement whereby on a set date – the *value or settlement* date – Bank A will sell to Bank B a nominal amount of securities in exchange for cash.[7] The price received for the securities is the market value of the stock on the value date. The agreement also demands that on the termination date Bank B will sell identical stock back to Bank A at the previously agreed price, and, consequently, Bank B will have its cash returned with interest at the agreed repo rate.

In essence, a repo agreement is a secured loan (or *collateralised loan*) in which the repo rate reflects the interest charged.

On the value date, stock and cash change hands. This is known as the start date, *first leg*, or *opening leg*, while the termination date is known as the *second leg* or *closing leg*. When the cash is returned to Bank B, it is accompanied by the interest charged on the cash during the term of the trade. This interest is calculated at a specified rate known as the *repo rate*. It is important to remember that, although in legal terms the stock is initially "sold" to Bank B, the economic effects of ownership are retained with Bank A. This means that if the stock falls in price it is Bank A that will suffer a capital loss. Similarly, if the stock involved is a bond and there is a coupon payment during the term of trade, this coupon is to the benefit of Bank A and, although Bank B will have received it on the coupon date, it must be handed over on the same day or immediately after to Bank A. This reflects the fact that, although legal title to the collateral passes to the repo buyer, the economic costs and benefits of the collateral remain with the seller.

A classic repo transaction is subject to a legal contract signed in advance by both parties. A standard document will suffice; it is not necessary to sign a legal agreement prior to each transaction.

---

[7]The two terms are not necessarily synonymous. The value date in a trade is the date on which the transaction acquires value, for example, the date from which accrued interest is calculated. As such it may fall on a non-business day, such as a weekend or public holiday. The settlement date is the day on which the transaction settles or clears, and so can only fall on a working day.

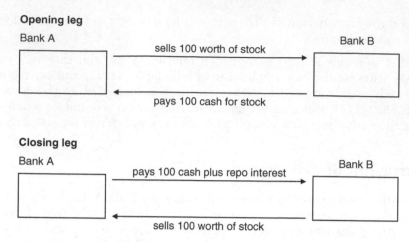

Figure 4.8   Classic repo transaction

Note that, although we have called the two parties in this case "Bank A" and "Bank B", it is not only banks that are involved in repo transactions – we have used these terms for the purposes of illustration only.

The basic mechanism is illustrated in Figure 4.8.

A seller in a repo transaction is entering into a repo, whereas a buyer is entering into a *reverse repo*. In Figure 4.8 the repo counterparty is Bank A, while Bank B is entering into a reverse repo. That is, a reverse repo is a purchase of securities that are sold back on termination. As is evident from Figure 4.8, every repo is a reverse repo, and the name given is dependent on whose viewpoint one is looking at the transaction from.[8]

Examples of classic repo

The basic principle is illustrated with the following example. This considers a specific repo – that is, one in which the collateral supplied is specified as a particular stock – as opposed to a general collateral (GC) trade in which a basket of collateral can be supplied, of any particular issue, as long as it is of the required type and credit quality.

---

[8]Note that the guidelines to the syllabus for the Chartered Financial Analyst examination, which is set by the Association for Investment Management and Research, defines repo and reverse repo slightly differently. Essentially, a "repo" is conducted by a bank counterparty and a "reverse repo" is conducted by an investment counterparty or non-financial counterparty. Another definition states that a "repo" is any trade where the bank counterparty is offering stock (borrowing cash) and a "reverse repo" is any trade where the non-bank counterparty is borrowing cash. The author believes this is artificial and so doesn't make this distinction; by definition every repo is a "reverse repo" for the other side.

We first consider a classic repo in the UK gilt market between two market counterparties in the 5.75% Treasury 2012 gilt stock as at 2 December 2005. The terms of the trade are given in Table 4.2 and the trade is illustrated in Figure 4.9.

The repo counterparty delivers to the reverse repo counterparty £10 million nominal of the stock, and in return receives the purchase proceeds. In this example, no margin has been taken, so the start proceeds are equal to the market value of the stock, which is £10,539,928. It is common for a rounded sum to be transferred on the opening leg. The repo rate is 4.50%, so the repo interest charged for the trade is:

$$10,539,928 \times 4.50\% \times \frac{7}{365}$$

Table 4.2   Terms of a classic repo trade

Trade date	2 December 2005
Value date	5 December 2005
Repo term	1 month
Termination date	5 January 2006
Collateral (stock)	UKT 5% 2012
Nominal amount	£10,000,000
Price	104.17
Accrued interest (89 days)	1.2292818
Dirty price	105.3993
Haircut	0%
Settlement proceeds (wired amount)	£10,539,928.18
Repo rate	4.50%
Repo interest	£40,282.74
Termination proceeds	£10,580,210.92

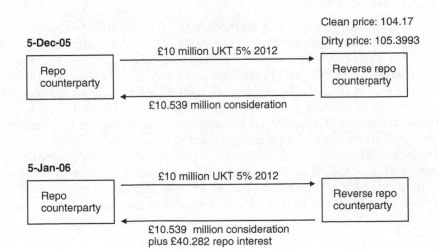

Figure 4.9   Classic repo trade example

or £40,282.74. The sterling market day-count basis is actual/365, so the repo interest is based on a 7-day repo rate of 4.50%. Repo rates are agreed at the time of the trade and are quoted, like all interest rates, on an annualised basis. The settlement price (dirty price) is used because it is the market value of the bonds on the particular trade date and therefore indicates the cash value of the gilts. By doing this, the cash investor minimises credit exposure by equating the value of the cash and the collateral.

On termination, the repo counterparty receives back its stock, for which it hands over the original proceeds plus the repo interest calculated above.

REPO COLLATERAL

The collateral in a repo trade is the security passed to the lender of cash by the borrower of cash. It is not always secondary to the transaction; in stock-driven transactions the requirement for specific collateral is the motivation behind the trade. However, in a classic repo or sell/buyback, the collateral is always the security handed over against cash.[9] In a stock loan transaction, the collateral against stock lent can be either securities or cash. Collateral is used in repo to provide security against default by the cash borrower. Therefore, it is protection against counterparty risk or credit risk, the risk that the cash-borrowing counterparty defaults on the loan. A secured or *collateralised* loan is theoretically lower credit risk exposure for a cash lender compared with an unsecured loan.

The most commonly encountered collateral is government bonds, and the repo market in government bonds is the largest in the world. Other forms of collateral include Eurobonds, other forms of corporate and supranational debt, asset-backed bonds, mortgage-backed bonds, money market securities such as T-bills, and equities.

In any market where there is a defined class of collateral of identical credit quality, this is known as *general collateral* (GC). So, for example, in the UK gilt market a GC repo is one where any gilt will be acceptable as repo collateral. Another form of GC might be "AA-rated sterling Eurobonds". In the US market, the term *stock collateral* is sometimes used to refer to GC securities. In equity repo it is more problematic to define GC and by definition almost all trades are specifics; however, it is becoming more common for counterparties to specify any equity being acceptable if it is in an established index – for example, a FTSE 100 or a CAC 40 stock – and this is perhaps the equity market equivalent of GC. If a specific security is required in a reverse repo or as the other side of a sell/buyback, this is known as a *specific* or *specific collateral*. A specific stock that is in high demand in the market, such that the

---

[9]So that even in a stock-driven reverse repo the collateral is the security handed over against the borrowing of cash by the repo seller.

repo rate against it is significantly different from the GC rate, is known as a *special*.

Where a coupon payment is received on collateral during the term of a repo, it is to the benefit of the repo seller. Under the standard repo legal agreement, legal title to collateral is transferred to the buyer during the term of the repo, but it is accepted that the economic benefits remain with the seller. For this reason, the coupon is returned to the seller. In classic repo (and in stock lending) the coupon is returned to the seller on the dividend date, or in some cases on the following date. In a sell/buyback the effect of the coupon is incorporated in the repurchase price. This includes interest on the coupon amount that is payable by the buyer during the period from the coupon date to the buyback date.

LEGAL TREATMENT

Classic repo is carried out under a legal agreement that defines the transaction as a full transfer of the title to the stock. The standard legal agreement is the PSA/ISMA GRMA, which we review in the book *An Introduction to Repo Markets 3e*. It is now possible to trade sell/buybacks under this agreement as well. This agreement was based on the PSA standard legal agreement used in the US domestic market, and was compiled because certain financial institutions were not allowed to borrow or lend securities legally. By transacting repo under the PSA agreement, these institutions were defined as legally buying and selling securities rather than borrowing or lending them.

MARGIN

To reduce the level of risk exposure in a repo transaction, it is common for the lender of cash to ask for a margin, which is where the market value of collateral is higher than the value of cash lent out in the repo. This is a form of protection should the cash-borrowing counterparty default on the loan. Another term for margin is *overcollateralisation* or a *haircut*. There are two types of margin: *initial margin* taken at the start of the trade and *variation margin*, which is called if required during the term of the trade.

Initial margin

The cash proceeds in a repo are typically no more than the market value of the collateral. This minimises credit exposure by equating the value of the cash to that of the collateral. The market value of the collateral is calculated at its *dirty* price, not *clean* price – that is, including accrued interest. This is referred to as *accrual pricing*. To calculate the accrued interest on the (bond) collateral we require the day-count basis for the particular bond.

The start proceeds of a repo can be less than the market value of the collateral by an agreed amount or percentage. This is known as the initial margin or haircut. The initial margin protects the buyer against:

- A sudden fall in the market value of the collateral;
- Illiquidity of collateral;
- Other sources of volatility of value (for example, approaching maturity);
- Counterparty risk.

The margin level of repo varies from 0–2% for collateral such as UK gilts, to 5% for cross-currency and equity repo, to 10–35% for emerging market debt repo.

In both classic repo and sell/buyback, any initial margin is given to the supplier of cash in the transaction. This remains the case in the case of specific repo. For initial margin, the market value of the bond collateral is reduced (or given a haircut) by the percentage of the initial margin and the nominal value determined from this reduced amount. In a stock loan transaction, the lender of stock will ask for margin.

There are two methods for calculating margin; for a 2% margin this could be one of the following:

- The dirty price of the bonds × 0.98;
- The dirty price of the bonds ÷1.02.

The two methods do not give the same value! The RRRA repo page on Bloomberg uses the second method for its calculations, and this method is turning into something of a convention.

For a 2% margin level, the PSA/ISMA GRMA defines a "margin ratio" as:

$$\frac{\text{Collateral value}}{\text{Cash}} = 102\%$$

The size of margin required in any particular transaction is a function of the following:

- The credit quality of the counterparty supplying the collateral: for example, a central bank counterparty, inter-bank counterparty, and corporate will all suggest different margin levels;
- The term of the repo: an overnight repo is inherently lower risk than a 1-year repo;
- The duration (price volatility) of the collateral: for example, a T-bill against the long bond;
- The existence or absence of a legal agreement: a repo traded under a standard agreement is considered lower risk.

However, in the final analysis, margin is required to guard against market risk, the risk that the value of collateral will drop during the course of the repo. Therefore, the margin call must reflect the risks prevalent in the market at the time; extremely volatile market conditions may call for large increases in initial margin.

Variation margin

The market value of collateral is maintained through the use of *variation margin*. So, if the market value of collateral falls, the buyer calls for extra cash or collateral. If the market value of collateral rises, the seller calls for extra cash or collateral. In order to reduce the administrative burden, margin calls can be limited to changes in the market value of collateral in excess of an agreed amount or percentage, which is called a *margin maintenance limit*.

The standard market documentation that exists for the three structures covered so far includes clauses that allow parties to a transaction to call for variation margin during the term of a repo. This can be in the form of extra collateral, if the value of collateral has dropped in relation to the asset exchanged, or a return of collateral, if the value has risen. If the cash-borrowing counterparty is unable to supply more collateral where required, he will have to return a portion of the cash loan. Both parties have an interest in making and meeting margin calls, although there is no obligation. The level at which variation margin is triggered is often agreed beforehand in the legal agreement put in place between individual counterparties. Although primarily viewed as an instrument used by the supplier of cash against a fall in the value of the collateral, variation margin can of course also be called by the repo seller if the value of the collateral has risen.

FOREIGN EXCHANGE

The market in foreign exchange is an excellent example of a liquid, transparent, and immediate global financial market. Rates in the foreign exchange (FX) markets move at a rapid pace and in fact trading in FX is a different discipline to bond trading or money markets trading. There is considerable literature on the FX markets, as it is a separate subject in its own right. However, some banks organise their forward desk as part of the money market desk and not the foreign exchange desk, necessitating its inclusion in this chapter. For this reason, we present an overview summary of FX in this chapter, both spot and forward.

Market conventions

The price quotation for currencies generally follows the ISO convention, which is also used by the SWIFT and Reuters dealing systems, and is the three-letter code used to identify a currency, such as USD for US dollar and GBP for sterling. The rate convention is to quote everything in terms of one unit of the US dollar, so that the dollar and Swiss franc rate is quoted as USD/CHF, and is the number of Swiss francs to one US dollar. The exception is for sterling, which is quoted as GBP/USD and is the number of US dollars to the pound. The rate for euros has been quoted both ways round, for example,

EUR/USD, although some banks, for example, RBS Financial Markets in the UK, quotes euros to the pound, that is GBP/EUR.

Spot exchange rates

A *spot* FX trade is an outright purchase or sale of one currency against another currency, with delivery 2 working days after the trade date. Non-working days do not count, so a trade on a Friday is settled on the following Tuesday. There are some exceptions to this, for example, trades of US dollar against Canadian dollar are settled the next working day. Note that in some currencies, generally in the Middle East, markets are closed on Friday but open on Saturday. A settlement date that falls on a public holiday in the country of one of the two currencies is delayed for settlement by that day. An FX transaction is possible between any two currencies. However, to reduce the number of quotes that need to be made the market generally quotes only against the US dollar or occasionally sterling or euro, so that the exchange rate between two non-dollar currencies is calculated from the rate for each currency against the dollar. The resulting exchange rate is known as the *cross-rate*. Cross-rates themselves are also traded between banks in addition to dollar-based rates. This is usually because the relationship between two rates is closer than that of either against the dollar, for example, the Swiss franc moves more closely in line with the euro than against the dollar, so in practice one observes that the dollar/Swiss franc rate is more a function of the euro/franc rate.

The spot FX quote is a two-way bid–offer price, just as in the bond and money markets, and indicates the rate at which a bank is prepared to buy the base currency against the variable currency; this is the "bid" for the variable currency, so is the lower rate. The other side of the quote is the rate at which the bank is prepared to sell the base currency against the variable currency. For example, a quote of 1.6245–1.6255 for GBP/USD means that the bank is prepared to buy sterling for $1.6245 and to sell sterling for $1.6255. The convention in the FX market is uniform across countries, unlike the money markets. Although the money market convention for bid–offer quotes is, for example, $5\frac{1}{2}$–$5\frac{1}{4}$%, meaning that the "bid" for paper – the rate at which the bank will lend funds, say in the CD market – is the higher rate and always on the left, this convention is reversed in certain countries. In the FX markets, the convention is always the same as the one just described.

The difference between the two sides in a quote is the bank's dealing spread. Rates are quoted to 1/100th of a cent, known as a *pip*. In the quote above, the spread is 10 pips; however, this amount is a function of the size of the quote number, so that the rate for USD/JPY at, say, 110.10–110.20 indicates a spread of 0.10 yen. Generally, only the pips in the two rates are quoted, so that, for example, the quote above would be simply "45–55". The "big figure" is not quoted.

> ### Example 4.5   Exchange cross-rates
>
> Consider the following two spot rates:
>
> EUR/USD   1.0566–1.0571
> AUD/USD   0.7034–0.7039
>
> The EUR/USD dealer buys euros and sells dollars at 1.0566 (the left side),
> while the AUD/USD dealer sells Australian dollars and buys US dollars at
> 0.7039 (the right side). To calculate the rate at which the bank buys euros
> and sells Australian dollars, we need:
>
> EUR/USD   1.0566–1.0571
> AUD/USD   0.7034–0.7039
>
> The EUR/USD dealer buys euros and sells dollars at 1.0566 (the left side),
> while the AUD/USD dealer sells Australian dollars and buys US dollars at
> 0.7039 (the right side). To calculate the rate at which the bank buys euros
> and sells Australian dollars, we need:
>
> $$1.0566/0.7039 = 1.4997$$
>
> which is the rate at which the bank buys euros and sells Australian dollars.
> In the same way, the rate at which the bank sells euros and buys Australian
> dollars is given by 1.0571/0.7034 or 1.5028.
>
> Therefore, the spot EUR/AUD rate is 1.4997–1.5028.
>
> The derivation of cross-rates can be depicted in the following way. If we
> assume two exchange rates XXX/YYY and XXX/ZZZ, the cross-rates are:
>
> $$YYY/ZZZ = XXX/ZZZ \div XXX/YYY$$
> $$ZZZ/YYY = XXX/YYY \div XXX/ZZZ$$
>
> Given two exchange rates YYY/XXX and XXX/ZZZ, the cross-rates are:
>
> $$YYY/ZZZ = YYY/XXX \times XXX/ZZZ$$
> $$ZZZ/YYY = 1 \div (YYY/XXX \times XXX/ZZZ)$$

Forward exchange rates

We consider forward exchange rates in the next two sections.

Forward outright

The spot exchange rate is the rate for immediate delivery (notwithstanding
that actual delivery is 2 days forward). A *forward contract* or simply *forward* is
an outright purchase or sale of one currency in exchange for another currency

for settlement on a specified date at some point in the future. The exchange rate is quoted in the same way as the spot rate, with the bank buying the base currency on the bid side and selling it on the offered side. In some emerging markets no liquid forward market exists, so forwards are settled in cash against the spot rate on the maturity date. These *non-deliverable forwards* are considered at the end of this section.

Although some commentators have stated that the forward rate may be seen as the market's view of where the spot rate will be on the maturity date of the forward transaction, this is incorrect. A forward rate is calculated on the current interest rates of the two currencies involved, and the principle of no-arbitrage pricing ensures that there is no profit to be gained from simultaneous (and opposite) dealing in spot and forward. Consider the following strategy:

- Borrow US dollars for 6 months starting from the spot value date;
- Sell dollars and buy sterling for value spot;
- Deposit the long sterling position for 6 months from the spot value date;
- Sell forward today the sterling principal and interest, which mature in 6 months' time into dollars.

The market will adjust the forward price so that the two initial transactions if carried out simultaneously will generate a zero profit/loss. The forward rates quoted in the trade will be calculated on the 6 months deposit rates for dollars and sterling; in general, the calculation of a forward rate is given as 2.1.

$$Fwd = Spot \times \frac{\left(1 + \text{Variable currency deposit rate} \times \frac{Days}{B}\right)}{\left(1 + \text{Base currency deposit rate} \times \frac{Days}{B}\right)} \tag{4.15}$$

The year day-count base B will be either 365 or 360 depending on the convention for the currency in question.

Example 4.6 Forward rate	
90-day GBP deposit rate:	5.75%
90-day USD deposit rate:	6.15%
Spot GBP/USD rate:	1.6315 (mid-rate)

The forward rate is given by:

$$1.6315 \times \frac{\left(1 + 0.0575 \times \frac{90}{365}\right)}{\left(1 + 0.0615 \times \frac{90}{360}\right)} = 1.6296$$

Therefore, to deal forward the GBP/USD mid-rate is 1.6296, so in effect £1 buys $1.6296 in 3 months' time as opposed to $1.6315 today. Under different circumstances, sterling may be worth more in the future than at the spot date.

Example 4.7   Forward rate arbitrage

The following rates are quoted to a bank:

USD/CHF	spot:	1.4810–1.4815
	3-month swap:	116–111
USD	3-month deposit rates:	7.56–7.43
CHF	3-month deposit rates:	4.62–4.50

The bank requires funding of CHF10 million for 3 months (91 days). It deals on the above rates and actions the following:

(i) It borrows USD 6,749,915.63 for 91 days from spot at 7.56%;

(ii) At the end of the 91 days the bank repays the principal plus the interest, which is a total of USD 6,880,324.00;

(iii) The bank "buys and sells" USD against CHF at a swap price of 11, based on the spot rate of 1.4815, that is:
   - The bank sells USD6,749,915.63/buys CHF 10 million spot at 1.4815;
   - The bank buys USD 6,880,324/sells CHF 10,116,828.42 for 3 months; forward at 1.4704.

The net USD cash flows result in a zero balance.

The effective cost of borrowing is therefore interest of CHF 116,828.41 on a principal sum of CHF 10 million for 91 days, which is:

$$\frac{116,828}{10,000,000} \times \frac{360}{91} = 4.57\%$$

The net effect is therefore a CHF 10 million borrowing at 4.57%, which is 5 basis points lower than the 4.62% quote at which the bank could borrow directly in the market. If the bank has not actually required funding but was able to deposit the Swiss francs at a higher rate than 4.57%, it would have been able to lock in a profit.

Forward swaps

The calculation given above illustrates how a forward rate is calculated and quoted in theory. In practice, as spot rates change rapidly, often many times even in 1 minute, it would be tedious to keep recalculating the forward rate so often. Therefore, banks quote a forward spread over the spot rate, which can then be added or subtracted to the spot rate as it changes. This spread is known as the *swap points*. An approximate value for the number of swap points is given by (4.16) below.

$$\text{Forward swap} \approx \text{Spot} \times \text{Deposit rate differential} \times \frac{Days}{B} \qquad (4.16)$$

The approximation is not accurate enough for forwards maturing more than 30 days from now, in which case another equation must be used. This is given as (4.17). It is also possible to calculate an approximate deposit rate differential from the swap points by rearranging (4.16).

$$\text{Forward swap} = \text{Spot} \times \frac{\left(\begin{array}{l}\text{Variable currency depo rate} \times \dfrac{\text{Days}}{B} \\[2mm] - \text{Base currency depo rate} \times \dfrac{\text{Days}}{B}\end{array}\right)}{\left(1 + \text{Base currency depo rate} \times \dfrac{\text{Days}}{B}\right)} \qquad (4.17)$$

Example 4.8　　Forward swap points

Spot EUR/USD:	1.0566–1.0571
Forward swap:	0.0125–0.0130
Forward outright:	1.0691–1.0701

The forward outright is the spot price + the swap points, so in this case:

$$1.0691 = 1.0566 + 0.0125$$

$$1.0701 = 1.0571 + 0.0130$$

Spot EUR/USD rate:	0.9501
31-day EUR rate:	3.15%
31-day USD rate:	5.95%

$$\text{Forward swap} = 0.9501 \times \frac{0.0595 \times \dfrac{31}{360} - 0.0315 \times \dfrac{31}{360}}{1 + 0.0315 \times \dfrac{31}{360}} = 0.0024$$

or +24 points.

The swap points are quoted as two-way prices in the same way as spot rates. In practice, a middle spot price is used and then the forward swap spread around the spot quote. The difference between the interest rates of the two currencies will determine the magnitude of the swap points and whether they are added or subtracted from the spot rate. When the swap points are positive and the forwards trader applies a bid–offer spread to quote a two-way price, the left-hand side of the quote is smaller than the right-hand side as usual. When the swap points are negative, the trader must quote a "more negative" number on the left and a "more positive" number on the right-hand side. The "minus" sign is not shown, however, so that the left-hand side may appear to be the larger number. Basically, when the swap price appears larger on the right, it means that it is negative and must be subtracted from the spot rate and not added.

Forwards traders are in fact interest-rate traders rather than foreign exchange traders. Although they will be left positions that arise from customer orders, in general they will manage their book based on their view of short-term deposit rates in the currencies they are trading. In general, a forwards trader expecting the interest-rate differential to move in favour of the base currency, for example, a rise in base currency rates or a fall in the variable currency rate, will "buy and sell" the base currency. This is equivalent to borrowing the base currency and depositing in the variable currency. The relationship between interest rates and forward swaps means that banks can take advantage of different opportunities in different markets. Assume that a bank requires funding in one currency but is able to borrow in another currency at a relatively cheaper rate. It may wish to borrow in the second currency and use a forward contract to convert the borrowing to the first currency. It will do this if the all-in cost of borrowing is less than the cost of borrowing directly in the first currency.

Forward cross-rates

A forward cross-rate is calculated in the same way as spot cross-rates. The formulas given for spot cross-rates can be adapted to forward rates.

Forward-forwards

A forward-forward swap is a deal between two forward dates rather than from the spot date to a forward date. This is the same terminology and meaning as in the bond markets, where a forward or a forward-forward rate is the zero-coupon interest rate between two points both beginning in the future. In the foreign exchange market, an example would be a contract to sell sterling 3 months forward and buy it back in 6 months' time. Here, the swap is for the 3-month period between the 3-month date and the 6-month date. The reason a bank or corporate might do this is to hedge a forward exposure or because of a particular view it has on forward rates, in effect deposit rates.

Example 4.9   Forward-forward contract

GBP/USD spot rate:	1.6315–20
3-month swap:	45–41
6-month swap:	135–125

If a bank wished to sell GBP 3 months forward and buy them back 6 months forward, this is identical to undertaking one swap to buy GBP spot and sell GBP 3 months forward, and another to sell GBP spot and buy it 6 months forward. Swaps are always quoted as the quoting bank buying the base currency forward on the bid side, and selling the base currency forward on the offered side; the counterparty bank can "buy and sell" GBP "spot against

3 months" at a swap price of –45, with settlement rates of spot and (spot –0.0045). It can "sell and buy" GBP "spot against 6 months" at the swap price of –125 with settlement rates of spot and (spot –0.0125). It can therefore do both simultaneously, which implies a difference between the two forward prices of (–125) – (–45) = –90 points. Conversely, the bank can "buy and sell" GBP "3 months against 6 months" at a swap price of (–135) – (–41) or –94 points. The two-way price is therefore 94–90 (we ignore the negative signs).

FX BALANCE SHEET HEDGING

The majority of the world's banks hold assets that are denominated in the domestic reporting currency. That said, many vanilla commercial banks originate assets and/or raise liabilities that are in a different currency to their reporting currency. This generates an element of structural balance sheet risk because the reporting currency is different and the FX rate impacts final reporting numbers. Where the asset is funded by liabilities in a different currency, this generates a further liquidity risk exposure.

The approach to hedging this first-order FX risk ("reporting risk", if you like) is orthodox as practised by most banks. We present the basic principles as a series illustration of a worked example, shown in Figures 4.10 to 4.13.

Other instruments that may be used in off-balance-sheet hedging include:

- Cross currency swaps;
- Options.

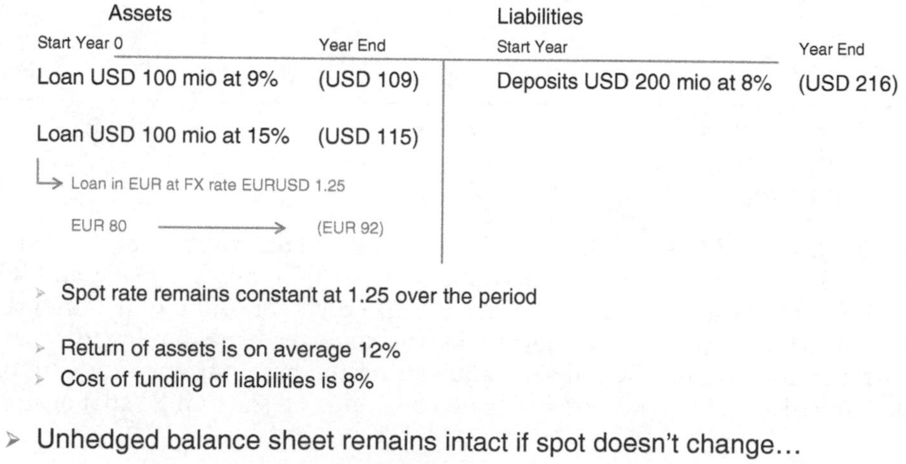

Assets		Liabilities	
Start Year 0	Year End	Start Year	Year End
Loan USD 100 mio at 9%	(USD 109)	Deposits USD 200 mio at 8%	(USD 216)
Loan USD 100 mio at 15%	(USD 115)		
↳ Loan in EUR at FX rate EURUSD 1.25			
EUR 80 ⟶	(EUR 92)		

➢ Spot rate remains constant at 1.25 over the period

➢ Return of assets is on average 12%
➢ Cost of funding of liabilities is 8%

➢ Unhedged balance sheet remains intact if spot doesn't change...

Figure 4.10   FX balance sheet hedging- part (i)

Assets		Liabilities	
Start Year 0	Year End	Start Year	Year End
Loan USD 100 mio at 9%	(USD 109)	Deposits USD 200 mio at 8%	(USD 216)
Loan USD 100 mio at 15%	(USD 105.8)		
	(USD 128.8)		
↳ Loan in EUR at FX rate EURUSD 1.15/1.40			
EUR 80 ——15%——→	(EUR 92)		

> Spot rate depreciates to 1.00 vs appreciates to 1.50 at the end of the period

> Return of assets is on average 7.4% ⬅⬛⬛⬛➡ 18.90%
> Cost of funding of liabilities is 8%

> Unhedged balance sheet will negatively affect returns in case of depreciation of foreign currency and vice versa.

Figure 4.11　FX balance sheet hedging- part (ii)

• On balance sheet hedging by matching the liabilities against the assets in terms of foreign exchange exposure.

Assets		Liabilities	
Start Year 0	Year End	Start Year	Year End
Loan USD 100 mio at 9%	(USD 109)	Deposits USD 100 mio at 8%	(USD 108)
Loan USD 100 mio at 15%	(USD 105.8)	Deposits USD 100 mio at 11%	(USD 102.12)
	(USD 128.8)		(USD 124.32)
↳ Loan in EUR at FX rate EURUSD 1.15/1.40		↳ Deposit in EUR at FX rate EURUSD 1.15/1.40	
EUR 80 ——————→	(EUR 92)	EUR 80 ——————→	(EUR 88.80)

> Spot rate depreciates to 1.00 vs appreciates to 1.50 at the end of the period

> Return of assets is on average 7.4% ⬅⬛⬛➡ 18.90%
> Cost of funding of liabilities is 5.06% 16.16%

> Not a perfect hedge but return remains positive.

Figure 4.12　FX balance sheet hedging- part (iii)

Exotic options such as knock-ins, knock-outs, digitals, or even window barriers will inject optionality into your hedge again but at a price.

It is safe to say that 95% of the world's banks' FX hedging requirements can be met with cash or plain vanilla derivative products. Hedging is as much art as science, so there is often little upside payoff in structuring a sophisticated hedge that costs you almost as much as it is meant to save you.

Assets		Liabilities	
Start Year 0	Year End	Start Year	Year End
Loan USD 100 mio at 9%	(USD 109)	Deposits USD 200 mio at 8%	(USD 216)
Loan USD 100 mio at 15%	(USD 115)		

↳ Loan in EUR at FX rate EURUSD 1.25

EUR 80   ——————→   (EUR 92)

➢ Bank enters (off-balance-sheet) into an FX swap (spot-forward) contract with maturity at year end

➢ E.g. forward curve EURUSD shows a discount of 500 points or FX FWD rate EURUSD 1.20

➢ Result: EUR 92 at EURUSD 1.20 converted is USD 110.4

➢ Return of assets is locked in at an on average rate of 9.70%
➢ Cost of funding of liabilities remains 8%

Figure 4.13   FX balance sheet hedging- part (iv)

CURRENCIES USING MONEY MARKET YEAR BASE OF 365 DAYS

- Sterling;
- Hong Kong dollar;
- Malaysian ringgit;
- Singapore dollar;
- South African rand;
- Taiwan dollar;
- Thai baht.

In addition, the domestic markets, but not the international markets, of the following currencies also use a 365-day base:

- Australian dollar;
- Canadian dollar;
- Japanese yen;
- New Zealand dollar.

To convert an interest rate i quoted on a 365-day basis to one quoted on a 360-day basis (i^*) we use the expressions given at (4.18):

$$\left.\begin{array}{l} i = i^* \times \dfrac{365}{360} \\[2mm] i^* = i \times \dfrac{360}{365} \end{array}\right\} \tag{4.18}$$

Chapter

5

....

THE YIELD CURVE

Understanding and appreciating the yield curve is, or should be, important to all finance market participants. It is especially important to debt capital market participants, and even more especially important to bank practitioners. So, for anyone reading this book, it is safe to assume that the yield curve is a very important subject! This is a long chapter but well worth getting to grips with. In it, we discuss the basic concepts of the yield curve, as well as its uses and interpretation. We show how to calculate the zero-coupon (or spot) and forward yield curve, and present the main theories that seek to explain its shape and behaviour. We will see that the spread of one different curve to another, such as the swap curve compared with the government curve, is itself important. We begin with an introduction to the curve and interest rates.

IMPORTANCE OF THE YIELD CURVE

Banks deal in interest rates and credit risk. These are two fundamental tenets of banking – just as fundamental today as they were when banking first began. The first of these – interest rates – is an explicit measure of the cost of borrowing money and is encapsulated in the yield curve. For bankers, understanding the behaviour and properties of the yield curve is an essential part of the loan pricing and asset-liability management (ALM) process. The following are some, but not all, of the reasons that this is so:

- Changes in interest rates have a direct impact on bank revenue, measured by net interest income (NII); the yield curve captures the current state of term interest rates and also presents the current market expectation of future interest rates;
- The interest-rate gap reflects the state of bank borrowing and lending; gaps along the term structure are sensitive to changes in the shape and slope of the yield curve;
- Current and future business strategy, including the asset allocation and credit policy decision, will impact interest-rate risk exposure and therefore will take into account the shape and behaviour of the yield curve.

We can see then that understanding and appreciating the yield curve is a vital part of banking and ALM operations. This chapter is a detailed look at the curve from the banker's viewpoint.

The yield curve is an important indicator and knowledge source of the state of a financial market. It is sometimes referred to as the *term structure of interest rates*, although strictly speaking this is not correct, as this expression should be reserved for the zero-coupon yield curve only. In other words, the two expressions are not synonymous. But we don't need to worry about this here.

The analysis and pricing activity that takes place in financial markets revolves around the yield curve. The yield curve describes the relationship between a particular yield and its term to maturity. So, plotting yields of a set of interest rates along the maturity structure will give us our yield curve. These interest rates can come from a variety of sources, including market instruments such as bonds or deposits. The primary curve in any domestic capital market is the government bond yield curve – for example, in the US market it is the US Treasury yield curve. Outside government bond markets, yield curves are plotted for Eurobonds, money market instruments, off-balance-sheet instruments – in fact, virtually all debt market products. So, it is always important to remember to compare like for like when analysing yield curves across markets.

USING THE YIELD CURVE

The yield curve tells us where the bond market is trading now. It also implies the level of trading for the future, or at least what the market thinks will be happening in the future. In other words, it is a good indicator of the future level of the market. It is also a much more reliable indicator than any other indicator used by private investors, and we can prove this empirically. But for the moment take my word for it!

As an introduction to yield curve analysis, let us first consider its main uses. All participants in debt capital markets will be interested in the current shape and level of the yield curve, as well as what this information implies for the future. The main uses are summarised below.

Setting the yield for all debt market instruments. The yield curve essentially fixes the price of money over the maturity structure. The yields of government bonds from the shortest maturity instrument to the longest set the benchmark for yields for all other debt instruments in the market, around which all debt instruments are priced. What does this mean? Essentially, it means that if a government 5-year bond is trading at a yield of 5.00%, all other 5-year bonds, whoever they are issued by, will be issued at a yield over 5.00%. The amount over 5.00% that the other bond trades is known as the spread. Therefore, issuers of debt use the yield curve to price bonds and all other debt instruments. Generally, the zero-coupon yield curve is used to price new issue securities, rather than the redemption yield curve.

The spread over the risk-free yield is composed of credit risk spread and term liquidity risk spread (see Figure 5.1). It is this risky curve that drives customer loan pricing.

Acting as an indicator of future yield levels. As we discuss later in this chapter, the yield curve assumes certain shapes in response to market expectations of future interest rates. Bond market participants analyse the present shape of the yield curve in an effort to determine implications regarding the direction of market interest rates. This is perhaps one of the most important functions of the yield curve. Interpreting it is a mixture of art and science. The yield curve is scrutinised for its information content not just by bond traders and fund managers but also by corporate financiers as part of their project appraisals. Central banks and government Treasury departments also analyse the yield curve for its information content, not just regarding forward

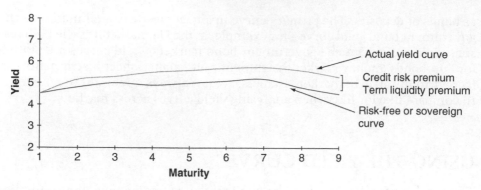

Figure 5.1   Risk-free and risky curves

interest rates but also inflation levels. They then use this information when setting interest rates.

Measuring and comparing returns across the maturity spectrum. Portfolio managers use the yield curve to assess the relative value of investments across the maturity spectrum. The yield curve indicates returns that are available at different maturity points and is therefore very important to fixed interest fund managers, who can use it to assist them to assess which point of the curve offers the best return relative to other points.

Indicating the relative value between different bonds of similar maturity. The yield curve can be analysed to indicate which bonds are "cheap" or "dear" (expensive) to the curve. Placing bonds relative to the *zero-coupon yield curve* helps to highlight which bonds should be bought or sold, either outright or as part of a bond spread trade.

Pricing interest-rate derivative instruments. The price of derivatives such as futures and swaps revolves around the yield curve. At the shorter end, products such as forward rate agreements are priced off the futures curve, but futures rates reflect the market's view on forward 3-month cash deposit rates. At the longer end, interest-rate swaps are priced off the yield curve, while hybrid instruments that incorporate an option feature such as convertibles and callable bonds also reflect current yield curve levels. The "risk-free" interest rate – one of the parameters used in option pricing – is the T-bill rate or short-term government repo rate, both constituents of the money market yield curve.

YIELD-TO-MATURITY YIELD CURVE

Yield curve shapes

The most commonly occurring yield curve is the yield-to-maturity (YTM) yield curve. The process of calculating a debt instrument's yield to maturity is described in countless finance textbooks. The curve itself is constructed by plotting yield to maturity against term to maturity for a group of bonds of the same class.

Curves assume many different shapes; Figure 5.2 shows three common types. Bonds used in constructing the curve will only rarely have an exact number of whole years to redemption; however, it is often common to see yields plotted against whole years on the X-axis. This is because once a bond is designated the *benchmark* for that term, its yield is taken to be the representative yield. A bond loses benchmark status once a new benchmark for that maturity is issued.

The yield-to-maturity yield curve is the most commonly observed curve simply because yield to maturity is the most frequent measure of return used. The business sections of daily newspapers – if they quote bond yield at all – usually quote bond yields to maturity.

The yield-to-maturity yield curve contains some inaccuracies. This is because the yield-to-maturity measure has one large weakness: the assumption of a constant discount rate for coupons during the bond's life at the redemption yield level. In other words, we discount all the cash flows of the bond at one discount rate. This is not a realistic assumption to make because we know, just as night follows day, that interest rates in 6 months' time (used to discount the coupon due in 6 months) will not be the same as the interest rate prevailing in 2 years' time (used to discount the 2-year coupon). To actually earn the YTM stated on a bond, one would have to purchase the bond at par and then be able to reinvest all of the bond's coupons at the same stated YTM. This is clearly never going to happen. But we make this assumption nevertheless – for the

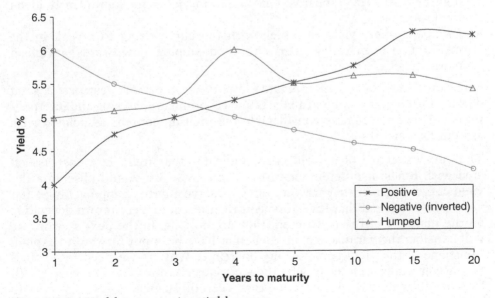

Figure 5.2   Yield-to-maturity yield curves

sake of convenience. However, the upshot of all this is that redemption yield is not the true interest rate for its particular maturity.

By the way, this gives rise to a feature known as reinvestment risk: the risk that – when we reinvest each bond coupon as it is paid – the interest rate at which we invest it will not be the same as the redemption yield prevailing on the day we bought the bond. We must accept this risk, unless we buy a strip or zero-coupon bond. Only zero-coupon bondholders avoid reinvestment risk as no coupon is paid during the life of their bond.

For the reasons we have discussed, the professional wholesale market often uses other types of yield curve for analysis when the yield-to-maturity yield curve is deemed unsuitable – usually, the zero-coupon yield curve. This is the yield curve constructed from zero-coupon yields; it is also known as the term structure of interest rates. We construct a zero-coupon curve from bond prices and redemption yields.

ANALYSING AND INTERPRETING THE YIELD CURVE

From observing yield curves in different markets at any time, we notice that a yield curve can adopt one of four basic shapes:

- *Normal or conventional*: in which yields are at "average" levels and the curve slopes gently upwards as maturity increases;
- *Upward sloping or positive or rising*: in which yields are at historically low levels, with long rates substantially greater than short rates;
- *Downward sloping or inverted or negative*: in which yield levels are very high by historical standards, but long-term yields are significantly lower than short rates;
- *Humped*: where yields are high with the curve rising to a peak in the medium-term maturity area, and then sloping downwards at longer maturities.

Sometimes yield curves incorporate a mixture of the above features. A great deal of effort is spent by bond analysts and economists analysing and interpreting yield curves. There is considerable information content associated with any curve at any time.

The very existence of a yield curve indicates that there is a cost associated with funds of different maturities, otherwise we would observe a flat yield curve. The fact that we very rarely observe anything approaching a flat yield curve suggests that investors require different rates of return depending on the maturity of the instrument they are holding. In the next section, we will consider the various explanations that have been put forward to explain the shape of the yield curve at any one time. Why do we need to do this? Because an understanding of why the yield curve assumes certain shapes will help us understand the information that a certain shape implies.

None of the theories can adequately explain everything about yield curves and the shapes they assume at any time, so generally observers seek to explain specific curves using a combination of accepted theories.

THEORIES OF THE YIELD CURVE

No one mathematical explanation of the yield curve explains its shape at all times. At the same time, some explanations are mutually exclusive. That said, practitioners often seek to explain the shape of a curve by recourse to a mixture of theories.

The expectations hypothesis

The *expectations hypothesis* suggests that bondholder expectations determine the course of future interest rates. There are two main competing versions of this hypothesis: the *local expectations hypothesis* and the *unbiased expectations hypothesis*. The *return-to-maturity expectations hypothesis* and *yield-to-maturity expectations* hypothesis are also quoted (see Ingersoll, 1987). The local expectations hypothesis states that all bonds of the same class – but differing in term to maturity – will have the same expected holding period rate of return. This suggests that a 6-month bond and a 20-year bond will produce the same rate of return, on average, over the stated holding period. So, if we intend to hold a bond for 6 months, we will get the same return no matter what specific bond we buy. The author feels that this theory is not always the case, despite being mathematically neat; however, it is worth spending a few moments discussing it and related points. Generally, holding period returns from longer dated bonds are on average higher than those from short-dated bonds. Intuitively, we would expect this, with longer dated bonds offering higher returns to compensate for their higher price volatility (risk). The local expectations hypothesis would not agree with the conventional belief that investors, being risk averse, require higher returns as a reward for taking on higher risk; in addition, it does not provide any insight into the shape of the yield curve. Essentially though, in theory, one should expect that the return from holding any bond for a 6-month period will be the same irrespective of the term to maturity and yield that the bond has at time of purchase.

In his excellent book *Modelling Fixed Income Securities*, Professor Robert Jarrow (1996, p. 50) states:

> "...in an economic equilibrium, the returns on similar maturity zero-coupon bonds cannot be too different. If they were too different, no investor would hold the bond with the smaller return. This difference could not persist in an economic equilibrium."

This is true, but in practice other factors can impact holding period returns between bonds that do not have similar maturities. For instance, investors have restrictions as to which bonds they can hold – for example, banks and building societies are required to hold short-dated bonds for liquidity purposes. In an environment of economic disequilibrium, these investors would still have to hold shorter dated bonds, even if the holding period return was lower.

This is noted by Mark Rubinstein (1999, pp. 84–85) who states in his book *Rubinstein on Derivatives*:

> "In the real world…it is usually the case that annualised shorter-term risk-less returns are lower than longer-term riskless returns…Real assets with shorter-term payouts will tend to have a "liquidity" advantage. In aggregate this advantage will be passed on to shorter-term financial claims on real assets [which results in them having a lower return]."

A related theory is the *pure or unbiased expectations hypothesis*, which states that current implied forward rates are unbiased estimators of future spot interest rates.[1] It assumes that investors act in a way that eliminates any advantage of holding instruments of a particular maturity. Therefore, if we have a positive-sloping yield curve, the unbiased expectations hypothesis states that the market expects spot interest rates to rise. Equally, an inverted yield curve is an indication that spot rates are expected to fall. If short-term interest rates are expected to rise, then longer yields should be higher than shorter ones to reflect this. If this were not the case, investors would only buy the shorter dated bonds and roll over the investment when they matured. Likewise, if rates are expected to fall, then longer yields should be lower than short yields. The unbiased expectations hypothesis states that the long-term interest rate is a geometric average of expected future short-term rates.

Using elementary mathematics we can prove this theory. Indeed, its premise must be so, to ensure no *arbitrage* opportunities exist in the market. The hypothesis can be used to explain any shape in the yield curve.

Therefore, a rising yield curve is explained by investors expecting short-term interest rates to rise. A falling yield curve is explained by investors expecting short-term rates to be lower in the future. A humped yield curve is explained by investors expecting short-term interest rates to rise and long-term rates to fall. *Expectations*, or views on the future direction of the market, are a function mainly of the expected rate of inflation. If the market expects inflationary pressures in the future, the yield curve will be positively shaped, while if inflation expectations are inclined towards disinflation, then the yield curve will be negative. Several empirical studies including one by Fama (1976) have shown that forward rates are essentially biased predictors of future spot interest rates, and often overestimate future levels of spot rates.

---

[1] For the original discussion, see Lutz (1940) and Fisher (1986), although the latter formulated his ideas earlier.

The unbiased hypothesis has also been criticised for suggesting that investors can forecast (or have a view on) very long-dated spot interest rates, which might be considered slightly unrealistic. As yield curves in most developed country markets exist to a maturity of up to 30 years or longer, such criticisms may have some substance. Are investors able to forecast interest rates 10, 20, or 30 years into the future? Perhaps not, nevertheless this is indeed the information content of, say, a 30-year bond. Since the yield on the bond is set by the market, it is valid to suggest that the market has a view on inflation and future interest rates for up to 30 years forward.

The expectations hypothesis is stated in more than one way; we have already encountered the local expectations hypothesis. Other versions include the *return-to-maturity* expectations hypothesis, which states that total return from holding a zero-coupon bond to maturity will be equal to total return that is generated by holding a short-term instrument and continuously rolling it over the same maturity period. A related version – the *yield-to-maturity* hypothesis – states that the periodic return from holding a zero-coupon bond will be equal to the return from rolling over a series of coupon bonds, but refers to annualised return earned each year rather than total return earned over the life of the bond. This assumption enables a zero-coupon yield curve to be derived from the redemption yields of coupon bonds. The unbiased expectations hypothesis of course states that forward rates are equal to the spot rates expected by the market in the future. Cox, Ingersoll and Ross (1981) suggest that only the local expectations hypothesis describes a model that is purely arbitrage free, as under the other scenarios it would be possible to employ certain investment strategies that would produce returns in excess of what was implied by today's yields. Although it has been suggested[2] that differences between the local and unbiased hypotheses are not material, a model that describes such a scenario would not reflect investors' beliefs, which is why further research is required in this area.

The unbiased expectations hypothesis does not in itself explain all the shapes of the yield curve or the information content contained within it, which is why it is often combined with other explanations when seeking to explain the shape of the yield curve, including the liquidity preference theory.

Liquidity preference theory

Intuitively, we might feel that longer maturity investments are more risky than shorter ones. An investor lending money for a 5-year term will usually demand a higher rate of interest than if she were to lend the same customer money for a 5-week term. This is because the borrower may not be able to repay the loan over the longer time period as he may, for instance, have gone bankrupt in that period. For this reason, longer dated yields should be higher

---

[2]For example, Campbell (1986) and Livingstone (1990).

than short-dated yields, to recompense the lender for higher risk exposure during the term of the loan.[3]

We can consider this theory in terms of inflation expectations as well. Where inflation is expected to remain roughly stable over time, the market would anticipate a positive yield curve. However, the expectations hypothesis cannot in itself explain this phenomenon, as under stable inflationary conditions one would expect a flat yield curve. The risk inherent in longer dated investments, or the *liquidity preference theory*, seeks to explain a positive-shaped curve. Generally, borrowers prefer to borrow over as long a term as possible, while lenders will wish to lend over as short a term as possible. Therefore, as we first stated, lenders have to be compensated for lending over the longer term; this compensation is considered a premium for a loss in *liquidity* for the lender. The premium is increased the further the investor lends across the term structure, so that longest dated investments will, all else being equal, have the highest yield. So, the liquidity preference theory states that the yield curve should almost always be upward sloping, reflecting bondholders' preference for the liquidity and lower risk of shorter dated bonds. An inverted yield curve could still be explained by the liquidity preference theory when it is combined with the unbiased expectations hypothesis. A *humped* yield curve might be viewed as a combination of an inverted yield curve together with a positive-sloping liquidity preference curve.

The difference between a yield curve explained by unbiased expectations and an actual observed yield curve is sometimes referred to as the *liquidity premium*. This refers to the fact that in some cases short-dated bonds are easier to transact in the market than long-term bonds. It is difficult to quantify the effect of the liquidity premium, because it is not static and fluctuates over time. The liquidity premium is so called because, in order to induce investors to hold longer dated securities, the yields on such securities must be higher than those available on short-dated securities, which are more liquid and may be converted into cash more easily. The liquidity premium is the compensation required for holding less liquid instruments. If longer dated securities then provide higher yields, as is suggested by the existence of the liquidity premium, they should generate on average higher total returns over an investment period. This is not consistent with the local expectations hypothesis.

Segmentation hypothesis

Capital markets are made up of a wide variety of users, each with different requirements. Certain classes of investors will prefer dealing at the shorter end of the yield curve, while others will concentrate on the longer end of the market. The *segmented markets* theory suggests that activity is concentrated in certain specific areas of the market and that there are no interrelationships between these parts of the market; the relative amounts of funds invested in

---

[3]For original discussion, see Hicks (1946).

each of the maturity spectra cause differentials in supply and demand, which results in humps in the yield curve. That is, the shape of the yield curve is determined by supply and demand for certain specific maturity investments, each of which has no reference to any other part of the curve.

For example, banks and building societies concentrate a large part of their activity at the short end of the curve, as part of daily cash management (known as *asset and liability management*) and for regulatory purposes (known as *liquidity* requirements). However, fund managers such as pension funds and insurance companies are active at the long end of the market. But, few institutional investors have any preference for medium-dated bonds. This behaviour on the part of investors will lead to high prices (low yields) at both the short and long ends of the yield curve and lower prices (higher yields) in the middle of the term structure.

According to the segmented markets hypothesis, a separate market exists for specific maturities along the term structure, hence interest rates for these maturities are set by supply and demand.[4] Where there is no demand for a particular maturity, the yield will lie above other segments. Market participants do not hold bonds in any other area of the curve outside their area of interest[5] so that short-dated and long-dated bond yields exist independently of each other. The segmented markets theory is usually illustrated by reference to banks and life assurance companies. Banks and building societies usually hold their funds in short-dated instruments for no longer than 5 years in maturity. This is because of the nature of retail banking operations, with a large volume of instant access funds being deposited at banks, and also for regulatory purposes. Holding short-term, liquid bonds enables banks to meet any sudden or unexpected demand for funds from customers. The classic theory suggests that – as banks invest their funds in short-dated bonds – the yields on these bonds are driven down. When they then liquidate part of their holding, perhaps to meet higher demand for loans, the yields are driven up and the prices of the bonds fall. This affects the short end of the yield curve but not the long end.

The segmented markets theory can be used to explain any particular shape of the yield curve, although it perhaps fits best with positive-sloping curves. However, it cannot be used to interpret the yield curve whatever shape it may be, and therefore offers no information content during analysis. By definition, the theory suggests that – for investors – bonds with different maturities are not perfect substitutes for each other. This is because different bonds would have different holding period returns, making them imperfect substitutes for one another.[6] As a result of bonds being imperfect substitutes, markets are segmented according to maturity.

---

[4] See Culbertson (1957).
[5] For example, retail and commercial banks hold bonds for short dates, while life assurance companies hold long-dated bonds.
[6] Ibid.

The segmentations hypothesis is a reasonable explanation of certain features of a conventional positive-sloping yield curve, but by itself is not sufficient. There is no doubt that banks and building societies have a requirement to hold securities at the short end of the yield curve, as much for regulatory purposes as for yield considerations; however, other investors are probably more flexible and will place funds where value is deemed to exist. Nevertheless, the higher demand for benchmark securities does drive down yields along certain segments of the curve.

A slightly modified version of the market segmentation hypothesis is known as the preferred habitat theory. This suggests that different market participants have an interest in specified areas of the yield curve, but can be induced to hold bonds from other parts of the maturity spectrum if there is sufficient incentive. Hence, banks may at certain times hold longer dated bonds once the price of these bonds falls to a certain level, making the return on the bonds worth the risk involved in holding. Similar considerations may persuade long-term investors to hold short-dated debt. So, higher yields will be required to make bondholders shift out of their usual area of interest. This theory essentially recognises the flexibility that investors have – outside regulatory or legal constraints (such as the terms of an institutional fund's objectives) – to invest in whatever area of the yield curve they identify value.

The flat yield curve

Conventional theories do not seek to explain a flat yield curve. Although it is rare – certainly for any length of time – to observe flat curves in a market, at times they do emerge in response to peculiar economic circumstances. In conventional thinking, a flat curve is not tenable because investors should in theory have no incentive to hold long-dated bonds over shorter dated bonds when there is no yield premium, so that the yield at the long end should rise as they sell off long-dated paper, producing an upward-sloping curve. In previous occurrences of a flat curve, analysts have produced different explanations for their existence. In November 1988 the US Treasury yield curve was flat relative to the recent past; researchers contended that this was the result of the market's view that long-dated yields would fall as bond prices rallied upwards.[7] One recommendation is to buy longer maturities when the yield curve is flat, in anticipation of lower long-term interest rates, which is diametrically opposite to the view that a flat curve is a signal to sell long bonds. In the case of the US market in 1988, long bond yields did in fact fall by approximately 2% in the following 12 months. This would seem to indicate that one's view of future long-term rates should be behind the decision to buy or sell long bonds, rather than the shape of the yield curve itself. A flat curve may well be more heavily influenced by supply and demand factors than anything else, with the majority opinion eventually winning out and forcing the curve to change into a more conventional shape.

---

[7] See Levy (1999).

Further views on the yield curve

At any one time a range of factors contribute to the yield curve being a particular level and shape. For instance, short-term interest rates are greatly influenced by the availability of funds in the money market. The slope of the yield curve (usually defined as 10-year yield minus 3-month interest rate) is also a measure of the degree of tightness of government monetary policy, as well as supply and demand for bonds at particular points along the curve. A low, upward-sloping curve is often thought to be a sign that an environment of cheap money, due to looser monetary policy, is to be followed by a period of higher inflation and higher bond yields. Equally, a high downward-sloping curve is taken to mean that a situation of tight credit, due to stricter monetary policy, will result in falling inflation and lower bond yields. Inverted yield curves have often preceded recessions; for instance, an article in *The Economist* in April 1998 remarked that in the US every recession since 1955 bar one has been preceded by a negative yield curve. The analysis is the same: if investors expect a recession they also expect inflation to fall, so the yields on long-term bonds will fall relative to short-term bonds. So, the conventional explanation of an inverted yield curve is that the markets and the investment community expect either a slowdown of the economy – if not an outright recession.[8] In this case, one would expect monetary policy to ease the money supply by reducing the base interest rate in the near future: hence, an inverted curve. At the same time, a reduction in short-term interest rates will affect short-dated bonds, which are then sold off by investors, further raising their yield.

There is therefore significant information content in the yield curve, and economists and bond analysts will consider the shape of the curve as part of their policy-making and investment advice. The shape of parts of the curve, whether the short end or long end, as well as that of the entire curve, can serve as useful predictors of future market conditions. As part of an analysis it is also worthwhile considering yield curves across several different markets and currencies. For instance, the interest-rate swap curve, and its position relative to that of the government bond yield curve, is also regularly analysed for its information content. In developed country economies, the interest-rate swap market is invariably as liquid as the government bond market – if not more so – hence, it is common to see the swap curve analysed when making predictions about, say, the future level of short-term interest rates.[9]

---

[8] A recession is formally defined as two successive quarters of falling output in the domestic economy.
[9] Interest-rate swaps are derivative instruments used in professional wholesale markets to change the basis of an interest-rate liability; they are also used for speculative trading purposes. We don't need to worry about them in this chapter.

Government policy will influence the shape and level of the yield curve, including its policy on public sector borrowing, debt management, and open-market operations. The market's perception of the size of public sector debt will influence bond yields – for instance, an increase in the level of debt can lead to an increase in bond yields across the maturity range. Open-market operations – that is, a central bank's daily operations to control the money supply (to which end the central bank may purchase short-term bills and also engage in repo dealing) – can have a number of effects. In the short term, they can tilt the yield curve both upwards and downwards; in the longer term, changes in the level of the base rate will affect yield levels. An anticipated rise in base rates can lead to a drop in prices for short-term bonds, whose yields will be expected to rise; this can lead to a temporary inverted curve. Finally, debt management policy will influence the yield curve. Much government debt is rolled over as it matures, but the maturity of the replacement debt can have a significant influence on the yield curve in the form of humps in the market segment in which the debt is placed, as long as the debt is priced by the market at a relatively low price and hence high yield.

THE ZERO-COUPON YIELD CURVE

The *zero-coupon* (or *spot*) *yield curve* plots zero-coupon yields (or spot yields) against the term to maturity. A zero-coupon yield is the yield prevailing on a bond that has no coupons. In the first instance – as long as there is a liquid zero-coupon bond market – we can plot the yields from these bonds if we wish to construct this curve. However, it is not necessary to have a set of zero-coupon bonds in order to construct this curve, as we can derive it from a coupon or par yield curve; in fact, in many markets where zero-coupon bonds are not traded, a spot yield curve is derived from the conventional-yield-to-maturity-yield curve. This is of course a *theoretical* zero-coupon (spot) yield curve, as opposed to a *market* or *observed* spot curve that can be constructed using the yields of actual zero-coupon bonds trading in the market.

Spot yields must comply with equation (5.1). This equation assumes annual coupon payments and that the calculation is carried out on a coupon date such that accrued interest is zero:

$$P_d = \sum_{n=1}^{N} \frac{C}{(1 + rs_n)^n} + \frac{M}{(1 + rs_T)^N}$$

$$= \sum_{n=1}^{N} C \times Df_n + M \times Df_N \qquad (5.1)$$

where

> rs_n = Spot or zero-coupon yield on a bond with t years to maturity;
> $Df_n \equiv 1/(1 + rs_n)^n$ = Corresponding *discount factor*.

In equation (5.1), rs_1 is the current 1-year spot yield, rs_2 is the current 2-year spot yield, and so on. Theoretically, the spot yield for a particular term to maturity is the same as the yield on a zero-coupon bond of the same maturity, which is why spot yields are also known as zero-coupon yields.

This last result is important. It means spot yields can be derived from redemption yields that have been observed in the market.

As with the yield-to-redemption yield curve, the spot yield curve is commonly used in the market. It is viewed as the true term structure of interest rates because there is no reinvestment risk involved; the stated yield is equal to actual annual return. That is, the yield on a zero-coupon bond of n years maturity is regarded as the true n-year interest rate. Because the observed government bond redemption yield curve is not considered to be the true interest rate, analysts often construct a theoretical spot yield curve. Essentially, this is done by breaking down each coupon bond being observed into its constituent cash flows, which become a series of individual zero-coupon bonds. For example, £100 nominal of a 5% 2-year bond (paying annual coupons) is considered equivalent to £5 nominal of a 1-year zero-coupon bond and £105 nominal of a 2-year zero-coupon bond.

Let us assume that there are 30 bonds in the market all paying annual coupons. The first bond has a maturity of 1 year, the second bond of 2 years, and so on out to 30 years. We know the price of each of these bonds, but we wish to determine what the prices imply about the market's estimate of future interest rates. We naturally expect interest rates to vary over time and that all payments being made on the same date are valued using the same rate. For the 1-year bond we know its current price and the amount of the payment (comprising one coupon payment and the redemption proceeds) we will receive at the end of the year; therefore, we can calculate the interest rate for the first year. Assume the 1-year bond has a coupon of 5%. If the bond is priced at par and we invest £100 today we will receive £105 in 1 year's time, hence the rate of interest is apparent and is 5%. For the 2-year bond we use this interest rate to calculate the future value of its current price in 1 year's time: *this is how much we would receive if we had invested the same amount in the 1-year bond*. However, the 2-year bond pays a coupon at the end of the first year; if we subtract this amount from the future value of the current price, the net amount is what we should be giving up in 1 year in return for the one remaining payment. From these numbers we can calculate the interest rate in Year 2.

Assume that the 2-year bond pays a coupon of 6% and is priced at 99.00. If 99.00 was invested at the rate we calculated for the 1-year bond (5%), it would accumulate £103.95 in 1 year, made up of the £99 investment and inter-est of £4.95. On the payment date in 1 year's time, the 1-year bond matures and the 2-year bond pays a coupon of 6%. If everyone expected the 2-year bond at this time to be priced at more than 97.95 (which is 103.95 minus 6.00), then no investor would buy the 1-year bond, since it would be more advan-tageous to buy the 2-year bond and sell it after 1 year for a greater return. Similarly, if the price was less than 97.95 no investor would buy the 2-year bond, as it would be cheaper to buy the shorter bond and then buy the longer dated bond with the proceeds received when the 1-year bond matures. There-fore, the 2-year bond must be priced at exactly 97.95 in 12 months' time. For this £97.95 to grow to £106.00 (the maturity proceeds from the 2-year bond, comprising the redemption payment and coupon interest), the interest rate in Year 2 must be 8.20%. We can check this using the present value for-mula covered earlier. At these two interest rates, the two bonds are said to be in equilibrium.

This is an important result and shows that there can be no arbitrage opportu-nity along the yield curve; using interest rates available today the return from buying the 2-year bond must equal the return from buying the 1-year bond and rolling over the proceeds (or reinvesting) for another year. This is known as the *breakeven principle*.

Using the price and coupon of the 3-year bond we can calculate the interest rate in Year 3 in precisely the same way. Using each of the bonds in turn we can link together the *implied 1-year rates* for each year up to the maturity of the longest dated bond. The process is known as *bootstrapping*. The "average" rate over a given period is the spot yield for that term: in the example given above, the rate in Year 1 is 5%, and in Year 2 is 8.20%. An investment of £100 at these rates would grow to £113.61. This gives a total percentage increase of 13.61% over 2 years, or 6.588% per annum. The average rate is not obtained by sim-ply dividing 13.61 by 2, but – using our present value relationship again – by calculating the square root of "1 plus the interest rate" and then subtract-ing 1 from this number. Thus, the 1-year yield is 5% and the 2-year yield is 8.20%.

In real-world markets it is not necessarily as straightforward as this; for instance, on some dates there may be several bonds maturing, with different coupons, and on some dates there may be no bonds maturing. It is most unlikely that there will be a regular spacing of bond redemptions exactly 1 year apart. For this reason, it is common for analysts to use a software model to calculate the set of implied spot rates that best fits the market prices of the bonds that do exist in the market. For instance, if there are several 1-year bonds, each of their prices may imply a slightly different rate of interest. We choose the rate that gives the smallest average price error. In practice, all bonds are used to find the rate in Year 1, all bonds with a term longer than 1 year are used to calculate the rate in Year 2, and so on. The zero-coupon curve can also be calculated directly from the coupon yield curve using a method similar to that described above; in this case, the bonds would be priced at par and their coupons set to par yield values.

The zero-coupon yield curve is ideal to use when deriving implied forward rates, which we consider next, and when defining the term structure of interest rates. It is also the best curve to use when determining the *relative value*, whether cheap or dear, of bonds trading in the market, and when pricing new issues, irrespective of their coupons.

Arithmetic

Having introduced the concept of the zero-coupon curve in the previous section, we can illustrate the mathematics involved more formally. When deriving spot yields from redemption yields, we view conventional bonds as being made up of an *annuity* (the stream of fixed coupon payments) and a zero-coupon bond (the redemption payment on maturity). To derive the rates we can use equation (5.1), setting $P_d = M = 100$ and $C = rm_N$, as shown in equation (5.2). This has coupon bonds trading at par, so that the coupon is equal to the yield:

$$100 = rm_N \times \sum_{n=1}^{N} Df_n + 100 \times D_N$$

$$= rm_N + A_N + 100 \times D_N \tag{5.2}$$

where rm_N is par yield for a term to maturity of N years, the discount factor Df_N is the fair price of a zero-coupon bond with a par value of £1 and a term to maturity of N years, and

$$A_N = \sum_{n=1}^{N} Df_n = A_{N-1} + Df_N \tag{5.3}$$

is the fair price of an annuity of £1 per year for N years (with $A_0 = 0$ by convention). Substituting equation (5.3) into equation (5.2) and rearranging will give us the expression for the N-year discount factor shown in equation (5.4):

$$Df_N = \frac{1 - rm_N \times A_{N-1}}{1 + rm_N} \tag{5.4}$$

If we assume 1-year, 2-year, and 3-year redemption yields for bonds priced at par to be 5%, 5.25%, and 5.75%, respectively, we will obtain the following solutions for the discount factors:

$$Df_1 = \frac{1}{1+0.05} = 0.95238$$

$$Df_2 = \frac{1-(0.0525)(0.95238)}{1+0.0525} = 0.90261$$

$$Df_3 = \frac{1-(0.0575)(0.95238+0.90261)}{1+0.0575} = 0.84476$$

We can confirm that these are the correct discount factors by substituting them back into equation (5.2). This gives us the following results for the 1-year, 2-year, and 3-year par value bonds (with coupons of 5%, 5.25%, and 5.75%, respectively):

$$100 = 105 \times 0.95238$$
$$100 = 5.25 \times 0.95238 + 105.25 \times 0.90261$$
$$100 = 5.75 \times 0.95238 + 5.75 \times 0.90261 + 105.75 \times 0.84476$$

Now that we have found the correct discount factors it is relatively straightforward to calculate the spot yields using equation (5.1):

$$Df_1 = \frac{1}{(1+rs_1)} = 0.95238 \quad \text{which gives} \quad rs_1 = 5.0\%$$

$$Df_2 = \frac{1}{(1+rs_2)^2} = 0.90261 \quad \text{which gives} \quad rs_2 = 5.269\%$$

$$Df_3 = \frac{1}{(1+rs_3)^3} = 0.84476 \quad \text{which gives} \quad rs_3 = 5.778\%$$

Equation (5.1) discounts the n-year cash flow (comprising the coupon payment and/or principal repayment) by the corresponding n-year spot yield. In other words, rs_n is the *time-weighted rate of return* on an n-year bond. Thus, as we said in the previous section, the spot yield curve is the correct method for pricing or valuing any cash flow, including an irregular cash flow, because it uses the appropriate discount factors. That is, it matches each cash flow to the discount rate that applies to the time period in which the cash flow is paid. Compare this with the approach for calculating the yield-to-maturity, which discounts all cash flows by the same yield to maturity. This neatly illustrates why the n-period zero-coupon interest rate is the true interest rate for an N-year bond.

The expressions above are solved algebraically in the conventional manner, although those wishing to use a spreadsheet application such as Microsoft Excel® can input the constituents of each equation into individual cells and solve using the "Tools" and "Goal Seek" functions.

There is a very large literature on the zero-coupon yield curve. A small fraction of it – as referred to in this chapter – is given in the Bibliography at the end of the chapter.

CONSTRUCTING THE BANK'S INTERNAL YIELD CURVE[10]

The construction of an internal yield curve is one of the major steps in product pricing as well as in the implementation of the bank's internal funds pricing or "funds transfer pricing" (FTP – see Chapter 11) system in a bank. It should be done after the trading book and the banking book are split, but before internal funding methodologies for all balance sheet items and the internal bank result calculation methodology are approved and implemented in the balance sheet reporting metrics ("MIS").

As is pointed out in regulatory recommendations, "the transfer prices should reflect current market conditions as well as the actual institution-specific circumstances".[11] Put simply, that means the curve should contain a market component responsible for interest-rate risk and a bank-specific spread over the market that will reflect the term liquidity cost for the bank.

There are several approaches for construction of an FTP curve. The choice of the approach depends on the scale of your bank, as well as on the market where the bank operates. These main approaches are:

- **Market** approach (based on market interest rates): FTP rates reflect the rate of alternative placement of funds or borrowing in the market and change according to the market's dynamics;
- **Cost** approach (based on the borrowing rates): FTP rates motivate placement of funds at a higher rate than the rate at which the funds were raised;
- **Mixed** approach (based on the sum of the interest-rate curves): FTP rates take into consideration diversified contents of liabilities at different tenors;
- **Marginal** approach (based on the price of the following additional asset or liability): FTP rates represent the most relevant pricing levels. This approach can be based on:
  o Marginal rates of lending; or
  o Marginal rates of borrowing.

We consider each of these approaches in turn. We also show in the Appendix the ALCO submission prepared by one of the authors on implementing an internal curve methodology, when he was working in the investment banking division of a global multinational bank.

---

[10]This section was co-authored with Polina Bardaeva.
[11]Guidelines on Liquidity Cost Benefit Allocation. CEBS, October 2010.

Market approach for FTP curve construction

As it comes from the name and definition of the approach, both components of an FTP curve should be derived from the market quotes and indicators. There's a list of requirements towards characteristics of these market indicators:

- They should properly and in time reflect the market situation;
- The quotes should be published in well-known sources and should be available for all market participants (or calculated according to widely accepted formula);
- Instruments should allow one to define the spread to the market indicator to get the level of the funding cost for the bank.

Usually, as market indicators for FTP curve construction, we understand Libor (Euribor, etc.), interest-rate swap (IRS), cross-currency swap (CCS), and credit default swap (CDS). Although CDS is not available for each bank and sometimes is not representative when it is available, bond yields as market quotes can be used. An FTP curve based on bond yields can be constructed using several methods, which are deeply analysed in a special section (see Application of Ordinary Least Squares method and Nelson-Siegel family approaches).

The market approach can be applied by large banks that have a lot of operations in financial markets. The deep and developed market of financial instruments (including derivatives) is required.

The advantages of this approach are:

- Objectivity and transparency (as a consequence, high level of trust);
- Instant reflection of the level of the market rates;
- Possibility to define FTP rates even for those tenors at which no balance sheet items exist;
- Construction of a smoothed curve without distortions.

Although this method also has limitations:

- Too high volatility of the money market indicators;
- Sometimes lack of market indicators for the middle and long term;
- Sometimes low volume of deals with government bonds and as a result loss of marketability of quotes;
- Insufficient volume of deals and instruments for representativeness of the results for mathematical modelling.

Application of Ordinary Least Squares method and Nelson-Siegel family approaches

The topic of constructing a yield curve has been widely investigated in scientific literature and by practitioners of central banks. The reason for such a deep investigation for these researches was that each country that has government bonds needs to construct a realistic, trustworthy, and flexible zero-coupon yield curve to reflect the level of the country's debt cost. Such reasons and the grade of responsibility for fair curve construction do not stop debates around the best methods and approaches to use for curve building, although not all of them are of use for ALM purposes.

What are the main criteria for choosing the optimal approach? This approach should be *simple enough* to be executed without complicated technical packages, but at the same time reflect the market of a particular country, even when *bond quotes* are *available not for all tenors*.

According to the Bank for International Settlements survey about zero-coupon yield curve estimation procedures at central banks (2005), the most used approaches are spline-based (for example, McCulloch, 1971, 1975) and parametric (Nelson, Siegel, 1987 and Svensson, 1994) methods. Although the spline methods gain more positive assessments due to their provision of smoothness and accuracy, they are more complex. At the same time, Nelson and Siegel state in their work that their objective is simplicity rather than accuracy. The following part of this section is devoted to comparison and contrasting of parametric approaches and their practical implementation.

All the parametric methods are based on minimisation of the price/yield errors. Among parametric methods the most basic approach is the **Ordinary Least Squares (OLS) method**. This is the simplest parametric method, which applies calculation of squares of deviations of actual quotes from the calculated approximated values and minimisation of their sum. The formula used to construct the curve is:

$$f(x) = a * x^2 + b * x + c,$$

where

   x – duration;
$f(x)$ – yield.

Parameters a, b, and c should satisfy the following: sum of the squares of deviations from the mean should be minimal.

The implementation in practice consists of three steps:

- Collecting data from the information sources and placing in an Excel spreadsheet (on the graph the bond quotes with different durations would represent a so-called "starry sky");
- Calculation of approximations according to the formula with some initial values of parameters a, b, and c, deviations from the actual values, squares of deviations, and sum of squares; next through the "Goal Seek" in Excel determination of the most appropriate parameters a, b, and c;
- Solving the equation for some tenor in order to get the yield for this tenor.

The advantages of applying this method for ALM purposes are its simplicity and transparency.

There are, however, disadvantages that can significantly impact the result. The first and the main one is that the function that is used for approximation is parabolic – and, thus, is increasing in its first half, but after the extremum it starts to decline (see the graph). It's evident that this is not the best function to describe the market structure of interest rates – at least due to the reason that according to time value of money theory, in the long run the rates tend to increase.

This method can, however, be used by an ALM unit of a bank in the following cases:

(a) The market does not have long tenors (so the declining part of the curve won't be used);
(b) The market yield curve is increasing (which means that it is not inverted and does not have troughs);
(c) The ALM unit doesn't have resources to try to implement any more complicated method (usually in small banks).

Figure 5.3 shows an example of the difference in output of the Nelson-Siegel and OLS methodologies when using the same inputs.

In order to make the curve more flexible, **Nelson-Siegel family curves** are used.

For the first time the approach was suggested by **Nelson** and **Siegel (basic N-S)**. They use four parameters in the equation to describe the yield curve:

$$f(x) = \beta_0 + (\beta_1 + \beta_2) * \frac{\left(1 - e^{-\frac{x}{\tau}}\right)}{\frac{x}{\tau}} - \beta_2 * e^{-\frac{x}{\tau}}$$

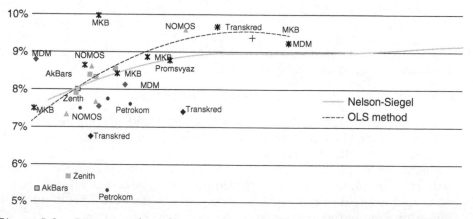

Figure 5.3   Curve results when employing Nelson-Siegel and OLS methods
Source: www.micex.ru, author's calculations.

where

β_0 – is a long-term interest rate;

β_1 – represents the spread between short-term and long-term rates (this parameter defines the slope of the curve: if the parameter is positive, then the slope is negative). $\beta_0 + \beta_1$– is the starting point of the curve at the short end;

β_2 – is the difference between the middle-term and the long-term rates, defining the hump of the curve (if $\beta_2 > 0$ then the hump is observed in period τ, if $\beta_2 < 0$ then the curve will have a "U" shape);

τ – a constant parameter, representing the tenor at which the maximum of the hump is achieved.

The main difference between the basic N-S approach and the OLS method is the addition of dependence between short-term and long-term rates, which tend to make the curve more flexible. This model assumes that long-term rates directly impact the short-term rates and, thus, some segments of the curve can't change while other segments are stable. Moreover, this basic approach provides a curve with only one hump or trough. And that is not always true in practice.

Svensson suggested an extension to the basic N-S approach: he implemented an additional component for better description of the first part of the curve:

$$f(x) = \beta_0 + (\beta_1 + \beta_2) * \frac{\left(1 - e^{-\frac{x}{\tau_1}}\right)}{\frac{x}{\tau_1}} - \beta_2 * e^{-\frac{x}{\tau_1}} + \beta_3 * \frac{\left(1 - e^{-\frac{x}{\tau_2}}\right)}{\frac{x}{\tau_2}} - \beta_3 * e^{-\frac{x}{\tau_2}}$$

Thus, the curve can have two extremums: β_3 determines the size and the form of the second hump, and τ_2 specifies the tenor for the second hump.

The advantages of the Svensson method in comparison to OLS and basic N-S approaches are even better flexibility and better accuracy. However, even two humps do not perfectly reflect the market curve. That is why in practice further adjustments were made.

One of them is the **adjusted Nelson-Siegel (adjusted N-S) approach** with a set of seven parameters. The vector of the curve's parameters is recalculated after each new bond/new quote is added. The first four parameters (β_S) are responsible for the level of yields on short-term, middle-term, and long-term segments of the yield curve (the shifts up and down). The remaining three parameters (τ_S) are responsible for convexity/concavity of the appropriate segments.

Such adjustment provides even more advantages: such flexibility that the yield curve by the adjusted N-S approach can have all types of forms: monotonous increasing or decreasing, convex, U-form, or S-form; memory, because the calculation is based on the previous parameters, so additional data doesn't change the form abruptly. This may be especially useful for markets with low liquidity of some bond issues – when on one day bonds are traded, there's a quote and the bond is included in the calculation, but on another day they are not traded, there's no quote and, thus, there's no input for calculation.

The disadvantage of all types of Nelson-Siegel approaches is their complexity in comparison with the OLS method. As far as one needs to assign initial values to parameters and then apply the "Goal Seek" function – there's the risk that at this moment a mistake is made and further calculations are incorrect.

Nevertheless, one of the Nelson-Siegel family approaches would be recommended to be used for ALM purposes in the following cases:

(a) For larger banks with bigger ALM units, equipped with automatic systems;
(b) On the markets where the curve is supposed to demonstrate several humps on different tenors;
(c) On bond markets with low liquidity.

To summarise, not all of the existing methods to construct a yield curve can be successfully applied by ALM units. Parametric approaches are most simple in their implementation. The choice between the most "plain vanilla" OLS method and the more complicated Nelson-Siegel family approaches should be done according to the size of the bank and market conditions and peculiarities.

Cost approach for FTP curve construction

In this method, an FTP rate is an average borrowing rate defined according to the current (or historic) contents of liabilities. It can be the only rate or several rates, calculated for different time periods. Just current interest rates (rates of deposits raised in the current accounting period) can be used. Or a moving average of historic interest rates on deposits can be applied in order to describe slow change of rates for the particular type of liabilities. When needed, the weights are used for construction of the moving average. (The older observation will have a smaller weight, while most recent ones will have higher weights.)

This method is applied on a calm non-European market with low volatility of rates and when widely accepted market indicators (for some currencies) do not exist. The better effect is achieved when the bank has a diversified liability structure and liabilities are of different tenors. This approach is recommended for use at a bank that has raised long-term funds at high rates in the past. An FTP curve constructed according to the cost approach will give the needed incentive to the lending units – to place money not at market rates (so the bank will face losses), but to place above the funding cost (and try to earn more for the bank).

This is probably the only case when the cost approach should be applied, as notwithstanding the advantages of the method (absolute objectivity and simplicity of calculation), its drawbacks are significant:

• Dependence on the rates in the past results in reaction to the market changes with a time lag;
• The yield curve can be distorted because liabilities on different tenors could be raised at different times in the past;

- When there are too many liabilities not placed into loans (on some tenors), this method doesn't provide an instrument for deposit volumes regulation;
- It doesn't allow for steering of risk.

Mixed approach for FTP curve construction

As it follows from the name of the method, it is a mixture of the market curve and the curve based on actual costs of liabilities.

The construction itself consists of the following steps:

Step 1 – Construction of the FTP curve based on market approach.

Step 2 – Analysis of stable funding sources for each tenor. Calculation of the weights of each type of liability in total liabilities of this time bucket.

Step 3 – Obtaining the weighted FTP curve as a result of summing up of yield curves of different liabilities.

The advantages of the method are:

- The current structure of liabilities and the costs of funding are taken into account;
- The market component helps to reflect the fluctuations of market conjuncture;
- The cost component helps to take the actual cost of funds into account.

The disadvantages include time-consuming calculation. Moreover, in case of a lack of long-term liabilities it is necessary to make assumptions about the cost of funding – thus, it brings some subjectivity and opacity into calculations.

Marginal approach for FTP curve construction

The marginal approach is the only approach recommended by a regulator (Commission for European Banking Supervision) to European banks. The attractiveness of this method is due to these perceived advantages:

- The curve overall reflects the market level of rates;
- Exhibits comparably fast reaction to market changes;
- Allows the bank to set an FTP rate for those tenors for which no balance sheet liabilities exist.

The fact that this method is considered the best one by the regulators doesn't mean that it lacks disadvantages. They are:

- Subjectivity of assessment;
- Severe dependence of this method adequacy on the depth of market of lending/borrowing instruments and the chosen instruments as benchmarks;
- Possibility of distortions of the yield curve;
- Limited opportunities to hedge interest-rate risk.

The marginal lending approach is less popular among bankers than the marginal borrowing approach. It is applied by small banks operating in rather developed local financial markets that don't use any other approach. For application of this method, a deep and diversified market of lending instruments should exist.

The marginal borrowing approach is much more often applied by banks, usually in developing countries with an insufficient level of development of the local financial market (and limited choice of money market indicators). Banks should have a diversified balance sheet structure. This requirement is due to the need to outline the core liabilities.

Core liabilities are such liabilities on the bank's balance sheet that satisfy the following:

- Deposited by customers of long standing;
- The funding volume is sufficiently high for the bank's financing needs;
- The overall structure of each funding source is stable.

The steps to construct a curve using this approach are as follows:

- Selection of the relevant funding sources (core liabilities) for the bank:
  ○ Analysis of all the sources of funding in place at the bank;
  ○ Assessment of the additional amount needed to be borrowed at the current moment;
  ○ If there's no need to raise funds at the moment – the rates are decreased to the level when no additional funds are raised.
- Gathering of information to obtain the rates:
  ○ That could be actual quotes at what level the bank can raise funds (for example, the rates for retail products published at the bank's website);
  ○ In some cases, it can be an assumption of the business at what rate it is possible to borrow the required amount of funds;
  ○ Determining weights, which reflect the marginal funding mix. The weights can be derived either from the actual balance sheet structure or from the budgeted balance sheet structure for the future period and should reflect the possibilities of a bank to raise these kinds of funds.

No matter which approach for yield curve construction is chosen, it should serve the principles of FTP and customer loan pricing in the bank.

CALCULATION ILLUSTRATIONS

In this section we illustrate some elementary uses of the yield curve by providing some example calculations.

Forward rates: breakeven principle

Consider the following spot yields:

1-year	10%
2-year	12%

Assume that a bank's client wishes to lock in *today* the cost of borrowing 1-year funds in 1 year's time. The solution for the bank (and the mechanism to enable the bank to quote a price to the client) involves raising 1-year funds at 10% and investing the proceeds for 2 years at 12%. The no-arbitrage principle means that the same return must be generated from both fixed rate and reinvestment strategies.

In effect, we can look at the issue in terms of two alternative investment strategies, both of which must provide the same return:

Strategy 1   Invest funds for 2 years at 12%.
Strategy 2   Invest funds for 1 year at 10%, and reinvest the proceeds for a
             further year at the forward rate calculated today.

The forward rate for Strategy 2 is the rate that will be quoted to the client. Using the present value relationship, we know that the proceeds from Strategy 1 are:

$$FV = (1 + r_2)^2$$

while the proceeds from Strategy 2 would be:

$$FV = (1 + r_1) + (1 + R)$$

We know from the no-arbitrage principle that the proceeds from both strategies will be the same, therefore this enables us to set:

$$(1 + r_2)^2 = (1 + r_1)(1 + R)$$
$$R = \frac{(1 + r_2)^2}{(1 + r_1)} - 1$$

This enables us to calculate the forward rate that can be quoted to the client (together with any spread that the bank might add) as follows:

$$(1 + 0.12)^2 = (1 + 0.10) \times (1 + R)$$
$$(1 + R) = (1 + 0.12)^2 / (1 + 0.10)$$
$$(1 + R) = 1.14036$$
$$R = 14.04\%$$

This rate is the 1-year forward-forward rate, or the implied forward rate.

Forward rates: calculating forward start yield

A highly rated customer asks you to fix a yield at which he could issue a 2-year zero-coupon USD Eurobond in 3 years' time. At this time the US Treasury zero-coupon rates were:

1 year	6.25%
2 year	6.75%
3 year	7.00%
4 year	7.125%
5 year	7.25%

(a) Ignoring borrowing spreads over these benchmark yields, as a market-maker you could cover the exposure created by borrowing funds for 5 years on a zero-coupon basis and placing these funds in the market for 3 years before lending them on to your client. Assume annual interest compounding (even if none is actually paid out during the life of the loans):

$$\text{Borrowing rate for 5 years} \left[\frac{R_5}{100}\right] = 0.0725$$

$$\text{Lending rate for 3 years} \left[\frac{R_3}{100}\right] = 0.0700$$

(b) The key arbitrage relationship is:

$$\text{Total cost of funding} = \text{Total return on investments}$$
$$(1 + R_5)^5 = (1 + R_3)^3 \times (1 + R_{3\times5})^2$$

Therefore, breakeven forward yield is:

$$(1 + R_{3\times5})^2 = \frac{(1 + 0.0725)^5}{(1 + 0.0700)^3}$$

$$(1 + R_{3\times5}) = \sqrt{\left[\frac{(1 + 0.0725)^5}{(1 + 0.0700)^3}\right]}$$

$$R_{3\times5} = \sqrt{\left[\frac{(1 + 0.0725)^5}{(1 + 0.0700)^3}\right]} - 1$$

$$= 7.63\%$$

UNDERSTANDING FORWARD RATES

Spot and forward rates calculated from current market rates follow mathematical principles to establish what the arbitrage-free rates for dealing *today* will be at some point in the future. In other words, forward rates and spot rates are actually saying the same thing. They are two sides of the same coin.

However, as we have already noted, forward rates are not a prediction of future rates. It is important to be aware of this distinction. If we were to plot the forward rate curve for the term structure in 3 months' time, and then compare it in 3 months with the actual term structure prevailing at the time, the curves would certainly not match. However, this has no bearing on our earlier statement: that forward rates are the mathematical *expectation* of future rates as of today. The main point to bear in mind is that we are not comparing like for like when plotting forward rates against actual current rates at a future date. When we calculate forward rates we use the current term structure. The current term structure incorporates all known information, both economic and political, and reflects the market's views.

This is exactly the same as when we say that a company's share price reflects all that is known about the company and all that is expected to happen with regard to the company in the near future, including expected future earnings. The term structure of interest rates reflects everything the market knows about relevant domestic and international factors. It is this information, then, that goes into forward rate calculation. An instant later, though, there will be new developments that will alter the market's view and therefore alter the current term structure. These developments and events were (by definition, as we cannot know what lies in the future!) not known at the time we calculated and used 3-month forward rates. This is why rates actually turn out to be different from what the term structure mathematically constructed at an earlier date. However, for dealing today we use today's forward rates, which reflect everything we know about the market today.

SONIA YIELD CURVE[12]

An important reference yield curve today is the overnight index swap (OIS) curve. This is similar to the conventional swap curve except it refers to the overnight rate on the floating leg of the swap, compared to the 3-month or 6-month rate on the floating leg of a conventional swap.

Prior to the 2008 crash, derivative pricing and valuations were based on the simple principle of the time value of money. A breakeven price was calculated such that when all the future implied cash flows were discounted back to today, the net present value (NPV) of all the cash flows was zero. The breakeven price was used for valuations or spread by a bid–offer price to create a trading price. Bid–offers would generally incorporate a counterparty-dependent mark-up to cover various costs and a return on capital in a fairly ill-defined way.

A breakeven price required the construction of a projection curve for the index being referenced, which could be a tenor of Libor, such as 3-month, for 3-month Libor swaps, or an overnight rate in the case of Overnight Index Swaps. The projection curve would use market observable inputs and various interpolation methodologies to derive market implied future rates used to project the future floating rate fixings. In other words:

- A conventional swap curve is a projection curve based on the 3-month (or 6-month) Libor fix; whereas
- An OIS curve is a projection curve based on the overnight rate.

Once the market implied future fixings are known, a discount curve will then be used to discount cash flow mismatches in such a way that the breakeven fixed rate gives a result where all the cash flow mismatches have a present value of zero. Historically, market practice was to discount cash flows using a Libor discount curve, the assumption being that all cash flow mismatches could be borrowed or reinvested at Libor. It was implicitly assumed that Libor was the risk-free rate at which these cash flow mismatches could be funded.

---

[12]This section was co-written with Kevin Liddy.

Figure 5.4 shows the GBP OIS (known as SONIA) and GBP swap curves as at 13 October 2016. The OIS curve lies below the conventional swap curve because of the term liquidity premium (TLP) difference between the two tenors (the TLP is higher the longer the tenor).

In the case of a collateralised trade transacted under the terms of a CSA, the posting of collateral ensures that the NPV of a trade is always zero net of collateral held or posted. All future funding mismatches are therefore explicitly funded directly by the exchange of collateral and as a result do not require any external funding. The collateral remuneration rate is defined by the CSA and is normally the relevant OIS rate. As it is the relevant OIS rate that becomes the applicable rate for funding cash flow mismatches, market practice has evolved to discount future cash flows using OIS rates when pricing or valuing a collateralised trade, so-called OIS discounting. It is impossible to determine when market practice changed but it is generally accepted that when the London Clearing House (LCH) (which clears derivative transactions) changed to OIS discounting in 2010, it was doing so to reflect best market practice.

Where multiple forms of collateral were permissible under a CSA, market practice evolved to take into account the embedded option for the collateral poster. Pricing assumed that a counterparty would always act rationally and post the cheapest to deliver collateral with the discount curve reflecting the relevant collateral OIS rate, so-called CTD or CSA discounting. A further enhancement

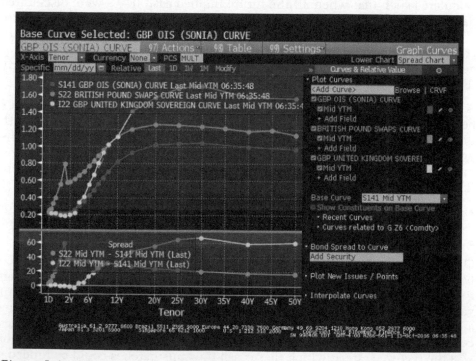

Figure 5.4   GBP SONIA and GBP swap curves, 13 October 2016

© Bloomberg LP. Reproduced with permission.

is often used where the collateral is non-cash such as a government bond. In these instances the discount curve reflects the price at which the bonds can be traded in the repo market. For complex CSAs where collateral was multicurrency, the discount curve is often a multicurrency hybrid curve that reflects that the CTD may change at a future date.

For uncollateralised trades, not only was the use of a Libor rate to discount cash flow mismatches clearly inappropriate given the increase in funding spreads during the 2008 crisis but also, in the absence of collateral, the NPV of an uncollateralised trade represented a potential funding requirement. Pricing for uncollateralised trades now generally contains an upfront adjustment to the price to take into account the expected funding costs of non-collateralisation referred to as the Funding Valuation Adjustment or FVA. FVA along with a Credit Valuation Adjustment CVA now represent a more rigorously defined part of the bid–offer adjustment.

Collateral posted at the LCH has no optionality allowed – it must be in cash and in the currency of the transaction. Hence, the swap screen price now reflects the price for a cleared swap at the LCH. Because the collateral is unambiguous (cash in the currency of the trade) remunerated at the relevant OIS, so the discount/funding rate is always known and is not counterparty dependent. Anything other than an LCH cleared trade means the price is different to take into account the impact of the type of collateral. This is an important point: observable swap rates are for LCH cleared trades only.

CONCLUSIONS

The yield curve is the best snapshot of the state of the financial markets. It is not the sole driver of customer prices in banking, but it is the most influential. Hence, it is important that all practitioners understand the behaviour of the curve and how to analyse and interpret it. Being aware of the relationship between spot rates, forward rates, and yield to maturity is also important. Ultimately, there should be no shortcuts when it comes to understanding the yield curve.

APPENDIX

ALCO submission paper

Author: Moorad Choudhry
          GBM Treasury   **Global Banking & Markets**
                                          135 Bishopsgate
                                          London EC2M 3UR

Date: 29 March 2011

Subject: **Formalising the procedure for constructing the GBM internal
          yield curve**

A significant risk management decision at every bank is selecting the internal yield curve construction methodology. The internal curve is an important tool in the pricing and risk management process, driving resource allocation, business line transaction pricing, hedge construction and RAROC analysis. It is given therefore that curve construction methodology should follow business best-practice. In this paper we describe a recommended procedure on curve formulation to adopt at GBM, as well as a secondary procedure to liaise with Group Treasury (GT) aimed at maintaining a realistic and market-accurate public issuance curve.

Background

Orthodox valuation methodology in financial markets follows the logic of risk-neutral no-arbitrage pricing [1].The same logic should apply when setting a bank's internal pricing term structure. The risk-free curve is given by sovereign bond prices, while the banking sector risky curve was traditionally the Libor or swap curve. Banks now fund at "cost of funds" as opposed to Libor-flat; therefore, the logic of the no-arbitrage approach dictates that a bank's risky pricing yield curve should be extracted from market prices, because the latter dictate the rate at which the bank can raise liabilities. Such an approach preserves consistency because the same no-arbitrage principles drive market prices in the first place. In other words, the logic behind setting a bank's yield curve would be identical to the logic used when pricing derivatives.

The practice at peer-group banks is to adopt an interpolation method that uses prices (yields) of the issuer's existing debt as model inputs, and extracts a discount function from these prices. The output is then used to derive a term structure that represents the issuer's current risky yield curve. To adopt such an approach requires a liquid secondary market in the issuer's bonds. This is a not unreasonable assumption in the case of RBS.

The two most common interpolation methods in use are the cubic spline approach and the parametric approach. The former produces markedly oscillating forward rates and is also less accurate at the short-end [2], [3].Therefore we propose adopting the parametric method. The original parametric model is Nelson-Siegel [4],which is a forward rate model; however we recommend an extension of Nelson-Siegel for use at GBM, the Svensson (94) model, which produces a smoother forward curve, partly as a result of incorporating one extra parameter [5].

Recommended procedure

In line with business best-practice we recommend immediate adoption of the following procedure:

1) Fit Svensson 94 to market data
2) Extract the RBS risky yield curve. This is the baseline EUR yield curve that determines the fixed coupon for a vanilla coupon fixed-maturity bond issued at par
3) Use the continuous discount function obtained from (2) above to create a par-par asset swap curve
4) This is the market-implied EUR Term Liquidity Premium (TLP) curve, which sets the spread for a vanilla FRN issued at par.

The curve at (4) is therefore the GBM TLP as dictated by market rates. By definition, under the no-arbitrage principles we refer to above, this curve is the baseline GBM pricing curve, and therefore will be used as such in GBM going forward.

The curve construction procedure logic is shown in the Appendix. It has been reviewed by the GBM Head of Front Office Risk Management and Quantitative Analytics.

Following approval at ALCO, we will implement the procedure via the Quantitative Analytics function, to create an application that can produce the RBS risky curve at the touch of a button.

The baseline EUR curve will be the source for creating all cross-currency funding curves. This procedure will be articulated formally in a later submission to GBM ALCO.

Maintenance in line with market: liaison with Group Treasury

One of the issues raised by the FSA during the recent ILAA review, and also as part of the KPMG s166 review, referred to the risks created by a bank's public funding curve falling out of line with market prices.

To manage this risk, we recommend that GBM liaise with Group Treasury on a regular basis to ensure that the public issuance curve set by GT remains within a 10-15 basis point range of the 2-week moving average of the GBM market-implied TLP curve.

The tolerance level will be reviewed on a quarterly basis (or as required by market events) by GBM ALCO and in liaison with GT.

REFERENCES

[1] The most appropriate references in this field are Feynman-Kac (1949), Ito (1951), Markowitz (1959), Fama (1970), Black-Scholes (1973) and Merton (1973).
[2] James, J., and N. Webber (2000), *Interest Rate Modelling*, Chichester: John Wiley & Co Ltd

[3] Choudhry, M. (2003), *Analysing and Interpreting the Yield Curve*, Singapore: John Wiley & Sons Pte Ltd

[4] Nelson, C., and A.F. Siegel, (1987), "Parsimonious Modeling of Yield Curves", *Journal of Business*, 60, pp. 473–489

[5] Svensson, Lars E. O. (1994), "Estimating and Interpreting Forward Rates: Sweden 1992-4," *National Bureau of Economic Research Working Paper #4871*

APPENDIX

We desire to extract the RBS credit-risky curve from market prices. To do this we require a liquid secondary market of RBS-issued bonds, and an interpolation model. Practitioners generally use either the cubic spline approach or a parametric model approach.

For the reasons cited above, we recommend using the parametric methodology. The original parametric model is Nelson-Siegel (1987), which suffers to an extent from oscillating forward curves, so we recommend Svensson (1994) which has one extra parameter, and reduced oscillation, and also produces smoother short-date forwards.

A working Svensson model with Excel front-end is available on request.

The procedure we implement involves the following:

1 – Extract the RBS risky yield curve using RBS money-market funding rates and prices of secondary market bonds. We set the model's Beta and Tau parameters ourselves, or otherwise allow for the model to extract the ordinary least-squares best fit. The parameters include the long-run expected interest rate, which in general would be user-specified. This will be set as part of regular discussion within GBM, co-ordinated by GBM Treasury, and in liaison with GT.

2 – Running the model produces a discount function in near-continuous time. (See Exhibit 1, which shows the function in annual time steps. This can be adjusted for monthly or daily time steps if desired). This is the Svensson discount function (DF). We convert this DF to match to EUR swap dates, and to spot settlement (this is because the EUR curve in the bank's common analytics function (CAF) is defined with spot settlement).

3 – We extract the par yield curve. We now have a set of discrete rates corresponding to the RBS fair value yield curve, which tells us the coupon to set on a vanilla fixed coupon bond we issue at par for the relevant tenor.

4 – We use these rates to construct a full yield curve in CAF. Note that until the CAF methodology is set up to incorporate the Svensson model, this part of the process will use cubic spline methodology. However the procedure will ensure that the CAF output matches the input precisely (that is, a 0.000% error) so we have preserved our market-determined Svensson curve.

From the curve at (4) we extract the implied TLP. (Exhibit 2) This shows the fair-value spread we should pay on an FRN we issue of relevant tenor with a

Maturity (year)	discount factor	forward rates	spot rates
0	1	0.48%	0.48%
1	0.981433988	3.10%	1.87%
2	0.942635953	4.85%	2.95%
3	0.892551064	5.98%	3.79%
4	0.837510049	6.68%	4.43%
5	0.781645775	7.08%	4.93%
6	0.727458537	7.26%	5.30%
7	0.676326573	7.30%	5.59%
8	0.628899097	7.23%	5.80%
9	0.585375249	7.10%	5.95%
10	0.545690715	6.93%	6.06%

Exhibit 1   Svensson discount function, annual time steps

floating re-set of 3 months Euribor. It is also the GBM internal private placement curve.

(Note: this also sets the rate we would pay on a fixed coupon bond issue that was asset-swapped, but for an unsecured swap [as this is the unsecured pricing curve]. Hence it would not be the correct fair-value spread to pay on an asset swap, because that would involve a secured derivative. If we assume an unsecured derivative, we now have the par-par asset swap curve.).

We should note that the above is the market-implied curve process. The model output extrapolates beyond the latest tenor of our issued bonds to as long a

Point	Basis Swap	implied 3m spreads
3m	##66.Unity.Swap	−17
6m	##67.Unity.Swap	−1
1y	##35.Unity.Swap	33
18m	##41.Unity.Swap	66
2y	##40.Unity.Swap	95
3y	##39.Unity.Swap	147
4y	##38.Unity.Swap	184
5y	##37.Unity.Swap	210
6y	##36.Unity.Swap	228
7y	##42.Unity.Swap	240
8y	##43.Unity.Swap	248
9y	##44.Unity.Swap	253
10y	##45.Unity.Swap	255

Exhibit 2   Extracted implied TLP

maturity as the user wishes, and as a function of the long-run expected forward rate. Exhibit 2 shows yields up to 10-year because that is within the life of existing RBS debt issuance. The user can set the model to extrapolate fair-value output to a tenor of its choice. Note that extrapolated rates represent the current secondary market-implied value, and hence the fair-value rate to pay for that tenor.

The implied TLP is the same curve that GBM would be feeding back to GT on a regular basis. The suggested procedure to GT is that they will set the RBS public curve to within a specified tolerance (such as plus/minus 15 bps) of the 2-week moving average of the GBM curve.

BIBLIOGRAPHY

Campbell, J. (1986). "A defence of traditional hypotheses about the term structure of interest rates", *Journal of Finance*, March, pp. 183–193.
Choudhry, M. (1998). "The information content of the United Kingdom gilt yield curve", unpublished MBA assignment, Henley Management College.
Choudhry, M. (2001). *The Bond and Money Markets*, Butterworth Heinemann, Chapters 51–53.
Choudhry, M. (2009). "The value of introducing structural reform to improve bond market liquidity: Experience from the U.K. gilt market", *European Journal of Finance and Banking Research*, 2(2).
Cox, J., Ingersoll, J.E., and Ross, S.A. (1981). "A re-examination of traditional hypotheses about the term structure of interest rates", *Journal of Finance*, **36**, September, pp. 769–799.
Culbertson, J.M. (1957). "The term structure of interest rates", *Quarterly Journal of Economics*, **71**, November, 485–517.
The Economist (1998). "Admiring those shapely curves", 4 April, p. 117.
Fama, E.F. (1976). "Forward rates as predictors of future spot interest rates", *Journal of Financial Economics*, **3**(4), October, pp. 361–377.
Fama, E.F. (1984). "The information in the term structure", *Journal of Financial Economics*, **13**, December, 509–528.
Fisher, I. (1986). "Appreciation of interest", *Publications of the American Economic Association*, August, pp. 23–39.
Hicks, J. (1946). *Value and Capital*, Oxford University Press, 1946.
Ingersoll, J. (1987). *Theory of Financial Decision Making*, Rowman & Littlefield, Chapter 18.
Jarrow, R. (1996). *Modelling Fixed Income Securities and Interest Rate Options*, McGraw-Hill.
Levy, H. (1999). *Introduction to Investments*, Second Edition, South-Western.
Livingstone, M. (1990). *Money and Capital Markets*, Prentice Hall.
Lutz, F. (1940). "The structure of interest rates", *Quarterly Journal of Economics*, November, pp. 36–63.
McCulloch, J.H. (1975). "An estimate of the liquidity premium", *Journal of Political Economy*, **83**, January/February, pp. 95–119.
Meiselman, D. (1962). *The Term Structure of Interest Rates*, Prentice Hall.
Rubinstein, M. (1999). *Rubinstein on Derivatives*, RISK Publishing.

Chapter

6

INTRODUCTION TO MONEY MARKET DEALING AND HEDGING

In this chapter we introduce some basics of trading and hedging as employed by a bank asset–liability management (ALM) or money market desk. The instruments and techniques used form the fundamental building blocks of ALM, so the reader can imagine that a full and comprehensive treatment of this subject would require a book in its own right.[1] Our purpose here is to acquaint the newcomer to the market with the essentials. The market yield curve and the bank's internal curve are paramount in this discipline, which is why we introduced that topic earlier. The next two chapters look at the ALM discipline in more detail.

The ALM and money market desk has a vital function in a bank, funding all the business lines in the bank. In some banks and securities houses it will be placed within the Treasury or money market areas, whereas other firms will organise it as an entirely separate function. Wherever it is organised, the need for clear and constant communication between the ALM desk and the other operating areas of the bank is paramount. But first we look at specific uses of money market products like deposits and repo in the context of the shape of the yield curve.

MONEY MARKET APPROACH

The yield curve and interest-rate expectations

When the yield curve is positively sloped, the conventional approach is to fund the book at the short end of the curve and lend at the long end. In essence, therefore, if the yield curve resembled that shown in Figure 6.1, a bank would borrow, say, 1-week funds while simultaneously lending out at, say, 3-month maturity. This is known as funding short. A bank can effect the economic equivalent of borrowing at the short end of the yield curve and lending at the longer end through repo transactions – in our example, a 1-week repo and a 6-month reverse repo. The bank then continuously rolls over its funding at 1-week intervals for the 6-month period. This is also known as creating a tail; here the "tail" is the gap between 1 week and 6 months – the interest-rate "gap" that the bank is exposed to. During the course of the trade – as the reverse repo has locked in a loan for 6 months – the bank is exposed to interest-rate risk should the slope or shape of the yield curve change. In this case, the bank may see its profit margin shrink or turn into a funding loss if short-dated interest rates rise.

As we noted in Chapter 5, a number of hypotheses have been advanced to explain the shape of the yield curve at any particular time. A steep positive-shaped curve may indicate that the market expects interest rates to rise over

[1]See Choudhry (2007).

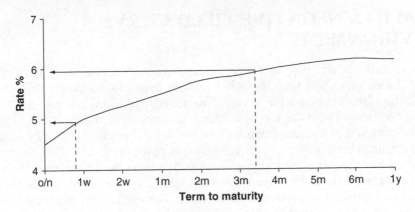

Figure 6.1   Positive yield curve funding

the longer term, although this is also sometimes given as the reason for an inverted curve with regard to shorter term rates. Generally speaking, trading volumes are higher in a positive-sloping yield curve environment, compared with a flat or negative-shaped curve.

In the case of an inverted yield curve, a bank will (all else being equal) lend at the short end of the curve and borrow at the longer end. This is known as *funding long* and is shown in Figure 6.2.

The example in Figure 6.2 shows a short cash position of 2-week maturity against a long cash position of 4-month maturity. The interest rate *gap* of 10 weeks is the book's interest-rate exposure. The inverted shape of the yield curve may indicate market expectations of a rise in short-term interest rates. Further along the yield curve, the market may expect a benign inflationary environment, which is why the premium on longer term returns is lower than normal.

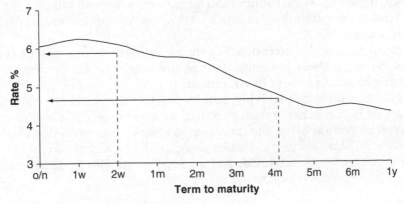

Figure 6.2   Negative yield curve funding

ALM IN A NEGATIVE YIELD CURVE ENVIRONMENT

In economic theory, negative interest rates should not exist, at least not for more than a very short time, or only because of specific technical reasons such as when individual bonds go "special" in the repo market, because individuals and corporations who are long cash have no incentive to place deposits with an institution that charges them for the privilege of lending it money. Again in theory, this is because one can always simply place one's cash "under the mattress" rather than at a bank that pays negative interest. In practice, of course, that is not possible and institutions are obliged to place their cash with banks even if a negative rate is charged, because it is not practical to place and transfer cash legitimately other than through the banking system.[2] In any case, unlike you or me, institutions can't really place their money under the mattress!

Since the banking crash in 2008, central banks have pursued very low or even negative interest-rate policies, and at the time of writing both the European Central Bank (ECB) and the Japanese central bank were operating a negative base interest-rate monetary policy. This extended into the capital markets tenor as well, principally because certain institutional investors are obliged to hold sovereign bonds irrespective of their yields, as shown, for example, in Figure 6.3 which is the Eurozone sovereign bond curve in June 2017. The rate does not become positive until the 7-year tenor area. The ECB charges –40 basis points for deposits placed with it by euro-area banks.

A continuous negative rates environment places difficulties on the ALM desk in a bank. In general, the approach to operating in these conditions may involve the following:

• Ideally, pass on the negative interest rate to deposit customers. This is not usually possible for relationship and reputation reasons, or for retail and small business customers, but is common for larger corporate customers;
• Within the constraints placed by sound liquidity risk management policy (see Chapter 9), avoid running too large surplus deposit balances and seek to lend surplus liabilities as much as possible within individual bank loan policy constraints;
• Seek to raise stable long-dated customer funding while deposit rates are low, paying a lower premium than would otherwise be the case in a conventional positive curve environment;
• Consider strategies involving exchanging the surplus domestic currency deposits into another currency so that there is no need to place them with the home central bank, and investing in assets denominated in the foreign currency. This, of course, creates associated FX market risk, which must be monitored and mitigated, and an appropriate risk appetite statement regarding this must be approved.

---

[2]This ignores the use of "crypto" currencies such as Bitcoin, but such payment mechanisms are not mainstream as yet, if indeed they ever will be.

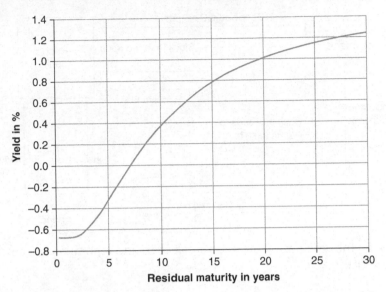

Figure 6.3 Eurozone AAA sovereign bond yield curve, 15 June 2017

Source: https://www.ecb.europa.eu/stats/financial_markets_and_interest_rates/euro_area_yield_curves/html/index.en.html

From the ALM desk perspective, the negative rates charged by the central bank will need to be considered for incorporation in the bank's funds transfer pricing policy (FTP – see Chapter 11), although as noted above in the retail customer space, where loans will still be made at a positive rate of interest, deposits will not necessarily be charged at a negative rate.

In general, while euro-area and Japanese banks will have learnt to operate in a negative rates environment, and despite the fact that the ECB has operated its negative base rate policy for some years, negative interest rates remain "non-normal" and are a sign of economic stagnation.

CREDIT INTERMEDIATION BY THE REPO DESK

In general, for banks with access to repo and bond stock loan markets, the government bond repo market will trade at a lower rate than other money market instruments, reflecting its status as a secured instrument with the best credit. This allows spreads between markets of different credits to be exploited. The following are examples of credit intermediation trades:

- A repo dealer lends general collateral (GC) currently trading at a spread below Libor and uses the cash to buy certificates of deposit (CDs) trading at a spread above Libor;
- A repo dealer borrows specific collateral in the stock-lending market – paying a fee – and sells the stock in the repo market at the GC rate; the cash is then lent in the inter-bank market at a higher rate – for instance, through the purchase of a clearing bank certificate of deposit. The CD is

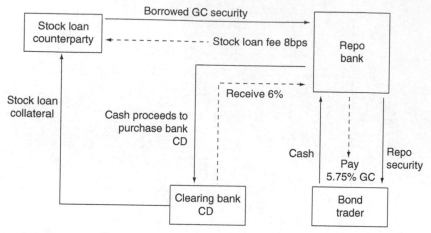

Figure 6.4 Intermediation between stock loan and repo markets; an example using UK gilts

used as collateral in the stock loan transaction. A bank must have dealing relationships with both the stock loan and repo markets to effect this trade. An example of the trade that could be put on using this type of intermediation is shown in Figure 4.3 for the UK gilt market. The details are given below and show that the bank would stand to gain 17 basis points over the course of the 3-month trade;

- A repo dealer trades repo in the GC market, and using the cash from this repo invests in emerging market collateral at a spread, say, 400 basis points higher.

These are but three examples of the way that repo can be used to exploit the interest-rate differentials that exist between markets of varying credit qualities and between secured and unsecured markets.

Figure 6.4 shows potential gains that can be made by a repo-dealing bank (market-maker) that has access to both the stock loan and general collateral repo market. It illustrates the rates available in the gilt market on 31 October 2000 for 3-month maturities, which were:

3-month GC repo   5.83–5.75%
3-month clearing bank CD   6132–6.00%

The stock loan fee for this term was quoted at 510 basis points, with the actual fee paid being 8 basis points. Therefore, the repo trader borrows GC stock for 3 months and offers this in repo at 5.75%.[3] The cash proceeds are then used

---

[3]A repo dealer is a market-maker, and so offers stock in repo at the offered side, which is 5.75%. However, this trade still turns in a profit if the bank dealt at another market-maker's bid side of 5.83%, with a profit of 9 basis points on the cash sum. Rates were quoted from King & Shaxson Bond Brokers Limited.

to purchase a clearing bank CD at 6.00%. This CD is used as collateral in the stock loan. The profit is market risk free as the terms are locked, although there is an element of credit risk in holding the CD. On these terms, the profit in £100 million stock for the 3-month period is approximately £170,000.

The main consideration for the dealing bank is the capital requirements of the trade. Gilt repo is zero weighted for capital purposes. Indeed, clearing bank CDs are accepted by the Bank of England for liquidity purposes, so the capital cost is not onerous. The bank will need to ensure that it has sufficient credit lines for the repo and CD counterparties.

Example 6.1   ALM considerations

Assume that a bank may access the markets for 3-month and 6-month funds, whether for funding or investment purposes. The rates for these terms are shown in Table 6.1. Assume no bid–offer spreads. The ALM manager also expects the 3-month Libor rate in 3 months' time to be 5.10%. The bank can usually fund its book at Libor, while it is able to lend at Libor plus 1%.

Table 6.1   Hypothetical money market rates

Term	Libor	Bank rate
90-day	5.50%	6.50%
180-day	5.75%	6.75%
Expected 90-day rate in 90 days' time	5.10%	6.10%
3v6 forward rate agreement (FRA)	6.60%	

The bank could adopt any of the following strategies, or a combination of them:

- Borrow 3-month funds at 5.50% and lend this out in the 3-month at 6.50%. This locks-in a return of 1% for a 3-month period;
- Borrow 6-month funds at 5.75% and lend in the 6-month at 6.75%; again this earns a locked-in spread of 1%;
- Borrow 3-month funds at 5.50% and lend this in the 6-month at 6.75%. This approach would require the bank to refund the loan in 3 months' time, which it expects to be able to do at 5.10%. This approach locks-in a return of 1.25% in the first 3-month period, and an expected return of 1.65% in the second 3-month period. The risk of this tactic is that the 3-month rate in 3 months' time does not fall as expected by the ALM manager, reducing profits and possibly leading to loss;
- Borrow in the 6-month at 5.75% and lend these for a 6-month period at 6.50%. After this period, lend the funds in the 3-month or 6-month. This strategy does not tally with the ALM manager's view, however, who

expects a fall in rates and so should not wish to be long of funds in 3 months' time;

- Borrow 3-month funds at 5.50% and again lend this in the 3-month at 6.75%. To hedge the gap risk, the ALM manager simultaneously buys a 3v6 FRA to lock-in the 3-month rate in 3 months' time. The first period spread of 1.25% is guaranteed, but the FRA guarantees only a spread of 15 basis points in the second period. This is the cost of the hedge (and also suggests that the market does not agree with the ALM manager's assessment of where rates will be 3 months from now!), the price the bank must pay for reducing uncertainty, the lower spread return. Alternatively, the bank could lend in the 6-month period, funding initially in the 6-month, and buy an interest-rate cap with a ceiling rate of 6.60% and pegged to Libor, the rate at which the bank can actually fund its book.

Although somewhat stylistic, these scenarios serve to illustrate what is possible, and indeed there are many other strategies that could be adopted. The approaches described in the last option show how derivative instruments can be used actively to manage the banking book, and the cost that is associated with employing them.

Example 6.2   Position management

Starting the day with a flat position, a money market interbank desk transacts the following deals:

£100 million borrowing from 16/9/09 to 7/10/09 (3 weeks) at 6.375%
£60 million borrowing from 16/9/09 to 16/10/09 (1 month) at 6.25%
£110 million loan from 16/9/09 to 18/10/09 (32 days) at 6.45%.

The desk reviews its cash position and the implications for refunding and interest-rate risk, bearing in mind the following:

- There is an internal overnight roll-over limit of £40 million (net);
- The bank's economist feels more pessimistic about a rise in interest rates than most others in the market, and has recently given an internal seminar on the dangers of inflation in the UK as a result of recent increases in the level of average earnings;
- Today there are some important figures being released including inflation (RPI) data. If today's RPI figures exceed market expectations, the dealer expects a tightening of monetary policy by *at least* 0.50% almost immediately;
- A broker's estimate of daily market liquidity for the next few weeks is one of low shortage, with little central bank intervention required, and hence low volatilities and rates in the overnight rate;

- Brokers' screens indicate the following term repo rates:

O/N	6.350–6.300%
1 week	6.390–6.340%
2 week	6.400–6.350%
1 month	6.410–6.375%
2 month	6.500–6.450%
3 month	6.670–6.620%

- The indication for a 1v2 FRA is:

1v2 FRA	6.680–6.630%

- The quote for an 11-day forward borrowing in 3 weeks' time (the "21v32 rate") is 6.50% bid.

The book's exposure looks like the illustration in Figure 6.5.

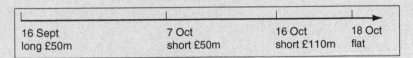

Figure 6.5 Position timeline

What courses of action are open to the desk, bearing in mind that the book needs to be squared off such that the position is flat each night?

Possible solutions

Investing early surplus

From a cash management point of view, the desk has a £50 million surplus from 16/9 up to 7/10. This needs to be invested. It may be able to negotiate a 6.31% loan with the market for overnight, or 6.35% term deposit for 1 week to 6.38% for 1 month.

The overnight roll is the most flexible but offers a worse rate, and if the desk expects the overnight rate to remain both low and stable (due to forecasts of low market shortages), it may not opt for this course of action.

However, it may make sense from an interest-rate risk point of view. If the desk agrees with the bank's economist, it should be able to benefit from rolling at higher rates soon – possibly in the next 3 weeks. Therefore, it may not want to lock in a term rate now, and the overnight roll would match this view. However, it exposes them to lower rates, if their view is wrong, which will limit the extent of the positive funding spread. The market itself appears neutral about rate changes in the next month, but appears to factor in a rise thereafter.

The forward "gap"

Looking forward, the book is currently on course to exceed the £40 million overnight position limit on 7/10, when the refunding requirement is £50 million. The situation gets worse on 16/10 (for 2 days) when the refunding requirement is £110 million. The desk needs to fix a term deal before those dates to carry it over until 18/10 when the funding position reverts to zero. A borrowing from 7/10 to 18/10 of £50 million will reduce the rollover requirement to within limit.

However, given that interest rates will rise, should the desk wait until the 7th to deal in the cash? Not if it has a firm view. They may end up paying as much as 6.91% or higher for the funding (after the 0.50% rate rise). So it would be better to transact now a forward starting repo to cover the period, thus locking in the benefits obtainable from today's yield curve. The market rate for a 21 × 32-day repo is quoted at 6.50%. This reflects the market's consensus that rates may rise in about a month's time. However, the desk's own expectation is of a larger rise, hence its own logic suggests trading in the forward loan. This strategy will pay dividends if their view is right, as it limits the extent of funding loss.

An alternative means of protecting the interest-rate risk alone is to BUY a 1v2 month Forward Rate Agreement (FRA) for 6.68%. This does not exactly match the gap, but should act as an effective hedge. If there is a rate rise, the book gains from the FRA profit. Note that the cash position still needs to be squared off. Should the desk deal before or after the inflation announcement? That is, of course, down to its judgement, but most dealers like, if at all possible, to sit tight ahead of releases of key economic data.

INTEREST-RATE HEDGING TOOLS

For bank dealers who are not looking to trade around term mismatch or other spreads, but who will run a tenor mismatch between assets and liabilities (which is, after all, what banking is: the practice of maturity transformation), there are a number of instruments they can use to hedge the resulting interest-rate risk exposure. We consider them briefly here.

Interest-rate futures

A forward term interest-rate gap exposure can be hedged using interest-rate futures. These are standardised exchange-traded derivative contracts, and represent a forward-starting 90-day time deposit. In the sterling market, the instrument will typically be the 90-day short sterling future traded on London's "LIFFE" futures exchange. A strip of futures can be used to hedge the term gap. The trader buys futures contracts to the value of the exposure and for the term of the gap. Any change in cash rates should be hedged by offsetting moves in futures prices.

Description

A *futures* contract is a transaction that fixes the price today for a commodity that will be delivered at some point in the future. Financial futures fix the price for interest rates, bonds, equities, and so on, but trade in the same manner as commodity futures. Contracts for futures are standardised and traded on recognised exchanges. In London, the main futures exchange is LIFFE, although other futures are also traded on, for example, the International Petroleum Exchange and the London Metal Exchange. Money markets trade short-term interest-rate futures that fix the rate of interest on a notional fixed term deposit of money (usually for 90 days or 3 months) for a specified period in the future. The sum is notional because no actual sum of money is deposited when buying or selling futures – the instrument being off-balance-sheet. Buying such a contract is equivalent to making a notional deposit, while selling a contract is equivalent to borrowing a notional sum.

The 3-month interest-rate future is the most widely used instrument for hedging interest-rate risk.

The LIFFE exchange in London trades short-term interest-rate futures for major currencies including sterling, euros, yen, and the Swiss franc. Table 6.2 summarises the terms for the short sterling contract as traded on LIFFE.

Futures contracts originally related to physical commodities, which is why we speak of *delivery* when referring to the expiry of financial futures contracts. Exchange-traded futures such as those on LIFFE are set to expire every quarter during the year. The short sterling contract is a deposit of cash, so as its price refers to the rate of interest on this deposit, the price of the contract is set as $P = 100r$ where P is the price of the contract and r is the rate of interest at the time of expiry implied by the futures contract. This means that if the price of

Table 6.2 Description of LIFFE short sterling futures contract

Name	**90-day sterling Libor interest-rate future**
Contract size	£500,000
Delivery months	March, June, September, December
Delivery date	First business day after the last trading day
Last trading day	Third Wednesday of delivery month
Price	100 minus interest rate
Tick size	0.01
Tick value	£12.50
Trading hours	LIFFE CONNECT™ 07:30–18:00 hours

Source: LIFFE.

the contract rises, the rate of interest implied goes down and vice versa. For example, the price of the June 2011 short sterling future (written as Jun11 or M11, from the futures identity letters of H, M, U, and Z for contracts expiring in March, June, September, and December, respectively) at the start of trading on 22 September 2010 was 99.05, which implied a 3-month Libor rate of 0.95% on expiry of the contract in June 2011. If a trader bought 20 contracts at this price and then sold them just before the close of trading that day, when the price had risen to 99.08, an implied rate of 0.92%, she would have made 3 ticks profit or £750. That is, a 3-tick upward price movement in a long position of 20 contracts is equal to £750. This is calculated as follows:

$$\text{Profit} = \text{Ticks gained} \times \text{Tick value} \times \text{Number of contracts}$$
$$\text{Loss} = \text{Ticks lost} \times \text{Tick value} \times \text{Number of contracts}$$

The tick value for the short sterling contract is straightforward to calculate. Since we know that the contract size is £500,000, there is a minimum price movement (tick movement) of 0.01% and the contract has a 3-month "maturity":

$$\text{Tick value} = 0.01\% \times £500,000 \times \frac{3}{12} = £12.50$$

The profit made by the trader in our example is logical because if we buy short sterling futures we are depositing (notional) funds and if the price of the futures rises, it means the interest rate has fallen. We profit because we have "deposited" funds at a higher rate beforehand. If we expected sterling interest rates to rise, we would sell short sterling futures, which is equivalent to borrowing funds and locking in the loan rate at a lower level.

Note how the concept of buying and selling interest-rate futures differs from FRAs: if we buy an FRA we are borrowing notional funds, whereas if we buy a futures contract we are depositing notional funds. If a position in an interest-rate futures contract is held to expiry, cash settlement will take place on the delivery day for that contract.

Short-term interest-rate contracts in other currencies are similar to the short sterling contract and trade on exchanges such as Deutsche Terminbörse in Frankfurt and MATIF in Paris.

In practice, futures contracts do not provide a precise tool for locking into cash market rates today for a transaction that takes place in the future, although this is what they are theoretically designed to do. Futures do allow a bank to lock in a rate for a transaction to take place in the future; this rate is the forward rate. The basis is the difference between today's cash market rate and the forward rate on a particular date in the future. As a futures contract approaches expiry, its price and the rate in the cash market will converge (the process is given the name convergence). This is given by the exchange delivery settlement price, and the two prices (rates) will be exactly in line at the precise moment of expiry.

Example 6.3   The Eurodollar futures contract

The Eurodollar futures contract is traded on the Chicago Mercantile Exchange. The underlying asset is a deposit of US dollars in a bank outside the US, and the contract is at the rate of dollar 90-day Libor. The Eurodollar future is cash settled on the second business day before the third Wednesday of the delivery month (London business day). The final settlement price is used to set the price of the contract, given by:

$$10,000(100-0:25r)$$

where r is the quoted Eurodollar rate at the time. This rate is the actual 90-day Eurodollar deposit rate.

The longest dated Eurodollar contract has an expiry date of 10 years. The market assumes that futures prices and forward prices are equal; this is indeed the case under conditions where the risk-free interest rate is constant and the same for all maturities. In practice, it also holds for short-dated futures contracts, but does not for longer dated futures contracts. Therefore, using futures contracts with a maturity greater than 5 years to calculate zero-coupon rates or implied forward rates will produce errors in results, which need to be taken into account if the derived rates are used to price other instruments such as swaps.

Hedging using interest-rate futures

Banks use interest-rate futures to hedge interest-rate risk exposure in cash and OBS instruments. Bond-trading desks often use futures to hedge positions in bonds of up to 2 or 3 years' maturity, as contracts are traded up to 3 years' maturity. The liquidity of such "far month" contracts is considerably lower than for "near month" contracts and the "front month" contract (the current contract for the next maturity month). When hedging a bond with a maturity of, say, 2 years' maturity, the trader will put on a strip of futures contracts that matches as near as possible the expiry date of the bond.

The purpose of a hedge is to protect the value of a current or anticipated cash market or OBS position from adverse changes in interest rates. The hedger will try to offset the effect of the change in interest rate on the value of his cash position with the change in value of his hedging instrument. If the hedge is an exact one the loss on the main position should be compensated by a profit on the hedge position. If the trader is expecting a fall in interest rates and wishes to protect against such a fall, he will buy futures (known as a long hedge) and will sell futures (a short hedge) if wishing to protect against a rise in rates.

Bond traders also use 3-month interest-rate contracts to hedge positions in short-dated bonds; for instance, a market-maker running a short-dated bond book would find it more appropriate to hedge his book using short-dated futures rather than the longer dated bond futures contract. When this happens it is important to accurately calculate the correct number of contracts to use for the hedge. To construct a bond hedge it will be necessary to use a strip of contracts, thus ensuring that the maturity date of the bond is covered by the longest dated futures contract. The hedge is calculated by finding the sensitivity of each cash flow to changes in each of the relevant forward rates. Each cash flow is considered individually and hedge values are then aggregated and rounded to the nearest whole number of contracts.

Examples 6.4 and 6.5 illustrate hedging with short-term interest-rate contracts.

Example 6.4 Hedging a forward 3-month lending requirement

On 1 June a corporate treasurer is expecting a cash inflow of £10 million in 3 months' time (1 September), which he will then invest for 3 months. The treasurer expects interest rates will fall over the next few weeks and wishes to protect himself against such a fall. This can be done using short sterling futures. The market rates on 1 June are as follows:

3-month Libor	$6\frac{1}{2}\%$
Sep futures price	93.220

The treasurer buys 20 September short sterling futures at 93.220, this number being exactly equivalent to a sum of £10 million. This allows him to lock in a forward *lending* rate of 6.78%, on the assumption there is no bid–offer quote spread:

$$\text{Expected lending rate} = \text{Rate implied by futures price}$$
$$= 100 - 93.220$$
$$= 6.78\%$$

On 1 September the market rates are as follows:

3-month Libor	612%
Sep futures price	93.705

The treasurer unwinds the hedge at this price.

$$\text{Futures P\&L} = +97\text{ticks}(93.705 - 93.22) \quad \text{or} \quad 0.485\%$$
$$\text{Effective lending rate} = \text{3-month Libor} + \text{Futures profit}$$
$$= 6.25\% + 0.485\%$$
$$= 6.735\%$$

The treasurer was quite close to achieving his target lending rate of 6.78% and the hedge has helped to protect against the drop in Libor rates from $6\frac{1}{2}$% to $6\frac{1}{4}$%, as a result of the profit from the futures transaction.

In the real world, the cash market bid–offer spread will impact the amount of profit/loss from the hedge transaction. Futures generally trade and settle near the offered side of the market rate (Libor), whereas lending, certainly by corporates, will be nearer the Libid rate.

Example 6.5   Hedging a forward 6-month borrowing requirement

---

A Treasury dealer has a 6-month borrowing requirement for EUR30 million in 3 months' time, on 16 September. He expects interest rates to rise by at least 12% before that date and would like to lock in a future borrowing rate. The scenario is:

Date	16 June
3-month Libor	6.0625%
6-month Libor	6.25
Sep futures contract	93.66
Dec futures contract	93.39

In order to hedge a 6-month EUR30 million exposure, the dealer needs to use a total of 60 futures contracts, as each has a nominal value of EUR1 million, and corresponds to a 3-month notional deposit period. The dealer decides to sell 30 September futures contracts and 30 December futures contracts. This is referred to as a strip hedge. The expected forward borrowing rate that can be achieved by this strategy, where the expected borrowing rate is rf, is calculated as follows:

$$1 + rf \times \frac{\text{Days in period}}{360} = \left(1 + \text{Sep implied rate} \times \frac{\text{Sep days period}}{360}\right)$$
$$\times \left(1 + \text{Dec implied rate} \times \frac{\text{Dec days period}}{360}\right)$$

Therefore, we have:

$$1 + rf \times \frac{180}{360} = \left(1 + 0.0634 \times \frac{90}{360}\right) \times \left(1 + 0.0661 \times \frac{90}{360}\right)$$
$$= 6.53\%$$

The rate rf is sometimes referred to as the "strip rate".

The hedge is unwound upon expiry of the September futures contract. Assume the following rates now prevail:

3-month Libor	6.4375%
6-month Libor	6.8125%
Sep futures contract	93.56
Dec futures contract	92.93

The futures P&L is:

September contract	+10 ticks
December contract	+46 ticks

This represents a 56-tick or 0.56% profit in 3-month interest-rate terms, or 0.28% in 6-month interest-rate terms. The effective borrowing rate is the 6-month Libor rate minus the futures profit, or:

$$6:8125\% - 0:28\% \quad \text{or} \quad 6:5325\%$$

In this case the hedge has proved effective because the dealer has realised a borrowing rate of 6.5325%, which is close to the target strip rate of 6.53%.

The dealer is still exposed to the basis risk when the December contracts are bought back from the market at the expiry date of the September contract. If, for example, the future was bought back at 92.73, the effective borrowing rate would only be 6.4325%, and the dealer would benefit. Of course, the other possibility is that the futures contract could be trading 20 ticks more expensive, which would give a borrowing rate of 6.6325%, which is 10 basis points above the target rate. If this happened, the dealer may elect to borrow in the cash market for 3 months, maintain the December futures position until the December contract expiry date, and roll over the borrowing at that time. The profit (or loss) on the December futures position will compensate for any change in 3-month rates at that time.

Forward rate agreements

Forward rate agreements (FRAs) are similar in concept to interest-rate futures and like them are off-balance-sheet instruments. Under an FRA a buyer agrees notionally to borrow and a seller to lend a specified notional amount at a fixed rate for a specified period – the contract to commence on an agreed date in the future. On this date (the "fixing date"), the actual rate is taken and, according to its position versus the original trade rate, the borrower or lender will receive an interest payment on the notional sum equal to the difference between the trade rate and the actual rate. The sum paid over is present valued as it is transferred at the start of the notional loan period, whereas in a cash market trade interest would be handed over at the end of the loan period. As FRAs are off-balance-sheet contracts no actual borrowing or lending of cash takes place, hence the use of the term "notional". In hedging an interest-rate gap in the cash period, the trader will buy an FRA contract that equates to the term gap for a nominal amount equal to his exposure in the cash market. Should rates move against him in the cash market, the gain on the FRA should (in theory) compensate for the loss in the cash trade.

Definition of an FRA

An FRA is an agreement to borrow or lend a notional cash sum for a period of time lasting up to 12 months, starting at any point over the next 12 months, at an agreed rate of interest (the FRA rate). The "buyer" of an FRA is borrowing a notional sum of money, while the "seller" is lending this cash sum. Note how this differs from all other money market instruments. In the cash market, the party buying a CD or bill, or bidding for stock in the repo market, is the lender of funds. In the FRA market, to "buy" is to "borrow". Of course, we use the term "notional" because with an FRA no borrowing or lending of cash actually takes place. The notional sum is simply the amount on which interest payment is calculated.

So, when an FRA is traded, the buyer is borrowing (and the seller is lending) a specified notional sum at a fixed rate of interest for a specified period – the "loan" to commence at an agreed date in the future. The *buyer* is the notional borrower, and so she will be protected if there is a rise in interest rates between the date that the FRA is traded and the date that the FRA comes into effect. If there is a fall in interest rates, the buyer must pay the difference between the rate at which the FRA was traded and the actual rate, as a percentage of the notional sum. The buyer may be using the FRA to hedge an actual exposure – that is, an actual borrowing of money – or simply speculating on a rise in interest rates. The counterparty to the transaction, the seller of the FRA, is the notional lender of funds, and has fixed the rate for lending funds. If there is a fall in interest rates the seller will gain, and if there is a rise in rates the seller will pay. Again, the seller may have an actual loan of cash to hedge or be a speculator.

In FRA trading only the payment that arises as a result of the difference in interest rates changes hands. There is no exchange of cash at the time of the trade. The cash payment that does arise is the difference in interest rates between that at which the FRA was traded and the actual rate prevailing when the FRA matures, as a percentage of the notional amount. FRAs are traded by both banks and corporates and between banks. The FRA market is very liquid in all major currencies and rates are readily quoted on screens by both banks and brokers. Dealing is over the telephone or over a dealing system such as Reuters.

The terminology quoting FRAs refers to the borrowing time period and the time at which the FRA comes into effect (or matures). Hence, if a buyer of an FRA wished to hedge against a rise in rates to cover a 3-month loan starting in 3 months' time, she would transact a "3-against-6-month" FRA, more usually denoted as a 3–6s or 3v6 FRA. This is referred to in the market as a "threes–sixes" FRA, and means a 3-month loan beginning in 3 months' time. So, correspondingly, a "ones–fours" FRA (1v4) is a 3-month loan in 1 month's time, and a "threes–nines" FRA (3v9) is a 6-month loan in 3 months' time.

Remember that when we buy an FRA we are "borrowing" funds. This differs from cash products such as a CD or repo, as well as interest-rate futures, where to "buy" is to lend funds.

Example 6.6   FRA hedging

A company knows that it will need to borrow £1 million in 3 months' time for a 12-month period. It can borrow funds today at Libor 50 basis points. Libor rates today are at 5% but the company's treasurer expects rates to go up to about 6% over the next few weeks. So, the company will be forced to borrow at higher rates unless some sort of hedge is transacted to protect the borrowing requirement. The treasurer decides to buy a 3v15 ("threes–fifteens") FRA to cover the 12-month period beginning 3 months from now. A bank quotes $5\frac{1}{2}\%$ for the FRA, which the company buys for a notional £1 million. After 3 months the rates have indeed gone up to 6%, so the treasurer must borrow funds at $6\frac{1}{2}\%$ (the Libor rate plus spread). However, she will receive a settlement amount that will be the difference between the rate at which the FRA was bought and today's 12-month Libor rate (6%) as a percentage of £1 million, which will compensate for some of the increased borrowing costs.

FRA mechanics

In virtually every market, FRAs trade under a set of terms and conventions that are identical. The British Bankers Association (BBA) has compiled standard legal documentation to cover FRA trading. The following standard terms are used in the market:

- *Notional sum*: the amount for which the FRA is traded;
- *Trade date*: the date on which the FRA is dealt;
- *Settlement date*: the date on which the notional loan or deposit of funds becomes effective; that is, is said to begin. This date is used, in conjunction with the notional sum, for calculation purposes only as no actual loan or deposit takes place;
- *Fixing date*: this is the date on which the *reference rate* is determined; that is, the rate with which the FRA dealing rate is compared;
- *Maturity date*: the date on which the notional loan or deposit expires;
- *Contract period*: the time between the settlement date and maturity date;
- *FRA rate*: the interest rate at which the FRA is traded;

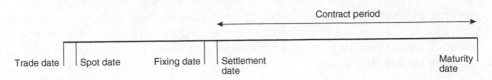

Figure 6.6 Key dates in an FRA trade

- *Reference rate*: the rate used as part of the calculation of the settlement amount, usually the Libor rate on the fixing date for the contract period in question;
- *Settlement sum*: the amount calculated as the difference between the FRA rate and the reference rate as a percentage of the notional sum, paid by one party to the other on the settlement date.

These dates are illustrated in Figure 6.6.

The spot date is usually 2 business days after the trade date; however, it can by agreement be sooner or later than this. The settlement date will be the time period after the spot date referred to by FRA terms – for example, a 1 × 4 FRA will have a settlement date 1 calendar month after the spot date. The fixing date is usually 2 business days before the settlement date. The settlement sum is paid on the settlement date and, as it refers to an amount over a period of time that is paid upfront at the start of the contract period, the calculated sum is a discounted present value. This is because a normal payment of interest on a loan/deposit is paid at the end of the time period to which it relates. Because an FRA makes this payment at the start of the relevant period, the settlement amount is also a discounted present value sum.

With most FRA trades the reference rate is the Libor setting on the fixing date.

The settlement sum is calculated after the fixing date, for payment on the settlement date. We may illustrate this with a hypothetical example. Consider the case where a corporate has bought £1 million notional of a 1v4 FRA and dealt at 5.75%, and that the market rate is 6.50% on the fixing date. The contract period is 90 days. In the cash market, the extra interest charge that the corporate would pay is a simple interest calculation:

$$\frac{6.50 - 5.75}{100} \times 1,000,000 \times \frac{91}{365} = £1,869.86$$

The extra interest that the corporate is facing would be payable with the interest payment for the loan, which (as it is a money market loan) is when the loan matures. Under an FRA, then, the settlement sum payable should be exactly equal to this if it was paid on the same day as the cash market interest charge. This would make it a perfect hedge. However, as we noted above, the FRA settlement value is paid at the start of the contract period – that is, at the beginning of the underlying loan and not the end. Therefore, the settlement sum has to be adjusted to account for this, and the amount of the adjustment is the value of the interest that would be earned if the unadjusted cash value was invested for the contract period in the money market. The settlement value is given by equation (6.1):

$$\text{Settlement} = \frac{(r_{ref} - r_{FRA}) \times M \times \frac{n}{B}}{1 + \left(r_{ref} \times \frac{n}{B}\right)} \tag{6.1}$$

where

r_{ref} = Reference interest fixing rate;
r_{FRA} = FRA rate or contract rate;
M = Notional value;
n = Number of days in the contract period;
B = Day-count base (360 or 365).

Equation (6.1) simply calculates the extra interest payable in the cash market, resulting from the difference between the two interest rates, and then discounts the amount because it is payable at the start of the period and not, as would happen in the cash market, at the end of the period.

In our hypothetical illustration, the corporate buyer of the FRA receives the settlement sum from the seller as the fixing rate is higher than the dealt rate. This then compensates the corporate for the higher borrowing costs that he would have to pay in the cash market. If the fixing rate had been lower than 5.75%, the buyer would pay the difference to the seller, because cash market rates will mean that he is subject to a lower interest rate in the cash market. What the FRA has done is hedge the interest rate, so that whatever happens in the market, it will pay 5.75% on its borrowing.

A market-maker in FRAs is trading short-term interest rates. The settlement sum is the value of the FRA. The concept is exactly the same as with trading short-term interest-rate futures; a trader who buys an FRA is running a long position, so that if $r_{ref} > r_{FRA}$ on the fixing date the settlement sum is positive and the trader realises a profit. What has happened is that the trader, by buying the FRA, "borrowed" money at an interest rate that subsequently rose. This is a gain, exactly like a *short* position in an interest-rate future, where if the price goes down – that is, interest rates go up – the trader realises a gain. Equally, a "short" position in an FRA, put on by selling an FRA, realises a gain if $r_{ref} < r_{FRA}$ on the fixing date.

FRA pricing

As their name makes clear, FRAs are forward rate instruments and are priced using standard forward rate principles.[4] Consider an investor who has two

---

[4] An introduction to the basics of spot and forward rates can be found in any number of finance textbooks; the author particularly likes Windas (1993), which is highly suitable for beginners.

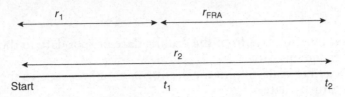

Figure 6.7 Rates used in FRA pricing

alternatives: either a 6-month investment at 5% or a 1-year investment at 6%. If the investor wishes to invest for 6 months and then roll over the investment for a further 6 months, what rate is required for the rollover period such that the final return equals the 6% available from the 1-year investment? If we view an FRA rate as the breakeven forward rate between the two periods, we simply solve for this forward rate. The result is our approximate FRA rate.

We can use the standard forward rate breakeven formula to solve for the required FRA rate. The relationship given in equation (6.2) connects simple (bullet) interest rates for periods of time up to 1 year, where no compounding of interest is required. As FRAs are money market instruments we are not required to calculate rates for periods in excess of 1 year,[5] where compounding would need to be built into the equation. The expression is:

$$(1 + r_2 t_2) = (1 + r_1 t_1)(1 + r_f t_f) \qquad (6.2)$$

where

r_2 = Cash market interest rate for the long period;
r_1 = Cash market interest rate for the short period;
r_f = Forward rate for the gap period;
t_2 = Time period from today to the end of the long period;
t_1 = Time period from today to the end of the short period;
t_f = Forward gap time period, or the contract period for the FRA.

This is illustrated diagrammatically in Figure 6.7.

The time period t_1 is the time from the dealing date to the FRA settlement date, while t_2 is the time from the dealing date to the FRA maturity date. The time period for the FRA (contract period) is t_2 minus t_1. We can replace the symbol "t" for time period with "n" for the actual number of days in the time periods themselves. If we do this and then rearrange the equation to solve for r_{FRA} (the FRA rate) we obtain:

$$r_{\text{FRA}} = \frac{r_2 n_2 - r_1 n_1}{n_{\text{FRA}} \left(1 + r_1 \frac{n_1}{365}\right)} \qquad (6.3)$$

---

[5]Although it is of course possible to trade FRAs with contract periods greater than 1 year, for which a different pricing formula must be used.

where

n_1 = Number of days from the dealing date or spot date to the settlement date;

n_2 = Number of days from the dealing date or spot date to the maturity date;

r_1 = Spot rate to the settlement date;

r_2 = Spot rate from the spot date to the maturity date;

n_{FRA} = Number of days in the FRA contract period;

r_{FRA} = FRA rate.

If the formula is applied to, say, US dollar money markets, the 365 in the equation is replaced by 360, the day-count base for that market.

In practice, FRAs are priced off the exchange-traded short-term interest-rate future for that currency, so that sterling FRAs are priced off LIFFE short sterling futures. Traders normally use a spreadsheet pricing model that has futures prices directly fed into it. FRA positions are also usually hedged with other FRAs or short-term interest-rate futures.

Example 6.7 Hedging an FRA position

An FRA market-maker sells a EUR100 million 3 × 6 FRA, i.e. an agreement to make a notional deposit (without exchange of principal) for 3 months in 3 months' time at a rate of 7.52%. He is exposed to the risk that interest rates will have risen by the FRA settlement date in 3 months' time.

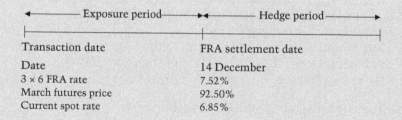

Transaction date	FRA settlement date
Date	14 December
3 × 6 FRA rate	7.52%
March futures price	92.50%
Current spot rate	6.85%

Action

The dealer first needs to calculate a precise hedge ratio. This is a three-stage process:

(i) Calculate the nominal value of a basis point move in Libor on the FRA settlement payment:

$$BPV = FRA_{nom} \times 0.01\% \times \frac{n}{360}$$

Therefore:

$$EUR100,000,000 \times 0.01\% \times 90/360 = EUR2,500$$

(ii) Find the present value of (i) by discounting it back to the transaction date using the FRA and spot rates:

Present value of a basis point move

$$= \frac{\text{Nominal value of basis point}}{\left[1 + \text{Spot rate} \times \frac{\text{Days in hedge period}}{360}\right] \times \left[1 + \text{FRA rate} \times \frac{\text{Days in hedge period}}{360}\right]}$$

Therefore:

$$\frac{\text{EUR2,500}}{\left[1 + 6.85\% \times \frac{90}{360}\right]\left[1 + 7.52\% \times \frac{90}{360}\right]}$$

(iii) Determine the correct hedge ratio by dividing (ii) by the futures tick value.

$$\text{Hedge ratio} = \frac{2,412}{25} = 96.48$$

The appropriate number of contracts for the hedge of a EUR100,000,000 3 × 6 FRA would therefore be 96 or 97, as the fraction is under one-half, 96 is correct.

To hedge the risk of an increase in interest rates, the trader sells 96 EUR 3 months futures contracts at 92.50. Any increase in rates during the hedge period should be offset by a gain realised on the futures contracts through daily variation margin receipts.

Outcome

Date	15 March
3-month Libor	7.625%
March EDSP	92.38

The hedge is lifted upon expiry of the March futures contracts. The 3-month Libor on the FRA settlement date has risen to 7.625%, so the trader incurs a loss of EUR25,759 on his FRA position (i.e. EUR26,250 discounted back over the 3-month FRA period at current Libor rate), calculated as follows:

$$\frac{(\text{Libor} - \text{FRA rate}) \times \frac{\text{Days in FRA period}}{360} \times \text{Contract nominal amount}}{1 + \text{Libor rate} \times \frac{\text{Days in FRA period}}{360}}$$

Therefore:

$$\frac{26,250 \left(\text{i.e. } 0.105\% \times \frac{90}{360} \times \text{ECU100,000,000}\right)}{1 + 7.625\% \times \frac{90}{360}} = \text{ECU25,759}$$

Futures P/L:

12 ticks (i.e. 92.50 − 92.38) × EUR25 × 96 contracts = EUR28,800

Conclusion

The EUR25,759 loss on the FRA position is more than offset by the EUR28,800 profit on the futures position when the hedge is lifted.

If the dealer has sold 100 contracts, his futures profit would have been EUR30,000, and, accordingly, been a less accurate hedge. The excess profit in the hedge position can mostly be attributed to the arbitrage profit realised by the market-maker (i.e. the market-maker has sold the FRA for 7.52% and in effect bought it back in the futures market by selling futures at 92.50 or 7.50% for a 2 tick profit).

Interest-rate swaps

An interest-rate swap is an off-balance-sheet agreement between two parties to make periodic interest payments to each other. Payments are on a predetermined set of dates in the future, based on a notional principal amount; one party is the *fixed-rate payer*, the rate agreed at the start of the swap, and the other party is the *floating-rate payer*, the floating-rate being determined during the life of the swap by reference to a specific market rate or index. There is no exchange of principal, only of the interest payments on this principal amount. Note that our description is for a plain vanilla swap contract; it is common to have variations on this theme – for instance, *floating–floating* swaps where both payments are floating-rate, as well as cross-currency swaps where there is an exchange of an equal amount of different currencies at the start dates and end dates of the swap.

An interest-rate swap can be used to hedge the fixed-rate risk arising from originating a loan at a fixed interest rate, such as a fixed-rate mortgage. The terms of the swap should match the payment dates and maturity date of the loan. The idea is to match the cash flows from the loan with equal and opposite payments in the swap contract, which will hedge the mortgage position. For example, if the retail bank has advanced a fixed-rate mortgage, it will be receiving fixed-rate coupon payments on the nominal value of the loan (together with a portion of the capital repayment if it is a repayment mortgage and not an interest-only mortgage). To hedge this position, the trader buys a swap contract for the same nominal value in which he will be paying the same fixed-rate payment; net cash flow is a receipt of floating interest-rate payments.

A borrower, on the other hand, may issue bonds of a particular type because of investor demand for such paper, but prefer to have the interest exposure on the debt in some other form. So, for example, a UK company issues fixed-rate bonds denominated in, say, Australian dollars, swaps the proceeds into sterling, and pays floating-rate interest on the sterling amount. As part of the swap the company will be receiving fixed-rate Australian dollars, which neutralises the exposure arising from the bond issue. On termination of the swap (which must coincide with the maturity of the bond), the original currency amounts are exchanged back, enabling the issuer to redeem the holders of the bond in Australian dollars.

For detailed coverage of interest-rate swaps and their application, see Choudhry (2014), which includes a discussion on post-crash swap pricing principles.

Description

Swaps are derivative contracts involving combinations of two or more interest-rate bases or other building blocks. Most swaps currently traded in the market involve combinations of cash market securities – for example, a fixed interest-rate security combined with a floating interest-rate security, possibly also combined with a currency transaction. However, the market has also seen swaps that involve a futures or forward component, as well as swaps that involve an option component. The market for swaps is organised by the International Swaps and Derivatives Association (ISDA).

Example 6.8   Comparative advantage and interest-rate swap structure

---

When entering into a swap either for hedging purposes or to alter the basis of an interest-rate liability, the opposite of a current cash flow profile is required. Consider a homeowner with a variable rate mortgage. The home-owner is at risk from an upward move in interest rates, which will result in her being charged higher interest payments. She wishes to protect her-self against such a move and in theory (don't try this with your building society!), as she is *paying floating*, she must *receive floating* in a swap. Therefore, she will pay fixed in the swap. The floating interest payments cancel each other out, and the homeowner now has a fixed-rate liability. The same applies in a hedging transaction: a bondholder *receiving fixed* coupons from the bond issuer – that is, the bondholder is a *lender* of funds – can hedge against a rise in interest rates that lowers the price of the bond by *paying fixed* in a swap with the same basis point value as the bond position; the bondholder receives floating interest. *Paying fixed* in a swap is concep-tually the same as being a *borrower of funds*; this borrowing is the opposite of a loan of funds to the bond issuer and therefore the position is hedged. Consider two companies' borrowing costs for a 5-year loan of £50 million:

- *Company A* can pay fixed at 8.75% or floating at Libor. Its desired basis is floating;
- *Company B* can pay fixed at 10% or floating at Libor + 100 basis points. Its desired basis is fixed.

Without a swap:

Company A borrows fixed and pays 8.75%.
Company B borrows floating and pays Libor + 100 basis points.

Let us say that the two companies decide to enter into a swap, whereby Company A borrows floating-rate interest and therefore receives fixed from Company B at the 5-year swap rate of 8.90%. Company B, which has borrowed at Libor + 100 basis points, pays fixed and receives Libor in the swap. Company A ends up paying floating-rate interest and Company B ends up paying fixed.

The result after the swap:

$$A \text{ pays } 8.75\% + Libor - 8.90\% = Libor - 15bp$$
$$B \text{ pays } Libor + 100bp + 8.90\% - Libor = 9.90\%$$

Company A saves 15 basis points (pays L–15bp rather than L flat) and B saves 10 basis points (pays 9.90% rather than 10%).

Both parties benefit from the *comparative advantage* of A in the fixed-rate market and B in the floating-rate market (spread of B over A is 125bp in the fixed-rate market but 100bp in the floating-rate market). Originally, swap banks were simply brokers, and charged a fee to both counterparties for bringing them together. In the example, Company A deals directly with Company B, although it is more likely that an intermediary bank would have been involved. As the market developed, banks became principals and dealt directly with counterparties, eliminating the need to find someone who had requirements that could be met by the other side of an existing requirement.

An interest-rate swap is an agreement between two counterparties to make periodic interest payments to one another during the life of the swap, on a predetermined set of dates, based on a notional principal amount. One party is the fixed-rate payer, and this rate is agreed at the time of trade of the swap; the other party is the floating-rate payer, the floating-rate being determined during the life of the swap by reference to a specific market index. The principal or notional amount is never physically exchanged, hence the term "off-balance-sheet", but is used to calculate interest payments. The fixed-rate payer receives floating-rate interest and is said to be "long" or to have "bought" the swap. The long side has conceptually purchased a floating-rate note (because it receives floating-rate interest) and issued a fixed coupon bond (because it pays out fixed interest at intervals) – that is, it has in principle borrowed funds. The floating-rate payer is said to be "short" or to have "sold" the swap. The short side has conceptually purchased a coupon bond (because it receives fixed-rate interest) and issued a floating-rate note (because it pays floating-rate interest).

So, an interest rate swap is:

an agreement between two parties to exchange a stream of cash flows calculated as a percentage of a notional sum and on different interest bases.

For example, in a trade between Bank A and Bank B, Bank A may agree to pay fixed semi-annual coupons of 10% on a notional principal sum of £1 million, in return for receiving from Bank B the prevailing 6-month sterling Libor rate on the same amount. The known cash flow is the fixed payment of £50,000 every 6 months by Bank A to Bank B.

Like other financial instruments, interest-rate swaps trade in a secondary market. The value of a swap moves in line with market interest rates, in exactly the same fashion as bonds. If a 5-year interest-rate swap is transacted today at a rate of 5% and 5-year interest rates fall to 4.75% shortly thereafter, the swap will have decreased in value to the fixed-rate payer, and correspondingly increased in value to the floating-rate payer, who has now seen the level of interest payments fall. The opposite would be true if 5-year rates moved to 5.25%. Why is this? Consider the fixed-rate payer in an interest-rate swap to be a borrower of funds. If she fixes the interest rate payable on a loan for 5 years and then this interest rate decreases shortly afterwards, is she better off? No, because she is now paying above the market rate for the funds borrowed. For this reason, a swap contract decreases in value to the fixed-rate payer if there is a fall in rates. Equally, a floating-rate payer gains if there is a fall in rates, as he can take advantage of the new rates and pay a lower level of interest; hence, the value of a swap increases to the floating-rate payer if there is a fall in rates.

The P&L profile of a swap position is shown in Table 6.3.

Example of vanilla interest-rate swap

Table 6.4 shows a "pay fixed, receive floating" interest-rate swap with the following terms.

Table 6.3   Impact of interest-rate changes

	Fall in rates	Rise in rates
Fixed-rate payer	Loss	Profit
Floating-rate payer	Profit	Loss

Table 6.4   Vanilla swap example terms

Trade date	3 December 2010
Effective date	7 December 2010
Maturity date	7 December 2015
Interpolation method	Linear
Day-count (fixed)	Semi-annual, actual/365
Day-count (floating)	Semi-annual, actual/365
Nominal amount	£10 million
Term	5 years
Fixed-rate	4.73%

The interest payment dates of the swap fall on 7 June and 7 December; the coupon dates of benchmark gilts also fall on these dates, so even though the swap has been traded for conventional dates, it is safe to surmise that it was put on as a hedge against a long gilt position. Fixed-rate payments are not always the same, because the actual/365 basis will calculate slightly different amounts.

The swap we have described is a plain vanilla swap, which means it has one fixed-rate and one floating-rate leg. The floating interest rate is set just before the relevant interest period and is paid at the end of the period. Note that both legs have identical interest dates and day-count bases, and the term to maturity of the swap is exactly 5 years. It is of course possible to ask for a swap quote where any of these terms have been set to customer requirements; for example, both legs may be floating-rate, or the notional principal may vary during the life of the swap. Non-vanilla interest-rate swaps are very common, and banks will readily price swaps where the terms have been set to meet specific require-ments. The most common variations are different interest payment dates for the fixed-rate leg and floating-rate leg, on different day-count bases, as well as terms to maturity that are not whole years.

Swap spreads and the swap yield curve

In the market, banks will quote two-way swap rates – on screens, on the tele-phone, or via a dealing system such as Reuters. Brokers will also be active in relaying prices in the market. The convention in the market is for the swap market-maker to set the floating leg at Libor and then quote the fixed-rate that is payable for that maturity. So, for a 5-year swap a bank's swap desk might be willing to quote the following:

Floating-rate payer: Pay 6-month Libor receive fixed-rate of 5.19%

Fixed-rate payer: Pay fixed-rate of 5.25% receive 6-month Libor

In this case, the bank is quoting an offer rate of 5.25%, which the fixed-rate payer will pay in return for receiving Libor flat. The bid price quote is 5.19%, which is what a floating-rate payer will receive fixed. The bid–offer spread in this case is therefore 6 basis points. Fixed-rate quotes are always at a spread above the government bond yield curve. Let us assume that the 5-year gilt yields 4.88%; in this case, then, the 5-year swap bid rate is 31 basis points above this yield. So, the bank's swap trader could quote swap rates as a spread above the benchmark bond yield curve, say 37–31, which is her swap spread quote. This means that the bank is happy to enter into a swap paying fixed 31 basis points above the benchmark yield and receiving Libor, and receiv-ing fixed 37 basis points above the yield curve and paying Libor. The bank's screen on, say, Bloomberg or Reuters might look something like Table 6.5, which quotes swap rates as well as the current spread over the government bond benchmark.

Table 6.5   Swap quotes

1 year	4.50	4.45	+17
2 year	4.69	4.62	+25
3 year	4.88	4.80	+23
4 year	5.15	5.05	+29
5 year	5.25	5.19	+31
10 year	5.50	5.40	+35

A swap spread is a function of the same factors that influence the spread over government bonds for other instruments. For shorter duration swaps – say, up to 3 years – there are other yield curves that can be used in comparison, such as the cash market curve or a curve derived from futures prices. For longer dated swaps, the spread is determined mainly by the credit spreads that prevail in the corporate bond market. Because a swap is viewed as a package of long and short positions in fixed-rate and floating-rate bonds, it is the credit spreads in these two markets that will determine the swap spread. This is logical; essentially, it is the premium for greater credit risk involved in lending to corporates that dictates that a swap rate will be higher than same maturity government bond yield. Technical factors will be responsible for day-to-day fluctuations in swap rates, such as the supply of corporate bonds and the level of demand for swaps, plus the cost to swap traders of hedging their swap positions.

Overnight interest-rate swaps

An interest-rate swap contract, which is generally regarded as a capital market instrument, is an agreement between two counterparties to exchange a fixed interest-rate payment in return for a floating interest-rate payment, calculated on a notional swap amount, at regular intervals during the life of the swap. A swap may be viewed as being equivalent to a series of successive FRA contracts, with each FRA starting as the previous one matures. The basis of the floating interest rate is agreed as part of the contract terms at the inception of the trade. Conventional swaps index the floating interest rate to Libor; however, an exciting recent development in the sterling money market has been the sterling overnight interest-rate average or SONIA. In this section, we review SONIA swaps, which are extensively used by sterling market banks.

SONIA is the average interest rate of inter-bank (unsecured) overnight sterling deposit trades undertaken before 15:30 hours each day between members of the London Wholesale Money Brokers' Association. Recorded interest rates are weighted by volume. A SONIA swap is a swap contract that exchanges a fixed interest rate (the swap rate) against the geometric average of overnight interest rates that have been recorded during the life of the contract. Exchange of interest takes place on maturity of the swap. SONIA swaps are used to speculate on or to hedge against interest rates at the very short end of the sterling yield curve; in other words, they can be used to hedge an exposure to overnight interest rates.[6] The swaps themselves are traded in maturities of 1 week to 1 year, although 2-year SONIA swaps have also been traded.

Conventional swap rates are calculated off the government bond yield curve and represent the credit premium over government yields of inter-bank default risk. In essence, they represent average forward rates derived from the government spot (zero-coupon) yield curve. The fixed-rate quoted on a SONIA swap represents the average level of overnight interest rates expected by market participants over the life of the swap. In practice, the rate is calculated as a function of the Bank of England's repo rate. This is the 2-week rate at which the Bank conducts reverse repo trades with banking counterparties as part of its open market operations. In other words, this is the Bank's base rate. In theory, we would expect the SONIA rate to follow the repo rate fairly closely, since the credit risk on an overnight deposit is low. However, in practice, the spread between the SONIA rate and the Bank repo rate is very volatile, and for this reason the swaps are used to hedge overnight exposures.

Example 6.9   Using an OIS swap to hedge a funding requirement

A structured hedge fund derivatives desk at an investment bank offers a leveraged investment product to a client in the form of a participating interest share in a fund of hedge funds. The client's investment is made up partly of funds lent to it by the investment bank, for which the interest rate charged is overnight Libor (plus a spread).

This investment product has an expected life of at least 2 years. As part of its routine asset–liability management operations, the bank's Treasury desk has been funding this requirement by borrowing overnight each day. It now wishes to match the funding requirement raised by this product by matching the asset term structure to the liability term structure. Let us assume that this product creates a USD1 billion funding requirement for the bank.

Current market depo rates are shown in Figure 6.8. The Treasury desk therefore funds this requirement in the following way:

Assets	$1 billion, >1-year term
Receiving overnight Libor (plus spread)	
Liabilities	$350 million, 6-month loan
Pay 1.22%	
$350 million, 12-month loan	
Pay 1.50%	
$300 million, 15-month loan	
Pay 1.70% (not shown in Figure 6.8)	

---

[6]Traditionally, overnight rates fluctuate widely during the day, depending on the day's funds shortage, and although volatility has reduced since the introduction of gilt repo it is still unpredictable on occasion.

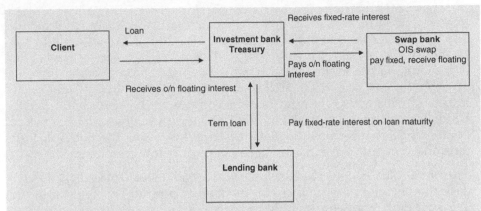

Figure 6.8 Illustration of interest basis mismatch hedging using the OIS instrument

```
GRAB                                                        M-Mkt  TTDE
11:37 TULLETT & TOKYO                               PAGE  1 / 1
      USD Cash  Non-Japanese                USD Cash   Japanese
      Deposits   Bid      Ask      Time     Deposits   Bid      Ask      Time
 1)  Spot      1.0000   1.0200   9:33  18)  T/N       1.0000   1.0300  11/07
 2)  T/N       1.0100   1.0300  11/07  19)  1 Week    1.0400   1.0600   9:33
 3)  1 Week    1.0300   1.0500   9:33  20)  2 Week    1.0500   1.0700   9:33
 4)  2 Week    1.0300   1.0500   9:33  21)  3 Week    1.0600   1.0800   9:33
 5)  3 Week    1.0300   1.0500   9:33  22)  1 Month   1.0800   1.1000   9:33
 6)  1 Month   1.0400   1.0500   9:33  23)  2 Month   1.1800   1.2100   9:33
 7)  2 Month   1.1200   1.1400   9:33  24)  3 Month   1.1900   1.2200   9:33
 8)  3 Month   1.1300   1.1500   9:33  25)  4 Month   1.2000   1.2300   9:33
 9)  4 Month   1.1400   1.1700   9:33  26)  5 Month   1.2100   1.2400   9:33
10)  5 Month   1.1600   1.1900   9:33  27)  6 Month   1.2300   1.2600   9:33
11)  6 Month   1.2000   1.2200   9:33  28)  7 Month   1.2700   1.3000   9:33
12)  7 Month   1.2300   1.2500   9:33  29)  8 Month   1.3100   1.3400   9:33
13)  8 Month   1.2700   1.2900   9:33  30)  9 Month   1.3800   1.4100   9:33
14)  9 Month   1.3300   1.3600   9:33  31)  10 Month  1.4600   1.4900   9:33
15)  10 Month  1.3800   1.4100   9:33  32)  11 Month  1.5300   1.5600   9:33
16)  11 Month  1.4500   1.4800   9:33  33)  12 Month  1.5500   1.5800   9:33
17)  12 Month  1.5000   1.5300   9:33

Australia 61 2 9777 8600      Brazil 5511 3048 4500       Europe 44 20 7330 7500      Germany 49 69 920410
Hong Kong 852 2977 6000 Japan 81 3 3201 8900 Singapore 65 6212 1000 U.S. 1 212 318 2000 Copyright 2003 Bloomberg L.P.
                                                                           G657-802-0 10-Nov-03 11:37:50
```

Figure 6.9 Tullet US dollar depo rates, 10 November 2003

This matches the asset structure more closely to the term structure of assets; however, it opens up an interest-rate basis mismatch in that the bank is now receiving an overnight Libor-based income but paying a term-based liability. To remove this basis mismatch, the Treasury desk transacts an OIS swap to match the amount and term of each of the loan deals, paying overnight floating-rate interest and receiving fixed-rate interest. The rates for OIS swaps of varying terms are shown in Figure 6.9, which shows two-way prices for OIS swaps up to 2 years in maturity. So, for the 6-month OIS, the hedger is receiving fixed interest at a rate of 1.085% and for the 12-month OIS he is receiving 1.40%. The difference between what he is receiving in the swap and what he is paying in term loans is the cost of removing the basis mismatch, but more fundamentally reflects a key feature of OIS swaps vs deposit rates: depo rates are Libor-related, whereas US dollar OIS rates are driven by the Fed Funds rate. On average, the Fed Funds rate lies approximately 8–10 basis points below the dollar deposit rate, and sometimes as much as 15 basis points below cash levels.

This action hedges out the basis mismatch and also enables the Treasury desk to match its asset profile with its liability profile. The net cost to the Treasury desk represents its hedging costs.

Figure 6.10 illustrates the OIS swap rates.

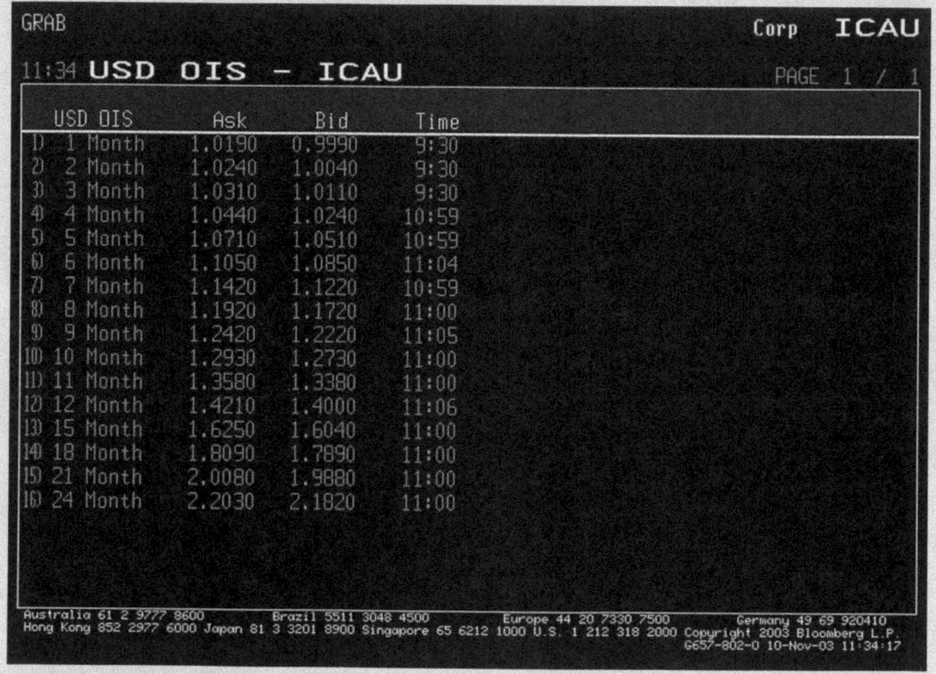

Figure 6.10   Garban ICAP OIS rates for USD, 10 November 2003

Example 6.10   Cash flows on OIS

Table 6.6 shows daily rate fixes on a 6-month OIS that was traded for an effective date of 17 October 2003, at a fixed-rate of 1.03%. The swap notional is USD200 million.

From Table 6.6 we see that the average rate for Fed Funds during this period was 0.99952%. Hence, on settlement the fixed-rate payer would have passed over a net settlement amount of USD30,480.

Table 6.6   OIS cash flows

Fix date	Maturity	Rate fix
17/10/2003	20/10/2003	0.98
20/10/2003	21/10/2003	1.02
21/10/2003	22/10/2003	1.02
22/10/2003	23/10/2003	0.99
23/10/2003	24/10/2003	0.99
24/10/2003	27/10/2003	1.02
27/10/2003	28/10/2003	1.01
28/10/2003	29/10/2003	0.98
29/10/2003	30/10/2003	0.98
30/10/2003	31/10/2003	0.97
31/10/2003	03/11/2003	1.02
03/11/2003	04/11/2003	1.02
04/11/2003	05/11/2003	1.02
05/11/2003	06/11/2003	0.98
06/11/2003	07/11/2003	0.98
07/11/2003	10/11/2003	0.98
10/11/2003	12/11/2003	0.98
12/11/2003	13/11/2003	0.99
13/11/2003	14/11/2003	1
14/11/2003	17/11/2003	0.99
17/11/2003	18/11/2003	1.04
18/11/2003	19/11/2003	1.04
19/11/2003	20/11/2003	0.98
20/11/2003	21/11/2003	1
21/11/2003	24/11/2003	1
24/11/2003	25/11/2003	0.98
25/11/2003	26/11/2003	0.98
26/11/2003	28/11/2003	1.02
28/11/2003	01/12/2003	1.01
01/12/2003	02/12/2003	1.03
02/12/2003	03/12/2003	0.97
03/12/2003	04/12/2003	0.97
04/12/2003	05/12/2003	0.98
05/12/2003	08/12/2003	0.98
08/12/2003	09/12/2003	0.98
09/12/2003	10/12/2003	0.99
10/12/2003	11/12/2003	0.97
11/12/2003	12/12/2003	0.99
12/12/2003	15/12/2003	0.99
15/12/2003	16/12/2003	0.99

Table 6.6   (Continued)

Fix date	Maturity	Rate fix
16/12/2003	17/12/2003	1.04
17/12/2003	18/12/2003	0.99
18/12/2003	19/12/2003	0.99
19/12/2003	22/12/2003	0.98
22/12/2003	23/12/2003	0.98
23/12/2003	24/12/2003	1.02
24/12/2003	26/12/2003	1
26/12/2003	29/12/2003	0.97
29/12/2003	30/12/2003	0.97
30/12/2003	31/12/2003	0.98
31/12/2003	02/01/2004	0.93
02/01/2004	05/01/2004	0.94
05/01/2004	06/01/2004	1.01
06/01/2004	07/01/2004	0.97
07/01/2004	08/01/2004	0.94
08/01/2004	09/01/2004	0.94
09/01/2004	12/01/2004	0.99
12/01/2004	13/01/2004	0.99
13/01/2004	14/01/2004	1
14/01/2004	15/01/2004	0.99
15/01/2004	16/01/2004	1.04
16/01/2004	20/01/2004	0.98
20/01/2004	21/01/2004	1.02
21/01/2004	22/01/2004	1
22/01/2004	23/01/2004	1.02
23/01/2004	26/01/2004	1
26/01/2004	27/01/2004	1
27/01/2004	28/01/2004	1.08
28/01/2004	29/01/2004	1.02
29/01/2004	30/01/2004	0.99
30/01/2004	02/02/2004	1.03
02/02/2004	03/02/2004	1.01
03/02/2004	04/02/2004	1.01
04/02/2004	05/02/2004	0.97
05/02/2004	06/02/2004	1
06/02/2004	09/02/2004	1.01
09/02/2004	10/02/2004	0.99
10/02/2004	11/02/2004	1
11/02/2004	12/02/2004	1
12/02/2004	13/02/2004	1.02
13/02/2004	17/02/2004	1.02
17/02/2004	18/02/2004	1.02
18/02/2004	19/02/2004	1
19/02/2004	20/02/2004	1

Table 6.6   (*Continued*)

Fix date	Maturity	Rate fix
20/02/2004	23/02/2004	0.99
23/02/2004	24/02/2004	0.99
24/02/2004	25/02/2004	1
25/02/2004	26/02/2004	0.99
26/02/2004	27/02/2004	1.02
27/02/2004	01/03/2004	1.04
01/03/2004	02/03/2004	1.04
02/03/2004	03/03/2004	1.04
03/03/2004	04/03/2004	1
04/03/2004	05/03/2004	0.99
05/03/2004	08/03/2004	0.99
08/03/2004	09/03/2004	1
09/03/2004	10/03/2004	0.99
10/03/2004	11/03/2004	0.99
11/03/2004	12/03/2004	1
12/03/2004	15/03/2004	0.99
15/03/2004	16/03/2004	1.05
16/03/2004	17/03/2004	1.05
17/03/2004	18/03/2004	1
18/03/2004	19/03/2004	1
19/03/2004	22/03/2004	0.99
22/03/2004	23/03/2004	1.01
23/03/2004	24/03/2004	1.01
24/03/2004	25/03/2004	0.99
25/03/2004	26/03/2004	0.99
26/03/2004	29/03/2004	1.02
29/03/2004	30/03/2004	1
30/03/2004	31/03/2004	1
31/03/2004	01/04/2004	0.98
01/04/2004	02/04/2004	1.05
02/04/2004	05/04/2004	1.03
05/04/2004	06/04/2004	1.01
06/04/2004	07/04/2004	1.01
07/04/2004	08/04/2004	1
08/04/2004	09/04/2004	1
09/04/2004	12/04/2004	1.02
12/04/2004	13/04/2004	1.01
13/04/2004	14/04/2004	1
14/04/2004	15/04/2004	1
15/04/2004	16/04/2004	1.01
16/04/2004	19/04/2004	0.99
	Average rate 0.99952	

BIBLIOGRAPHY

Choudhry, M. (2014). *Fixed Income Markets*, 2nd Edition, John Wiley Asia Ltd.

Cox, J., Ingersoll, J., and Ross, S. (1981). "The relationship between forward prices and futures prices", *Journal of Financial Economics*, **9**, December, pp. 321–346.

French, K. (1983). "A comparison of futures and forwards prices", *Journal of Financial Economics*, **12**, November, pp. 311–342.

Hull, J. (2017). *Options, Futures and Other Derivatives*, 10th Edition, Prentice-Hall.

Jarrow, R. and Oldfield, G. (1981). "Forward contracts and futures contracts", *Journal of Financial Economics*, **9**, December, pp. 373–382.

Kimber, A. (2004). *Credit Risk*, Oxford: Elsevier.

Merton, R.C. (1974). "On the pricing of corporate debt: The risk structure of interest rates", *Journal of Finance*, **29**(2), May, pp. 449–470.

Rubinstein, M. (1999). *Rubinstein on Derivatives*, RISK Publishing, Chapter 2.

Windas, T. (1993). *An Introduction to Option-Adjusted Spread Analysis*, Bloomberg Publishing, Chapter 3.

Unfortunately Vic came off rather badly [in the squadron], as he suffered from two career-limiting character faults: firstly he was outspokenly honest and always said what he really thought, and secondly he was invariably right.

—Michael Napier, *Tornado Over the Tigris: Recollections of a Fast Jet Pilot*, Pen & Sword Books, 2015.

PART II

Asset–Liability Management and Liquidity Risk

Part II gets into the nitty-gritty of balance sheet risk management, with a detailed look at asset–liability management (ALM), liquidity risk management, and interest-rate risk in the banking book (IRRBB). The remaining tenet of ALM, regulatory capital management, we save for Part III.

As part of the review of liquidity risk, we consider best-practice processes in the following areas:

- Managing the liquid asset buffer;
- Optimum liabilities mix strategy;
- Individual liquidity adequacy assessment process (ILAAP);
- Funds transfer pricing;
- Analysing net interest margin (NIM); and
- Securitisation for balance sheet management.

There is also a chapter on asset–liability committee (ALCO) governance framework best practice, which is important for all banks, be they large or small.

Chapter
7

BANK ASSET AND LIABILITY MANAGEMENT I

A sset–liability management (ALM) is a generic term that can mean different things in subtly distinct ways, depending on what type of financial market participant one is. For bankers, the term is used to denote high-level management of a bank's balance sheet assets and liabilities; in other words, it refers to the process of managing the balance sheet. As such it is a strategy level discipline but at the business line level, it is also a tactical one.

The art of asset and liability management is essentially one of balance sheet risk management and capital management, and although the day-to-day activities are run at the desk level, overall direction should be given at the highest level of a banking institution. The risk exposures in a banking environment are multidimensional, and as we have seen they encompass interest-rate risk, liquidity risk, credit risk, and operational risk.

Traditionally, asset and liability management covered the set of techniques used to manage interest-rate and liquidity risks; it also dealt with the structure of the bank's balance sheet, which is heavily influenced by funding and regulatory constraints and profitability targets. Interest-rate risk is one type of market risk. Risks associated with moves in interest rates and levels of liquidity are those that result in adverse fluctuations in earnings levels due to changes in market rates and bank funding costs. By definition, banks' earnings levels are highly sensitive to moves in interest rates and the cost of funds in the wholesale market.

One of the major areas of decision-making in a bank involves the maturity of assets and liabilities. Typically, longer term interest rates are higher than shorter-term rates; that is, it is common for the yield curve in the short term (say, 0–3 year range) to be positively sloping. To take advantage of this, banks usually raise a large proportion of their funds from the short-dated end of the yield curve and lend out these funds for longer maturities at higher rates. The spread between the borrowing and lending rates is the bank's profit. The obvious risk from such a strategy is that the level of short-term rates rises during the term of the loan, so that when the loan is refinanced the bank makes a lower profit or a net loss. A more critical risk is that funding no longer becomes available when a deposit is rolled over. Managing this risk exposure is the key function of an ALM desk.

Another risk factor is liquidity. From a banking and Treasury point of view, the term liquidity means funding liquidity, or the "nearness" of money. The most liquid asset is cash money. Banks bear several interrelated liquidity risks, including the risk of being unable to pay depositors on demand, an inability to raise funds in the market at reasonable rates, and an insufficient level of funds available with which to make loans. Banks keep only a small portion of their assets in the form of cash, because this earns only a very low return for them, but must make other arrangements to ensure continuous liquidity at all times.

Despite its name, throughout history since the term was first described in the early 1970s, the principal function of the ALM desk has been to manage interest-rate risk and liquidity risk. This is hardly managing everything to do with the bank's "assets and liabilities". In some banks the ALM discipline will also encompass the setting of overall policy for credit risk and credit risk management, with tactical level credit policy being set at a lower level within credit committees. But this is rare – in most banks the ALM function (and indeed the asset and liability committee (ALCO)) gets nowhere near credit risk policy and credit risk management. The author considers this not to be best practice, and later on we will provide the rationale why a bank's ALCO oversight remit should extend to credit risk as well, thus living up to the committee's name.

In this chapter we introduce the basic tenets of traditional bank ALM and the key ALM concepts of liquidity, interest-rate risk, and ALM policy. A subsequent chapter describes modern-day best practice principles and organisation of the Asset and Liability Committee (ALCO), the paramount balance sheet risk management committee in a bank.

BASIC CONCEPTS

In the era of stable interest rates that preceded the breakdown of the Bretton–Woods agreement, ALM was a more straightforward process, constrained by regulatory restrictions and the saving and borrowing pattern of bank customers. The introduction of the negotiable Certificate of Deposit (CD) by Citibank in the 1960s enabled banks to diversify both their investment and funding sources. With this there developed the concept of the interest margin, which is the spread between the interest earned on assets and that paid on liabilities. This led to the concept of the interest gap and the management of the gap, which is the cornerstone of modern-day ALM. The increasing volatility of interest rates, and the rise in absolute levels of rates themselves, made gap management a vital part of running the banking book. This development meant that banks could no longer rely permanently on the traditional approach of borrowing short (funding short) to lend long, as a rise in the level of short-term rates would result in funding losses. The introduction of derivative instruments such as FRAs and swaps in the early 1980s removed the previous uncertainty and allowed banks to continue the traditional approach while hedging against medium-term uncertainty.

In financial markets, two important strands of risk management are interest-rate risk and liquidity risk. ALM practice is concerned with managing this risk. Interest-rate risk exists in two strands. The first strand is the more obvious one: the risk of changes in asset–liability value due to changes in interest rates. Such a change impacts the cash flows of assets and liabilities as well as their present value because financial instruments are valued with reference to market interest rates. The second strand is that associated with optionality, which arises with products such as early-redeemable loans. The other main type of risk that ALM seeks to manage is liquidity risk, which refers to both the liquidity of markets and an ability to maintain funding of assets and deposit withdrawals, but also to the ease with which assets can be translated into cash. The former is the primary concern of all banks large and small.

ALM is conducted primarily at an overview, balance sheet level. The risk that is managed is an aggregate, group level risk. This makes sense because one could not manage a viable banking business by leaving interest-rate and liquidity risk management at individual operating levels. We illustrate this in Figure 7.1, which illustrates the cornerstones of traditional ALM. Essentially, interest-rate risk exposure is managed at the group level by the Treasury desk. The drivers are the different currency interest rates, with each exposure being made up of the net present value (NPV) of cash flow as it changes with changes in interest rates. The discount rate used to calculate NPV is the prevailing market rate for each time bucket in the term structure.

Interest-rate exposure arises because rates fluctuate from day to day, and continuously over time. The primary risk is that of interest-rate reset for floating-rate assets and liabilities. The secondary risk is liquidity risk: unless assets and liabilities are matched by amount and term, assets must be funded on a continuous rolling basis. Equally, the receipt of funds must be placed on a continuous basis. Whether an asset carries a fixed- or floating-rate, reset will determine its exposure to interest-rate fluctuations. Where an asset is marked at a fixed-rate, a rise in rates will reduce its NPV and so reduce its value to the bank. This is intuitively easy to grasp, even without recourse to financial arithmetic, because we can see that the asset is now paying a below-market rate of interest. Or we can think of it as a loss due to opportunity cost foregone, since the assets

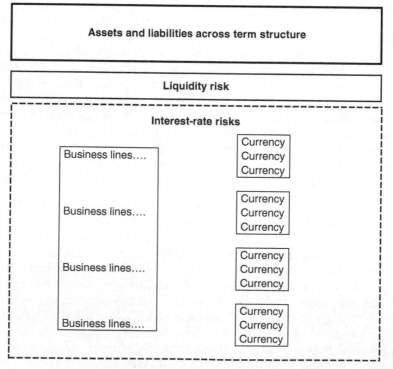

Figure 7.1   Cornerstone of traditional ALM philosophy

are earning below what they could earn if they were employed elsewhere in the market. The opposite applies if there is a fall in rates: this causes the NPV of the asset to rise. For assets marked at a floating-rate of interest, the exposure to fluctuating rates is much less, because the rate receivable on the asset will reset at periodic intervals, which will allow for changes in market rates.

We speak of risk exposure as being for the group as a whole. This exposure must therefore aggregate the net risk of all the bank's operating business. Even for the simplest banking operation, we can see that this will produce a net mismatch between assets and liabilities, because different business lines will have differing objectives for their individual books. This mismatch will manifest itself in two ways:

- The mismatch between the different terms of assets and liabilities across the term structure;
- The mismatch between the different interest rates that each asset or liability contract has been struck at.

This mismatch is known as the ALM *gap*. The first type is referred to as the *liquidity gap*, while the second is known as the *interest-rate gap*. We value assets and liabilities at their NPV; hence, we can measure the overall sensitivity of balance sheet NPV to changes in interest rates. As such, then, ALM is an art that encompasses aggregate balance sheet risk management at the group level.

Figure 7.2 shows the aggregate group level ALM profile for a derivatives trading house based in London. There is a slight term mismatch as no assets are deemed to have "overnight" maturity, whereas a significant portion of funding (liabilities) is in the overnight term. One thing we do not know from looking at Figure 7.2 is how this particular institution defines the maturity of its assets. To place them in the relevant maturity buckets, one can adopt one of two approaches, namely:

- Actual duration of the assets;
- "Behavioural" tenor or expected life of the assets;

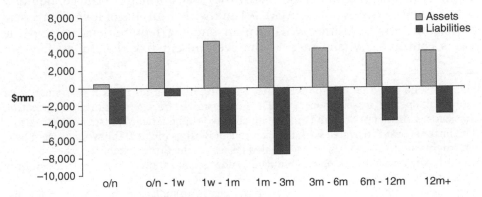

Figure 7.2   A derivatives trading house's ALM profile

- "Liquidity duration", which is the estimated time it would take the firm to dispose of its assets in an enforced or "firesale" situation, such as a withdrawal from business.

Each approach has its adherents. It is up to the individual institution to adopt one method and then adhere consistently to it. The third approach has the disadvantage, however, of being inherently subjective – estimating the time taken to dispose of an asset book is not an exact science and is little more than educated guesswork. Nevertheless, for long-dated and/or illiquid assets, it is at least a workable method that enables practitioners to work around a specified ALM framework with regard to structuring the liability profile.

LIQUIDITY GAP

There is clearly risk exposure as a result of liquidity mismatches between assets and liabilities. Maturity terms will not match, thereby creating a liquidity gap. The amount of assets and liabilities maturing at any one time will also not match (although overall, by definition, assets must equal liabilities). Liquidity risk is the risk that a bank will not be able to refinance assets as liabilities become due for any reason.[1] To manage this, the bank will hold a portion of its assets in very liquid form.[2] A surplus of assets over liabilities creates a funding requirement. If there is a surplus of liabilities, the bank will need to find efficient uses for these funds. In either case, the bank has a liquidity gap. This liquidity can be projected over time so that one knows what the situation is each morning, based on net expiring assets and liabilities. The projection will change daily, of course, due to the new business undertaken each day.

We could eliminate liquidity gap risk by matching assets and liabilities across each time bucket. Actually, at the individual loan level this is a popular strategy: if we can invest in an asset paying 5.50% for 3 months and fund this with a 3-month loan costing 5.00%, we have locked in a 50bp gain that is interest-rate risk free. However, this is not what banks actually do, as they are in the business of undertaking maturity transformation. Hence, liquidity risk is a key consideration in ALM. A bank with a surplus of long-term assets over short-term liabilities will have an ongoing requirement to fund the assets continuously, and there is the ever-present risk that funds may not

---

[1] The reasons could be macro-level ones, affecting most or all market participants, or more firm specific or sector specific. The former might be a general market correction that causes the supply of funds to dry up, and would be a near-catastrophic situation. The latter is best illustrated with the example of Barings plc in 1995: when it went bust overnight due to large, hitherto concealed losses on the Simex exchange, the supply of credit to similar institutions was reduced or charged at much higher rates – albeit only temporarily – as a result.

[2] Such assets should be very short-term, risk-free assets such as cash at the central bank, Treasury bills, and such like.

be available as and when they are required. The concept of a future funding requirement is itself a driver of interest-rate risk, because the bank will not know the future interest rates at which it will deal.[3] So a key part of ALM involves managing and hedging this forward liquidity risk.

The liquidity gap is the difference, at all future dates, between assets and liabilities of the banking portfolio. Gaps generate liquidity risk. When liabilities exceed assets, there is an excess of funds. An excess does not of course generate liquidity risk, but it does generate interest-rate risk, because the present value of the book is sensitive to changes in market rates. When assets exceed liabilities, there is a funding deficit and the bank has long-term commitments that are not currently funded by existing operations. The liquidity risk is that the bank requires funds at a future date to match the assets. The bank is able to remove any liquidity risk by locking in maturities, but of course there is a cost involved as it will be dealing at longer maturities.[4]

Definition and illustration

To reiterate then, the liquidity gap is the difference in maturity between assets and liabilities at each point along the term structure. Because ALM in many banks concerns itself with medium-term management of risk, this may be a 5-year horizon. Note from Figure 7.2 how the longest dated time bucket in the ALM profile extended out to only "12 months+", hence all liabilities longer than 1 year were grouped in one time bucket. This recognises the fact that most liabilities are shorter than 1 year, although a proportion of funding will be longer term – an average of 5 years or so.

For each point along the term structure at which a gap exists, there is (liquidity) gap risk exposure. This is the risk that funds cannot be raised as required, or that the rate payable on these funds is prohibitive.[5] To manage this risk, a bank must:

- Disperse the funding profile (the liability profile) over more than just a short period of time. For example, it would be excessively risky to concentrate funding in just the overnight to 1-week time bucket, so a bank will spread the profile across a number of time buckets. Figure 7.3 shows the liability profile for a European multi-currency asset-backed commercial paper programme, with liabilities extending from 1 month to 1 year;
- Manage expectations such that large-size funding requirements are diarised well in advance – not planned for times of low liquidity such as the Christmas and New Year period;

---

[3] It can of course lock in future funding rates with forward-starting loans, which is one way to manage liquidity risk.

[4] This assumes a conventional upward-sloping yield curve.

[5] Of course, the opposite applies when the gap risk refers to an excess of liabilities over assets.

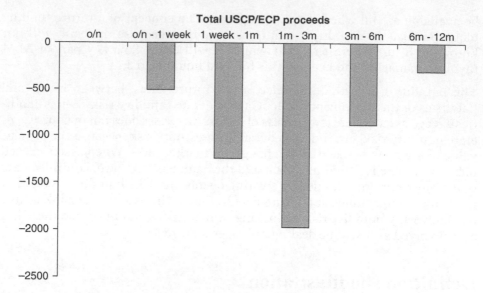

Figure 7.3 Commercial paper programme liability profile

- Hold a significant proportion of assets in the form of very liquid instruments such as very-short-term cash loans, Treasury bills, and high-quality short-term bank certificates of deposit (CDs).

Following these guidelines leads to a reserve of liquidity that can be turned into cash at very short notice in the event of a funding crisis.

The size of the liquidity gap at any one instant is never more than a snapshot in time, because it is constantly changing as new commitments are entered into on both the asset and liability size. For this reason, some writers speak of a "static" gap and a "dynamic" gap, but in practice one recognises that there is only ever a dynamic gap, because the position changes daily. Hence, we will refer only to a liquidity gap.

A further definition is the "marginal" gap, which is the difference between the change in assets and liabilities during a specified time period. This is also known as the "incremental" gap. If the change in assets is greater than the change in liabilities, this is a positive marginal gap, while if the opposite applies it is a negative marginal gap.[6]

We illustrate these values in Table 7.1 and graphically at Figure 7.4. This is a simplified asset–liability profile from a regional European bank, showing gap and marginal gap at each time period. Note that liabilities have been structured to produce an "ALM smile", which is recognised as following prudent business practice. Generally, no more than 20% of total funding should be in the overnight to 1-week time bucket – similarly for the 9-to-12-month bucket.

---

[6]Note that this terminology is not universally held.

Table 7.1   Simplified ALM profile for a regional European bank

	1 week	1 month	3 month	6 month	9–12 month	>12 months	Total
Assets	10	90	460	710	520	100	1,890
Liabilities	100	380	690	410	220	90	1,890
Gap	90	290	230	300	300	10	
Marginal	gap	200	60	530	0	290	

The marginal gap is measured as the difference between the change in assets and liabilities from one period to the next.

Liquidity risk

Liquidity risk exposure arises from normal banking operations. That is, it exists irrespective of the type of funding gap, be it excess assets over liabilities for any particular time bucket or an excess of liabilities over assets. In other words, there is a funding risk in any case: either funds must be obtained or surplus assets laid off. The liquidity risk in itself generates interest-rate risk as a result of uncertainty about future interest rates. This can be managed through interest-rate hedging, which is discussed in Chapter 12.

If assets are floating-rate, there is less concern over first-order interest-rate risk because of the nature of interest-rate reset. This also applies to floating-rate liabilities, but only insofar as they match floating-rate assets. Floating-rate liabilities issued to fund fixed-rate assets create forward risk exposure to rising interest rates. Note that even if both assets and liabilities are floating-rate, they can still generate interest-rate risk. For example, if assets pay 6-month Libor and liabilities pay 3-month Libor, there is an interest-rate spread risk

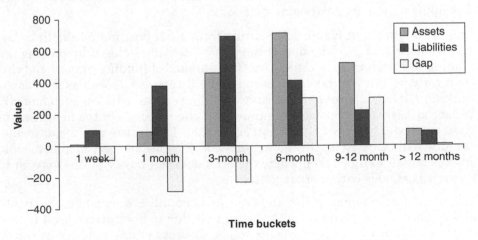

Figure 7.4   Shows the graphical profile of the numbers in Table 7.1

between the two terms. Such an arrangement has eliminated liquidity risk, but not interest-rate spread risk. This is termed second-order interest-rate risk or basis risk.

Liquidity risk can be managed by matching assets and liabilities, or by setting a series of rolling term loans to fund a long-dated asset. Generally, however, banks have a particular view of future market conditions and manage the ALM book in line with this view. This would leave in place a certain level of liquidity risk.

MANAGING LIQUIDITY

Managing liquidity gaps and the liquidity process is both continuous and dynamic because the ALM profile of a bank changes on a daily basis. Liquidity management is the term used to describe this continuous process of raising and laying off funds, depending on whether one is long or short cash that day.

The basic premise is a simple one: the bank must be "squared off" by the end of each day, which means ensuring the net cash position is zero. Thus, liquidity management is both very short term as well as projected over the long term, because every position put on today creates a funding requirement in the future on its maturity date. The ALM desk must be aware of its future funding or excess cash positions and act accordingly, whether this means raising funds now or hedging forward interest-rate risk.

The basic case: the funding gap

A funding requirement is dealt with on the day it occurs. The decision on how it will be treated will factor the term that is put on – it also has to allow for any new assets put on that day. As funding is arranged, the gap on that day will be zero. The next day there will be a new funding requirement or a surplus depending on the net position of the book.

This is illustrated in Figure 7.5. Starting from a flat position on the first day (t_0), we observe a gap (the dotted line) on t_1, which is closed by putting on funding to match the asset maturity. The amount of funding to raise and the term for it to run will take into account the future gap as well as that day's banking activities. So, at t_2 we observe a funding excess, which is then laid off. We see at t_3 that invested assets run beyond the maturity of the liabilities at t_2, so we have a funding requirement again at t_3. The decision on the term and amount will be based on the market view of the ALM desk. A matched book approach may well be taken where the desk does not have a strong view or if its view is at odds with market consensus.

There are also external factors to take into account. For instance, the availability of funds in the market may be limited, due to both macro-level issues and to the bank's own ability to raise funds. The former might be during times of market correction or recession (a "credit crunch"), while the latter might include the bank's credit lines with market counterparties. Moreover, some

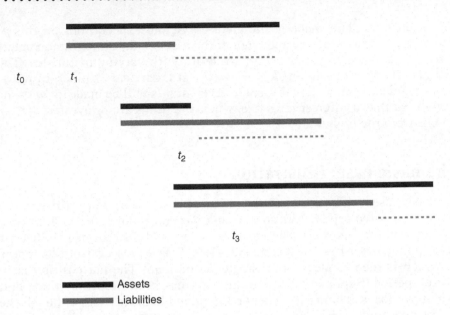

t_0 t_1

t_2

t_3

Assets
Liabilities

Figure 7.5 Funding position on a daily basis

funds will have been raised in the capital markets and this cash will cover part of the funding requirement. In addition, the ALM desk must consider the cost of the funds it is borrowing – for example, if it thought that interest rates in the short term, or for short-term periods, were going to fall, it might cover the gap with only short-term funds so that it can then refinance at expected lower rates. The opposite might be done if the desk thought rates would rise in the near future.

Running a liquidity gap over time, beyond customer requirements, would reflect a particular view of the ALM desk. So, maintaining a consistently underfunded position suggests that interest rates are expected to decline, and so longer term funds can be taken at cost. Maintaining an overfunded gap would imply that the bank thinks rates will be rising, and so longer term funds are locked in now at lower interest rates. Even if the net position is dictated by customer requirements – for example, customers placing more on deposit than they take out in loans – the bank can still manage the resultant gap in the wholesale market.

Generally, excess liabilities at a bank are a rare occurrence and, under most circumstances, such a position is clearly undesirable. This is because the bank will have to achieve target return on capital ratios, and this requires funds to be put to work, so to speak, by acquiring assets. In the case of equity capital it is imperative that these funds are properly employed.[7] The exact structure of the asset book will depend on the bank's view on interest rates and the yield

---

[7]The bank's capital will be invested in risk-free assets such as government T-bills or, in some cases, bank CDs. It will not be lent out in normal banking operations because the ALM desk will not want to put capital in a credit-risky investment.

curve generally. The shape of the yield curve and expectations on this will also influence the structure and tenor of the asset book. The common practice is to spread assets across the term structure with varying maturities. There will also be investments made with a forward start date to lock in rates in the forward curve now. Equally, some investments will be made for very short periods, so that if interest rates rise, when the funds are reinvested they will benefit from the higher rates.

The basic case: illustration

The basic case is illustrated in Table 7.2 in two scenarios. In the first scenario, the longest dated gap is −130, so the bank puts on funding for +130 to match this tenor of three periods. The gap at period t_2 is 410, so this is matched with a two-period tenor-funding position of +280. This leaves a gap of 180 at period t_1, which is then funded with a single-period loan. The net position is zero at each period ("squared off"), and the book has been funded by three bullet fixed-term loans. The position is not a matched book as such, although there is now no liquidity risk exposure.

In the second case, the gap increases from Period 1 to Period 2. The first period is funded by a three-period and a two-period borrow of +50 and +200, respectively. The gap at t_2 needs to be funded by a position that is not needed now. The bank can cover this with a forward start loan of +390 at t_1 or can wait

Table 7.2   Funding the liquidity gap: two examples

Time	t_1	t_2	t_3
Scenario (i)			
Assets	970	840	1,250
Liabilities	380	430	1,120
Gap	−590	−410	−130
Borrow 1: three-period tenor	130	130	130
Borrow 2: two-period tenor	280	280	
Borrow 3: single-period tenor	180		
Total funding	+590	+410	+130
Squared off	0	0	0
Scenario (ii)			
Assets	970	840	1,250
Liabilities	720	200	1,200
Gap	−250	−640	−50
Borrow 1: three-period tenor	50	50	130
Borrow 2: two-period tenor	200	200	
Borrow 3: single-period tenor	0	390	
Total funding	+250	+640	+50
Squared off	0	0	0

and act at t_2. If it does the latter it may still wish to hedge the interest-rate exposure.[8]

Example 7.1   UK gilt portfolio

Commercial banks and building societies are natural holders of government bonds such as gilts. They do so for the following reasons:

- Because gilts are the most liquid instruments in the UK market;
- As an instrument in which to invest the firm's capital reserves;
- For income generation purposes, given the favourable funding costs of gilt repo as well as zero credit and liquidity risk;
- To intermediate between gilt, stock loans, and inter-bank markets in CDs;
- To benefit from being long in gilts that go special and can be funded at anything from 25bp to 2–3% cheaper than GC repo;
- To establish an asset pool that receives favourable capital treatment (0% risk-weighted under Basel I and Basel II).

The benefits to XYZ of holding such a portfolio include some of the above, as well as the following:

- Earning the spread between yield and funding cost;
- Using the business to set up dealing relationships with bank counter-parties that could then be used as sources of additional funding if required, adding to the diversity of funding (required as part of the Treasury desk's remit);
- Assisting the Treasury desk in undertaking ALM objectives.

Business line

A UK government bond portfolio at XYZ's Treasury desk has the objective of maintaining an income stream that is diversified from current sources and that is also relatively low risk, but stable. This is achieved by:

- Establishing a portfolio of very short-dated gilts and gilt strips on the balance sheet (maximum maturity recommended 1 year, the majority in 3 to 6 months). The expected makeup of the book might be:
  - 125 million 3 months;
  - 200 million 6 months;
  - 25 million 1 year;
  - The average maturity of the portfolio in the first year would be around 6 months.
- Funding these in gilt repo – under the GMRA agreement – and funding using TRS – under ISDA – if required. The repo-funding margin for gilts in the wholesale market is often 0%. With a zero or very low margin – that is, a haircut – all positions will be virtually fully funded;

---

[8]We look at the mechanics of this, using different derivative instruments, in Chapter 12.

- Holding gilts and gilt strips to maturity to generate a steady income stream. With ultra-short-dated strips, we also benefit from the pull-to-par effect.

Market rates

Table 7.3 shows income yields and funding rates as at 2 June 2004. This shows where value was obtained from holding a book of gilts in the first instance. For example, all the following positions yielded funding profit:

- Hold gilts and fund in GC; depending on the specific stock and the term of funding arranged, a gain ranging from 15bp to 50–60bp;
- Hold strips to maturity. For example, a gain of approximately 35bp for a Dec 04 principal strip at 1-week or 2-week funding; and a locked-in funding gain of 9bp for a Dec 04 strip (buy a 6-month strip and fund in 6 months) – this is risk-free income;
- Hold strips at 3-month, 6-month, and 9-month maturities as longer dated bills and hold to maturity. Funding will be locked in if available or rolled.
  - For example, as at 2 June 2004, XYZ purchased a Sep 04 coupon strip at 4.34% and funded in the 1-week term at 4.15% (and ran the resultant funding gap risk – but this gilt had a strong pull-to-par effect. If funding is no longer profitable in short dates, XYZ would have sold the gilt for a probable realised mark-to-market profit);
  - Coupon strips are bid for in repo by the main market-makers, thereby reducing liquidity risk in these products.
- Take advantage of special rates for the stocks XYZ is long in. On 2 June 2004, a position in 9.5% 2005 gilt was funded cheaper as a result of its special status, from 35bp (down from 50bp the week before). The 6.75% 2004 gilt was being funded at 100bp cheaper than GC. So, the gain on holding that stock would be significant, as our funding cost in repo would be very low. It would be an objective of the Treasury desk to be aware of stocks expected to go special and act accordingly.

Risks

The principal risk is funding rollover (gap risk). Where possible, we will lock in funding to match expected holding period of positions, but will also look to take advantage of market rates as appropriate and roll over funding. Gap risk will be managed in the normal way as part of overall Treasury operations. Gaps will be put on to reflect the interest rate and yield curve view of the desk.

There is no credit risk.

Interest-rate risk and gap risk are managed as a standard banking ALM or cash book. The objective is to set up an income stream position at low risk, but if necessary DV01 risk would be managed where deemed necessary using 90-day sterling futures, OIS, or short-dated swaps. XYZ can also sell out of positions where it expects significant market movement – for example, a central bank base rate hike. The main objective, however, is to establish an income stream, in line with a view on short-term interest rates. Hedging would only be carried out when necessary for short-term periods (say, ahead of a data release or anticipated high volatility).

As the positions would be on the trading book – not the banking book – they will be marked-to-market. The desk expects volatility in short-dated gilts to be considerably lower than for medium-dated and long-dated gilts, but volatility is a risk exposure and there may be periods when the desk will experience mark-to-market losses.

The interest-rate risk for longer dated stocks is shown in Table 7.3, measured as DV01. Longer dated stocks expose the bank to a greater interest-rate risk position when marking-to-market.

Table 7.3   Market rates as at 2 June 2004

	GC rates	
1w	4.15	4.10
2w	4.25	4.15
3w	4.25	4.15
1m	4.25	4.15
2m	4.28	4.18
3m	4.32	4.22
4m	4.40	4.30
5m	4.43	4.33
6m	4.50	4.40
9m	4.67	4.57
1y	4.78	4.68

Source: HBOS screen.

Gilt yields

	GRY%	DV01	Special rates
5% Jun 04	4.05		
6T Nov 04	4.33	0.00416	100bp
9H Apr 05	4.668	0.00817	35bp cheaper than GC
8H Dec 05	4.818 0.014	25bp cheaper, down from 1.5%	
7T Sep 06	4.945 0.02141		
7H Dec 06	4.966	0.02364	10bp

Source: Butler Securities/KSBB screens.

Gilt strip yields

	GRY%	DV01
P Jun 04	3.78	
C Sep 04	4.342	0.00195
C Dec 04	4.509	0.00432
C Mar 05	4.633	0.00664
C Jun 05	4.744	0.00888
C Sep 05	4.829	0.01107
P Dec 05	4.85	0.01321

Source: Bloomberg.

Gap risk and limits

Liquidity gaps are measured by taking the difference between outstanding balances of assets and liabilities over time. At any point a positive gap between assets and liabilities is equivalent to a deficit, and this is measured as a cash amount. The *marginal gap* is the difference between the changes of assets and liabilities over a given period. A positive marginal gap means that the variation of value of assets exceeds the variation of value of liabilities. As new assets and liabilities are added over time, as part of the ordinary course of business, the gap profile changes.

The gap profile is tabulated or charted (or both) during and at the end of each day as a primary measure of risk. For illustration, a tabulated gap report is shown at Figure 7.1 and is an actual example from a UK banking institution. It shows the assets and liabilities grouped into maturity *buckets* and the net position for each bucket. It is a snapshot today of the exposure, and hence funding requirement of the bank for future maturity periods.

Table 7.1 is very much a summary figure, because the maturity gaps are very wide. For risk management purposes the buckets would be much narrower, for instance the period between 0 and 12 months might be split into 12 different maturity buckets. An example of a more detailed gap report is shown at Figure 7.7, which is from another UK banking institution. Note that the overall net position is zero, because this is a balance sheet and therefore, not surprisingly, it balances. However, along the maturity buckets or grid points there are net positions that are the gaps that need to be managed.

Limits on a banking book can be set in terms of gap limits. For example, a bank may set a 6-month gap limit of £10 million. The net position of assets and maturities expiring in 6 months' time could then not exceed £10 million.

Table 7.4 Example gap profile

	Total		0–6 months		6–12 months		1–3 years		3–7 years		7+ years	
							Time periods					
Assets	40,533	6.17%	28,636	6.08%	3,801	6.12%	4,563	6.75%	2,879	6.58%	654	4.47%
Liabilities	40,533	4.31%	30,733	4.04%	3,234	4.61%	3,005	6.29%	2,048	6.54%	1,513	2.21%
Net cumulative positions	**0**	**1.86%**	**(2,097)**		**567**		**1,558**		**831**		**(859)**	
Margin on total assets:	2.58%											
Average margin on total assets:	2.53%											

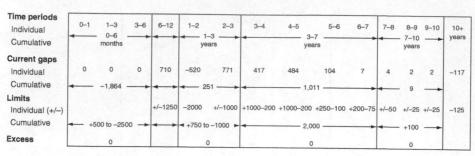

Figure 7.6   Gap limit report

An example of a gap limit report is shown at Figure 7.6, with the actual net gap positions shown against the gap limits for each maturity. Again, this is an actual limit report from a UK banking institution.

The maturity gap can be charted to provide an illustration of net exposure, and an example is shown at Figure 7.9 from yet another UK banking institution. In some firms' reports both the assets and the liabilities are shown for each maturity point, but in our example only the net position is shown. This net position is the gap exposure for that maturity point. A second example, used by the overseas subsidiary of a Middle Eastern commercial bank, which has no funding lines in the inter-bank market and so does not run short positions, is shown at Figure 7.10, while the gap report for a UK high-street bank is shown at Figure 7.11. Note the large short gap under the maturity labelled "non-int"; this stands for *non-interest bearing liabilities* and represents the balance of current accounts (cheque or "checking" accounts), which are funds that attract no or very low interest and are in theory very short dated (because they are demand deposits, so may be called at instant notice). In behavioural terms, however, such deposits are treated as "stable" long-term funding.

Gaps represent cumulative funding required at all dates. The cumulative funding is not necessarily identical to the new funding required at each period, because the debt issued in previous periods is not necessarily amortised at subsequent periods. The new funding between, for example, months 3 and 4 is not the accumulated deficit between months 2 and 4 because the debt contracted at month 3 is not necessarily amortised at month 4. Marginal gaps may be identified as the new funding required or the new excess funds of the period that should be invested in the market. Note that all the reports are snapshots, at a fixed point in time and the picture is of course a continuously moving one. In practice, the liquidity position of a bank cannot be characterised by one gap at any given date, and the entire gap profile must be used to gauge the extent of the book's profile.

The liquidity book may decide to match its assets with its liabilities. This is known as *cash matching* and occurs when the time profiles of both assets and liabilities are identical. By following such a course, the bank can lock in the spread between its funding rate and the rate at which it lends cash, and run a

	Total (£m)	Up to 1 month	1–3 months	3–6 months	6 months to 1 year	1–2 years	2–3 years	3–4 years	4–5 years	5–6 years	6–7 years	7–8 years	8–9 years	9–10 years	10+ years
ASSETS															
Cash & Interbank Loans	2,156.82	1,484.73	219.36	448.90	3.84	0.00	0.00	0.00	0.00	0.00	0.00	0.00	0.00	0.00	0.00
Certificates of Deposit purchased	1,271.49	58.77	132.99	210.26	776.50	92.96	0.00	0.00	0.00	0.00	0.00	0.00	0.00	0.00	0.00
Floating-Rate Notes purchased	936.03	245.62	586.60	12.68	26.13	45.48	0.00	0.00	19.52	0.00	0.00	0.00	0.00	0.00	0.00
Bank Bills	314.35	104.09	178.36	31.90	0.00	0.00	0.00	0.00	0.00	0.00	0.00	0.00	0.00	0.00	0.00
Other Loans	13.00	0.00	1.00	0.00	0.00	7.00	0.00	1.00	0.00	0.00	2.00	2.00	0.00	0.00	0.00
Debt Securities/Gilts	859.45	0.00	25.98	7.58	60.05	439.06	199.48	26.81	100.50	0.00	0.00	0.00	0.00	0.00	0.00
Fixed-Rate Mortgages	4,180.89	97.72	177.37	143.13	964.98	1,452.91	181.86	661.36	450.42	22.78	4.30	3.65	3.10	2.63	14.67
Variable & Capped Rate Mortgages	14,850.49	14,850.49	0.00	0.00	0.00	0.00	0.00	0.00	0.00	0.00	0.00	0.00	0.00	0.00	0.00
Commercial Loans	271.77	96.62	96.22	56.52	0.86	2.16	1.12	3.64	8.85	1.06	0.16	0.17	0.16	4.23	0.00
Unsecured Lending and Leasing	3,720.13	272.13	1,105.20	360.03	507.69	694.86	400.84	195.19	79.98	25.45	14.06	10.03	10.44	10.82	33.42
Other Assets	665.53	357.72	0.00	18.77	5.00	0.00	0.00	0.00	0.00	0.00	0.00	0.00	0.00	0.00	284.03
TOTAL CASH ASSETS	29,239.95	17,567.91	2,523.06	1,289.77	2,345.05	2,734.43	783.31	888.00	659.26	49.28	20.53	15.85	13.71	17.68	332.12
Swaps	9993.28	3,707.34	1,462.32	1,735.59	1,060.61	344.00	146.50	537.60	649.00	70.00	5.32	200.00	75.00	0.00	0.00
Forward Rate Agreements	425.00	0.00	50.00	0.00	220.00	5.00	150.00	0.00	0.00	0.00	0.00	0.00	0.00	0.00	0.00
Futures	875.00	0.00	300.00	0.00	175.00	400.00	0.00	0.00	0.00	0.00	0.00	0.00	0.00	0.00	0.00
TOTAL	40,533.24	21,275.24	4,335.38	3,025.36	3,800.66	3,483.43	1,079.81	1,425.60	1,308.26	119.28	25.84	215.85	88.71	17.68	332.12
LIABILITIES (£m)															
Bank Deposits	3,993.45	2,553.85	850.45	233.03	329.06	21.07	1.00	0.00	5.00	0.00	0.00	0.00	0.00	0.00	0.00
Certificates of Deposit issued	1,431.42	375.96	506.76	154.70	309.50	60.00	20.00	3.50	1.00	0.00	0.00	0.00	0.00	0.00	0.00
Commercial Paper – CP & Euro	508.46	271.82	128.42	108.21	0.00	0.00	0.00	0.00	0.00	0.00	0.00	0.00	0.00	0.00	0.00
Subordinated Debt	275.00	0.00	0.00	0.00	0.00	0.00	0.00	0.00	0.00	0.00	0.00	200.00	0.00	0.00	75.00
Eurobonds + Other	2,582.24	768.75	1,231.29	121.94	53.86	9.77	13.16	150.43	150.53	0.00	7.51	0.00	75.00	0.00	0.00
Customer Deposits	17,267.55	15,493.65	953.60	311.70	340.50	129.10	6.60	24.90	0.00	7.50	0.00	0.00	0.00	0.00	0.00
Other Liabilities (incl capital/reserves)	3,181.83	1,336.83	0.00	0.00	741.72	0.00	0.00	0.00	0.00	0.00	0.00	0.00	0.00	0.00	1,103.28
TOTAL CASH LIABILITIES	29,239.96	20800.86	3,670.52	929.58	1,774.64	219.93	40.76	178.83	156.53	7.50	7.51	200.00	75.00	0.00	1,178.28
Swaps	9,993.28	1,754.70	1,657.59	1,399.75	1,254.24	1,887.97	281.44	905.06	770.52	15.76	6.48	7.27	8.13	13.06	31.30
FRAs	425.00	0.00	150.00	70.00	55.00	150.00	0.00	0.00	0.00	0.00	0.00	0.00	0.00	0.00	0.00
Futures	875.00	0.00	0.00	300.00	150.00	425.00	0.00	0.00	0.00	0.00	0.00	0.00	0.00	0.00	0.00
TOTAL	40,533.24	22555.56	5,478.11	2,699.33	3,233.89	2,682.90	322.20	1,083.90	927.05	23.26	13.99	207.27	83.13	13.06	1,209.58
Net Positions	0.00	-1,280.32	-1,142.73	326.03	566.77	800.53	757.61	341.70	381.21	96.02	11.85	8.58	5.58	4.62	-877.46

Figure 7.7 Example of detailed gap profile

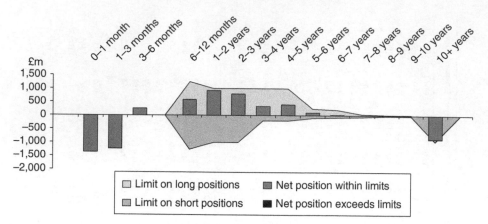

Figure 7.8   Gap maturity profile in graphical form

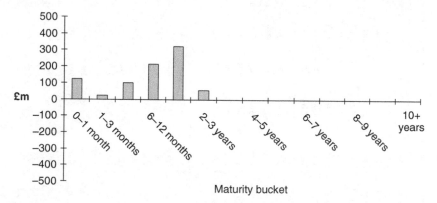

Figure 7.9   Gap maturity profile, bank with no short funding allowed

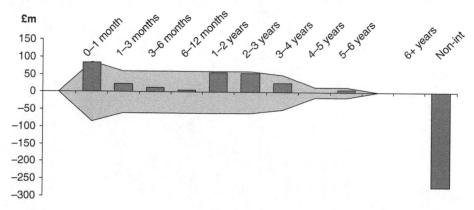

Figure 7.10   Gap maturity profile, UK high-street bank

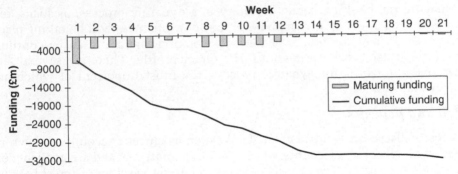

Figure 7.11   Liquidity analysis – example of UK bank profile of maturity of funding

guaranteed profit. Under cash matching the liquidity gaps will be zero. Matching the profile of both legs of the book is done at the overall level; that is, cash matching does not mean that deposits should always match loans. This would be difficult as both result from customer demand, although an individual purchase of, say, a CD can be matched with an identical loan. Nevertheless, the bank can elect to match assets and liabilities once the net position is known, and keep the book matched at all times. However, it is highly unusual for a bank to adopt a cash matching strategy.

LIQUIDITY MANAGEMENT

The continuous process of raising new funds or investing surplus funds is known as liquidity management. If we consider that a gap today is funded, thus balancing assets and liabilities and squaring-off the book, the next day a new deficit or surplus is generated, which also has to be funded. The liquidity management decision must cover the amount required to bridge the gap that exists the following day, as well as position the book across future dates in line with the bank's view on interest rates. Usually, in order to define the maturity structure of debt a target profile of resources is defined. This may be done in several ways. If the objective of ALM is to replicate the asset profile with resources, the new funding should contribute to bringing the resources profile closer to that of the assets, that is, more of a matched book looking forward. This is the lowest-risk option. Another target profile may be imposed on the bank by liquidity constraints. This may arise if, for example, the bank has a limit on borrowing lines in the market so that it could not raise a certain amount each week or month. For instance, if the maximum that could be raised in 1 week by a bank is £10 million, the maximum period liquidity gap is constrained by that limit. The ALM desk will manage the book in line with the target profile that has been adopted, which requires it to try to reach the required profile over a given time horizon.

Managing the banking book's liquidity is a dynamic process, as loans and deposits are known at any given point, but new business will be taking place continuously and the profile of the book looking forward must be continuously rebalanced to keep it within the target profile. There are several factors that influence this dynamic process, the most important of which are reviewed below.

Demand deposits

Deposits placed on demand at the bank, such as current accounts (known in the US as "checking accounts") have no stated maturity and are available on demand at the bank. Technically, they are referred to as "non-interest bearing liabilities" because the bank pays no or very low rates of interest on them, so they are effectively free funds. The balance of these funds can increase or decrease throughout the day without any warning, although in practice the balance is quite stable. There are a number of ways that a bank can choose to deal with these balances, which are:

- To group all outstanding balances into one maturity bucket at a future date that is the preferred time horizon of the bank, or a date beyond this. This would then exclude them from the gap profile. Although this is considered unrealistic because it excludes the current account balances from the gap profile, it is nevertheless a fairly common approach;
- To rely on an assumed rate of amortisation for the balances, say 5% or 10% each year;
- To divide deposits into stable and unstable balances, of which the core deposits are set as a permanent balance. The amount of the core balance is set by the bank based on a study of the total balance volatility pattern over time. The excess over the core balance is then viewed as very short-term debt. This method is reasonably close to reality as it is based on historical observations;
- To make projections based on observable variables that are correlated with the outstanding balances of deposits. For instance, such variables could be based on the level of economic growth plus an error factor based on the short-term fluctuations in the growth pattern.

Preset contingencies

A bank will have committed lines of credit, the utilisation of which depends on customer demand. Contingencies generate outflows of funds that are by definition uncertain, as they are contingent upon some event, for example, the willingness of the borrower to use a committed line of credit. The usual way for a bank to deal with these unforeseen fluctuations is to use statistical data based on past observation to project a future level of activity.

Prepayment options of existing assets

Where the maturity schedule is stated in the terms of a loan, it may still be subject to uncertainty because of prepayment options. This is similar to the prepayment risk associated with a mortgage-backed bond. An element of prepayment risk renders the actual maturity profile of a loan book to be uncertain; banks often calculate an "effective maturity schedule" based on prepayment statistics instead of the theoretical schedule. There are also a range of prepayment models that may be used, the simplest of which use constant prepayment ratios to assess the average life of the portfolio. The more sophisticated models incorporate more parameters, such as one that bases the prepayment rate on the interest rate differential between the loan rate and the current market rate, or the time elapsed since the loan was taken out.

Interest cash flows

Assets and liabilities generate interest cash inflows and outflows, as well as the amortisation of principal. The interest payments must be included in the gap profile as well.

Interest-rate risk and source

Interest-rate risk

Put simply, interest-rate risk is defined as the potential impact, adverse or otherwise, on the net asset value of a financial institution's balance sheet and earnings resulting from a change in interest rates. Risk exposure exists whenever there is a maturity date mismatch between assets and liabilities, or between principal and interest cash flows. Interest-rate risk is not necessarily a negative thing; for instance, changes in interest rates that increase the net asset value of a banking institution would be regarded as positive. For this reason, active ALM seeks to position a banking book to gain from changes in rates. The Bank for International Settlements splits interest-rate risk into two elements: *investment risk* and *income risk*. The first risk type is the term for potential risk exposure arising from changes in the market value of fixed interest-rate cash instruments and off-balance-sheet instruments, and is also known as *price risk*. Investment risk is perhaps best exemplified by the change in value of a plain vanilla bond following a change in interest rates, and from Chapter 2 we know that there is an inverse relationship between changes in rates and the value of such bonds (see Example 2.2). Income risk is the risk of loss of income when there is a non-synchronous change in deposit and funding rates, and it this risk that is known as gap risk.

ALM covering the formulation of interest-rate risk policy is usually the responsibility of what is known as the asset-liability committee or ALCO, which is made up of senior management personnel including the Finance Director and the heads of Treasury and Risk Management. ALCO sets bank policy for balance sheet management and the likely impact on revenue of various scenarios that it considers may occur. The size of ALCO will depend on the complexity of the balance sheet and products traded, and the amount of management information available on individual products and desks.

The process employed by ALCO for ALM will vary according to the particular internal arrangement of the institution. A common procedure involves a monthly presentation to ALCO of the impact of different interest-rate scenarios on the balance sheet. This presentation may include:

- An analysis of the difference between the actual net interest income (NII) for the previous month and the amount that was forecast at the previous ALCO meeting. This is usually presented as a gap report, broken by maturity buckets and individual products;
- The result of discussion with business unit heads on the basis of the assumptions used in calculating forecasts and impact of interest-rate changes; scenario analysis usually assumes an unchanging book position between now and 1 month later, which is essentially unrealistic;
- A number of interest-rate scenarios, based on assumptions of (a) what is expected to happen to the shape and level of the yield curve, and (b) what may happen to the yield curve, for example, extreme scenarios. Essentially, this exercise produces a value for the forecasted NII due to changes in interest rates;
- An update of the latest actual revenue numbers;
- Specific new or one-off topics may be introduced at ALCO as circumstances dictate; for example, the presentation of the approval process for the introduction of a new product.

Sources of interest-rate risk

Assets on the balance sheet are affected by absolute changes in interest rates as well as increases in the volatility of interest rates. For instance, fixed-rate assets will fall in value in the event of a rise in rates, while funding costs will rise. This decreases the margins available. We noted that the way to remove this risk was to lock-in assets with matching liabilities; however, this is only not always possible, but also sometimes undesirable, as it prevents the ALM manager from taking a view on the yield curve. In a falling interest-rate environment, deposit-taking institutions may experience a decline in available funds, requiring new funding sources that may be accessed at less favourable terms. Liabilities are also impacted by a changing interest-rate environment.

There are five primary sources of interest-rate risk inherent in an ALM book, which are described below.

- **Gap risk** is the risk that revenue and earnings decline as a result of changes in interest rates, due to the difference in the maturity profile of assets, liabilities and off-balance-sheet instruments. Another term for gap risk is *mismatch risk*. An institution with gap risk is exposed to changes in the level of the yield curve, a so-called *parallel shift*, or a change in the shape of the yield curve or *pivotal shift*. Gap risk is measured in terms of short-term or long-term risk, which is a function of the impact of rate changes on earnings for a short or long period. Therefore, the maturity profile of the book, and the time to maturity of instruments held on the book, will influence whether the bank is exposed to short-term or long-term gap risk.

- **Yield curve risk** is the risk that non-parallel or pivotal shifts in the yield curve cause a reduction in NII. The ALM manager will change the structure of the book to take into account their views on the yield curve. For example, a book with a combination of short-term and long-term asset-maturing or liability-maturity structures[9] is at risk from a yield curve inversion, sometimes known as a *twist* in the curve.

- **Basis risk** arises from the fact that assets are often priced off one interest rate, while funding is priced off another interest rate. Taken one step further, hedge instruments are often linked to a different interest rate to that of the product they are hedging. In the US market, the best example of basis risk is the difference between the Prime rate and Libor. Term loans in the US are often set at Prime, or a relationship to Prime, while bank funding is usually based on the Eurodollar market and linked to Libor. However, the Prime rate is what is known as an "administered" rate and does not change on a daily basis, unlike Libor. While changes in the two rates are positively correlated, they do not change by the same amount, which means that the spread between them changes regularly. This results in the spread earning on a loan product changing over time. Figure 7.12 illustrates the change in spread during 2009–2010.

- Another risk for deposit-taking institutions such as clearing banks is **run-off risk**, associated with the non-interest bearing liabilities (NIBLs) of such banks. The level of interest rates at any one time represents an opportunity cost to depositors who have funds in such facilities. However, in a rising interest-rate environment, this opportunity cost rises and depositors will withdraw these funds, available at immediate notice, resulting in an outflow of funds for the bank. The funds may be taken out of the banking system completely, for example, for investment in the stock market. This risk is significant and therefore sufficient funds must be maintained at short notice, which is an opportunity cost for the bank itself.

- Many banking products entitle the customer to terminate contractual arrangement ahead of the stated maturity term; this is sometimes referred to as **option risk**. This is another significant risk as products such as CDs, cheque account balances, and demand deposits can be withdrawn or liquidated at no notice, which is a risk to the level of NII should the option inherent in the products be exercised.

Gap and net interest income

We noted earlier that gap is a measure of the difference in interest-rate sensitivity of assets and liabilities that revalue at a particular date, expressed as a cash value. Put simply it is:

$$Gap = A_{ir} - L_{ir} \qquad (9.1)$$

where A_{ir} and L_{ir} are the interest-rate sensitive assets and interest-rate sensitive liabilities. When $A_{ir} > L_{ir}$ the banking book is described as being

---

[9]This describes a *barbell* structure, but this is really a bond market term.

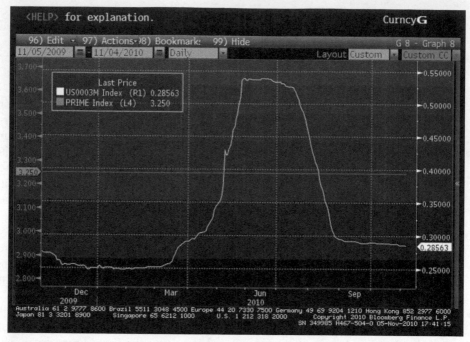

Figure 7.12 Change in spread between 3-month Prime rate and 3-month Libor 2009–2010
Source: Bloomberg.

positively gapped, and when $A_{ir} < L_{ir}$ the book is said to be *negatively gapped*. The change in NII is given by:

$$\Delta NII = Gap \times \Delta r \tag{9.2}$$

where r is the relevant interest rate used for valuation. The NII of a bank that is positively gapped will increase as interest rates rise, and will decrease as rates decline. This describes a banking book that is asset sensitive; the opposite, when a book is negatively gapped, is known as liability sensitive. The NII of a negatively gapped book will increase when interest rates decline. The value of a book with zero gap is immune to changes in the level of interest rates. The shape of the banking book at any one time is a function of customer demand, the Treasury manager's operating strategy, and view of future interest rates.

Gap analysis is used to measure the difference between interest-rate-sensitive assets and liabilities, over specified time periods. Another term for this analysis is *periodic gap*, and the common expression for each time period is maturity *bucket*. For a commercial bank the typical maturity buckets are:

- 0–3 months;
- 3–12 months;

- 1–5 years;
- 5 years;

although another common approach is to group assets and liabilities by the buckets or grid points of the *Riskmetrics* Value-at-Risk methodology. Any combination of time periods may be used, however. For instance, certain US commercial banks place assets, liabilities, and off-balance-sheet items in terms of *known maturities, judgemental maturities,* and *market-driven maturities.* These are defined as:

- **Known maturities:** fixed-rate loans and CDs;
- **Judgemental maturities:** passbook savings accounts, demand deposits, credit cards, non-performing loans;
- **Market-driven maturities:** option-based instruments such as mortgages, and other interest-rate sensitive assets.

The other key measure is *cumulative gap,* defined as the sum of the individual gaps up to 1 year maturity. Banks traditionally use the cumulative gap to estimate the impact of a change in interest rates on NII.

Assumptions of gap analysis

A number of assumptions are made when using gap analysis, assumptions that may not reflect reality in practice. These include:

- The key assumption that interest-rate changes manifest themselves as a parallel shift in the yield curve; in practice, changes do not occur as a parallel shift, giving rise to basis risk between short-term and long-term assets;
- The expectation that contractual repayment schedules are met; if there is a fall in interest rates, prepayments of loans by borrowers who wish to refinance their loans at lower rates will have an impact on NII. Certain assets and liabilities have option features that are exercised as interest rates change, such as letters of credit and variable rate deposits; early repayment will impact a bank's cash flow;
- That repricing of assets and liabilities takes place in the mid-point of the time bucket;
- The expectation that all loan payments will occur on schedule; in practice, certain borrowers will repay the loan earlier.

Recognised weaknesses of the gap approach include:

- No incorporation of future growth, or changes in the asset–liability mix;
- No consideration of the time value of money;
- Arbitrary setting of time periods.

Limitations notwithstanding, gap analysis is used extensively. Gup and Brooks (1993, page 59) state the following reasons for the continued popularity of gap analysis:

- It was the first approach introduced to handle interest-rate risk, and provides reasonable accuracy;

- The data required to perform the analysis is already compiled for the purposes of regulatory reporting;
- The gaps can be calculated using simple spreadsheet software;
- It is easier (and cheaper) to implement than more sophisticated techniques;
- It is straightforward to demonstrate and explain to senior management and shareholders.

Although there are more sophisticated methods available, gap analysis remains in widespread use.

THE ALM DESK

The ALM desk or unit is a specialised business unit that fulfils a range of functions. Its precise remit is a function of the type of activities of the financial institution that it is a part of. Let us consider the main types of activities that are carried out.

If an ALM unit has a profit target of zero, it will act as a cost centre with a responsibility to minimise operating costs. This would be consistent with a strategy that emphasises commercial banking as the core business of the firm, and where ALM policy is concerned purely with hedging interest-rate and liquidity risk.

The next level is where the ALM unit is responsible for minimising the cost of funding. That would allow the unit to maintain an element of exposure to interest-rate risk, depending on the view that was held as to the future level of interest rates. As we noted above, the core banking activity generates either an excess or shortage of funds. To hedge away all of the excess or shortage, while removing interest-rate exposure, has an opportunity cost associated with it since it eliminates any potential gain that might arise from movements in market rates. Of course, without a complete hedge, there is an exposure to interest-rate risk. The ALM desk is responsible for monitoring and managing this risk, and of course is credited with any cost savings in the cost of funds that arise from the exposure. The saving may be measured as the difference between the funding costs of a full hedging policy and the actual policy that the ALM desk adopts. Under this policy, interest-rate risk limits are set that the ALM desk ensures the bank's operations do not breach.

The final stage of development is to turn the ALM unit into a profit centre, with responsibility for optimising the funding policy within specified limits. The limits may be set as *gap* limits, *Value-at-Risk* limits or by another measure, such as level of earnings volatility. Under this scenario, the ALM desk is responsible for managing all financial risk.

The final development of the ALM function has resulted in it taking on a more active role. The previous paragraphs described the three stages of development that ALM has undergone, although all three versions are part of the "traditional" approach. Practitioners are now beginning to think of ALM as extending beyond the risk management field, and being responsible for adding value to the net worth of the bank, through proactive positioning of the book and hence the balance sheet. That is, in addition to the traditional function of managing liquidity risk and interest-rate risk, ALM should be concerned additionally with managing the regulatory capital of the bank and with actively positioning the balance sheet to maximise profit. The latest developments mean that there are now financial institutions that run a much more sophisticated ALM operation than that associated with a traditional banking book.

Let us review the traditional and developed elements of an ALM function.

Traditional ALM

Generally, a bank's ALM function has in the past been concerned with managing the risk associated with the banking book. This does not mean that this function is now obsolete, rather that additional functions have now been added to the ALM role. There are a large number of financial institutions that adopt the traditional approach, indeed the nature of their operations would not lend themselves to anything more. We can summarise the role of the traditional ALM desk as follows:

- **Interest-rate risk management:** This is the interest-rate risk arising from the operation of the banking book, as described above. Overall the ALM desk is responsible for hedging the interest-rate risk or positioning the book in accordance with its view;
- **Liquidity and funding management:** As described above; also there are regulatory requirements that dictate the proportion of banking assets that must be held as short-term instruments;
- **Reporting on hedging of risks:** The ALM fulfils a senior management information function by reporting on a regular basis on the extent of the bank's risk exposure. This may be in the form of a weekly hardcopy report, or via some other medium;
- **Setting up risk limits:** The ALM unit will set limits, implement them, and enforce them, although it is common for an independent "middle office" risk function to monitor compliance with limits;
- **Capital requirement reporting:** This function involves the compilation of reports on capital usage and position limits as percentage of capital allowed, and reporting to regulatory authorities.

All financial institutions will carry out the activities described above.

Example 7.2 Gap analysis

Maturity gap analysis measures the cash difference or *gap* between the absolute values of the assets and liabilities that are sensitive to movements in interest rates. Therefore, the analysis measures the relative interest-rate sensitivities of the assets and liabilities, and thus determines the risk profile of the bank with respect to changes in rates. The *gap ratio* is given as (33.1):

$$\text{Gap ratio} = \frac{\text{Interest} - \text{Rate-sensitive assets}}{\text{Interest} - \text{Rate-sensitive liabilities}} \qquad (33.1)$$

and measures whether there are more interest-rate-sensitive assets than liabilities. A gap ratio higher than one, for example, indicates that a rise in interest rates will increase the net present value of the book, thus raising the return on assets at a rate higher than the rise in the cost of funding. This also results in a higher income spread.

A gap ratio lower than one indicates a rising funding cost. *Duration gap* analysis measures the impact on the net worth of the bank due to changes in interest rates by focusing on changes in market value of either assets or liabilities. This is because duration measures the percentage change in the market value of a single security for a 1% change in the underlying yield of the security (strictly speaking, this is *modified duration* but the term for the original "duration" is now almost universally used to refer to modified duration). The duration gap is defined as (33.2):

$$\text{Duration gap} = \text{Duration of assets} - w(\text{Duration of liabilities}) \qquad (33.2)$$

where w is the percentage of assets funded by liabilities. Hence, the duration gap measures the effects of the change in the net worth of the bank. A higher duration gap indicates a higher interest-rate exposure. As duration only measures the effects of a linear change in interest rate, that is a parallel shift yield curve change. Banks with portfolios that include a significant amount of instruments with elements of optionality, such as callable bonds, asset-backed securities, and convertibles, also use the *convexity* measure of risk exposure to adjust for the inaccuracies that arise in duration over large yield changes.

Generic "traditional" ALM policy for different-sized banks

ALM discipline as practised traditionally in banks could be summarised as follows:

- The preparation and adoption of a high-level interest-rate risk and liquidity risk policy at managing board level; this sets general guidelines on the type and extent of risk exposure that can be taken on by the bank;
- Setting limits on the risk exposure levels of the banking book; this can be by product type, desk, geographic area, and so on, and will be along the maturity spectrum;
- Actively measuring the level of interest-rate risk exposure at regular, specified intervals;

- Reporting to senior management on general aspects of risk management, risk exposure levels, limit breaches, and so on;
- The monitoring of risk management policies and procedures by an independent "middle office" risk function.

The risk management approach adopted by banks will vary according to their specific markets and appetite for risk. Certain institutions will have their activities set out or proscribed for them under regulatory rules. For instance, building societies in the UK are prohibited from trading in certain instruments under the regulator's guidelines. In this section we present, purely for the purposes of illustration, the ALM policies of three hypothetical banks, called Bank S, Bank M, and Bank L. These are, respectively, a small banking entity with assets of £500 million, a medium-sized bank with assets of £2.5 billion and a large bank with assets of £10 billion. The following serves to demonstrate the differing approaches that can be taken according to the environment that a financial institution operates in.

ALM policy for Bank S (assets = £500 million)

The aim of the ALM policy for Bank S is to provide guidelines on risk appetite, revenue targets, and rates of return, as well as risk management policy. Areas that may be covered include capital ratios, liquidity, asset mix, rate-setting policy for loans and deposits, and investment guidelines for the banking portfolio. The key objectives should be:

- To maintain capital ratios at the planned minimum, and to ensure safety of the deposit base;
- To generate a satisfactory revenue stream, both for income purposes and to further protect the deposit base.

The responsibility for overseeing the operations of the bank to ensure that these objectives are achieved is lodged with the ALM Committee. This body monitors the volume and mix of the bank's assets and funding (liabilities), and ensures that this asset mix follows internal guidelines with regard to banking liquidity, capital adequacy, asset base growth targets, risk exposure, and return on capital. The norm is for the committee to meet on a monthly basis; at a minimum the membership of the committee will include the finance director, head of Treasury, and risk manager. For a bank the size of Bank S, the ALM committee membership will possibly be extended to the chief executive, the head of the loans business, and the chief operating officer.

As a matter of course, the committee will wish to discuss and review the following on a regular basis:

- Overall macroeconomic conditions;
- Financial results and key management ratios such as share price analysis and rates of return on capital and equity;
- The house view on the likely direction of short-term interest rates;
- The current lending strategy and suggestions for changes to this, as well as the current funding strategy;

- Any anticipated changes to the volume and mix of the loan book, and that of the main sources of funding; in addition, the appropriateness or otherwise of alternative sources of funding;
- Suggestions for any alteration to the bank's ALM policy;
- The maturity gap profile and anticipated and suggested changes to it.

The committee will also wish to consider the interest rates offered currently on loans and deposits, and whether these are still appropriate.

Interest-rate sensitivity is monitored and confirmed as lying within specified parameters; these parameters are regularly reviewed and adjusted if deemed necessary according to changes in the business cycle and economic conditions. Measured using the following ratio:

$$A_{ir}/L_{ir},$$

typical risk levels would be expected to lie between 90 and 120% for the maturity period 0–90 days, and between 80 and 110% for the maturity period over 90 days and less than 365 days.

Put simply, the objective of Bank S would be to remain within specified risk parameters at all times, and to maintain as consistent level of earnings as possible (and one that is immune to changes in the stage of the business cycle).

ALM policy for Bank M (assets = £2.5 billion)

Bank M is our hypothetical "medium-sized" banking institution. Its ALM policy would be overseen by an Asset–Liability Management Committee or ALCO. Typically, the following members of senior management would be expected to be members of ALCO:

- Deputy chief executive;
- Finance director;
- Head of retail banking;
- Head of corporate banking;
- Head of Treasury;
- Head of risk management;
- Head of internal audit;

together with others such as product specialists who are called to attend as and when required. The finance director will often chair the meeting.

The primary responsibilities of ALCO are detailed below.

Objectives

ALCO is tasked with reviewing the bank's overall funding strategy. Minutes are taken at each meeting, and decisions taken are recorded on the minutes and circulated to attendees and designated key staff. ALCO members are responsible for undertaking a regular review of the following:

- Minutes of the previous meeting;

- The ratio of the interest-rate-sensitive assets to liabilities, gap reports, risk reports, and the funding position;
- The bank's view on expected level of interest rates and how the book should be positioned with respect to this view; and related to this, the ALCO view on anticipated funding costs in the short term and medium term;
- Stress testing in the form of "what if?" scenarios to check the effect on the banking book of specified changes in market conditions; and the change in parameters that may be required if there is a change in market conditions or risk tolerance;
- The current interest rates for loans and deposits to ensure that these are in accordance with the overall lending and funding strategy;
- The maturity distribution of the liquidity book (expected to be comprised of T-bills, CDs, and very short-dated government bonds); the current liquidity position and the expected position in the short term and medium term.

As ALCO meets on a regular monthly basis, it may not be the case that every aspect of their responsibility is discussed at every meeting; the agenda is set by the chair of the meeting in consultation with committee members. The policies adopted by ALCO should be dynamic and flexible, and capable of adaptation to changes in operating conditions. Any changes will be made on agreement of committee members. Generally, any exceptions to agreed policy can only be with the agreement of the CEO and ALCO itself.

Interest-rate risk policy

The objective will be to keep earnings volatility resulting from an upward or downward move in interest rates to a minimum. To this end, at each ALCO meeting members will review risk and position reports and discuss these in the light of the risk policy. Generally, the 6-month and 12-month A_{ir}/L_{ir} cumulative ratio will lie in the range 90–110%. A significant move outside this range will most likely be subject to corrective action. The committee will also consider the results of various scenario analyses on the book, and if these tests indicate a potential earnings impact of greater than, say, 10%, instructions may be given to alter the shape and maturity profile of the book.

Liquidity policy

A primary responsibility of ALCO is to ensure that an adequate level of liquidity is maintained at all times. We define liquidity as:

> " ... the ability to meet anticipated and unanticipated operating cash needs, loan demand, and deposit withdrawals, without incurring a sustained negative impact on profitability."

> (Gup and Brooks, 1993, page 238)

Generally, a Bank M-type operation would expect to have a target level for loans to deposits of around 75–85%, and a loans to core deposits ratio of 85–95%. The loan/deposit ratio is reported to ALCO and reviewed on a monthly basis, and a reported figure significantly outside these ranges (say, by 5% or more) will be reviewed and asked to be adjusted to bring it back into line with ALCO policy.

ALM policy for Bank L (assets = £10 billion)

The management policy for ALM at a larger entity will build on that described for a medium-sized financial institution. If Bank L is a group company, the policy will cover the consolidated balance sheet as well as individual subsidiary balance sheets; the committee will provide direction on the management of assets and liabilities, and the off-balance-sheet instruments used to manage interest-rate and credit risk. A well-functioning management process will be proactive and concentrate on direction in response to anticipated changes in operating conditions, rather than reactive responses to changes that have already taken place. The primary objectives will be to maximise shareholder value, with target returns on capital of 15–22%.

The responsibility for implementing and overseeing the ALM management policy will reside with ALCO. ALCO will establish the operating guidelines for ALM, and review these guidelines on a periodic basis. The committee will meet on a more frequent basis than would be the case for Bank M, usually on a fortnightly basis. As well as this, it will set policies governing liquidity and funding objectives, investment activities, and interest-rate risk. It will also oversee the activities of the investment banking division. The head of the ALM desk will prepare the interest-rate risk sensitivity report and present it to ALCO.

Interest-rate risk management

ALCO will establish an interest-rate risk policy that sets direction on acceptable levels of interest-rate risk. This risk policy is designed to guide management in the evaluation of the impact of interest-rate risk on the bank's earnings. The extent of risk exposure is a function of the maturity profile of the balance sheet, as well as the frequency of repricing, the level of loan prepayments, and funding costs. Managing interest-rate risk is, in effect, the adjustment of risk exposure upwards or downwards, which will be in response to ALCO's views on the future direction of interest rates. As part of the risk management process, the committee will monitor the current risk exposure and duration gap, using rate sensitivity analysis and simulation modelling to assess whether the current level of risk is satisfactory.

Measuring interest-rate risk

Notwithstanding the widespread adoption of Value-at-Risk as the key market risk measurement tool, funding books such as repo books continue to use the gap report as a key measure of interest-rate risk exposure. This enables ALCO to view the risk sensitivity along the maturity structure. Cumulative gap positions and the ratio of assets revaluation to liabilities revaluation are calculated and compared to earnings levels on current the asset–liability position. Generally, the 90-day, 6-month, and 1-year gap positions are the most significant points along the term structure at which interest-rate risk exposure is calculated. The ratio of gap to earnings assets will be set at the ±15% to ±20% level.

As it is a traditional duration-based approach, gap reporting is a static measure that measures risk sensitivity at one specific point in time. For this reason, banks combine a Value-at-Risk measure as well, or only use Value-at-Risk. It is outside the scope of this book to consider Value-at-Risk but we cite a useful introductory reference in the Bibliography at the end of this chapter.

Simulation modelling

Simulation modelling is a procedure that measures the potential impact on the banking book, and hence earnings levels, of a user-specified change in interest rates and/or a change in the shape of the book itself. This process enables senior management to gauge the risk associated with particular strategies. Put simply, the process is:

* Construct a "base" balance sheet and income statement as the starting point (this is derived from the current shape of the banking book, and any changes expected from current growth trends that have been projected forward);
* Assess the impact on the balance sheet of changes under selected scenarios; these might be no change in rates; a 100 basis point and 250 basis point upward parallel shift in the yield curve; a 100 basis point and 250 basis point downward parallel shift; a 25 basis point steepening and flattening of the yield curve, between the 3-month and the 3-year maturity points; a combination of a parallel shift with a pivotal shift at a selected point; an increase or decrease in 3-month T-bill yield volatility levels; and a 20 basis point change in swap spreads;
* Compare the difference in earnings resulting from any of the scenarios to the anticipated earnings stream under the current environment.

Generally, the committee will have set guidelines about the significance of simulation results; for example, there may be a rule that a 100 basis point change in interest rates should not impact NII by more than 10%. If results indicate such an impact, ALCO will determine if the current risk strategy is satisfactory or whether adjustments are necessary.

CRITIQUE OF THE TRADITIONAL APPROACH TO ALM

Traditionally, the main approach of ALM concentrated on interest sensitivity and net present value sensitivity of a bank's loan–deposit book. The usual interest sensitivity report is the maturity gap report, which we reviewed briefly earlier. The maturity gap report is not perfect, however, and can be said to have the following drawbacks:

- The repricing intervals chosen for gap analysis are ultimately arbitrary, and there may be significant mismatches within a repricing interval. For instance, a common repricing interval chosen is the 1-year gap and the 1–3-year gap; there are (albeit extreme) circumstances when mismatches would go undetected by the model. Consider a banking book that is composed solely of liabilities that reprice in 1 month's time, and an equal cash value of assets that reprice in 11 months' time. The 1-year gap of the book (assuming no other positions) would be zero, implying no risk to net interest income. In fact, under our scenario the net interest income is significantly at risk from a rise in interest rates;
- Maturity gap models assume that interest rates change by a uniform magnitude and direction. For any given change in the general level of interest rates, however, it is more realistic for different maturity interest rates to change by different amounts, what is known as a non-parallel shift;
- Maturity gap models assume that principal cash flows do not change when interest rates change. Therefore, it is not possible effectively to incorporate the impact of options embedded in certain financial instruments. Instruments such as mortgage-backed bonds and convertibles do not fall accurately into a gap analysis, as only their first-order risk exposure is captured;
- Notwithstanding these drawbacks, the gap model is widely used as it is easily understood in the commercial banking and mortgage industry, and its application does not require a knowledge of sophisticated financial modelling techniques.

But perhaps the biggest drawback of the traditional approach to ALM in banks is that it is reactive in nature. The department(s) that are responsible for managing ALM risk in banks are not responsible for originating most of the assets and liabilities that are on the balance sheet at any time. In effect, Treasury is given a balance sheet to manage, after the fact, for interest-rate and liquidity risk purposes. This makes strategic planning less of a practical exercise and often more of just a budgeting one.

STRATEGIC ALM

The twenty-first century approach to ALM in banks must, given the operating environment post-2008, be more proactive in nature rather than reactive as it has been traditionally. Strategic ALM is a single, integrated aggregate approach to balance sheet management that ties in asset origination with the liabilities raising. It attempts to break down "silos" in the organisation, in that asset type is relevant and appropriate to funding type and source (and vice versa).

Strategic ALM addresses a three-dimensional optimisation problem that we summarise as follows, in line with the requirements of the three key stakeholders of a bank:

- The liquidity and regulatory requirement aspects (Regulator);

- The NII/NIM aspects (Shareholder);
- The customer franchise aspects (Customer);

and must be a high-level, strategic discipline driven from the top down. It is by nature proactive and not reactive.

A key operating model decision is whether the ALM function should be a profit centre or a cost centre.

- If an ALM unit has a profit target of zero, it will act as a cost centre with a responsibility to minimise operating costs. This would be consistent with a strategy that emphasises commercial banking as the core business of the firm, and where ALM policy is concerned purely with hedging interest-rate and liquidity risk;
- The next stage is where the ALM unit is responsible for minimising the cost of funding. Any saving is measured as the difference between the funding costs of a full hedging policy and the actual policy that the ALM desk adopts. Under this policy, interest-rate risk limits are set that the ALM desk ensures the bank's operations do not breach;
- The final stage of development is to turn the ALM unit into a profit centre, with responsibility for optimising the funding policy within specified limits.

The op model decision is a key part of business development.

For a bank's funding structure to be assessed on an aggregate balance sheet approach, it must measure the quality and adequacy of the funding structure (liabilities) alongside the capital and asset side of the balance sheet. This gives a more holistic picture of the robustness and resilience of the funding model under stress. The robustness of funding is almost as much a function of the liquidity, maturity, and product type of the asset base as it is of the type and composition of the liabilities.

The following are key considerations of the ALM function:

- Liquid assets vs illiquid assets share;
- How much illiquid assets are funded by unstable and/or short-term liabilities;
- Breakdown of liabilities:
  o Retail deposits: stable and less stable;
  o Wholesale funding: secured, senior unsecured;
  o Capital: subordinated/hybrid; equity.

On the liability side, the ALCO will look at:

- Debt buybacks, especially of expensive instruments issued post-crash;
- Wider investor base;
- Private placement programme;
- Fit-for-purpose allocation of liquidity costs to business lines (FTP);
- Design and use of adequate stress testing policy and scenarios;

- Adequate risk management of intra-day liquidity risk;
- Strong public disclosure to promote market discipline.

On the asset side, strategic action could include:

- Increasing liquid assets as a share of the balance sheet (although liquidity and ROE concerns must be balanced);
- De-linking the bank – sovereign risk exposure connection;
  - The LCR doesn't have to be all sovereign debt;
- Avoiding lower loan origination standards as the cycle moves into the bull market phase;
- Addressing asset quality problems:
  - Ring-fenced NPLs and impaired loans? (A sort of "non-core" part of the balance sheet that indicates you are addressing the problem and looking at disposal);
- Review the bank's operating model. Retail/wholesale mix? Franchise viability? Comparative advantage?;
- Limit asset encumbrance: this contradicts pressure for secured funding.

Hedging

In theory hedging allows the bank to limit or offset losses in income arising from fluctuations in interest rates. From an "interest-rate risk" perspective, interest-rate swaps are the main hedging tool that a bank uses to "hedge" its balance sheet.

The "ponderous" orthodox hedging procedure is to use a "gross" approach:

- All fixed-rate assets are hedged via "pay fixed" and "receive floating" interest-rate swaps;
- All fixed-rate liabilities are hedged via "receive fixed" and "pay floating" interest-rate swaps.

Under a more strategic ALM approach, pairs of assets and liabilities are hedged individually. For example:

- An internal IRS together with the funding ticket for the asset is generated; OR
- The net exposure of the asset and corresponding liability is hedged, after allowing for behaviouralisation and tenor matching.

This benefits from natural hedges already in place, such as fixed-rate loans vs fixed-rate deposits and variable rate loans vs floating-rate deposits.

CONCLUSIONS

Asset-liability management is a discipline that is as old as banking itself, even if it was only articulated in formal terms fairy recently. The traditional approach to it was essentially reactive in nature, however, with business lines originating assets and liabilities that were then "risk managed" for interest-rate and liquidity risk by Treasury and Risk (and in some cases Finance) departments. As we noted in the chapter, this is not fit for purpose in the twenty-first century. In a bank, the balance sheet is everything, because the very survival of the institution depends on the balance sheet being robust and long-term viable. So for an ALM function to be able to carry out its function effectively, banks need to change practices in two areas:

- Bring credit risk policy under the aegis of the ALM function; and
- Move from a reactive to a more proactive ALM process whereby the origination of balance sheet assets and liabilities is more integrated and also under ALCO direction.

We term this more proactive approach Strategic ALM.

BIBLIOGRAPHY

Bitner, J. (1992). *Successful Bank Asset-Liability Management*, Wiley.

Butler, C. (1998). *Mastering Value-at-Risk*, FT Prentice Hall.

Cornyn, A., Mays, E. (eds.) (1997). *Interest Rate Risk Models: Theory and Practice*, Glenlake Publishing/Fitzroy Dearborn Publishers, Chapter 6, p. 15.

Greenbaum, S., Thakor, A. (1995). *Contemporary Financial Intermediation*, Dryden Press.

Gup, B., Brooks, R. (1993). *Interest Rate Risk Management*, Bankers Publishing Company and Probus Publishing Company.

Gup, B., Brooks, R. (1993). *Interest Rate Risk Management*, Irwin Professional Publishing.

Howe, D. (1992). *A Guide to Managing Interest-Rate Risk*, New York Institute of Finance.

Johnson, H. (1994). *Bank Asset/Liability Management*, Probus Publishing.

Kamakura Corporation (1998). *Asset & Liability Management: A Synthesis of New Methodologies*, Risk Publications.

Koch, T. (1988). *Bank Management*, Dryden Press.

Marshall, J., Bansal, V.K. (1992). *Financial Engineering*, New York Institute of Finance, Chapter 20.

Schaffer, S. (1991). "Interest Rate Risk", *Business Review*, Federal Reserve Bank of Philadelphia, May–June, pp. 17–27.

Sinkey, J. (1992). *Commercial Bank Financial Management*, 4th edition, Macmillan.

Stevenson, B., Fadil, M. (1995). "Modern Portfolio Theory: can it work for commercial loans?", *Commercial Lending Review*, 10(2), Spring, pp. 4–12.

Toevs, A., Haney, W. (1984). *Measuring and Managing Interest Rate Risk*, Morgan Stanley Publication.

Toevs, A., Haney, W. (1986). "Measuring and managing interest rate risk: a guide to asset/liability models used in banks and thrifts", in Platt, R. (ed.), *Controlling Interest Rate Risk, New Techniques and Applications for Money Management*, Wiley.

Wilson, J.S.G. (ed.) (1988). *Managing Banks' Assets and Liabilities*, Euromoney Publications.

Chapter

8

....

ASSET AND LIABILITY MANAGEMENT II: THE ALCO

We continue the discussion on bank asset-liability management (ALM) with a review of the asset–liability management committee (ALCO). ALCO has a specific remit to oversee all aspects of asset–liability management, from the front-office money market function, to back-office operations, and middle-office reporting and risk management. In the author's opinion it is the most important risk management committee in a bank because it is concerned wholly and solely with the balance sheet, more critically the long-term viability of the balance sheet. For this reason, an effective ALCO governance process is vital for every bank, irrespective of size or business model.

In this chapter we consider the traditional role of ALCO and then go on to present recommended best-practice principles, which may be applied in any bank.

TRADITIONAL ALCO MISSION

The ALM reporting process is overseen by the bank's ALCO. It is responsible for setting and implementing ALM policy. Its composition varies in different banks but usually includes heads of business lines as well as director-level staff such as the finance director. It also oversees direction on issues such as strategy and risk hedging policy.

Table 8.1 is a summary overview of the traditional responsibilities of ALCO.

ALCO will meet on a regular basis; the frequency depends on the type of institution but is usually once a month. The composition of ALCO varies by institution but may comprise the heads of Treasury, trading, and risk management, as well as the finance director. Representatives from the credit committee and loan syndication may also be present. A typical agenda would consider all the elements listed in Table 8.1. Thus, the meeting will discuss and generate action points on the following:

- Management reporting: this will entail analysing various management reports and either signing them off or agreeing items to be actioned. The issues to consider include the lending margin, interest income, variance from last projection, customer business, and future business. Current business policy with regard to lending and portfolio management will be reviewed and either continued or adjusted;
- Business planning: existing asset (and liability) books will be reviewed and future business directions drawn up. This will consider the performance of existing business, most importantly with regard to return on capital. The existing asset portfolio will be analysed from a risk–reward perspective, and a decision taken to continue or modify all lines of business. Any proposed new business will be discussed and – if accepted – in principle will

Table 8.1   ALCO traditional mission

Mission	Components
ALCO management and reporting	Formulating ALM strategy
	Management reporting
	ALCO agenda and minutes
	Assessing liquidity, gap, and interest-rate risk reports
	Scenario planning and analysis
	Interest income projection
Asset management managing	Bank liquidity book (CDs, bills)
	Managing FRN book
	Investing bank capital
ALM strategy	Yield curve analysis
	Money market trading
Funding and liquidity management	Liquidity policy
	Managing funding and liquidity risk
	Ensuring funding diversification
	Managing lending of funds
Risk management	Formulating hedging policy
	Interest-rate risk exposure management
	Implementing hedging policy using cash and derivative instruments
Internal Treasury function	Formulating transfer-pricing system and level
	Funding group entities
	Calculating the cost of capital

be moved on to the next stage.[1] At this stage, any new business will be assessed for projected returns, revenue, and risk exposure;

- Hedging policy: overall hedging policy will consider acceptable levels of risk exposure, existing risk limits, and use of hedging instruments. Hedging instruments also include derivative instruments. Many bank ALM desks find that their hedging requirements can be met using plain vanilla products such as interest-rate swaps and exchange-traded short-money futures contracts. The use of options and especially vanilla instruments such as FRAs[2] is much lower than one might think. Hedging policy takes into account the cash book revenue level, current market volatility levels, and

[1] New business will follow a long process of approval, typically involving all the relevant front-office, middle-office, and back-office departments of the bank and culminating in a "new products committee" meeting, at which the proposed new line of business will be either approved, sent back to the sponsoring department for modification, or rejected.
[2] See Chapter 6.

the overall cost of hedging. On occasion, certain exposures may be left unhedged because the costs associated with hedging them are deemed prohibitive. (This includes the actual cost of putting on the hedge as well as the opportunity cost associated with expected reduced income from the cash book.) Of course, hedging policy is formulated in coordination with overall funding and liquidity policy. Its final form must consider the bank's views of the following:

o Expectations on the future level and direction of interest rates;
o Balancing the need to manage and control risk exposure with the need to maximise revenue and income;
o Level of risk aversion, and the level of risk exposure the bank is willing to accept.

ALCO is dependent on management reporting from the ALM or Treasury desk – reports may be compiled by the Treasury middle office. The main report is the overall ALM report, showing the composition of the bank's ALM book. Other reports will look at specific business lines and consider the return on capital generated by these businesses. These reports will need to break

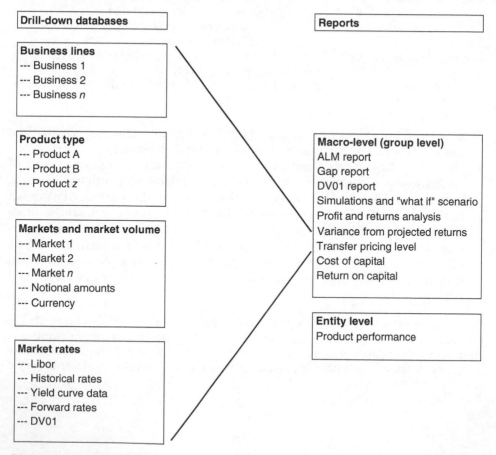

Figure 8.1   ALCO reporting input and output

down aggregate levels of revenue and risk by business line. Reports will also drill down by product type across business lines. Other reports will consider the gap, gap risk, the Value-at-Risk (VaR) or DV01 report, and credit risk exposures. Overall, the reporting system must be able to isolate revenues, return, and risk by country sector, business line, and product type. There is usually an element of scenario planning as well, which is expected performance under various specified macro-level and micro-level market conditions.

Figure 8.1 illustrates the general reporting concept.

ALCO GOVERNANCE BEST-PRACTICE PRINCIPLES

We consider here the role and best-practice governance structure for the bank's asset-liability committee or ALCO. But before we do, consider this question:

What executive committees have a responsibility for oversight of balance sheet risk?

- Executive committee;
- Risk management committee (CRO chaired);
- Credit risk committee;
- ALCO.

It is arguable that the only executive committee that is concerned wholly with balance sheet risk on a *strategic* and *integrated* basis (both sides of the balance sheet) is the Asset-Liability Committee (ALCO). No other executive committee focuses solely on balance sheet risk management. In essence, given its mandate, membership and expertise, it should be ALCO.

As well as considering ALCO itself, banks should also seek to ensure the most effective way to ensure above-satisfactory and effective governance of the bank from the Board's perspective.

ALCO principles

It is recommended that ALCO be constituted as a committee with Board-delegated authority, ranking on a par with the executive committee, responsible for management of a bank's balance sheet with respect to liquidity, funding, capital, interest rate, and foreign exchange (FX) risk. Ideally, it would also have an oversight or policy overview function for credit risk, but this recommendation is controversial among some bankers.

The main responsibilities of ALCO are:

- Approves policy and direction with respect to all aspects of balance sheet management;
- Provides strategy and direction with respect to balance sheet structure and shape;

- Approval authority for new products and processes (delegated to the new products committee);
- Guides the management of the bank's liquid asset buffer;
- Responsible for ensuring the bank complies with all regulatory requirements on liquidity and funding;
- Held monthly with exceptions in stressed environments when frequency can be increased.

The author's template ALCO Terms of Reference (ToR) is given at Appendix 8.1.

The asset-liability committee is mandated by executive authority to act as the primary risk committee responsible for asset–liability, liquidity, funding, and balance sheet management.

Managing risks: Liquidity, funding, capital, interest-rate, and FX risk management:

- Effectively understanding, valuing, and managing risks on the balance sheet;
- Production of data measures and monitoring of positions against limits set by ALCO;
- Managing risk exposure through effective execution;
- External market access function;
- Management of liquid asset buffer;
- Review of limit breaches and remedial action.

Providing Treasury support:

- Design and implementation of Treasury policies across the business and ensuring compliance;
- Producing analysis and papers for monthly ALCO.

Providing Treasury services:

- Proactive support and involvement to new product development and pricing decisions;
- Prudent management of risk in line with bank policies.

Reporting, responsibility, and transparency

- For oversight of balance sheet risk to be effective throughout the cycle, the operating model has to be transparent and **has to make clear who is responsible**;
- The balance sheet triumvirate approach (see Chapter 7), together with the authority of ALCO as operating *either* with Board-delegated authority *or* as a subcommittee of the Board, is the most effective because it is the only way to ensure that balance sheet metrics and exposure are at the forefront of governance culture *throughout the cycle*;
- The Board risk appetite statement (see Chapter 9) is the start of this process.

Organisation structure

The recommended organisation structure governing ALCO authority is shown in Figure 8.2.

The Board and technical competence

- Board members must be thoroughly attuned to balance sheet risk;
- The chairperson is not exempt (regulators note);
- Sustained through-the-cycle bank risk management dictates that the ultimate guardian of the balance sheet, ALCO, must not only be the premier executive risk committee of the bank but also the main driver of strategy and acceptable risk appetite;
- Approach strategy making by means of an integrated balance sheet approach – looking at both sides of the balance sheet;
- For the risk triumvirate, note that Treasury is the only part of the bank that oversees the whole balance sheet and crucially is both inward and outward facing.

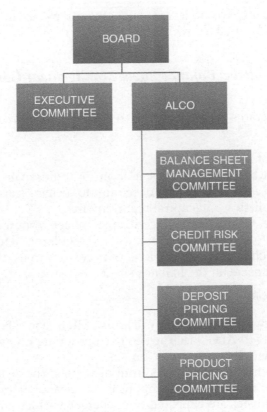

Figure 8.2   ALCO governance organisation

ALCO membership

Members include:
- Chief Executive Officer;
- Chief Financial Officer (Chair);
- Head of Treasury (Deputy Chair);
- Head of Corporate Banking;
- Head of Retail Banking;
- Head of Private Banking;
- CRO;
- Head of Strategy.

In attendance are:
- Head of ALM/Money Markets;
- Head of Liquidity Risk;
- Head of Valuation Control/Product Control;
- MD, Products & Marketing;
- Internal Auditor;

Secretariat: Business Manager to Head of Treasury or Liquidity Manager

In addition there are two important subcommittees of ALCO (for all but the smallest banks), detailed below.

ALCO subcommittee: Balance Sheet Management Committee (BSMCO)

The BSMCO operates as a subcommittee of ALCO. It is a technical ALM forum.

- The purpose of BSMCO is to:
  - Review the bank's balance sheet, monitor trends in deposits and earning assets, and assess the impact of economic scenarios on the group's NIM, assets, liabilities, and capital requirements;
  - Determine actions to manage balance sheet resources in the light of economic forecasts, market trends, and regulatory demands;
  - Discuss technical considerations with respect to capital, liquidity, and funding impacts on the balance sheet.

ALCO authorises BSMCO to:

- Investigate any activity within its Terms of Reference (ToR) and make recommendations to ALCO that it deems appropriate on any area within its remit where action is needed;
- Seek any information it requires from or request the attendance at any of its meetings of any director or employee of the bank (or group) and all directors and employees are expected to cooperate with any requests made by the committee.

In essence, BSMCO is necessary because ALCO has at most perhaps 2 hours a month to review the entire balance sheet (except where extraordinary ALCOs are called) ...

... this is not necessarily sufficient to review the detail or – paradoxically – see the wood for the trees.

The existence of BSMCO is designed to ensure that the detail does not "fall through the cracks". The membership may be comprised as:

- Head of Treasury (Chair);
- Deputy CFO;
- Deputy CRO;
- Head of Research or Strategy;
- Ad hoc as required from the business.

ALCO subcommittee: Deposit/Product Pricing Committee

The other recommended technical subcommittee of ALCO is the Product Pricing Committee/Deposit Pricing Committee. This is a smaller committee whose remit is to ensure that, as per the recommended model, "all pricing decisions are made by ALCO".

It is a committee operating as a subcommittee of ALCO, which has ultimate responsibility for all liabilities/products pricing decisions.

The products in question would in the first instance be customer deposit products.
This may be extended to customer asset products if deemed necessary.
The Product Pricing Committee/Deposit Pricing Committee has delegated authority to approve specific changes to standard rates for one-off transactions (for example, to improve a rate paid to a customer to retain a deposit).

Membership comprises:

- Treasury representative;
- Finance representative;
- Business line representative (retail and corporate banking).

Hedging policy

Overall hedging policy will consider the acceptable risk exposure, existing risk limits, and use of hedging instruments.

Hedging policy takes into account the cash book revenue level, current market volatility levels, and the overall cost of hedging. On occasion, certain exposures may be left unhedged because the cost associated with hedging them is deemed prohibitive. (This includes the actual cost of putting on the hedge as well as the opportunity cost associated with expected reduced income from the cash book.)

Hedging policy is formulated in coordination with overall funding and liquidity policy. Its final form will reflect the ExCo's views of the following:

- Expectations on the future level and direction of interest rates;
- Balancing the need to manage and control risk exposure with the need to maximise revenue and income;
- The level of risk aversion, and how much risk exposure the bank is willing to accept.

Best practice guidelines

The following PRA guidelines issued in January 2011 articulate best practice guidelines encouraged to be applied to ALCOs:

- Proactively controls the business in line with the firm's objectives; focuses on the entire balance sheet;
- Ensures risks remain within risk appetite;
- Considers the impact on earnings volatility of changing economic and market conditions;
- Ensures an appropriate funds transfer pricing mechanism that aligns to the firm's strategic objectives and risk appetite, and regularly reviews this mechanism;
- Acts as the arbitrator in the debate and challenge process between business lines;
- Focuses on effects of future plans/strategy at bank and business line level;
- Takes decisions to manage ALM risks or escalates issues to ExCo, rather than simply "observing" the risks;
- Ensures issues are fully articulated and debated;
- Considers recommendations from a tactical subcommittee (the ABC Bank BSMCO) that excludes the CEO and other ExCo members;
- Engages in active dialogue among various members and displays a strong degree of challenge;
- Minutes insight into the discussions and extent of challenge; does not only list action points.

Policy approval process

For non-small banks, it is recommended to submit technical issues to a "technical ALCO" or "Balance Sheet Management Committee" (BSMCO) first – provided this adds value to ALCO itself!

- Papers submitted by business lines should include a section that covers off all Treasury-related issues (capital, liquidity, funding, IRR, etc.):
  - All new business or new limits to make explicit reference and detail to Treasury funding implications (see over).
- "Socialisation" of paper to members:
  - Pre-positioning.
- Discussion and debate at ALCO followed by approval (or not).

Forward agenda

Certain items (such as liquidity policy, LAB policy, FTP policy, etc.) should be reviewed on a regular basis at ALCO, say every 6 or 12 months.

To facilitate adequate time for discussion, papers, analysis, etc. these should be part of a forward agenda that is set at the start of the year so that everyone is aware of what is coming up when.

Dates should also be set on the same day each month and diarised in advance.

Holding ALCO in the last week of the month rather than the first or second means at least that the ALCO deck will be for last month's data rather than the data from the month before.

Figure 8.3 is an example of a bank forward ALCO agenda; only a sample of standing items are shown here. A bank would have its specific list added to this template, at the frequency required.

The ALCO pack

Key pointers for the ALCO MI deck are:

- Make it succinct and as accessible as possible;
- Relegate detailed MI to an appendix and just have key indicators and summaries at the front;
- Compare packs and agendas where possible (not easy ...);
- Have a key message summary on each slide;
- Have forward agenda items;
- Include market data in summary fashion ... see the following examples.

ALCO and the Board paper summary

Ideally, the main ALCO pack (minus the papers and the appendices with a note "available on request") would be part of the Board papers – i.e. the balance sheet metrics and exposures with a 1-page summary of "main messages". If not, then ALCO delegated to Treasury should prepare a summary of 3–4 pages based on the main deck.

Revisit the MI pack

- Is it succinct, accessible, easy to read?
- Does it give the latest balance sheet information, within the first 5–6 pages, in a way that enables the reader to ascertain quickly what the current balance sheet risks are?
- *Does it help ALCO/ExCo do its job?*
- Is every item within it completely relevant and completely necessary?
- Is it completely bereft of spurious or surplus-to-requirement content?
- Is the summary risk metrics still fit for purpose? (regularly updated as relevant to bank business model and its current and expected environment)?

	Jan-15	Feb-15	Mar-15	Apr-15	May-15	Jun-15	Jul-15	Aug-15	Sep-15	Oct-15	Nov-15	Dec-15
Agenda item												
Market MI	x	x	x	x	x	x	x	x	x	x	x	x
RWA	x	x	x	x	x	x	x	x	x	x	x	x
Liquidity MI	x	x	x	x	x	x	x	x	x	x	x	x
Credit VaR	x	x	x	x	x	x	x	x	x	x	x	x
FTP curve			x				x			x			x
For review and approval												
FTP policy	x								x			
LAB policy		x									x	
LAB IRR limits			x						x			
Securities issuance policy												
For 2-weekly Treasury review												

Figure 8.3   Template for ALCO forward agenda planning

CONCLUSIONS

A bank is managed from the top down. The cultural attitude towards risk is driven from the top down. Hence, efficient management at operating levels requires clear strategy and direction from Board level. Once this is communicated, ALCO should be trusted to oversee operations and to have the final say on strategy and risk appetite. Clear direction must be set on what the bank is here to do. Of course, shareholders should proactively approve the Board's direction – not passively sign off on it – but the delegation is from the Board to ALCO. Therefore, the Board should set guidelines on risk appetite and delegate authority to ALCO to ensure this is carried out.

APPENDIX 8.1:

ALCO RECOMMENDED TERMS OF REFERENCE

Terms of Reference

Chair	• Chief Financial Officer In the absence of the Chief Financial Officer, the Head of Treasury will act as the meeting Chair. [If the Head of Treasury is unavailable, a suitable alternative for the Chair shall be appointed by the Chief Executive Officer.]
Members	• Chief Financial Officer • Chief Executive Officer • Head of Treasury • Global Head of Balance Sheet Management, Group Treasury, GROUP (or alternate) • Head of Corporate Banking • Head of Retail Banking • Head of Private Banking and Advice • Chief Risk Officer • Head of Strategy • MD Products and Marketing
Attendees	• Head of ALM/Money Markets • Head of Liquidity Risk • Head of Valuation Control/Product Control • [Head of Internal Audit]
Additional invitees	As appropriate.
Deputies	If a Member is unable to attend a meeting, he/she shall appoint a deputy to attend on his/her behalf. Such deputy's attendance shall not count towards the quorum and the deputy shall not hold the right to vote.
Quorum	Three members, at least one of whom shall be the Chief Financial Officer or the Chief Executive Officer and at least one of whom shall be either the MD Corporate or MD Retail.

Meeting frequency	Monthly and ad hoc as required by any member. Ad hoc meetings are permitted to take place via email if necessary. Rules regarding decision making and quorum remain the same as for face to face meetings.
Secretary	Provided by Treasury.
Committee authority	ALCO operates as a sub-committee of the Board.
Authority delegated by the Committee	ALCO may delegate any of its powers to a sub-committee consisting of two or more ALCO members. Any sub-committee so formed shall conform to any regulations that may be imposed on it by ALCO and the acts and proceedings of a sub-committee shall be reported to ALCO. ALCO shall review and approve the ToR of those committees to which it has delegated authority at least annually and on an ad hoc basis should material amendment be proposed. The ABC Bank Products Pricing Committee will report as a sub-committee of ALCO. The ABC Balance Sheet Management Committee will operate as a sub-committee of ALCO. Specific delegated authorities are set out within "Scope of the Board/Committee's oversight and responsibility".
Committee accountability	ALCO operates as a sub-committee of the Board and reports to the [Executive Committee/Board].
Escalation	Management decisions beyond this Committee's authority and matters which this Committee deems necessary for escalation will be escalated to the Board or appropriate other Board committees where relevant.
Purpose of the Committee	It is responsible for identifying, managing and controlling the bank's balance sheet risks and capital management in executing its chosen business strategy. Balance sheet risks are managed by setting limits monitoring exposures and implementing controls across the dimensions of capital, funding, and liquidity and non-traded interest rate risk. It is responsible for the implementation of ALCO strategy and policy for the bank's balance sheet.

Scope of the Committee's oversight and responsibility

Strategic overview
- Provide a single forum where the balance sheet risks of the bank can be monitored and managed.
- Ensure a consistency of approach across a range of Treasury issues.
- Establish risk appetite for the individual business lines and monitor exposures against limits.
- Provide oversight of business line Stress Testing.
- Provide a single forum to consider developments in Treasury policy and regulation.
- Approve significant transactions where appropriate.
- Ensure that the decisions and policies from the Board are fully adhered to.
- Ensure compliance with regulatory requirements.

Capital
- Monitor long-term RWA trends and oversee actions to optimise RWA levels.
- Monitor and review capital usage and return on capital metrics for each business against targets.
- Review capital budgets/forecasts by business to ensure compliance with Board strategy.
- Approve allocation of capital between businesses where appropriate.
- Review strategic transactions as required.
- Review proposed changes in bank risk policy and drive action as required.

Non-Trading Interest Risk and Foreign Currency Exposure
- Establish risk appetite and set appropriate business limits.
- Review principle positions, hedging strategies, and approve excesses as required.
- Review proposed changes in Board policy and drive action as required.
- Review the effects of stress tests and the potential impact of significant external events on interest rate and FX exposure.

Liquidity and funding
- Establish liquidity risk appetite and set appropriate business limits (where measurable) and targets.
- Set liquidity risk tolerances via specific metric limits, at bank, corporate banking, retail banking, and business line level.
- Review liquidity and funding positions by business (where possible) against limits and approve excesses as required.
- Review liquidity and funding budgets/forecasts by business to ensure compliance with Group strategy.
- Review stress testing and underlying assumptions. Consider whether alterations to modelling scenarios are required.
- Approve and sign off on the bank's Contingency Funding Plan.
- Approve the sign off Treasury Funding Policy statements.

Pricing
- Support business pricing strategy through transparent identification and communication of liquidity, funding and capital costs.
- Review and monitor portfolio pricing initiatives and implications for strategic balance sheet management.
- Review and challenge margin trends/ movements.
- Ensure that pricing methodologies remain appropriate, including the FTP and RAROE pricing model (where appropriate), particularly the assumptions of funding costs.

Intra Group Limits (IGLs)
- [For GROUP entities] Oversight, approval and monitoring of all intra-group limits and limit usage by business lines and [subsidiaries for GROUP entities]

Internal funds pricing regime
- Approve the Bank's internal funds pricing regime ("FTP") and sign off the FTP policy on a semi-annual basis.
- Delegate authority for FTP implementation to Treasury.
- Approve and sign off FTP policy statements for Retail Banking and Corporate Banking.

Other

- Approve all funding cost re-charge mechanisms.
- Other issues relating to the management of financial risk and the balance sheet, as the Chair and members identify from time to time.
- Credit risk is within the scope of ALCO governance to the extent that it entails high level reporting and review of key credit risk parameters which have implications for RWA reporting and trends.
- Promote and ensure a culture of good corporate governance.
- Escalation of issues to the Board where necessary.

Board Administration/ Secretariat

The Treasury team is responsible for meeting administration.

The draft agenda for each meeting is agreed with the Head of Treasury [and the Chief Financial Officer] in advance of meetings. Papers are circulated to Members and Attendees a minimum of two business days before each meeting. Draft minutes and agreed actions are circulated for approval as soon as possible after each meeting, preferably within a period of one week.

The minutes of the meeting shall include:

- A record of all material issues discussed and agreed by the Committee;
- All agreed actions and items approved by the Committee; and
- Any matters which require escalation.

The Chair of the meeting has responsibility for ensuring the meeting minutes are reviewed before circulation to the Members and Attendees for review and comment. The minutes from the previous Committee meeting will be submitted for formal approval at its next meeting.

Copies of the approved minutes and record sets for all meetings are retained by the secretary.

Chapter

9

....

BANK LIQUIDITY RISK MANAGEMENT I[1]

---

[1] This chapter was co-written with Chris Westcott.

The western world's banking system was, in some jurisdictions at least, on the brink of collapse in September and October 2008, in the wake of the Lehman bankruptcy. Intervention by governments, which in some cases extended to a blanket guarantee of banks' complete liabilities, prevented this collapse from taking place. In the aftermath of the crisis, national regulators and the Bank for International Settlements (BIS) circulated consultative papers and recommendations that addressed new requirements on bank capital, liquidity, and risk management. The United Kingdom's Financial Services Authority (FSA) was perhaps most demanding; in its Policy Statement 09/16, which was issued in October 2009, it outlined measures on capital treatment, liquidity requirements, and stress testing that implied a fundamental change in the bank's business model for the future.

In this chapter, we discuss the implications for banks of the new emphasis on risk management of the regulators and the BIS committee, the latter of whom issued "Basel III" rules in September 2010 for implementation from 2015 onwards. We also provide our recommendations on how banks can go about meeting these requirements in a way that generates sustained return on capital. This chapter looks at the fundamentals of liquidity risk management, and what its basic principles need to be in the light of current central bank and regulatory requirements.

BEST-PRACTICE LIQUIDITY RISK MANAGEMENT FRAMEWORK

The first step in undertaking effective and fit-for-purpose liquidity risk management is to understand precisely what it is. We define liquidity risk as:

> the risk that a bank may be unable to meet its obligations as and when they fall due.

At all times a bank must be able to service its obligations as they arise, on both sides of the balance sheet. This means having the ability to be able to fund assets throughout their life, and being able to meet demand for withdrawals of liabilities as and when they arise. With respect to the former, these can be very long-dated assets such as residential mortgages and project finance loans, as well as committed but as yet undrawn assets such as credit cards or contingency funding lines. A large proportion of customer liabilities are demand deposits, current accounts ("checking accounts" or money transmission accounts – MTAs), or instant-access savings accounts, so a bank needs to be able to meet requests for withdrawals.

The challenge of bank liquidity management is a simple one to understand: have available funding for very long periods (a project finance loan may have a 50-year maturity) and be able to meet requests for withdrawal of that funding at immediate notice.

It is important to make the distinction between liquidity and funding. Funding is a point in time concept:

- The liquidity characteristics of an asset or liability *also* take into account *term* and *marketability* considerations;
- A portfolio of 10-year mortgages could be funded by either 1-month inter-bank deposits or the proceeds of long-term senior debt issuance;
- The inter-bank deposits may well provide cheap funding, but they create a liquidity risk;
- Long-term senior debt is a good source of both funding and liquidity to a bank, but is likely to be expensive.

This trade-off between risk and reward is at the heart of the liquidity risk management challenge facing bank Treasurers.

The starting point of a bank's liquidity risk management framework must be the Board risk appetite statement. This will be the document approved by the Board that states what appetite the bank has for risk exposures across the balance sheet, including liquidity risk. It will describe both qualitative and quantitative appetites and limits. An example of a Board risk appetite summary template created by the author is shown as Figure 9A. The limits for liquidity risk appetite are shown in the third box.

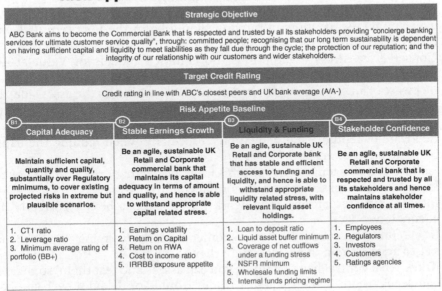

Risk appetite framework overview template

Strategic Objective			
ABC Bank aims to become the Commercial Bank that is respected and trusted by all its stakeholders providing "concierge banking services for ultimate customer service quality", through: committed people; recognising that our long term sustainability is dependent on having sufficient capital and liquidity to meet liabilities as they fall due through the cycle; the protection of our reputation; and the integrity of our relationship with our customers and wider stakeholders.			
Target Credit Rating			
Credit rating in line with ABC's closest peers and UK bank average (A/A-)			
Risk Appetite Baseline			
B1 Capital Adequacy	B2 Stable Earnings Growth	B3 Liquidity & Funding	B4 Stakeholder Confidence
Maintain sufficient capital, quantity and quality, substantially over Regulatory minimums, to cover existing projected risks in extreme but plausible scenarios.	Be an agile, sustainable UK Retail and Corporate commercial bank that maintains its capital adequacy in terms of amount and quality, and hence is able to withstand appropriate capital related stress.	Be an agile, sustainable UK Retail and Corporate bank that has stable and efficient access to funding and liquidity, and hence is able to withstand appropriate liquidity related stress, with relevant liquid asset holdings.	Be an agile, sustainable UK Retail and Corporate commercial bank that is respected and trusted by all its stakeholders and hence maintains stakeholder confidence at all times.
1. CT1 ratio 2. Leverage ratio 3. Minimum average rating of portfolio (BB+)	1. Earnings volatility 2. Return on Capital 3. Return on RWA 4. Cost to income ratio 5. IRRBB exposure appetite	1. Loan to deposit ratio 2. Liquid asset buffer minimum 3. Coverage of net outflows under a funding stress 4. NSFR minimum 5. Wholesale funding limits 6. Internal funds pricing regime	1. Employees 2. Regulators 3. Investors 4. Customers 5. Ratings agencies

Figure 9A   Template for Board risk appetite statement

Source: Choudhry (2012).

Principles of bank liquidity

A bank's funding structure should be assessed on an aggregate balance sheet approach. The quality and adequacy of the funding structure (liabilities) should be measured alongside the capital and asset side of the balance sheet. This gives a more holistic picture of the robustness and resilience of the funding model, under "business as usual" AND in stress.

Robustness of funding is almost as much a function of the liquidity, maturity, and product type of the asset base as it is of the type and composition of the liabilities.

The list below details some of the key principles of bank liquidity:

- Fund illiquid assets with core customer deposits;
- Where core customer deposits are not available, use long-term wholesale funding sources;
- Maintain "liquidity buffers" to cater for both firm-specific and market-wide stresses;
- All legal entities and geographies are required to be "stand-alone" with regard to liquidity and funding;
- Policy is centralised. The liquidity risk management framework is "owned" by Group Management Board;
- Liquidity contingency plans are required for all legal entities and geographies;
- Create your deposit base and raise your deposits BEFORE you start your lending. The traditional principle of banking … ;
- Do not overrely on wholesale funding. Run a sensible term structure wherever you do use it: more of funding should be in the long term (>1 year) rather than in the short term;
- Conservative stress assumptions: no complex models or Value-at-Risk models to model future risk losses;
- Be aware of all exposures (on the *liability* side as well as the asset side). For example, sponsoring an SPV creates a reputational, rather than contractual obligation to provide funding;
- Be aware of reputational obligations, especially when lending the bank's name to another entity;
- Collateral management and optimisation: be aware of the liquidity of collateral under stressed as well as normal conditions;
- Internal transfer pricing framework ("FTP") must be set correctly and adequately;
- Be careful when attracting core customer deposits. If paying above the market to attract them, how "core" are they?;
- Know what central bank facilities you can assess and test them, so that you can access them instantly (and without trouble or delay) if ever you need them;
- Liquidity risk is NOT a single metric. It is an array of metrics, and all are needed to get the most accurate picture. This is especially true for multinational banks and/or banks with multiple business lines. Regularly review the suite and ask the question: does it tell what is necessary to know about balance sheet risk?

Liquidity risk management

The objective of liquidity risk management is to ensure that there is always enough cash available or assets that can be readily converted into cash to meet both withdrawals by depositors and/or drawdowns on assets.

Successful liquidity management provides answers to the following questions:

- Are assets held in a form to enable them to be readily converted into cash to meet demands for repayment from depositors?
- Does the bank have enough cash available to meet customer drawdowns on loan commitments?
- Does the bank have enough cash available to fund increased drawdowns under revolving credit facilities?

While liquidity risk management is a straightforward conceptual challenge, there are many questions to answer, such as:

- How do you treat assets and liabilities with no fixed maturity?
- What do you do with undrawn commitments?
- How do you act in normal and stressed situations?
- How long should the liquidity time horizon be?
- How do you decide which assets can be readily converted into cash?
- How do you measure the liquidity position of a bank on an ongoing basis?
- How much liquidity risk should banks take?
- What is the role of regulators?

Effective liquidity risk management must do all of the following:

- Define and understand liquidity risk;
- Learn lessons about liquidity management from past crises;
- Understand the role of liquidity risk management;
- Put in place effective strategy, policy, and process;
- Define and establish liquidity risk tolerance limits and know regulatory expectations;
- Have an effective funding strategy;
- Specify and report liquidity risk exposure metrics;
- Forecast institution-specific and market-wide stress scenarios.

Liquidity: pre-2008 crisis

It was generally accepted that banks should hold a buffer of high quality assets that they could transfer into cash at any time to cover the fallout from firm-specific or market-wide stresses.

However, with the assumption of continuous liquidity, the amount of the buffer maintained by banks just kept on falling. This is shown for UK banks in Figure 9.1.

Bank liquidity risk management was characterised by:

- *Leverage*: a small capital base is levered up into an asset pool that can be 10, 20, 30 times greater, or even higher;

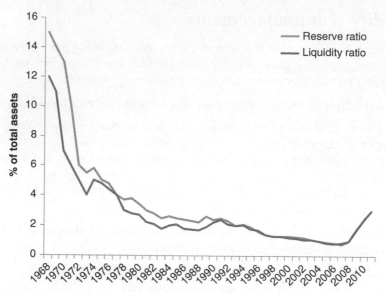

Figure 9.1   UK banks' liquidity ratios 1968–2010
Source: Bank of England.

- *Maturity transformation*, or the "gap": essentially funding short to lend long. A function of the conventional positively sloping yield curve. Which by definition requires an assumption of … ;
- *Continuous liquidity*: the assumption that one will always be able to rollover funding as due;
- *Liquidity asset buffer*: not big or liquid enough.

In the bull market, the focus shifted from liabilities (if ever that was the focus) to assets and lower loan origination standards. Liquidity was assigned a lower and lower priority because it is assumed to be continuous. Basel I and II addressed risky assets and capital in detail, but not liquidity. There were very few bank failures between the early 1990s and 2007–2008, as shown in the histogram below – convincing regulators that their approach was right.

The Basel Committee did not completely ignore liquidity risk though, as a paper on Sound Practices for Liquidity Management was issued in 2000, as summarised in Figures 9.2 and 9.3.

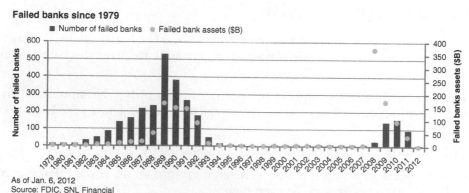

As of Jan. 6, 2012
Source: FDIC, SNL Financial

Risk management area	Specific principle – each bank should...
Developing a structure for managing liquidity	✓ have an agreed strategy for the day to day management of liquidity and the strategy should be communicated throughout the organisation ✓ The Board should approve the strategy and policies related to the management of liquidity ✓ have a management structure in place to execute the liquidity strategy ✓ have adequate information systems for measuring, monitoring, controlling, and reporting liquidity risk
Measuring and monitoring net funding requirements	✓ establish a process for the ongoing measuring and monitoring of net funding requirements ✓ analyse liquidity using a variety of "what-if" scenarios ✓ review frequently the assumptions utilised in managing liquidity to determine that they continue to be valid
Managing market access	✓ periodically review its efforts to establish and maintain relationships with liability holders to maintain the diversity of liabilities and aim to ensure its capacity to sell assets

Figure 9.2   Basel Committee principles from 2000, part I

Risk management area	Specific principle
Contingency planning	✓ have contingency plans in place that address the strategy for handling liquidity crises
Foreign currency liquidity management	✓ have a measurement, monitoring and control system for its liquidity positions for each major currency in which it is active ✓ set and regularly review limits on the size of its cash flow mismatches over particular time horizons for foreign currencies in aggregate and for each significant individual currency in which the bank operates
Internal controls	✓ have an adequate system of internal controls over its liquidity risk management process
Public disclosure	✓ have in place a mechanism for ensuring that there is an adequate level of disclosure about the bank to manage public perception of the organisation and its soundness
Role of supervisors	✓ Supervisors should conduct an independent evaluation of a bank's strategies, policies, procedures, and practices related to the management of liquidity

Figure 9.3   Basel Committee principles from 2000, part II

What was lacking was:

- An internationally harmonised set of standards establishing minimum liquidity requirements (including metrics) and a level playing field;
- Reference to establishing a liquidity risk tolerance (and appetite);
- The design and use of *severe*, but plausible, stress test scenarios;
- The need for a robust and operational contingency funding plan;
- The management of intra-day liquidity risk and collateral;
- The identification and management of the full range of liquidity risks including contingent liquidity risks;
- A funding strategy that provides effective diversification;
- The necessity to allocate liquidity costs, benefits, and risks to all significant business activities;
- A bank should actively monitor and control liquidity risk exposures across legal entities, currencies, and business lines;
- Supervisors that are prepared to intervene when necessary.

Liability side of the balance sheet

On the liability side, a bank should:

- Have a genuinely robust capital and funding management policy and procedure;
- Higher capital levels allow banks to withstand loan losses. A better quality balance sheet reduces the probability of loan defaults and lower loss given default. Both increase investor confidence and lead to lower funding costs.

Manage active liabilities, including:

- Debt buybacks, especially instruments:
  - Issued expensively post-crash;
  - No longer qualifying as Tier 2 capital;
- Develop and widen its investor base;
- Develop a private placement programme;
- Not necessarily "sustainable" funding but is a term funding outlet that diversifies the liability base;
- Liability and funding strategy tied in with the impacts of Basel III liquidity metrics.

It must be noted that funding is *not* a substitute for capital.

Naturally, approaches to liquidity management vary from bank to bank and market to market, although the following goals are common to many banks when it comes to asset management and liquidity:

- Increase liquid assets as share of balance sheet;
- De-link the bank to avoid the sovereign risk exposure connection;
- Reduce leverage;
- Consider reducing balance sheet size;
- Review the bank's operating model;

- Address asset quality problems;
- Limit asset encumbrance: this contradicts pressure for secured funding.

One possible approach could be to ring-fence non-performing and impaired loans. This indicates the bank is addressing the problem and looking at disposal of low quality assets.

Sources of liquidity

Bank funding instruments and sources of liquidity vary considerably depending on the operating model of the bank in question, but in essence they fall into two types: customer funds and wholesale funds. We would not need to make any further distinction if the different types within each category all exhibited similar behavioural characteristics with respect to their tenor. However, they do not, which is why a proper understanding of customer and wholesale types is necessary.

Banks fund their balance sheet using a variety of liability types. The liquidity value of each type is different, and in some cases the behavioural aspect of a certain type of liability renders it a more stable and long-term form of funding than would be implied by its contractual maturity. For this reason, regulators review liquidity management principles on both a contractual and behavioural basis.

When supplying liquidity metrics to the regulator, banks include historical analysis of types of liabilities – such as retail current accounts – to demonstrate their stability. Basel III guidelines refer to "stable" and "non-stable" funds, whereas the UK Prudential Regulatory Authority speaks of "sticky" and "non-sticky" funds (termed by it as Type B and Type A funds, respectively).

Retail current accounts are the best example of this. They are contractually payable on demand (immediate maturity), but observation of their behaviour reveals that typically customers maintain large stable balances in such accounts over a long time period. Therefore, it is necessary to treat a proportion of the amount of such liabilities as "term funding". The exact amount and tenor is a function of the historical statistical behaviour specific to each bank. The Treasury and Risk functions need to understand their different liabilities behaviour and observe over time before they can draw conclusions.

It is apparent that some forms of liabilities have greater term liquidity value for a bank than others. At one end of the scale are retail current accounts. At the other end are short-term unsecured wholesale liabilities, sourced in the inter-bank market, which have much more volatile characteristics in stressed market conditions and therefore are less valuable for liquidity management purposes. This assumption is based on historical observation, when such funds were seen to flow out much more aggressively than other funding types during stress events, and also because of a perception that wholesale market or "professional" depositors are deemed to be savvier when it comes to anticipated stress events.

THE LIQUIDITY POLICY STATEMENT

Business best practice dictates that a bank formally documents its liquidity policy. This will articulate the bank's approach to and appetite for liquidity risk, the actions it should follow to maintain liquidity safety, and the contingent actions to follow in the event of stressed conditions in the financial markets. We provide a template for bank liquidity policy here with a series of illustrations. They are self-explanatory and applicable to a conventional medium-sized commercial bank.

The basic principles of the policy statement are shown in Figures 9.4 to 9.8. Figure 9.5 shows the alternative actions that can be taken in the event of liquidity stress. Figure 9.9 is the summary liquidity risk reporting template.

Measuring bank liquidity risk: key metrics

As we noted above, given that bank asset–liability management is as much an art as a science, it is vital that banks use a range of liquidity measures for risk estimation and forecasting. In this section, we list seven baseline liquidity metrics, which all banks, irrespective of their size or line of business, should adopt and monitor as a matter of course. These are:

- Liquidity ratio;
- Loan-to-deposit ratio;
- 1-week and 1-month liquidity ratios;

The liquidity policy statement is the go-to reference that explains and demonstrates how a bank's integrated approach to liquidity management is performed.

Liquidity objective: To ensure that the bank will always be able to maintain or generate sufficient cash resources to meet its payment obligations in full as they fall due, on acceptable terms.

- Reflects the bank's liquidity strategy.
- Reflects the bank's specific risk appetite.

Requirement to review and update policy on stress testing and scenario analysis:
- Reliability of its assumptions
- Basis on which the set is used.

Test assumptions on readily available liquidity. These might include:
- Repo – government bonds, bank-name securities, etc.
- Sales of such securities
- Sales of less liquid assets.

| Liquidity policy statement |
| Organisational structure |
| Roles and responsibilities |
| Procedures |
| Methodologies |
| Underlying assumptions |
| Reporting |

Figure 9.4   Liquidity policy statement: basic framework

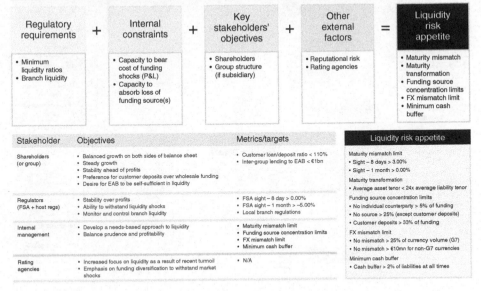

Figure 9.5 Liquidity policy statement: basic framework

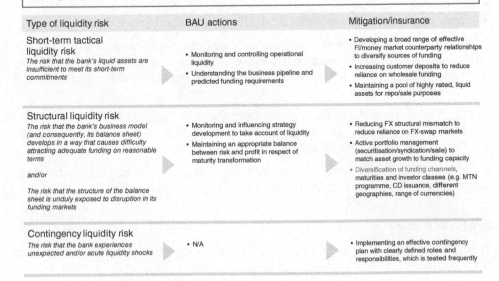

Figure 9.6 Liquidity policy statement: basic framework

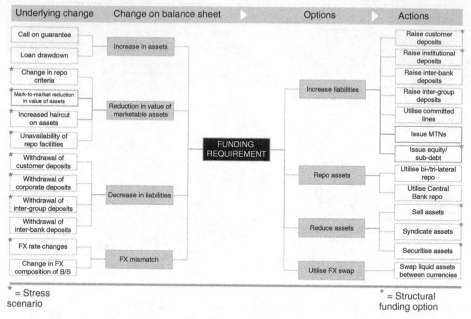

Beware: any changes in the composition of the balance sheet determine the bank's short-term and long-term funding requirements, which can be met in a variety of ways depending on the magnitude and urgency.

Figure 9.7 Liquidity policy statement: basic framework

- Cumulative liquidity model;
- Liquidity risk factor;
- Concentration report;
- Inter-entity lending report.

These reports measure and illustrate different elements of liquidity risk. For consolidated or group banking entities, reports must be at country level, legal entity level, and group level. Taken together, on aggregate the reports should provide sufficient detail on:

- The exposure of the bank to funding rollover or "gap" risk;
- The daily funding requirement, and what it is likely to be at a forward date;
- The extent of "self-sufficiency" of a branch or subsidiary.

Liquidity reports also help in providing early warning of any likely funding stress points. We examine them individually.

Liquidity ratio

A bank's liquidity ratio is the basic asset–liability gap ratio. A liquidity report for a commercial bank is shown in Figure 9.10.

The liquidity gap value shown in the report is the assets minus the liabilities for each tenor bucket. The "total available funds" number is the liquidity

Structural liquidity management should be carried out by ALCO, within the parameters set out in this liquidity policy statement. Tactical liquidity management is performed by Treasury under delegated authority from ALCO (Head of Treasury is member of ALCO).

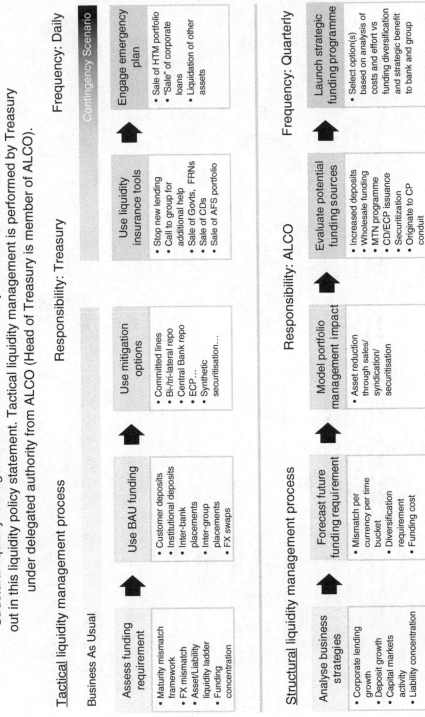

Figure 9.8 Liquidity policy statement: basic framework

Executive summary liquidity risk reporting template

Maturity mismatch

Purpose: To measure the net funding requirement (or surplus) per maturity bucket. This is the main regulatory requirement for liquidity measurement.

Measure: Measures the net cash flow for each maturity bucket.

Analysis: In the short term, when commitments (cash outflows) exceed liquid assets (cash inflows), the money markets desk needs to raise additional funding. In the longer term, structural imbalances, ALCO will determine the appropriate funding strategy.

Maturity mismatch ladder

	Sight	8 day	1 month	3 months	6 months	1 year	3 years	5 years	5 years+	TOTAL
Inflows	805	383	273	268	143	129	276	657	742	3,675
Outflows	980	813	838	1,563	277	52	11	0	0	4,533
Mismatch	(175)	(430)	(570)	(1,295)	(134)	77	265	657	742	(858)

FX mismatch

Purpose: To measure the gap between funding and lending in each currency.

Measure: Funding minus lending, per currency.

Analysis: By measuring FX mismatch, the bank gains an understanding of its exposure to the risk that FX swap markets become illiquid which could force a large open FX position or make it difficult to meet commitments in a particular currency.

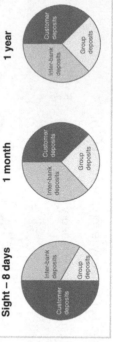

Funding − Lending = FX mismatch

Currency	Mismatch
USD	956
EUR	(150)
GBP	(450)

Asset/liability liquidity ladder

Purpose: To measure the asset liquidity and likely stickiness of liabilities.

Measure: Each asset/liability type (per COA) is rated based on size of holding, contractual maturity, behavioural stickiness, yield, cost to liquidate.

Analysis: A detailed understanding of the attributes and behaviour of the bank's balance sheet allows ALCO to make better informed strategic choices.

Liquid — Illiquid

Asset: Cash, Gilts, FI FRNs, CDS, ECB Eligible ABS, Other ABS, Corp Loans, LGS, Property

Liability: Bank deposits, Customer deposits (10%), Institutional deposits, Customer deposits (90%)

Short-term — Long-term

Funding concentration

Purpose: To measure the relative concentration of each funding source.

Measure: % concentration of each funding source per maturity bucket.

Analysis: Analysing funding concentration risk allows the bank to develop effective diversification strategies.

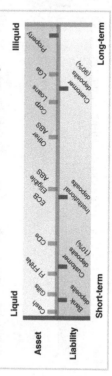

Sight – 8 days   1 month   1 year

Figure 9.9 Liquidity policy statement: basic framework

EUR '000
Bank Liquidity Report
28-Nov-10

	Sight	2 - 8 Days	9 Days - 1 Month	1 - 3 Months	3 - 6 Months	6 Mths to 1 Yr	1 - 3 Years	3 - 5 Years	+5 Years	Total
Corporate Current / Call	24,289	0	0	0	0	0	0	0	0	24,289
Corporate Time Loan	28,433	14,203	151,471	106,637	98,959	47,608	357,872	573,993	642,563	2,021,738
Government Current/Call	342	0	0	0	0	0	0	0	0	342
Government Time Loan	250	3	805	63	3,383	2,942	12,656	7,016	76,853	103,971
Interbank Current / Call	41,752	0	0	0	0	0	0	0	0	41,752
Interbank Time Loan	339,276	201,745	6,251	31,906	18,704	28,428	11,971	0	0	638,281
Repos	0	0	0	47,500	0	0	0	0	0	47,500
Intergroup Current / Call	4,445	0	0	0	0	0	0	0	0	4,445
Intergroup Time Loan	210,177	348,414	277,964	76,268	13,981	30,047	156	101	0	957,108
Marketable Secs & CDs - <1Mth to Mat	5,009	0	55,358	0	0	0	0	0	0	60,367
Retail Current / Call	8,215	0	0	0	0	0	0	0	0	8,215
Retail Time Loan	238	41	221	2,643	2,427	310	6,294	38,755	10,204	61,133
Additional Corporate Time Lending	0	8	1,313	43	624	0	21,608	7,857	75,724	107,177
Receivables	0	0	0	0	0	0	0	0	0	0
Total Assets	**662,426**	**564,414**	**493,383**	**265,060**	**138,078**	**109,335**	**410,557**	**627,722**	**805,344**	**4,076,318**
Corporate Current / Call	51,033	0	0	12,758	0	0	0	0	0	63,791
Corporate Time Deposit	32,303	122,955	114,627	299,551	28,387	928	0	0	0	598,751
Government Current / Call	1,946	0	0	0	0	0	0	0	0	1,946
Government Time Deposit	2,056	8,112	24,391	23,503	22,687	1,200	0	0	0	81,949
Interbank Current / Call	82,087	0	0	0	0	0	0	0	0	82,087
Interbank Time Deposit	83,898	83,684	349,461	86,979	23,967	1,205	0	0	0	629,194
Repos	0	0	0	50,000	0	0	0	0	0	50,000
Intergroup Current / Call	47,095	0	0	0	0	0	0	0	0	47,095
Intergroup Time Deposit	302,879	418,383	629,609	225,314	88,464	78,769	375	0	0	1,743,993
Retail Current / Call	65,273	0	0	16,318	0	0	0	0	0	81,591
Retail Time Deposit	203	54,128	167,090	683,288	27,925	13,273	9,224	0	0	955,131
Additional Govt / Local Authority Time Deposits	8,656	9,319	50,508	82,531	15,252	8,500	1,000	0	0	175,766
Share Capital	0	0	0	0	0	0	0	0	0	0
Payables	0	0	0	0	0	0	0	0	0	0
Total Liabilities	**677,429**	**696,581**	**1,335,886**	**1,480,242**	**206,682**	**103,875**	**10,599**	**0**	**0**	**4,511,294**

0.17313541781

-0.0136

Ratio Calculation

	O/N	8 Day	1 Month
Marketable Securities		630,536	630,536
Repos		0	0
CD'S		353,219	353,219
Unutilised Commitments	39,000	(55,520)	(55,520)
Liquidity Gap	(55,520)	(15,003) (147,170)	(989.63)
Total Available Funds	(70,523)	(61,438) 781,065	4,511,294
Total Liabilities	4,511,294	4,511,294	4,511,294

Liquidity Ratio

		O/N	8 Day	1 Month
Liquidity Ratio		-1.56%	17.31%	-1.36%
Internal Limit			3.00%	3.00%	-3.00%
Regulatory Authority Limit			0.00%	0.00%	-5.00%

Figure 9.10 Bank liquidity report showing 8-day and 1-month liquidity ratios

gap, plus "marketable securities" such as government bonds, bank bonds, and CDs, minus any committed facilities that are as yet undrawn. The liquidity ratio calculation itself is the "total available funds" value, which is +781,065 for the 8-day bucket and –61,438 for the 30-day bucket, divided by the "total liabilities" value, which is 4,511,294. This gives ratios of 17.31% and –13.6% for the two buckets, respectively, which are above the bank regulators limits of 0.00% and –5.00%. In the case of this bank, the liquidity ratios must not fall below these limit levels.

Note that it is the "liquidity gap" element that drives the 30-day ratio to a lower level than the 8-day ratio. In other words, the bigger the gap, the lower the ratio; this is why regulators place limits on liquidity ratios, so that banks are required to maintain asset–liability gaps at manageable levels.

Loan-to-deposit ratio (LTD)

This is the standard and commonly used metric, typically reported monthly. It measures the relationship between lending and customer deposits, and is a measure of the self-sustainability of the bank (or the branch or subsidiary). A level above 100% is an early warning sign of excessive asset growth; of course, a level below 70% implies excessive liquidity and a potentially inadequate return on funds.

The LTD is a good measure of the contribution of customer funding to the bank's overall funding; however, it is not predictive and does not account for the tenor, concentration, and volatility of funds. As such, it is insufficient as a liquidity risk measure on its own and must be used in conjunction with the other measures.

1-week and 1-month liquidity ratios

These are standard liquidity ratios that are commonly measured against a regulatory limit requirement. An example of a report for a group-type entity comprised of four subsidiaries is shown in Figure 9.11.

Country	1-week gap USD mm	1-week liquidity This week	Limit excess	1-month liquidity This week	Limit excess
F	–1,586	–22.83%	–30.00%	–39.11%	–50.00%
D	188	15.26%	0.00%	1.62%	–5.00%
H	786	22.57%	0.00%	19.12%	–5.00%
G	550	53.27%	25.00%	69.83%	25.00%
Regional total	–62	–0.48%		–10.64%	

Figure 9.11   Sample liquidity ratio report

Liquidity ratios are an essential measure of "gap" risk. They show net cash flows, including the cash effect of liquidating "liquid" securities, as a percentage of liabilities, for a specific maturity "bucket". These are an effective measure of structural liquidity, with early warning of likely stress points.

A more detailed liquidity ratio report is shown in Figure 9.12. This shows the breakdown of cash inflows and outflows per time bucket, and also the liquidity ratio. The ratio itself is calculated by dividing the selected time bucket liability by the cumulative liability. So in this example the 30-day ratio of 17.3% is given by the fraction [781,065/4,511,294].

Cumulative liquidity model

This is an extension of the liquidity ratio report and is a forward-looking model of inflows, outflows, and available liquidity, accumulated for a 12-month period. It recognises and predicts liquidity stress points on a cash basis. A report such as this, like the liquidity ratios, will be prepared daily at legal entity level and group level.

Figure 9.13 is an example of a cumulative outflow output graph rising from the cumulative liquidity model. This gives a snapshot view of forward funding stress points.

Liquidity risk factor (LRF)

This measure shows the aggregate size of the liquidity gap: it compares the average tenor of assets to the average tenor of liabilities. It is also known as a "maturity transformation report". The ratio can be calculated using years or days, as desired. For example, Figure 9.14 is an example of the risk factor for a hypothetical bank, where the unit of measurement is days. In this example, (262/19) is slightly below 14.

The higher the LRF, the larger the liquidity gap, and the greater the liquidity risk.

It is important to observe the trend over time and the change to long-run averages, so as to get early warning of the build-up of a potentially unsustainable funding structure.

Concentration report and funding source report

This report shows the extent of reliance on single sources of funds. An excess concentration to any one lender, sector, or country is an early-warning sign of potential stress points in the event of a crash event.

An example of a concentration report is shown at Figure 9.15. In this example, Customer 1 is clearly the focus of a potential stress point, and a bank would need to put in a contingency in the event that this source of funds dried up.

EURO's
XYZ Bank, London - Liquidity Report
28-Nov-09

	Sight	2 - 8 Days	9 Days - 1 Month	1 - 3 Months	3 - 6 Months	6 Mths to 1 Yr	1 - 3 Years	3 - 5 Years	+5 Years	Total
Corporate Current / Call	24,289	0	0	0	0	0	0	0	0	24,289
Corporate Time Loan	28,433	14,203	151,471	106,637	98,959	47,608	357,872	573,993	642,563	2,021,738
Government Current/Call	342	0	0	0	0	0	0	0	0	342
Government Time Loan	250	3	805	63	3,383	2,942	12,656	7,016	76,853	103,971
Interbank Current / Call	41,752	0	0	0	0	0	0	0	0	41,752
Interbank Time Loan	339,276	201,745	6,251	31,906	18,704	28,428	11,971	0	0	638,281
Repos	0	0	0	47,500	0	0	0	0	0	47,500
Intergroup Current / Call	4,445	0	0	0	0	0	0	0	0	4,445
Intergroup Time Loan	210,177	348,414	277,964	76,268	13,981	30,047	156	101	0	957,108
Marketable Secs & CDs - <1Mth to Mat	5,009	0	55,358	0	0	0	0	0	0	60,367
Retail Current / Call	8,215	0	0	0	0	0	0	0	0	8,215
Retail Time Loan	238	41	221	2,643	2,427	310	6,294	38,755	10,204	61,133
Additional Corporate Time Lending	0	8	1,313	43	624	0	21,608	7,857	75,724	107,177
Receivables	0	0	0	0	0	0	0	0	0	0
Total Assets	**662,426**	**564,414**	**493,383**	**265,060**	**138,078**	**109,335**	**410,557**	**627,722**	**805,344**	**4,076,318**
Corporate Current / Call	51,033	0	0	12,758	0	0	0	0	0	63,791
Corporate Time Deposit	32,303	122,955	114,627	299,551	28,387	928	0	0	0	598,751
Government Current / Call	1,946	0	0	0	0	0	0	0	0	1,946
Government Time Deposit	2,056	8,112	24,391	23,503	22,687	1,200	0	0	0	81,949
Interbank Current / Call	82,087	0	0	0	0	0	0	0	0	82,067
Interbank Time Deposit	83,698	83,684	349,461	86,979	23,967	1,205	0	0	0	629,194
Repos	0	0	0	50,000	0	0	0	0	0	50,000
Intergroup Current / Call	47,095	0	0	0	0	0	0	0	0	47,095
Intergroup Time Deposit	302,879	418,383	629,809	225,314	88,464	78,769	375	0	0	1,743,993
Retail Current / Call	65,273	0	0	16,318	0	0	0	0	0	81,591
Retail Time Deposit	203	54,128	167,090	683,288	27,925	13,273	9,224	0	0	955,131
Additional Govt / Local Authority Time Deposits	8,656	9,319	50,508	82,531	15,252	8,500	1,000	0	0	175,766
Share Capital	0	0	0	0	0	0	0	0	0	0
Payables	0	0	0	0	0	0	0	0	0	0
Total Liabilities	**677,429**	**696,581**	**1,335,886**	**1,480,242**	**206,682**	**103,875**	**10,599**	**0**	**0**	**4,511,294**

Ratio Calculation

	Sight	Sight - 8 Days	Sight - 1 M
Marketable Securities	0	630,536	630,536
Repos Adj*	0	0	0
CD'S	0	353,219	353,219	GBP Denominated 39,000
Unutilised Commitments	(55,520)	(55,520)	(55,520)
Liquidity Gap	(15,003)	(147,170)	(989,273)
Total Available Funds	(70,523)	781,065	(61,438)
Total Liabilities	4,511,294	4,511,294	4,511,294

Liquidity Ratio	-1.56%	17.31%	-1.36%
Internal Limit	45	45	45
FSA Limit	3.00%	3.00%	-3.00%
	0.00%	0.00%	-6.00%
Stress testing 10% Fall in Marketable Securities		15.13%	-3.54%
Stress testing 10% Fall in Stickiness		17.32%	-2.79%
Stress testing Combined Effect of above		15.14%	-4.97%

LIQUIDITY GAP IS ASSETS MINUS LIABILITIES IN RELEVANT TENOR BUCKET

TOTAL AVAILABLE FUNDS IS LIQUIDITY GAP, PLUS MARKETABLE SECURITIES (FRNs), CDs AND COMMITTED FACILITIES THAT ARE AS YET UNDRAWN (WHICH IS SUBTRACTED)

434,976 TOTAL ALM GAP ALL TENORS

Figure 9.12 Liquidity report and liquidity ratio calculation

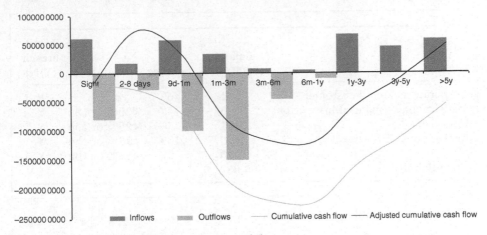

Figure 9.13 Cumulative liquidity model

Report date	Average liabilities tenor (days)	Average assets tenor (days)	Maturity transformation effect	Limit
30/09/2009	19	262	14	24

Figure 9.14 Liquidity risk factor

Customer	Deposit amount	Percentage of bank funding	Percentage of group external funding
	000s		
Customer 1	836,395	17.1%	2.6%
Customer 2	595,784	7.9%	1.8%
Customer 3	425,709	5.8%	1.3%
Customer 4	241,012	0.6%	0.7%
Customer 6	214,500	1.2%	0.7%
Customer 21	190,711	4.5%	0.6%
Customer 17	123.654	2.9%	0.4%
Customer 18	97,877	2.3%	0.3%
Customer 14	89,344	2.1%	0.3%
Customer 15	88,842	2.1%	0.3%
Customer 31	83,272	2.0%	0.3%
Customer 19	74,815	0.5%	0.2%
Customer 10	64,639	1.5%	0.2%
Customer 29	59,575	1.4%	0.2%
Customer 16	58,613	1.4%	0.2%
Total	6,562,116	53.3%	20.1%

Figure 9.15 Large depositors as percentage of total funding report

Source	Balance (€000,000s)	% Funding	Limit	Limit breach (Y/N)
Corporate and retail customer	1,891	46%	>40%	Y
Institutional – financial institutions	675	17%	<25% or 1bn	Y
Inter-bank	301	7%	<25% or 1bn	Y
Inter-group (NET balance)	400	10%	<25% or 1bn	Y
Other	20	0%	<25% or 1bn	Y
Total liabilities	**4,087**			

Figure 9.16　Funding source report

A related report is the funding source report, an example of which is shown in Figure 9.16.

This is a summary of the share of funding obtained from all the various sources, and should be used to flag potential concentration risk by sector.

Inter-entity lending report

This report is relevant for group and consolidated banking entities. As intra-group lending is common in banking entities, this report is a valuable tool used to determine how reliant a specific banking subsidiary is on group funds. An example of a report for a group entity is shown in Figure 9.17.

We have described the range of reports that represent essential metrics in the measurement of liquidity risk. They are the minimum management information that banks and group Treasuries will wish to prepare, both as business best practice and as part of adherence to new regulatory standards.

	Group Treasury		
As at (date)	Total borrowing	Total lending	Net intergroup lending
London	1,713,280	883,133	−830,157
Paris	3,345,986	978,195	−2,367,617
Frankfurt	17,026	195,096	178,089
Dublin	453,490	83,420	−370,070
HK	0	162,000	162,000
NY	690,949	1,516,251	825,302

Figure 9.17　Sample inter-company lending report

Summary liquidity report

For executive summary reporting to senior management, a bank may provide a one-sided report of the main liquidity metrics. An example of this is shown in Figure 9.18.

MONTHLY LIQUIDITY SNAPSHOT – Bank "D"

CUMULATIVE LIQUIDITY REPORT ($ '000)

Cumulative Liquidity Report									
	1 Day	2 Day	1 Week	2 Week	1 Month	2 Months	3 Months	6 Months	1 Year
Cumulative Net Cash Balance	80	80	-1,260	-1,260	-1,180	-1,408	-1,150	-850	-850
Other Forecast Inflows									
Other Forecast Outflows									
Cumulative Cash Gap	80	80	-1,260	-1,260	-1,180	-1,408	-1,150	-850	-850
Counterbalancing Capacity	180	180	635	640	748	748	1,238	1,238	1,238
Liquidity Gap	260	260	-625	-620	-432	-660	88	388	388
Limit									
Variance	260	260	-625	-620	-432	-660	88	388	388

* Cash gap turns negative between 2-day and 1-week
* Liquidity gap turns negative between 2-day and 1-week

LIQUIDITY RATIOS – THREE MONTH VIEW

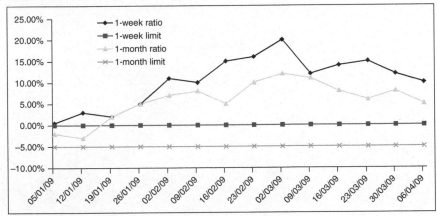

* Ratios are above the limit

	Current month	Previous month	Change
LIQUIDITY RISK FACTOR	22.2	25.1	▼
LOAN-TO-DEPOSIT RATIO	96%	93%	▲
NET INTERGROUP LENDING	(1,228)	(1,552)	▼

Figure 9.18   Summary liquidity snapshot

CONCLUSION

In this chapter we have considered the essential principles of bank liquidity risk management. The events of 2007–2008 served to reiterate the importance of sound ALM practice in banks. For this reason, it is important that a bank's ALCO be set up as an effective management entity at every bank, empowered to ensure correct business practice for asset–liability management. The framework set out in this chapter can be viewed as the best-endeavours approach to the operation of the ALCO function at a bank.

The next chapter looks at key technical issues that are part of an effective liquidity risk management framework.

Chapter

10[1]

LIQUIDITY RISK
MANAGEMENT II:
BASEL III LIQUIDITY,
LIABILITIES
STRATEGY, STRESS
TESTING,
COLLATERAL
MANAGEMENT
AND THE HQLA

[1]This chapter was co-written with Jamie Paris and Chris Westcott.

In this chapter we consider an important part of the liquidity risk management process, that of quantifying and reporting liquidity risk exposure as required by the universal "Basel III" rules on bank supervision. We also consider all related ingredients of a best-practice liquidity risk management framework. This makes Chapter 10 rather a long one, but worth working through as it is possibly the most important in the book!

BASEL III LIQUIDITY METRICS

Strong capital requirements are a necessary condition for banking sector stability but by themselves are not sufficient. A strong liquidity base reinforced through robust supervisory standards is of equal importance. Prior to 2010, there were no internationally harmonised standards in this area. To complement the other elements of its liquidity framework (*Principles for Sound Liquidity Risk Management and Supervision and Additional Monitoring Metrics*), the Basel Committee developed two minimum liquidity standards:

- The Liquidity Coverage Ratio (LCR): to promote short-term funding resilience;
- The Net Stable Funding Ratio (NSFR): to provide a sustainable maturity structure of assets and liabilities.

In Europe, a minimum LCR was introduced in October 2015. Implementation of the NSFR, however, is not due until 2018, to give global regulators sufficient time to conduct parallel run exercises to enable proper calibration of the ratio.

Liquidity coverage ratio

The LCR focuses on the short term and is designed to ensure that a financial institution has sufficient unencumbered high-quality liquid resources to survive a severe liquidity stress scenario lasting for 1 month. The ratio is calculated as:

Stock of high-quality liquid assets/Total net cash outflows over the next 30 days (in a stress situation) $\geq$ *100%*

The highest quality liquid assets (for example, cash or government bonds) are included in the calculation at their market value. Assets of a slightly lower quality, such as covered bonds and securitisation paper, may also be counted if their ratings are above minimum thresholds, but will be subject to a haircut.

Run-off factors are applied to liabilities and off-balance-sheet commitments based on their likelihood of withdrawal/drawdown in a stress. Figure 10.1 provides a simplified overview of the initial assumptions published by the Basel Committee in 2010.

Simplified overview of LCR (per BCBS 2010)

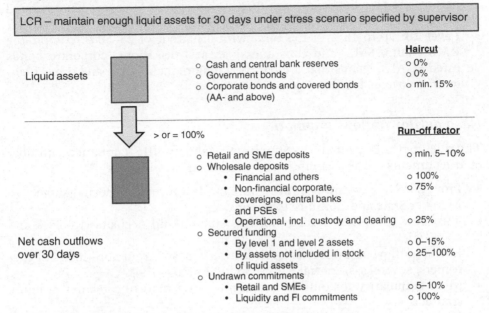

LCR – maintain enough liquid assets for 30 days under stress scenario specified by supervisor

Haircut

Liquid assets
- Cash and central bank reserves — o 0%
- Government bonds — o 0%
- Corporate bonds and covered bonds — o min. 15%
  (AA- and above)

> or = 100%

Run-off factor

Net cash outflows over 30 days
- Retail and SME deposits — o min. 5–10%
- Wholesale deposits
  - Financial and others — o 100%
  - Non-financial corporate, — o 75%
    sovereigns, central banks
    and PSEs
  - Operational, incl. custody and clearing — o 25%
- Secured funding
  - By level 1 and level 2 assets — o 0–15%
  - By assets not included in stock — o 25–100%
    of liquid assets
- Undrawn commitments
  - Retail and SMEs — o 5–10%
  - Liquidity and FI commitments — o 100%

Figure 10.1   Simplified overview of the LCR calculation

© Chris Westcott 2017. Used with permission.

Liquidity stress scenario

The assumptions are provided by the regulatory authorities based upon a combined market and idiosyncratic stress, which incorporates many of the shocks experienced during the financial crisis. They should be viewed as a minimum supervisory requirement for banks. Banks are expected to conduct their own stress tests to assess the level of liquidity they should hold beyond this minimum, and construct their own scenarios that could cause difficulties for their specific business activities. The results of these additional stress tests should be shared with supervisors (Individual Liquidity Adequacy Process and Liquidity Supervisory Review and Evaluation Process are covered in Section 19 of the handbook).

Liquid assets

Liquid assets eligible for inclusion in the calculation were initially split into two categories (Level 1 and Level 2), but this was subsequently increased to three (Level 1, Level 2A, and Level 2B) to capture a broader range of securities:

- **Level 1:** up to 100% of the total, comprising cash, deposits at the central bank government/government guaranteed bonds, and covered bonds rated ECAI 1 (External Credit Assessment Institutions – EU rating system) that meet certain conditions (subject to a 7% haircut and a 70% cap in the liquidity buffer);

- **Level 2A:** up to 40% of the total with a minimum haircut of 15%, comprising government bonds with 20% risk weight, EU covered bonds rated ECAI 2, and non-EU covered/corporate bonds rated ECAI 2;
- **Level 2B:** up to 15% of the total with a haircut of 25–50%, comprising RMBS, auto, SME, and consumer loan securitisations, corporate bonds rated ECAI 3, shares that are part of a major stock index, and other high-quality covered bonds.

Cash outflow/inflow assumptions

The rules for the EU, which were finalised in January 2015, contained a number of amendments to the assumptions on cash outflows/inflows:

- From 2019, a new lower outflow rate of 3% for retail deposits (subject to Member State and Commission approval);
- Two new risk buckets for other less stable retail deposits (10–15% and 15–20%);
- Lower outflow assumptions for maturing deposits from non-financial customers, sovereigns, central banks, and PSEs (20–40%);
- More granularity for outflow assumptions on maturing secured funding transactions;
- Higher outflow assumptions (30–40%) for undrawn committed liquidity facilities to non-financial corporates provided to replace funding that cannot be obtained in the financial markets;
- More favourable outflow assumptions on deposits from credit unions and undrawn credit or liquidity facilities for members of a group or institutional protection scheme.

The overall effect of the assumption changes has been a net relaxation of the rules, making it easier for banks to comply. As at 31 December 2012, Group 1 Banks (those with Tier 1 capital >€3 bn and internationally active) had an average LCR of 95% based on the 2010 BCBS rules and 119% based on the January 2013 version. As at the same date, Group 2 Banks had an average LCR of 99% based on the 2010 BCBS rules and 126% based on the January 2013 version.

LCR implementation in the US and Switzerland

The US has introduced an LCR that is consistent with that applying in Europe, although it differs in a number of respects. There is an additional feature called a "maturity mismatch add-on" – it requires institutions to identify the largest single-day maturity mismatch within the 30-day period by calculating the daily difference in cumulative outflows and inflows that have set maturity dates. The maturity mismatch add-on is the difference between the peak day amount and the net cumulative outflow amount on the last day of the 30-day period. This is illustrated in Figure 10.2 – although the institution in question has a 100% LCR, there is an additional liquid asset holding requirement of US$230m due to the maturity mismatch add-on.

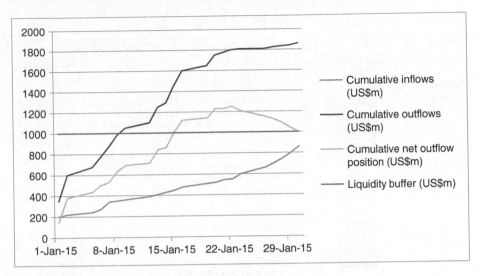

Figure 10.2   The US maturity mismatch add-on

The LCR rule only applies to the largest, internationally active US banks. The final rule has been effective since 1 January 2015 (min. 80% compliance), though there is a transitional phase with full application from 1 January 2017 (earlier than under the Basel Committee framework). The LCR rule will be complemented by the NSFR in 2019.

Due to the low level of public debt in Switzerland, "Alternative Liquidity Approaches" are available to enable compliance with minimum ratio requirements. Outflows in Swiss francs can be covered up to a defined portion in foreign currency assets. Also, a higher proportion of Category 2 assets may be permitted and short-term repo transactions against high-quality assets with a maturity of less than 30 days may be treated as non-existent.

The Net Stable Funding Ratio

In contrast to the LCR, the NSFR is a measure of structural liquidity and focuses on the longer-term horizon by placing a formal limit on the amount of maturity transformation that banks are able to undertake. The required ratio is calculated as:

Available amount of stable funding/Required amount of stable funding ≥100%

All assets (required amount of stable funding) and liabilities (available amount of stable funding) are weighted according to their likelihood of still being on the balance sheet 12 months into the future.

Figure 10.3 gives a simplified overview of the assumptions used in the NSFR calculation based upon the Basel III document. Since the initial calibration, the Basel Committee proposed a number of amendments to the Available

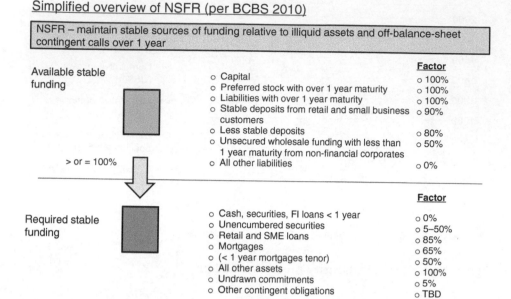

Note: The RSF factors assigned to various types of assets are parameters intended to assess the amount of a particular asset that could not be monetised in the NSFR scenario.

Figure 10.3 Simplified overview of the NSFR calculation
© Chris Westcott 2017. Used with permission.

Stable Funding (ASF) and Required Stable Funding (RSF) factors in January and October 2014. Some of the main changes were:

- The ASF factor on operational deposits was increased from 0% to 50%;
- The ASF factor on stable retail and SME deposits was increased from 90% to 95%;
- The RSF factor was increased from 0% to 50% on both non-renewable loans to non-bank financial institutions with a maturity of less than 1 year and inter-bank lending for a period of 6 months to 1 year;
- Net derivative liabilities are included in the 0% ASF category and 20% of derivative liabilities captured in the 100% RSF category (as well as net derivative assets);
- Two new RSF categories have been introduced at 10% and 15% for unencumbered loans to financial institutions (previously 0%).

The implications of the Basel liquidity metrics for banks' funding and lending strategies

The new rules combined with banks' own desire to reduce liquidity risk have resulted in material changes in balance sheet structures. The adjustment process began in 2008, so is now well advanced. Initially, LCR/NSFR presented a compliance issue, but satisfying the ratios on an ongoing basis is increasingly becoming an efficiency issue.

Some of the main impacts have included:

- Customer loan/deposit ratios moving more into balance;
- A reduction in inter-bank loan/deposit market and repo activity (except in government securities);
- A focus on retail/SME deposits, including the introduction/relaunch of deposit products, such as 35-day notice accounts;
- Simplification of balance sheet structures to reduce trapped liquidity in branches and/or subsidiaries;
- Higher liquid asset holdings and disposal of traded securities that do not count towards the LCR;
- Tighter control of undrawn commitments, particularly liquidity facilities, where the treatment is asymmetric;
- Increased consideration of the currency denomination of activities;
- The generation of liquidity from long-term assets.

For efficient balance sheet optimisation, a bank should consider how the above impacts its business model and specific business lines, and seek to concentrate on those areas that provide efficiency in both return and regulatory compliance.

OPTIMUM LIABILITIES STRATEGY AND MANAGING THE HIGH-QUALITY LIQUID ASSETS (HQLA) PORTFOLIO

In this section we examine the interdependency between the liability strategy and the link that it has to the HQLA, known in pre-Basel III days as the liquidity book or liquid asset buffer (LAB), requirement.

Liabilities strategy

As part of an integrated liquidity risk management framework, a bank should articulate an optimum liabilities strategy. This sits at the heart of the balance sheet planning process. The liabilities strategy of an organisation needs to take into consideration the diversification of the liability base to ensure that it is not concentrated in any particular aspect such as tenor, client, industry sector, or product type.

Under the strategic asset-liability management (ALM) umbrella, there are a few core components that are directly relevant to the liabilities strategy:

- A single, integrated balance sheet approach that ties in asset origination with liabilities raising;
- Thus, asset type must be relevant and appropriate to funding type and source … ;
- … and the funding type and source must be appropriate to the asset type.

In order to apply these three key principles, it is important to undertake a comprehensive review of the bank's balance sheet liabilities as a first step towards determining both the optimum liability profile and then the overall liabilities strategy.

This exercise is more involved in the larger and more complex businesses, but critical nonetheless.

The strategy setting is not a static or one-off process. The objective is to arrive at a balance sheet liability mix and structure by design, and one which is optimum from a strategic ALM perspective, rather than one that is a result simply of history and business line BAU activity – in other words, a passive inherited liability shape.

The changing liabilities structure of banks

Let's examine how bank balance sheets have evolved over time in order to better understand the context of a liabilities strategy. Figure 10.4 shows the changes in breakdown of funding types that took place with UK banks between 2007 and 2012.

The liability structure of many EU and MENA banks have changed since 2007–2008 and have focused on moving away from wholesale funds, both short term (supply) and long term (demand), and move towards more non-interest bearing liabilities (NIBLs) and equity. This has largely been driven by the introduction of the ILAS regime and subsequent LCR stress testing regulatory metrics. Both of these stress tests penalise the use of wholesale funding and hence banks have diversified and focused on retail and NIBLs balances. For one high street UK bank, NIBLs rose from 28% of liabilities and equity in 2007 to 41% in 2012.

	UK banks' average	
	2007	**2012**
Deposits by banks	6.00%	3.80%
Customer accounts	31%	31%
Debt securities	12.30%	10.60%
NIBLs	24.30%	27.50%
Equity	4.40%	5.00%
Other	21.90%	22.10%
Total liabilities and equity	100%	100%

(*Source*: SEC 20-F filings)

Figure 10.4   Funding breakdown of UK banks' average, 2007 and 2012

The liability structure: what is the optimum mix?

In compiling the optimum liability mix targets, there are some important considerations that need to be applied in the planning process. These revolve around:

- Regulation;
- Liquidity value (to what extent is a type of customer deposit or type beneficial towards the final LCR or NSFR metric?);
- Funding diversification/concentration;
- Impact to net interest income (NII) and net interest margin (NIM);
- NII sensitivity;
- How to build the customer franchise;
- Set up costs of new products.

Figure 10.5 highlights the detailed considerations that need to be applied during the planning process.

Banks fund their balance sheets using a variety of liability types. The liquidity value of each type is different. Ideally, a funding type has high liquidity value as well as high NII value, customer franchise value, etc. This is essentially the "strategic ALM" optimisation problem, attempting to structure the balance sheet mix, in this case with respect to liabilities, that best serves the competing requirements of the regulator, the customer stakeholder, and the shareholder.

In practice, there is usually a trade-off among these factors as some liabilities have greater term liquidity value for a bank than others. At one end of the

Factor	Consideration
Regulation	Deposit Guarantee Scheme? Is a regulated sales force required to distribute the product?
Liquidity	What is the liquidity value of the deposit?
Concentration	Does the deposit type improve the diversity of the funding base?
NII/NIM	Contribution to NII per funds transfer pricing (FTP) system, not gross cost?
NII sensitivity	Does the deposit act as a natural hedge for assets? Some banks do not use derivatives to manage NII sensitivity
Customer franchise	Does the product reinforce the franchise value of the organisation? E.g., Santander 123 account
Other costs	Explicit costs associated with the product?

Figure 10.5   Considerations during the liabilities strategy setting stage

**High Liquidity Value –
Long Term, Low Volatility**

Retail current accounts
Retail deposit accounts
Corporate cash flow accounts/call accounts
Retail savings accounts
Retail fixed term deposits
Private bank deposits
Corporate savings accounts
Corporate fixed term deposits
Wholesale market fixed term deposits
Money market term funding (CD/CP)
Money market deposits/inter-bank deposits

**Low Liquidity Value –
Short Term, High Volatility**

Figure 10.6   Liquidity value of liabilities
Source: Choudhry (2012)

scale are retail current accounts; at the other end are short-term unsecured wholesale liabilities, sourced in the inter-bank market, which have much more volatile characteristics in stressed market conditions and therefore are less valuable for liquidity management purposes.

Figure 10.6 illustrates the hierarchy of value of different types of liabilities. From a liquidity value perspective, a bank should seek to maximise funding from customer relationship balances and minimise its reliance on wholesale inter-bank funding.

The mix of these should be arrived at through design as much as possible and a bank's FTP process may be used to help drive liabilities raising of the "right" type and through incentivising businesses by rewarding them with a higher commission or sales credit for the higher value liquidity type.

Peer group analysis

In the UK, the Bank of England (BoE) publishes monthly data showing effective interest-rate paid on (sterling) deposit balances of UK household and UK non-FI corporate sectors, split by deposit type. It is a measure of back-book deposit costs (in the UK), not front book (i.e. marginal cost of new funds).

Through this peer review, one can compare the current bank levels to peer levels to establish whether your bank is paying above the sector-wide average and to establish a better understanding of what your bank is paying for its deposits and assess if this can be improved.

From Figure 10.7, we observe that for UK banks, 2-year fixed-rate bonds have reduced by ~200bp since 2010, from an average of 3.25% to 1.46%. For instant access liability products, this has reduced by ~90bp from 1.44% to 0.54%.

In addition to data published by central banks, a bank should survey the market itself to determine the current pricing associated with certain liability products. In Figure 10.8 we present the results of such a comparison. We note that

Bank of England Statistics					
	2-year fixed-rate bonds (%)	Instant access including bonus (%)	Instant access excluding bonus (%)	ISA including bonus (%)	ISA excluding bonus (%)	1-year fixed-rate ISA (%)
2010	3.25					
2011	3.27	1.44	0.51	2.48	1.25	2.56
2012	3.02	1.45	0.48	2.46	1.35	2.54
2013	1.99	0.86	0.50	1.46	0.71	1.77
2014	1.60	0.67	0.46	1.17	0.86	1.49
2015	1.46	0.54	0.39	1.00	0.82	1.41

Figure 10.7 BoE comparative rates statistics example

Deposit terms	ABC Bank	XYZ Bank	County Bank	Friendly Bank	Life Bank	Trust Bank
Instant access	0.10		1.50	0.50	0.95	0.90
30-day notice	1.25	0.60	1.00	1.35	1.10	1.00
90-day notice		1.55	2.00	1.75	0.95	1.35
95-day notice	1.95		2.00			1.35
3-month		1.55		2.00		
6-month	2.00	1.75	2.25		2.25	1.75
12-month	2.20	2.15		2.50	2.65	2.00
2-year		2.35				2.50
3-year				2.60		
5-year		2.65				

Figure 10.8 Deposit rates peer comparison

"XYZ bank" is exactly where it most probably wishes to be, in the middle of the range among its peers and not an outlier for rates at either end. The highest deposit rate payers are sometimes perceived by customers to be struggling to raise deposits, and such a customer perception would not be welcome for a bank.

An analysis of front-book deposit prices vs competitors would provide additional colour to the liabilities review. This information should also be presented regularly to either the Products Pricing Committee or Deposits Pricing Committee (subcommittee of asset–liability committee (ALCO)). As noted above, the general rule of thumb is not to be an outlier at either end.

Product volume sensitivity to interest-rate movements

Some liability products are sensitive to movements in interest rates and are referred to as NII-sensitive products. A high volume sensitivity may not be a good thing as this could lead to certain challenges, notably cannibalisation from other product types and "hot money".

Cannibalisation from other deposit products offered by the bank can lead to a dramatically different impact on NII than originally anticipated, especially if large volumes of deposits switch to the new/repriced product from high margin accounts. Placing restrictions on who can apply for certain products can attract the attention of the regulators.

"Hot money" from interest-rate seekers (stand-alone customers): if a new/repriced account attracts deposits from customers who are only interested in the rate being paid, then you may finish up with expensive funding that has no liquidity value. For this reason, many banks have withdrawn from offering offshore instant access Internet-based accounts.

The same can also be said of products that have been offered at below par rate. Deposit products often have tiered rates and/or customer relationship managers are given the discretion to pay a higher rate to protect/attract business. Average product margins can mask underlying trends. Figure 10.9 is an example of this type of review in more detail.

As part of the liability strategy, a bank should conduct a granular review to understand which deposits are being written at negative margins and consider the options to reduce the size of this segment of business as it is value destroying.

Output of the liability review

The result of the liabilities mix review should be a medium-term (for example, 3- to 5-year) strategy that specifies a precise target for:

- The liabilities mix: how much do we wish of each funding type, and why;
- What the drivers are;

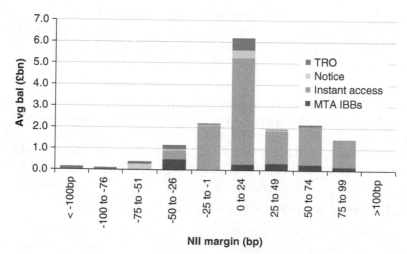

Figure 10.9   Deposit product analysis

- What, if any, funding types are of less value and should be reduced or with-drawn from;
- Plan for implementation.

This liabilities strategy review would be presented for ALCO approval and subsequent implementation. This plan could include a series of initiatives that would be tracked at ALCO on a regular basis to ensure that the balance sheet is tracking in the right direction and is being measured by some key performance indicators.

Initiatives could include any or all of those listed in Figure 10.10.

Tracking progress through ALCO

The liabilities strategic review output should articulate the high-level deposits strategy. For example, this could be a simple statement such as "The 2016 strategy is to retain current balances and enhance the value of those retained balances for NIM" or "The medium-term strategy is to grow the deposit book by £2 billion".

The ALCO review should have a level of product emphasis aligned to the specific initiatives that the plan has identified such as focus on instant access savings or term deposits.

There should be a regular competitive analysis, as previously described, to ensure that pricing is still relevant in the market and that process against key performance indicators is tracked monthly and any variations clearly understood.

	Initiative
Customer optimisation	Target specific sectors, e.g. universities, charities. Package an offering to growing customer segments Rationalise geographies Volume caps on retail customer business (e.g. £1m) Remove from sale any products offering lifetime guarantees
Margin improvement	Increase range of managed rate products by reducing those that price according to a fixed formula (e.g. base rate + ..%)
Other initiatives	Stand-alone customers: target reduction in "rate chaser" customers acquired during periods of aggressive balance sheet growth Lengthen notice period on notice accounts, from 7/14 days to 90+ Remove the facility to break fixed-rate deposits early Stop paying liquidity premia on accounts without liquidity value

Figure 10.10   Range of liabilities strategies

Summary

A balance sheet funding review is an essential start to the bank's drafting of its optimum funding mix and liabilities strategy. The larger and more complex the bank (IB, corporate, retail), the more complex the review. It is important to understand the share of the balance sheet, and costs currently, and review these in the context of what the balance sheet should look like in 1 to 3 years' time.

The overall optimum liabilities strategy will consist of a series of tactical/strategic initiatives that will help the bank re-engineer the funding profile to achieve an optimal mix.

This is the start of a more logical and coherent approach to balance sheet funding.

THE LIQUID ASSET BUFFER

We consider now the liquid asset buffer (LAB), which can be a sizeable item on the asset side of the balance sheet. The size of the LAB is determined purely by the quality of the liabilities mix on the balance sheet, as it is required to offset the potential outflow of liabilities in a time of stress, for example, a financial crisis.

All firms are required to hold buffers of liquid assets and it forms a key part of the PRA requirement for liquidity, and this is now enshrined in global regulation by Basel III (the High Quality Liquid Assets (HQLA) portfolio). These assets must be uncorrelated to the institution – so it cannot be the bank's own debt issued – nor can they be repo funded (i.e. unencumbered) and should preferably be funded by long-term (>90 days) liabilities.

Liquid assets are those that can be easily converted to cash at any time (including times of stress), with little or no loss of value. They have certain characteristics that need to be fulfilled in order to qualify as liquid assets. These characteristics can be divided into fundamental and market components.

The fundamental characteristics of LAB asserts are described as:

- Low Credit and Market Risk:
  - Low degree of subordination, low duration, low volatility, low inflation risk, and denominated in a convertible currency;
- Ease and Certainty of Valuation:
  - Pricing formula must be easy to calculate with no strong assumptions and inputs must be publicly available;
- Low Correlation with Risky Assets:
  - Should not be subject to wrong way risk;
- Listed on a Developed and Recognised Exchange Market:
  - Increases transparency;
- The market characteristics are described as:
- Active and sizeable market:
  - Outright sale and repo markets at all times. Historical evidence of market breadth and market depth;

- Presence of Committed Market-makers:
  - Quotes are always available for buying and selling the asset Low Market Concentration;
  - Diverse group of buyers and sellers in the assets' market;
- Flight to Quality:
  - Historic evidence of these types of asset being traded in a systemic crisis.

Under the Basel III LCR calculation, the liquidity value of differing types of liquid assets is predetermined within the confines of the stress test. Figure 10.11 highlights what these haircuts are and highlights that a minimum of 60% of the portfolio would need to be made up of Level 1 assets (most liquid).

Hedging the liquid asset buffer

Part of the LAB will be comprised of longer term securities and so ALCO must agree an interest-rate risk (and credit risk) hedging approach, particularly for those assets that are fixed rate.

Interest-rate risk hedges may be transacted using interest-rate swaps, short sterling futures (fixed-rate instruments up to 3 years), or LIFFE gilt futures (fixed-rate instruments of over 3 years). The pros and cons of each instrument are considered in Figure 10.12.

HQLA Eligibility Criteria	Cap	Haircut
Level 1 • Cash at Central Banks _(Min 60%)_ • Central Bank Reserves • Government Bonds issued or guaranteed by ECB, member state government or central bank • Government Bonds (AAA to AA-) • Public Sector Debt guart'd by sovereign (AAA to AA-) • Government Bonds (<A+) for CCY specific stress • Multinational Banks		0%
• Covered Bonds (EEA) (AAA to AA-)[1]	70%	7%
Level 2 A • Government Bonds (A+ to A-) • Public Sector Debt guart'd by sovereign (A+ to A-) • Covered Bonds (Non EEA) (AAA to AA-)[2] • Corporate Bonds (AAA to AA-)[3]		15%
• Covered Bonds (EEA) (A+ to A-)[4]	40%	
Level 2 B • Corporate Bonds (A+ to BBB-) _(Max 15%)_		50%
• Major Index Equities		50%
• Covered Bonds (Unrated)[5]		30%
• Restricted Use Central Bank Committed Liquidity Facility[6]		35%
• Asset Backed Securities (AAA to AA-)	15%	
• RMBS		25%
• Auto-ABS		25%
• CMBS – SME		35%
• Consumer Loans ABS		35%

Figure 10.11 Requirements for LAB (or HQLA) eligibility

Source: BCBS.

> **IR Swap – Pros**
> * A liquid instrument – GBP swap market is transparent and served by a large number of market makers
>
> * An accurate hedge can be achieved by matching asset tenor precisely

> **IR Swap – Cons**
> * Remain exposed to the counterparty risk of the swap bank (mitigated in part by the use of collateral via a CSA)
> * Uses up precious swap lines which may be better saved for other books
> * Difficult to use for dynamic hedging (loss of bid–offer spread on unwind)

> **IR Futures – Pros**
> * No counterparty risk
> * Liquid instant market with narrow bid–offer spread
> * Dynamic hedging is straightforward – adjust the hedge by buying or selling additional contracts as necessary
> * Does not use swap lines

> **IR Futures – Cons**
> * Requires account at clearing house and daily margining
> * Requires rollover each time the "front month" is reached, which is on or before the 1st of the delivery month

Figure 10.12 Pros and cons of the different interest-rate risk hedging instruments

A point worth noting is that, in the UK, there is a requirement that LAB be demonstrated to be truly liquid through an element of "churn" (sold and repurchased), so the assets will be designated as available for sale (AFS) and not the held to maturity (HTM) from an accounting perspective.

Liquid asset buffer policy

Given the importance of the LAB, it is important to ensure that investment criteria are established in line with the Board risk appetite of the firm. An integral part of the Board-approved liquidity risk management policy is that all banks must maintain a portfolio of high-quality genuinely liquid assets to act as a funding reserve against liabilities outflow in times of stress.

The amount of liquid assets should cover the outflows projected from the bank's liquidity stress tests, provide collateral for payment systems, and satisfy minimum regulatory requirements.

The Liquid asset buffer policy sets out the parameters in respect of the ownership, size, maturity, and composition of the liquidity portfolio.

This policy document is approved by ALCO and reviewed on an annual basis.

The policy will set out some key principles around the governance of the portfolio. These principles are typically as follows:

* The LAB policy will be proposed by the treasurer and approved by ALCO;
* ALCO will review the parameters within the policy on a semi-annual or ad-hoc basis as required;
* Internal audit and risk will oversee implementation of the policy;
* To ensure segregation of duties, the quantum of the portfolio and breaches will be reported through finance to the treasurer (or delegated authority);

- The liquidity portfolio policy applies to all high-quality liquid assets held by Treasury for the provision of liquidity to prudential, operational (for example, to support payment systems), and regulatory requirements;
- The sell-down test must be representative of the constitution of the LAV and must be randomly tested in size at least once a quarter via a sale or repurchase agreement;
- The relevant Discount Window Facilities operated by the central banks should be tested in size and regularity. This exercise should be prenotified to the Central Bank and only done if there is no market stigma associated with the testing.

Summary

The LAB is an integral part of the balance sheet and is predominantly derived from the quality of the liability base through the lens of stress tests. It needs to be representative of the risk appetite of the Board and commensurate with the underlying breakdown of the balance sheet. The LAB needs to be easily and quickly liquefiable and this needs to be tested regularly via sale or repo of a test sample of the portfolio.

LIQUIDITY REPORTING, STRESS TESTING, ILAAP, AND ASSET ENCUMBRANCE POLICY

We continue our detailed look into the liquidity risk management process. We consider first the regulatory aspect and the process of the "individual liquidity adequacy assessment process" (ILAAP). We also review intra-day liquidity risk and the importance of understanding the liquidity risk aspects of having encumbered assets on the balance sheet.

Liquidity reporting

Liquidity reporting is necessary because:

- It obliges banks to monitor their liquidity risk on a daily or intra-day basis;
- The data required by the regulator would normally be required by firms for their own purposes in undertaking prudent liquidity risk management (regulatory guidance);
- It enables the regulator to identify and challenge outliers;
- Supervisors can apply their own stress testing scenario analysis to data provided by a firm;
- It enables the regulator to form firm, specific, sector, and industry-wide views on liquidity risk during good and bad times, and provide feedback to firms on their liquidity positioning within their peer group.

In the UK, in 2009–2010, in the wake of the financial crisis, the Financial Services Authority (FSA, now Prudential Regulation Authority) introduced a series of new liquidity reports. The most well known of these reports are the FSA 047 (Daily Flows) and the FSA 048 (Enhanced Mismatch Report), which show, respectively, contractual liquidity flows out to 3 months (for the analysis of survival periods and potential liquidity squeezes), and liquidity mismatch positions across the whole maturity spectrum.

Other key reports include: FSA 050 (Liquidity Buffer Qualifying Securities), FSA 051 (Funding Concentration), FSA 052 (Pricing Data), FSA 053 (Retail, SME and Large Enterprise Type B (Stable Funding)), FSA 054 (Currency Analysis), and FSA 055 (Systems and Controls Questionnaire). These too are all based upon contractual maturities, where relevant.

Reporting frequency ranged between daily and quarterly depending upon: the size and complexity of the bank, the nature of the report (for example, money/financial market updates were required more often than those on retail/corporate accounts), and the market conditions (reporting frequency was increased in a stress situation).

The FSA reports were required to be submitted at a consolidated group level, as well as for key banking subsidiaries.

Since October 2015, the FSA suite of reports has largely been replaced by EU Common Reporting or COREP. COREP is a standardised reporting framework issued by the European Banking Authority for the Capital Requirements Directive. It covers credit risk, market risk, operational risk, own funds capital adequacy, and liquidity risk. The reporting framework has been adopted by c30 countries in the EU (including the UK) and applies to all banks (credit institutions), building societies, and investment firms (and, in some cases, significant branches of credit institutions).

COREP requires data to be reported at a more granular level than hitherto. Separate reports must be prepared for all "significant" currencies, which make up more than 5% of the total balance sheet.

As illustrated in Figure 10.13, the FSA reports (apart from FSA 047 and 048, which may be retained) are being replaced by four returns on the Liquidity Coverage Ratio, two on the Net Stable Funding Ratio and six reports on Additional Monitoring Metrics. The LCR and Additional Monitoring Metrics reports must be submitted each month, while the NSFR templates are required on a quarterly basis.

The Additional Monitoring Metrics cover a range of data, which helps supervisors to identify potential liquidity difficulties for a single institution or across the market as a whole and to take pre-emptive action if necessary:

- **Contractual Maturity Ladder**: provides an insight into the extent to which an organisation relies on maturity transformation and provides advance warning of potential future liquidity stress;

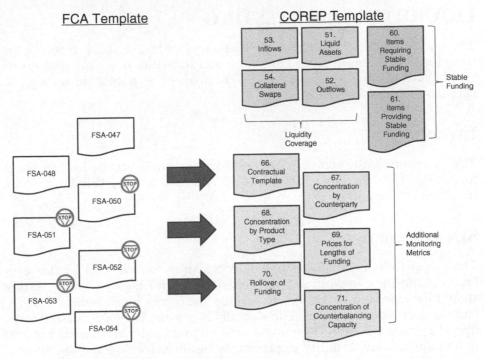

Figure 10.13 Transition to COREP in the EU

- **Concentration of Funding by Counterparty**: the top 10 largest counterparties from which funding obtained exceeds 1% of total liabilities – identifies those sources of wholesale and retail funding of such significance that their withdrawal could trigger liquidity problems;
- **Concentration of Funding by Product Type**: the total amount of funding received from each product category when it exceeds a threshold of 1% of total liabilities – identifies those sources of wholesale and retail funding of such significance that their withdrawal could trigger liquidity problems;
- **Concentration of Counterbalancing Capacity by Issuer/Counterparty**: the 10 largest holdings of assets or liquidity lines granted – demonstrates potential borrowing capacity in a stress;
- **Prices for Various Lengths of Funding**: average transaction volume and prices paid by institutions for funding with different maturities – provides advanced warning of a deteriorating liquidity position through a peer group comparison;
- **Rollover of Funding**: volume of funds maturing and new funding obtained on a daily basis over a monthly time horizon – provides a validation for behavioural assumptions and advance warning of a deteriorating liquidity position through a peer group comparison.

LIQUIDITY STRESS TESTING

The liquidity stress testing process (illustrated in Figure 10.14) involves the modelling of **assumptions** on how assets and liabilities of a bank (**inventory**) will behave in various **stress scenarios**, to produce an **output** for **review** and action by senior management.

Inventory

The inventory is the composition and maturity profile of the balance sheet (including off-balance-sheet exposures) on a given date – a basic building block for all modelling activity.

Stress scenarios

The calculation of the LCR is based upon a stress scenario set by the regulatory authorities. In contrast, the scenarios used for liquidity stress testing should be generated by banks and include a range of idiosyncratic, market, and macroeconomic stresses. These should be severe, but plausible and focus upon key vulnerabilities. Examples could include: a sustained period of systems failure, a vulnerability to previously liquid markets becoming illiquid (for example, commercial paper or securitisation), and heavy reliance on a particular sector for funding that becomes no longer available (local authorities in a credit downgrade scenario).

Assumptions

Assumptions about the response of assets and liabilities to a given stress scenario are based on their historic behaviour in both normal and stressed

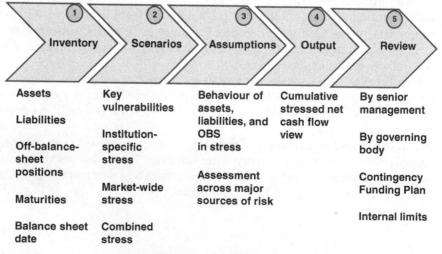

Figure 10.14   End-to-end liquidity stress testing process

conditions. The level of sophistication adopted will depend on the amount of historic data available to support the modelling process. For example, if there is little or no history, assumptions might be developed at a product level only. Alternatively, if the product data can be broken down by customer type and cohort (by account opening date), a more advanced modelling approach may be adopted.

In forming behavioural assumptions, banks should consider the likely consequences of the stress scenario for the major sources of risk they face, which include: Retail Funding Risk, Wholesale Secured and Unsecured Funding Risk, Correlation and Concentration of Funding, Additional Contingent Off-Balance-Sheet Exposures, Funding Tenors, Intra-day Liquidity Risk, Deterioration in the Firm's Credit Rating, Foreign Exchange Convertibility and Access to Foreign Exchange Markets, Ability to Transfer Liquidity Across Entities, Sectors and Countries, Future Balance Sheet Growth, Impact on a Firm's Reputation and Franchise, Marketable and Non-Marketable Asset Risk, and Internalisation Risk (which relates to the potential close-out of customer short positions leading to outflows).

Output

A key output from the stress testing process is the calculation of a cash flow survival period. This details how many days a bank's sources of liquidity (liquid assets, cash inflows, and drawdown of contingent liquidity facilities) will be able to offset the outflows that are assumed in a stress scenario. Banks will set a minimum acceptable survival period as part of their Liquidity Risk Appetite Statements.

Review

The output of the stress testing process should be shared with ALCO and be included in periodic updates to the Board. If the cash flow survival period exceeds the bank's risk appetite, then no further action is necessary, other than continuously reviewing the stress testing process and investing in areas like data collection to improve the quality of outputs over time. Alternatively, if the cash flow survival period is less than the risk appetite, then some form of corrective action is required, such as:

- Reduce exposures to certain products and markets;
- Reduce limits applied to contractual outflows (i.e. the amount of maturity transformation undertaken by the bank);
- Review strategies to address liquidity shortfalls in the Contingency Funding Plan. The Contingency Funding Plan is a statement setting out a bank's strategies for addressing liquidity shortfalls in emergency situations; it will demonstrate how a bank will survive a given stress scenario. Quick, decisive, preplanned action is important in times of great uncertainty when confidence is low and may make the difference between bank survival and failure.

INDIVIDUAL LIQUIDITY ADEQUACY ASSESSMENT PROCESS

A bank should undertake a regular review of whether its liquidity resources are sufficient to cover the major sources of risk to the firm's ability to meet its liabilities as and when they fall due. This "Individual Liquidity Adequacy Assessment Process" (ILAAP) should incorporate:

- A clearly articulated risk appetite defining the duration and type of stress the firm aims to survive;
- A range of stress scenarios focusing upon key vulnerabilities of the firm;
- The results of stress tests; and
- Those measures set out in the Contingency Funding Plan that it would implement.

The ILAAP should also be:

- Recorded in a document approved by the Board;
- Proportionate to the nature, scale, and complexity of a bank's activities; and
- Updated annually or more frequently if the business model of the firm changes.

In the UK the PRA has published a suggested contents structure for the ILAAP; however, in most jurisdictions there is no pre-prescribed format for an ILAAP. The headings included in Figure 10.15 provide an example of what a bank may choose to include. Above all, banks must ensure that their ILAAP informs decision-making and risk management and are not seen to be just a compliance exercise.

---

1 Executive Summary (including ILAA scope and purpose)
2 Institution Strategy
3 Funding Profile
4 Forecast Balance Sheet
5 Liquidity Risk Management Framework (including ownership and risk appetite)
6 ILAA Coverage
7 Stress scenarios
8 Stress Testing Results (covering all major sources of risk)
9 Liquidity Risk Assessment
10 High-Quality Liquid Assets/Collateral Management
11 Other sources of funding/mitigants
12 ILAA Challenge and Internal Approval Process
13 Use of ILAA in the firm
14 Individual Liquidity Guidance
15 Recovery and Resolution
16 Internal Funds Transfer Pricing Policy
17 Appendix A. Outflow Assumptions
18 Appendix B. Contingency Funding Plan

Figure 10.15 Specimen ILAAP contents

Liquidity supervisory review and evaluation process (L-SREP)

In the UK, this is the review of the ILAAP by the regulator. It is a broad assessment that will also capture items such as:

- Whether the institution has an appropriate framework and IT system for identifying liquidity risk;
- Whether the governance framework around the liquidity risk management process is sufficient;
- Whether there is an adequate transfer pricing mechanism for liquidity;
- Whether there are adequate controls over the liquid asset buffer;
- Whether the institution defines and communicates its liquidity risk strategy and tolerance;
- Whether there is a comprehensive internal limit and control framework for liquidity risk management.

Individual liquidity guidance

Following the L-SREP, the PRA (in the UK) will give individual liquidity guidance to banks. Typically, this will cover whether the quantity and quality of liquid assets held by the bank are sufficient, whether the firm's funding profile is appropriate, and any further qualitative arrangements the firm should undertake to mitigate its liquidity risk. Note, the quantitative guidance extends beyond the liquidity buffer the firm is required to maintain under the LCR and will cover liquidity risks to which the firm is exposed, but which are not captured by the LCR.

A similar process exists in other jurisdictions subject to the Basel regulations.

INTRA-DAY LIQUIDITY RISK

Principle 8 of the Basel Committee Principles for Sound Liquidity Risk Management and Supervision states:

"A bank should actively manage its intraday liquidity positions and risks to meet payment and settlement obligations on a timely basis under both normal and stressed conditions and thus contribute to the smooth running of payment and settlement systems."

Intra-day liquidity is defined as funds that can be accessed during the business day to enable firms to make payments in real time. Intra-day liquidity risk is the risk that a bank fails to manage its intra-day liquidity effectively, which could leave it unable to meet a payment obligation at the time expected, thereby affecting its own liquidity position and that of other parties.

Intra-day sources of liquidity include:

- Reserve balances and collateral pledged at central banks;
- Unencumbered liquid assets that can be freely transferred to the central bank;

- Secured or unsecured committed or uncommitted credit lines available intra-day;
- Balances with other banks that can be used for settlement on the same day;
- Payments received from other payment system participants and ancillary systems.

Intra-day liquidity needs arise from:

- Payments needing to be made to other system participants and ancillary systems;
- Contingent payments (for example, as an emergency liquidity provider) relating to a payment system's failure to settle procedures;
- Contingent intra-day liquidity liabilities to customers;
- Payments arising from the provision of correspondent banking services.

The Basel Committee and the EU recommend that a bank's usage of and requirement for intra-day liquidity are monitored in both normal and stressed conditions via eight metrics:

1. Daily Maximum Liquidity Requirement;
2. Available Intra-day Liquidity at the Start of the Business Day;
3. Total Payments;
4. Time Specific and Other Critical Obligations;
5. Value of Payments Made on Behalf of Correspondent Bank Customers;
6. Intra-day Credit Lines Extended to Customers;
7. Timing of Intra-day Payments;
8. Intra-day Throughput.

In the EU, firms have been required to provide quarterly reports on the above measures since October 2015.

Of particular note are the Daily Maximum Liquidity Requirement, Time Specific and Other Critical Obligations, and Intra-day Throughput.

The daily maximum liquidity requirement

Banks need to calculate their net intra-day liquidity position (the difference between the total value of payments received and payments made at any point in the day) during the course of the day. The bank's largest net cumulative position during the day will determine its maximum intra-day requirement on that day. If a bank runs a negative net cumulative position at some point during the day, it will need to access intra-day liquidity to fund this balance. In the example in Figure 10.16, this is just over 10 currency units.

Time-specific and other critical obligations

Banks must identify the volume and value of time-specific obligations and any missed payments. This enables supervisors to assess whether these obligations are being effectively managed. Examples include payments required to settle positions in payment and settlement systems and those related to

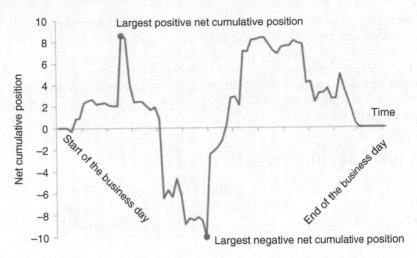

Figure 10.16   Specimen daily maximum liquidity requirement

market activities, such as the delivery or return of money market transactions or margin payments. A bank's failure to settle such obligations on time could result in financial penalty, reputational damage, or loss of future business.

Intra-day throughput

This metric shows the proportion, by value, of a bank's outgoing payments that settle by specific times during the day (for example, by 9.00 a.m., by 10.00 a.m., etc.) and enables supervisors to identify specific times during the day when a bank may be more vulnerable to liquidity or operational stresses and any changes in its payment and settlement behaviour.

Intra-day liquidity stress testing

The monitoring tools discussed provide supervisors with information on a bank's intra-day liquidity profile in normal conditions. However, the availability and usage of intra-day liquidity can change markedly in times of stress. As guidance, the Basel Committee has developed four stress scenarios relating to own financial stress: customer stress, counterparty stress, and market-wide credit or liquidity stress. Banks should use the scenarios to assess how their intra-day liquidity profile in normal conditions would change in a stressful situation and discuss with their supervisors how any adverse impact would be addressed either through contingency planning and/or the wider intra-day liquidity risk management framework.

How are the intra-day liquidity rules influencing banks?

The intra-day liquidity rules have encouraged banks to focus on IT development to generate the required metrics and real-time information flows. Senior management understanding of sources and uses of intra-day liquidity has improved rapidly and banks are employing their available liquidity resources more efficiently, for example, through payment scheduling to reduce maximum intra-day liquidity usage and ensuring that liquid assets are held in the right place to support payment systems as necessary. Also, banks have considered what might happen in a stress situation and put plans in place to mitigate the outcomes.

The total liquidity requirement

Liquid assets required to manage a bank's intra-day obligations cannot also be available to support the LCR buffer. So, a bank's total liquidity requirement must include an allowance for all of the items identified in Figure 10.17.

ASSET ENCUMBRANCE

Asset encumbrance, also known as earmarking or pledging assets, refers to a situation where assets secure liabilities in the event that an institution fails to meet its financial obligations. It originates from transactions such as repurchase agreements, securitisations, covered bonds, or derivatives. Asset encumbrance is critical to the asset and liability manager because unsecured creditors are unable to benefit from the liquidation of encumbered assets in the case of insolvency, and encumbered assets are not available to obtain emergency liquidity in the case of an unforeseen stress event.

Since the 2007–2008 global financial crisis, the level of encumbrance among financial institutions has increased rapidly. According to the European Systemic Risk Board, encumbrance in the EU rose from 11% in 2007 to 32% in 2011. Since the end of 2014, the European Banking Authority has

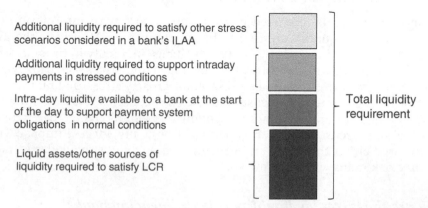

Figure 10.17   The total liquidity requirement

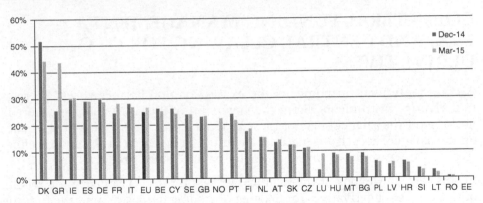

Figure 10.18   Weighted average asset encumbrance by country
Source: EBA.

been collecting data from 200 banks across 29 countries – in March 2015 this revealed an encumbrance position that was still high relative to historic norms at 27.1%.

As illustrated in Figure 10.18, the challenge for regulators is the very different levels of encumbrance across the countries in the EU. The asset encumbrance ratio ranges from 0% in Estonia to 44% in the case of both Denmark and Greece. Higher encumbrance ratios are driven by a variety of factors, such as:

- Large and established covered bond markets (for example, Sweden and Denmark);
- A high share of central bank funding in countries affected by the sovereign debt crisis (for example, Greece);
- A high share of repo financing and collateral requirements for over-the-counter (OTC) derivatives (for example, UK and Belgium).

Due to the disparity across EU institutions, there are no formal limits imposed by the EU authorities as a whole. (Note, in the UK, the PRA has applied capital add-ons if the asset encumbrance level of a firm exceeds 20%.) However, a clear framework should be adopted by institutions containing the following components:

- Establishment of an approach to asset encumbrance by the governing body, including regular review;
- Monitoring and active management of the asset encumbrance position;
- Incorporation of asset encumbrance into stress testing scenarios;
- Provision of information to the governing body on contingent encumbrance requirements from stress scenarios;
- Incorporation of strategies to address asset encumbrance into contingency funding and recovery and resolution plans.

This is more important for banks whose funding profile employs a material amount of secured funding, via repo, securitisation, covered bonds, and so on.

COLLATERAL FUNDING MANAGEMENT, FVA, AND CENTRAL CLEARING FOR OTC DERIVATIVES[2]

A commonly used misnomer is the expression "off-balance-sheet" to refer to derivative instruments. From the viewpoint of the ALM manager, there is nothing off the balance sheet of these products: they have a cash flow impact on the balance sheet that is material and must be managed as closely and effectively as any cash flows arising out of on-balance-sheet products.

In this section we look at the practical impact on the ALM discipline arising out of the use of derivatives for hedging or trading purposes; first, the funding value adjustment (FVA), and then the use of central clearing counterparties (CCP) to clear over-the-counter (OTC) derivatives.

Derivative risks and CVA

Entering into a derivative transaction creates a number of balance sheet risks for both counterparties. A key one is counterparty risk, namely:

- Derivatives are typically entered free of payment at zero initial cost;
- The value can go up (buyer has performance risk on seller) or down (seller has performance risk on buyer) through the whole life of the contract.

Counterparty risk remains live for a long period of time. For this reason, most derivatives business is undertaken under a Credit Support Annexe (CSA), which dictates that collateral must be passed from the counterparty offside on the trade to the party onside. CSA agreements are mostly standardised with the following terms:

- Cash collateral and no substitution option;
- Zero threshold;
- Zero minimum transfer amount;
- Daily continuous margining.

Certain counterparties (such as some sovereign authorities and central banks) do not enter into CSAs and their trades remain uncollateralised to the market-maker.

Banks apply a credit valuation adjustment (CVA) to the price of the derivative contract, which is an adjustment to the risk-neutral derivative price. It allows for the chance that a loss might result if the counterparty defaults, that is, the bank has a receivable on a derivative that the counterparty cannot pay.

---

[2]Acknowledgements and special thanks to Stephen Laughton for his FVA presentation at BTRM Cohort 4 and Cohort 5, which has been used as a source for some of the data in this chapter.

Exposures and CVA

A vanilla interest-rate swap (IRS) exhibits the following characteristics:

- No exchange of principal at inception;
- Parties exchange fixed for floating (i.e. a variable rate such as Libor) throughout the life;
- No re-exchange or principal at termination.

A cross-currency swap (XCY) has the following characteristics:

- Full exchange of principal at inception, one currency vs another;
- Exchange of floating payments, one currency for the other throughout the life;
- Full re-exchange or principal at termination.

The counterparty risks on the IRS are as follows:

- Traded "at market" at inception, hence no net counterparty risk on day 1;
- Unless yield curves are (exactly) flat, IRS has implied payments throughout the life: as time passes payments are made;
- Net payable/receivable remain on structure;
- Interest rates fluctuate throughout the life:
  - Expected payments on floating leg vary;
  - Discounting of implied cash flows varies.

The counterparty risks on the XCY are:

- Traded "at market" at inception, hence no net counterparty risk on day 1;
- Unless yield curves are (exactly) flat, XCY has implied payments through-out its life:
  - As time passes, payments are made;
  - Net payable/receivable remains on structure.
- Interest rates fluctuate throughout the life:
  - Expected payments on floating leg vary;
  - Discounting of implied cash flows varies.
- FX rates fluctuate throughout the life:
  - Value of the re-exchange of principal varies.

The fact that market rates vary from day 1 onwards throughout the life of the contract presents the problem with estimating counterparty risk exposure. "At market" derivatives start with a zero net present value; however, over time and the movement of markets, the structure will develop a present value (PV); but we don't know how much, because we don't know how market prices will evolve. Therefore, the amount of our counterparty exposure is uncertain. The questions to answer are (1) How do we know how much to price for counterparty risk at inception? And (2) How can we hedge this counterparty risk?

We don't know exactly how (i.e. in which direction) market prices will evolve but we do know (can hypothesise) their dynamics and distribution. For example, under the Black-Scholes model assumption we assume a log-normal

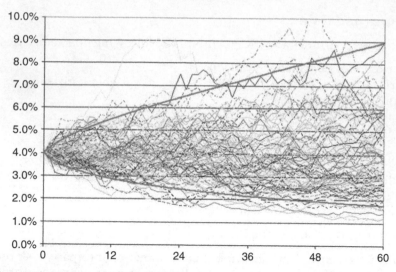

Figure 10.19   Interest-rate simulations

interest rate and foreign exchange rate movements profile. Hence, the most common approach is to simulate the variation in PV. For instance, how will interest rates develop? Figure 10.19 shows a set of interest-rate simulations, where we assume a yield curve flat at 4%, and a set of possible profiles on how the remaining maturity swap rate may develop over the next 5 years. Solid lines are one standard deviation move.

The future distribution of possible market rates and FX rates expands at a decreasing rate (the $\sqrt{T}$ law), converging to a log-normal distribution. But what about the remaining mark-to-market (MtM) value on the swap, and hence the counterparty risk? Over time, fewer cash flows remain on the IRS as duration shortens, and on the XCY the exposure is dominated by the principal occurring in one bullet payment at maturity. So again we run the simulation; expected exposure on an IRS peaks at between 18 and 30 months, then falls back towards zero at maturity. Figure 10.20 shows an example of remaining maturity IRS MtM simulations.

However, with an XCY the expected exposure grows throughout the life, peaking at maturity (due to the bullet exchange of principal on maturity). We show this at Figure 10.21.

To reiterate, XCY swaps involve principal exchange, whereas interest rate swaps involve only coupon exchanges; therefore, expected exposures are much larger on the XCY than on the IRS, as we compare in Figure 10.22.

So how do we use these PV MtM distributions to calculate counterparty risk, and hence the counterparty credit valuation adjustment (CVA)? The most common approach involves:

1. Price the cost of insuring expected exposure on day 1;
2. Only increase the hedge if realised exposure exceeds expected exposure.

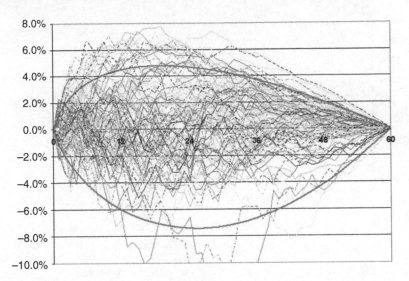

Figure 10.20 IRS MtM PV simulations

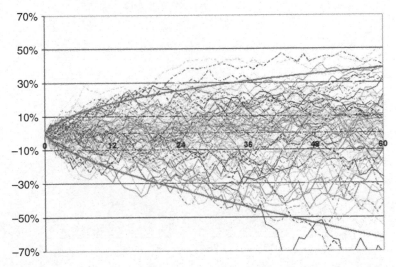

Figure 10.21 Cross-currency swap mark-to-market PV simulations

Using this approach, CVA is therefore the cost of insuring the area under the curve shown at Figure 10.23, given by:

$$CVA = LGD_C \sum_{i=1}^{T} EPE(t_i) Q_C(t_{i-1}, t_i) D(t_i)$$

where

LGD_C is the counterparty loss given default;
$Q_C(t_{i-1}, t_i)$ is the counterparty default probability.

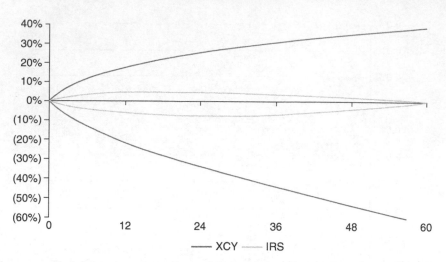

Figure 10.22   Comparing IRS and XCY expected exposures

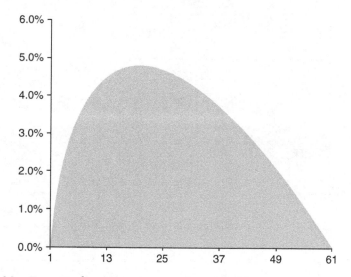

Figure 10.23   Expected swap exposure through life

LGD and Q can be estimated from market credit curves (CDS) or estimated from fundamental credit analysis. So we see that CVA is the cost of hedging expected counterparty credit exposure.

We should be aware that there are some obvious problems with the standard CVA approach:

- Where one party has a positive mark, the other has a negative mark:
  - Both should be charging each other CVA;
  - No agreed, open market price, therefore no trade;

- o   In reality, there is usually a significant disparity between (bank) dealer credit and customer credit, which partly explains the need for collateralisation between inter-dealer/trading counterparties;
- o   Dealers are typically unable to monetise a negative market (their own payable).
- Exposure is not capped at the expected exposure:
- o   This is only an arbitrarily chosen percentile exposure (normally one standard deviation);
- o   Exposures (and hence potential losses) can be much higher.
- Credit curves may be unobservable and/or untradable.

As one can appreciate, there is more than way to approach this issue!

While CVA relates to the credit exposures from derivatives, FCA relates to funding costs. An uncollateralised derivative hedged with a collateralised one can give rise to a funding requirement: if markets move such that the collateralised trade has a negative MtM, then collateral must be posted. There would be no offsetting flows on the uncollateralised derivative, thus giving rise to a net funding requirement. At the same time, the CVA will increase due to the net counterparty exposure. So we see that CVA and FCA operate in the same direction. We consider FVA next.

Derivatives funding policy

As part of sound liquidity management policy, all banks should have articulated funding policies in place for each of their business lines. These set out the liquidity and funding treatment of each product type within the businesses, including FTP rates, required tenor of funding, and so on. The treatment of the derivatives book can sometimes be particularly problematic. But if we stop using the misnomer "off-balance-sheet", and treat the funding requirement that arises out of derivatives business in exactly the same way we should be treating the cash business, then the issue regains clarity.

In practice, this means that banks that run derivatives portfolios, generally the derivatives dealers plus large users of derivatives, must treat the cash flow requirements arising out of this business with the same discipline and liquidity risk principles as they do any other business line. The divergence in bank cost of funds (COF) from Libor since 2008 confirms the importance of valuing and risk managing derivatives using such an approach, in a way that recognises the bank's term funding rates.

First principles

Inter-bank derivatives trading takes place under the CSA arrangement in the standard ISDA agreement. This means that the mark-to-market value of each derivative contract is passed over as collateral, usually in the form of cash but sometimes as risk-free sovereign securities. In general, the collateral requirements under a two-way CSA agreement should result in a netted zero cash flow position, because what a bank needs to pass over as collateral on a derivative that is offside, it will receive from the counterparty to the hedge on this derivative. However, a number of counterparties, such as corporates, sovereign authorities, sovereign debt management offices, and central banks, do not sign CSA agreements. This one-way CSA arrangement will create a funding requirement for a bank, as it will have to transfer cash if it is MtM negative, while it will not receive any cash if it is MtM positive.

To incorporate the correct discipline with regard to the liquidity effects generated by uncollateralised derivatives business, the funding policy needs to incorporate an appropriate liquidity premium charge. This will apply to the net MtM value of all uncollateralised derivatives on the balance sheet. By charging the right rate, the business lines are incentivised to work towards reducing uncollateralised business wherever possible.

A bank will fund its balance sheet at its specific COF, which splits into four categories:

- Secured short-term funding costs: the rate at which the bank borrows against collateral. This is generally the OIS curve, and thus the lowest funding rate available (OIS lies below Libor). It is not relevant in an uncollateralised derivative context, because such instruments cannot be used as collateral (even if they are positive MtM);
- Secured long-term funding costs: the rate at which the bank can borrow by issuing term secured liabilities such as covered bonds and mortgage-backed securities;
- Short-term unsecured funding costs: the bank's COF for short-dated (0–12-month) tenors. At its lowest this will be around Libor, although many banks' short-term unsecured borrowing rate is at a spread above Libor. That said, for certain banks the short-term unsecured funding will be at zero, for example, retail deposits such as current ("checking") account balances;
- Long-term unsecured funding costs: the bank's COF for long-dated (2–10-year) tenors, also referred to as the term liquidity premium (TLP).

A general position of OIS, Libor, and TLP curves is shown in Figure 10.24.

The above of course is in the "wholesale" or investment bank space. In reality, derivatives dealers are often part of "universal" banking groups that also include retail and corporate business lines. A large part of the balance sheet will be funded therefore by low-cost liabilities of contractual short-dated but behaviourally long-dated maturity. These also need to be factored into the pricing curve in a way that is appropriate. One approach might be to derive the derivatives COF off a "weighted average cost of funds" (WACF) curve that is an average of all balance sheet liabilities. Either way, care needs to be taken that business lines in the wholesale bank, which includes the derivatives desk, are charged an appropriate price and not necessarily the retail or corporate COF rate, particularly since customer deposits have short contractual tenors but long behavioural tenors, and so do not inflict a term liquidity premium (TLP) on the bank.

Derivative liabilities and assets

Derivative liabilities correspond to what is termed an overall expected negative exposure (ENE), the most basic example of which is a deposit. A derivative asset corresponds to an overall expected positive exposure or EPE and at its simplest would be a loan.

An appreciation of the terms of a derivatives funding policy requires an understanding of credit valuation adjustment (CVA), debt value adjustment (DVA), and funding value adjustment (FVA). Following existing literature (for example, see Picault (2005) and Gregory (2009)), under a set of simplifying assumptions we have:

$$CVA = EPE \times PD \times LGD$$
$$= EPE \times \text{Counterparty credit spread}$$

where EPE is expected positive earnings, and PD and LGD are standard credit analyst expressions for default probability and loss given default. More formally we write:

$$CVA = (1 - R) \int_{t=0}^{T} q(t)v(t)dt$$

where R is the recovery rate, q is the probability density function of counterparty default, and v is the value of the derivative payoff. In discrete time we write:

$$CVA = (1 - R) \sum_{i=1}^{n} q_i v_i$$

where q_i is the probability of default between times t_{i-1} and t_i:

$$DVA = ENE \times \text{RBS credit spread}$$

and

$$\text{Funding cost} = (EPE + ENE) \times \text{Derivative funding spread}$$

In other words, the discounting to be applied for valuation is at the appropriate tenor bank funding cost.

The funding cost to apply to the derivatives portfolio cash flows may sometimes be selected depending on what assumption we make about the ease of unwinding the portfolio:

- Assume no easy unwind: if we cannot unwind the portfolio without punitive costs, we must assume we will have to fund the transaction for the full term. The funding cost of this commitment is given by the bank's long-term COF. If we fund (value) at short-term COF we run the risk that sudden spikes in the short-term COF will create funding losses, or that a liquidity squeeze in general will impact our ability to roll over funding for the position. To avoid this risk, we would fund with long-term borrowing, and discount unsecured derivatives off the long-term COF (TLP) curve;

- Assume easy unwind: if we can unwind the position with no extraneous cost, we can apply the short-term COF, say the 1-year TLP. The assumption of easy unwind means that we are not committed to rolling over funding; in the event of liquidity stress we would simply unwind the portfolio and eliminate the funding commitment. This is a strong assumption to make, particularly at a time of stress, and would be a high-risk policy.

Therefore, in theory we recommend that the derivative asset be discounted at TLP and the funding for collateral postings be substantially term funded. That said, in some cases the funding generated from a derivative book (assuming no counterparty default) is contractually for a long maturity, and so the case may be made that this should be charged for or receive the secured funding rate as opposed to the unsecured COF rate. That being the case, the derivatives funding curve then sits below the bank's COF curve and closer to the secured funding curve. This is shown at Figure 10.24.

In general, when applying derivatives funding policy we assume no netting arrangements are in place, but in practice these are quite common and will have an impact on the bank's collateral funding position in the event of default.

Derivative portfolio maturity

The tenor period to apply when applying the correct funding cost to derivative book cash flows can be the contractual maturity of the derivative in question, but not necessarily so. An alternative approach is to split the portfolio into

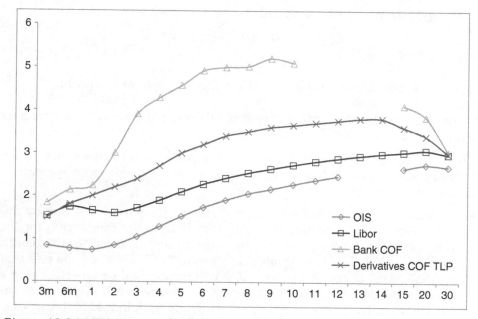

Figure 10.24   Derivatives funding curve as secured funding COF

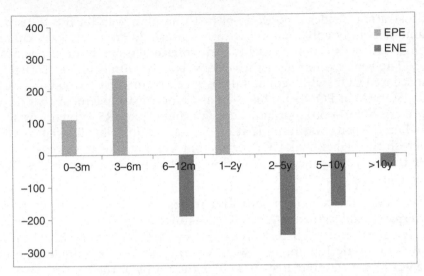

Figure 10.25   Uncollateralised derivatives net position FTP pricing

tenor buckets commensurate with the tenors at which we wish to fund the cash flows, with each bucket funded at the appropriate tenor COF.

Placing the derivative portfolio cash flows into appropriate term tenor buckets is a logical position on which to base how we choose to fund these cash flows. In practice, the derivative valuation model itself can be used to produce this tenor bucket breakdown, in the form of a "funding risk per basis point" (FR01) delta ladder. Using this model output removes the need for a subjective analysis of the maturity profile of the portfolio. In other words, the maturity profile of the portfolio is given by the model output. The appropriate tenor TLP is charged on the amount in each bucket.

This is shown at Figure 10.25.

In practice of course the profile is unlikely to look like the one in Figure 10.25 (although it might do). Rather, it is more likely to be all one way – either net long or short across most if not all tenor buckets.

In summary, cash flows arising out of the derivatives business, both contractual and collateral, must be funded at the appropriate TLP COF for their tenor. This means term funding a large part of the portfolio cash flows.

Funding valuation adjustment

Funding value adjustment is as important in derivative pricing as CVA, if not more so, and a vital part of an effective derivatives funding policy. When incorporating CVA, FVA, and where desired the cost of associated regulatory capital ("CRC") into a transaction, we take a portfolio view with each individual counterparty. FVA represents the value adjustment made for the funding and liquidity cost of undertaking a derivative transaction.

To illustrate, consider a portfolio of just one plain vanilla IRS transaction. Assume it is fully collateralised with no threshold and daily cash collateral postings. This means that on a daily basis collateral is posted or received (MtM value). The bank exhibiting negative MtM borrows funds to post collateral at its unsecured COF, while collateral posted earns interest at the OIS rate (Fed Funds, SONIA, or EONIA). This is an asymmetric arrangement that impacts the pre-crash norm of Libor-based discounting of the IRS, which was acceptable when the bank was funding at Libor or at the inter-bank swap curve. But post-crash the higher bank COF means that funding adds to the cost of transacting the swap. The magnitude of this cost is a function of [OIS% – COF%] for the bank.

If we consider now a book of derivative transactions, the funding cost for the counterparty banks ("Banks A and B") is a function of the size of the net MtM for the entire portfolio. Therefore, exactly as with CVA, to calculate the impact of the asymmetric funding cost we need to consider the complete portfolio value with each counterparty, as well as the terms of the specific CSA. This means in practice that when pricing the single swap, unless Banks A and B have the same funding costs – unlikely unless one is being very approximate – we see that the banks will not agree on a price for the instrument, irrespective of their counterparty risk and CVA.

That means a bank can choose to use FVA for a profitability-type analysis only, not impacting swap MtM, or it can choose to cover this cost, in which case it will impact swap valuation. The decision may depend on the counterparty and the product/trade type, or it can be a universal one. But not passing it on or adjusting the price for FVA means the derivatives business line is not covering its costs correctly.

The position is not markedly different with uncollateralised derivatives, generally ones where one counterparty is a "customer", for example, a corporate that is using the swap to hedge interest-rate risk. The bank providing the swap will hedge this exposure with another bank, and this second swap will be traded under a CSA. This is shown in Figure 10.26.

The first swap has no collateral posting flows, but the second one does. This is in itself an asymmetric CSA position; moreover, the second swap cost will include an FVA element. The bank may wish to pass on this FVA hedge cost into the customer pricing, which means making the FVA adjustment to the swap price.

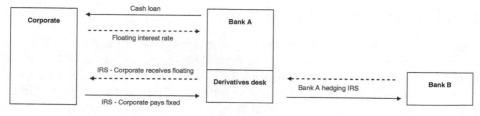

Figure 10.26 Customer IRS and hedging IRS

In both of the above illustrations, at any time the transaction (or hedge transaction) or portfolio MtM is negative, the bank will be borrowing cash to post as collateral. This borrowing is at the bank's cost of funds (COF), which we denote Libor + s where s is the funding spread. (Ignore specific tenor at this point.) If we look at FVA intuitively, it is an *actual* cost borne by the derivatives desk (and therefore the bank) as part of maintaining the derivatives portfolio – no different in cost terms than funding the cash asset side of the balance sheet. So at the very least, a bank needs to incorporate FVA into its derivatives business returns and profitability analysis. Ideally, the governance of FVA will be incorporated alongside all collateral management functions, including CVA, and overseen by the bank's Treasury/ALM function.

Notwithstanding the strategic objective of a balanced portfolio policy, the net impact of uncollateralised derivatives transactions or any asymmetric derivatives and hedging arrangement is to generate an ongoing unsecured funding requirement. We should expect this funding requirement to be in place as long as a bank is a going concern, in other words as ordinary business. Therefore, it should be funded in long-term tenors, with only a minority proportion funded in short-term tenors.

The cost of funding a derivatives portfolio, whether as a market-maker or simply for hedging purposes, is an important part of the overall profitability of a bank and needs to be treated exactly as would the funding cost of a cash asset. FVA is one approach to measure funding cost. It can be passed on in customer pricing or the bank can choose to wear it, but the business line still needs to be charged for it (exactly as with cash asset funding).

The magnitude of FVA is a direct function of a bank's COF, which fluctuates, and so it is important for FVA to reflect current reality. By definition, banks with the highest COF (highest s and lowest perceived credit quality) will suffer a competitive disadvantage in this space.

Centralised clearing and ALM[3]

One of the policy decisions taken in the wake of the 2008 bank crash was the demand from regulators that hitherto "over-the-counter" (OTC) derivative transactions be settled, or "cleared", through a centralised clearing counterparty (CCP), in the same way that exchange-traded derivatives are settled at the clearing house. This would remove bilateral counterparty risk because every transaction participant would, in effect, be dealing with the clearing house. In theory, this removes counterparty credit risk, because the clearing house would be sufficiently collateralised so as never to go bankrupt.[4]

---

[3]Thanks to Kevin Liddy, BTRM Faculty, for assistance with this section.

[4]Or, as one might say, in their rush to remove the liability of the taxpayer to "Too Big To Fail" (TBTF) banks, the regulators have created an institution that is, if not necessarily the largest TBTF institution in existence, certainly one of the most systemically important ...

A bigger role for CCPs
- CCPs have been growing in importance for many years
- A particularly important boost to growth came after the financial crisis, with the G20 requirement that standardised OTC derivatives should be centrally cleared
- CCPs are, in effect, being tasked with helping to mitigate the effects of the next financial crisis

Are CCPs safe enough?
- This question has been increasingly asked over the past year
- Whatever the *potential* advantages, if *in practice* CCP risk management is not good enough those advantages won't be realised
- Concern about banks' large and growing exposures to CCPs...
- ...and what is seen as the resulting "concentration" of risk and "single points of failure"

Financial stability: advantages of CCPs over bilateral clearing
De facto advantages
- More risk absorbed by the defaulter itself (i.e. higher "initial margin" or "defaulters-pay collateral")
- More rigorous risk management processes (e.g. re collection of margin, transparency)

Intrinsic advantages
- Multilateral netting
- Mutualisation of risk – risk borne by the non-defaulting clearing members (e.g. through the default fund)

Largely an empirical issue
CCPs are subject to international standards, the CPMI-IOSCO *Principles for financial market infrastructures* (PFMI), issued in 2012
- Are the standards being observed?
  - Lags in adopting and enforcing the standards
  - Differences in interpreting the standards
- Are the standards enough? Are they effective?

Figure 10.27 (i) Centralised clearing counterparty key points

The role of CCP is being carried out by existing clearing houses such as London Clearing House in the European Union. While there are technical issues to consider when dealing in, say, USD IRS (because of the basis that exists between IRS cleared in the US and the EU), from an ALM perspective the issues that should be addressed may include:

- What price FVA to consider? The bank's TLP vs capital arbitrage;
- Who "owns" the collateral in the bank?;
- Impact on the Basel III NSFR liquidity requirement: all market participants will have to post a significant amount of "initial margin" with the CCP (or their agent bank). Thus, IM will act as a permanent drain of funding, with negative impact on the NSFR metric value;
- Optimising collateral (placing the cheapest available, in the cheapest currency, to the bank as collateral at the CCP);

A key difference between CCPs and banks
- CCPs are not like banks. In particular, capital plays a different role.
- CCPs exist to provide protection against member default.
  - They <u>don't</u> do this primarily by absorbing the loss themselves through their capital
  - Rather, it's more accurate to see a CCP as being there to help the market *manage* risk effectively
  - Specifically, they try to ensure that, if the losses are so great that they exceed the collateral put up by the defaulter itself, they are *mutualised* by the surviving members in a safe and effective way
- In this sense, CCPs are risk "distributors" more than "concentrators"

Should capital play a bigger role?
- In principle, you can imagine a world where CCP capital <u>does</u> play the primary role in absorbing losses from participant default
- We'd need to think carefully about whether this was:
  - "fair"
  - realistic
- But even if CCPs don't become like banks in their use of capital, capital <u>is</u> nevertheless important:
  - "skin in the game" (incentive for good CCP risk management)
  - other risks (e.g. business risk), where a CCP <u>is</u> more like a bank
  - even for absorbing losses from participant default, could play a *bigger* role than today

Optimal allocation of losses
May need to focus more broadly on two issues simultaneously:
- Quantity (and quality) of the prefunded financial resources the CCP should have *in total* to deal with clearing member default? How extreme an event should be assumed?
- Who provides those resources:
  - the defaulting clearing member(s)?
  - the surviving clearing members (i.e. mutualisation)?
  - the owners (i.e. capital)?
  - others (e.g. insurance)?
It seems clear that clearing members themselves will continue to play the primary role in absorbing the risk that they create. The issue is how best that can be done.

Figure 10.27 (ii) Centralised clearing counterparty key points

- Impact on securities financing;
- The role of the XVA desk;
- Incentivising the right behaviour at business lines.

The collateral management impact of dealing via CCPs is considerable, and the orthodox treatment would be to place collateral management as a direct responsibility of the Treasury department.

Figure 10.27 (i) and (ii) summarise the key issues for consideration surrounding CCPs.

CONCLUSIONS

Today the practice of liquidity risk management in banks is heavily prescribed by the regulatory regime in every jurisdiction. This was a natural response to the bank crash of 2008, and it places onerous requirements, in terms of resources and reporting, on all banks. As this chapter has shown, the liquidity risk discipline combines everything from cash management and funding to intra-day liquidity and asset encumbrance. It is important that all banks have a deep and thorough understanding of all the drivers of liquidity risk exposure on the balance sheet, which is why the governance structure for liquidity management must run from ALCO downwards via Treasury. All aspects must be included (for example, traditionally collateral management was often placed in a back-office operational function or outside Treasury: this would not be best practice today).

Liquidity risk management must remain the most important function in any bank at any time.

Chapter
11

....

BUSINESS BEST-PRACTICE BANK INTERNAL FUNDS TRANSFER PRICING POLICY

Internal bank funds pricing or "FTP" is a key element in liquidity risk management. It is also a devil of a topic to teach, because there is no "one size fits all" and different banks set different objectives for it. As befits what should be viewed as a key pillar of the liquidity risk management framework, but is as often as not treated as an internal accounting exercise, there are many nuances and the FTP process can be as frustrating to implement and monitor as it is to set policy for. That said, an inappropriate or artificial internal funds pricing policy may lead to poor business decision-making, and could generate excessive liquidity and funding risk exposure. It is therefore imperative for banks to operate a robust and disciplined internal funding mechanism, one that is integrated into the overall liquidity risk management framework.

In this chapter we review the rationale behind the internal term liquidity premium (TLP) and present a recommended best-practice policy template for internal funds pricing.

BACKGROUND

Bank internal funds pricing mechanism – called variously funds transfer pricing (FTP), firm liquidity pricing (FLP), liquidity transfer pricing (LTP), or term liquidity premium (TLP), although these terms are not actually synonymous – is invariably operated via the Treasury function. This is logical given that all banks operate essentially the same internal funding arrangement, as illustrated in Figure 11.1. Treasury is also responsible for external balance sheet liquidity risk management, as well as interest-rate risk.

FTP – the price at which an individual business line raises funds from or places deposits at its own Treasury desk – is essential to the risk management process. It is the key parameter in business decision-making, the driving of sales, asset allocation, and customer product pricing. It is also a key hurdle rate behind the product approval process and in an individual business line's performance measurement. Just as capital allocation decisions affecting front-office business units need to account for the cost of that capital (in terms of return on regulatory and economic capital), so funding decisions exercised by corporate treasurers carry significant implications for sales and trading teams at the trade level.

The problem arises because banks undertake maturity transformation, funding long-dated assets with shorter dated liabilities. Moreover, certain assets such as mortgages and corporate loans are frequently illiquid in nature. The combination of a funding gap and illiquid asset base makes it imperative that, each time an asset is originated, business lines correctly price in the term liquidity risk they are generating. Conversely, a business line that raises funds can also be valued at the internal TLP.

Hence, the internal funding rate is important to the discipline driving business decision-making. For example, a uniform cost of funds (something practised by many banks during the lead-up to the 2008 financial crisis) will mean that the

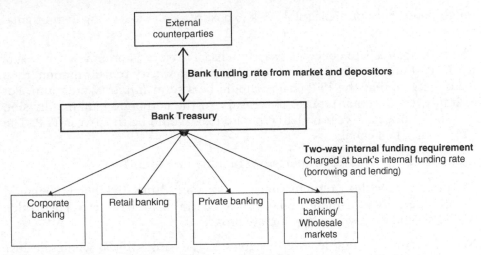

Figure 11.1   Bank internal funding arrangement

different liquidity stresses on the balance sheet, created by different types of asset, are not addressed adequately at the aggregate funding level. Different asset types place different liquidity pressures on the Treasury funding desk, thereby demanding a structurally sound internal funding pricing policy that is appropriate to the type of business line being funded.

SETTING THE BANK POLICY STANDARD

A formal internal funding policy is necessary in order to make explicit to business lines the need for the bank to cover the cost of its liquidity risk. The objectives of the policy are to:

- Ensure consistent liquidity pricing behaviour among each business line;
- Remove interest-rate risk from business lines; and
- Include the bank's cost of liquidity in product pricing.

The policy must also seek to ensure that business lines recognise the impact of asset and liability pricing on the balance sheet of the bank, and allow for these costs accordingly. The policy document should be formalised and approved at the asset–liability committee (ALCO) level, and Treasury should review the document on a semi-annual basis. The policy should include the treatment for each product asset class in which the bank deals.

THE TERM LIQUIDITY PREMIUM

It is important, then, that all banks put in place an internal funding structure that correctly charges for the term liquidity risk placed on the balance sheet by each business line. An artificially low funding rate can create as much potentially unmanageable risk exposure as a risk-seeking loan origination culture.

The principal debate concerns exactly what Treasury is pricing when it sets the FTP. If one accepts that a bank undertakes maturity transformation, then logic dictates that the FTP charge should be a term *liquidity* premium. For example, the internal rate from Treasury to the corporate banking division looking to price a 5-year bullet corporate loan would be the 5-year TLP. The FTP would then equal:

$$\text{FTP} = \text{Short-term funding rate} + \text{TLP}$$

The proxy for the short-term funding rate is usually 3-month Libor, but it could equally logically be 1-month Libor or the central bank base rate. The bank's ALCO should approve the appropriate proxy.

Note that this does not necessarily equate to the bank's 5-year wholesale cost of funds (COF). The bank's funding rate will incorporate an element of its own credit risk to the market, as well as the term liquidity premium, and it is only the liquidity premium that should be passed on to the business line in the internal FTP.

If we discount the reality of maturity transformation and assume matched funding, then in this example we would have:

$$\text{FTP} = \text{COF}$$

While it is always important to ensure that the correct cost of liquidity is allowed for in the internal funding model, it needs to be set in line with commercial and practical reality.

Calculating the term liquidity premium

The TLP, when used in the way we have defined it here, is not a straightforward exercise when extracting from market and customer rates. Often one needs to have recourse to proxies, and instead of one specific value being available, one may need to be satisfied with a range and/or average.

The base case scenario would be for a bank to have access to the wholesale markets at Libor across the entire term structure. There is a case here for saying that the FTP can be Libor-flat; however, this is the current state *now*, with the future state of the markets being unknown. Thus, a zero FTP spread can be justified only on a match-funded basis. Given this logic, a bank needs to determine its cost of liquidity. There may be more than one answer, so an element of judgement is called for.

The starting point is the rate at which the bank can raise funds in the market. For a large bank, its primary issuance level will, in a stable market, lie above the secondary market level. If we ignore this difference for the time being, a logical first step would be to take the cost of its funds in the market as the primary input to its internal funding curve. Two things must be considered: (i) this funding rate includes the credit risk of the bank, which needs to be stripped out, and (ii) not every bank has a public funding curve. It is necessary then to consider proxies to establish the cost of liquidity.

While a number of proxy measures can be considered, we recommend the following:

- The difference between the funded and the unfunded rate for the bank; that is, the swap rate vs the bond rate paid by the bank. In other words, what it pays floating in an interest-rate swap against what it pays floating in an asset swap on a bond it issues (of the same tenor);
- The difference between:
  o Paying fixed on a term interest-rate swap; and
  o Paying fixed on the same-tenor money market swap or overnight index swap (OIS) swap.
- The increase in the cost of funds for the bank for each incremental upward change in tenor. For example, a bank's cost of borrowing along the term structure, as a spread over Libor, may look like this:
  o 1-year: 20bp;
  o 2-year: 30bp;
  o 3-year: 35bp;
  o 4-year: 40bp;
  o 5-year: 50bp.

While the above approach assumes a flat credit term structure for the bank (which from observation of the credit derivative market we know not to be accurate), it does still give some idea of the liquidity premium.

- The difference between the bank's credit default swap (CDS) spread and the asset swap spread (ASW) for the bank. This is the CDS basis, and in theory represents the cost of cash borrowing and liquidity premium for the bank against its pure credit risk. Since a CDS is, theoretically, the price of credit only, the basis should represent its liquidity premium.

The FTP charge can be based on a simple average of the above measures. Alternatively, given an individual bank's structure, it may choose to give higher weight to certain proxies. Since there is no transparent explicit cost of liquidity, a bank will have to exercise some judgement when setting the rate.

A worked example of this calculation will be presented in the next issue of iRisk.

Funds transfer pricing curve

The actual internal funding curve template, be it the TLP or all-in FTP curve, should be included in the bank's funding policy document and reviewed on a regular basis. While it is common for the FTP rates to be posted as a grid (as shown in Figure 11.2), this is not recommended because of the implied linear

Tenor	GBP
<3M	0
6M	7
12M	14
2Y	25
3Y	32
4Y	40
5Y	42
7Y	68
10Y	99

Figure 11.2   Bank FTP grid

interpolation relationship between odd-date tenors. Instead, the FTP curve should be drawn as a curve such as shown in Figure 11.3. Here we illustrate an example for a bank that operates across the retail, corporate, and wholesale banking space and has also calculated a "weighted average" funding curve (WACF). Many banks choose the grid presentation, however. When a grid is used, assets or liabilities with maturities that are not exact full years, and thus fall in between the tenors on the grid, should be priced on a straight-line interpolation basis between the shorter and longer date prices.

The FTP curve will state explicitly the rate paid or received by the business lines for assets and liabilities across the term structure. If the FTP policy assumes matched funding, and applies full marginal cost (FMC) pricing, then this disregards the fact that, in reality, the bank is engaging in maturity

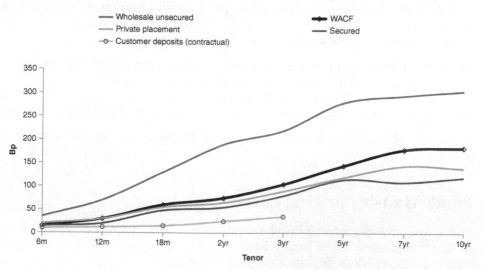

Figure 11.3   Bank FTP curve and other funding curves

transformation. While this is logically tenable, it may not be practical for commercial or economic reasons. This is why the more robust regime is for Treasury FTP to apply the TLP add-on to the short-term funding rate, rather than FMC. The final customer pricing would incorporate cost of capital, required margin, and an add-on for customer credit risk.

Of course, the final choice for the FTP policy is a matter of individual bank judgement, and again should be decided by ALCO.

As previously noted, where behavioural analysis indicates that the term to maturity of an item differs from its contractual term to maturity, the expected maturity is used to set the appropriate FTP rate. For assets and liabilities, the best example is as follows:

Residential mortgages: in the UK, the legal final maturity of such assets is 25 years. However, from observation and behavioural analysis the expected life is around 7 years, hence we would apply a 7-year rate, or lower, for new asset origination pricing.

Current accounts: this product has a 1-day (or 0-day) contractual maturity but balances are sticky and, typically, at least half of the aggregate balance is static over 2, 3, or even 5 years. It is logical to assign such tenors for FTP purposes. In a similar vein, if a call account balance is shown to be 50% sticky for 1 year, the 1-year FTP would be earned on 50% of the funds.

For trading book assets, which are generally assumed to be liquid and expected to be sold within 6 months of being bought, the FTP charge would be set according to the expected holding duration and not the legal maturity of the traded asset. Typically, this will be at the 6-month FTP rate; however, this depends on the type of asset and the level of liquidity. In general, a bank will set different tiers of liquidity, with Tier 1 (such as G7 government bonds) being the most liquid and thus attracting a 1-week or 1-month FTP, down to Tier 3 for the least liquid and attracting the 6-month internal funds rate.

TEMPLATE FTP REGIMES

Though there is no "one size fits all" FTP regime, we present here best-practice guidelines for the FTP approach in retail, corporate, and wholesale market business lines.

The guidelines assume a standard internal funding arrangement, whereby internal funding operations are arranged via a bank account in Treasury. When a loan is made, this internal account is overdrawn and then funded on an overnight basis to the business line. The standard overnight FTP charge is 3-month Libor, but it could be 1-month Libor or 6-month Libor, or the central bank base rate, depending on the opinion of the bank's ALCO. Assets or liabilities are set at the relevant tenor FTP, although another option is to operate a net rather than gross funding basis and either charge or pay the net position long or short in each relevant tenor bucket at the relevant FTP.

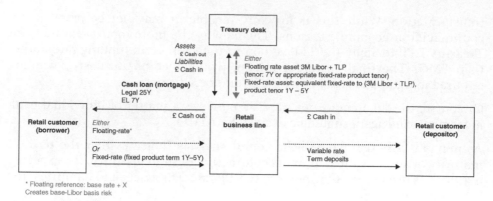

Figure 11.4   Retail banking FTP regime

Retail Bank FTP regime

A retail bank is stable funded, and in large part funded by zero-rate or low-rate liabilities (termed non-interest-bearing liabilities or NIBLs). The asset FTP tenor can generally be set safely at less than the contractual tenor, often the expected life (EL) tenor. This preserves competitive position. Liabilities are also priced at behavioural tenor. So here FTP = TLP and not COF. For residential mortgage assets we assume capital and repayment products, with no interest-only mortgages. The main principles are shown in Figure 11.4.

Note here that tenors quoted are behavioural or, as is common, can be adjusted downwards for competitive reasons. If operating a net charging regime, it is possible to set and net nearly matching tenors, for example, 3-year deposits against 3-year assets.

From Figure 11.4, for the floating-rate asset, FTP is 3M Libor + TLP. The TLP tenor will be the behavioural life of the asset, so we have suggested 7-year. For the fixed-rate asset, FTP is the fixed-rate equivalent to 3M Libor plus TLP where the TLP tenor matches the product life. (For example, a 2-year fixed-rate in a mortgage that moves to floating variable or can be refixed at a new rate after 2 years.) This transfers interest-rate risk from the business line and centralises it in Treasury, which is recommended.

Figure 11.6 shows our recommended template behavioural tenors, but it must be emphasised that each bank should set the level appropriate to its own product analysis.

The reality of FTP policy is that it must reflect the two-way relationship between assets and customers. We summarise, with reference to Figure 11.5, that the practical considerations for FTP should reflect:

- Actual rates paid by both sides;
- Competitive position;

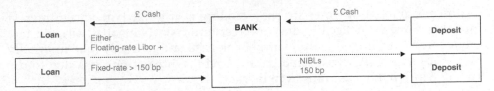

Figure 11.5 Retail banking asset–liability interconnection

Retail bank product	<1Y	1Y	2Y	3Y	4Y	5Y
Personal loans	20%		40%	40%		
Mortgages						100%
Overdrafts	10%	10%	80%			
Credit cards	20%		70%	10%		
Savings accounts	20%	20%	60%			
Current accounts	20%					80%

(*Source*: Choudhry, 2012)

Figure 11.6 Template retail bank behavioural tenors, percentage of balances

- Properly priced products:
  - in the Figure 11.5 illustration, deposits pay 150bps, so loans must earn above this rate.
- Behavioural match funding where applicable, for example, match funded or not:
  - Banks that treat current account balances as 5Y or even longer tenor;
  - Banks that treat such liabilities as shorter tenor.

The longer dated assumption allows a retail bank to consider itself as "almost match funded". This is the attraction, from a liquidity risk management point of view, of stable customer deposits ("stable" liabilities as opposed to "non-stable" in the Basel III terminology).

Corporate bank FTP regime

Compared to retail banking, corporate banking encompasses a wider range of products that attract FTP. As noted above, the treatment of specific product types will be articulated in the detailed funding policy statement.

Per the orthodox approach, business lines originating assets or raising liabilities will have funding and interest-rate risk transferred to Treasury and made up to an equivalent interest basis. In the process, the model assumes that all assets are funded at the short-term FTP rate, let us again assume 3M Libor, and all liabilities are rewarded at 3M Libor. The key consideration here, which also applies in retail banking but to a lesser extent, is the hedging side, as a significant amount of corporate bank lending is at a fixed or capped interest rate that must be hedged against interest-rate risk. Note that variable rate products that are linked to the central bank base rate generally fund internally on a 3M Libor basis, but often are unhedged for interest-rate risk due to the lack of depth in the base rate swap market.

This raises a key management point. Since internal FTP-base rate-Libor basis risk cannot be hedged externally, a bank's origination policy should dictate that fixed-rate, fixed-term assets are hedged with cash fixed-rate liabilities, in order to match repricing tenor and matching interest rates bases. In other words, the bank's IRR hedging policy document should influence product origination strategy to ensure basis risk is minimised at the point of origination.

The recommended corporate bank FTP regime is illustrated in Figure 11.7. Figure 11.8 shows a template tenor convention.

Note that there are two alternative approaches here, shown in Figure 11.7: (i) the internal FTP that Treasury charges the business for funds lent out at a fixed-rate to the customer is also at a fixed-rate for the (behavioural) life of the loan, or (ii) the internal FTP is at a floating-rate. Option 2 does not remove the interest-rate risk for the business line and so Treasury then also has to put in place an internal swap hedge with the business line.

For the business lines, approach (i) is the most transparent, consequently that is the one recommended by the author.

Wholesale bank FTP regime

The wholesale banking business model, where one exists in a bank, requires a more prescribed FTP regime. There is little, if any, concept of a "customer deposits" funding business and the asset side is funded with repo (secured funding) and wholesale funding (money markets and capital markets).

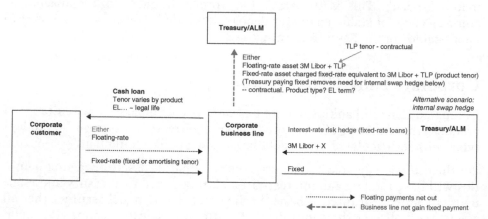

Figure 11.7   Corporate banking FTP regime, asset example

Corporate bank product	<1Y	1Y	2Y	3Y	4Y	5Y	Contractual tenor
Base rate loans		20%	20%	10%			50%
Libor-linked loans			20%	30%			50%
Overdrafts		25%	75%				
Interest-only loans				25%			75%
Repayment loans		10%	20%	20%			50%
Variable tenor (revolving facility)		10%					90%
Savings accounts				50%		50%	
Current accounts			20%	30%		50%	

(*Source*: Choudhry, 2012)

Figure 11.8 Corporate banking product tenor behaviour, percentage of balance

This makes the FTP model more straightforward to implement. For example, a summary template might look like this:

- **Trading book**: funded in repo at repo rate. Any unsecured funding is funded at 6-month or 12-month Libor. However, not all trading book assets are of an equal liquidity level. The funding policy may break down the asset types into the following:
  - Tier 1 G7 currency bonds;
  - Tier 2 bonds denominated in AUD, CHF, DKK, HKD, NOK, NZD, SEK, SGD;
  - Tier 3 bonds rated below A-/A3.

Most banks will not have FTP grids for currencies other than their domestic currency and USD and EUR. The base currency grid can be converted to a required currency rate by applying the FX basis swap rate to it – not an exact science but the approach should be sufficient for most purposes.

- **Securitisable assets**: origination of assets that are eligible for securitisation often receive a lower funding rate, say a specified reduction in basis points, because in theory they do not expose the bank to a need for more unsecured wholesale funding;
- **Derivatives book**: contractual and collateral funding cash flows are modelled into tenor buckets, as expected positive exposure (EPE) and expected negative exposure (ENE), with the net number ("expected exposure" or EE) charged or credited with the appropriate wholesale market COF, rather than the TLP. (See section on Funds Transfer Pricing.)

A bank that operates across all markets will need to consider carefully how to construct its FTP curve and whether there should be one unified curve across the bank or variations by business line.

Example 11.1   Calculating the term liquidity premium (TLP): worked example

---

A key element of the FTP regime is the specific term liquidity premium (TLP) that a bank's Treasury desk incorporates into the FTP whenever it prices funds, either lent or borrowed, for the internal business lines.

The true or "fair value" TLP is difficult, if not impossible, to observe. Banks' COF, whether raised in the customer or the wholesale markets, incorporate both the bank's perceived credit risk as well as an element of term premium, so the task here is to extract the term liquidity element from the overall cost. As there is no direct observable TLP, we have to use proxies. Earlier in this chapter we detailed the types of proxies that one can consider. Here we use these proxies to determine an estimate for a bank's 5-year TLP.

Consider the following market rates for EUR, observed for an A+ rated European bank in January 2013:

5-year rates

CDS	97bp
Asset swap (actual bond) interpolated	103bp
Interest-rate swap	95bp
Risk free	52bp

The above imply a 5-year TLP of 6bp (against the CDS) and 8bp (against the swap). Note that the combined credit and liquidity cost as implied by spread over risk free is 51bp. Further implied TLP by proxy can be gleaned from the following:

Pay fixed in 5-year swap

Vanilla IRS	95bp
OIS	56bp

This implies a 5-year TLP of 39bp. Note this is the 5-year TLP and not the overnight 3-month TLP. For the 1-year TLP we would use the 1-year swap.

Cost of funds term structure (wholesale market bonds)

3-month	50bp
1-year	61bp
2-year	79bp
5-year interpolated	103bp

This implies a 5-year TLP of 53bp.

New issue premium

New issue   132bp
Secondary market asset swap   103bp

This implies a 5-year TLP of 29bp.

From the foregoing we have five inputs for the 5-year TLP in the range of 6–53bp. The average is 27bp and the median is 29bp. If we remove the outlier highest and lowest, the average is 25.3bp. We conclude that a logical rate to set for the 5-year TLP is of the order of 25–30bp. This calculation should be updated periodically, say every quarter.

At first sight this may appear insufficient value for a 5-year liquidity premium. But bear in mind that the bank's 5-year asset swap is trading at 103bp, and it is able to issue new 5-year wholesale market FRNs at 132bp. If the bank's COF for this tenor is in this range, it is not unexpected that the pure liquidity premium element of this cost should appear to be around one-third of this figure, with the balance representing the issuer credit risk of the bank.

CONCLUSIONS

The concept of internal funds pricing and the term liquidity premium is quite a complicated one, and there is no "one size fits all". It is important that the mechanism put in place is the one most appropriate to the business model of the bank in question, and set up to reflect the type of business that the bank's shareholders and Board want it to do.

Implementing an internal funds pricing policy that explicitly charges each business line for its cost of liquidity is not always a painless task, due in part to inertia and resistance from the business lines themselves. This is particularly acute when the businesses have historically always paid a Libor-flat or Libor + fixed spread charge. The bank's FTP policy, whether it is an update or it is being set up for the first time, should always be owned by the Board, delegated to ALCO, and implemented by the Treasury and Finance departments.

Chapter

12[1]

....

NET INTEREST INCOME (NII), NET INTEREST MARGIN (NIM) AND THE MANAGEMENT OF INTEREST-RATE RISK IN THE BANKING BOOK

---

[1]This chapter was co-written with Chris Westcott.

For conventional commercial banks, net interest income (NII) is their core form of revenue. For this reason, it is important for asset–liability committee (ALCO) to understand its drivers and behaviour, so that it is able to manage it and plan forward for its performance. NII itself is exposed to movements in interest rates, so this makes managing interest-rate risk in the banking book (IRRBB) important as well. This chapter considers behaviour and characteristics of NII and net interest margin (NIM), before moving on to key principles of IRRBB management.

NET INTEREST INCOME

Net Interest Income or NII is defined as the interest income received from lending activities or debt instruments held (for example, subordinated debt, senior debt, or certificates of deposit issued by other financial institutions) less the interest expense incurred on deposits or issued debt instruments. It is expressed as a currency amount over a period of time, normally 3, 6, or 12 months in line with reporting frequencies.

Examples of banking products that would typically contribute to NII include: loans, mortgages, overdrafts, credit cards, asset finance, instant access deposits, savings accounts, and fixed- or variable-rate bonds. Income earned from activities such as asset management, broking, insurance, corporate finance, investment management, and trusts and estate planning are classified under Fees and Commissions Receivable/Payable. Dividends received on equity positions held are classified as Other Income. Figure 12.1 illustrates the major components of bank P&L. NII is a key element and can often make up the largest constituent part.

An analysis of the accounts of the major UK banks reveals that NII accounted for between approximately half and three-quarters of their Total Income in 2014, as illustrated in Figure 12.2.

NET INTEREST MARGIN

NIM is a key bank profitability metric, given by the gap between interest income and interest expense, divided by assets. (UK and US banks use "average interest earning assets"; Eurozone banks usually use average total assets.) Average interest-earning assets is an average of all of a bank's assets that generate interest income during a specific time period. This excludes certain assets that are not interest bearing, like cash holdings and fixed assets, but includes non-performing assets.

NIM is normally expressed as an annual percentage rate. Figure 12.3 illustrates that the NIMs for the major UK banks ranged between 1.8 and 3.6% in 2014.

Which banking products affect NIM?

Figure 12.4A is an extract from the HSBC annual report and accounts for 2014. We indicate with a tick or a cross which banking products would impact the firm's NIM.

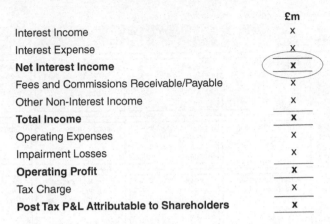

	£m
Interest Income	x
Interest Expense	x
Net Interest Income	**x**
Fees and Commissions Receivable/Payable	x
Other Non-Interest Income	x
Total Income	**x**
Operating Expenses	x
Impairment Losses	x
Operating Profit	**x**
Tax Charge	x
Post Tax P&L Attributable to Shareholders	**x**

Figure 12.1   Components of bank P&L

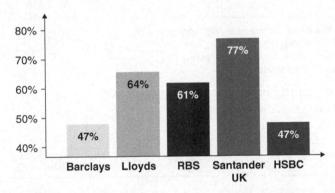

Figure 12.2   NII as a percentage of Total Income – major UK banks, 2014 accounts
Source: Published Accounts.

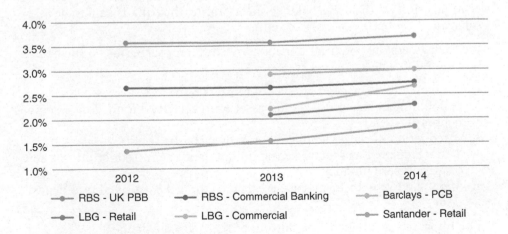

Source: Banks' annual reports, CMA analysis.
Note: NIM for HSBC RBWM and CMB not reported in published accounts. 2012 NIM for Barclays PCB not reported in published accounts. 2012 NIM for LBG Retail and Commercial Banking not reported in published accounts. NIM for Santander Retail is for Santander UK plc.

Figure 12.3   UK bank NIMs, 2012–2014

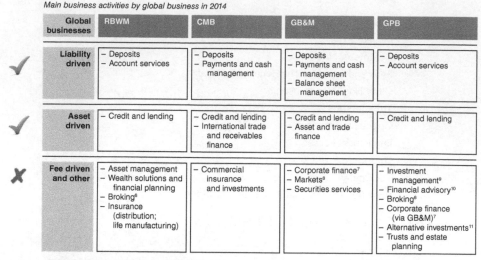

Main business activities by global business in 2014

Global businesses	RBWM	CMB	GB&M	GPB
Liability driven	– Deposits – Account services	– Deposits – Payments and cash management	– Deposits – Payments and cash management – Balance sheet management	– Deposits – Account services
Asset driven	– Credit and lending	– Credit and lending – International trade and receivables finance	– Credit and lending – Asset and trade finance	– Credit and lending
Fee driven and other	– Asset management – Wealth solutions and financial planning – Broking[6] – Insurance (distribution; life manufacturing)	– Commercial insurance and investments	– Corporate finance[7] – Markets[8] – Securities services	– Investment management[9] – Financial advisory[10] – Broking[6] – Corporate finance (via GB&M)[7] – Alternative investments[11] – Trusts and estate planning

RBWM = Retail Bank and Wealth Management
CMB = Commercial Banking
GB&M = Global Banking and Markets
GPB = Global Private Banking

Figure 12.4A   Bank products that influence NIM

Source: HSBC plc, 2014 Annual Report and Accounts

Example 12.1   NIM sensitivity example

We examine various scenario impacts on the NIM position of our hypothetical WestChoud Bank. The initial balance sheet position is shown at Figure 12.4B. If we make the (admittedly very strong!) assumption that the position will remain unchanged for a year, we see at the bottom the NII and NIM position. With such a balance sheet profile, the bank is said to be asset sensitive.

We then assess the potential impact of five different scenarios on the bank's NII and NIM. The scenarios are:

1. An increase in the general level of interest rates;
2. A doubling in size of the liquid asset buffer (HQLA) funded by a senior debt issue;
3. A reduction in the general level of interest rates;
4. The relaunch of an instant access product and the introduction of a new 0% credit card product;
5. Significant growth in mortgage balances funded by a fixed-rate deposit issue.

The impacts are shown at the bottom of the revised balance sheet for each of these scenarios, at Figures 12.4C, 12.4D, 12.4E, 12.4F, and 12.4G.

WestChoud Bank - Balance Sheet

5% Rate Environment (flat yield curve - same at all tenors)

Assets

	£m	Rate	Interest Income (£m)
Cash	100	-	-
Central Bank Deposits	250	1.00%	2.50
Loans to Banks	1,000	5.00%	50.00
Loans and Advances to Customers			
Credit Cards	1,000	12.00%	120.00
Personal Loans (Fixed Rate)	1,500	8.00%	120.00
Retail Overdrafts	500	9.00%	45.00
Fixed Rate Mortgages	5,000	5.25%	262.50
Variable Rate Mortgages	2,500	5.50%	137.50
Small Business Loans and Overdrafts	500	7.50%	37.50
Corporate Loans and Overdrafts	2,000	6.50%	130.00
Bad Debts Net of Provisions	250	0.00%	0.00
Debt Securities	1,500	4.50%	67.50
Equity Shares	500	-	-
Fixed Assets	400	-	-
Goodwill/Intangible Assets	300	-	-
Prepayments and Accrued Income	200	-	-
Total	17,500		972.50

Liabilities

	£m	Rate	Interest Expense (£m)
Deposits by Banks	2,000	4.80%	96.00
Customer Accounts			
Retail Non-Interest Bearing Current Accounts	3,000	0.00%	0.00
Retail Instant Access Deposit Accounts	2,000	2.50%	50.00
Retail Notice Accounts	500	3.50%	17.50
Retail Fixed Rate Bonds	1,000	4.50%	45.00
Corporate/Small Business Non-Interest Bearing Current Accounts	2,000	0.00%	0.00
Corporate Variable Rate Savings Accounts	1,000	2.00%	20.00
Small Business Variable Rate Savings Accounts	800	1.00%	8.00
Debt Securities in Issue (floating rate)	1,000	7.50%	75.00
Subordinated Liabilities (fixed rate)	2,000	10.00%	200.00
Accruals and Deferred Income	200	-	-
Equity Capital	2,000	-	-
Total	17,500		511.50

	£m
Interest Income	972.50
Interest Expense	511.50
Interest Earning Assets	16,000
Net Interest Income	461.00
NIM	2.88%

(after 12 months assume stable balance sheet)

Figure 12.4B WestChoud Bank starting balance sheet position, showing NII and NIM

WestChoud Bank - Balance Sheet

Scenario 1: Interest rates rise and there is an increased incidence of bad debts. No Funds Transfer Pricing Process. NIM increases from base scenario

8% Rate Environment (flat yield curve - same at all tenors)

Assets

	£m	Rate	Interest Income (£m)
Cash	100	-	-
Central Bank Deposits	250	4.00%	10.00
Loans to Banks	1,000	8.00%	80.00
Loans and Advances to Customers			
Credit Cards	990	18.00%	178.20
Personal Loans (Fixed Rate)	1,475	8.00%	118.00
Retail Overdrafts	485	12.00%	58.20
Fixed Rate Mortgages	4,975	5.25%	261.19
Variable Rate Mortgages	2,475	8.50%	210.38
Small Business Loans and Overdrafts	450	10.50%	47.25
Corporate Loans and Overdrafts	1,900	9.50%	180.50
Bad Debts Net of Provisions	500	0.00%	0.00
Debt Securities	1,500	7.50%	112.50
Equity Shares	500	-	-
Fixed Assets	400	-	-
Goodwill/Intangible Assets	300	-	-
Prepayments and Accrued Income	200	-	-
Total	**17,500**		**1,256.21**

Liabilities

	£m	Rate	Interest Expense (£m)
Deposits by Banks	2,000	7.80%	156.00
Customer Accounts			
Retail Non-Interest Bearing Current Accounts	3,000	0.00%	0.00
Retail Instant Access Deposit Accounts	2,000	5.50%	110.00
Retail Notice Accounts	500	6.50%	32.50
Retail Fixed Rate Bonds	1,000	4.50%	45.00
Corporate/Small Business Non-Interest Bearing Current Accounts	2,000	0.00%	0.00
Corporate Variable Rate Savings Accounts	1,000	5.00%	50.00
Small Business Variable Rate Savings Accounts	800	4.00%	32.00
Debt Securities in Issue (floating rate)	1,000	10.50%	105.00
Subordinated Liabilities (fixed rate)	2,000	10.00%	200.00
Accruals and Deferred Income	200	-	-
Equity Capital	2,000	-	-
Total	**17,500**		**730.50**

	£m
Interest Income	1,256.21
Interest Expense	730.50
Interest Earning Assets	16,000
Net Interest Income	525.71
versus Base Scenario	64.71
NIM	3.29%
versus Base Scenario	0.40%

Figure 12.4C   WestChoud Bank, Scenario 1 potential impact on NII/NIM

WestChoud Bank - Balance Sheet

Scenario 2: Liquid asset buffer doubled, funded by a senior debt issue. No Funds Transfer Pricing Process. NIM declines from base scenario

5% Rate Environment (flat yield curve - same at all tenors)

Assets

	£m	Rate	Interest Income (£m)
Cash	100	-	-
Central Bank Deposits	250	1.00%	2.50
Loans to Banks	1,000	5.00%	50.00
Loans and Advances to Customers			
Credit Cards	1,000	12.00%	120.00
Personal Loans (Fixed Rate)	1,500	8.00%	120.00
Retail Overdrafts	500	9.00%	45.00
Fixed Rate Mortgages	5,000	5.25%	262.50
Variable Rate Mortgages	2,500	5.50%	137.50
Small Business Loans and Overdrafts	500	7.50%	37.50
Corporate Loans and Overdrafts	2,000	6.50%	130.00
Bad Debts Net of Provisions	250	0.00%	0.00
Debt Securities	3,000	4.50%	135.00
Equity Shares	500	-	-
Fixed Assets	400		
Goodwill/Intangible Assets	300		
Prepayments and Accrued Income	200		
Total	**19,000**		**1,040.00**

Liabilities

	£m	Rate	Interest Expense (£m)
Deposits by Banks	2,000	4.80%	96.00
Customer Accounts			
Retail Non-Interest Bearing Current Accounts	3,000	0.00%	0.00
Retail Instant Access Deposit Accounts	2,000	2.50%	50.00
Retail Notice Accounts	500	3.50%	17.50
Retail Fixed Rate Bonds	1,000	4.50%	45.00
Corporate/Small Business Non-Interest Bearing Current Accounts	2,000	0.00%	0.00
Corporate Variable Rate Savings Accounts	1,000	2.00%	20.00
Small Business Variable Rate Savings Accounts	800	1.00%	8.00
Debt Securities in Issue (floating rate)	2,500	7.50%	187.50
Subordinated Liabilities (fixed rate)	2,000	10.00%	200.00
Accruals and Deferred Income	200		
Equity Capital	2,000		
Total	**19,000**		**624.00**

	£m
Interest Income	1,040.00
Interest Expense	624.00
Interest Earning Assets	17,500
Net Interest Income	416.00
versus Base Scenario	-45.00
NIM	2.38%
versus Base Scenario	-0.50%

Figure 12.4D WestChoud Bank, Scenario 2 potential impact on NII/NIM

WestChoud Bank - Balance Sheet

Scenario 3: Interest rates fall. No Funds Transfer Pricing Process. NIM declines from base scenario

4% Rate Environment (flat yield curve - same at all tenors)

Assets

	£m	Rate	Interest Income (£m)
Cash	100	-	-
Central Bank Deposits	250	0.00%	0.00
Loans to Banks	1,000	4.00%	40.00
Loans and Advances to Customers			
Credit Cards	1,000	10.00%	100.00
Personal Loans (Fixed Rate)	1,500	8.00%	120.00
Retail Overdrafts	500	8.00%	40.00
Fixed Rate Mortgages	5,000	5.25%	262.50
Variable Rate Mortgages	2,500	4.50%	112.50
Small Business Loans and Overdrafts	500	6.50%	32.50
Corporate Loans and Overdrafts	2,000	5.50%	110.00
Bad Debts Net of Provisions	250	0.00%	0.00
Debt Securities	1,500	3.50%	52.50
Equity Shares	500	-	-
Fixed Assets	400	-	-
Goodwill/Intangible Assets	300	-	-
Prepayments and Accrued Income	200	-	-
Total	17,500		870.00

Liabilities

	£m	Rate	Interest Expense (£m)
Deposits by Banks	2,000	3.80%	76.00
Customer Accounts			
Retail Non-Interest Bearing Current Accounts	3,000	0.00%	0.00
Retail Instant Access Deposit Accounts	2,000	1.50%	30.00
Retail Notice Accounts	500	2.50%	12.50
Retail Fixed Rate Bonds	1,000	4.50%	45.00
Corporate/Small Business Non-Interest Bearing Current Accounts	2,000	0.00%	0.00
Corporate Variable Rate Savings Accounts	1,000	1.00%	10.00
Small Business Variable Rate Savings Accounts	800	0.00%	0.00
Debt Securities in Issue (floating rate)	1,000	6.50%	65.00
Subordinated Liabilities (fixed rate)	2,000	10.00%	200.00
Accruals and Deferred Income	200	-	-
Equity Capital	2,000	-	-
Total	17,500		438.50

	£m
Interest Income	870.00
Interest Expense	438.50
Interest Earning Assets	16,000

Net Interest Income	431.50
versus Base Scenario	–29.50

NIM	2.70%
versus Base Scenario	–0.18%

Figure 12.4E WestChoud Bank, Scenario 3 potential impact on NII/NIM

WestChoud Bank - Balance Sheet

Scenario 4: Instant access product relaunched at a higher rate and new 0% credit card introduced for balance transfers leading to growth in the balance sheet and paydown of Deposits by Banks. No Funds Transfer Pricing Process. Marginal decline in NIM from base scenario

5% Rate Environment (flat yield curve - same at all tenors)

Assets

	£m	Rate	Interest Income (£m)
Cash	100	-	-
Central Bank Deposits	250	1.00%	2.50
Loans to Banks	1,000	5.00%	50.00
Loans and Advances to Customers			
0% Credit Cards for Balance Transfers	500	0.00%	0.00
Credit Cards	1,000	12.00%	120.00
Personal Loans (Fixed Rate)	1,500	8.00%	120.00
Retail Overdrafts	500	9.00%	45.00
Fixed Rate Mortgages	5,000	5.25%	262.50
Variable Rate Mortgages	2,500	5.50%	137.50
Small Business Loans and Overdrafts	500	7.50%	37.50
Corporate Loans and Overdrafts	2,000	6.50%	130.00
Bad Debts Net of Provisions	250	0.00%	0.00
Debt Securities	1,500	4.50%	67.50
Equity Shares	500	-	-
Fixed Assets	400	-	-
Goodwill/Intangible Assets	300	-	-
Prepayments and Accrued Income	200	-	-
Total	**18,000**		**972.50**

Liabilities

	£m	Rate	Interest Expense (£m)
Deposits by Banks	1,500	4.80%	72.00
Customer Accounts			
Retail Non-Interest Bearing Current Accounts	3,000	0.00%	0.00
Retail Instant Access Deposit Accounts	3,000	3.50%	105.00
Retail Notice Accounts	500	3.50%	17.50
Retail Fixed Rate Bonds	1,000	4.50%	45.00
Corporate/Small Business Non-Interest Bearing Current Accounts	2,000	0.00%	0.00
Corporate Variable Rate Savings Accounts	1,000	2.00%	20.00
Small Business Variable Rate Savings Accounts	800	1.00%	8.00
Debt Securities in Issue (floating rate)	1,000	7.50%	75.00
Subordinated Liabilities (fixed rate)	2,000	10.00%	200.00
Accruals and Deferred Income	200	-	-
Equity Capital	2,000	-	-
Total	**18,000**		**542.50**

	£m
Interest Income	972.50
Interest Expense	542.50
Interest Earning Assets	16,500
Net Interest Income	430.00
versus Base Scenario	–31.00
NIM	2.61%
versus Base Scenario	–0.28%

Figure 12.4F WestChoud Bank, Scenario 4 potential impact on NII/NIM

WestChoud Bank - Balance Sheet

Scenario 5: Mortgage growth funded by deposits by banks and a fixed rate bond issue. No Funds Transfer Pricing Process. NIM declines from base scenario although NII increases

5% Rate Environment (flat yield curve - same at all tenors)

Assets

	£m	Rate	Interest Income (£m)
Cash	100		-
Central Bank Deposits	250	1.00%	2.50
Loans to Banks	1,000	5.00%	50.00
Loans and Advances to Customers			
Credit Cards	1,000	12.00%	120.00
Personal Loans (Fixed Rate)	1,500	8.00%	120.00
Retail Overdrafts	500	9.00%	45.00
Fixed Rate Mortgages	6,000	5.25%	315.00
Variable Rate Mortgages	3,000	5.50%	165.00
Small Business Loans and Overdrafts	500	7.50%	37.50
Corporate Loans and Overdrafts	2,000	6.50%	130.00
Bad Debts Net of Provisions	250	0.00%	0.00
Debt Securities	1,500	4.50%	67.50
Equity Shares	500	-	-
Fixed Assets	400	-	-
Goodwill/Intangible Assets	300	-	-
Prepayments and Accrued Income	200	-	-
Total	**19,000**		**1,052.50**

Liabilities

	£m	Rate	Interest Expense (£m)
Deposits by Banks	3,000	4.80%	144.00
Customer Accounts			
Retail Non-Interest Bearing Current Accounts	3,000	0.00%	0.00
Retail Instant Access Deposit Accounts	2,000	2.50%	50.00
Retail Notice Accounts	500	3.50%	17.50
Retail Fixed Rate Bonds	1,500	4.50%	67.50
Corporate/Small Business Non-Interest Bearing Current Accounts	2,000	0.00%	0.00
Corporate Variable Rate Savings Accounts	1,000	2.00%	20.00
Small Business Variable Rate Savings Accounts	800	1.00%	8.00
Debt Securities in Issue (floating rate)	1,000	7.50%	75.00
Subordinated Liabilities (fixed rate)	2,000	10.00%	200.00
Accruals and Deferred Income	200	-	-
Equity Capital	2,000	-	-
Total	**19,000**		**582.00**

	£m
Interest Income	1,052.50
Interest Expense	582.00
Interest Earning Assets	17,500
Net Interest Income	**470.50**
versus Base Scenario	9.50
NIM	**2.69%**
versus Base Scenario	-0.19%

Figure 12.4G   WestChoud Bank, Scenario 5 potential impact on NII/NIM

This sort of analysis and scenario planning should be an integral part of both asset–liability management (ALM) as well as the new product development and product marketing campaign process.

Is there a NIM gold standard, a level to which all banks should aspire? The answer is "no". Comparisons between banks are not really valid as NIMs will differ due to factors such as:

- The amount of equity capital held: a high level will tend to boost the NIM as this form of capital is non-interest bearing, so will tend to reduce a bank's interest expense;
- The amount of credit and/or interest-rate risk: a bank that engages in risky lending may generate more interest income relative to competitors, but may also carry more non-performing assets, which would act as a drag on the NIM;
- The proportion of non-interest-bearing liabilities (for example, current accounts): these may be good for NIM as they do not carry any interest expense, but there are other issues to consider (cost of attracting/maintaining these accounts via branches, handling complaints, etc.);
- The relative sizes of small and medium-sized enterprise and retail business vs corporate and wholesale business: the former would tend to be associated with a higher NIM;
- The amount of residential mortgage lending: often associated with a lower NIM as this type of business is low risk.

While there is not a NIM level that all banks should aim for, it is important for this measure of profitability to be relatively constant over time. Stable sources of income are more highly valued than volatile income streams by the investment community and can be built into valuation models for future years, while items like abnormal trading profits cannot be assumed to recur.

According to *Forbes Magazine* in November 2014: "The importance of NIM figures for banks is demonstrated by the fact that the share price of every single US bank jumped last month after the Federal Reserve hinted at a hike in benchmark interest rates in early 2015."

The objective for all banks therefore is to preserve and maximise whatever NIM they have. Careful management of interest-rate risk in the banking book can help to achieve this objective.

INTEREST-RATE RISK IN THE BANKING BOOK

Interest-rate risk in the banking book refers to the current or prospective risk to a bank's capital and earnings arising from movements in interest rates.

When interest rates change, the present value and timing of future cash flows change. This in turn affects the underlying value of a bank's assets, liabilities, and off-balance-sheet instruments, and hence its economic value. Changes in interest rates also influence a bank's earnings by altering interest income and expense from assets and liabilities that reprice within a 12-month time horizon, affecting its NII. This risk is inherent to the banking business and its successful management can have an important impact on the NIM and shareholder value. Excessive interest-rate risk can pose a significant threat to a bank's current capital base and/or future earnings if not properly managed.

There are a number of different types of interest-rate risk faced by banks in their banking books:

- **Gap risk**: which occurs when the price of assets and liabilities, expressed in the interest rate receivable or payable, changes at different times;
- **Basis risk**: arises when assets and liabilities price off different benchmark rates at the same tenor or the same benchmark rate at different tenors;
- **Option risk**: is present when the characteristics of financial market option products are embedded in normal banking products. Examples include prepayment options on fixed-rate loans, early redemption options on fixed-rate deposits, drawdown options on fixed-rate loans or deposits, deposit floors, and loan caps.

The interest-rate gap report

A static interest-rate gap report is used as a basis to assess gap risk, whether it is in relation to the effect of interest-rate movements on income (NII sensitivity) or economic value.

The report has separate columns for assets and liabilities and is divided into a number of distinct time buckets, ranging from 0–1 month to a period normally in excess of 10 years. All cash items in the balance sheet (not accounting adjustments) are included in the report according to when they reprice or, in the case of fixed-rate items, when they mature.

The difference between the assets and liabilities repricing in a given period is known as the interest-rate gap. The cumulative gap captures the net position on all the assets and liabilities that reprice between 0 months and a given time bucket.

A specimen interest-rate gap report is illustrated in Figure 12.5.

Within a given time bucket, a bank may have a positive, negative, or neutral gap. The gap is positive when more assets reprice or mature than liabilities. In this case, the bank is said to be asset sensitive for the time band. An asset-sensitive bank is generally expected to benefit from rising interest rates because its assets are expected to reprice more quickly than its liabilities. A similar situation applies to the cumulative gap; if this is positive out

Repricing Bucket	Assets	Liabilities	Interest-Rate Gap	Cumulative Gap
Currency (£m)				
0–1 month	500	4,600	−4,100	−4,100
1–2 months	443	324	119	−3,981
2–3 months	156	1,781	−1,625	−5,606
3–4 months	342	430	−88	−5,694
4–5 months	213	24	189	−5,505
5–6 months	224	69	155	−5,350
6–9 months	356	17	339	−5,011
9–12 months	324	46	278	−4,733
12–15 months	614	32	582	−4,151
15–18 months	459	123	336	−3,815
18–24 months	875	275	600	−3,215
2 years–3 years	1,365	135	1,230	−1,985
3 years–4 years	845	86	759	−1,226
4 years–5 years	725	58	667	−559
5 years–6 years	413	0	413	−146
6 years–7 years	45	0	45	−101
7 years–10 years	89	0	89	−12
10 years +	12	0	12	0
Total	8,000	8,000		

Figure 12.5   Specimen interest-rate gap report

to a given time bucket, a bank will gain for that period from any rise in interest rates.

The converse is true for a negative gap, which occurs when more liabilities than assets mature in a given time bucket. A bank in this situation will be liability sensitive for the time band and expected to gain from falling rates (but lose from rising rates) as in this instance its liabilities would reprice downwards more quickly than its assets. A bank with an interest-rate gap report like that illustrated in Figure 12.5 would be liability sensitive.

If the gap is zero in all time buckets, the NII of the bank would not be subject to any gap risk.

What should be included in a static interest-rate gap report?

A static interest-rate gap report is focused on the assets and liabilities making up the balance sheet at a particular point in time. It takes no account of future levels of business or how the interest-rate gap is likely to develop over time in response to different levels of interest rates. (The section on Simulation Analysis will cover dynamic modelling of the balance sheet in more detail.)

	A Assets	B Liabilities	A-B Net Position	C Discount Factor Weighting	(A-B)*C
1 Overnight					
2 Overnight - 1 month					
3 1 month - 3 months					
4 3 months - 6 months					
5 6 months - 9 months					
6 9 months - 1 year					
7 1 year - 18 months					
8 18 months - 2 years					
9 2 years - 3 years					
10 3 years - 4 years					
11 4 years - 5 years					
12 5 years - 6 years					
13 6 years - 7 years					
14 7 years - 8 years					
15 8 years - 9 years					
16 9 years - 10 years					
17 10 years - 15 years					
18 15 years - 20 years					
19 20 years +					
					Sum = EVE

Figure 12.6 Maturity schedule time buckets for EVE calculation

All principal balances must be included in the gap report (though see later discussion on the treatment of non-interest-bearing balances in the calculation of NII sensitivity). When it comes to interest flows though, there is a trade-off between technical accuracy and practicality. Technically speaking, banks should include interest payments on tranches of principal that have not yet been repaid or repriced and the spread component of floating-rate instruments, but capturing and reporting this data is no easy task and the majority of gap risk, in most interest-rate environments, tends to arise from principal rather than interest flows.

While the static interest-rate gap report has the benefit of being relatively simple and easy to calculate, it is not readily able to capture basis and option risks, though the Basel Committee has sought to address the problem in their latest framework for the management of interest-rate risk in the banking book.

For the purposes of simplification, the product treatments discussed below will focus on the representation of principal balances in the static interest-rate gap report.

The treatment of variable rate products

Variable rate products are normally linked to a benchmark rate that either does (for example, 1-month or 3-month LIBOR) or can (for example, bank base rates or standard variable rates) reprice in the short term. As a result, principal balances on variable rate products will generally be shown in the repricing buckets of 2–3 months or below.

The treatment of fixed maturity products

The principal amounts of fixed-rate loans and deposits, with market-related early repayment/redemption charges, should be reflected in the interest-rate gap report according to their contractual repayment profile. These would normally be associated with wholesale, corporate, or commercial clients.

For bullet repayment loans, the entire principal balance should be shown in the gap report in a time bucket corresponding to the maturity of each loan. In the case of amortising loans, though, the regular repayments of principal are allocated to the time period in which they are scheduled to occur.

When it comes to fixed-rate retail bank products, these tend to be homogeneous and are characterised by early repayment charges that do not reflect the potential underlying funding cost to banks. Given the nature of the products and the desire to avoid losses from early repayment/redemption, banks often build models to estimate the behavioural run-off profile of the loans and deposits (how they expect it to happen in practice, which may be different to the run-off profile agreed with the customer in the contract) and this is what should be captured in the interest-rate gap report.

The treatment of non-interest-bearing balances

Typical examples of items in this category include non-interest-bearing deposits and cash (notes and coin) balances. Neither of them carries an interest rate, so cannot reprice as such. However, the items need to be included in the gap report if it is being used to calculate the economic value sensitivity of the balance sheet.

Earlier in the chapter, we concluded that banks should aim for a stable NIM over time. With these balance sheet items, this will be best achieved by treating them as long term as possible in the gap report.

We have already noted that a commercial bank seeking to run an interest-rate neutral position will aim to minimise the size of both the gaps in each repricing bucket, as well as the overall cumulative gap. So, with this in mind, representing non-interest-bearing balances as notionally repricing in the long term will require the bank to obtain matching assets and liabilities at the same long-term tenor on the other side of the balance sheet (see the later section on the Management of Gap Risk).

Using non-interest-bearing current accounts as an example, a time series analysis will reveal that a proportion of the aggregate balance is volatile and between 5 and 20% of accounts are closed each year due to demographic factors, switching to competitors, etc. So, even if a bank continues to offer this product ad infinitum, it would be unwise to treat the balances as having a notional repricing maturity beyond 5 years (as they could disappear from the balance sheet altogether in that timeframe).

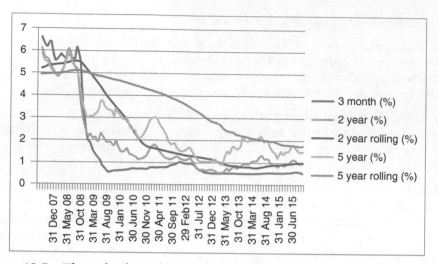

Figure 12.7   The volatility of UK interest rates over time

Source: Bank of England Bank Liability Curve Estimates (cash and interest rate swap rates) 2007–2015.

Figure 12.7 illustrates that 5-year interest rates are more stable over time than either 3-month or 2-year interest rates. In addition, if choosing to invest or borrow over 5 years, with a potential requirement to extend the arrangement after 5 years, it is better to do so on a rolling basis (by spreading the borrowing or investment over 5 years and renewing a proportion each year) to avoid any potential "cliff effects" (for example, the 5-year swap rate in May 2008 was 5%, but only 1% by May 2013).

Putting all of these factors together, banks will often decide to represent a proportion (say 20%) of non-interest-bearing deposits as notionally repricing in the short term and spread the remainder between 1 month and 3 or 5 years in the interest-rate gap report. This will ensure that a relatively stable return, which is insensitive to interest-rate movements, is generated on the core element of the balances.

The treatment of managed rate products

Examples of products in this category include credit cards, interest-bearing current accounts, and obsolete accounts that are no longer on sale. In these instances, a bank may not reprice these products in line with an established market benchmark rate.

This is where production of the static interest-rate gap report becomes part art and part science. To establish the treatment of managed rate products in the gap report, the ALM manager must estimate which market benchmark rate their interest rate correlates most closely to. Also, he (or she) must consider how long the balances are likely to remain on the balance sheet.

Based on these two factors, a notional repricing treatment is allocated. Akin to non-interest-bearing accounts, to avoid "cliff risk" with the corresponding asset or liability, it is preferable to spread the balances over all the time buckets within the repricing maturity than allocate the full sum to the time bucket corresponding to the agreed repricing maturity.

NII sensitivity

There are a range of different mechanisms used by banks to calculate the sensitivity of their NII to movements in interest rates.

In its simplest form, the repricing profile of assets and liabilities, established in the production of the interest-rate gap report, is subjected to a parallel shock of 1% or 2%, either upwards or downwards, in the level of interest rates across the yield curve, which is assumed to be sustained for 12 months.

If, by way of example, interest rates are currently 5% at all tenors, that will result in a given level of forecast NII for a bank over the next 12 months. In this analysis, we are not concerned with the forecast itself, but want to estimate how it would change if interest rates at all tenors were to move to 6% or 7% or alternatively were to fall to 3% or 4%.

In the basic calculation, we would multiply the gap in each period out to 12 months by the rate shock and the number of months between the repricing bucket and 1 year, divided by 12, for example, instruments repricing between 4 and 5 months' time could only affect NII for between 7 and 8 months over the next year, so we would calculate: gap × rate shock × 7.5/12. Note, it is assumed that the repricing of the assets and liabilities occurs at the mid-point of each repricing bucket.

In Figure 12.8, an NII sensitivity analysis has been performed on the specimen interest-rate gap report from Figure 12.5. This reveals that the NII for the bank in question would fall by £48.1m in the event of a parallel 1% upward shift in the yield curve sustained for 12 months.

For the purposes of this analysis, non-interest-bearing balances should be removed from the interest-rate gap report before the calculation is performed, as they do not reprice in response to interest-rate movements.

This basic calculation contains a number of simplifying assumptions, and therefore in this form only provides a rough guide to an organisation's NII sensitivity. In reality:

- Bank balance sheets are seldom constant over time, which is the implication here;
- Parallel shifts in the yield curve are rare: more often than not, the movement at the short end of the yield curve will exceed that at the long end;
- Not all assets and liabilities will reprice by the exact amount of the shock in rates.

Repricing Bucket	Interest- Rate Gap	IR Gap × Rate Shock × Remaining Months/12		(£m)
Currency (£m)				
0–1 month	−4,100	−4,100 × 1% × 11.5/12	=	−39.29
1–2 months	119	119 × 1% × 10.5/12	=	1.04
2–3 months	−1,625	−1,625 × 1% × 9.5/12	−	−12.86
3–4 months	−88	−88 × 1% × 8.5/12	=	−0.62
4–5 months	189	189 × 1% × 7.5/12	=	1.18
5–6 months	155	155 × 1% × 6.5/12	=	0.84
6–9 months	339	339 × 1% × 4.5/12	=	1.27
9–12 months	278	278 × 1% × 1.5/12	=	0.35
12–15 months	582			
15–18 months	336			
18–24 months	600			
2 years–3 years	1,230			
3 years–4 years	759			
4 years–5 years	667			
5 years–6 years	413			
6 years–7 years	45			
7 years–10 years	39			
10 years +	12			
				−48.10

Figure 12.8   Specimen NII sensitivity calculation

Limits on NII sensitivity, which will be discussed and approved by a bank's Asset and Liability Committee, are normally expressed as a currency amount or percentage of NII relative to a given rate shock. For example, Bank X might wish to restrict NII sensitivity to + or − £10m (or 5% of NII) to a parallel shock of + or − 1% in the level of interest rates at all tenors.

As a first step to developing the analysis, banks will look to factor in how much and when products are likely to be repriced in response to a given rate shock:

- Depending upon the competitive environment and P&L and market share aspirations, management may choose to reprice managed rate products by either more than, less than, or by the same amount as the underlying market interest-rate movement;
- Leads or lags that management may choose to impose on when managed rate products are repriced.

Economic value of equity (EVE) sensitivity

The starting point for an EVE sensitivity calculation is also the static interest-rate gap report. In this case, the gaps in each time bucket are turned into a net present value (NPV) by discounting using discount factors based upon the current level of interest rates. As a second step, the NPVs for each time bucket are summed to produce a high-level estimate of the bank's economic value.

The exercise is repeated for a given interest-rate shock, for example, a 1% parallel upward movement in the yield curve. Note, application of the rate shock will give rise to a new set of discount factors and a revised estimate of economic value.

It is the difference between the two sums that gives rise to the EVE sensitivity. In this example, we would say calculation 2 minus calculation 1 is the EVE sensitivity of the balance sheet to a 1% parallel upward shock in interest rates. An example template is shown at Figure 12.6.

Typically, banks will evaluate their EVE sensitivities to a variety of different shock scenarios (see the section on Interest-Rate Shock Scenarios). Based on risk appetite, a bank's ALCO will set limits on the change in EVE it is prepared to accept to a sudden movement in interest rates.

Interest-rate shock scenarios

The interest-rate shocks employed should reflect a stressful rate environment that is both plausible and severe.

The relatively simple NII sensitivity calculations rely only on parallel shifts in the yield curve, for example, + or − 2% at all tenors.

EVE sensitivity calculations do not face these constraints. To capture a full range of scenarios, banks often choose to assess the consequences of a steepening or flattening in the yield curve or material shocks to short-term rates, in addition to the parallel shifts. ALCOs will focus upon those scenarios that lead to the biggest negative effect on EVE, as this may influence capital requirements under Pillar II of the Basel framework.

SIMULATION ANALYSIS

Simulation models, adopted by some banks, can be used to assess either NII or economic value sensitivities. Rather than relying upon a constant or static balance sheet, these models allow management to introduce assumptions on how prepayment/early redemption, levels of new business, and margins will be affected by interest-rate movements. Also, they allow multiple interest-rate shocks or rate paths to be modelled using Monte Carlo analysis.

The key steps in the analysis are:

- Develop a bottom-up forecast of NII for the next 1–5 years;
- Capture assumptions for all conceivable interest-rate environments on:
  o How all products would be repriced;
  o New business volumes;
  o Forecast prepayments/early redemptions;
  o The level of loan defaults.

- Run a simulation to evaluate the impact of multiple different interest-rate paths on NII and economic value;
- Review the distribution of NII and economic value outputs;
- Focus on outlying values, particularly on the downside. If these are of concern to management, consider what mitigants can be put in place to reduce the exposure.

THE MANAGEMENT OF GAP RISK

There are a number of tools at the disposal of banks to reduce NII or EVE sensitivities if they are operating close to or in excess of approved limits. These may be categorised as either "cash hedges" or "derivative hedges".

Cash hedges

Banks may write assets or liabilities at specific repricing maturities to reduce the size of gap exposures. For example, a 2-year fixed-rate deposit bond product might be offered to customers to offset the interest-rate risk arising on 2-year fixed-rate mortgages. Alternatively, fixed-rate amortising business loans might provide a useful match for a book of non-interest-bearing current accounts that is spread over 5 years in the interest-rate gap report.

Derivative hedges

The main derivative instruments used to manage gap risk are Forward Rate Agreements, futures and interest-rate swaps. Interest-rate derivatives are more flexible than cash hedges and will be the instrument of choice of most medium/larger banks. Smaller banks, on the other hand, may prefer to maintain all operations in cash instruments, either for simplicity and/or to avoid the additional accounting (for example, potential P&L volatility if hedge accounting arrangements are not put in place) and operational challenges (for example, collateral posting for negative mark-to-market positions) posed by derivatives.

By way of an illustration, if a bank had a 5-year fixed-rate loan of £100m funded by a 3-month deposit, it would have a cumulative interest-rate gap exposure between 3 months and 5 years, as shown in Figure 12.9.

This position could be hedged by writing a 5-year pay fixed, receive 3-month Libor interest-rate swap, with a notional principal of £100m.

From the perspective of the interest-rate gap report, writing the swap creates an asset of 100 in the 3-month repricing bucket and a liability of 100 in the 5-year repricing bucket, which would eliminate the bank's gap risk and NII would equate to the margin above the 5-year rate on the customer loan, plus the margin below the 3-month rate on the customer deposit, as illustrated in Figures 12.10 and 12.11.

Repricing Bucket	Assets	Liabilities	Interest-Rate Gap	Cumulative Gap
Currency (£m)				
0–1 month	0	0	0	0
1–2 months	0	0	0	0
2–3 months	0	100	−100	−100
3–4 months	0	0	0	−100
4–5 months	0	0	0	−100
5–6 months	0	0	0	−100
6–9 months	0	0	0	−100
9–12 months	0	0	0	−100
12–15 months	0	0	0	−100
15–18 months	0	0	0	−100
18–24 months	0	0	0	−100
2 years–3 years	0	0	0	−100
3 years–4 years	0	0	0	−100
4 years–5 years	100	0	100	0
5 years–6 years	0	0	0	0
6 years–7 years	0	0	0	0
7 years–10 years	0	0	0	0
10 years +	0	0	0	0

Figure 12.9 Specimen interest-rate gap report for a 5-year fixed-rate bullet loan funded by a 3-month deposit

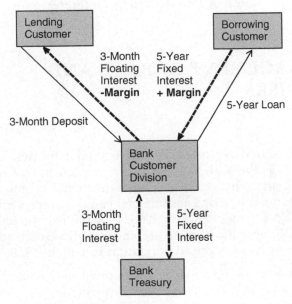

Figure 12.10 Interest rate swap schematic

Repricing Bucket	Assets	Liabilities	Interest-Rate Gap	Cumulative Gap
Currency (£m)				
0–1 month	0	0	0	0
1–2 months	0	0	0	0
2–3 months	100	100	0	0
3–4 months	0	0	0	0
4–5 months	0	0	0	0
5–6 months	0	0	0	0
6–9 months	0	0	0	0
9–12 months	0	0	0	0
12–15 months	0	0	0	0
15–18 months	0	0	0	0
18–24 months	0	0	0	0
2 years–3 years	0	0	0	0
3 years–4 years	0	0	0	0
4 years–5 years	100	100	0	0
5 years–6 years	0	0	0	0
6 years–7 years	0	0	0	0
7 years–10 years	0	0	0	0
10 years +	0	0	0	0

Figure 12.11 Specimen interest-rate gap report for a 5-year fixed-rate bullet loan funded by a 3-month deposit hedged by an interest-rate swap

THE MANAGEMENT OF BASIS AND OPTION RISKS

Basis risk

As a reminder, basis risk is present when assets and liabilities price off different benchmark rates at the same tenor or the same benchmark rate at different tenors. The risk arises because these rates might not all move by the same amount at the same time. For a commercial bank, examples might include an asset written off the Bank of England Bank Rate funded by a liability linked to short-term LIBOR rates or, alternatively, an asset priced in relation to 3-month LIBOR funded by a liability priced in relation to 1-month LIBOR.

In normal market conditions, basis risk is often overlooked; the index you receive is assumed to be correlated to the index you pay, and the risk is regarded as small. As Figure 12.12 shows however, it can often be material.

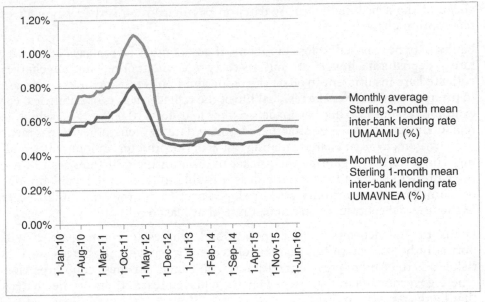

Notes:

[a] Data provided is for general reference purposes. Every effort is made to ensure that it is up to date and accurate. The Bank of England does not warrant, or accept responsibility/liability for, the accuracy/completeness of content, or loss/damage, whether direct, indirect or consequential, which may arise from reliance on said data. We reserve the right to change information published, including timing and methods used. We give no assurance that data currently published will be in the future.

Figure 12.12   A comparison between sterling 1-month and 3-month interbank lending rates

Source: Bank of England Statistics.

Basis risk cannot be measured by the static interest-rate gap report. However, the Basel Committee has developed a methodology based upon historic differentials between the various reference rates. Banks faced with basis risk can manage their exposure using a variety of different techniques, such as:

• Develop products pricing off the same underlying interest rate on both sides of the balance sheet to provide a natural hedge;
• Hedge the exposure with basis swaps;
• Adjust product pricing.

Option risks

Commercial banks face a range of option risks that are embedded in the products they offer to customers. We will concentrate on three types:

Prepayment or early redemption risk: applies on fixed-rate loans and deposits, where customers have the right (or an option) to repay loans or redeem deposits ahead of the scheduled maturity date, on payment of an early repayment or redemption charge.

Banks may be exposed to loss of income if assets must be replaced at a lower rate or deposits at a higher rate and any early repayment or redemption charges collected are insufficient to offset the reduction in interest income or increase in interest expense over the residual life of the replaced assets or liabilities. For example, assume a bank has made a 5-year loan for £10,000 at 7%, which is repaid 2 years before its contractual maturity date by a customer on payment of an early repayment charge equating to 1% of the principal amount outstanding. For simplicity, ignoring the impact of discounting on future cash flows, the bank will suffer a loss of NII unless it is able to relend the repaid amount to a similar customer (from a credit risk perspective) for the remaining 2 years of the original contract at an interest rate of at least 6.50%.

Loans to and deposits from corporate and wholesale counterparties will normally be subject to full market-related early repayment charges, so this risk tends to be more prevalent with retail and small business counterparties, where governments or regulators may have placed restrictions on the charges that banks are able to levy.

Pipeline risk: also applies on fixed-rate loans and deposits and occurs when customers have an option (but not a contractual obligation) to draw down on a fixed-rate loan or enter into a fixed-rate deposit at a given interest rate. In the case of certain fixed-rate loans, such as mortgages, the borrower may be required to pay a booking or commitment fee to secure the option.

Similar to prepayment risk, pipeline risk is most in evidence with retail products. Banks may be exposed to loss of income if interest rates move, either upwards or downwards, between the time when the fixed-rate offer is made to customers and the time when loan drawdown takes place or the deposit is received. Consider a 2-year fixed-rate deposit bond offered to customers at 3%. If interest rates rise during the offer period, customers may be able to obtain better rates from depositors, with the result that bond sales are below expectations and the bank is required to close out a surplus hedging position (normally achieved with forward-starting interest-rate swaps) at a loss. Alternatively, if interest rates fall during the offer period, the bond starts to look particularly attractive in the market place, relative to those offered by competitors, with the result that the bank may be flooded with applicants and forced to undertake more hedging activity at a reduced or negative margin.

The Basel Committee has recommended a methodology for banks to use to measure prepayment and pipeline option risks. Under the framework, the cash flows on fixed-rate loans and deposits captured in the interest-rate gap report are reworked for each predetermined interest-rate shock scenario using scaling factors to recognise that the amount drawn down and the level of prepayments will be affected by movements in interest rates.

Cap and floor risk: the former relates to loans that are offered to customers with a maximum rate and the latter to deposits (and possibly loans) that cannot be repriced downwards in response to a reduction in the general level of interest rates, for example, when interest rates are low.

In both cases, banks are exposed to a reduction in NII and NIM. With cap risk, as interest rates rise, interest-sensitive liabilities reprice upwards, but the interest rates on corresponding assets that have reached their rate ceiling (for example, capped rate loans) remain at existing levels. Alternatively, with floor risk, the margin is squeezed as interest-rate-sensitive assets reprice in response to a downward movement in the general level of interest rates, but deposits that would normally be interest-rate sensitive may not be capable of repricing if the interest rate being paid is close to zero %.

THE MANAGEMENT OF PREPAYMENT RISK

Prepayment or early redemption occurs either due to social factors (such as death, divorce, etc.) or when the customer has a financial incentive (for example, he or she can borrow more cheaply elsewhere taking into account any early repayment charges payable). Figures 12.13, 12.14 and 12.15 illustrate examples of run off profiles.

In respect of the financial incentive, there is no naturally offsetting item on the other side of the balance sheet; if rates fall, fixed-rate borrowers may be encouraged to prepay, but fixed-rate depositors are much more likely to be happy with their existing arrangements in this situation. Equally, if interest rates rise, fixed-rate depositors may consider moving to other products available in the market, but fixed-rate borrowers will face a negative financial incentive to do the same.

In theory, at least, banks could purchase derivative products called swaptions, giving them the right to enter into an interest-rate swap during the life of a

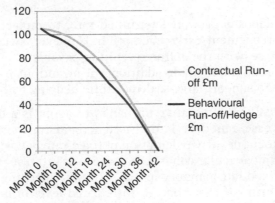

Figure 12.13 Period 1 – Amortising pay fixed swap hedge aligned to anticipated behavioural run-off profile of a loan cohort

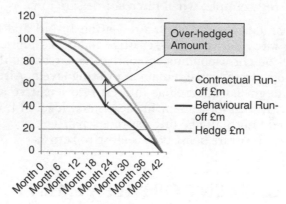

Figure 12.14   Period 2 – General level of interest rates falls so loans anticipated to repay quicker than original assumption

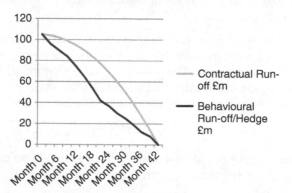

Figure 12.15   Period 2 – Balloon receive fixed swap is written to realign swap
hedge to behavioural loan run-off profile

cohort of loans/deposits at a predetermined rate, to replace lost cash flows
from customer prepayment/early redemption. However, swaptions tend to be
relatively expensive, with the upfront premium payable likely to make a serious dent in the product margin. In addition, the swaptions market is not deep
or liquid enough to support large-scale portfolio hedging by banks.

Another, more realistic alternative for banks to adopt is a dynamic hedging
approach. In this case, a model is built, based upon historic experience of fixed-
rate loan prepayment or early redemption of fixed-rate deposits, to predict the
run-off profile of a particular cohort in a variety of interest-rate scenarios. At
inception of the fixed-rate loans or deposits, a funding/hedging profile is aligned
to their expected run-off based on the anticipated level of interest rates over
the life of the cohort. Each month, the expected run-off profile is re-evaluated
according to the latest expectation for interest rates and the level of balances
outstanding and the funding/hedging position adjusted accordingly.

Banks will tend to impose levels of tolerance, so that the funding/hedge is only amended for material movements in the expected run-off profile of the loans/deposits. In following this approach, they hope that the cost of periodically realigning the funding hedge is less than any early repayment or redemption fees collected.

The dynamic hedging process is illustrated in Figures 12.13 to 12.15.

THE MANAGEMENT OF PIPELINE RISK

Conceptually, the management of pipeline risk is similar to that of prepayment risk.

In both cases, there is no natural hedge between loans and deposits and although the drawdown risk faced by banks could be hedged by the use of swaptions, this is expensive and will tend to offset most if not all of any prospective interest margin.

So, as with the management of prepayment risk, banks tend to adopt a dynamic hedging approach. Based upon historical experience and management's assessment of competitive conditions, a forward starting hedge (such as an interest-rate swap) will be booked when the loan or deposit is first offered to customers, based upon the anticipated level of drawdowns or product take-up. As the offer period progresses, regular reassessments of likely drawdowns will be made and the hedge adjusted accordingly. Again, similar to the position with prepayment risk, any hedge realignment is likely to carry a cost and management will be hoping that this is less than or equal to any booking or commitment fees collected.

For fixed-rate mortgages, the final amount of any drawdowns may not be known until up to 9 months after the terms of the offer are first developed by the product marketing department. This is illustrated in Figure 12.16.

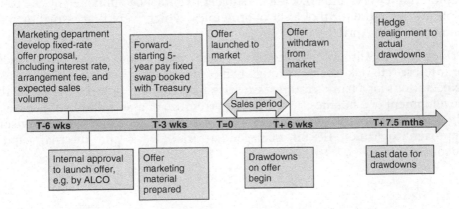

Figure 12.16 Typical timeline for a fixed-rate mortgage offer

THE MANAGEMENT OF CAP AND FLOOR RISK

Historically, it was common for banks in the UK to offer loan products with published minimum rates that would act as a natural hedge to floor risk on deposits. However, this type of product is no longer prevalent in the marketplace, as it was not favoured by the regulatory authorities. As a result, banks must look to interest-rate caps and interest-rate floors offered in the financial markets, if they wish to hedge their exposures to caps and floors that are embedded in the products they offer.

Interest-rate caps and floors are generally based on money market interest rates (such as LIBOR) and pay out if interest rates move above (for caps) or below (for floors) pre-agreed levels or strike prices. The payout is determined by the notional principal of the contract and the amount by which the strike price is breached. Banks pay an upfront premium to secure protection for a specific period of time.

The amount of protection sought by a bank will depend on factors such as:

- The internally held view on future interest-rate movements (the likelihood that embedded product caps and floors will be triggered);
- The bank's risk appetite (the amount it can afford to lose if embedded product caps and floors are triggered);
- The depth of the financial markets in the provision of interest-rate caps and floors;
- The accounting treatment of the arrangement: a lesser factor, which should nevertheless be understood by management.

BASEL COMMITTEE: HIGH-LEVEL PRINCIPLES FOR INTEREST-RATE RISK IN THE BANKING BOOK

Interest rate risk in the banking book (IRRBB) is part of Pillar II in the Basel capital framework. This risk area is subject to guidance published by the Basel Committee in the form of a set of principles, which were first issued in 2004 and updated in April 2016.

Principles 1 to 9 are intended to be of general application for the management of interest-rate risk arising through banks' non-trading activities. They cover expectations for a bank's interest-rate risk management process, including the development of a business strategy, the structure of assets and liabilities, and the system of internal controls. Principles 10 to 12 focus on the supervisory approach to banks' IRRBB management framework and internal capital adequacy.

Each of the principles is summarised below:

Principle 1: IRRBB is an important risk for all banks that must be specifically identified, measured, monitored, and controlled. In addition, banks should monitor and assess credit spread risk in the banking book (CSRBB).

It is essential that an adequate control system is in place to identify the interest-rate risk inherent in both new and existing products/services and to approve hedging/risk-taking strategies. CSRBB refers to any kind of asset/liability spread risk of credit-risky instruments that is not explained by IRRBB and the expected credit/jump to default risk, i.e. the risk of loss associated with the deterioration of an entity that remains a going concern.

Principle 2: The governing body of each bank is responsible for oversight of the IRRBB management framework, and the bank's risk appetite for IRRBB. Monitoring and management of IRRBB may be delegated by the governing body to senior management, expert individuals, or an asset and liability committee. Banks must have an adequate IRRBB management framework, involving regular independent reviews and evaluations of the effectiveness of the system.

In most banks, it will be the Board of Directors that has ultimate responsibility and must ensure that senior management have the requisite skills to manage IRRBB. The Board should receive updates on a semi-annual basis as a minimum. Also, monitoring and control processes should be reviewed regularly by an independent party (for example, internal or external auditor).

Principle 3: The bank's risk appetite for IRRBB should be articulated in terms of the risk to both economic value and earnings. Banks must implement policy limits that target maintaining IRRBB exposures consistent with their risk appetite.

A risk appetite statement is a written articulation of the levels and types of IRRBB exposures that a bank will accept or avoid. The policy framework should delineate delegated powers, lines of responsibility, and accountability over IRRBB management decisions and clearly define limits, authorised instruments, hedging strategies, risk-taking opportunities, and the procedure for exceptions. Limits should be appropriate to the nature, size, and complexity of the organisation. Policies should be reviewed at least annually and be approved by the Board.

Principle 4: Measurement of IRRBB should be based on outcomes of both economic value and earnings-based measures, arising from a wide and appropriate range of interest-rate shock and stress scenarios.

The economic value measure should focus on instruments already on the balance sheet (static approach). The earnings measure, in addition to the static view, may incorporate future business flows (dynamic view). Interest-rate shock scenarios assessed should include: internally selected rate shock scenarios to comply with the Internal Capital Adequacy Assessment Process (ICAAP), the six supervisory prescribed interest-rate shock scenarios, and any additional rate shock scenarios required by the supervisor. The bank should estimate how interest rates that are administered or managed will reprice in each of the scenarios.

Principle 5: In measuring IRRBB, key behavioural and modelling assumptions should be fully understood, conceptually sound, and documented. Such assumptions should be rigorously tested and aligned with the bank's business strategies.

Key behavioural assumptions are required for items such as: expected prepayments of loans/early redemption of deposits, non-maturity deposits, and pass through assumptions for market interest-rate changes. The most significant assumptions should be documented, together with supporting evidence and regularly reviewed.

Principle 6: Measurement systems and models used for IRRBB should be based on accurate data, and subject to appropriate documentation, testing, and controls to give assurance on the accuracy of calculations. Models used to measure IRRBB should be comprehensive and covered by governance processes for model risk management, including a validation function that is independent of the development process.

As every risk measurement system has its limitations, the Basel Committee recommends that banks should rely on a variety of measures; both earnings and economic value based with both static and dynamic views. An effective validation framework should include: evaluation of conceptual soundness, ongoing monitoring, including process verification and benchmarking, and outcomes analysis including back-testing.

Principle 7: Measurement outcomes of IRRBB and hedging strategies should be reported to the governing body or its delegates on a regular basis, at relevant levels of aggregation (by consolidation level and currency).

Reports prepared for the Board and various levels of management should include: summaries of the bank's aggregate exposures, reports demonstrating compliance with policies and limits, key assumptions, results of stress tests, and summaries of findings of internal and external auditors.

Principle 8: Information on the level of IRRBB exposure and practices for measuring and controlling IRRBB must be disclosed to the public on a regular basis.

Banks should notify their supervisors ahead of any significant changes planned for: internal limits, internal modelling systems, or methodologies and behavioural assumptions on options. Public disclosure should cover economic value and earnings measures using the bank's internal model as well as the standardised framework (if appropriate), together with key assumptions across both processes.

Principle 9: Capital adequacy for IRRBB must be specifically considered as part of the Internal Capital Adequacy Assessment Process approved by the governing body, in line with the bank's risk appetite on IRRBB.

Banks should not only rely on supervisory measures of capital required for IRRBB, but should also develop their own methodologies for internal capital allocation. In determining the appropriate level of capital, banks should consider both the amount and quality of capital needed.

Principle 10: Supervisors should, on a regular basis, collect sufficient information from banks to be able to monitor trends in banks' IRRBB exposures, assess the soundness of banks' management and identify outlier banks that should be subject to review and/or should be expected to hold additional regulatory capital.

The information collected by supervisors should be consistent across the banks they supervise and may include: the modelling of non-maturity deposits, the impact of the assumptions used on products with embedded options, the treatment of own equity in a bank's internal calculations of IRRBB, repricing gaps, the exposure to automatic interest-rate options, the change in EVE in each interest-rate shock scenario under the standardised framework, and EVE and earnings-based sensitivities under both prescribed and bank internal stress scenarios.

Principle 11: Supervisors should regularly assess banks' IRRBB and the effectiveness of the approaches that banks use to identify, measure, monitor, and control IRRBB. Supervisory authorities should employ specialist resources to assist with such assessments. Supervisors should cooperate and share information with relevant supervisors in other jurisdictions regarding the supervision of banks' IRRBB exposures.

When assessing a bank's IRRBB, supervisors are guided to consider, as a minimum:

- The complexity and level of risk posed by a bank's assets, liabilities, and off-balance-sheet activities;
- The adequacy of governance oversight;
- Knowledge and ability to identify and manage IRRBB;
- The adequacy of both internal validation of IRRBB measures and internal monitoring;
- The effectiveness of risk limits and of the bank's IRRBB stress testing programme;
- The adequacy and effectiveness of internal review, audit, and IRRBB management practices as evidenced by past and projected financial performance;
- The effectiveness of hedging strategies; and
- The appropriateness of the level of IRRBB in relation to a bank's capital, earnings, and risk management systems.

Principle 12: Supervisors must publish their criteria for identifying outlier banks. Banks identified as outliers must be considered as potentially having undue IRRBB. When a review of a bank's IRRBB exposure reveals inadequate management or excessive risk relative to capital, earnings, or general risk profile, supervisors must require mitigation actions and/or additional capital.

When a national supervisor concludes that a bank has undue interest-rate risk in the banking book relative to its capital or earnings (for example, change in EVE under any of the six prescribed scenarios exceeds 15% of Tier 1 capital), it should require the bank to undertake one or more of the following actions within a specified timeframe: reduce interest-rate exposure, improve its risk management framework, raise additional capital, and/or set constraints on the internal risk parameters used until improvements have been made.

CONCLUSIONS

The principal revenue indicator for most commercial banks is net interest income. Given this fact, an understanding of NII and NIM are important when reviewing strategy and forward planning in the bank. All ALCO members should have a good understanding of the drivers of NIM and its sensitivities, and some idea of how a change in one or more of a number of factors – such as interest rates, FX rates, customer behaviours, product changes, and so on – will impact NII/NIM going forward.

Interest-rate risk in the banking book is now a driver of Pillar II capital in a bank, as given by the Basel Committee directive of 2016, hence steps to mitigate IRRBB exposure and hedge it effectively are a key objective of ALCO.

Chapter

13[1]

SECURITISATION MECHANICS FOR BALANCE SHEET MANAGEMENT

[1] This chapter was co-written with Chris Westcott and also reproduces with permission material written by Suleman Baig for the BTRM Certificate.

S ecuritisation is a financing technique that involves the conversion of certain types of assets with predictable cash flows into marketable securities. Generally speaking, it is the process of creating securities backed by pools of assets that are then sold to institutional investors. The conversion process usually involves a special purpose vehicle (SPV) whose only purpose is to buy assets and raise funding through issuance of asset-backed securities ("ABS").

Other short-term methods of financing utilising securitisation technology are available. In the case of mortgages it is known as warehousing (as it is only short term); this is usually financed either on a balance sheet or using asset-backed commercial paper (ABCP financing).

Banks and other financial institutions undertake securitisation as a means of raising long-term funding, diversifying the funding base, freeing up balance sheet capacity, and, in some instances, also to achieve a regulatory capital benefit through the transfer of credit risk to another party.

THE PARTIES TO A SECURITISATION

Figure 13.1 illustrates a vanilla securitisation structure and the various parties involved; the roles performed by each are discussed in more detail below.

Underlying assets: These can be any assets with a predictable cash flow. Examples include: residential mortgages, credit cards, pub tenant lease payments, ticket receivables (for example, Arsenal Football Club), song royalties (for example, David Bowie's "Bowie Bonds"), etc.

Assets included in securitisation transactions may be subject to eligibility criteria. These will be designed to meet the originator's own origination criteria to maximise the funding availability. Typical mortgage eligibility criteria might include:

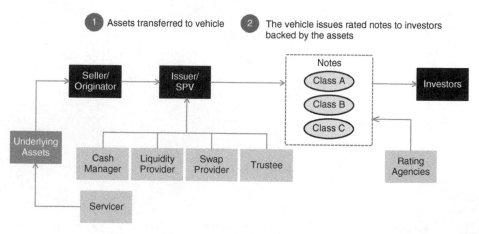

Figure 13.1   Vanilla securitisation structure

- Maximum mortgage balance < £500,000;
- Maximum loan to value ratio < 95%;
- The current balance of mortgages in arrears for at least 3 months as a percentage of the total pool < 4%;
- No mortgage has a term greater than 35 years;
- Each borrower has made at least one payment;
- Loans are originated in line with credit and collection policies;
- The properties are located in England, Scotland, and Wales (and possibly Northern Ireland).

Seller/Originator: The entity with funding/capital needs and assets suitable for securitisation. Figure 13.2 gives examples of originators who have securitised assets in Europe.

Issuer/Special Purpose Vehicle (SPV): The issuing entity is structured to be a bankruptcy-remote vehicle and is created especially for the purpose of securitisation. Bankruptcy remoteness allows the notes (see below) to delink from the seller and achieve a higher rating than that of the seller. Provisions are put in place to restrict the purpose of the issuer and its ability to incur additional liabilities or expenses. Legal opinions are also obtained to provide comfort that the issuer's assets are unlikely to be considered as part of the seller's estate in the case of originator bankruptcy. Issuer profiles vary according to jurisdiction and asset type, for example, standalone SPV or trust in the UK, stichtings in the Netherlands, Law 130 company in Italy, etc.

Issuance structure: A variety of issuance structures exist to accommodate different types of asset, the most common of which are static pool/pass-through and revolving pool/master-trust.

Originator	Assets	Examples
Commercial Banks	✓ Mortgages ✓ Credit cards, consumer loans, auto loans ✓ Corporate bonds/loans	✓ Abbey National, Northern Rock ✓ MBNA International ✓ Deutsche Bank
Investment Banks/ Managers	✓ Corporate loans/bonds ✓ Commercial mortgages (conduits)	✓ Deutsche Bank ✓ MS Mortgage Capital
Finance Companies	✓ Auto loans, consumer loans ✓ Sub-prime mortgages/loans	✓ Ford Credit Europe, Fiat Bank ✓ GMAC-RFC, Kensington
Government/ Agencies	✓ Student loans ✓ Export credits, tax liens ✓ Social security payments	✓ UK Student Loan Company ✓ Italian Treasury ✓ Portugal
Corporates	✓ Trade receivables ✓ Inventory ✓ Real estate operating (whole business) income	✓ Glencore ✓ Cruise Ship Finance ✓ Telecom Italia ✓ Madame Tussauds
Real Estate Operators	✓ Tenant lease payments ✓ Operating income	✓ Punch Taverns ✓ Canary Wharf

Figure 13.2   Originators and asset classes used for securitisation in Europe

In a static pool transaction, the asset pool is fixed, with no substitution. Products with redraw facilities must be excluded. The notes, starting with those that are most highly rated, amortise in conjunction with the underlying assets. Typical static pool assets include, but are not restricted to: residential mortgages, commercial mortgages, student loans, home equity loans, personal loans, and leases.

Alternatively, in a master trust structure, underlying assets are transferred to a trust. Both investors and the seller participate in the economic benefits arising from the performance of the trust according to their respective shares. New assets, meeting eligibility requirements, may be transferred to the trust to replace redeemed assets and/or to enable new issuance. Multiple issuance of notes at different times is possible. Due to the revolving nature of the trust, notes require a predefined amortisation schedule. Credit cards, residential mortgages, and trade receivables are examples of assets that may be securitised in a master trust structure.

Notes: The SPV issues securities or notes to investors to fund the purchase of the receivables from the originator. To optimise the risk profile of the securities and therefore maximise the range of investors to whom they can be sold, the notes are divided into different classes. These typically consist of several sequential tranches with differing priorities as to payment of principal and interest (from the cash flows on the underlying receivables) and carrying differing rates of interest. The more senior tranches have the right to priority of payment over more junior tranches, but the more junior tranches carry a higher rate of interest. Each tranche is generally given a rating by a credit rating agency (for example, "AAA", "A", "BBB", unrated, etc.).

Rating agencies: Such as Moody's, Standard and Poor's, and Fitch, play a key part in the execution process. Similar to a corporate rating process, the rating agencies will take a close look at all aspects of the transaction. In particular, they will focus on:

- *Due diligence*: Examination of the assets and servicing capabilities of the originator/seller;
- *Credit/asset analysis*: Sizing the exposure to defaults and losses on the assets in a "worst case scenario";
- *Structural analysis*: Modelling of the income stream generated from the assets to pay debt in a "stress case";
- *Legal analysis*: Legal soundness of the structure reviewed to ensure that there are no disruptions to the timely servicing of debt.

Historical performance is the key driver of the credit assessment process. Using consumer loans as an example, the focus is upon defaults and recovery. Loans are tracked from origination to repayment. Those loans originated at similar times can be grouped to construct vintage curves as illustrated in Figure 13.3. Credit assessment looks at historical peaks of cumulative default/recovery to determine the maximum likely net loss on the portfolio. Historical behaviour also informs the appropriate level for performance triggers.

Data Table

	Months Since Origination				
Vintage	12	24	38	48	60
2009 H2	1.00%	4.47%	5.80%	6.11%	6.15%
2010 H1	2.04%	4.56%	5.57%	5.58%	
2010 H2	2.04%	4.25%	5.20%	5.59%	
2011 H1	1.90%	3.94%	4.87%		
2011 H2	1.40%	3.46%	4.78%		
2012 H1	1.58%	3.05%			
2012 H2	1.36%	2.83%			

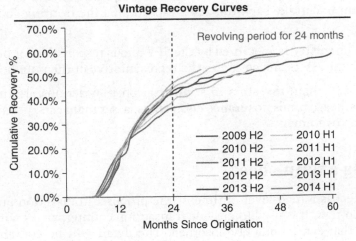

Figure 13.3   Consumer loan vintage analysis

Servicer: The main responsibility of the servicer is to manage the asset pool to maximise cash flows for the benefit of the note-holders. This includes the administration of delinquencies and ensuring that investors retain a first perfected security interest in the assets and their associated collateral throughout the life of the transaction. Generally, the servicing function will be performed by the seller/originator, but it is also possible to enlist the services of a specialist third-party servicer, in either case in exchange for a fee.

Cash manager: The rating agencies will require protection within the transaction to ensure that any collections on securitised receivables are ring-fenced in the case of the bankruptcy of the originator/seller. Where the seller collects into its own bank accounts and wants to continue this process after a securitisation (as opposed to moving collection accounts), this will be subject to rating agency minimum short-term ratings criteria: P-1 for Moody's, F-1 for Fitch, and A-1 for Standard and Poor's.

Liquidity provider: The liquidity provider covers any temporary (i.e. timing) mismatches in cash flow, usually to enable the payments of interest to the note-holders by the SPV.

Swap provider: A floating-rate term securitisation is almost always financed by notes issued at a spread to 3-month Libor (or its equivalent in other jurisdictions). There will be an interest-rate risk to manage in the structure if the assets are linked to any other benchmark rate, for example, 5-year fixed rate, bank base rate, standard variable mortgage rate, etc. Gap risk must be hedged and basis risk, for example, between 3-month Libor on the notes and bank base rate on a securitisation of mortgage assets will be looked upon negatively by rating agencies unless it is mitigated by swaps. The rating agencies will require that any hedges provided to the transaction meet their minimum rating tests (similar to cash management above). To the extent that the originator is already hedging this risk and is sufficiently rated, it can undertake back-to-back swaps and be the fronting counterparty to the SPV.

Trustee: The trustee is appointed by the SPV and is responsible for holding the security of the assets and acting as the representative of the note-holders.

Investors: The main investors in securitisation transactions are investment companies/hedge funds, insurance companies, asset managers, pension funds, banks, and governments.

Building a term-sheet

A term-sheet is a high-level outline of the proposed transaction and will be prepared upfront. It is used to provide transaction counterparties with a quick summary that can be quickly absorbed. The detail will be contained in an offering circular/prospectus and myriad legal documents prepared by lawyers to the transaction.

Audit

All securitisations are subject to upfront audit procedures, mainly relating to the assets sold to the SPV or trust. In the case of loans, the "pool audit" (alternatively known as "agreed-upon procedures") and "loan file due diligence", performed by a firm of accountants and lawyers to the transaction, respectively, are designed to ensure that the representations made about the pool are true at the time of the offering to investors.

The pool audit constitutes a range of checks on a random sample of loans selected for the securitisation. The confidence level for the audit is set by the rating agencies and for most issuers will be established at 99%. There are a number of parties that are interested in the results of the pool audit:

- *Rating agencies*: who base their credit enhancement/note tranching on the pool data provided. If the tests reveal that the data provided in a data tape is not a reliable representation of the underlying assets, then the rating agencies will assume that the credit profile is weaker than presented and increase the amount of lower rated notes in the structure to provide more protection to the higher rated notes. This will result in more expensive funding for the originator;
- *Underwriters/arrangers*: as the investment banks maintain relationships with investors, they will want to ensure that the information portrayed in the offering document is accurate in all material respects;
- *The trustee*: as it is acting on behalf of note-holders, it will be looking for comfort that the security is as represented in the offering circular.

STRUCTURAL FEATURES OF ABS

Many of the structural features of ABS provide both flexibility for originators and additional protection for note-holders:

Revolving period (used in master trust transactions): provides originators with bullet financing for the length of the revolving period and the revolving period allows the issuer to use principal repayments from the existing pool to purchase new assets.

Performance triggers: used in a transaction to protect note-holders against adverse credit performance, for example, early amortisation (repayment) if defaults rise above a specified percentage. Historical data is key in establishing the performance triggers.

Eligibility criteria: used to ensure that all current and future assets in the pool exhibit similar credit and legal characteristics, which can be described in the offering circular to investors.

Subordination: enables highly rated (senior) tranches to be protected from loss of principal and interest by lower rated (junior) tranches. Under EU legislation,

	Asset-backed Securitisation	Bank/Bond
Description	■ Non-recourse financing backed by assets	■ Secured or unsecured debt of the company
Issuer	■ Newly formed bankruptcy-remote SPV, wholly owned by the company	■ Company
Ratings	■ Senior-subordinated tranche structure ■ Senior notes potentially rated higher than unsecured rating	■ Corporate ratings
Bond Structure	■ Amortising bond that could be deferred with a revolving period ■ Can be structured as a bullet maturity	■ Varies
Debtholder Protections	■ If portfolio performances are triggered; early amortisation of the notes ■ Limitations on SPV activities, and requirement that the company continues to manage the collateral	■ Financial and operational convenants including pledges, ratios, and restricted activity
Expected Maturity	■ Varies; typically 3 to 5 years ■ Can be shorter if in loan format	■ Varies
Funding	■ Issuing vehicle is typically fully funded	■ Bonds are fully funded
Optional Redemption	■ Usually allowed with make-whole or after a non-call period	■ Varies; generally significant flexibility with bank financing ■ Bond financing typically involves prepayment premium
Covenants	■ Avoid restrictive convenants, especially dividend and acquisition restrictions	■ Limited flexibility subject to agreed baskets or carve-outs
Other Considerations	■ Structurally complex with longer time to market ■ By pledging most assets to separate SPV, other debtholders, if any, are effectively subordinated	■ Often easiest to execute upfront, subject to market conditions ■ Typically more volatile issuing market ■ Bank markets typically provide maximum structural flexibility (e.g. prepayment)

Figure 13.4   ABS vs traditional bond finance

originators must retain 5% of any issued ABS to align their interests with those of investors.

Cash reserves: as well as to provide liquidity (to cover mismatches in the timing of payments), certain types of asset require a dedicated cash reserve to address their specific characteristics. For example, trade receivables typically need a dilution reserve to mitigate non-cash reduction of payable invoices.

Excess spread: is available when interest and fee payments on the underlying assets are greater than interest payable on the notes and fees payable to the transaction counterparties. Excess spread provides credit enhancement to note-holders and additional liquidity to the structure. The extra cash flows down the established payment waterfalls (priorities), topping up cash reserves in the structure as necessary. Any surplus is paid to the party holding unrated notes or equity.

Asset-backed securities vs traditional finance: Figure 13.4 provides a tabular comparison between ABS and more traditional bond finance.

PRACTICAL ISSUES WITH ORIGINATING AN OWN-ASSET SECURITISATION TRANSACTION

Securitisation is a complex technique. This section focuses on the operational issues that may be encountered when originating a traditional static pool mortgage securitisation.

Initial transaction preparations

Launching a successful securitisation requires involvement and input from many parts of an organisation. It is essential that all parties referred to in Figure 13.5 are involved in the process at the outset by the deal team and there is a clearly defined governance structure in place.

Multiple external transaction counterparties also need to be engaged:

- Rating agencies: at least two of Moody's, Fitch, Standard and Poor's, and DBRS;
- Arranger: an investment bank;
- Lawyers for the seller and arranger: two major city law firms;
- A servicer, swap provider (if applicable), liquidity provider (if applicable), collection account bank, trustee, cash manager, corporate services provider, and potentially others depending upon the deal structure.

End-to-end delivery of a first-time transaction for an originator will take 6–9 months to complete. The main workstreams are: deal set-up, engagement of transaction counterparties, deal structuring and rating, due diligence, legal documentation, systems and data, regulatory approvals, transaction launch, investor roadshows, transaction closure, and investor reporting.

Deal structuring and rating

The structuring process requires the originator and arranger to discuss and agree on many structural factors such as:

- The currency of notes issued;
- The classes of notes issued;
- The amount and type of reserve funds established;

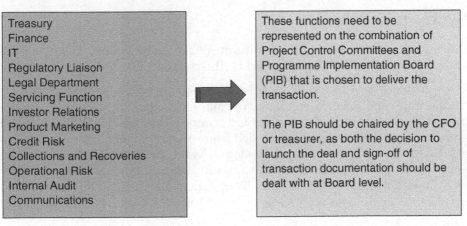

Treasury
Finance
IT
Regulatory Liaison
Legal Department
Servicing Function
Investor Relations
Product Marketing
Credit Risk
Collections and Recoveries
Operational Risk
Internal Audit
Communications

These functions need to be represented on the combination of Project Control Committees and Programme Implementation Board (PIB) that is chosen to deliver the transaction.

The PIB should be chaired by the CFO or treasurer, as both the decision to launch the deal and sign-off of transaction documentation should be dealt with at Board level.

Figure 13.5   Engagement across the organisation and transaction governance

- Requirement for interest-rate swaps;
- Treatment of product switchers;
- Whether the transaction will support further advances;
- Whether substitution is allowed;
- Treatment of fee income (such as early repayment charges);
- Treatment of overpayments on mortgage accounts;
- Process for segregating securitisation cash flows from bank cash flows and frequency of separation;
- The first transaction interest payment date.

There will not always be a right or wrong answer (it may just come down to the preferences of the originator), but the legal documentation supporting the transaction must be aligned to what is agreed.

Multiple other factors will influence the rating/tranching of the transaction and will need to be thoroughly researched by the originator:

- *Set-off*: may exist if the seller/originator has deposits in the same names as the assets being securitised. The rating agencies will want to establish whether the SPV would receive full value for the outstanding mortgages in the event of the liquidation of the seller;
- *Staff lending*: are any of the loans in the securitisation pool to staff members? The concern is potential contagion effects in the case of the liquidation of the seller;
- *Prepayment trends*: will help the rating agencies and investors to determine the likely amortisation profile of the securitisation notes and the coupon on them;
- *Payment holidays on loans*: will affect the ability of the SPV to meet coupon payments on the notes;
- *Arrears, loss, and delinquency data, ideally by cohort*: will affect the proportions of different notes (for example, "AAA", "AA", "A", "BBB", etc.) sold in the transaction.

Systems and data

Rating agencies need a significant volume of account level data to rate a transaction. A subset of the data required is illustrated in Figure 13.6.

Data provided to the rating agencies for analysis of the deal structure and "tranching" and used to populate summary statistics published in the deal prospectus should be both complete and accurate. Account level data with gaps and obvious errors should be excluded from the pool of eligible securitisation assets, for example, property postcode not valid, property valuation is only a small percentage of the original loan amount, loan amount and/or maturity are outside established lending criteria. Poor data quality could reduce the portfolio of assets eligible for securitisation by up to 50%, so many first-time issuers

Pool Cut-off Date	Property Identifier	Borrower's Employment Status	Secondary Income	Loan Origination Date	Original Balance	Geographic Region List
Pool Identifier	Borrower Type	First-time Buyer	Income Verification for Secondary Income	Date of Loan Maturity	Current Balance	Property Postcode
Loan Identifier	Foreign National	Right to Buy	Resident	Account Status Date	Fractioned/ Subrogated Loans	Occupancy Type
Regulated Loan	Borrower Credit Quality	Right to Buy Price	Number of County Court Judgements or Equivalent - Satisfied	Origination Channel / Arranging Bank or Division	Repayment Method	Property Type
Originator	Borrower Year of Birth	Class of Borrower	Value of County Court Judgements or Equivalent - Satisfied	Purpose	Payment Frequency	New Property
Servicer Identifier	Number of Debtors	Primary Income	Number of County Court Judgements or Equivalent - Unsatisfied	Shared Ownership	Payment Due	Construction Year
Borrower Identifier	Second Applicant Year of Birth	Income Verification for Primary Income	Value of County Court Judgements or Equivalent - Unsatisfied	Loan Term	Payment Type	Property Rating

Figure 13.6 Extract of the type of account level data required to support a mortgage transaction

need to establish a data quality initiative to correct the position to maximise securitisation capacity.

In a true sale, securitisation loans will be equitably assigned to an SPV. Ideally, there should be a securitisation transaction identifier or *flag* recorded on the bank's source system, as all cash flows due to the vehicle must be tracked and there are ongoing loan level and aggregate reporting requirements. The *flag* must be installed before the closing date of the transaction. Close liaison with the bank's IT function is required to plan the *flagging* date and alternatives, for example, if market conditions affect the launch. There must be a capability to buy loans out of the securitisation pool (i.e. remove *flags*) once the transaction is up and running (for example, post launch discovery that certain loans have failed representation and warranty tests), and potentially to *flag* new accounts (for example, if substitution is allowed).

A system must be built to track cash flows (for example, loan repayments, interest payments, fee income (?), proceeds from repossession proceedings, etc.) on all securitised accounts. Rating agencies will assess the risk arising from the "co-mingling" of securitisation and seller cash flows. Cash transfers to an account in the name of the securitisation SPV may need to be daily – the required frequency will depend on the servicer/seller rating.

Legal documentation

Legal documentation describes how the transaction will operate in all conceivable situations, and includes the specific requirements of the transaction counterparties.

The main provisions are summarised in the prospectus, but there will be myriad transaction agreements (possibly 100+), prepared by the lawyers to the deal, which will be signed by relevant transaction counterparties on deal closure. In a mortgage securitisation, the key documents are the mortgage sale agreement, the cash management agreement, the trust deed, the subscription agreement, and the servicing agreement.

At the outset, "boiler plate" documentation will be provided by the lawyers to the transaction, which will be adapted to the specific circumstances of the deal. All parties to the transaction must check that the legal documents deliver exactly what has been agreed and/or what has been asked for. Paragraphs are often complex and take a few reads to interpret. Any errors should be "picked up" before launch of the transaction and become progressively more difficult to change after this point.

Agreeing a name for a securitisation SPV is not as straightforward as it may seem, as sellers need to create the right image for the transaction. The name chosen is often linked to the underlying seller, for example, Northern Rock's "Granite" Programme, Lloyds Bank's "Arkle Master Trust", and KBC's Belgian connection to Tintin titles such as "Calculus Master Trust".

Due diligence

The agreed-upon procedures and loan file due diligence have been referred to in the earlier section on audit. Due diligence for a transaction is extensive and other key checks include:

- **Rating agency due diligence**: to support the rating agency assessment of the transaction and disclosures in pre-sale reports issued to prospective investors;
- **Legal due diligence**: conducted by the lawyers to confirm that disclosures in the legal documentation for the transaction are accurate;
- **Bring down call at launch**: a discussion between senior management of the seller, transaction counterparts, and lawyers to confirm there have been no changes or omissions from the disclosures in the prospectus.

Regulatory approvals and opinions

A number of other sign-offs/approvals need to be in place before the transaction can be launched, such as:

- **Prospectus**: UK Listing Authority. The Official List is a definitive record of whether a company's securities are officially listed or not;
- **Regulator**: PRA. A letter of non-objection should be sought if the bank is aiming to achieve capital relief on the deal;
- **Note ratings**: based on rating agencies' statistical analysis of default probabilities;
- **Legal opinion**: Required from every jurisdiction in which securitisation assets have been originated. Note, Scotland and Northern Ireland are separate from England and Wales;
- **Tax opinion**: What taxes may arise from the transaction?;
- **Accounting opinion**: How should the transaction be accounted for?

Transaction launch and close

Provided that market conditions permit, once all preparatory activities are complete, the deal can be "launched" and announced to the market. This will be followed by meetings with prospective investors (roadshow) supported by an "investor presentation". During this period, representatives of the seller/originator will respond to investor queries and the arranger will "book build" (line up purchasers of the notes). To "close" the transaction, closing cash flows will take place (investors buy notes, SPV buys assets from seller/originator, etc.), all legal documents must be signed, and securitised accounts must be flagged on the seller's source system.

As illustrated in Figure 13.7, if market conditions deteriorate, the deal may need to be temporarily suspended or pulled from the market altogether.

The cost of preparing a securitisation for the market can easily spiral out of control, so needs to be carefully budgeted and tightly controlled, in particular:

- **Legal costs**: especially if there is an unforeseen challenge to overcome;
- **Project costs**: resources will be sucked into the project near the time of the launch to ensure delivery;
- **System costs**: when are these less than anticipated?;
- **Rating agencies**: will need to pay all for review work even if one or more of the agencies is not chosen to rate the deal.

Post transaction close

The transaction needs to be supported on an ongoing basis. Key activities include: investor reporting, cash flow management (application of revenue and principal waterfalls built into the transaction), and checking status on all procedural triggers built into the deal, for example, ratings downgrade triggers.

UK 3-5 Yr AAA RMBS Spreads

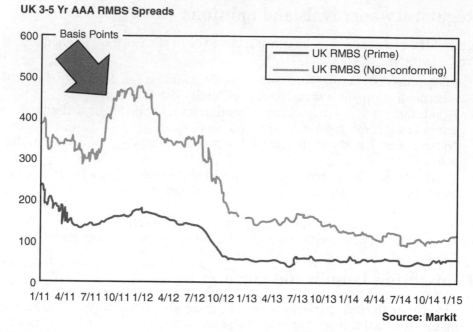

Figure 13.7   Market conditions could adversely affect transaction launch

SUMMARY AND CONCLUSIONS

Securitisation is a long-established technique that enables banks to manage their balance sheets with greater flexibility and precision. By employing it, a bank can work toward ensuring optimum treatment of its assets for funding, regulatory capital, and credit risk management purposes. In addition, in the post-crash era the securitisation tool continues to be used to create tradable notes that can then be used as collateral at the central bank.

The primary driver behind the decision to securitise part of the asset side of the balance sheet is one or more of the following:

- Funding: Assets that are unrepo-able may be securitised, which enables the bank to fund them via the capital market, or by creating notes that can be used as collateral at the central bank;
- Regulatory capital: This is a rarer reason driving securitisation in the post-crash, Basel III era;
- Risk management: Assets on the balance sheet expose the originator to credit risk, and this can be managed (either reduced, removed, or hedged) via securitisation.

A secondary driver is client demand. The process of securitisation creates bonds that can be sold, and investor demand for a note of specified credit risk, liquidity, maturity, and underlying asset class may well cause a bond to be created, via securitisation, to meet this specific investor requirement. Whether a transaction is demand driven or issuer driven, it will always be created to meet at least one of the preceding requirements.

The process of securitisation, which we cover in detail in subsequent chapters, can take anything from a few months to up to a year. The most important parts of the process are the legal review and drafting of transaction documents, and the rating agency review. The involvement of third parties, such as lawyers, trustees, agency services providers, and the rating agencies, is the key driver behind the cost of closing a securitisation deal, and these costs are covered either by the deal itself or direct by the originating institution.

A wide range of asset classes can be securitised, with the most common being residential mortgages and corporate loans. Other asset classes include auto loans and credit card receivables. When assessing the risk exposure and performance of different types of ABS, investors will consider the behaviours and characteristics of the specific type of underlying asset. Some performance metrics are of course common to all types of assets, such as delinquency rate or the percentage of non-performing loans.

A type of securitisation unknown before the 2008 crash but now common is the in-house transaction. In this process, the originating bank will undertake all the usual steps to structure the deal, but will buy the ABS notes itself. These notes, which would be rated by a rating agency in the normal way, are then available to the bank to use as collateral, either in a repo transaction or to place with the central bank. The deal has thereby transformed illiquid assets on the bank's balance sheet into liquid notes that can then be used to raise funding.

BIBLIOGRAPHY

Baig, S., and Choudhry, M. 2013. *The Mechanics of Securitization*. Hoboken, NJ: John Wiley & Sons Limited.

Choudhry, M. 2007. *Bank Asset and Liability Management*. Singapore: John Wiley & Sons Limited.

It was clear to me that many Naval Academy graduates and senior officers did whatever it took to please their bosses. Such sycophants taught me one of the most important lessons I learned from my Vietnam experience: there will always be people who pursue power by ingratiating themselves with those in power without pausing to assess the goals of those leaders. I came to understand this as a POW, but I have witnessed it in all institutions ever since: corporations, bureaucracies, schools, churches, you name it.

—Robert Wideman, *Unexpected Prisoner: Memoir of a Vietnam POW*, 2016.

PART

III

Strategy, Regulatory Capital and Case Studies

Having established the basics and the technicals in Parts I and II, we can now tackle the essential "top level" topics, namely, strategy setting, regulatory capital and Basel III (and ICAAP), and operational risk.

We then "bring it all together" in the last chapter, which is a selection of real-world case studies where particular risk, governance, operating model, or Board-level issues were discussed and solutions implemented.

Chapter

14

STRATEGY SETTING

This chapter provides an overview of the development of a strategy for a bank, as well as the identification of the likely key elements of a strategic plan. Strategy is a big topic, and those wishing to have a deeper understanding may consider some of the writings by leading thinkers in this domain.

The development of an effective bank strategy is as much an art as it is a science. Fundamental analytic work is a key element of the process; however, the crafting of an effective strategy requires more input still. Equally important is a deep understanding of the organisation itself – its key strengths ("core competencies", which we will return to later) and its key weaknesses in the environment within which the entity operates – the markets, the competitors, and the regulatory framework – and the emerging trends and forces likely to shape the future environment. The art lies in the integration of all this information and the distillation of the relevant actions that the organisation needs to implement to improve its competitive positioning – the essence of strategy.

Many different methodologies are employed to assist with this process. Robust analytics assist with the understanding of internal financial dynamics (for example, the profitability of business units or products) and some elements of market and consumer dynamics. Insightful analysis of competitor performance can also be of value in the process. However, strategy is all about changing course for some preferred future positioning of the organisation (strategy is seldom, if ever, about what needs to be done to maintain the current "status quo" of an organisation), and this is where intuition is often as powerful as logic. The preferred future positioning needs to be identified and articulated, and a bridge needs to be built from where the organisation currently stands to that future positioning. An overview of this process is discussed in this chapter.

For most organisations, the lack of an effective strategy is likely to lead to a "slow death" – the gradual loss of a commercial franchise in its chosen market place, as it succumbs to the efforts of its competitors – unless it is in the unusual position of being a monopoly, without any threat of substitution! This effect leads to attrition – loss of clients, loss of profitability, loss of talented staff, consolidation, and eventual closure.

A similar process may happen with a bank as well, but there is one key aspect of a bank that normally hastens this process: banking is built on trust and confidence and when that erodes, the effects can be and usually are a "rapid death". When a bank loses the trust of its clients and the market, deposits are withdrawn, new funding dries up, and bad debts may increase. Sometimes it is the increase in bad debts (credit losses) to unforeseen levels that erodes confidence in a bank, and if the bank has insufficient capital to withstand this, it will experience a rapid demise. Similarly, a bank with an unsustainable asset/liability mismatch may suddenly suffer a liquidity crisis, the triggering of which may also lead to a credit crisis, which will be followed by an equally rapid demise. The failure of a bank is seldom a slow process, but rather a rapid one and is usually led by a liquidity or credit crisis, but often by the latter.

For this reason, it is essential that the strategic plan of a bank includes at its centre robust capital and liquidity management plans that can deal with all challenges through the various expected (and unexpected) phases of the business cycle – it has to be financially robust through the business cycle. The strength of the bank's balance sheet throughout the business cycle lies at the heart of any effective strategic plan for a bank.

In this chapter we distinguish between the annual business plan or budget and the strategic plan. A strategic plan typically describes a process of development or change in the entity, including high level financial outcomes over an extended period of time (say, 3 to 5 years). The business plan or budget captures the planned set of activities and expected financial outcomes for the next year, by month/quarter, and possibly for the following year. The annual business plan or budget is the year by year roll-out of the longer term strategic plan and must therefore be structured to deliver the strategic plan 1 year at a time for the duration of the strategic plan period. This chapter will focus on the development and shape of an effective strategic plan and not the annual business plan.

THE STRATEGIC PLANNING PROCESS

This subject has a large scope; here we set out the key ingredients of a successful outcome.

Strategy is about defining a path from where an organisation is at present to where it would prefer to be in the future and preparing a plan to get there. This involves the enquiry and development of responses to a number of basic, but complex, questions:

- Where are we today? What is the imperative to change? (Often described as the "Current Reality");
- What should we aim to become? Why? (The "Preferred Future" or "Vision");
- What do we need to do to take us from our "Current Reality" to our "Preferred Future" ("Strategic Initiatives")?;
- What enablers are required to ensure that we can execute the planned "Strategic Initiatives"?

This is the start of a multi-year commitment to some form of organisational change, sometimes of significant magnitude, and the importance thereof is reflected in the fact that the Board must agree and drive the strategic plan.

It is often said that 80% of strategic plans fail to deliver their expected results; much of this is due to execution failure, where the combination of lack of resources, change fatigue, and executive impatience undermine the implementation of the strategic plan. Frequently, this is a direct result of a lack of executive commitment to the plan in the face of various difficulties that are encountered. Consequently, the commitment of both the Board and executive management to the desired outcome and the associated strategic plan is critical to a successful execution of the plan.

Step 1:

The first stage in the process is an honest and open interrogation of the "current reality" of the enterprise: How are we performing? What is being done well? What are the weaknesses? Where do our strengths lie? What are our customers saying? What are our competitors doing to improve their position? How well are we responding to changes in our environment/market/industry? This is not a simple exercise, as it requires insight and honesty and is based on an in-depth analysis, which together leads to a thoughtful assessment.

There are three key outputs from this stage of the process:

- Firstly, a good understanding of the imperative for change – why we must do something other than "business as usual". This is crucial to ensuring internal alignment with the strategic objectives;
- Secondly, a clear view of aspects of the business around which future developments can take place ("core competencies"), or where changes need to be made, or where new skills may be needed;
- Thirdly, how the entity's current market positioning affects its ability to realise its goals.

Step 2:

Based on this assessment, the next step is to consider what the entity should become, for example, over the following 5 years. This is often crafted in the form of a "vision statement", which describes the organisation in 5 years' time (or it may be a longer term vision). It articulates what the organisation strives to be and the manner it intends to operate, specifically at a higher level, and the statement should further be crafted in a form that captures the imagination of both internal and external stakeholders. It is always short on detail (the "how"): this is explained later. There is no template: such statements can be brief or one page long, depending on the organisation and audience, but what it has to do is articulate a preferred high level future state for the entity.

Sometimes, as this is organisation dependent, a vision statement will precede or be in existence prior to the assessment of the current reality, and it may be that failure to achieve the previously crafted vision is what drives re-evaluation of the strategy. It is also possible that the vision statement exists in the form of a "grand ambition" – "to be the best/biggest. . ."– to the extent that such a statement is far removed from the organisation's current reality. It is most likely to encounter many difficulties in executing a plan that has been developed to advance such a vision.

It remains important, however, that any "vision statement" is built on a deep and thorough understanding of the organisation and the environment within which it operates. In the absence of this, any "vision statement" runs the real risk of being no more than wishful thinking, detached from reality and doomed to failure. This risks turning the statement, and the bank itself, into something of a farce.

Few strategic plans survive in the absence of a compelling "vision statement", simply because without a vision statement in one form or other, the strategic plan lacks a motive.

Step 3:

The third stage involves identifying those developments that the entity needs to undertake to enable it to approximate the organisation described in the vision or "preferred future". These often take the form of high level "strategic initiatives" that in turn are supported by many detailed projects spread throughout the organisation. It may not be important to scope or identify all the supporting projects at the outset, but it is imperative that the eventual outcome is kept clearly in mind throughout. These strategic initiatives in turn define the strategic priorities throughout the organisation and should also shape the allocation of resources. Annual business plans/budgets should also make it clear how they intend to advance the agreed strategic initiatives.

The definition of the strategic initiatives is seldom a trivial matter; appropriate scoping must always be based on a deep understanding of the resource base available to support an initiative – for example, if a strategic initiative within a bank calls for geographical expansion, problems are foreseen if the bank has minimal scalable and transportable business processes or significant depth of management, or, especially, if the bank has little risk management experience in the targeted region.

Step 4:

Finally, careful consideration should be applied to which resources and support needs are to be provided to enable the strategic initiatives. Day to day business activities will continue for most of the organisation, and simply to add strategic initiative work to the workload of people responsible for normal operations will most often result in failure. How to resource for the strategic initiatives and type of support needed by those involved is also a key consideration. Often, this aspect of a plan needs to consider and address matters such as corporate culture and the relationship the entity has with its employees, because such "soft" matters will often define the manner in which employees respond to the challenges in the strategic plan.

Of fundamental importance to the strategic plan is the commitment of senior management up to and including the Chief Executive and the Board. Operational management may resent changes that affect their daily lives and there will inevitably be resistance to requirements for change or additional effort. Management at all levels must find ways to test the commitment of senior management to a plan, and any evidence of hesitation or ambivalence on the part of executive management will initiate the process of erosion for the foundations of a strategic plan. It is thus vital that the commitment of the executive

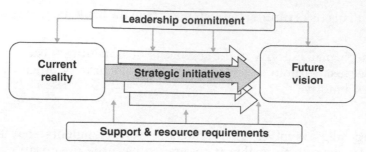

Figure 14.1   Leadership commitment

management be seen continuously by everyone throughout the entity for the strategic plan to have any chance of success.

The overall process may be represented diagrammatically by Figure 14.1.

There are many tools, approaches, and techniques that can be of help with the development of an integrated strategy as described above. It is beyond the scope of this chapter to review these, but the output of such a process must cover all five aspects of Figure 14.1 if it is to be successful.

CONSIDERATIONS IN THE DEVELOPMENT OF STRATEGY

The previous section considered the *process* involved in the development of a strategic plan; in this section we consider briefly the *key influencers and drivers* of a strategic plan, particularly in the context of a bank. These are the factors that will have to be analysed and understood in order to develop the plan as described previously.

Stakeholder expectations

What is expected of the entity by its various stakeholders, including shareholders, regulators, and clients? Shareholder expectations assist in defining financial targets. Client expectations – considering both current and future clients – should also influence in defining product and service delivery expectations. The expectations (and requirements) of regulators, particularly in the banking industry, may have a significant impact on what is possible, and the resources, both financial (often in the form of capital) and people, are required to support a particular plan.

Within a banking environment (also generally), these expectations provide an important input into the development of a bank's "risk appetite", which will in turn provide an important overlay to the development of the bank's strategic plan. The overall "risk appetite" will also be guided by a number of other factors, and further comments are made on this below.

The macro (economic) and micro (market and market segment) environment

Views on development with regard to future macro-economic and market developments will play a significant role in the shaping of the plan. However, one has to bear in mind that predictions can be dangerous and therefore any chosen business strategy should be robust under various scenarios. For a bank, this is particularly important, where capital and liquidity management under various scenarios is a key aspect of any plan.

The competitive landscape

No entity, including a bank, operates in a vacuum. Competitors, both direct and indirect, are continuously seeking some form of competitive advantage and any strategic plan will have to take into account any changing competitive landscape. This will include a deep understanding of the customer franchise and its changes in response to both the entity's actions and those of its competitors. This analysis will suggest product and market segment developments, or perhaps some form of geographical expansion or change; it may also suggest marketing initiatives designed to reposition the entity within its chosen market and market segments.

The entity is in control of its response to its environment and the changing competitive landscape: for a bank, all actions should be designed to reinforce an image of trustworthiness and stability, whatever other attributes they may seek to highlight. In addition, dramatic changes to how or where the bank operates are likely to be viewed negatively.

Internal "core competencies"

The concept of "core competencies" was developed in an article by Prahalad and Hamel in 1990 ("The Core Competence of the Corporation": *Harvard Business Review*: May–June 1990), but is used here in a more general sense. As previously noted, a deep understanding of what the entity does well, including those areas where its skill or competence is at best average – or worse – is paramount to the development of an effective strategy. It enables better strategic choices, and potentially avoids unwise ventures into areas (geographic and product/business) where the entity has little expertise.

Competencies that really do exist within an entity can be used as platforms for new developments; where these are lacking they could be bought in or developed. When they are bought in and are embodied in people (as compared to the acquisition of a technology, for example), the "cultural fit" is important; when they are developed internally, the process is usually a lengthy one and quite likely to test the patience of leadership.

To properly implement a coherent, articulate strategy, a bank needs to be aware of its exact lack or possession of expertise when undertaking and operating in products or markets in which it has no genuine knowledge base.

Resource capacity

This asks the question: Does the entity have the resources to undertake this plan? We will separately (see below) consider the balance sheet implications because this is such an important matter for banks in particular – here we limit the question to people, skills, and processes. This is linked to the question of core competencies, but also addresses the issue of "capacity". This will inform the assessment for the resources required to support the plan, covering aspects as varied as financial/budgets, people and training, management support and communication, and equipment. Failure to address this adequately will fuel employee discontent and build resistance to the implementation of the plan.

Organisational structure

It has been said that "structure follows strategy", and for good reason. A key element in the development of the overall plan is the organisational structure required to properly support the plan. Structure should be shaped by a number of factors that emerge from the strategic plan, and would typically address how the entity should be structured:

- To best engage with its chosen markets;
- To best deliver the products/services to the chosen markets;
- To best leverage and/or build the identified "core competencies"; and
- To operate within acceptable cost and pricing constraints.

Within an entity as complex as a bank, the resultant structures are seldom simple, and care needs to be taken to ensure that the principle of clear accountability is maintained, given its importance to both governance and effective execution.

This also suggests the need for clarity of purpose: the future of business units that do not naturally fit into the defined strategy should be considered with care as such entities are often management diversions and potential sources of unwanted problems. Similar care needs to be taken with acquisitions and alignment with strategy.

Capital and funding

For most organisations, the question of capital and funding is limited to access to sufficient funding and capital to enable the execution of the strategy. There may also be questions of risk management should there be reliance on third parties for the funding. For banks, however, capital and funding are central to any strategic plan. The bank should be able to demonstrate its robustness, within the context of its chosen strategy, throughout a full business cycle, as well as under extreme stress scenarios. Such a consideration is a regulatory requirement in most jurisdictions, and needs to cover both the sufficiency of capital and access to liquidity under both "fair weather" and adverse business conditions.

For this reason, capital and liquidity management (in effect the structure of the bank's balance sheet) must lie at the heart of the bank's strategic plan and will guide the bank's capacity for embarking on the strategic plan. For many banks, post Basel III, the issue will be building their capital base to meet the new requirements and restructuring their depositor and funding base to improve their liquidity profile; for some banks it may be more an issue of maintenance of appropriate capital levels and funding profiles. Whatever the position of a bank, these issues remain central to the development of their strategic plan and any plan will continuously be tested against its potential impact on capital levels and liquidity profiles. Similarly, the strategic plan will have to take an account of the bank's ability to attract appropriate duration funding, and where necessary to raise capital over the entire planning period. Hence, the capital management plan and liquidity management plan will both be core elements of any bank's strategic plan.

Risk appetite

An articulated risk appetite statement is a key factor that shapes bank strategy. Risk appetite is shaped by a number of factors, including:

- Board and shareholder appetite for variations in financial performance and expected levels of profitability (for example, return on equity or return on capital – see below);
- Absolute and relative levels of loss absorption of capital and regulatory requirements;
- Funding structures and liquidity profiles;
- Reputational and market positioning of the bank;
- Operational robustness and managerial capacity.

However, risk appetite will impact on strategic choices. Rapid growth of the balance sheet is unlikely to be a choice for a bank with a low tolerance for credit risk surprises, while geographical expansion might not be a top priority for a bank with a low tolerance for operational risk. However, this may well be a strategic option for a bank with significant capital buffers, robust operational processes, and a deep pool of managerial talent.

For this reason, the strategic plan will have to be assessed against the framework of the risk appetite for the bank as approved by the Board. An element of this includes the capital and liquidity management plans as discussed previously.

STRATEGY AND THE BANK BUSINESS MODEL

The basic bank business model has remained largely unchanged since banks were first introduced in modern society. In essence, banking involves taking risks in order to facilitate intermediation between providers and consumers of finance, and then applying effective management of that risk to ensure continuing viability as a going concern continuously over the business cycle. The model parameters themselves are set to suit the specific strategy of the individual bank, depending on its customer franchise and whether the bank operates at a higher or lower risk–reward profile. However, the basic model is identical across all banks.

We summarised the basic ingredients of the historical bank business model in Chapter 1. These fundamentals remain unchanged. The critical issue for bank management, however, is that some of the assumptions behind the application of these fundamentals have changed, as demonstrated by the crash of 2007–2008. The business landscape in the wake of the crisis has resulted in some hitherto "safe" or profitable business lines being viewed as risky. Although more favourable conditions for banking will return in due course, for the foreseeable future the challenge for banks will be to set their strategy only after first arriving at a true and full understanding of economic conditions as they exist today. There also needs to be an understanding of the drivers that are likely to shape the economic conditions over the planning period and beyond, enabling a better appreciation of the potential impacts of adverse conditions on the capital position of the bank.

It is perhaps interesting to compare the approaches of banks and life assurers to the management of the balance sheets. Given the definition of "leverage", both manage a balance sheet where total assets are a significant multiple of the capital or equity of the entity. The fundamental difference between the two is the degree of "mismatch" found on the bank's balance sheet – a function largely of the role they play within the economy. This mismatch is found both in terms of duration – banks lend long and borrow short – and liquidity – liabilities that can be called up at short notice backed by assets that, in the main, do not normally trade in the open market. The behavioural aspects that play such an important part in the changing value of a bank's assets (credit risk) are also a much less significant factor on the balance sheet of a life assurer. For this reason, risk management is more developed (to date) within a bank because of the ability of the bank, via its own internal processes, to influence the value of its assets; for a life assurer, the value of its assets is more likely to be influenced by external asset market movements, and it is also more likely to have some measure of "control" over the value of its liabilities in extreme circumstances.

As a result, a bank's strategic plan will always require robust management of the following two core focus areas:

- Managing the bank's capital;
- Managing the balance sheet funding or "liquidity" mismatch: a fundamental ingredient of banking is "maturity transformation", the impact on the balance sheet of the fact that loans (assets) generally have a longer tenor than deposits (liabilities).

Universal objectives

It is unsurprising that there are a number of strategic objectives that will be found universally within banking, particularly following the implementation of the Basel III regulatory regime. These may be summarised as:

- To **ensure adequate capital buffers**, in terms of both quantity and quality, to meet the requirements of Basel III; for many banks, this called for an increase in capital, a process that is not complete at the time of writing this chapter. It also requires effective ongoing management of capital buffers;
- To **improve capital efficiency** via, for example, existing loan book restructuring and "optimising" collateral management;
- To investigate **"capital-light" growth opportunities** within the existing knowledge and resource base;
- To **lower cost structures** via a combination of improving business processes to reduce operational costs, simplifying operating models, headcount reduction, or outsourcing;
- To **review the portfolio of business units** within the bank; this may lead to the disposal of unprofitable or non-core business lines for reasons such as strategic fit or failure to achieve target risk-adjusted return on capital;
- To implement more **robust and stable funding structures**, particularly with respect to higher-cost longer term funds.

The first and last of these are demanded explicitly in the Basel III regime, in the form of higher capital buffers of varying types (see Chapter 8) and adherence to structural liquidity metrics (see Chapter 9). Of course the first three are essentially platitudes – all businesses would seek to maximise capital efficiency and minimise the cost–income ratio at all times, simply as good operating practice.

However, to be considered a genuine long-term contender in banking requires more than this in fact: no less than a specific defined customer-orientated differentiation of one's business model. The competitive environment for banks remains challenging. This is particularly the case for banks domiciled in countries that experienced a sovereign bail-out, where there is additional pressure associated with continuing poor public image and brand association. Under such circumstances, it is unsurprising that differentiating oneself from the competition presents difficulties for bank Boards and senior management, particularly in view of the commoditised nature of the basic bank product.

The requirements of Basel III standards and those of national regulators will play a major role in influencing bank strategy. Of course, the Board must have its own view on sustainable banking, and consider the regulatory standards to be a minimum requirement. The specific areas of capital and liquidity, as well as sound asset origination policy, must be set by the Board in line with its own beliefs and understanding. To summarise, the basic strategy is identical for all banks in that it must ensure that the entity meets regulatory requirements. At the individual bank level, strategy should reflect core competence and risk appetite strengths.

Bank strategy

The most important function that a bank's Board and senior executives can undertake is to set the firm's strategy. It is vital that banks put in place a coherent, explicit, and articulated strategy that sets the culture for the entire business from the top down. The process that should be followed, at least in broad outline, is as described earlier in this chapter. In the following section we will discuss certain specific aspects of a bank strategic plan.

The first subject for discussion is to consider what a realistic, sustainable return on capital target level should be, and that it is commensurate with the level of risk aversion desired by the Board as defined in the risk appetite statement. Setting these targets at appropriate levels and in a manner that does not encourage behaviour that is inconsistent with the risk appetite or general ethos of the bank is very important. It is also important that the target be clearly understood as a "through the cycle" target – on average, through both good and bad years!

Investment markets relate more easily to Return on Equity (RoE) and Return on Assets (ROA) targets, but they suffer because they are not "risk adjusted", as the unsustainably high RoEs generated by many banks prior to the 2008 crash revealed; as a result, the use of RoE and RoA has been questioned by regulators. There are a number of ways to approach the question of an appropriate risk-adjusted return metric that reflects the changing risk profile of the bank's underlying business:

- "Return on Capital" (RoC) could be defined as return on the total regulatory capital required for the bank, combining both Pillar I and Pillar II requirements. By definition, this is a "risk-adjusted" metric. However, a bank may, and often does, choose to keep a higher level of capital, including its own defined capital buffers; if such additional capital margins are included in the "C", as they are at the discretion of the bank, the robustness of the definition of "C" should be carefully considered;
- Alternatively, one could use "risk-adjusted" return or capital metrics; this calls for the use of "economic profit" rather than accounting profit, or "economic capital" rather than regulatory capital. These approaches would provide "risk-adjusted return on capital" (RARoC) and return on risk-adjusted capital (RoRAC or RoEC) measures, respectively. Both would need careful definition and to satisfy the challenge of both robustness and transparency;
- Return on Risk-Weighted Assets (RoRWA) is also a commonly used risk-adjusted metric.

Ultimately, both RoC (and the other variations) and RoRWA link to "equity", as the bank needs sufficient "equity" to back the capital implicit in both numbers; in addition, the quite natural question from investors is: "What return is the bank generating on the funds we, as investors, have left in the bank?" Even if the bank uses RoE targets in discussion with the investment community, it would be wise to adopt a risk-adjusted measure for strategic plan purposes, and deal with the link between "equity" held and "capital" requirements as a separate investor discussion.

As can be seen from this brief discussion, choice of the target return metric is not simple and is evidently a very important part of the strategy formulation process; the target chosen (form and level) will influence much of the bank's culture and ethos.

The Board should also consider the bank's capital availability, including the capital generated by operations over the planning period, and what sustained amount of business this would realistically support. The ability of a bank to generate free capital from its existing book of business is a key consideration over any planning period.

These two key issues, the return target – both unadjusted and adjusted for risk – and the availability of capital to support business within the bank's risk appetite, need to be addressed before the remainder of the bank's strategy can be considered.

A bank cannot formulate strategy without a clear and genuine understanding of the environment in which it operates. The regulatory environment has become a major factor in all banks' strategic deliberations; often, an actual or even anticipated regulatory environment will be a major factor shaping a bank's strategy. The Board must take into account the current regulatory environment, as well as trends and developments likely to shape future activities. This includes, of course, the requirements of Basel III, as well as any specific requirements of the national regulator.

It will also consider carefully its competitive environment and the developments within the markets it serves (and does not!). To assist with the decision as to its chosen product/market focus areas, the bank will need to consider where its genuine expertise resides and the extent of its capacity – its "core competencies".

To properly implement a coherent, articulate strategy, a bank needs to be aware of exactly what it does and does not have an expertise for undertaking, and not operate in products or markets in which it has no genuine knowledge base. The experience of the crash showed that many banks found themselves with balance sheet risk exposures that they did not realise they had, and did not understand. This may have been simply the holding of assets (such as structured finance securities) whose credit exposures, valuation, and secondary market liquidity they did not understand, or otherwise embarking on investment strategies such as cash-synthetic negative basis trading without being aware of all the risk measurement parameters of such strategies.

An interesting but unsurprising observation in the immediate aftermath of the 2008 global financial crisis was that US, UK, and European banks withdrew from or reduced their exposure to lending in overseas markets, irrespective of whether these were deemed peripheral or not, and concentrated on core markets. This reflects informational advantages in core markets compared to overseas and non-core markets. The UK corporate lending sector makes a case in point: between 2002 and 2009, lending volume from UK banks fell by approximately 16% (the figure between 2006 and 2009 was a decline of 14%). However, the equivalent figures for foreign subsidiaries was a fall of 10.5% and 20%, while for foreign branches the decline was even more dramatic, at 17% and 46%. Foreign banks would, on average, have less depth and breadth of corporate relationships, while branches would be expected to have even less developed relationships in the domestic market.

The lessons for the bank business model and strategy setting are clear: during an expansionary phase, it is important to remain focused on areas of core competence and those sectors in which the bank possesses genuine knowledge and understanding. Concentrating on areas in which the bank carries competitive advantage makes it less likely that loan origination standards will decline, resulting in lower losses during an economic downturn. There is also a technical reason for ensuring that overseas lending standards are strictly maintained, and limits set carefully, because it is often undertaken in foreign currency. Where no customer funding base exists in the overseas location, a bank's ability to fund such lending is more dependent on external markets and wholesale counterparties relative to domestic lending, thus making the bank more vulnerable to a market downturn.

Based on this capacity assessment (including capital availability), the bank needs to make strategic choices such as what markets it should operate in, what products it sells, and what class of customer it wishes to serve. This defines the specific target markets and product suites chosen by the bank as the basis of its strategy, after taking into account what resources are currently in place, and if these are insufficient, what additional resources are needed before embarking on the strategy.

Individual business lines should be set up to operate in alignment with the overall strategy. In other words, all the business lines exist as ingredients of the same one strategy. If a business line is not a fit with the current or future strategy, it should be exited. Equally, if a bank wishes to enter into new business where the fit with the agreed strategy is not clear, either the strategy or the acquisition should be challenged; put simply, it is difficult, if not impossible, to "ride two horses at once". This sounds obvious, but there are many cases of banks entering piecemeal into different businesses, or maintaining unsuitable lines that have been inherited through previous growth or acquisition, all usually leading to some future difficulty.

As previously noted, to compete effectively in most banking markets, a clearly defined customer-orientated differentiation of one's business model that is experienced by customers in the target markets is required. There are many elements to this, but all will be underpinned by the "core competencies" of the bank if they are to be robust and sustainable.

One element of this may be the pricing strategy applied by the bank. Banks charge for their products and services in many different ways; in some countries, banking is portrayed as being "free", which, of course, it is not. Elsewhere bank charges are more explicit and have become a competitive element. Pricing also relates to the setting of interest-rate margins and fees, and the extent to which these prices reflect the risk of a particular product and client – applied at client level, this is an element of the so-called "use test" applied by regulators since the introduction of Basel II – while appropriate pricing to match the cost of longer duration funding that may be required for specific products helps balance the supply of and demand for longer dated funds and hence the bank's overall matching. Most of the deliberations around pricing naturally take place at business unit and/or product owner level, but from time to time, pricing may be a component of the overall strategic plan. Ultimately, there needs to be a clear link of pricing into the returns objectives of the plan.

Finally, a comment on the "cost to income" ratio. The cost to income ratio is a widely used measure of the efficiency of a bank, and there is a natural and ongoing drive to improve efficiency; there are always new demands being placed on how a bank interacts with its customers, and there seems to be a constant upgrading of the technology at play. Regulation, too, plays a part in the need for additional technology, whether because of growing regulation relating to customer information or additional information required by the regulator for oversight purposes. However, the construct of this measure within a bank needs to be carefully understood before setting targets, as different parts of a bank's operation may have distinctly different cost structures. This also suggests some caution before simply comparing one bank's cost to income ratio with another, as the relative sizes and structures of the different business units may differ.

Bank strategy-setting cycle

Figure 14.2 is a stylised representation of the typical bank strategy (and typically, budget-setting) cycle as practised by banks for many years. However, the crash showed the obvious flaw in this paradigm, in that it is too heavily skewed towards a profit and unconstrained Return on Equity (RoE) incentive without regard to or adjustment for risks being undertaken by the bank. This in turn leads to "market share" targets set by senior executives.

The problem with this approach to strategy formulation is that it pays insufficient attention to the risks being undertaken by the bank and the impact on the balance sheet itself, including capital and liquidity risk management – with results that were apparent in 2008 and 2009 in the US and Europe, as well as a number of banks in the MENA and GCC regions. The direction of strategy setting – with the unconstrained RoE target driving the process in a clockwise direction – also results in business lines extending into areas of the market that they may not necessarily possess any genuine expertise in. The obvious flaw in the process lies in the dangerous assumption it makes about capital and funding liquidity: *that they will always be available*. Such an approach

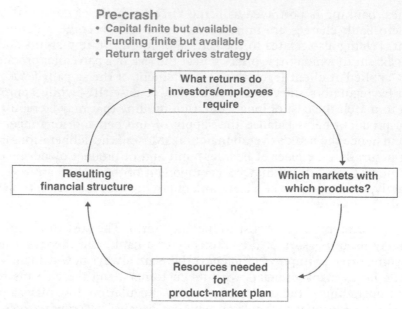

Figure 14.2   Strategy-setting cycle, pre-crash
Source: Choudhry, 2012.

means that balance sheet risk management is secondary to profit and growth ambitions.

An alternative approach to strategy formulation emphasises the primacy of balance sheet risk management in the process when it comes to bank strategy setting. This reflects more prudent management practices, and is illustrated in Figure 14.3. It shows clearly the change in strategy-setting culture that has been demanded as a result of the crash. The cycle is now resource-constraint driven, and anticlockwise in direction on the diagram, compared to the clockwise process that was heavily influenced by return target, often unadjusted for risk, in the pre-crash era.

Figure 14.3 states that a bank's resource base, and its ability to grow it over the economic cycle, including the availability of funding from capital markets, should drive the strategy forward, rather than the other way round. In practice, the process is more iterative than may be suggested in Figure 14.3, and the stages may be considered simultaneously during the strategy-setting cycle. The key point is that this approach recognises the importance of the balance sheet and its shape and structure over the economic cycle (and indeed in perpetuity – unless the bank has an objective to wind itself up at some point in the future), and the critical resource constraints that may arise with respect to capital and liquidity from time to time.

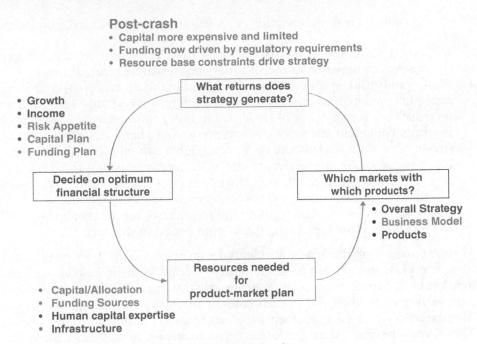

Figure 14.3   Strategy-setting cycle, post-crash
Source: Choudhry, 2012.

Strategy setting: sustainable banking through the cycle

Inherent to the strategic framework for a bank is the belief that strategy should be *sustainable*. That is, it should focus on preserving returns and capital strength through the business cycle. This belief needs to be a genuine part of the Board's thinking. In other words, the bank needs to stick to its core strengths and not be overly influenced by KPIs, which emphasise growth, such as balance sheet growth or market share, over resilience during a bull market phase in the economic cycle.

Allied to this is governments' and regulators' conversion to the idea of "macro-prudential" strategy: although the practical impact of this sort of thinking is not new, it had just been forgotten in recent years.

As a result, bank strategy needs to consider two key aspects of sustainable banking:

- **Macro-prudential:** banks should strengthen their balance sheets and liquidity ratios during the expansionary period of the economic cycle while profits are growing and conditions are benign. This can be done by:
  o Limiting the asset-side growth of their balance sheet;

○ Retaining a greater proportion of profits as reserves during the bull market phase;
○ Setting a leverage ratio limit (the Basel III leverage ratio limit of 3% can be set as an upper bound with a more conservative internal limit).

• **Micro-prudential:** at all times, banks should maintain an appropriate level and quality of capital and liquid asset buffers; they should also seek to increase the average tenor of liabilities in order to improve the mismatch position. Both elements work towards preserving a bank as a going concern irrespective of the state of the economy. Higher capital ratios and absolute levels per se should act as a more effective buffer to cushion the impact of an economic downturn, when business volumes decrease and loan losses increase. At the same time, a more conservative liquidity regime, with limits on the use of wholesale funding and larger gaps, means that a bank will be less able to grow rapidly during a boom period in the cycle.

The importance of the macro-prudential aspect of a bank's strategy arises from the phenomenon of "herd mentality", found in all industries and not just banking. Senior executives, inexplicably, often find it difficult to resist a prevailing trend even if that runs counter to one's better instincts. This is illustrated in Figure 14.4, sourced with data from the European Central Bank. This shows the increase in the funding gap, measured as customer loans less customer deposits, on an aggregate basis for four large UK banks during the period 1997–2009. The worsening "loan to deposit" (LTD) ratio during this time, which was mirrored across the individual banks, is a perfect example of how banks can end up adopting the same approach when the latest fad is

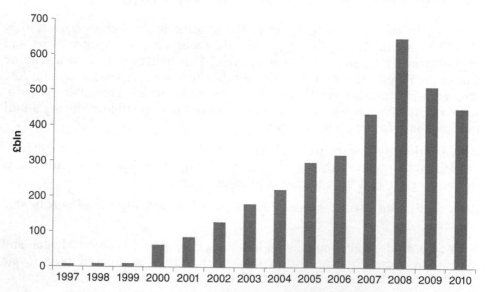

Figure 14.4   UK banks customer funding gap, 1997–2009
Source: ECB.

mistaken for business best practice. Bank management needs to be mindful of this danger during a bull market.

In assessing what factors should form part of strategy formulation, it is also worth noting those factors that should be viewed with extreme caution when they make an appearance as part of a bank's strategy. The bank crisis of 2007–2008, as well as previous banking failures such as the US bank crash of 1980–1982 and the zombie-like experience of Japanese banks in the 1990s, all resulted from banks adopting a management approach that allowed them to become overextended through:

- Ever greater risk-taking and leverage levels;
- Over-reliance on wholesale funding;
- Increasing exposure to higher-risk product classes, such as 100% LTV mortgages, adjustable-rate mortgages, buy-to-let mortgages, or derivatives trading;
- Poor management decisions involving overly ambitious acquisitions or expansion of new business lines;
- Emphasis on market share and high RoE as KPI targets, thereby driving excessive risk-taking.

Evidence of any of the above in a bank's strategic plan should serve as a warning light with regard to the sustainability of the plan through the cycle.

Capital management as part of the strategic plan

As noted above, capital management is an integral part of a bank's strategic plan. The capital strategy follows on from the overall strategy, and describes how and what capital is allocated to each business line. Capital strategy is a coherent, articulated, and formal plan of action that builds on a regular review of the business, allocation of capital to those businesses, and the desired return on capital, adjusted and unadjusted for risk. This should all be documented as part of the bank's capital strategy that feeds into the overall strategy.

As a key part of the strategy, the capital management framework at a bank should address the requirements of all the various stakeholders. It should be communicated in a transparent fashion to all internal and external stakeholders, articulating:

- How the risk appetite is aligned to their needs and expectations;
- How and why capital allocation and capital constraints are integrated with funding capabilities and assigned to each business line;
- The extent of tolerance for earnings volatility;
- The framework in which each of the business lines operates with respect to risk exposure and the type of business undertaken;
- Strategy and implications on business plans.

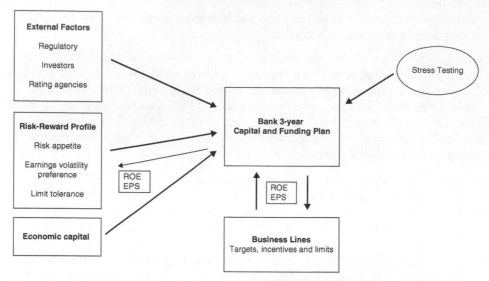

Figure 14.5   Formulation of capital management strategy
Source: Choudhry 2012.

Figure 14.5 is a stylised representation of this strategy formulation process. It reiterates that a bank's capital management process is part of overall strategy and is encompassed in a "capital management framework". This process must be the right way round; in other words, it should reflect the priorities for the bank to maintain confidence, deliver on its customer-focus strategy, and optimise risk-adjusted return on capital – **and in that order**.

As will be seen from the above, stress testing is an important part of the process; the results of this testing feed into an assessment of the robustness of the plan through different business conditions, as well as testing the plan against the bank's risk appetite.

However, capital management is as much about the quality of the capital as it is about the quantity; while regulators have raised the amount of capital required by a bank significantly, post-2008, they have also required significant changes to the quality of the capital, with a much stronger focus on the accessibility of the capital in times of crisis. Accordingly, capital management strategy also has to address the structure of the capital base over the planning period, ensuring the maintenance of the quality of the capital.

Typical elements of a bank's strategic plan

This section considers what might be expected in a typical bank's strategic plan. Some would consider this an ambitious goal because one finds in practice so many different presentations and areas of focus. What follows therefore can best be described as an attempt to highlight those features that should be present in some form or other, if the plan is to succeed.

Objectives

As discussed above, the strategic objectives of the bank should be framed by a vision statement that is embraced by the Board and executive management. This should set the tone and the long-term goal of the bank in very broad terms. With this in place, the strategic plan then outlines the strategic objectives that define more specific objectives for the bank over a shorter period – now perhaps 3 to 5 years.

These strategic objectives will range in nature and in character, but there are a few that should be found in all plans, due to the nature of banking. We would expect to find strategic objectives covering the following four aspects of a bank's operations at least, and under each we set out some of the issues that may be specifically addressed; note the points are not exhaustive:

Financial objectives:

- Capital strength: what capital the bank will have as it executes its strategy, both quantity and quality; target ratios; sources of capital; steps to be taken to ensure the maintenance of confidence in the bank by customers, markets, and regulators;
- Profitability: what profitability/return targets the bank has and the key drivers of the planned change in return; business actions to be taken to impact the drivers;
- Balance sheet structure: planned changes in the nature and structure of the bank's balance sheet with a specific focus on liquidity management; funding strategies; limits to balance sheet growth;
- Cost structures: planned cost targets (for example, cost to income); specific cost reduction targets or planned extraordinary expenditure;
- Sources of income: plans for improving the "quality" of the bank's income – annuity vs once off; net interest income vs fee income;
- Risks to the planned financial outcomes and actions to mitigate the risks;
- Customers and the competitive environment:
  - Which markets the bank intends to serve and segments within those markets, and why;
  - The positioning of the bank within those markets and segments and how it will achieve this;
  - The differentiation of the bank's market propositions;
  - Business objectives and targets for the targeted segments and markets;
  - Dealing with challenges from competitors (both current and potential);
  - Improving the bank's relationship with customers;
  - Positioning the bank as a "good corporate citizen".
- Business capacity and capabilities:
  - What core competencies are to be leveraged and how;
  - Structure of the organisation; acquisition and divestment plans;
  - How the bank intends dealing with changes in the regulatory environment and other environmental impacts such as market changes, technology, and even climate change;

- ○ Information technology infrastructure development (critical within a bank);
- ○ Revisions to major product/business lines;
- ○ Expense reduction activities.
- Skills and people:
  - ○ Development and retention of the talent pool within the bank;
  - ○ Development of new core competencies;
  - ○ Major training and development programmes;
  - ○ Support activities for major strategic initiatives.

The above categorisation of potential issues within a typical strategic plan is based on the "Balanced Scorecard" approach developed by Kaplan and Norton and elaborated in their book *The Strategy-Focused Organization* (Harvard Business School Press, 2001).

Financial targets and metrics (KPIs)

Table 14.1 illustrates a set of key metrics and targets that should be covered in a bank's strategic plan, as well as the annual budgets. Within the strategic

Table 14.1   Strategic metrics and KPIs.

Metric/KPI	Bank overall	Treasury	Corporate banking	Retail banking
Tier 1 Capital ratio				
Core Tier 1 ratio				
Return on Capital (RoC)				
Return on Risk Weighted Assets				
Loan to Deposit ratio				
Loan growth				
Deposit growth				
Risk Weighted Assets				
Wholesale Funding ratio				
Leverage ratio (Assets/Capital)				
Liquidity ratio				
Net Stable Funding ratio				
Unfunded Asset growth				
Cost/Income ratio				
FO/BO cost ratio				
Non-interest income percent revenue				
Credit Loss ratio				
VAR limits				
Securities growth (yoy)				

plan, explicitly longer term targets for certain of the key metrics should be set. The table also shows how the metrics might apply to a bank with three lines of business: Treasury, Corporate banking, and Retail banking.

Strategy as a dynamic process

Notwithstanding that "strategy" is geared towards the medium term and long term, the process by which it is formulated and approved needs to be flexible in order to respond quickly and efficiently to changing events. This includes changes in the competitive arena, changes enforced by regulatory fiat, market events that result in higher balance sheet resource costs, and so on.

Part of the strategy will therefore have to include the so-called "Plan B" or action to be taken in the event of any of these types of occurrences. A good example would be the contingency funding plan (CFP) that is part of the liquidity risk management regime (nowadays by regulatory requirement). Although the CFP is not part of a bank's strategy, the part of the strategy document that deals with liquidity and funding strategy would refer to it.

Larger banks and banking groups are also now required by regulators to develop and maintain "recovery and resolution" plans. The recovery plan describes in some detail how the bank would respond to an event that had a major negative impact on its capital position while remaining solvent. This may include responses like major cost reduction exercises and the sale of non-core assets/businesses, and would also have to deal with the market repercussions of such an event (for example, liquidity and credit issues). The resolution plan, which belongs as much to the regulator as it does to the individual bank, would consider the necessary steps to be taken in the event that recovery is no longer an option – i.e. solvency is an issue.

In addition to balance sheet management and related risk management activities, the customer franchise and the (hopefully "unique") customer proposition that the bank is offering will be an important part of the overall strategy. To ensure that this remains relevant, the bank must be aware of its marketplace and what is happening within it, both at the macro and the individual customer-facing level. For this to happen, the senior executives cannot be too far removed from the "coal face". For large banks, this becomes a practical difficulty, but it is incumbent on the bank's leadership that they remain in touch with the marketplace through whatever means best suits their circumstances. This is an important aspect of keeping the strategy and risk appetite in tune with changes in the operating environment.

Internal communication and management involvement are key elements of ensuring the continued relevance of the strategic plan; all key players must be involved in both the development of the plan as well as its monitoring and review. Within a banking environment, this often means that the process is owned and driven by the Finance Director (CFO), given the centrality of the financial, capital, and liquidity issues, but this does not minimise the importance of the contributions required of other functional and business unit leaders.

An analogy may be drawn between the strategic planning process and the actuarial control cycle: they both begin with an analysis phase, a solution is proposed and implemented, and the results are monitored and examined with a view to adjusting the proposed solution. It is a process well known to actuaries – as is the understanding that the ongoing review of outcomes is an essential part of the process.

A final observation is that while some flexibility is called for, it should be remembered that tactical process setting exists to handle short-term adjustments. A strategy that was regularly modified would not be much of a strategy. Consider the following text, taken from the website of a MENA-based commercial bank:

> The Directors set the strategic direction of the Bank (with due consideration given to risk tolerance, shareholder expectations, business development opportunities and other macro-economic factors) which senior management then uses to design the Bank's annual strategic plan and prepare the annual budget for Board approval. Thereafter, quarterly updates are provided by senior management to the Board of Directors to monitor progress and permit any necessary modifications or adjustments in strategic direction.

This description appears text book and has much to commend it – it sets essentially the right tone and is largely unarguable as an appropriate description. One could place it on one's strategy-setting template. However, the reference to quarterly updates should not be interpreted to suggest a quarterly adjustment to the strategic plan; strategy is forward looking and long term. Therefore, stakeholders should consider the long term. Quarterly aberrations in performance should not necessarily be a reason to change strategic direction.

EVALUATION OF THE STRATEGIC PLAN

It is perhaps useful to consider a number of questions that may be asked as part of the interrogation of a proposed strategic plan. The questions set out below are far from exhaustive and the reader should consider what additional questions he or she may ask in such a position. However, understanding the type of questions to be asked also helps to better understand the key elements of the plan and what needs to be in place to facilitate the execution of the plan.

The questions asked should include:

- How helpful is the vision statement that frames the strategic plan? Are the two congruent and aligned?

- Would the execution of the strategy advance the realisation of the vision? How quickly?
- How realistic is the evaluation of the "current reality" of the bank? Is there a clear understanding of the strengths and weaknesses of the bank? Does the bank understand its "core competencies"?
- Are the proposed strategic initiatives grounded in reality? Can they be achieved? Is there adequate resourcing and support? Does the bank have the skills and competencies to deliver?
- Are the strategic targets and objectives clear?
- Is there clear accountability for delivery?
- Does management have the capacity to focus on the initiatives amidst "business as usual"? Where will pressure be felt in the delivery of the plan?
- Can progress be monitored effectively and how will "success" be measured?
- Is leadership committed to the plan? How well are the plan and its implications understood by management and other staff?
- Will the bank have sufficient capital to fund the initiatives, as well as the balance sheet to support the planned book of business? Where will this capital come from? Will the bank's capital targets be realised?
- Will any of the new initiatives – for example, new business units and/or lines of business – impact on the risk profile of the bank?
- What can be done to make the balance sheet more robust over the planning period – restructuring of liabilities; restructuring of debt; improving the liquidity profile?
- What is the risk profile of the planned new balance sheet and does this fit within the agreed risk appetite of the bank?
- Do the pricing policies in place adequately reflect the underlying risk of the key product areas, both financial and operational? Do the transfer pricing policies properly reflect the cost of funds and the duration of the liabilities?

There are clearly many more questions that may be asked, depending on the particular circumstances, but the above list provides an indication of what might be covered.

CONCLUSION

Developing a strategy for a bank is a complex task as banks are complex institutions operating within a complex industry. Banks are also potentially fragile, notwithstanding their often formidable-looking balance sheets. The imperative for effective strategic planning that is found in any business is therefore of greater importance within banking, and particular attention has to be focused on the sustainability of the bank through an entire business cycle as part of the strategic planning process. The banking regulators take a specific interest in both the process as well as the outcome, which adds a further dimension to the process within the banking industry.

For that reason, while banks need to deal with all the usual strategic issues in the planning process, the balance sheet and its robustness take central stage – everything takes a cue from the evolving balance sheet, and the health of the bank, which is measured by capital and liquidity metrics, remains of the utmost importance. As noted, banking rests on trust and confidence, and unfortunately banking is a business where perceptions can drive reality with undesirable consequences. The strategic plan has to take all this into account, and at the same time meet the expectations of the various stakeholder groups, including most importantly the shareholders. Stakeholders generally care for a constant and sustainable performance from the bank. That is why we have emphasised the "balance sheet as everything" tone for the strategy-setting process. This will prove ultimately beneficial for shareholder and wider society interests.

Banking is also a difficult industry in which to carve out a distinctive "niche", due to the commoditised nature of the products and services offered. This is not to say it is an impossible quest as there are numerous examples of banks that have achieved this. However, this invariably takes time, suggesting that if the goal of the strategy is to build a distinctive positioning for itself as a bank, it is going to entail perseverance. This makes the commitment of executive management and the Board even more important.

The strategy-setting process requires input at both the conceptual and detail level; it is a process requiring clear logical analysis and thinking, as well as creative and lateral thinking. The end result has to contain both the "call to arms" – the vision statement, as well as the much more detailed "battle plan" – and be supported by regular reports from the business lines and progress reviews.

BIBLIOGRAPHY

Choudhry, M., (2012), *The Principles of Banking*, Singapore: John Wiley & Sons Ltd.

Chapter

15

BANK REGULATORY CAPITAL, BASEL RULES AND ICAAP

A bank's strategy is closely linked to its capital position. That said, a bank's capital position also drives its strategy. Like all commercial enterprises, the return shareholders receive for their investment in a bank or financial holding company is of critical importance when considering the value generated. Furthermore, the regulators and society in general require banks to be well capitalised to reduce friction to the financial system. Well-regulated and strongly capitalised banks are fundamental to a robust financial system.

Bank capital is a concept that is central to the understanding, and management, of a bank's business strategy and the risk exposure associated with that strategy. In the business media, it is often suggested that capital is the most important aspect of bank risk management, but although such a view is not wholly correct (liquidity and funding are as important certainly, if not more so), it is indeed the case that effective capital management is essential if a bank is to continue to deliver shareholder returns through the economic cycle. Put simply, understanding capital is key to understanding what banks do, the risks they take, and how best these risks should be managed.

Often capital is spoken of as being "held" or "put aside" by a bank in order to support lending operations, as if it was some kind of asset. This is an unfortunate turn of phrase. Far from being an asset, capital is a liability, alongside all the other forms of liability the bank has, and as such a form of funding for the bank. However, unlike the other forms of liability it has no fixed interest cost, indeed given that core capital is not obliged to pay out any form of coupon at any time it has no explicit interest cost. Moreover, because it has no repayment date it is able to absorb losses. Such losses could otherwise threaten a bank's solvency, so it is easy to see why a sufficient capital base to cover all eventualities is essential for every bank. Alternative sources of "non-core Tier 1" capital with contractual costs and different levels of loss absorption are also available to banks. In this chapter, the core issues of capital management from both a bank governance viewpoint as well as the regulatory requirement viewpoint are discussed. Then the issues surrounding the delivery and presentation of the internal capital adequacy assessment process, or ICAAP, and stress testing issues associated with the ICAAP are presented.

THE BANKING MODEL AND CAPITAL

This chapter describes the best-practice framework within which capital should be planned and managed within a bank, including the internal processes undertaken to ensure regulatory compliance (perhaps best exemplified by the "ICAAP" process, which is covered later in the chapter). Before that, however, the concepts of capital and its purpose are introduced. The best-practice recommended approach to use of capital is also presented.

The business model and capital

The importance of capital to a bank and an appropriate appreciation of its importance requires a genuine understanding of what banks actually do. In essence they:

1. Provide transaction services for customers, primarily payments, which enable them to settle commercial transactions;
2. Provide funding, in the form of credit, to customers to enable them to enter into commercial transactions; and
3. Provide risk management services to customers, ranging from the simple current account ("checking account") to more complex services that enable customers to manage and hedge their foreign exchange and interest-rate risk exposures.

Services 2 and 3 require a bank to undertake two fundamentally contradictory things: lend money for as long a period as the customer requires, and accept deposits on an "instant access" basis from customers. This is the process of "maturity transformation", the very definition of the banking business model, and it is the risk exposures generated by operating this model that make capital and liquidity so important for a bank. Liquidity was covered in Chapters 10 and 11.

A stylised bank balance sheet is shown in Figure 15.1.

Bank balance sheet

The balance sheet is a snapshot in time of the bank's financial strength. Note that the capital amount must, at all times, be more than sufficient to absorb customer loan losses (or losses incurred for other reasons, such as the result of proprietary trading losses or ineffective hedging resulting in unexpected losses). However, the reality of government regulation, which every bank in the world is subject to, means that banks don't need sufficient capital to absorb only losses. They also need sufficient capital to absorb losses *and* still, after such absorption, be able to demonstrate capital levels that are above the regulatory minimum. Banking is all about confidence. If customers have confidence in the bank, they will continue to place their funds on deposit there. If they do not, they will not. A bank that dips below its regulatory minimum capital ratios, even if it has still absorbed all its losses to date, will not be able to maintain that confidence.

In other words, good capital management, and indeed considered by some practitioners as best-practice capital management, is all about managing capital on a *going concern* basis. The Board of a bank takes responsibility to articulate its risk appetite such that this requirement is met. It is generally considered bad practice to manage capital on a gone concern basis. *The available capital*, the actual amount that can be used to absorb losses, is the surplus above the minimum required by the regulator. Capital that meets the

Bank balance sheet

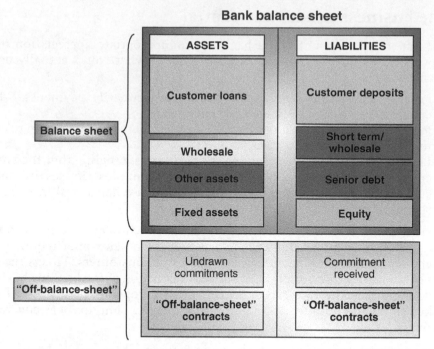

Figure 15.1 Stylised representation of a typical commercial bank balance sheet

regulator's requirement is not, in truth, available to absorb losses on a going concern basis. It is essential that bank Boards and executive directors manage the institution on this basis.

Invariably banks may fail. In such circumstances the capital sources must be adequate to recover the bank or, if this is not possible, resolve the bank without undue stress to the financial system. This, however, is more feasible in theory than in practice. If a bank fails, one can assume, to a reasonable and safe extent, that its capital base will be insufficient to recover it, and for large banks to resolve it either.

Treatment of bank capital

The core Tier 1 capital base of a bank comprises its initial capital, or start-up capital, and retained earnings that have been placed in the reserves. Generally, the simplest and most transparent model is to consider that the complete capital base is used as part of a leveraged business model in which it represents equity backing for borrowed funds, which are invested in assets. The return on the assets covers for the cost of borrowing, and the surplus over this and all other costs is the shareholder value-added for the equity owner.

In its simplest form, the bank's capital should not be exposed to risk. Ideally, it must be placed in an instantly liquid risk-free asset, with zero counterparty risk, so that it itself is not in danger of erosion and can be retrieved easily if needed, either to cover losses or to fund further expansion and investment. The only assets that fit this category are a deposit at the central bank or an investment in the sovereign bonds of the same currency. All other investments carry an element of counterparty and/or liquidity risk and may be considered unsuitable assets in which to invest the bank's capital.

The logic is straightforward: given that capital available must be sufficient to cover unexpected losses, as well as expected losses, if the capital itself was placed at risk, then there would be no guarantee that it would be able to absorb all losses at any one time. A loss elsewhere in the portfolio may occur at the same time as losses from assets that were funded with capital. This is what is meant when managing capital on a going concern basis is referred to.

The equity and funding provide the sources of funding to invest in assets. The bank has to hold sufficient liquid assets and cash to ensure liquidity pressures can be met immediately. Given that capital is generally only returned through dividends, the capital therefore has a very long behavioural term. The Treasury of the bank acts as the "bank to the bank", that is, to provide funding to all assets and pay for all liabilities. From an accounting perspective, the cost of funding of capital is nil. An endowment benefit therefore arises as no expense is incurred for this funding. In order to ensure that businesses in a bank group do not unduly benefit from such capital structures, the central Treasury charges a funding cost on all assets and pays a funding cost to all liabilities, including capital.

So the capital base itself should not be expected to generate a return. Where it does, for example, the coupon return from a holding of government bonds, this income on capital should accrue to a central book or asset–liability committee "ALCO" book, and not to any business line. Neither is it allocated on a pro-rata basis to the business lines, otherwise the calculation of shareholder value-added by the businesses will be skewed. The business lines are assumed to utilise matched funding instruments to fund their operations. Certain banks also charge a capital risk premium, which will also accrue to the "ALCO" book. Views vary on the treatment of this endowment benefit. Some banks keep the benefit in the ALCO book and implement an economic profit type of management account framework, while others allocate some or all of the benefit to incentivise business, hence there is no cost to allocate.

The target return on equity, set by the shareholder and therefore the Board as their representatives, sets the hurdle rate for the business or the legal entities in the group. Senior management generally then translate these hurdles for each of the business lines, who benefit indirectly from the existence of the capital base. This hurdle rate can be a minimum for all the businesses (which is very unlikely as the returns per line of business vary greatly, for example, between asset and liability lines), or it can be modified to suit the differing requirements of each business. It is imperative to note how important it is for the bank's return on capital (RoC) target to be set at a Board level, reflecting the needs of the shareholder and thereby the "cost" of that equity.

The example below describes the treatment of share capital further.

Example 15.1   Treatment of share capital

In other words, the share capital of a legal entity represents a source of funding like any other, except it has one main defining characteristic – it bears no real actual interest cost. That said, there is a cost that is imputed in it, this being the shareholder's targeted return on equity. This "cost" must be attributed to the equity base, otherwise there is a risk that it ends up representing "free capital" to the benefit of the business lines. This would result in an incorrect and inaccurate reporting of genuine shareholder valued-added.

There are different approaches as to where the share capital is booked and where the benefit of this free source of funding is assigned. That said, in reality because the share capital is a specific type of external funding source, it is often booked in the Treasury books of the entity in which the capital resides, with the cash forming part of the general cash funding pool of the entity that is then managed by Treasury.

The net interest benefit of the utilisation of this "free" cash should then be subject to the same internal funds pricing (transfer pricing) rules as any other funding in the bank (see Chapter 10). In any case, the treatment of capital should be consistent with the treatment of retained earnings: since retained earnings and share capital are both similar sources of funding in that neither have a real interest cost. It is important that the benefit of retained earnings is allocated to a central ALCO book, and not to any of the business lines.

The treatment and allocation of capital described here represents what is considered business best practice at the one bank observed. However, it is not universal. In some cases, a deviation from the above is justified where a portion of the capital base is allocated for use as "working capital", for example, in a start-up situation to cover cash requirements such as rental and salary expenses. In this case, the amount to be allocated should be identified in advance and once the business has declared a profit, then the same amount should be restored to the capital base or the bank needs to adjust its reported capital base. So there could well be other treatments of the capital base that are justified, hence some banks may still deviate from the above.

Expected and unexpected losses

Banks' normal course of business involves exposing themselves to risk of loss due to customer loan default. Losses will vary from one year to the next, unsurprisingly closely correlated to the economic cycle. The extent of exposure also varies, from "AAA"-rated exposure to lower-rated exposure, by type of customer, and product. The extent of collateral provided by a loan customer also dictates the level of loss.

Obviously, it is not possible to know in advance what the extent of loss in the next 12 months (or any time period) will be. Banks estimate the average level of losses they expect to incur over the next budgeting period based on their historical experience. This is the bank's *expected losses*. The level of expected loss dictates the nature of future business. For example, since it can be seen as part of the cost of doing business, expected loss levels will influence:

- The level of future balance sheet expansion and lending levels;
- The rate of interest charged to customers.

Banks must also, however, account for *unexpected losses*. This should be self-evident: it would not be possible to estimate accurately what future losses will be. It is common for actual loss rates to far exceed expected loss rates, especially if historical rates were used to estimate expected losses and the last 5 years had seen the economy booming with the central bank raising interest rates. It is these unexpected losses that banks require a buffer of capital to absorb, and as was said earlier, if the bank is to manage itself on a going concern basis, this buffer must be sufficient to absorb losses and still remain above the regulatory minimum. Otherwise of course it would no longer be a going concern. This is because a bank that falls even 1 basis point below the regulator's minimum will suffer a loss of confidence and a run on the bank (as well as the inevitable credit rating downgrade to junk status).

Unexpected losses are harder to estimate than expected losses. The way it is approximated is the basis of the orthodox credit risk management methodology process in banks. Figure 15.2 provides a stylised illustration of the distribution of credit losses.

Area B is the extent of unexpected losses, and the bank will calculate the probability of such losses and the amount.

Understanding the difference between capital and liquidity

It is evident then that a bank's capital base and its holding of genuinely liquid assets are of equal importance in helping to mitigate against its main bank balance sheet risks. Arguably, liquidity risk is of greater importance because a failure of liquidity sourcing can kill a bank in an instant, compared with a

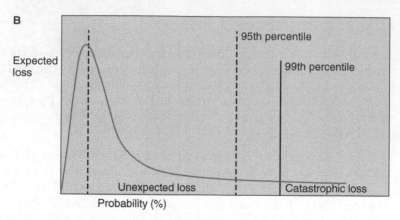

Figure 15.2   Expected and unexpected losses

shortage of capital that may take longer to force the bank into failure. But this aside, it should be noted that in the same way as banks operating models differ, so does the type of risk exposure that capital and liquidity are used to manage against differ. We reiterate that capital is a liability, on the same side of the balance sheet as all other liabilities, and is a source of funding. The balance sheet has to balance of course, and liquid assets are on the other side of the balance sheet as a use of funding. (The most liquid asset is a deposit at the central bank, or failing that the domestic sovereign Treasury bill.) The requirement to have both sufficient capital and sufficient liquid assets requires balance sheet managers to be aware of the details surrounding the source of funds and the use of funds. In other words, how much capital is available capital that is perpetual (it has no repayment date), has no obligation to pay dividends, and can absorb losses on a going concern basis? And how truly liquid are the liquid assets?

Capital regulation

As will be seen later in this chapter, how much minimum capital a bank needs is determined by legislation – so the answer to this question is straightforward. Indeed, Basel III enshrines in law a limit on how much balance sheet leverage a bank can employ. But it is a useful exercise to determine what the capital requirement would look like if there was no regulator.

Certain key ratios (including the leverage ratio) help to provide an estimate answer to this question. This is because not all assets on a bank's balance sheet are the same – some assets are (credit) riskier than others, so each asset type is assigned a risk weight to reflect how risky it is deemed to be. These weights are then applied to the bank's assets to give a risk-weighted asset (RWA) value. This is then used to calculate the capital ratio, the bank's capital amount as a percentage of the RWA amount. It is seen that it is easy enough to alter the capital ratio value by adjusting either the numerator or the denominator – or both.

In such an instance the capital requirement would be based on the internal view of risk and the level of financial resources required to ensure the bank remains a going concern within the tolerances set by its risk appetite. This is the economic capital requirement of the bank.

KEY CAPITAL CONSIDERATIONS

For a bank to ensure that it has adequate capital to support its business, it must consider the following:

- Regulatory requirements;
- Risk appetite and risk profile;
- Rating agency (for example, S&P) considerations;
- Equity investor expectations.

Regulatory requirements will be the primary driver of the bank's capital structure, involving consideration for a number of metrics across the regulatory spectrum. The Board sets the risk appetite of the firm. One of the risk appetite metrics will consider the level of friction the bank wishes to endure before breaching regulatory requirements. Capital will be held as a buffer on the regulatory buffer to minimise regulatory friction. Also, from an S&P perspective, risk-adjusted capital (RAC) is an important ratings score determinant and is key in influencing the achievable optimum capital mix. Equity investor considerations around dividend capacity and RoC expectations would influence the capital mix. The importance of each factor will vary according to the risk appetite of each firm.

Regulatory requirements are those of the national regulator and international regulatory considerations as set by the Basel capital rules. In the UK, for example, the requirements would include the Capital Requirements Directive IV (CRDIV) (the European Union's legislative implementation of Basel III), the buffer requirements of the UK Prudential Regulatory Authority (PRA), the leverage ratio, and also any relevant ring-fencing rules. For a bank in South Africa, the considerations are similar as the South African Reserve Bank (SARB) is a member of the Basel Committee. The SARB compares the capital strategies of banks by type of bank with smaller banks having considerably higher capital requirements than their larger counterparts, given the lack of diversification in the portfolio.

A rating agency will consider issues including: access to bank financing, issuance capability in the capital markets, implicit support for government or a foreign parent, and the price the bank has to pay to raise long-term funding.

Equity investors will be concerned with the "value vs growth" equity outlook, the formal dividend policy, and their expectations for RoC. These are considered in further detail below.

Regulatory capital requirements

In the first instance, capital structure considerations are essentially given by the Capital Requirements Regulation (CRR)/CRDIV (in the EU) and in other jurisdictions by the local interpretation of Basel III. Figure 15.3 is a summary of this requirement.

For Basel III, paper BCBS 189 (June 2011) footnote 47 states:

> Common Equity Tier 1 must first be used to meet the minimum capital requirements (including the 6 per cent Tier 1 and 8 per cent Total capital requirements if necessary) before the remainder can contribute to the capital conservation buffer.

For banks in the EU, the requirement of CRDIV as stated in Article 124 (July 2011) is that:

> Institutions shall meet the requirement imposed by the Countercyclical Capital Buffer with Common Equity Tier 1 capital, which shall be additional to any Common Equity Tier 1 capital maintained to meet the own finds requirement imposed by Article 87 of Regulation [total capital ratio of 8 per cent], the requirement to maintain a Capital Conservation Buffer ...

The buffers set in the capital requirements can be utilised during times of stress. However, in such circumstances distributions to shareholders and staff will be restricted.

Sources of capital

Core equity Tier 1 capital consists in principle of share capital, share premium, and retained earnings attributed as regulatory capital. Certain deductions apply.

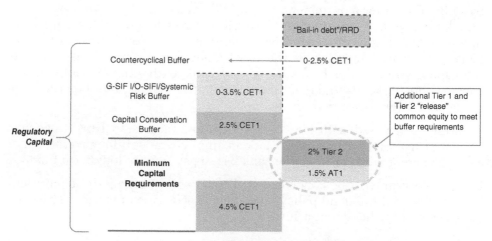

Figure 15.3   Capital structure considerations under CRR/CRDIV

The features that make a long-dated liability eligible as Additional Tier 1 (AT1) and Tier 2 (T2) are as follows:

AT1:
- Perpetual; not callable prior to year 5;
- Non-cumulative, discretionary distributions;
- Deeply subordinated;
- Conversion to equity or principal write-down at a trigger of CET1 < 5.875% (or higher);
- Conversion or write-down at the point of non-viability, where the point of non-viability is determined at the discretion of the SARB prior to the failure of the bank.

T2:
- Minimum maturity of 5 years (with capital credit amortising 20% per year 5 years prior to maturity);
- Subordinated;
- Conversion or write-down at the point of non-viability.

Given the requirements of Basel III, at a strategic level the main ingredients of capital planning are essentially given: that is, the attachment points for maximum distributable amounts can be set quite easily. The most transparent way to illustrate this is to assume that one is setting up a bank from scratch, as shown in Table 15.1, with the theoretical illustration at Figure 15.4 and 15.6.

The Pillar 2A add-on is stipulated by the national regulator.

In other jurisdictions, as in the UK, the PRA has stated that the Pillar IIA add-on of up to 2% must comprise at least 56% CET1 and the remainder of a combination of AT1 and T2. For a new bank, the minimum capital requirement would allow the requirements under Basel III to be met, as well as to allow for sufficient capital should a countercyclical buffer requirement be implemented by the regulator SARB.

Hypothetical example: vanilla commercial bank

To illustrate the considerations involved from a first-principles basis, an assumed example of a UK commercial bank that is being set up from scratch, with an inherited portfolio, is considered. What would be the primary factors driving the capital planning process? The balance sheet RWA breakdown is shown in Figure 15.5.

The main factors that (say) a ratings agency review would consider include: asset mix (for example, whether there is a concentration in assets such as commercial real estate (CRE)); advanced – vs foundation – IRB being applied; Pillar II impacts; stress buffers required; and any capital release opportunities. With a total balance sheet RWA of just over GBP 13 billion, the bank is below 1% of UK GDP in size, so the countercyclical, globally systemically important institutions (G-SIFIs), and ring-fence buffers do not apply. Hence, the capital considerations that must be accounted for are shown below.

Table 15.1 Capital framework based on the Basel III framework: hypothetical bank start-up

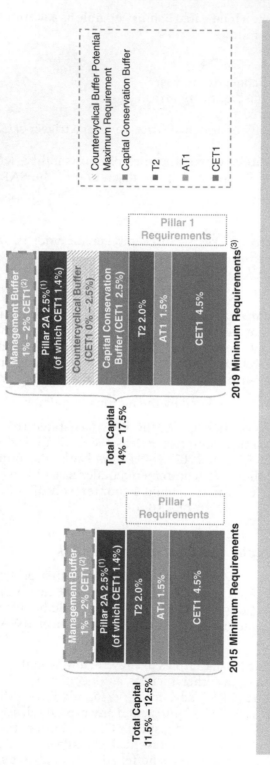

Basel III capital framework, phase-in and final

- Pillar 1 represents the regulatory minimum capital (8%) requirement under CRD IV – Pillar 1 can be comprised entirely of CET1, but AT1 and Tier 2 cannot exceed the proportion illustrated for minimum requirement purposes
- Additional capital buffers over and above the minimum regulatory capital levels (e.g. capital conservation buffer, countercyclical buffer) were phased in between 2016 and 2019
- Management buffer above minimum requirement assumed to be in the range of 1% – 2% - to be discussed

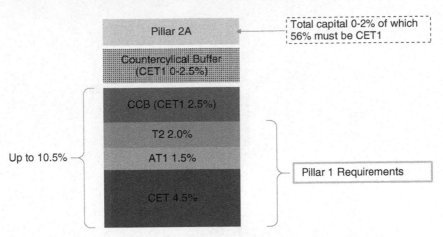

Figure 15.4 Combined buffer requirement for a bank under Basel III

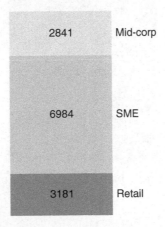

Figure 15.5 RWA breakdown

This argues for an indicative capital structure of 15%. However, as this is a fairly small portfolio, the individual capital guidance received from the regulator will more likely impose a higher requirement. This would be a working assumption taking into account:

- Regulator feedback (for example, the requirement for the amount of total loss-absorbing capacity);
- Potential impact of stress tests on the capital plan. Such stresses are then accounted for to a certain level of confidence using economic capital principles;
- Peer-group analysis;
- Market expectations;
- Rating agency feedback.

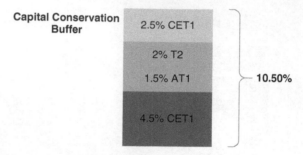

Figure 15.6   Capital considerations

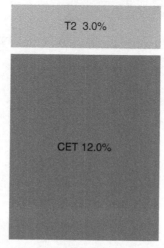

Figure 15.7   Hypothetical new bank capital structure minimum compliance with Basel III

Assuming the 15% capital base is accepted as a minimum requirement, there are two main scenarios that present themselves. The first is Scenario 1, the all-equity scenario, while Scenario 2 describes an equity plus other capital structure. The latter is shown in Figure 15.7.

A capital base as shown in Figure 15.7 would enable the bank to meet both the standing buffer requirements and the macro-prudential one. Note that the PRA has stipulated that CET1 must be used to fill Pillar IIA requirements prior to the combined capital buffer. The residual 3.0% of CET1 would be available to meet any remaining capital or buffer requirements, including the Pillar IIA requirements.

What factors should guide the capital planning process with respect to the structure of the capital base? The all-equity scenario presents the following features:

•   The most robust form from a regulatory perspective;
•   It may result in an incremental (one-notch) rating benefit;

- As the most expensive structure, it is least efficient from a shareholder return perspective;
- Compared to the equity plus other capital format, there is a substantial decrease in RoC.

The equity plus other capital liability structure has the following features:

- It is a more efficient capital structure;
- Ultimately, it remains subject to national regulatory approval;
- The rating agency position towards this structure is neutral to negative;
- The T2 issuance would of course be subject to investor demand for this paper;
- The structure allows for further gearing/leverage of the capital base. The level of leverage is restricted under Basel III and in particular in South Africa as discussed below.

Table 15.2 is a summary of the requirements for capital instruments to be AT1 and T2 eligible. In its capital planning, a bank may consider the following rationale for issuance of one or both of these instruments:

- Free up common equity to count towards buffer requirements (capital buffers are additive to minimum total capital requirements);
- Pillar II or bail-in capital requirements;
- Non-dilutive (absent conversion);

Table 15.2 AT1 and T2 instrument requirements

	Additional Tier 1	Tier 2
Tenor	Perpetual	May be dated. Must have minimum 5 years maturity
Subordination	Subordinated to depositors, general creditors, and subordinated debt of the bank	Subordinated to depositors and general creditors of the bank
Distribution	Bank must have full discretion to cancel payments (non-cumulative)	No requirement for deferral/cancellation of coupon
Call features	May be callable by the issuer after a minimum of 5 years (subject to regulatory approval)	May be callable by the issuer after a minimum of 5 years (subject to regulatory approval)
Going concern loss absorption	Must have principal loss absorption through either conversion to shares or a write-down mechanism	N/a
Gone concern loss absorption	Write-off or conversion if required by the regulator	Write-off or conversion if required by the regulator

- Tax deductible;
- Able to be sold to a fixed income investor base;
- Acts as a cushion for senior debt investors;
- Supports credit rating requirements (S&P RAC eligible).

In undertaking its capital planning, a bank must consider the Pillar II requirements. When conducting its Pillar II review (that is the review of the bank's Internal Capital Adequacy Assessment Process or ICAAP), the local regulator will consider both those risks to banks that are not fully captured under Pillar IIA and those risks a firm may be exposed to in future, for example, regulatory changes (Pillar IIB). The key considerations are:

- Pillar IIA: in addition to the Pillar I requirements of Basel III (in the EU, CRR/CRDIV), certain regulators including the PRA regard Pillar IIA capital as the minimum level of regulatory capital a bank should maintain at all times to cover against risks, with the implication being that CET1 must be used to fill the Pillar IIA requirement prior to being used for the capital conservation buffer (CCB);
- Pillar IIB: Pillar IIB buffers will be required for firms where the regulator (PRA included) deems that the Basel III or CRDIV buffers may not be sufficient to enable a firm to meet its capital requirements under stress. The Pillar IIB buffer will replace the existing (in the UK jurisdiction) capital planning buffer (CPB), and will be set based upon a range of factors, including firm-specific stress test results.

Leverage ratio

The leverage ratio limit is a Basel III requirement. It will initially be implemented as a Pillar II measure, although from January 2016 it will be a binding measure. However, prior to harmonisation, at this point national regulators are free to apply the leverage ratio requirements as they see fit. The Bank of England has already applied the 3.33% ratio limit, and the numerator is given by Tier 1 capital.

In CRDIV the leverage ratio is defined as T1 capital divided by a total exposure measure; the simplest form is given by:

$$\text{Leverage ratio} = \frac{\text{Tier 1 capital}}{\text{Funded assets}} \quad (15.1)$$

Credit rating considerations

In proceeding with issuance of an AT1 or T2 hybrid capital instrument, the capital planning process will also consider the treatment of the instrument by the international credit rating agencies (S&P, Moody's, Fitch). Ideally, the instrument will be eligible as capital, therefore strengthening the capital base to the benefit of the bank's final rating. S&P, for instance, issue guidelines for eligibility as RAC capital.

CAPITAL MANAGEMENT POLICY

Bank capital management should be articulated formally in a policy standard in the same way that liquidity management is (described in Chapters 8, 9, and 10). The objective of the policy is to describe how the bank will:

- Meet its regulatory and other legal obligations;
- Maintain its capital resources and buffer as required and in line with the stated risk profile of the business;
- Manage its capital planning in an efficient and cost-effective manner;
- Recover from stress events.

A benchmark standard template for a bank's capital management policy is given here.

Capital management

The starting point for the capital management policy is the regulatory capital ratios. The requirements of any overseas regulators, from jurisdictions that the bank also operates in, are also included. The next step is a consideration of internal capital requirements (economic capital) as the Board has a duty to meet regulatory requirements but where these requirements are inadequate, as indicated by the internal risk assessment, to demand higher capital ratios. The buffers on regulatory ratios are required to reduce the likelihood of a limit breach and form the basis of the capital risk appetite of the bank. This is followed by a description of the monitoring process and escalation process for limit breaches.

The policy template would cover:

Capital targets

The bank will monitor and report its forecast regulatory capital base and risk-weighted assets (RWAs) per business line to Finance, Risk, and Treasury. The responsibility for regulatory reporting lies typically with the Regulatory Reporting department within Finance. The bank's current operational targets are:

Core Tier 1:   [ ] %
Total Tier 1:   [ ] %
Total capital: [ ] %

The Finance department will maintain a 3-year rolling forecast and report this to ALCO. Forecast or actual breaches of the internal capital ratios and ultimately the regulatory capital ratios will be reported to the Head of Treasury and to ALCO as well as the regulatory authority. A regulatory breach should be very rare and the bank's risk management processes will require escalation prior to such an event. Upon escalation, management actions will be considered to rectify the position.

The Treasury department will undertake capital stress testing to assess the potential capital impact of changes in firm-specific and market-wide business conditions. Where the test results indicate a potential breach of target ratios, this must be reported to ALCO. Mitigating action should then be undertaken after approval from ALCO.

The actions considered to rectify any capital adequacy positions will also be tested during the stress testing exercises. There, actions range from the improvement of business processes, the sell-down of assets, and the change in balance sheet strategy, to a rights issue to obtain more capital. Each action will have wide ranging impact and therefore needs to be considered in detail.

Risk-weighted assets and economic capital demand

RWA balances (i.e. the regulatory Pillar I view of risk) and economic capital demand (the internal view of risk) must be reported to Finance, Treasury, and the business lines. The frequency of reporting may vary from inter-day to monthly depending on the type of risks. RWA forecasts are prepared at month-end; any inconsistency with the Finance general forecast must be reported to ALCO. The RWA forecast should be in line with the bank's capital allocation process. The impact of any business line transaction, whether asset or liability, that is likely to result in a reduction in capital must be reported immediately to ALCO. The process applied is similar in nature to the actuarial control cycle.

Business line profit

The net profit after direct and indirect costs of each business line must be transferred to the central book at year-end. This is a direct cash transfer.

Capital resource management

A subset of the capital management policy is the capital resource management policy. The object of this document is to articulate formally how each business line will meet its requirements with regard to adherence to the capital management policy standard, and to ensure that use of capital at the business level is at an optimum in terms of allocation, planning, and management. The efficient use of capital is also a metric in business performance evaluation. The capital resource management policy is part of the process to ensure that capital is allocated efficiently and as part of the bank's strategy.

Capital allocation

Each business line prepares a business case for capital demand, based on RWAs and economic capital. Each business case contains key metrics, including RoC, net generation of equity, and economic profit. The Balance Sheet Management department sets targets for RWAs and capital usage as part of the budget forecast and allocation process. Capital is allocated to produce optimum return, in line with the strategy and risk appetite of the bank. The strategy and risk appetite will drill down to each business line. Treasury Balance Sheet Management will present capital usage limits at month-end, for approval by ALCO (see Chapter 10 for template Treasury organisation structure). Treasury Balance Sheet Management will report current and forecast capital usage to ALCO on a weekly basis.

If a forecast exceeds a limit, the business line will submit a request for mitigating action to be taken, or for an increase in limit.

Performance metrics

The Board, having delegated authority to the executive management committee (ExCo), will set performance metrics targets for each business line. This will include RoC and capital usage (RWA) metrics, against which performance of each business is evaluated. Some banks also consider economic profit or profit after regulatory capital cost, depending on which view of risk is more onerous.

Portfolio credit risk management

ALCO is responsible for reviewing and approving the asset pool for credit risk management purposes. This is to ensure that provisions are signed off in a consistent manner, that all transactions are in line with the business strategy and risk profile, and that they follow policy on capital usage and regulatory requirements.

Capital management strategy

We conclude that bank strategy should focus on serving customers and driving the business via this customer focus. This strategy will be articulated in terms of a financial plan containing all key metrics. It should include a return on equity target set in advance, which is aligned to the bank's risk–reward preference. The capital strategy follows on from the overall strategy, and describes how and what capital is allocated to each business line. The plans are then stress tested. The outcomes indicate the potential frictions that may be experienced by each business area. At that point, the bank sets its core Tier 1 capital target level to achieve in line with the risk appetite set by the Board. The point being made here is that capital strategy is a coherent, articulated, and formal plan of action that builds on a regular review of the business, allocation of capital to those businesses, and desired return on capital. This should all be documented as part of the bank's capital strategy, which feeds into the overall strategy. This may sound obvious, but the layperson would be surprised by how few banks actually do this.

A bank's management may think that the core Tier 1 ratio to have in place is the starting point of the strategy. In fact, almost the contrary could be true: the desired core equity Tier 1 ratio should be arrived at after consideration of the business lines, the results of stress testing, and the share of capital allocated to each to support the revenue and return on equity target that is desired. The bank should compile an annual, 3-year, and 5-year capital ratio target, aligned to a strategic funding plan, and then target the optimum Tier 1 ratio through setting optimal capital structures. This will be achieved through management of dividends (regular or special), rights issues for significant opportunities, AT1 and T2 issuances, or repurchases and liability management exercises.

As a key part of strategy, the capital management framework at a bank should address the requirements of all the various stakeholders. It should be communicated in a transparent fashion to all internal and external stakeholders, articulating:

- How the risk appetite is aligned to their needs and expectations;
- How and why capital allocation and capital constraints are integrated with funding capabilities and assigned to each business line;
- The extent of tolerance for earnings volatility;
- The framework in which each of the business lines operates, with respect to risk exposure and the type of business undertaken.

Figure 15.8 is a reprise of the capital management strategy process. Bank's capital management is part of the overall strategy and is encompassed in a "capital management framework".

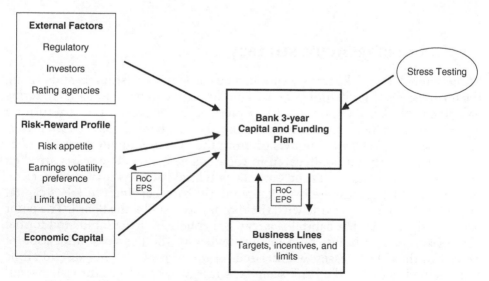

Figure 15.8   Formulating capital management strategy
Source: Choudhry 2012.

Stress testing, as part of the regulatory capital adequacy process, is considered in a later section.

CAPITAL ADEQUACY AND STRESS TESTING

To recap, Pillar I of the Basel regulatory capital framework describes the capital requirements for credit, market, and operational risk, while Pillar II focuses on the economic and internal perspective of banks' capital adequacy. Banks are required to employ satisfactory procedures and systems in order to ensure their capital adequacy is sufficient over the long term, with due attention to all material risks. These procedures are referred to collectively as the *internal capital adequacy assessment process* or ICAAP. The standard process by which the regulator determines whether a bank is managing capital on a satisfactory basis is also referred to, almost universally, as the ICAAP, which sometimes is taken to refer to the *individual* capital adequacy assessment process. It is known by other terms in certain jurisdictions, but irrespective of the name, we refer here to the process by which a bank stress tests its capital level for sufficiency through a range of scenarios and presents its results to the regulator. The regulatory authority will determine if it agrees with the results and thereby determine the level of capital required.

The ICAAP enables them to identify, measure, and aggregate all material risk types and calculate the economic, or internal, capital necessary to cover these risks. As such, the ICAAP process is key to the preservation of financial stability and is subject to a high degree of supervisory scrutiny, which does on the other hand make the process very bureaucratic and administrative. That said, because banks come in many different shapes and sizes, and a variety of balance sheet risk exposures, a number of different approaches may be observed when it comes to the ICAAP process. Business best practice for a vanilla commercial banking institution is described here.

ICAAP primer

In essence, the Basel Accord and its amendments form the basis for the ICAAP. In the EU, the legislative framework was described in CRD2. Further guidance was provided by CEBS (2006), which published 10 principles for the implementation of a consistent and comprehensive ICAAP. In short, all banks are required to document and specify fully the ICAAP, integrate it into the regular risk management process, and review it continuously to ensure it remains fit for purpose.

The ICAAP needs to be a risk-based document, comprehensive and detailed, as well as forward looking. Of course, the results of the ICAAP process need to be consistent with the bank remaining a going concern – if they are not, the bank's Board must implement management actions to redress the matter before presenting results to the regulator. While there is considerable commonality, each ICAAP is ultimately unique to the bank in question, reflecting its specific balance sheet structure and exposure.

Risk taxonomy and quantification

Before quantifying balance sheet risk exposure, it is important to categorise it, or as some banks term it, compile a taxonomy of risk. Not all banks exhibit all identified risk type exposures. Under Pillar II, all material risk types need to be quantified, and thereby covered with adequate capital provision. Certain types of risk (conduct risk, reputation, etc.) are not straightforward to quantify, so banks will apply a qualitative assessment. Typically, banks and, crucially, certain regulators employ the Value-at-Risk (VaR) technique to estimate risk exposure on the balance sheet. For those familiar with VaR, the logic of its methodology is consistent with a trading book, or a pool of assets that are repriced on a regular basis. However, this logic is less consistent in a banking book. Nevertheless, the VaR approach remains the one that is most in use and often demanded by the regulator to assess the VaR to the firm. The actual methods vary from simple risk weights to detailed economic risk assessments. In addition, regulators use peer group comparisons as well and any outliers per business area are interrogated further.

Table 15.3 summarises the Level 1 risks within the risk taxonomy for a vanilla UK commercial bank, with 1st and 2nd line-of-defence (LoD) responsibilities indicated.

It is common to see the variance-covariance ("parametric"), historical simulation, and Monte Carlo simulation approaches used in equal measure among banks. Typically, banks apply a 1-year holding period and one-sided confidence levels of 95% or 99%. For market risk, banks often apply a 1-day and 10-day holding period. Note that most banks classify interest-rate risk in the banking book (IRRBB) as a market risk, albeit a non-traded market risk. Again, it is common to observe VaR as the preferred measurement technique for IRRBB as well; however, the author's recommended approach is to supplement this with traditional modified duration analysis ("gap" analysis) as well.

Stress tests

In the post-2008 era, all banks, except perhaps the very smallest, specify a large number and variety of stress tests. That said, there is considerable commonality in approach. Generally, the primary focus is on scenario analyses, often based on 5-year historical worst-case values or hypothetical scenarios. The latter are sometimes also required to include a "reverse stress test", which is a hypothetical scenario that would break the bank. In theory, as stress tests allow for the identification of sensitivities to specific risk factors, they should be a worthwhile exercise as they provide value-added input to

Table 15.3 Level 1 risk taxonomy

Level 1 Risk Taxonomy
The table below summarises the Level 1 risks within the risk taxonomy for Rainbow

Level 1 Risk	1st LoD Risk Owners	2nd LoD Risk Owner	Definition
CREDIT	MDs of each business area/MD Sales and Marketing	CRO	Risk of loss from the failure of a customer to meet their obligation to settle outstanding amounts, including concentration risk.
OPERATIONAL	COO, Head of HR, Legal and CFO		The risk of loss resulting from inadequate or failed internal processes, people, or from external events, including legal risk and supplier risk.
IT	Head of IT		Loss of technology services due to loss of data, system, or data centre including, where applicable, failure of back-up processes and/or a third party to restore services.
COMPLIANCE	ExCo members		The risk of material financial costs (including rectification and remediation costs), legal and regulatory sanctions, or reputational damage the bank may suffer as a result of its failure to comply with relevant laws, regulations, principles, rules, standards, and codes of conduct applicable to its activities, in letter and spirit. Within compliance: • Conduct is the risk that actions undertaken by the bank and/or its staff could lead to customer detriment, employee detriment (outside of appetite), inappropriate control of financial crime and related activity, or negative impact on market stability; • Prudential compliance is the risk of material loss or liability, legal or regulatory sanctions, or reputational damage arising from breaching existing relevant prudential policy, laws, or regulations, in any jurisdiction in which the entity operates.

(Continued)

Table 15.3   (Continued)

Level 1 Risk Taxonomy

Level 1 Risk	1st LoD Risk Owners	2nd LoD Risk Owner	Definition
NON-TRADED MARKET RISK	Head of Treasury		The market risk arising in non-trading assets and liabilities.
CAPITAL AND STRESS TESTING	CFO		The risk of not being able to conduct business in base or stress conditions due to insufficient qualifying capital as well as the failure to assess, monitor, plan, and manage capital adequacy requirements.
FUNDING AND LIQUIDITY	Head of Treasury		The risk that the company is not able to meet its liabilities as they fall due, or has insufficient resources to repay withdrawals.
REPUTATIONAL	ExCo members		The risk of brand damage and/or financial cost due to the failure to meet stakeholder expectations of the company's conduct and/or performance.
BUSINESS	CFO/(+MDs of business areas)		The risk that the company suffers losses as a result of adverse variance in its revenues and/or costs relative to its business plan and strategy.
STRATEGIC	CEO (Board)		The risk that the company will make inappropriate strategic choices, is unable to successfully implement selected strategies, or changes arise that invalidate strategies. This includes all divestment programme-related risks.
GROUP	CEO		The dependency of the company on the group for key support areas, e.g. funding, liquidity, capital, and other back office functions, etc.

the bank's risk management process and subsequent management actions. The danger, as with all exercises subject to considerable regulatory supervision, is that the stress testing process becomes an excessively bureaucratic one and more of a "box-ticking" exercise. This must be avoided and ALCO is the appropriate forum to review the process and ensure this does not happen.

ICAAP process guidelines

To recap, Basel II introduced the three-pillar architecture for capital and risk management (see Figure 15.9, as reproduced from the BCBS document).

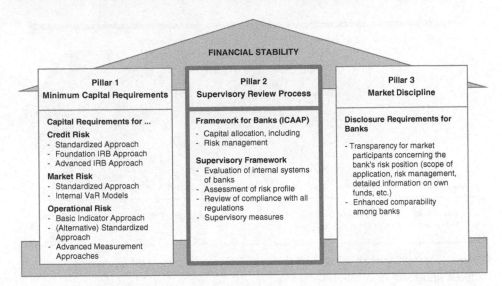

Figure 15.9   The three pillars of capital and risk management

On the one hand, Pillar II (Supervisory Review and Evaluation Process) requires banks to implement a process for assessing their capital adequacy in relation to their risk profiles as well as a strategy for maintaining their capital levels. This is the ICAAP. On the other hand, Pillar II also requires the regulatory authority to review all banks for their capital adequacy and to impose any necessary supervisory measures following such review. So there are two parts to this process:

- The ICAAP, which comprises all of a bank's procedures and measures designed to ensure that there exists:
  - The appropriate identification and measurement of all balance sheet risks;
  - An appropriate level of internal capital in relation to the bank's risk profile;
  - The application and further development of suitable risk management systems.
- The supervisory review process or SRP (sometimes SREP), which covers the processes and measures defined in the principles listed above, including the review and evaluation of the ICAAP process, an independent assessment of the bank's risk profile, and where necessary instructing the bank to undertake further prudential measures.

ICAAP implementation

Before a bank can begin designing its ICAAP, it should first define its relevant target state. The steps involved are those illustrated in Figure 15.10.

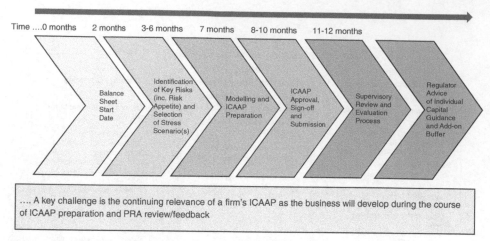

Time ....0 months   2 months   3-6 months   7 months   8-10 months   11-12 months

| | | | | | |
| Balance Sheet Start Date | Identification of Key Risks (inc. Risk Appetite) and Selection of Stress Scenario(s) | Modelling and ICAAP Preparation | ICAAP Approval, Sign-off and Submission | Supervisory Review and Evaluation Process | Regulator Advice of Individual Capital Guidance and Add-on Buffer |

.... A key challenge is the continuing relevance of a firm's ICAAP as the business will develop during the course of ICAAP preparation and PRA review/feedback

Figure 15.10   Steps involved in the ICAAP production and approval process
© Chris Westcott 2017. Used with permission.

What does Figure 15.10 mean in practice? Each step is considered in turn below.

Definition of bank-specific requirements (target state): In the first step, the bank compiles its strategy based on its goal or vision. It will test this strategy against a list of requirements based on national regulator statements, for example, the EU CRDIV. Next, these requirements have to be specified for the individual bank, thus in the course of a self-assessment the bank should identify its material risks, which arise from the implementation of its strategy. The ICAAP therefore facilitates assessing the sensitivity and risks in a firm's strategy. The requirements with regard to ICAAP methods should be defined in light of the bank's risk profile, as they need to be fit for purpose but also meet regulatory rigour. Typically, the introduction of new methods begins with relatively simple, robust solutions which are then developed and refined on an ongoing basis. The full list of requirements then represents the target state for ICAAP purposes and defines requirements with regard to methods, procedures, processes, and organisation.

Gap analysis: Once the target state has been defined, the bank should analyse those requirements that are currently not (or not completely) fulfilled. These gaps pertain both to the execution of strategy as well as the capital assessment process. It is the business team's responsibility to address the former and its risk management teams would survey the current state of methods, processes, and organisation in place in the internal risk management system. This might include the regulator's requirements for calculating capital amounts, or activities aimed at fulfilling the minimum standards for the credit origination business. The process is not restricted to risk managers. In terms of the three lines of defence model, the process starts with all business lines, which should analyse their current state and report it centrally to Risk (and ALCO). Gaps in implementation can then be identified by comparing the requirements with the current state. This comparison of target and actual states could be carried out in the course of a workshop attended by representatives from the business lines, with the results documented and reported to all relevant stakeholders. The bank can then assess the significance and consequences of the gaps identified as well as identify the necessary management actions as a result.

Implementation planning: In implementation planning, the first step is to prioritise the required measures identified in the previous process. This way a clear ranking can be defined in order to deploy implementation resources effectively. Measures identified should be combined in individual work packages and coordinated with business lines; this process requires that specific roles and responsibilities be identified and assigned. As part of the process, the bank should set binding deadlines, which reflect resource and capacity available within the firm.

Implementation: Put simply, this stage involves undertaking and delivering on the process measures identified in the previous stage. This includes employing human resources as well as IT capacity as required by the ICAAP. The process-related aspects and responsibilities within the ICAAP can then be defined and documented. This may involve quantifying and aggregating risks and coverage capital, monitoring limits, or taking measures in the *ex-post* control process. The ICAAP is integrated into the bank's strategic and operational control mechanisms (for example, annual budgeting and planning on the basis of risk indicators and coverage capital). Once implementation is completed, the bank should have in place adequate methods, processes, and systems to ensure its risk-bearing capacity over the long term.

What makes a good ICAAP?

In essence, the ICAAP process and its published output as presented to the national regulator should be a value-added exercise that reflects the interests of all stakeholders in the long-term viability of the bank as a going concern. This is not a platitude. However, because of the onerous regulation and reporting process in place in most jurisdictions, the process often boils down to producing something that the regulator signs off on. This is not the best approach to ICAAP production. To the question "What makes a good ICAAP?" the obvious answer is a document that presents the firm's strategy with all material risk exposures, on a forward-looking basis, and demonstrates that these exposures are covered by adequate capital levels, risk management systems, and management actions to rectify stresses in order to ensure the successful implementation of the strategy.

As a checklist, we should note that the following factors are crucial in the actual implementation and successful presentation of an ICAAP:

- *Early detection of gaps in fulfilment:*
    A bank should make efforts to detect gaps in the fulfilment of requirements as early as possible so that it can take the appropriate measures in a timely and economical manner. Closing these gaps quickly will improve

the bank's internal risk management and thus enhances its ability to ensure its risk-bearing capacity.

- *Selection of methods:*

    The bank should determine the methods and procedures that best suit its needs, as these determine the validity of the ICAAP as well as the required implementation resources. In the course of selecting methods, the bank should not only consider its current risk profile but also anticipate planned developments in individual risk types. If, for example, a decision has already been made that trading will be expanded in the medium term, then it makes sense to introduce more advanced procedures from the outset when designing the ICAAP.

- *Master plan and project management:*

    The bank should develop a master implementation plan that covers planning, budgeting, and a prioritisation of all ICAAP implementation tasks. There should be one overall, dedicated project manager (most probably someone within Risk or Treasury). This master plan forms the basis for requesting internal and external capacities and may well involve planning resources over a period of several years. For example, implementation might already be well under way for the most important risk types, while measures for other risk types are still being planned. Once it reaches a certain scale, the master plan should be transformed into a detailed project plan, which serves to reduce complexity and create transparency with regard to the current implementation status. It is also important to set binding deadlines and responsibilities on the basis of this plan. A project manager should then monitor and control the performance of individual tasks. Project management should seek to prevent any conflicts of interest between the business lines involved in implementation and to maintain an aggregate and holistic view of the project.

- *Communication:*

    The need for, and benefits of, the ICAAP have to be clearly communicated to all staff. The fundamental concept of the ICAAP is not something for senior executives only to appreciate, but for all business lines. An example is a newly designed limit allocation system or a change to the organisation chart, more likely to be supported by staff if they are informed about the need for these measures in a transparent and understandable manner. Insufficient communication in implementation projects often results in low levels of identification or even rejection and demotivation. By applying an appropriate communication policy and setting a good example, senior executives should generate the employee acceptance necessary for successful implementation of the ICAAP.

- *Know-how and resources:*

    One major objective of the ICAAP is to foster the development of an appropriate internal risk management culture. For this reason, expertise in this area is a key success factor in the implementation of the ICAAP. It is important for the bank to have the necessary resources (employees, systems) at its disposal in the ICAAP implementation process. Resource requirements will depend on the bank's size and risk profile as well as the difference between the current status and the defined requirements.

- *Data quality and IT systems:*

Data quality (completeness, availability) is especially important because it determines the reliability and accuracy of calculated results (for example, risk indicators and coverage capital). The process of data quality assurance begins with accurate data capture and goes as far as ensuring data availability in the ICAAP. Especially for risk management, it is necessary and worthwhile to ensure timely automated evaluations due to the large data quantities involved and the sometimes complex calculation algorithms used. In its ICAAP, the bank can rely on existing risk management systems (risk measurement, limit monitoring) if they meet the defined requirements. Historically, maintaining and updating the IT structures of many banks requires copious resources. It is a required investment, however, because the lack of uniform data pools can create considerable difficulties in assessing the true extent of balance sheet risk.

Principal ICAAP requirements

Based on supervisory requirements and the benefits from a business perspective, the basic requirements to be taken into account in the production of an ICAAP are:

- *Securing capital adequacy*: Banks should define a risk strategy that contains descriptions of its risk policy instruments and objectives. This is a Board-level statement. The explicit formulation of such a risk strategy aids in the early detection of deviations from appetite and tolerance;
- *ICAAP as an internal management tool:* The ICAAP should form an integral part of the management and decision-making process;
- *Responsibility of the management:* The overall responsibility for the ICAAP is assigned to the Board and senior executive, which must ensure that the bank's risk-bearing capacity is secured and that all material risks are identified, measured, and limited;
- *Assessment of all material risks:* The ICAAP focuses on ensuring bank-specific internal capital adequacy from a business perspective. For this purpose, all material risks must be assessed. Therefore, the focus is laid on those risks that are (or could be) significant for the individual bank;
- *Processes and internal review procedures:* Merely designing risk assessment and control methods is not sufficient to secure a bank's risk-bearing capacity. It is only in the implementation of appropriate processes and reviews that the ICAAP is actually brought to bear. This ensures that every employee knows which steps to take in various situations. For the sake of improving risk management on an ongoing basis, the development of an ICAAP should be regarded not as a one-time project but as a continuous development process. In this way, input from ongoing experience can be used to develop simpler methods into a more complex system with enhanced control functions.

Risk indicators

The ICAAP should present all relevant material balance sheet risk through a series of risk exposure indicators. These are specific to the risk types. Indicators presenting the aggregate view are also required, i.e. the firm's capital adequacy ratios as well as risk-adjusted performance indicators.

Credit risk indicators

The structure of the credit portfolio provides initial indications of a bank's risk appetite. A large share of loans in a certain asset class (for example, CRE) may point to increased risk. In addition, the presence of complex financing transactions such as specialised lending (project finance, for instance) may also indicate a larger risk appetite. For an approximate initial assessment, in the EU a bank can use the asset classes defined in Directive 2000/12/EC, or the asset classes outlined in the BA200 submission to the SARB, to examine the distribution of its credit portfolio. A bank can use credit assessments (such as credit ratings) to measure the share of borrowers with poor creditworthiness in its portfolio; this provides an indication of default risk. The bank will also consider the portfolio in terms of delinquency and impairment. The amount of available collateral – and thus the unsecured volume – also plays a role in this context. The lower the unsecured volume is, the lower the risk generally is; this relationship is also reflected in future supervisory regulations for calculating capital requirements. In this context, however, the type and quality of collateral are decisive; this can be assessed by asking the following questions:

- To what extent is the retention or liquidation of the collateral legally enforceable?
- How will the value of the collateral develop?
- Is there any correlation between the value of the collateral and the creditworthiness of the debtor?

A close inspection of the credit portfolio will provide further insights with regard to any existing concentration risks. In order to assess the size structure or granularity of its portfolio, the bank can also assess the size and number of large exposures. The bank should also consider the distribution of exposures among industries (for example, construction business, transport, tourism, and so on) in assessing its concentration risk. If a bank conducts extensive operations overseas (share of foreign assets), it is appropriate to take a close look at the risks associated with those activities as well, such as country and transfer risks. The share of foreign currency loans in a bank's credit portfolio can also point to concentration risks. If the share of foreign currency loans is very high, exchange rate fluctuations can have adverse effects on the credit quality of the borrowers. If the foreign currency loans are serviced using a repayment vehicle that is heavily exposed to market risks, this indicates an additional source of risk that should be monitored accordingly and controlled as necessary.

Market risks in the trading book, foreign exchange risks at the overall bank level

This exposure is calculated using a VaR approach. A bank can determine its sensitivity to foreign exchange fluctuations on the basis of its open foreign exchange positions and (in the broadest sense) open term positions. The influence of foreign exchange fluctuations on the default probability of borrowers with foreign currency loans is also considered.

Interest-rate risk in the banking book

The results reported in interest-rate risk statistics (part of regulatory reporting requirements) constitute an essential indicator of the level of interest rate risk in the banking book. The traditional approach here is to apply modified duration analysis such as parallel yield curve shifts (for example, the effects of a 200 basis point interest-rate shock on the present value of the balance sheet). Of course, if this method demonstrates that material interest-rate risks exist in the banking book, regulators usually require more "sophisticated" risk measurement methods to be applied, with output including a precise quantification of risks in terms of their effects on the income statement. Another risk indicator should cover proprietary trading both on- and off-balance-sheet. In accordance with the proportionality principle in the ICAAP (larger, more sophisticated balance sheets require larger, more sophisticated ICAAPs), the corresponding requirements increase in line with the scale of derivatives trading activities. Even in cases where a bank primarily uses derivatives to hedge other transactions or portfolios, the effectiveness of hedging transactions (the hedge effectiveness) should be examined in order to avoid undesirable side effects. In the case of on-balance-sheet proprietary transactions, the need for more precise risk control grows along with the scale and complexity of the positions held, for example, "alternative investments" or structured bonds.

Operational risk indicators

Two important indicators of operational risk are the size and complexity of a bank. As the number of employees, business partners, customers, branches, systems, and processes at a bank increases, its risk potential also tends to rise. Another risk indicator in this category is process intensity, for example, the number of transactions and volumes handled in payments processing, loan processing, securities operations, and proprietary trading. Failures (for example, due to overloaded systems) can bring about severe economic losses in banks with high levels of process intensity.[1] The number of lawsuits filed against a bank can also serve as an indicator of operational risks. A large number of lawsuits suggests that there are substantial sources of risk within

---

[1] A good example of this was the failure of Royal Bank of Scotland's ATM machines over a 3-day period in June 2012. In 2014, the UK Financial Conduct Authority imposed a several hundred million pound fine on the bank for this IT failure.

the bank, such as inadequate system security or insufficient care in processes and control mechanisms. In cases where business operations (for example, the processing activities mentioned above) are outsourced, the bank cannot automatically assume that operational risks have been eliminated completely. This is because a bank's dependence on an outsourcing service provider means that risks incurred by the latter can have negative repercussions for the bank. Therefore, the content and quality of the service level agreement, as well as the quality and creditworthiness of the outsourcing service provider, can also serve as risk indicators in this context.

The risk indicators may be presented as per the following template (note that more than one bank has been amalgamated to reflect different approaches), as illustrated in Table 15.4.

For Bank A, the risk types mentioned above would have little significance under the proportionality principle. The bank shows a low level of complexity and low risk levels. Besides, Bank A does not have any trading positions. For the purpose of measuring its risks and calculating its internal capital

Table 15.4 Example risk indicator levels

Risk indicator	Risk subtype	Bank A	Bank B	Bank C	Bank D
General risk indicators (e.g. size)		small	small	medium	large
Specific risks					
	Credit risk				
	Equity risk				
	Concentration risk				
	- Foreign currency loans				
	- Industries				
	- Size classes				
	- Country risks				
Market risks					
Interest-rate risk in the banking book					
Operational risks					
Liquidity risks					
Other risks					

	High significance
	Medium significance
	Low significance

needs, Bank A could calculate its capital requirements using the Standardised Approach, or the Basic Indicator Approach in the case of operational risk.

In terms of its total assets and number of employees, Bank B is comparable to Bank A, but Bank B's transactions show a markedly higher risk level. In addition, concentration risks exist with regard to size classes (for example, several relatively large loans to medium-sized businesses), borrowers in the same industry, and foreign currency loans. In this bank, methods that go beyond the Standardised Approach should be employed and/or adequate qualitative measures (monitoring/reporting) should be set. Furthermore, Bank B should pay attention to concentration risks, for example, by adhering to suitable individual borrower limits based on creditworthiness or by implementing minimum standards for foreign currency loans. In this example, using more advanced systems may be appropriate in other areas, such as interest rate risk in the banking book.

Bank C shows high credit exposures to SMEs and has also granted a number of relatively large loans. This results in a certain degree of concentration risk. In addition, the bank is exposed to relatively high interest-rate risks. In fact, Bank D has large exposures to almost all risk types. The bank's size and structure can be described (such as a VaR model) for interest-rate risk at Banks C and D; Bank D should also use a more sophisticated model for market risk. Due to the higher risk level and the existing complexity with regard to credit risk, the bank may use other risk-sensitive techniques based on the internal ratings-based (IRB) approach or a credit portfolio model.

The individual institutions in this example have to define the scale and type of risk management system that is appropriate to their activities, with due attention applicable to the regulator's requirements. The choice of suitable risk measurement procedures to determine risks and internal capital needs plays a key role in this context. Moreover, the proportionality concept also has effects on process and organisational design: banks that demonstrate a high level of complexity or a large risk appetite have to fulfil more comprehensive requirements.

An example of the presentation of the risk indicators is given in Table 15.5.

Documentation requirements

The ICAAP is a living document. That means the Board must use the ICAAP document to familiarise and challenge risk as well as capital management processes in the bank. The ICAAP has to be designed in a transparent and comprehensible manner. This will not only aid bank staff in understanding, accepting, and applying the defined procedures, it will also make it easier for the bank to review the adequacy of its methods and rules regularly and to enhance them on an ongoing basis. Critically, it makes the SRP (or SREP) process by the regulator a smoother one.

Table 15.5   Sample incorporation of an institution's relevant risk types in the ICAAP

Risk type	Risk subtype	Risk level	Justification (if immaterial)	Risk assessment procedure used
Credit risk	Counterparty/default risk	Very high		Foundation IRB Approach
	Equity risk	Immaterial	Equity investments as share of total assets < 0.5%	Foundation IRB Approach
	Country/transfer risk	Medium		Strict limitation (structural limit)
	Securitisation risk	Immaterial	No involvement in securitisation programmes (neither as originator nor as investor)	Not considered
	Credit risk concentration	High		Strict limitation (structural limit) and increased monitoring
	Residual risk from credit risk mitigation techniques	Medium		Qualitative assessment, process-based reduction of risk (use of standard contracts, "four eyes" principle, regular revaluation of collateral, etc.)
Market risk	Market risks in the trading book	Low		Standard supervisory methods
	Foreign exchange risks in the banking book	Medium		Standard supervisory methods
Interest-rate risks in the banking book		High		Value-at-Risk model
Operational risk		Medium		Basic Indicator Approach
Liquidity risk		Low		Qualitative measures
Other risks	Strategic risk	Medium		Cushion
	Reputation risk	Low		Cushion
	Capital risk	Medium		Cushion
	Earnings risk	Medium		Cushion

For this reason, it is necessary to compile formal written documentation on all essential elements of the ICAAP. In creating the required documentation, the bank should ensure that the depth and scope of its explanations are tailored to the relevant target group. It is sensible to use various levels of detail in the actual implementation of documentation requirements. For illustration purposes, a sample scenario with three levels is shown in Figure 15.11.

At the top level, it is advisable to articulate the bank's fundamental strategic attitude toward risk management. This will reflect the institution's basic orientation and guide all ICAAP-related decisions. The basic strategic attitude can be documented in the form of the firm's strategy – that is, the purpose and objectives of the bank and how it executes on this purpose. This will be executed via a business plan. The business plan will be delivered subject to a risk strategy. The essential components of such a strategy include:

- Risk policy principles;
- Statements as to the bank's appetite;
- A description of the bank's fundamental orientation with regard to individual risk types;
- Comments on the current business strategy and future development of the business;
- Areas of risk and uncertainty in the business strategy, and how these risks are managed in terms of the risk policy principles and the bank's risk appetite.

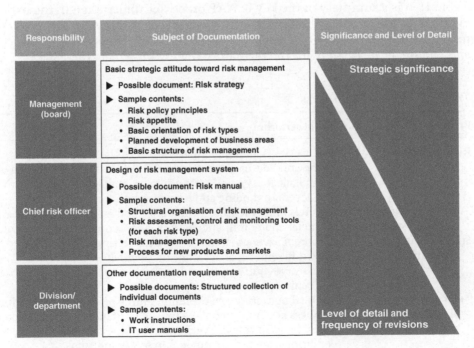

Figure 15.11   Three-level scenario

The risk strategy should be approved by the entire management Board of the bank and so it should be in summary form. At the next level down, the bank should provide a more detailed explanation of the methods and instruments employed for risk control and management. In practice, such a document is frequently referred to as the bank's risk management policy manual. Essentially, the risk manual contains a description of the risk management process, definitions of all relevant risk types, explanations of evaluation, control, and monitoring procedures for risk positions (separate for each risk type), and a discussion of the process of launching new products or entering new markets. In general, the depth of these explanations also implies that it will be necessary to revise at least certain parts of the document on a regular basis.

This level of detail will be contained in the executive summary of the report. Further outline will be provided in the body, while all technical detail required will be provided in appendices to the document.

ICAAP PROCESS – WORKED EXAMPLE OF PRESENTATION

In this section, a worked example of a typical ICAAP presentation to a regulator is presented. The bank in question is a vanilla UK commercial bank with retail and corporate business line exposure, and with a balance sheet of approximately £22 billion.

Table 15.6 is a summary of the key ICAAP processes undertaken in the bank. Figure 15.12 illustrates the governance structure of the ICAAP framework, mapping the components of the ICAAP to the internal processes, governance, and approvals, ultimately for the regulatory review known as the "SREP".

Table 15.6 ICAAP process

Process	Short description
Risk appetite	Risk appetite is an integral part of ABC's risk management framework, designed to deliver the strategic risk objectives of capital adequacy, market confidence, stable earnings growth and access to funding and liquidity.
Material integrated risk assessment	An exercise that identifies, evaluates, and assesses all material financial and non-financial risks whether quantifiable or not.
Stress testing programme	A comprehensive programme of stress testing that is designed to ensure senior management involvement, is aligned to regulatory requirements, and is integrated into the budgeting and capital planning processes.
9+3 capital planning and budgeting	An annual budgeting and capital planning process incorporating business and financial plans for the current year and project at least an additional 2 years under a base case (normal conditions) and 3 years under stressed conditions.

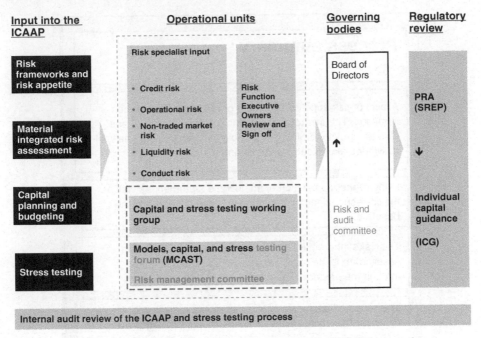

Figure 15.12   ICAAP governance process: the commonly observed process

The framework described in the foregoing could be said not to meet the "use test", which requires that the process and planning are to be derived from the business strategy, and that the business lines take an active part in the process. Figure 15.13 is an illustration of an all-embracing process for ICAAP preparation and submission, in that it shows the incorporation of the business lines. Figure 15.14 is a qualitative description of the process.

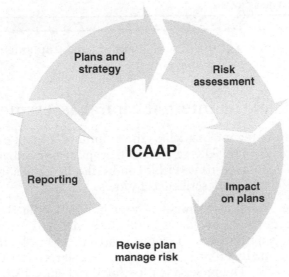

Figure 15.13   All-embracing ICAAP governance process

Process summary

A level of risk appetite will be set or revised from previous iterations. The **strategy** drivers include balance sheet and revenue growth, profitability and capital consumption, as well as wider stakeholder objectives and a strategic ALM focus.

In the **plans** a projection of the income statement as well as the corresponding change in the balance sheet forms the **baseline.**

The **risks** inherent in the business (as articulated by the baseline) must be identified, measured, and monitored through the process. These risks are tested to appetite.

The impact of each risk on the plan must be assessed. In particular this assessment will drive the **capital required** both on an internal and regulatory basis as well as the **funding profile** to support the business.

Based on the risk assessment, their impact will be tested through scenario analysis and stress testing. **Plans or risk appetite may be revised** to optimise the strategy or contingent management action plans developed.

The results of the risk assessment, capital requirement assessment, and consequential value metrics will be **reported** to the business areas. Analysis of change forms part of this process.

Figure 15.14   Summary of the ICAAP planning and implementation process, linking strategy and capital management

Components of the internal capital assessment

The Basel regulatory regime prescribes three "pillars" of risk exposure capital input (see Chapter 2). In the UK, generally the capital assessment process combines two views: a point-in-time (Pillar I and Pillar IIA) and a forward-looking (Pillar IIB) view. These are described as follows:

- Point-in-time capital assessment (1-year horizon) Pillar I and Pillar IIA: these form part of an Individual Capital Guidance (ICG), which is the minimum capital requirements the bank has to meet at all times. Pillar IIA assesses risks not in Pillar I or risks not adequately captured under the Pillar I framework. The process is illustrated in Figure 15.15.

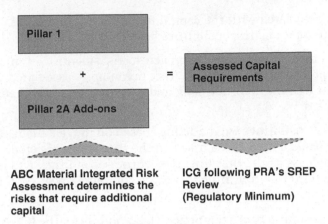

Figure 15.15 Point-in-time capital assessment (1-year horizon) Pillar I and Pillar IIA

In an emerging market economy such as South Africa, a similar approach is used. Pillar I is fundamentally the same but Pillar IIA refers to an emerging market minimum capital requirement deemed by the SARB to be appropriate for South African banks. Banks prepare their own internal view of risk towards capital for the Pillar I requirement. This is based on internal economic capital models evaluated in aggregate rather than per individual risk type. Pillar IIB refers to the individual capital guidance and is set for each bank, based on the output of the bilateral SREP process where the regulatory capital requirement is compared to the internal/economic capital requirement.

• The capital planning buffer (CPB): which is part of the internal capital target, is the amount of capital to be held in addition to the ICG such that it can be used in stress to absorb losses in order to prevent the bank from breaching its ICG. It reflects the change in the capital surplus/deficit and is illustrated in Figure 15.16.

The governance of this process is not cast in stone: different banks will organise it in different ways. Certainly, there is no one single correct way to approach this, but the governance structure must be fit for purpose in a way that provides confidence to the regulator and clearly articulates the risk appetite to the Board. The author's recommendation is first to compile a "risk

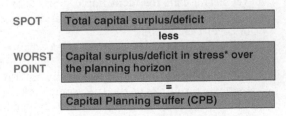

Figure 15.16 Capital surplus/deficit

taxonomy" associated with the capital management and ICAAP process, and then allocate roles and responsibilities based on this taxonomy.

In order to ensure a consistent approach to risk identification and measurement, it is preferable to compile a "risk taxonomy" associated with the risk management framework of the bank and used in the capital management and ICAAP process.

Roles and responsibilities will be defined based on the risk management framework of the bank. This is often based on the three lines of defence framework, based on business as the first line, risk as the second line, and audit and the Board as the third line, affirming that the second line review process functions properly.

Table 15.7 is a summary of a template risk taxonomy for the ICAAP and capital stress testing process.

Table 15.7   Capital management risk taxonomy

Aspect	Key facts
Definition	The risk taxonomy is a catalogue of the inherent risks associated with the ABC Bank business, its customers, and the regulatory environment in which it operates.
Rationale	In order to establish and maintain the risk framework and its various components, it is important to agree a list of risks (risk taxonomy) and associated accountabilities around which the framework is designed and built. The risk taxonomy provides a common risk language for all stakeholders whether internal or external.
Preparation	The group taxonomy has been used as a starting point and then tailored to the ABC Bank business based on discussion with business and risk stakeholders (subject matter experts), coupled with a review of ABC Bank's strategy, including product strategy, profit and loss account, and balance sheet and other related information/documentation. This will need to change and evolve as the company's internal and external environments change.
Structure	There are three levels of risks as follows: Level 1: These are the headline risk types common to most financial institutions, e.g. credit, market, and operational. Level 2: These are the identifiable subrisks of the Level 1, e.g. core lending risk and concentration risk are subrisks of Level 1 credit Risk. Level 3: These arise where Level 2 risks require to be subdivided further into specific risks requiring risk management.
Status	ExCo have approved the risk taxonomy and this will now be used when rolling out the risk framework.
Importance for ICAAP	The risk taxonomy is an important starting point for the MIRA process outlined on the next slide, which in turn is used in the capital assessment process.

The MIRA

The material integrated risk assessment (MIRA) is a key part of the ICAAP process. It helps to place the key drivers of the ICAAP in context. It is a basic "top-down" risk assessment tool across all risk types. It identifies material risks and assesses the risk and control framework in place to mitigate those risks. The MIRA is an important input to the capital assessment process because it identifies material risks and then assesses the capital treatment required for each of those risks. Material risks are either managed and have capital set aside or else they are managed away, not requiring capital. An example illustration of the output is given in the next section.

Capital treatment of material risks

In our example illustration, the MIRA material risks are summarised below. These are used to determine whether the risk is either "managed and cap-italised" or else just "managed". In this case, the MIRA has identified that the material add-on risks are for credit risk concentration, operational risk, and non-traded market risk and these are then discussed in more detail in Table 15.8.

Pillar II add-on

From the above, the bank in question has to calculate its Pillar II add-on for credit risk concentration and non-traded interest-rate risk. The relevant points here are:

- *Single name concentration (SNC):*
  One methodology to address this is the Pythkin approach, which is aligned with the theoretical (Vašíček) approach underlying the regulatory capital formula. The alternative Gordy approach, which is sometimes advocated, is also used although it is based on a different underlying model. In our example the add-on for SNC is highest for large exposures with high PD.
- *Sector concentrations (SRC):*
  This is an add-on for excess concentration in certain sectors such as CRE.
- *Non-traded market risk (NTMR) – method of assessment:*
  The bank does not incur traded market risk. Non-traded market risk arises from:
  - Repricing risk: arises from timing differences in the maturity (for fixed-rate) and repricing (for floating-rate) of assets and liabilities. There repricing mismatches can expose net interest income and economic value to fluctuations in interest rates.
  - Yield curve risk: arises when yield curve shifts differently between the short end and the long end and this can have adverse effects on a bank's economic value where repricing mismatches exist. The Liquid Asset Buffer (LAB) of £3.5bn is expected to be held in gilts for

Table 15.8 MIRA material risks

Risk type	Pillar I	Pillar IIA
Credit Risk	Advanced Internal Ratings Based (subject to PRA approval) and Standardised approaches are utilised.	Single Name, Sector, Geographical-Methodology to calculate capital charges is work in progress.
Operational Risk (including IT risk)	The Standardised Approach (TSA) is utilised. The 3-year average gross income grouped by business line is multiplied by a % factor (12%, 15%) depending on business line.	ABC Bank is developing a comprehensive scenario analysis programme from now and throughout 2014. In the interim, ABC Bank will adopt a scaling approach based on the Group operational risk economic capital model, which takes into account internal loss event experience, relevant scaled scenario analyses from the Group, scenario analyses outputs, and relevant external loss event data. ABC Bank will scale itself against the Group UK Retail and Corporate Banks based on Gross Income as at year end 2012.
Compliance Risk	Conduct and prudential compliance risks	
	Covered through the Operational Risk capital charge.	
Non-Traded Market Risk	Not covered in Pillar I	VaR approach is adopted for capital assessment.
Liquidity and Funding Risk	Liquidity and Funding risk is covered by the ILAA.	
Capital and Stress Testing Risk	Capital and Stress Testing Risk is managed through the capital planning process, stress testing, and scenario analysis.	
Strategic Risk	Not covered in Pillar I	Managed through the Business and Risk strategy and not capitalised.
Reputational Risk	Not covered in Pillar I	Any financial losses related to reputational risk are covered by the capital treatment relevant to the risk type through which the loss manifests. For non-financial events the relevant capital treatment is predominantly covered by the operational risk capital charge.
Business Risk	Not covered in Pillar I	The risk is managed and taken into account under integrated stress testing where income and expenses are stressed. For capital purposes this risk is captured through the Capital Planning Buffer (Pillar IIB).

Key:
Risk is managed and capitalised
Risk is managed
Pillar IIA Risk

an average duration of 4 to 7 years, and this would be subject to fluctuating gilts prices if unhedged or to swap spread risk if hedged with swaps. For the purpose of an interim capital assessment, NTMR is measured using a VaR model based on a 99% confidence interval over a 1-year holding period. In addition, a parallel shift of +/–100 and +/–200 basis point parallel shifts are also calculated and reported to ALCO. Non-traded market risk (NTMR) – estimates of exposure: The risk exposure on the estimated LAB is a PV01 of *circa* £820k for an average 4-year duration. The VaR estimated on a hedged or unhedged basis (using a 99% confidence interval for a 1-year holding period) is between £50 and £80m. Thus, the Pillar II add-on will be £80mm.

Operational risk

In normal circumstances, to calculate a robust Pillar II operational risk capital charge, a bank would use a variety of data including internal loss event data, external loss event data, key risk indicators, and the output of scenario analyses. For a new bank, there may be insufficient internal loss event data specific to its operations to be able to undertake any meaningful modelling capability. As a consequence, such a bank (as in our case study here) would develop a comprehensive programme for scenario analysis, which it would use until such time as 3 years' worth of loss event data was accumulated.

In the meantime, while the scenario analysis approach is being developed, the example bank here adopts a scaling approach based on the Group operational risk economic capital model, which considers Group internal loss event experience, its own programme of scenario analyses outputs, and relevant external loss event data.

ICAAP approach

In order to deliver a credible Pillar IIA operational risk capital charge, the bank takes its five largest risks based on its Material Integrated Risk Assessment (MIRA) and subjects them to workshopped scenario analysis. All other MIRA risks will be reviews to ensure that their exclusion from this process would not have a meaningful impact on the capital number generated by the five largest risks. These are:

- Technology/business process change/system failure;
- Third-party supplier failure (RBS);
- Customer retention;
- AML and sanctions; and
- Change management.

The outcomes of these scenarios will be subjected to a scenario analysis economic capital model.

Even though the internal risk assessment may be higher, banks in South Africa will only hold more capital if the aggregate internal risk view is higher than the regulatory view. Alternatively, the regulator may give guidance requesting increases under Pillar IIB.

STRESS TESTING

Stress tests show the effects of events that cannot (or not sufficiently) be accounted for under business as usual circumstances. Banks are repeatedly confronted with these exceptional scenarios: market crashes, country crises, critical political events, or major bankruptcies, for example. For situations of this kind, the assumptions of the usual assessment methods do not appear sufficient, which can lead to substantial underestimation of risk. For this reason, it is important for a bank to define relevant stress scenarios.

For example, fluctuations on international financial markets will have a different effect on a bank with high market risks than on a regional bank that primarily focuses on customer business. Nevertheless, it is necessary to account for the fact that these shocks can also have a noticeable impact on banks operating in more remote segments. After a market crisis, interest in funds and equities diminishes, which in turn brings about a decline in fee and commission income for many banks (even those that only operate regionally). For this reason, it may be helpful to define relevant stress scenarios for all of a bank's material risk types and to analyse the effect the simultaneous occurrence of such exceptional situations would have on the bank's risk-bearing capacity. The institution-specific business focuses can be taken into account by assigning different weights, for example. Banks that assume correlations in their ICAAP calculations should not assume any diversification effects in their stress scenarios. In practice, banks will apply systemic stress tests where the correlation between risk types is implicit in the risk factors evaluated in the macro-economic scenario. Banks also use specific stress events and reverse stress tests to obtain a broad understanding of the impact of individual risks and the interplay between them on the business plans and their inherent risk profiles.

Moreover, tests prescribed by supervisory authorities also have to be integrated into the design of relevant stress scenarios (for example, when certain methods are used to calculate capital requirements or large exposures). A bank can depict the effects of stress scenarios within the framework of risk-bearing capacity analysis. In this context, the bank should consider stress scenarios on the risk side as well as the effects of exceptional situations on the capital side. The results of the stress tests provide indications that may be helpful in identifying any existing weaknesses. This information can be used to develop countermeasures such as restricting dividend payouts, raising additional forms of capital, limiting certain business lines, redeveloping business architectures or in terms of certain specific risk criteria, limiting certain asset concentrations or introducing security checks and access authorisations in order to reduce operational risks, or drawing up general contingency plans.

ICAAP stress testing framework: worked example

For the example UK commercial bank, the templates used to describe the stress testing framework used as part of the ICAAP are presented.

Stress testing is a key internal risk management tool and is used as an input into a number of bank key business processes (including strategic planning, risk appetite, ICAAP, ILAA, and so on). This section summarises the different objectives of stress testing within the bank, structured across four main areas as follows:

- Strengthen risk management:
  1. Assess the impact of certain macro-economic and systemic events on a portfolio and bank as a whole;
  2. Identify a variety of hidden, unmatured risks at a group, portfolio, and divisional level;
  3. Formulate risk appetite and better manage the business through improved understanding of the underlying risks and sensitivities;
  4. Reverse stress testing: test the vulnerabilities of the business model and the resulting actions would improve the resilience of the entity under stress.
- Inform capital and liquidity requirements:
  1. Support the assessment of capital and liquidity requirements for the bank;
  2. Contribute to continuous improvement of the bank's capital and liquidity models.
- Maintain confidence in the bank's resilience to stress:
  1. Evaluate all of the material consequences of stress events, across all risk classes;
  2. Facilitate the development of risk mitigation plans and implement a framework of early warning indicators.
- Meet regulatory requirements:
  1. Respond promptly and effectively to regulator-mandated stresses;
  2. Support regulatory assessment of capital and liquidity requirements (for example, the UK PRA ICG and ILG requirements).

Stress testing approaches

Table 15.9 is a slide that would be presented at the start of the ICAAP deck to the regulator during the SREP, with initial capital assessment shown at Table 15.10 and projection at Table 15.11.

The stress testing framework should emphasise integrated stress testing for the aggregate balance sheet. Remember that the ICAAP is designed to be a forward-looking process, so that the anchor point for start of testing would be today and then built around scenarios over the next 1, 3, and 5 years.

Table 15.9   SREP slide
Three types of stress testing are applied:

Type of stress testing	Objectives	Type of activities
Entity-wide or integrated stress testing	• Assess the impact of certain macro-economic and systemic events on a portfolio and the banks as a whole. • Support the assessment of capital and liquidity requirements for the bank. • Facilitate the development of risk mitigation plans and implement a framework of early warning indicators. • Support regulatory assessment of capital and liquidity requirements (i.e. CPB, ICG, and ILG requirements).	• Top-down, integrated, macro-economic stress testing to support the following: – ICAAP and other supervisory mandated stress tests (e.g. CPP) – Risk appetite setting – Sensitivity analysis of the business plan (covering business and strategic risk).
Risk specific	• Better manage the business through improved understanding of the underlying risks and sensitivities. • Contribute to continuous improvement of the bank's capital and liquidity models.	• Bottom-up, risk-specific stress testing to cover the risk types defined in the ABC Bank risk taxonomy: – Credit risk; – Non-traded market risk; – Funding and liquidity risk; – Operational risk (including compliance and reputational risk).
Reverse stress testing	• Identify a variety of hidden, unmatured risks at a total, portfolio, and divisional level. • Identify the circumstance where the business model fails. • Remain in line with regulatory requirements related to stress testing, including completing regulator-mandated stresses.	• Developing scenarios that would threaten the bank's business model. • Calibrating a level of stress that would lead to bank failure. • Complementing setting of risk appetite and recovery and resolution planning.

Table 15.10   Initial capital assessment

Assessment as at 30 June 2013, £mn

	RWAs Mixed	Capital @8% Mixed	RWAs Standardised	Capital @8% Standardised
Pillar 1				
Credit	11,279	902.3	13,380	1,070.4
Credit Counterparty Risk (Derivatives)	295	23.6	295	23.6
Non-Credit Assets (Fixed Assets)	106	8.5	106	8.5
Operational Risk	1,576	126.1	1,576	126.1
Total Pillar 1	**13,256**	**1,060.5**	**15,357**	**1,228.6**
Pillar 2A Add-ons				
Single Name Concentration		10.0		10.0
Sector Concentration		267.0		267.0
Non-Traded Market Risk		80.0		80.0
Operational Risk		90.0		90.0
Total Pillar 2A		**447.0**		**447.0**
Total Pillar 1 and Pillar 2A Capital		**1,507.5**		**1,675.6**
ICG Multiplier		42%		36%

For the case study here on the UK commercial bank, the top-level scenario planning looked like this:

- A recession for the first 2 years, triggered by contagion from a re-intensification of Eurozone sovereign concerns; this scenario is relevant for the UK bank as it is a UK-based recession although the trigger is outside the UK. The scenario addresses the key vulnerabilities in the bank's portfolio, being UK focused affecting CRE and mortgage exposures with the key economic parameters below:
  - UK real GDP falls at an annualised rate of 5.7% at the trough of the recession;
  - Unemployment peaks at the highest to 11.4%, affecting household consumption and business consumption;
  - House prices fall by more than 20% over the first two scenarios and remain volatile thereafter;
  - M4 lending and holdings contract but at different rates;
  - Interest rates (3-month Libor) increase in the first 3 years and then fall for the next 2 years.
- The contraction is followed by a slow recovery, with growth eventually returning close to trend towards the end of the scenario.

Table 15.11   Base case scenario projection

£m	Base Case				
	2014	2015	2016	2017	2018
Required					
RWAs	12,647	12,870	13,387	13,877	14,488
Pillar 1 – Capital	1,012	1,030	1,071	1,110	1,159
Pillar 2A (proposed ICG) – Capital	426	434	451	468	489
Total Required Capital	**1,438**	**1,464**	**1,522**	**1,578**	**1,648**
Total CT1	1,748	1,970	2,206	2,478	2,757
Deductions	−230	−290	−268	−246	−225
Total Tier 1/CT1	1,518	1,680	1,938	2,231	2,532
Tier 2	374	374	374	374	374
Total Available Capital (T1 and T2)	**1,892**	**2,054**	**2,312**	**2,605**	**2,906**
Surplus	453	591	790	1,027	1,258
Ratios					
Core Tier 1 (based on Pillar 1 RWAs)	12.0%	13.1%	14.5%	16.1%	17.5%
Total Capital (based on Pillar 1 RWAs)	15.0%	16.0%	17.3%	18.8%	20.1%

Of course, banks would design their stress test relevant to their operating environment. A South African bank would concentrate on the economic impact of recession in South Africa.

The scenario is then subject to drilldown to see the impact on financials:

- Balance sheet under stress:
  - Asset balances decline under stress due to debt flow, fall in new lending, and in consumer/household spending as reflected in the relevant economic parameters;
  - Additional assumptions are being taken with regard to CRE decline as shown in scenario 3.
- Operating and funding costs:
  - Balance sheet decline will cause a corresponding fall in income in the first 2 years of the stress and then picks up the following 3 years;
  - Net interest margin declines compared to base case and remains low in the first few years of the recovery;
  - Costs will follow the base balance sheet forecast and any cost cutting will be taken as a management action;
  - Funding costs would reflect the scenario interest rates but would increase if the funding gap increases.
- Impairments:
  - Impairments are equal to EL and taken into the P&L;

- o The scenario has a negative effect on unemployment, house prices, and CRE index and this has a significant impact on impairments during the stress period as creditworthiness deteriorates. Consequently, PDs and expected losses increase causing impairments to more than double during the stress period;
  - o Similarly, an economic recovery would result in lower impairments.
- RWA credit:
  - o The effects of a decline in house prices and property values during stress would decrease the value of the security of the loan and hence increase LGDs. This and the increase in PDs would cause a sharp increase in RWAs and this is offset by debt flow (defaults) and contraction of the balance sheet.
- Operational risk losses and RWAs:
  - o It is assumed that certain operational risk losses (for example, external fraud) crystallise under stress;
  - o Operational risk RWAs are recalculated according to the Standardised Approach and would decline in line with income.
- Capital plans:
  - o Capital deductions remain although there will be no excess provisions over EL as provisions are equal to or greater than EL;
  - o The assets in the Liquid Asset Buffer (LAB), also termed Available For Sale (AFS), are revalued and profits/losses taken against capital and not P&L in line with accounting rules;
  - o The combined effects of a deterioration in P&L and an increase in RWAs causes CT1 and total capital ratios to decline compared to base. This will then be assessed against regulatory minima.

The above summary is presented as a template as to how a bank could set the stress testing framework for impact on financials.

Impact of Basel III/CRDIV capital buffers

The capital buffers described earlier in the chapter are not all relevant to all banks (as we discussed). Individual banks would have to determine which ones applied and then integrate the requirements of relevant buffers into their capital planning.

To recap, for banks in the EU, CRDIV specifies five new buffers:

- A micro-prudential buffer – the CCB set at 2.5%;
- Macro-prudential buffers – the CCB set buffers for Global Systemically Important Institutions (G-SIFIs), the buffer for other Systemically Important Institutions (O-SIIs), and the Systemic Risk Buffer.

These buffers are all additive and only the G-SIFI buffer takes into account the size of the financial situation. The UK PRA specifies a firm-specific PRA buffer to ensure firms are meeting capital requirements in line with the PRA's risk appetite, which may result in capital requirements over and above the other capital buffers. These combined requirements and, in particular, the increase in proportion of CET1, are super-equivalent and could put UK banks at a competitive disadvantage to overseas banks operating through UK branches.

The increase in the proportion of CET1 may disproportionately increase the cost of capital for UK banks and, hence, result in additional costs for borrowers. For smaller banks, who arguably already face reduced access to capital, this effect would potentially be exacerbated and could consequently become a deterrent to entry into the banking sector contrary to the OFT and ICB intentions of encouraging new challenger banks to compete in the industry.

For the case study here on the UK commercial bank, which has a balance sheet of approximately £22 billion, and is not a "G-SIFI" bank, its capital planning process would include the possibility of the PRA buffer being required to be maintained, thus increasing its capital requirements.

DIVIDEND POLICY

As part of its capital management and capital planning process, it is important for a bank to have in place a formal dividend policy statement. This should reflect the bank's overall risk appetite and be referred to in the risk appetite statement. Dividend policy is a critical part of the capital management process, because it is part of the process by which its capital buffers are built up and retained.

For example, where one has observed a dividend payment made to the shareholder, which was in excess of 50% of the reported post-tax profit, this would suggest a Board that was not placing capital preservation as a priority. Such an approach would not be a common one for, for instance, a "challenger" bank. Typically, banks that are in some form of challenger mode, such as start-ups, niche players, or those operating under a revised business model, pay little or no dividend for the first few years. A good example of this is TSB Bank in the UK, which was divested in 2014 from Lloyds Banking Group, with a balance sheet of approximately £25 billion. It stated on listing that it expected to pay no dividend for at least the next 5 years. The statement went on to describe the rationale for this policy, which included the desire to build up regulatory capital buffers to above peer group levels. A policy similar to that of TSB would be more in line with what one would expect to observe at most banks under competitive or other stress.

In the EU, Article 141 of the CRDIV (paragraph 2) states that institutions that fail to meet the combined buffer requirement shown in Exhibit 3 must calculate a "maximum distributable amount" (MDA). If a bank falls below its combined buffer capital requirement, it must reduce discretionary distributions of earnings (including dividend payments, share buybacks, discretionary cash payments on AT1 instruments, and bonus payments) in accordance with its MDA calculations. Hence, equity and AT1 investors must assume that AT1 distributions would be cancelled at the point of MDA breach and should focus on this calculation attachment point, in addition to any CET1 write-down or conversion trigger embedded in AT1 instruments. In essence, banks that fail to meet the combined buffer required are prohibited from distributing more than the MDA through any (a) distribution in connection with CET1, (b) bonus payments, or (c) payments on AT1.

The MDA is given by after-tax profits generated since the most distribution referred to in (a)–(c) above, multiplied by the appropriate "factor". This factor ranges from 0% to 60%, and is based on the quartile of the combined buffer requirement in which the bank's CET1 ratio falls. If CET1 falls in the upper quartile, 60% of the MDA may be distributed, falling in 20% increments to 0% in the lowest quartile.

CASE STUDY: INTERNAL CAPITAL ASSESSMENT

The quantitative output from an "internal capital assessment" (ICA) exercise at an EU commercial bank ("ABC Bank") is illustrated. It is a baseline input to the ICAAP process (the headings are the same as would be used in the ICAAP) as well as valuable management information in its own right, provided the output is used to inform management actions. An example of the list of possible management actions in stress is also illustrated. This output would be for senior management and the Board to approve before its content was submitted to the regulator. The key balance sheet objectives are those shown in Figure 15.17, with the base case capital projection shown at Figure 15.18.

Assessment of capital buffers

As there is more than one approach that can be taken when determining the capital buffer requirement, in most banks the process will involve running a range of different scenarios, such that one will be left with a range of different capital buffer requirements. It is a Board and/or senior executive decision as to which approach one should adopt finally.

In our case study example of the same bank that has been considered in the previous section, the following approaches were considered:

1. Assessment of capital buffers: mixed approach;
2. Forward-looking capital assessment: standard approach;
3. Assessment of capital buffers: standard approach.

The results for each approach are shown at Figures 15.19, 15.20 and 15.21.

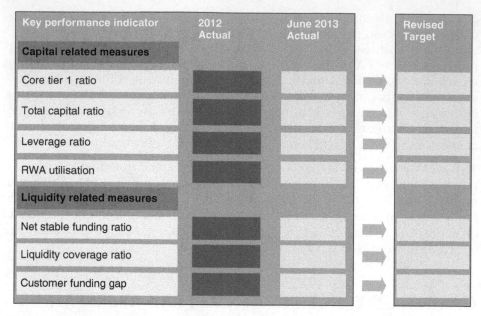

Figure 15.17   Progress towards key strategic balance sheet objectives

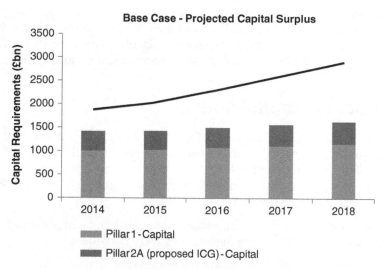

Figure 15.18   Base case capital projection

The results for each are presented in Figures 15.19 to 15.21.

Approach (1): Assessment of capital buffers: mixed approach

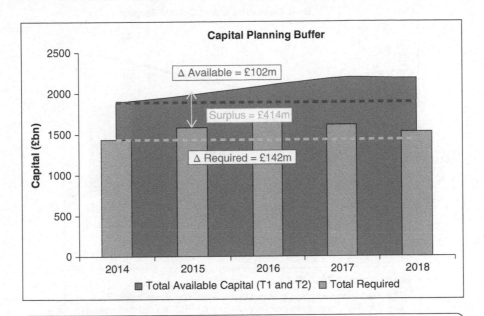

Capital planning buffer (CPB)

- The capital planning buffer (CPB) is based on a forward-looking analysis, identified during normal times so it can be used to absorb losses and/or to cover increasing capital requirements in adverse circumstances that are outside the firm's control
- ABC will have a total capital surplus in 2014 of £454m under the mixed approach. At the lowest point of the stress (2015), this surplus will fall to £414m, requiring a CPB of £40m (i.e. £454m - £414m)

Capital conservation buffer (CCoB) and Domestic Systemically Important Financial Institution buffer (D-SIFI)

- The capital conservation buffer (CCoB) is a CRDIV buffer to be phased in from 2016
- The D-SIFI is a CRDIV buffer which has been assumed to be 0.5% from 2016

Conclusions on PRA Required Capital Buffer

- PRA Required Capital Buffer has been assumed to be equal to the greater of the CPB and the CCoB + D-SIFI in any given year, with any excess capital in addition to this capital amount held to cover other regulatory buffers
- Under the mixed approach, ABC will be required to hold a CPB of £40m in 2014, and a higher capital amount equal to CCoB + D-SIFI thereafter

Figure 15.19   Assessment of capital buffers mixed approach

Approach (2): Forward-looking capital assessment: standard approach

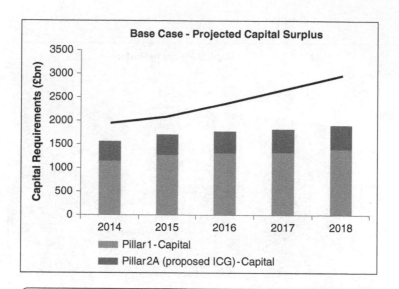

Base case with 2013 ICG

- The results on this page assume that the starting point capital is equal to that under the mixed approach (i.e. £1,518 post deductions). This means that starting point CET1 is 10.6% (instead of 12%) and that the total capital ratio is 13.6% (instead of 15%)

- The 2014 proposed ICG is based on the Pillar 2A calculations presented on slide 8. These Pillar 2A items have been projected as a fixed percentage (36%) of Pillar 1 capital requirements over the time horizon for the standardised approach

- The retained earnings grow through the forecast period leading to a significant increase in the capital surplus (£1,014m in 2018)

- The base case shows a sizeable surplus throughout the 5-year projection period with the lowest surplus in the first year (2014) reflecting ABC's starting point capital position

- During the forecast period the CT1 ratio steadily increases to attain 14.6% in 2018 under this approach

Figure 15.20   Forward-looking capital assessment: standard approach

Approach (3): Assessment of capital buffers: standard approach

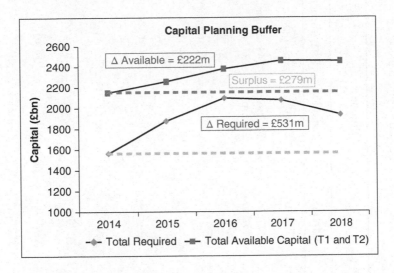

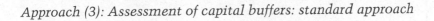

Capital planning buffer (CPB)

- The capital planning buffer (CPB) is based on a forward-looking analysis, identified during normal times so it can be used to absorb losses and/or to cover increasing capital requirements in adverse circumstances that are outside the firm's control

- ABC's will have a total capital surplus in 2014 of £588m at end 2014 under the standardised approach. At the lowest point of the stress (2016), this surplus will fall to £279m, requiring a CPB of £309m (i.e. £588m - £279m)

Capital conservation buffer (CCoB) and Domestic Systemically Important Financial Institution buffer (D-SIFI)

- The capital conservation buffer (CCoB) is a CRDIV buffer to be phased in from 2016

- The D-SIFI is a CRDIV buffer which has been assumed to be 0.5% from 2016

Conclusions on PRA Required Capital Buffer

- PRA Required Capital Buffer has been assumed to be equal to the greater of the CPB and the CCoB + D-SIFI in any given year, with any excess capital in addition to this capital amount held to cover other regulatory buffers

- Under the standardised approach, ABC will be required to hold a CPB of £309m until 2016 and a higher capital amount equal to CCoB + D-SIFI thereafter

Figure 15.21   Assessment of capital buffers: standard approach

Summary of management actions in stress

Table 15.12 is a summary of the analysis on management action in stress, which is an Appendix to the ICA and also an integral part of the ICAAP submission. The table is the complete list of possible capital related management and recovery actions that could be put in place at ABC Bank, including a summary

Table 15.12 Summary of management actions in stress

Management actions in stress

The table below is the complete list of possible capital related management and recovery actions that could be put in place, including a summary of their impact on capital, liquidity, and P&L

Management options	Description	Damage to franchise	Numbers		
			Capital	Liquidity	P&L impact
A. Stop selling					
A.1 Business lending	Cease all new business lending via loans and overdrafts	High	£202m	£2bn	£60m pa
A.2 Mortgages	Cease all new mortgages	Low	£17.2m	£1.2bn	£44.4m pa
A.3 Personal lending	Cease all new personal loans. This is normally unsecured borrowing and carries significant RWA	Medium	£45.1m	£376m	£37m pa
A.4 Stop renewals	Loans, commercial bullet facilities that do not contractually require renewal	Medium	£9.6m	£80m	£2.4m pa
B. Capital maximisation					
B.1 Adjust limits	Cancel all undrawn limits on accounts including utilised overdrafts	High	£50.4m	Nil	£21m
B.2 RWA	Stop high RWA items	Medium	See A1	See A1	See A1
C. Capital raising					
C.1 Sell a stake in the business	Seek buyers for element of the business via private placement	Low	£200m	£200m	£30m pa
C.2 Debt	Convert debt to shares. (Bail in senior debtholders)	Low	£200m	Nil	£18m
C.3 Rights issue	Launch rights issue	Low	£200m	£150m	Nil
D. Debt buyback					
D.1 Debt	Buy back own debt if opportunity for capital gain	Low	£129m (in retained profits)	£180m	£129m

E. Capital retention						
E.1	Dividends	Withhold any unpaid dividends, stop new ones	Low	£45m	£45m	Nil
F. Fixed asset sales						
F.1	Property	Sale and leaseback or sublease	Low	Net negligible	£32m	Nil
G. Sell assets						
G.1	Operations	Outsource with "free" period up front	Medium	£20.2m (in retained profits)	£26m	£26m
G.2	Mortgage book	Sell mortgage book	Medium	£104.4m	£5,800m	£435m
G.3	Credit card book	Sell receivables	Low	£36m	£300m	£6m
G.4	Data	Sell marketing data	Medium	£0.78m	£1m	£1m
G.5	Sale "tall trees" debt	Sell off debt for customers over £30m debt	Low	£187.5m	£1,860m	£56m
H. Repricing						
H.1	Deposits	Increase rate paid to customers to enhance liquidity	None	**Corporate:** £0.58m **Retail:** £1.55m	**Corporate:** £100m **Retail:** £100m	**Corporate:** £0.75m **Retail:** £2m
H.2	Lending	Increase pricing to enhance profitability and retain liquidity by reducing demand	Medium	£211.4m	£2,860.8m	−£113.1m
H.3	MTA	Increase pricing to enhance profitability	Medium	£1.0m	£1.3m	£1.3m

(Continued)

Table 15.12 (Continued)

Management options	Description	Damage to franchise	Numbers		
			Capital	Liquidity	P&L impact
H. Repricing					
H.4 LOBO	Exercise review clause under "lender option–borrower option" contracts (LOBO)	Low	?	?	?
I. Radical cost cutting					
I.1 Bonus/incentives	Stop all discretionary salary elements	Low	£12.4m (in retained profits)	£16m	£16m
I.2 Pay cut	10% pay cut for staff	Low	£13.2m (in retained profits)	£17m	£17m
I.3 Non-staff	Stop all discretionary payments, e.g. marketing, travel, etc.	Low	£14.9m (in retained profits)	£19.2m	£19.2m
I.4 Reduce footprint	Close branches	High	0	–£2.5m	£0.3m
I.5 Recruitment	Stop all recruitment activity including in-flight. Give notice to terminate consultants/agency, etc. Stop all recruitment	Low	£0.38m (in retained profits)	£0.5m	£0.5m
I.6 Cost reduction	Impose flat 10% budget reduction across all areas	Low	£38.75m (in retained profits)	£50m	£50m

of their impact on capital, liquidity, and P&L. Of course, the exact content of the table will differ by type of banking institution and specific business model. In reality, some of these actions will not be on a "going concern" basis, or would so damage the franchise as to render the firm moribund. The emphasis must be on realistic going concern management actions.

Example 15.2   Capital calculations[2]

Total capital requirement = Pillar I requirement + Pillar IIA requirement + Pillar IIB requirement

Pillar I consists of the following components:

- Credit risk (standardised method, as detailed below);
- Operational risk (15% of the average over 3 years of the "relevant indicator" that is the sum of interest income and non-interest income);
- Interest-rate risk (capital held on hedging positions that do not qualify for hedge accounting, i.e. trading positions – probably non-existent).

Pillar I Credit RWAs are calculated in the standardised method as follows:

- All non-property related loans to SME and retail clients (Start-up loan, Term loan, Property bridge finance, Invoice finance, Personal loan, Credit cards):
  - 100% for loans >€1.5m;
  - 75% for loans <€1m and where the customer is "Retail".
- Loans secured by mortgages on residential real estate:
  - 35% on eligible loans;
  - 100% on non-eligible loans.
- Loans secured by mortgages on commercial real estate:
  - 50% on eligible loans;
  - 150% on non-eligible loans.
- All non-performing loans require 150% of risk weight;
- 20%/50% credit conversion factor (CCF) has been assumed on undrawn balances of remaining maturity ≤1y or >1y;
- Surplus cash placed with global financial institutions (tenor <3 months): 20%, assuming rating of A–;
- Surplus cash placed with Bank of England/gilts held in LAB: 0%;
- All other assets (for example, fixed): 100%.

---

[2]This section was co-authored with Soumya Sarkar.

Pillar I capital for credit risk is then calculated at 8% of credit RWAs. In line with CRDIV CRR, a 0.7619 SME supporting factor has been applied to the capital weighting of 8% applied to credit RWAs for SME loans that meet the qualifying criteria.

Pillar IIA needs to account additionally for the following (PRA's methodology for setting Pillar II capital):

- Credit risk – specific to the nature of the loan book of CoLC;
- Credit concentration risk – to capture regional/sectoral/size concentrations in the loan book;
- Operational risk – basic indicator approach (probability weighting of loss register × 12.5);
- Interest rate risk in the banking book (IRRBB) – assessment based on 200bp stress (FSA017).

Pillar IIB capital has the following components (PRA's methodology for setting Pillar II capital):

- Severe stress covering credit risk, concentration risk, operational risk, business risk, liquidity risk, compliance risk, and IRRBB to assess if the bank's capital would drop below the P1 + P2A CET1 requirement;
- Capital Planning Buffer (CPB) to cover increased capital requirements in adverse circumstances and will be calculated as operating cost incurred over the next 12 months in winding down;
- Capital Conservation Buffer (CCB) at 1.875% of RWA in 2018 and 2.5% of RWA from 2019 onwards;
- Counter-cyclical Buffer (CCyB) is dependent on UK economic conditions, and will be set at a maximum of 2.5% of RWA. CoLC assumes CCyB at a conservative 2% all through.

The following extracts show the treatment for capital in 12 different cases, reproduced with permission from the Basel CRR document.

1. Government securities/exposure (0%)

(d) the institutional protection scheme conducts its own risk review which is communicated to the individual members;

(e) the institutional protection scheme draws up and publishes on an annual basis, a consolidated report comprising the balance sheet, the profit-and-loss account, the situation report and the risk report, concerning the institutional protection scheme as a whole, or a report comprising the aggregated balance sheet, the aggregated profit-and-loss account, the situation report and the risk report, concerning the institutional protection scheme as a whole;

(f) members of the institutional protection scheme are obliged to give advance notice of at least 24 months if they wish to end the institutional protection scheme;

(g) the multiple use of elements eligible for the calculation of own funds (hereinafter referred to as "multiple gearing") as well as any inappropriate creation of own funds between the members of the institutional protection scheme shall be eliminated;

(h) the institutional protection scheme shall be based on a broad membership of credit institutions of a predominantly homogeneous business profile;

(i) the adequacy of the systems referred to in points (c) and (d) is approved and monitored at regular intervals by the relevant competent authorities.

Where the institution, in accordance with this paragraph, decides not to apply the requirements of paragraph 1, it may assign a risk weight of 0 %.

Table 1

Credit quality step	1	2	3	4	5	6
Risk weight	0 %	20 %	50 %	100 %	100 %	150 %

3. Exposures to the ECB shall be assigned a 0 % risk weight.

4. Exposures to Member States' central governments, and central banks denominated and funded in the domestic currency of that central government and central bank shall be assigned a risk weight of 0 %.

6. For exposures indicated in Article 495(2):

(a) in 2018 the risk weight applied to the exposure values shall be 20 % of the risk weight assigned to these exposures in accordance with paragraph 2;

(b) in 2019 the risk weight applied to the exposure values shall be 50 % of the risk weight assigned to these exposures in accordance with paragraph 2;

(c) in 2020 and onwards the risk weight applied to the exposure values shall be 100 % of the risk weight assigned to these exposures in accordance with paragraph 2.

7. When the competent authorities of a third country which apply supervisory and regulatory arrangements at least equivalent to those applied in the Union assign a risk weight which is lower than that indicated in paragraphs 1 and 2 to exposures to their central government and central bank denominated and funded in the domestic currency, institutions may risk weight such exposures in the same manner.

Section 2

Risk weights

Article 114

Exposures to central governments or central banks

1. Exposures to central governments and central banks shall be assigned a 100 % risk weight, unless the treatments set out in paragraphs 2 to 7 apply.

2. Exposures to central governments and central banks for which a credit assessment by a nominated ECAI is available shall be assigned a risk weight in accordance with Table 1 which corresponds to the credit assessment of the ECAI in accordance with Article 136.

For the purposes of this paragraph, the Commission may adopt, by way of implementing acts, and subject to the examination procedure referred to in Article 464(2), a decision as to whether a third country applies supervisory and regulatory arrangements at least equivalent to those applied in the Union. In the absence of such a decision, until 1 January 2015, institutions may continue to apply the treatment set out in this paragraph to the exposures to the central government or central bank of the third country where the relevant competent authorities had approved the third country as eligible for that treatment before 1 January 2014.

2. Start-up loan, Unsecured term loan, Term loan secured against collateral other than immovable property, Property bridge finance, Invoice finance, Fixed assets (everything else: 100%)

Article 113

Calculation of risk-weighted exposure amounts

1.   To calculate risk-weighted exposure amounts, risk weights shall be applied to all exposures, unless deducted from own funds, in accordance with the provisions of Section 2. The application of risk weights shall be based on the exposure class to which the exposure is assigned and, to the extent specified in Section 2, its credit quality. Credit quality may be determined by reference to the credit assessments of ECAIs or the credit assessments of export credit agencies in accordance with Section 3.

2.   For the purposes of applying a risk weight, as referred to in paragraph 1, the exposure value shall be multiplied by the risk weight specified or determined in accordance with Section 2.

3.   Where an exposure is subject to credit protection the risk weight applicable to that item may be amended in accordance with Chapter 4.

4.   Risk-weighted exposure amounts for securitised exposures shall be calculated in accordance with Chapter 5.

5.   Exposures for which no calculation is provided in Section 2 shall be assigned a risk-weight of 100 %.

6.   With the exception of exposures giving rise to Common Equity Tier 1, Additional Tier 1 or Tier 2 items, an institution may, subject to the prior approval of the competent authorities, decide not to apply the requirements of paragraph 1 of this Article to the exposures of that institution to a counterparty which is its parent undertaking, its subsidiary, a subsidiary of its parent undertaking or an undertaking linked by a relationship within the meaning of Article 12(1) of Directive 83/349/EEC.

the institution;

(e) there is no current or foreseen material practical or legal impediment to the prompt transfer of own funds or repayment of liabilities from the counterparty to the institution.

Where the institution, in accordance with this paragraph, is authorised not to apply the requirements of paragraph 1, it may assign a risk weight of 0 %.

7.   With the exception of exposures giving rise to Common Equity Tier 1, Additional Tier 1 and Tier 2 items, institutions may, subject to the prior permission of the competent authorities, not apply the requirements of paragraph 1 of this Article to exposures to counterparties with which the institution has entered into an institutional protection scheme that is a contractual or statutory liability arrangement which protects those institutions and in particular ensures their liquidity and solvency to avoid bankruptcy where necessary. Competent authorities are empowered to grant permission if the following conditions are fulfilled:

(a) the requirements set out in points (a), (d) and (e) of paragraph 6 are met;

(b) the arrangements ensure that the institutional protection scheme is able to grant support necessary under its commitment from funds readily available to it;

(c) the institutional protection scheme disposes of suitable and uniformly stipulated systems for the monitoring and classification of risk, which gives a complete overview of the risk situations of all the individual members and the institutional protection scheme as a whole, with corresponding possibilities to take influence; those systems shall suitably monitor defaulted exposures in accordance with Article 178(1);

3. Deposit held with commercial banks (rating and maturity dependent, 20%/50%) https://www.fca.org.uk/publication/archive/fsa-ecais-standardised.pdf

Article 120

Exposures to rated institutions

1. Exposures to institutions with a residual maturity of more than three months for which a credit assessment by a nominated ECAI is available shall be assigned a risk weight in accordance with Table 3 which corresponds to the credit assessment of the ECAI in accordance with Article 136.

Table 3

Credit quality step	1	2	3	4	5	6
Risk weight	20 %	50 %	50 %	100 %	100 %	150 %

2. Exposures to an institution of up to three months residual maturity for which a credit assessment by a nominated ECAI is available shall be assigned a risk-weight in accordance with Table 4 which corresponds to the credit assessment of the ECAI in accordance with Article 136:

Table 4

Credit quality step	1	2	3	4	5	6
Risk weight	20 %	20 %	20 %	50 %	50 %	150 %

(¹) OJ L 250, 2.10.2003, p. 10.

ment for short-term exposures shall not be used and all unrated short-term claims shall be assigned the same risk weight as that applied by the specific short-term assessment.

Article 121

Exposures to unrated institutions

1. Exposures to institutions for which a credit assessment by a nominated ECAI is not available shall be assigned a risk weight in accordance with the credit quality step to which exposures to the central government of the jurisdiction in which the institution is incorporated are assigned in accordance with Table 5.

Table 5

Credit quality step to which central government is assigned	1	2	3	4	5	6
Risk weight of exposure	20 %	50 %	100 %	100 %	100 %	150 %

2. For exposures to unrated institutions incorporated in countries where the central government is unrated, the risk weight shall be 100 %.

3. For exposures to unrated institutions with an original effective maturity of three months or less, the risk weight shall be 20 %.

4. Retail unsecured exposure (personal loan, credit card) – 75%
5. Retail/commercial mortgage exposure – 35% and 50%

4.   Notwithstanding paragraphs 2 and 3, for trade finance exposures referred to in point (b) of the second subparagraph of Article 162(3) to unrated institutions, the risk weight shall be 50 % and where the residual maturity of these trade finance exposures to unrated institutions is three months or less, the risk weight shall be 20 %.

Article 122

Exposures to corporates

1.   Exposures for which a credit assessment by a nominated ECAI is available shall be assigned a risk weight in accordance with Table 6 which corresponds to the credit assessment of the ECAI in accordance with Article 136.

Table 6

Credit quality step	1	2	3	4	5	6
Risk weight	20 %	50 %	100 %	100 %	150 %	150 %

2.   Exposures for which such a credit assessment is not available shall be assigned a 100 % risk weight or the risk weight of exposures to the central government of the jurisdiction in which the corporate is incorporated, whichever is the higher.

Article 123

Retail exposures

Exposures that comply with the following criteria shall be assigned a risk weight of 75 %:

(a) the exposure shall be either to a natural person or persons, or to a small or medium-sized enterprise (SME);

(b) the exposure shall be one of a significant number of exposures with similar characteristics such that the risks associated with such lending are substantially reduced;

(c) the total amount owed to the institution and parent undertakings and its subsidiaries, including any exposure in default, by the obligor client or group of connected clients, but excluding exposures fully and completely secured on residential property collateral that have been assigned to the exposure class laid down in point (i) of Article 112, shall not, to the knowledge of the institution, exceed EUR 1 million. The institution shall take reasonable steps to acquire this knowledge.

Securities shall not be eligible for the retail exposure class.

Exposures that do not comply with the criteria referred to in points (a) to (c) of the first subparagraph shall not be eligible for the retail exposures class.

The present value of retail minimum lease payments is eligible for the retail exposure class.

Article 124

Exposures secured by mortgages on immovable property

1.   An exposure or any part of an exposure fully secured by mortgage on immovable property shall be assigned a risk weight of 100 %, where the conditions under Article 125 or 126 are not met, except for any part of the exposure which is assigned to another exposure class. The part of the exposure that exceeds the mortgage value of the immovable property shall be assigned the risk weight applicable to the unsecured exposures of the counterparty involved.

The part of an exposure treated as fully secured by immovable property shall not be higher than the pledged amount of the market value or in those Member States that have laid down rigorous criteria for the assessment of the mortgage lending value in statutory or regulatory provisions, the mortgage lending value of the property in question.

2.   Based on the data collected under Article 101, and any other relevant indicators, the competent authorities shall periodically, and at least annually, assess whether the risk-weight of 35 % for exposures secured by mortgages on residential property referred to in Article 125 and the risk weight of 50 % for exposures secured on commercial immovable property referred to in Article 126 located in their territory are appropriately based on:

(a) the loss experience of exposures secured by immovable property;

(b) forward-looking immovable property markets developments;

Competent authorities may set a higher risk weight or stricter criteria than those set out in Article 125(2) and Article 126(2), where appropriate, on the basis of financial stability considerations.

For exposures secured by mortgages on residential property, the competent authority shall set the risk weight at a percentage from 35 % through 150 %.

For exposures secured on commercial immovable property, the competent authority shall set the risk weight at a percentage from 50 % through 150 %.

6. SME supporting factor – 0.7619

5.   The competent authorities may, after consulting EBA, waive the application of point (b) of paragraph 1 to institutions provided that all the requirements for the IRB Approach set out in Part Three, Title II, Chapter 3, Section 6 or the qualifying criteria for the use of the Advanced Measurement Approach set out in Part Three, Title III, Chapter 4, as applicable, are met.

6.   By 1 January 2017, the Commission shall submit a report to the European Parliament and the Council on whether it is appropriate to extend the application of the Basel I floor beyond 31 December 2017 to ensure that there is a backstop to internal models, taking into account international developments and internationally agreed standards. That report shall be accompanied by a legislative proposal if appropriate.

Article 501

Capital requirements deduction for credit risk on exposures to SMEs

1.   Capital requirements for credit risk on exposures to SMEs shall be multiplied by the factor 0,7619.

2.   For the purpose of this Article:

(a) the exposure shall be included either in the retail or in the corporates or secured by mortgages on immovable property classes. Exposures in default shall be excluded;

(b) an SME is defined in accordance with Commission Recommendation 2003/361/EC of 6 May 2003 concerning the definition of micro, small and medium-sized enterprises ([1]). Among the criteria listed in Article 2 of the Annex to that Recommendation only the annual turnover shall be taken into account;

(c) the total amount owed to the institution and parent undertakings and its subsidiaries, including any exposure in default, by the obligor client or group of connected clients, but excluding claims or contingent claims secured on residential property collateral, shall not, to the knowledge of the institution, exceed EUR 1,5 million. The institution shall take reasonable steps to acquire such knowledge.

3.   Institutions shall report to competent authorities every three months on the total amount of exposures to SMEs calculated in accordance with paragraph 2.

4.   The Commission shall, by 28 June 2016, report on the impact of the own funds requirements laid down in this Regulation on lending to SMEs and natural persons and shall submit that report to the European Parliament and to the Council, together with a legislative proposal, if appropriate.

5.   For the purpose of paragraph 4, EBA shall report on the following to the Commission:

(a) an analysis of the evolution of the lending trends and conditions for SMEs over the period referred to in paragraph 4;

___
([1]) OJ L 124, 20.5.2003, p. 36.

(b) an analysis of effective riskiness of Union SMEs over a full economic cycle;

(c) the consistency of own funds requirements laid down in this Regulation for credit risk on exposures to SMEs with the outcomes of the analysis under points (a) and (b).

TITLE II

REPORTS AND REVIEWS

Article 502

Cyclicality of capital requirements

The Commission, in cooperation with EBA, ESRB and the Member States, and taking into account the opinion of the ECB, shall periodically monitor whether this Regulation taken as a whole, together with Directive 2013/36/EU, has significant effects on the economic cycle and, in the light of that examination, shall consider whether any remedial measures are justified.

By 31 December 2013, EBA shall report to the Commission on whether, and if so how, methodologies of institutions under the IRB Approach should converge with a view to more comparable capital requirements while mitigating pro-cyclicality.

Based on that analysis and taking into account the opinion of the ECB, the Commission shall draw up a biennial report and submit it to the European Parliament and to the Council, together with any appropriate proposals. Contributions from credit taking and credit lending parties shall be adequately acknowledged when the report is drawn up.

By 31 December 2014, the Commission shall review, and report on, the application of Article 33(1)(c) and shall submit that report to the European Parliament and the Council, together with a legislative proposal, if appropriate.

With respect to the potential deletion of Article 33(1)(c) and its potential application at the Union level, the review shall in particular ensure that sufficient safeguards are in place to ensure financial stability in all Member States.

Article 503

Own funds requirements for exposures in the form of covered bonds

1.   The Commission shall, by 31 December 2014, after consulting EBA, report to the European Parliament and to the Council, together with any appropriate proposals, on whether the risk weights laid down in Article 129 and the own funds requirements for specific risk in Article 336(3) are adequate for all the instruments that qualify for these treatments and whether the criteria in Article 129 are appropriate.

7. Eligibility for applying 35% risk weight to Retail mortgage (owner occupied or BTL where the valuation of the property and the credit quality of the borrower are not intricately linked)

Within these ranges, the higher risk weight shall be set based on loss experience and taking into account forward-looking markets developments and financial stability considerations. Where the assessment demonstrates that the risk weights set out in Article 125(2) and Article 126(2) do not reflect the actual risks related to one or more property segments of such exposures, fully secured by mortgages on residential property or on commercial immovable property located in one or more parts of its territory, the competent authorities shall set, for those property segments of exposures, a higher risk weight corresponding to the actual risks.

The competent authorities shall consult EBA on the adjustments to the risk weights and criteria applied, which will be calculated in accordance with the criteria set out in this paragraph as specified by the regulatory technical standards referred to in paragraph 4 of this Article. EBA shall publish the risk weights and criteria that the competent authorities set for exposures referred to in Articles 125, 126 and 199(1)(a).

3. When competent authorities set a higher risk weight or stricter criteria, institutions shall have a 6-month transitional period to apply the new risk weight.

4. EBA shall develop draft regulatory technical standards to specify:

(a) the rigorous criteria for the assessment of the mortgage lending value referred to in paragraph 1;

(b) the conditions referred to in paragraph 2 that competent authorities shall take into account when determining higher risk-weights, in particular the term of "financial stability considerations".

EBA shall submit those draft regulatory technical standards to the Commission by 31 December 2014.

Power is delegated to the Commission to adopt the regulatory technical standards referred to in the first subparagraph in accordance with Articles 10 to 14 of Regulation (EU) No 1093/2010.

5. The institutions of one Member State shall apply the risk-weights and criteria that have been determined by the competent authorities of another Member State to exposures secured by mortgages on commercial and residential property located in that Member State.

Article 125

Exposures fully and completely secured by mortgages on residential property

1. Unless otherwise decided by the competent authorities in accordance with Article 124(2), exposures fully and completely secured by mortgages on residential property shall be treated as follows:

(a) exposures or any part of an exposure fully and completely secured by mortgages on residential property which is or shall be occupied or let by the owner, or the beneficial owner in the case of personal investment companies, shall be assigned a risk weight of 35 %;

(b) exposures to a tenant under a property leasing transaction concerning residential property under which the institution is the lessor and the tenant has an option to purchase, shall be assigned a risk weight of 35 % provided that the exposure of the institution is fully and completely secured by its ownership of the property.

2. Institutions shall consider an exposure or any part of an exposure as fully and completely secured for the purposes of paragraph 1 only if the following conditions are met:

(a) the value of the property shall not materially depend upon the credit quality of the borrower. Institutions may exclude situations where purely macro-economic factors affect both the value of the property and the performance of the borrower from their determination of the materiality of such dependence;

(b) the risk of the borrower shall not materially depend upon the performance of the underlying property or project, but on the underlying capacity of the borrower to repay the debt from other sources, and as a consequence, the repayment of the facility shall not materially depend on any cash flow generated by the underlying property serving as collateral. For those other sources, institutions shall determine maximum loan-to-income ratios as part of their lending policy and obtain suitable evidence of the relevant income when granting the loan;

(c) the requirements set out in Article 208 and the valuation rules set out in Article 229(1) are met;

(d) unless otherwise determined under Article 124(2), the part of the loan to which the 35 % risk weight is assigned does not exceed 80 % of the market value of the property in question or 80 % of the mortgage lending value of the property in question in those Member States that have laid down rigorous criteria for the assessment of the mortgage lending value in statutory or regulatory provisions.

8. Eligibility for applying 50% risk weight to commercial mortgage (valuation of the property and credit quality of the borrower are not intricately linked)

3. Institutions may derogate from point (b) of paragraph 2 for exposures fully and completely secured by mortgages on residential property which is situated within the territory of a Member State, where the competent authority of that Member State has published evidence showing that a well-developed and long-established residential property market is present in that territory with loss rates which do not exceed the following limits:

(a) losses stemming from lending collateralised by residential property up to 80 % of the market value or 80 % of the mortgage lending value, unless otherwise decided under Article 124(2), do not exceed 0,3 % of the outstanding loans collateralised by residential property in any given year;

(b) overall losses stemming from lending collateralised by residential property do not exceed 0,5 % of the outstanding loans collateralised by residential property in any given year.

4. Where either of the limits referred to in paragraph 3 is not satisfied in a given year, the eligibility to use paragraph 3 shall cease and the condition contained in point (b) of paragraph 2 shall apply until the conditions in paragraph 3 are satisfied in a subsequent year.

Article 126

Exposures fully and completely secured by mortgages on commercial immovable property

1. Unless otherwise decided by the competent authorities in accordance with Article 124(2), exposures fully and completely secured by mortgages on commercial immovable property shall be treated as follows:

(a) exposures or any part of an exposure fully and completely secured by mortgages on offices or other commercial premises may be assigned a risk weight of 50 %;

(b) exposures related to property leasing transactions concerning offices or other commercial premises under which the institution is the lessor and the tenant has an option to purchase may be assigned a risk weight of 50 % provided that the exposure of the institution is fully and completely secured by its ownership of the property.

2. Institutions shall consider an exposure or any part of an exposure as fully and completely secured for the purposes of paragraph 1 only if the following conditions are met:

(a) the value of the property shall not materially depend upon the credit quality of the borrower. Institutions may exclude situations where purely macro-economic factors affect both the value of the property and the performance of the borrower from their determination of the materiality of such dependence;

(b) the risk of the borrower shall not materially depend upon the performance of the underlying property or project, but on the underlying capacity of the borrower to repay the debt from other sources, and as a consequence, the repayment of the facility shall not materially depend on any cash flow generated by the underlying property serving as collateral;

(c) the requirements set out in Article 208 and the valuation rules set out in Article 229(1) are met;

(d) the 50 % risk weight unless otherwise provided under Article 124(2) shall be assigned to the part of the loan that does not exceed 50 % of the market value of the property or 60 % of the mortgage lending value unless otherwise provided under Article 124(2) of the property in question in those Member States that have laid down rigorous criteria for the assessment of the mortgage lending value in statutory or regulatory provisions.

3. Institutions may derogate from point (b) of paragraph 2 for exposures fully and completely secured by mortgages on commercial immovable property which is situated within the territory of a Member State, where the competent authority of that Member State has published evidence showing that a well-developed and long-established commercial immovable property market is present in that territory with loss rates which do not exceed the following limits:

(a) losses stemming from lending collateralised by commercial immovable property up to 50 % of the market value or 60 % of the mortgage lending value, unless otherwise determined under Article 124(2), do not exceed 0,3 % of the outstanding loans collateralised by commercial immovable property;

(b) overall losses stemming from lending collateralised by commercial immovable property do not exceed 0,5 % of the outstanding loans collateralised by commercial immovable property.

4. Where either of the limits referred to in paragraph 3 is not satisfied in a given year, the eligibility to use paragraph 3 shall cease and the condition contained in point (b) of paragraph 2 shall apply until the conditions in paragraph 3 are satisfied in a subsequent year.

9. NPL at 150% risk weight

Article 127

Exposures in default

1.   The unsecured part of any item where the obligor has defaulted in accordance with Article 178, or in the case of retail exposures, the unsecured part of any credit facility which has defaulted in accordance with Article 178 shall be assigned a risk weight of:

(a) 150 %, where specific credit risk adjustments are less than 20 % of the unsecured part of the exposure value if these specific credit risk adjustments were not applied;

(b) 100 %, where specific credit risk adjustments are no less than 20 % of the unsecured part of the exposure value if these specific credit risk adjustments were not applied.

2.   For the purpose of determining the secured part of the past due item, eligible collateral and guarantees shall be those eligible for credit risk mitigation purposes under Chapter 4.

3.   The exposure value remaining after specific credit risk adjustments of exposures fully and completely secured by mortgages on residential property in accordance with Article 125 shall be assigned a risk weight of 100 % if a default has occurred in accordance with Article 178.

4.   The exposure value remaining after specific credit risk adjustments of exposures fully and completely secured by mortgages on commercial immovable property in accordance with Article 126 shall be assigned a risk weight of 100 % if a default has occurred in accordance with Article 178.

Article 128

Items associated with particular high risk

1.   Institutions shall assign a 150 % risk weight to exposures, including exposures in the form of shares or units in a CIU that are associated with particularly high risks, where appropriate.

2.   Exposures with particularly high risks shall include any of the following exposures:

(a) investments in venture capital firms;

(b) investments in AIFs as defined in Article 4(1)(a) of Directive 2011/61/EU except where the mandate of the fund does not allow a leverage higher than that required under Article 51(3) of Directive 2009/65/EC;

(c) investments in private equity;

(d) speculative immovable property financing.

3.   When assessing whether an exposure other than exposures referred to in paragraph 2 is associated with particularly high risks, institutions shall take into account the following risk characteristics:

(a) there is a high risk of loss as a result of a default of the obligor;

(b) it is impossible to assess adequately whether the exposure falls under point (a).

EBA shall issue guidelines specifying which types of exposures are associated with particularly high risk and under which circumstances.

Those guidelines shall be adopted in accordance with Article 16 of Regulation (EU) No 1093/2010.

Article 129

Exposures in the form of covered bonds

1.   To be eligible for the preferential treatment set out in paragraphs 4 and 5, bonds as referred to in Article 52(4) of Directive 2009/65/EC (covered bonds) shall meet the requirements set out in paragraph 7 and shall be collateralised by any of the following eligible assets:

(a) exposures to or guaranteed by central governments, the ESCB central banks, public sector entities, regional governments or local authorities in the Union;

(b) exposures to or guaranteed by third country central governments, third-country central banks, multilateral development banks, international organisations that qualify for the credit quality step 1 as set out in this Chapter, and exposures to or guaranteed by third-country public sector entities, third-country regional governments or third-country local authorities that are risk weighted as exposures to institutions or central governments and central banks in accordance with Article 115(1) or (2), or Article 116(1), (2) or (4) respectively and that qualify for the credit quality step 1 as set out in this Chapter, and exposures within the meaning of this point that qualify as a minimum for the credit quality step 2 as set out in this Chapter, provided that they do not exceed 20 % of the nominal amount of outstanding covered bonds of the issuing institutions;

(c) exposures to institutions that qualify for the credit quality step 1 as set out in this Chapter. The total exposure of this kind shall not exceed 15 % of the nominal amount of outstanding covered bonds of the issuing institution. Exposures to institutions in the Union with a maturity not exceeding 100 days shall not be comprised by the step 1 requirement but those institutions shall as a minimum qualify for credit quality step 2 as set out in this Chapter;

10. Off-balance-sheet items (Credit Conversion Factor or CCF of 20% or 50%)

(d) for other credit lines, note issuance facilities (NIFs), and revolving underwriting facilities (RUFs), a conversion factor of 75 % shall apply.

Institutions which meet the requirements for the use of own estimates of conversion factors as specified in Section 6 may use their own estimates of conversion factors across different product types as mentioned in points (a) to (d), subject to permission of the competent authorities.

9. Where a commitment refers to the extension of another commitment, the lower of the two conversion factors associated with the individual commitment shall be used.

10. For all off-balance sheet items other than those mentioned in paragraphs 1 to 8, the exposure value shall be the following percentage of its value:

(a) 100 % if it is a full risk item;

(b) 50 % if it is a medium-risk item;

(c) 20 % if it is a medium/low-risk item;

(d) 0 % if it is a low-risk item.

For the purposes of this paragraph the off-balance sheet items shall be assigned to risk categories as indicated in Annex I.

Section 6

Requirements for the IRB approach

Sub-Section 1

Rating systems

Article 169

General principles

1. Where an institution uses multiple rating systems, the rationale for assigning an obligor or a transaction to a rating system shall be documented and applied in a manner that appropriately reflects the level of risk.

2. Assignment criteria and processes shall be periodically reviewed to determine whether they remain appropriate for the current portfolio and external conditions.

3. Where an institution uses direct estimates of risk parameters for individual obligors or exposures these may be seen as estimates assigned to grades on a continuous rating scale.

Article 170

11. Risk classification for CCF

2. Medium risk:

(a) trade finance off-balance sheet items, namely documentary credits issued or confirmed (see also "Medium/low risk");

(b) other off-balance sheet items:

   (i) shipping guarantees, customs and tax bonds;

   (ii) undrawn credit facilities (agreements to lend, purchase securities, provide guarantees or acceptance facilities) with an original maturity of more than one year;

   (iii) note issuance facilities (NIFs) and revolving underwriting facilities (RUFs);

   (iv) other items also carrying medium risk and as communicated to EBA.

3. Medium/low risk:

(a) trade finance off-balance sheet items:

   (i) documentary credits in which underlying shipment acts as collateral and other self-liquidating transactions;

   (ii) warranties (including tender and performance bonds and associated advance payment and retention guarantees) and guarantees not having the character of credit substitutes;

   (iii) irrevocable standby letters of credit not having the character of credit substitutes;

(b) other off-balance sheet items:

   (i) undrawn credit facilities which comprise agreements to lend, purchase securities, provide guarantees or acceptance facilities with an original maturity of up to and including one year which may not be cancelled unconditionally at any time without notice or that do not effectively provide for automatic cancellation due to deterioration in a borrower's creditworthiness;

12. Operational risk

(b) the criteria set out in Article 320 and the standards set out in Articles 321 and 322 are fulfilled for the part of activities covered by the Standardised Approach and the Advanced Measurement Approaches respectively.

3. For institutions that want to use an Advanced Measurement Approach in combination with either the Basic Indicator Approach or the Standardised Approach competent authorities shall impose the following additional conditions for granting permission:

(a) on the date of implementation of an Advanced Measurement Approach, a significant part of the institution's operational risks are captured by that Approach;

(b) the institution takes a commitment to apply the Advanced Measurement Approach across a material part of its operations within a time schedule that was submitted to and approved by its competent authorities.

4. An institution may request permission from a competent authority to use a combination of the Basic Indicator Approach and the Standardised Approach only in exceptional circumstances such as the recent acquisition of new business which may require a transitional period for the application of the Standardised Approach.

A competent authority shall grant such permission only where the institution has committed to apply the Standardised Approach within a time schedule that was submitted to and approved by the competent authority.

5. EBA shall develop draft regulatory technical standards to specify the following:

(a) the conditions that competent authorities shall use when assessing the methodology referred to in point (a) of paragraph 2;

(b) the conditions that the competent authorities shall use when deciding whether to impose the additional conditions referred to in paragraph 3.

EBA shall submit those draft regulatory technical standards to the Commission by 31 December 2016.

Power is delegated to the Commission to adopt the regulatory technical standards referred to in the first subparagraph in accordance with Articles 10 to 14 of Regulation (EU) No 1093/2010.

CHAPTER 2

Basic Indicator Approach

Article 315

Own funds requirement

1. Under the Basic Indicator Approach, the own funds requirement for operational risk is equal to 15 % of the average over three years of the relevant indicator as set out in Article 316.

Institutions shall calculate the average over three years of the relevant indicator on the basis of the last three twelve-monthly observations at the end of the financial year. When audited figures are not available, institutions may use business estimates.

2. Where an institution has been in operation for less than three years it may use forward-looking business estimates in calculating the relevant indicator, provided that it starts using historical data as soon as it is available.

3. Where an institution can prove to its competent authority that, due to a merger, an acquisition or a disposal of entities or activities, using a three year average to calculate the relevant indicator would lead to a biased estimation for the own funds requirement for operational risk, the competent authority may permit the institution to amend the calculation in a way that would take into account such events and shall duly inform EBA thereof. In such circumstances, the competent authority may, on its own initiative, also require an institution to amend the calculation.

4. Where for any given observation, the relevant indicator is negative or equal to zero, institutions shall not take into account this figure in the calculation of the average over three years. Institutions shall calculate the average over three years as the sum of positive figures divided by the number of positive figures.

Article 316

Relevant indicator

1. For institutions applying accounting standards established by Directive 86/635/EEC, based on the accounting categories for the profit and loss account of institutions under Article 27 of that Directive, the relevant indicator is the sum of the elements listed in Table 1 of this paragraph. Institutions shall include each element in the sum with its positive or negative sign.

Table 1

1	Interest receivable and similar income
2	Interest payable and similar charges
3	Income from shares and other variable/fixed-yield securities
4	Commissions/fees receivable
5	Commissions/fees payable
6	Net profit or net loss on financial operations
7	Other operating income

CONCLUSIONS

Capital management is a critical part of managing a bank. Indeed, to suggest it is "risk management" is to somehow underplay its importance; capital along with liquidity is the lifeblood of banking and must be managed on a conservative basis, with a going concern outlook throughout the economic cycle.

This chapter has presented the role of capital management within the business of banking. The ICAAP process has been designed to ensure that long-term through-the-cycle capital planning is an inherent part of banking, but with any regulatory supervision process it tends to be downgraded to a bureaucratic "tick-box" exercise. This is an undesirable route for any bank to take.

Risk is a significant aspect of business activities in a market economy. As risk taking or transformation of risks constitutes a major characteristic of the banking business, it is especially important for banks to address risk management issues. The necessity from a business perspective has arisen from developments on the financial markets and the increasing complexity of the banking business. These circumstances call for functioning systems that support the limitation and control of risk exposure. The implementation of an ICAAP is not rooted exclusively in regulatory considerations; rather it is in the best interests of all stakeholders of an institution. The owners are inherently interested in the continued existence of the bank as they expect a reasonable return on their investment and wish to avoid capital losses. But certainly, a bank's employees, customers, and lenders also have an interest in its survival. The individual interests of these groups are not mutually exclusive; in fact, all stakeholders should be interested in ensuring that the institution does not take on risk positions that might endanger its continued existence. The main motive for the ICAAP can therefore be seen in ensuring a viable risk position by dealing with risks in the appropriate manner. In particular, it is important to detect developments that may endanger the institution as early as possible in order for the bank to take suitable management action in response. In this regard, delivering an ICAAP serves the interests of all the internal and external stakeholders of the bank.

This raises two issues: first, when calculating the bank's risk-bearing capacity, it is necessary to determine the extent to which a bank can afford to take certain risks at all. For this purpose, the bank needs to ensure that the available risk coverage capital is sufficient at all times to cover the risks taken. Second, the bank must review the extent to which risks are worth assuming; that is, it is necessary to analyse the opportunities arising from risk taking (evaluation of the risk/return ratio, typically a risk-adjusted measure such as RARoC). The main objective of the ICAAP is to confirm the bank's risk-bearing capacity. Comprehensive risk/return management follows as a next step. The ICAAP thus constitutes a comprehensive package that delivers significant benefits from a business perspective.

BIBLIOGRAPHY

BIS Enhancements to the Basel II framework, http://www.bis.org/publ/bcbs157.pdf

BIS Principles for sound stress testing practices and supervision, http://www.bis.org/publ/bcbs155.pdf

Choudhry, M. (2012). *The Principles of Banking*, Singapore: John Wiley & Sons Ltd., Chapters 2, 16, 17.

Churm and Radia (2012). "The Funding for Lending Scheme", *Bank of England Quarterly Bulletin*, Q4. Available at http://www.bankofengland.co.uk/publications/Documents/quarterlybulletin/qb120401.pdf

De La Mora, Matten and Barfield (2010). "Capital management in banking: the way forward", *The Journal*, PWC, December. Available at http://www.pwc.com/gx/en/banking-capital-markets/pdf/capital-management.pdf

EBA (2013). *Guidelines on retail deposits*. Available at http://www.eba.europa.eu/regulation-and-policy/liquidity-risk/guidelines-on-retail-deposits-subject-to-higher-outflows-for-the-purposes-of-liquidity-reporting

Freer, J. (2011). "Capital management: banking's trickiest juggling act", *Bank Director*, 3 June. Available at: www.bankdirector.com/magazine/archives/4th-quarter-2009/capital-management-bankings-trickiest-juggling-act

Gropp, R. and Heider, F. (2009). *The determinants of bank capital structure*. Available at www.ecb.europa.eu/pub/pdf/scpwps/ecbwp1096.pdf

Marshall, P. (2012). *Capital management in stressful times: taking a holistic approach*. Available at http://businessfinancemag.com/article/capital-management-stressful-times-taking-holistic-approach-0106

Chapter

16

MANAGING OPERATIONAL RISK

In this chapter we introduce the concept of operational risk management in banking. Operational risk is as old as banking, but its management has only recently been given some of the focus afforded to credit, interest rate, market, and liquidity risk due to regulator attention. In the past, operational risk was often simply placed in the same category as credit risk, despite it being different conceptually.

Measurement, modelling, and capital allocation associated with operational risk are challenging and are the topic of much debate. However, operational risk management continues to grow and be refined as a discipline in the face of losses in an increasingly complex banking environment driven by globalisation, regulation, and technology.

As with other risks, the Board of Directors should approve appropriate limits for specific and overall operational risk in the risk appetite statement.

OPERATIONAL RISK OVERVIEW

Whether huge and headline making or relatively small, banks suffer losses regularly from risks outside of credit, interest rates, and markets. In the 1990s, once the Basel Committee had determined that operational risk should be formalised as a concept in Basel II – with capital allocated against it – market participants made attempts to create a working definition. For many, operational risk was simply "other" risk, or a residual category for difficult to measure risk. Presently, most accept the Basel II definition of "the risk of direct or indirect loss resulting from inadequate or failed internal processes, people and systems or from external events". For regulatory capital purposes, this includes legal risk but not reputational and strategic risks.

Operational risk is a test of management and corporate governance and can stem from:

- Internal processes: must have clear, orderly, and complete processes to meet responsibilities to clients, manage risk, control payments, protect against fraud, and comply with regulation;
- People: must communicate and enforce rules, minimise conflicts of interest, and set proper incentives to maintain an ethical culture;
- Systems: must have adequate technology resources that are backed up and protected from security breaches;
- External events: must know and monitor clients to guard against fraud and protect people and facilities.

Operational risk management encompasses quality, change, and business continuity management disciplines, and also crisis management in adverse situations. While not included in the regulatory definition of operational risk or capital allocation, operational risk failings affect reputation, client satisfaction, business and earnings volatility, as well as shareholder value.

Basel II specified seven Level 1 categories of operational risk: Internal Fraud; External Fraud; Employment Practices and Workplace Safety; Clients, Products, and Business Practices; Damage to Physical Assets, Business Disruption, and System Failures; and Execution, Delivery, and Process Management. These are further broken down into Level 2 and Level 3 categories. Examples of actual operational risk failures are shown in Figure 16.1.

Type	Category	Description	Bank	Year
Internal Fraud	Fraud/unauthorised trading	Derivatives	Barings	1995
	Fraud/unauthorised trading	US Treasury bonds	Daiwa	1995
	Fraud/unauthorised trading	Commodities	Sumitomo	1996
	Fraud/unauthorised trading	Foreign exchange	Allied Irish	2002
	Fraud/unauthorised trading	Foreign exchange	National Australia Bank	2004
	Fraud/unauthorised trading	Proprietary trading	Société Générale	2008
	Fraud/unauthorised trading	Exchange traded funds	UBS	2011
External Fraud	Accounting fraud/ Parmalat	Overstated earnings	Numerous	2003
	Accounting fraud/ World Com	Overstated earnings	Numerous	2004
	Accounting fraud/ Enron	Overstated earnings	Numerous	2004
Employment	Discrimination	Racial bias	Merrill Lynch	2013
Business Practices	Mutual funds trading abuse	Late trading	Bank of America	2003
	Market manipulation	European Treasury bonds	Citi	2006
	ABS mis-selling	CDOs	Goldman Sachs	2007
	Libor rigging	Collusion	Numerous	2008
	Discriminatory lending	Racial bias	Wells Fargo	2012
	Aid tax evasion	Inadequate reporting	Swiss banks	2013
	Swaps mis-selling	Overselling	UK banks	2013
Physical	Terrorist attack – 9/11	Disruption, destruction	Numerous	2011
Systems/ Execution	Faulty mortgage underwriting	Incomplete data, records	Numerous	2008
	Payment processing failure	No client access to funds	RBS	2012
	Trading risk controls failure	Proprietary trading	J.P. Morgan	2012
	Money laundering risk controls failure	Inadequate checks	Numerous	2013
	Accounting failure	Capital position	Bank of America	2014

Figure 16.1   Operational risk failure: types and examples

Banks extend the grouping loss events along eight business lines to create a matrix. Business lines include commercial banking, retail banking, payment and settlement, agency services, trading and sales, corporate finance, asset management, and retail brokerage. Regulators have worked with banks to map business activities to business lines to avoid distortions and arbitrage.

Unlike lending or trading, new operational risks are not acquired to build revenue and profits. Operational risks can be more difficult to foresee and cannot be diversified, sold off, or hedged in the banking market. The only potential mitigation and pricing tool is insurance, which depends on availability. While operational risk cannot be eliminated, the goal must be to keep it within acceptable limits and prevent it from surpassing potential gains. Improvement to processes is necessary and protection increased when benefits are likely to exceed costs.

When the concept of operational risk was first formulated, some banks drew on inspiration from other institutions that had extensive experience monitoring operational risk, such as the military, in building their own methodologies.

CONDUCT RISK

While not an explicit part of the Basel framework, the concept of conduct risk has gained intensive focus following the financial crisis. The OECD has published multilaterally agreed, government backed guidelines for corporate behaviour, as well as guidelines for consumer financial protection. When the UK's Financial Conduct Authority (FCA) was launched in 2013, it placed conduct risk at the centre of its agenda. While not formally defined, conduct risk is the risk that a bank's performance will result in poor outcomes for customers. From the perspective of shareholders, this could be an issue as serious as market risk because such a negative outcome could have an impact as extreme as any other risk exposure and ultimately result in the bank's collapse.

Simply stated, banks must demonstrate fair regard for the interests of their customers in order to maintain the integrity of markets.

The FCA defines drivers of conduct risk as:

• Inherent: information asymmetries, biases and heuristics, inadequate financial capability;
• Structures and behaviours: ineffective competition, culture, and incentives, conflicts of interest;
• Environmental: regulatory and policy changes, technological developments, economic and market trends.

Negative behaviours the FCA is working to eradicate include:

• Putting profits ahead of ethics and customer interests;

- Taking tick-box and legalistic approaches in dealing with customers, where compliance is limited to the letter rather than the spirit of the law;
- Treating disclosure at the point of sale as the end of responsibility to ensure a good outcome for the customer.

The FCA is striving to keep "the wrong products from ending up in the wrong hands" and avoiding "people not being able to get access to the right products, to the detriment of society".

While much of the focus of conduct risk pertains to consumers, the principles apply to wholesale business as well.

Products with high growth and margins have potentially high conduct risk, and warrant added management scrutiny.

The management of conduct risk falls to the Chief Risk Officer's (CRO) department.

OPERATIONAL RISK MEASUREMENT

The key to developing operational risk management has been the building of operational risk measurement. To achieve this, historical data is gathered and organised into an internal loss database. Consequently, operational risk measurement and therefore management has become more robust, objective, and credible. Rather than relying simply on "expert" opinion, data is measured and audited. Risk can be replicated, referred to, and compared. This leads to a greater understanding of business area processes and can further highlight the risks to back up hard decisions on resources, limits, and capital.

The data process must consider:

- Automation: makes for ease of access and consistency;
- Frequency: some data can be collected daily (for example, transaction processing) while other data (for example, fraud or losses) can only be collected in a more meaningful way on a monthly or quarterly basis, etc.;
- Detail: some types of data can be collected more easily (for example, legal fees, customer compensation, fines) than others (for example, increased funding costs for failed trades).

Once risk is identified and classified, data can be collected and modelling can begin.

OPERATIONAL RISK MEASUREMENT CONCEPTS

Data capture should include gross loss amounts, dates, and any recoveries, as well as qualitative descriptions of events and causes.

Loss definition

Gross loss is the loss from an operational risk before recoveries. The loss may be recorded for risk management purposes prior to the consequences that this will have on the financial statements. Net loss is the loss after recoveries that could be amended over time. Insurance should be treated as a special recovery category, otherwise it will obscure the measurement of the riskiness of the activity.

Loss data thresholds

Loss collection thresholds are the minimum values above which loss amounts must be collected and recorded in the internal loss database. In setting thresholds, banks must ensure that all material exposure is captured.

Thresholds are a supervisory requirement. Levels may vary across business lines, but regulators seek consistency among peer banks.

Banks generally use judgement rather than statistical evidence to set thresholds. However, the level can affect modelling of expected losses. Losses must not be disregarded only because they are relatively small, and in fact recording "near losses" can be valuable. The higher the threshold, the more difficult it may be to reconcile operational risk totals within the financial statements.

A simple test of the appropriateness of the current threshold is to calculate the total subthreshold losses as a percentage of all losses.

Date of loss allocation

Losses from operational risk often build up over time and are not identified for months or years. The Daiwa unauthorised trading scandal proceeded for more than 10 years ("incurred") before it was exposed ("reported"). Legal settlements and regulatory fines are generally incurred well after events. Recognition of loss may vary for risk measurement and financial statement purposes.

Losses may best be modelled when assigned to a wider timeframe.

Grouping of loss events

Banks sometimes group a number of losses into a single loss for purposes of efficiency. If the individual losses are small and unrelated, the group should be excluded in the modelling process to prevent distortion of the results.

Model granularity, model validation, and monitoring

Limiting the number of loss groupings makes for a critical mass of data and overall simplicity. This may be unsatisfactory if risks within groups are substantially different and independent. According to the Basel text, measurement "must be sufficiently 'granular' to capture the major drivers of operational risk affecting the shape of the tail of the loss estimates". If data is limited, external data sources or different modelling techniques are required.

As with other types of risks, methods and models must be monitored and validated on a periodic basis, and if necessary reviewed by specialist external parties. This includes:

- Integrity of inputs, assumptions, processes, and outputs;
- Independence from business lines;
- Relevance and soundness of model through testing;
- Consistency with policies approved by the Board of Directors.

The monitoring and validation process should ask whether the framework is a realistic reflection of the operational risk position and highlight any issues or deficiencies.

Distribution assumptions

Distribution assumptions form the basis of all operational risk models, and are made for severity and frequency. Banks use a range of distributions to estimate severity, including generalised power law Pareto distributions of extreme value theory, empirical distributions, and lognormal distributions.

In estimating frequency, there is a consensus among most banks that a Poisson distribution should be used, but some assume a negative binomial distribution. In using a Poisson distribution, banks must consider how capital needs could be met if loss frequency exceeds what would seem the most reasonable of conservative assumptions.

It is important not to restrict the analysis to one type of distribution, but to rather test and parameterise several based on the available data.

Banks can model "working" (expected losses/provisioning) and "non-working" (unexpected) losses separately.

Data integration

Data integration involves combining internal loss, external loss, scenario, and control factor data to quantify operational risk. Bayesian inference can be used to update loss estimates as new data is acquired. Many banks began operational risk measurement relying on external loss data, given that internal loss data was limited. As internal loss data is accumulated and its variation with other sources decreased, credibility models could be used to increase its weighting. This allows for a greater focus on bank-specific rather than industry-wide and less relevant risk data over time.

Regardless, it must be remembered that using data is backward looking and is only a guide for the future.

BASEL OPERATIONAL RISK FRAMEWORK

Based on the original Basel Accord, the Basic Indicator Approach (BIA) used a single indicator (gross income) as the proxy for overall operational risk exposure. Banks held capital for operational risk equal to the average over the previous 3 years of a fixed percentage of annual gross income ("alpha" – typically 15%). Any year that showed a negative or zero annual gross income would be excluded.

Gross income is net interest and non-interest income before deduction of operational losses.

The Basic Indicator Approach was the simplest of Basel II operational risk approaches and often used by smaller banks with limited international operations. However, all approaches are to be replaced under Basel III final form with a single standardised approach.

STANDARDISED APPROACH

In its publication of the "final chapter" of Basel III, which some commentators refer to erroneously as "Basel IV", the Basel Committee acknowledged that the Advanced Measurement Approach (AMA) for operational risk regulatory capital had not worked. Operational risk capital held by banks had been insufficient to cover operational risk losses and internal models had proved ineffective in assessing capital requirements for risks such as misconduct and inadequate systems and controls.

Thus, the *AMA and the 3 standardised methods will be replaced with a single standardised approach. From 2022 onwards*, operational risk capital will be a function of:

- A three year average of certain Business Indicators (BI), for example, interest, lease and dividends, services and financial;
- A Marginal Coefficient, which will increase as the BI rises (0.12 - 0.18);
- An Internal Loss Multiplier (based upon 15 x a bank's average historical losses over the preceding 10 years).

This approach means that the internal models developed and implemented up to now will no longer be required from 2022 onwards, when there will be a single standardised approach for operational risk regulatory capital.

QUALITATIVE INPUT AND MODEL VALIDATION

Even after extensive use of quantitative methods, qualitative analysis is important in evaluating results and validating models. After sophisticated statistical modelling and simulation, the curve and severity of low probability, high impact events need to be debated. Discussions on the estimates as to how correlated these risk events are within the bank must follow.

Quantitative methods are most straightforward in analysing high probability, low impact areas like transaction processing. These methods are less useful in assessing risks related to areas such as governance, organisation, and incentives.

Banks, markets, regulations, and products change. Banks merge, restructure, and undergo shifts in organisation and culture. Business processes and technology evolve rapidly. Data can only be backward looking, so it is important for banks to use qualitative input from senior managers as well as risk and business experts. Risk events must be viewed within context as to how the individual bank would be affected, depending on circumstances. Potential severity may vary enormously, particularly if a number of events occur at once. High impact but rare events must be evaluated for general characteristics, but also uniqueness.

Banks organise regular internal workshops to discuss operational risk, with managers completing risk scorecards by business line and event. Besides frequency and financial severity, impacts such as reputation and employee retention and morale can be scored in a broader assessment of operational risk.

Just as with quantitative input, qualitative input must be assessed for quality. Risk management must attempt to ensure it is asking the right people when calling for expert opinion. Depending on the bank's culture, vested interest can bias and affect responses. Finally, some respondents may fail to grasp extreme circumstances.

Qualitative inputs should be converted into metrics for scenario analysis. Estimates from respondents on the distribution of the uncertainty of variables must be collated to anchor and adjust models. Scenario analysis should be forward looking, as clearly defined as possible, and repeatable.

Key risk indicators

As described earlier, business environment control factors are risk metrics and statistics used to monitor drivers of risk exposure.

- Key Performance Indicators (KPIs): monitor operational efficiency (for example, system downtime, staff turnover);
- Key Control Indicators (KCIs): monitor effectiveness of controls (for example, outstanding confirmations, audit exceptions);
- Key Risk Indicators (KRIs): a selection of KPIs and KCIs (typically 10–15) used to warn of escalating risk to trigger management attention and action. Composite KRIs can be rolled up to top management.

Indicators must be measurable and not complicated so as not to become a control issue in and of themselves, as well as a representative of the business line and its risk. If an indicator is broken down to the lowest level and assigned a cost centre, it can be kept in use throughout organisational changes.

The Basel Committee assumes the use of risk indicators to be subjective in nature and cautions against overweighting.

OPERATIONAL RISK MANAGEMENT FRAMEWORK

The Basel Committee has outlined 11 principles for operational risk management. These are intended to be a high-level operating framework that should set the culture for management of operational risk at the right level.

They are as follows:

1. The Board of Directors should establish a strong risk management culture that provides appropriate standards and incentives for responsible behaviour throughout the bank;
2. Banks should develop, implement, and maintain a framework that is fully integrated into the bank's overall risk management processes;
3. The Board of Directors should establish, approve, and periodically review the framework and oversee senior management to ensure effective implementation;
4. The Board of Directors should approve an operational risk appetite and tolerance statement;
5. Senior management should develop a clear and robust governance structure for Board approval with well-defined lines of responsibility;
6. Senior management should ensure identification and assessment of risk;
7. Senior management should ensure an approval process for new products and systems;
8. Senior management should implement a process for monitoring and reporting to support proactive management of operational risk;
9. Banks should have a strong control environment to utilise processes and systems, internal controls, and risk mitigation and transfer;
10. Bank should have continuity plans for severe business disruption;
11. Bank public disclosures should allow stakeholders to assess operational risk management.

Governance structure involves three lines of defence: business line management, risk management, and independent review (for example, audit). The latter two report to Board level committees. Risk management encompasses a number of areas including: compliance, legal, IT and data protection, new account opening, health and safety, HR screening, and building security.

Further defence comes from national supervisors and shareholders.

A good test of an operational risk management system is whether it addresses causes, events, and impact:

- Causes: classifies reasons for losses, helps perform "root cause" analysis, seeks prevention;
- Events: ensures risks are captured, integral to the Advanced Measurement Approach;
- Impact: helps set priorities and mitigation strategies.

Banks will want to assess whether their approach to operational risk is more "top-down" or "bottom-up" orientated. "Top-down" allows management to drive strategy and policy, unify standards, use firm-wide experience, and mitigate risk on an aggregated basis. "Bottom-up" fully utilises the dynamic, "real world" knowledge of those closest to the business and emphasises personal responsibility and ownership. The best approach is a combination of the two with neither overemphasised.

Mervyn King, the chair of South Africa's internationally respected King Committee on Corporate Governance, stated memorably that "the tone at the top, the tune in the middle, and the beat at the bottom" are all crucial.

CONCLUSIONS

The addition of an operational risk regulatory capital charge at the time of Basel II focused attention on this aspect of risk management in banks. Operational risk covers a wide range of exposures, from technology and physical security risk to employee fraud risk and beyond. The governance structure in place at a bank must be adequate to ensure satisfactory monitoring and mitigation of such risks. That said, similarly to the interest-rate risk in the banking book exposure in a bank, there are few if any examples of a bank failing due to operational risk issues (Barings in 1995 is a good example), and the multibillion dollar fines received by banks for issues such as compliance lapses, customer mis-selling, and sanctions busting in the years following 2008, none of which broke any bank, suggest that this state of affairs will continue. That said, given that operational risk drives a regulatory capital charge, it remains an important area for the bank's risk management department.

Chapter

17

ADVICE AND
PROBLEM SOLVING:
CASE STUDIES

In this chapter we aim to bring together all the elements of principle and sound best-practice approach that we described in earlier chapters, and join them in as coherent and user-friendly a format as possible. To do this we will use real-world case studies to illustrate how these principles can be applied to solve real-world problems as they arise. Banks, like all corporate entities, are collections of people with diverse backgrounds and experience. The process undertaken to effect change and/or improvement, principally in the balance sheet risk management space, must take into account the culture and operating process in place at the firm. That said, the aim of the case studies described here is to show that adherence to logical, unemotional best-practice principles is almost invariably the most effective way to approach problem solving. This calls for a certain level of technical expertise and experience in finance, emphasising at all times that the importance of a sound balance sheet structure remains the most reliable way to ensure a sustainable, through-the-cycle banking operation.

The foregoing chapters have shown that the art of banking over the long-term is essentially that of managing capital and liquidity in such a way that external market crashes or internal stress events do not "sink" the bank. This is the long-term objective. In the short and medium term, the challenge is to ensure that day-to-day processes and procedures remain fit for purpose, be they in the arena of interest-rate risk, risk committee governance framework, or funds transfer pricing (FTP). By approaching bank management in this way, the bank is better placed to survive continuously, throughout the economic cycle, and in perpetuity – or at least as long as the bank's managers and shareholders wish it to remain a going concern.

HOW TO STUDY THIS CHAPTER

This chapter has a different structure to the rest of this book. It is comprised of real-world case studies, selected to illustrate problem solving of specific operational or other issues that have been identified, discussed, analysed, and ultimately fixed though application of a chosen solution. The case studies all illustrate specific technical issues that are of the kind addressed in Chapters 1–16. The exception to this is Case Study 1, from the UK bank Northern Rock, as this is an excellent illustration for the need to have sound overall asset–liability management (ALM) principles in place. As such it is a good introduction to this chapter.

Readers should also be familiar with the additional reading listed for each case study. The **Core Text** referred to is the author's book *The Principles of Banking* (2012).

Case Study 1: The pitfalls of a risky liquidity risk management regime

Northern Rock plc, UK commercial banking institution with primary business line focus on residential mortgages

The UK bank Northern Rock was originally a mutually savings-and-loan organisation, with no shareholders. The organisation had operated for over a century when it changed itself into a bank in 1997. Alongside the change in legal entity type was a change in business philosophy, one that emphasised aggressive asset growth. Its main product was residential mortgages, which it marketed nationwide. However, its retail deposit base was still confined to its original home area in the north-east of England, so the new loans were funded via recourse to the wholesale market. Figure 17.1 shows the growth in wholesale and capital markets funding as a share of its total balance sheet liabilities during the 10 years from its transformation to its ultimate demise and government bailout. Figure 17.2 shows the change in its credit default swap (CDS) price during its last few months.

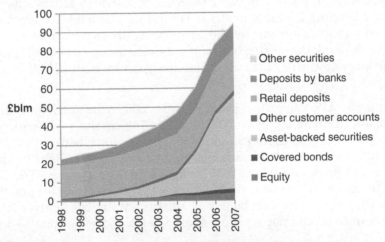

Figure 17.1 Northern Rock funding types 1998–2007

Figure 17.2 Northern Rock CDS price history April–September 2007
© Bloomberg LP. Reproduced with permission.

The case of Northern Rock highlights the pitfalls of a business model based on:

- Rapid asset growth in pursuit of market share (residential real estate), with asset pool far outstripping its retail deposit base;
- Use of securitisation to support asset growth, rather than as funding diversification tool;
- Increasing reliance on an unsustainable funding source.

In fact "market share" is an inappropriate performance indicator for banks to adopt. While it may have its value in other industries such as supermarket retail, in a banking business model it is vital for the bank to have adequate and robust liabilities support for the assets being originated. In other words, it is vital for the bank to consider both sides of the balance sheet at all times. This is the primary objective of the asset-liability management (ALM) function in a bank.

Following the US sub-prime crash in July 2007, the quality of its asset pool became the subject of rumours circulating in the inter-bank market; banks began reducing the term and size of their inter-bank lines. One day in September 2007, the bank was not able to roll its overnight funding and turned to the Bank of England (BoE), the lender of last resort. The BoE was obliged to report the borrowing. This news led to media headlines the next day, resulting in a high-street bank run, the first in the UK for over 100 years. The government could not countenance a default and so nationalised it.

The lessons of Northern Rock for all banks are to:

- Term out funding;
- Monitor liquidity ratios and the customer funding base;
- Arrange diversified funding and also have alternative sources of funds available;
- Grow slower during a bull market and set aside reserve liquidity for a "rainy day".

Reading: Core text, Part III

Castagna, A., and Fede, F., *Measuring and Managing Liquidity Risk*, Hoboken, NJ: John Wiley & Sons 2013

European Banking Authority, http://www.eba.europa.eu/regulation-and-policy/liquidity-risk

The British Bankers Association, http://www.bba.org.uk/advanced-liquidity-risk-management

US Federal Reserve, http://www.federalreserve.gov/bankinforeg/topics/liquidity_risk.htm

Case Study 2: Fixing the internal yield curve construction process

UK multinational integrated bank

In 2010 during a review of the internal liquidity adequacy assessment (ILAA) of a high-street UK bank, the UK regulatory authority made the following observations:

- A reference to the risks created by the bank's public funding curve falling out of line with market prices;
- A material difference between the Group and wholesale banking internal rates and the need for a consistent curve to be applied across the businesses.

This issue was raised by Treasury with the business lines, and it was discovered that the wholesale bank divisional ALM desk did not construct the internal funding curve by any recognised best-practice interpolation method. This had created the risk that the internal prices would not reflect the genuine market (external) prices, and therefore became a sufficient risk management issue to be cited specifically by the regulatory authority.

In response to the ILAA review, the Group Treasury (GT) function seconded an individual to the wholesale division ALM desk who would review the curve interpolation procedure existing at the wholesale bank and thereafter make recommendations for improvement. This individual found that no recognised interpolation method was in place, and that the ALM desk was not considered sufficiently influential to dictate procedure to the business lines.

The person seconded by GT addressed this issue by formulating a process that was logical and consistent, and based on theoretical principles that were robust in academic terms. He then discussed this at a meeting he chaired, which included representatives from all the business lines and the ALM desk. By holding a discussion on this so publicly, with all business lines in the room, it was difficult for any individual business to object to anything other than what seemed like partisan grounds. In other words, if a proposed solution is demonstrably (a) impartial, (b) based on logic that is proven in the academic literature, and (c) shown not to favour any one product or business line, and then discussed at a public forum, it will be difficult for any reasonable objection to be raised.

Following the meeting, the GT-appointed person drafted and presented a paper to the wholesale bank asset–liability committee (ALCO), where it was subsequently approved. Some extracts of the ALCO memo are reproduced here:

A significant risk management decision at every bank is selecting the internal yield curve construction methodology. The internal curve is an important tool in the pricing and risk management process, driving resource allocation, business line transaction pricing, hedge construction and RAROC analysis. It is given therefore that curve construction methodology should follow business best-practice. In this paper we describe the formal procedure on curve formulation in place at [investment bank ALM desk], as well as the secondary procedure to liaise with Group Treasury (GT) aimed at maintaining a realistic and market-accurate public issuance curve.

This set the scene for the discussion to follow.

The practice at peer-group banks is to adopt an interpolation method that uses prices (yields) of the issuer's existing debt as model inputs, and extracts a discount function from these prices. The output is then used to derive a term structure that represents the issuer's current risky yield curve. To adopt such an approach requires a liquid secondary market in the issuer's bonds. This is a not unreasonable assumption in the case of [bank].

The two most common interpolation methods in use are the cubic spline approach and the parametric approach. The former produces markedly oscillating forward rates and is also less accurate at the short-end. Therefore we have adopted the parametric method. The original parametric model is Nelson-Siegel, which is a forward rate model; however we recommend an extension of Nelson-Siegel for use at [bank], the Svensson (94) model, which produces a smoother forward curve, partly as a result of incorporating one extra parameter.

Treasury was able to provide a solution that was a neutral one, as well as one that was academically and technically robust. This undoubtedly helped approval and implementation.

In the field of balance sheet risk management, or indeed any aspect of risk management including customer and conduct risk, a bank will have in place internal procedures that ensure that potential pitfalls are picked up by its staff, rather than highlighted by the regulatory authority. This was not the case at this UK bank. Both the central (Group) and divisional Treasury functions were not aware that the method employed for constructing the internal yield curve, a vital input parameter to customer product pricing, was not a best-practice one (in that no firm methodology of any kind was in place). Subsequent to the regulator review, the bank implemented a regular curve procedure methodology.

Reading: Choudhry (2012), Chapter 5

Choudhry, M. (2003), *Analysing and Interpreting the Yield Curve*, Singapore: John Wiley & Sons Pte Ltd

James, J., and N. Webber (2000), *Interest Rate Modelling*, Chichester: John Wiley & Co. Ltd.

Nelson, C., and A.F. Siegel (1987), "Parsimonious Modeling of Yield Curves", *Journal of Business*, **60**, pp. 473–489

Svensson, Lars E.O. (1994), "Estimating and Interpreting Forward Rates: Sweden 1992–4," *National Bureau of Economic Research* Working Paper #4871

Case Study 3: Implementing a fit-for-purpose internal funds transfer pricing (FTP) process

Europe Arab Bank plc (EAB), UK subsidiary of Arab Bank Group, commercial banking entity

The UK-registered and regulated bank Europe Arab Bank plc (EAB) is a wholly-owned subsidiary of Arab Bank Group, which is domiciled in Jordan. In 2009 it had a balance sheet of just over GBP 10bln.

EAB comprises three business lines, Treasury, corporate bank, and private bank. These conduct the following activities:

- Treasury: responsible for managing the money market desk and the bank's liquidity portfolio, as well as a Treasury sales desk that worked with the corporate bank to provide risk management solutions to corporate clients;
- Corporate bank: provided a vanilla commercial bank service to EU-based corporate clients that had a particular interest in the Middle East. The product range included corporate loans, trade finance such as letters of credit, bridging loans, and stand-by liquidity lines. Its client base was essentially medium-sized corporates based in the UK;
- Private bank: provided a private banking service to high net-worth individuals (HNWI) domiciled in Western Europe, including expatriate citizens of the Gulf state, who had a connection of any kind with the Middle East.

Treasury therefore acted as a front-line business with a P&L target, but crucially also acted as the balance sheet management department of the bank. This meant that it was responsible for capital and liquidity risk management, as well as acting as the internal "clearing house" of the bank providing funding for the corporate and private bank business lines.

Like many banks, at the time of the global financial crash of 2008–09 the bank operated an FTP methodology that was not a true internal funding pricing mechanism, in that all internal funds were transacted between Treasury and the other business lines at Libor-flat. This was simply a tradition that was common at banks around the world, reflecting an assumption – usually unchallenged by the Treasury and Risk departments – that the bank could fund across the term structure at zero spread over Libor. While this assumption was reasonably accurate for large banks during 1998–2008, it was not universally the case and by 2008 was unrealistic.

This was recognised by the Treasury department at the beginning of 2009, which observed that the existing FTP framework was not fit for purpose, because at this time EAB was funding at significantly in excess of Libor. As well as facilitating excess liquidity risk creation on the balance sheet, it created artificially high business line returns and did not incentivise customer product pricing that was a true reflection of the cost of raising term liquidity by EAB.

The business lines themselves reflect an understandable but flawed process that concentrated on one side of the balance sheet only. By 2008 corporate banking operated at a loan-deposit ratio (LDR) approaching 180%, while private banking was overweight in customer deposits reflecting the interests of its customers: it operated at approximately 60% LDR. The deposit rates as at January 2009 are shown in Table 17.1.

Table 17.1 EAB deposit rates as at January 2009

Jan-09	Basis points
Base rate	100
3M Libor	118
Current account	40
Call account	25
30-day notice account	60
1-year	75
2-year	85

During Q1 and Q2 2009 Treasury carried out the following steps, in the order shown, that culminated in the FTP methodology being changed and a new best-practice model being implemented:

- Drafted a paper explaining the concept of liquidity risk, how it arises, and the negative consequences of ignoring and/or mispricing it;
- Presented "teach-ins" on the role of Treasury in the bank, and the concept of asset-liability management and liquidity risk management;
- Drafted a paper, to be presented at the bank's ALCO, on the recommended new FTP methodology, in conjunction with the Finance and Risk departments;
- Met bilaterally with the heads of corporate banking and private banking to discuss the ALCO paper. At these meetings, a strong (and at times emotional) objection was raised by the business lines, used to funding at Libor-flat for as long as anyone could remember, along the lines that Treasury was simply adding a term liquidity premium (TLP) to boost its own P&L from a captive audience that could not fund elsewhere. This objection was addressed in the following way: Treasury confirmed with the IT department that all internal deal tickets, conducted with the business lines, would be identified by a system flag. Finance was asked to ensure that all flagged tickets would not count towards the Treasury P&L. Faced with this fact, the business agreed to the new FTP regime.
- Presented the FTP paper to ALCO, where it was approved.

The paper presented to ALCO, which was co-sponsored by Treasury and Finance, stated the following:

- FTP will be changed (a) by introducing a "liquidity premium" into the FTP and (b) by increasing the liquidity premium as a function of the tenor;

- A liquidity-premium-enhanced transfer pricing will transfer more earnings to the liability generating activities and force corporate banking to more accurately price (and reprice) loan assets. It will also incentivise corporate banking to attract more customer deposits;
- More crucially, it will reduce chances of an artificial funding profit helping to drive the investment decision.

The new FTP regime was implemented at EAB from 1 January 2010. This proved to be timely, as the UK regulator started reviewing bank FTP mechanisms from 2010 onwards.

At first a very simple regime was implemented at the London subsidiary for GBP, EUR, and USD, as shown in Table 17.2.

Table 17.2 Regime implemented at the London subsidiary

	Old Bid	Old Offer	New Bid	New Offer	Liquidity Premium
O/N to 2 weeks:	Libor – 12.5 bp	Libor	Libor	Libor + 12.5 bp	+ 12.5 bp
2 weeks to 1 month:	Libor – 12.5 bp	Libor	Libor + 5 bp	Libor + 17.5 bp	+ 17.5 bp
> 1 and up to 3 months:	Libor – 12.5 bp	Libor	Libor + 10 bp	Libor + 22.5 bp	+ 22.5 bp
> 3 and up to 12 months:	Libor – 12.5 bp	Libor	Libor + 20 bp	Libor + 32.5 bp	+ 32.5 bp

The private bank rates benefited and raised net positive liabilities. Note that the rates are shown in Table 17.3.

Table 17.3 EAB deposit rates as at June 2009

Jun-09	Basis points
Base rate	50
3M Libor	66
Current account	60
Call account	40
30-day notice account	75
1-year	100
2-year	150

The fixed term deposits were "loss making" to the private bank but reflected the need to raise liquidity friendly customer term deposits for the bank as a whole. The impact on corporate banking included:

- Stopped writing back-stop liquidity facilities;
- Term loans now less competitive to market.

The crucial operational issue was the need to demonstrate explicitly that Treasury – a front office P&L department – did not generate and report P&L based on the FTP regime. Because all internal tickets were flagged as such by the IT booking system and enabled Finance month-end management accounts to be adjusted for Treasury (to strip out the impact of internal tickets), this was not an issue. The P&L of FTP tickets was held in a central "ALCO book".

Ultimately, the process at EAB transformed into a best-in-class FTP regime with a curve updated monthly by Treasury, and TLP rates calculated using market observed external parameters. The full curve appears similar to Table 17.4.

Table 17.4 Final EAB FTP monthly curve

Term	GBP	EUR	USD
<3mo	0	0	0
6mo	30	25	30
12mo	85	80	95
18mo	160	145	180
2yr	230	205	235
3yr	250	255	255
4yr	255	265	260
5yr	270	280	285
6yr	275	290	300
7yr	280	295	305
8yr	285	300	310
9yr	295	305	315
10yr+	305	310	320

The lessons learned for all banks are to:

- Be aware of one's actual TLP, what term funding is available, and how it impacts the balance sheet if borrowed at the rate offered;
- Approach ALCO because it is the appropriate forum for such debate, Treasury having previously obtained "buy-in" from all affected parties;
- Ensure adequate support from the business lines ahead of the ALCO presentation. Highlight how the FTP regime does not support Treasury P&L, if arranged to be treated appropriately, so there is no conflict of interest here;
- Demonstrate FTP via a genuine co-written effort from Finance and Treasury. Education is a big priority whenever a bank wants to introduce a new idea.

The above approach was subsequently adapted by the author of the FTP paper and presented at other UK conferences and banks, where its studied objective rationale ensured it became a confirmed success.

Reading: Choudhry (2012), Chapter 15

Accenture, http://www.accenture.com/us-en/Pages/insight-liquidity-transfer-pricing-challenges.aspx

Barbican Consulting, http://www.barbicanconsulting.co.uk/ftp

Pushkina, N., *A Simple Funds Transfer Pricing Model for a Commercial Bank*, Faculty of Law and Commerce, University of the Witwatersrand, February 2013

Case Study 4: Securities trading house funding mix and reporting implementation

UK securities and derivatives trading house pre-2008, no Treasury function

This firm was a former hedge fund that was acquired by a commercial banking entity in 2000. However, it retained its own internal procedures and culture, because the parent bank did not make any changes to its internal structure and it virtually retained its full autonomy. This meant that as the firm grew, the culture and business direction remained one that emphasised balance sheet growth and maximising return on capital. Three years after becoming part of a bank group, the entity comprised a number of business lines (convertibles market making, equity derivatives, hedge fund derivatives, structured finance origination, and small-cap equities) but no dedicated Treasury or cash management function. Funding was arranged with the parent bank by a single individual in the middle office, who rolled over all funding in the overnight – despite the fact that the balance sheet was at this time over GBP 3 billion. This person was a junior member of staff who reported to a level below that of the head of operations. There was no reporting of the liquidity stress on the firm's (and therefore ultimately the Group's) balance sheet.

The parent bank became aware of this fact in the middle of 2003 but only recommended that the subsidiary should recruit a Treasurer. It did not make any other recommendations or suggest any preferred operating model for the management of balance sheet risk.

The new "Treasury" function initially comprised the one individual recruited in 2003. This person recognised that the management of liquidity risk was severely inadequate. The first requirement was to highlight this to senior management in the form of a report, compiled as quickly as possible and containing only essential, unarguable information. The risk that was emphasised stated that "the present operating infrastructure runs a high risk of being censured by the regulatory authority".

The report highlights were as follows:

The key objective of the Treasury desk in any bank or non-bank financial is to undertake prudent management of the funding requirement with regard to liquidity management, interest-rate management, and funding diversification. This process includes management information and reporting. The primary deliverable of the Treasury desk is the ALM report. This is presented at Figure 17.3.

	o/n	o/n–1w	1w–1m	1m–3m	3m–6m	6m–12m	12m+	TOTAL
Assets	481	4,104	5,325	6,954	4,478	3,845	4,128	29,315
Liabilities	−3,947	−844	−5,107	−7,579	−5,053	−3,799	−2,986	(29,315)
Gap	3466	3260	218	625	575	46	1142	9332
Percent of total funding	13%	3%	17%	26%	17%	13%	10%	100%
Gap as % of total Gap	37%	35%	2%	7%	6%	0%	12%	100%
Gap as % of total Funding	**12%**	**11%**	**1%**	**2%**	**2%**	**0%**	**4%**	
Gap Limit	**20%**	**20%**	**20%**	**20%**	**20%**	**20%**	**20%**	
Limit breach	–	–	–	–	–	–	–	
Cumulative Assets	481	4585	9910	16864	21342	25187	29315	
Cumulative Liabilities	−3947	−4791	−9898	−17477	−22530	−26329	−29315	
Net Gap	−3466	−206	12	−613	−1188	−1142	0	

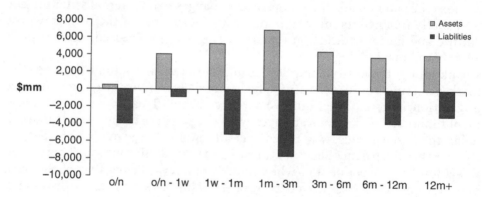

Figure 17.3　Proposed ALM report in table and graph formats

Historically, the funding of the firm's business was concentrated overwhelmingly on a very short-term basis. The motivation for this was primarily the short-term trading nature of its assets, which meant that the asset profile was effectively changing on a high frequency. Over the last 2 years, the business has evolved into dealing more in longer term asset classes and as a consequence the firm must begin a process of rolling out funding into longer term to match its asset profile more adequately. The Treasury aim going forward is based on the following reasoning:

- As much as possible to match asset profile with liability profile and to minimise forward gap;

- To term out the funding away from the very short-dated tenors used hitherto;
- To construct an ALM profile that recognises the differing requirements of individual business lines. For example, the market making businesses are expected to have a more flexible liquidity profile than the asset management business. Hence, the liability profile of the former will be concentrated along the short end of the funding term structure when compared to the latter;
- To even out the liability profile such that no one maturity bucket contains more than 20% of the total funding requirement. This will be treated as a funding limit.

The 20% limit will apply to the overall XYZ funding requirement.

The objective of ALM policy will be to apply market-standard guidelines to the business and to follow prudent market practice. It is also to make the whole funding process more transparent with regard to management reporting and to centralise funding onto one desk within the group.

Recommendations included to formalise a Treasury middle office function and to ensure that Treasury reported to the CEO. The report also highlighted the need to implement management reporting as shown in Figures 17.3 and 17.4, including the need for management to see individual business line funding usage.

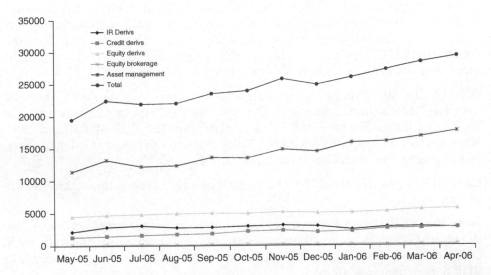

Figure 17.4   Business line funding usage

On review of the report the senior executive approved all of the recommendations. This process took 12 months to embed but at its conclusion the institution had in place a first-class infrastructure for the risk management, monitoring, reporting, and mitigation of balance sheet risk.

The key lessons learned from this study are:

- Do not allow management strategy to be overwhelmed by the revenue side of the balance sheet. Before embarking on a growth strategy, ensure first that the risk management infrastructure is in place (note that this requirement is explicit now in one of the UK PRA);
- The funding function must report to a person of sufficient seniority in the bank, to ensure that any concerns it has can be aired at the right level;
- The quickest way to ensure management attention and management action on any issue is to highlight what the regulatory authorities would say if they were to be aware of any relevant facts.

Reading: Choudhry (2007), Chapter 5

Case Study 5: Improving ALCO governance framework

European universal banking institution

The bank in question was comprised of three operating divisions: wholesale, corporate, and retail. Each of these was a large banking institution in its own right, with further operating breakdowns within each. For example, as well as the Group CEO each division had its own CEO, and within the division there was a further breakdown into business units, again each with its own "CEO". This case study looks at the operating framework for the asset-liability committee (ALCO) process in place at the corporate banking division (CBD). Note that the bank as a whole also operated a Group ALCO (GALCO).

CDB in this European bank was a large institution, with a balance sheet of over GBP 180 billion. It was split into two parts: Corporate & Institutional Banking (CIB) and Business & Commercial banking (B&C). Both CIB and B&C were run by their respective "CEOs". The framework in place for balance sheet risk management at CBD is shown in Figure 17.5.

Each ALCO had its own ALCO MI pack. The other arrangements are shown in Table 17.5.

Note that "CBD" is not a separate legal entity; it is the same legal entity as the wider Group. However, there was a triplication in management staff, with each operating business line having its own CEO, CFO, Finance department, Risk department, and so on.

It does not take a McKinsey or BCG-trained consultant (not that that is necessarily any measure of value) to see that such an operating infrastructure for risk management is not only grossly inefficient and wasteful in terms of resources, it is also risky. With so many operating committees and separate staff, there is a material danger of specific exposures "falling through the cracks" and not being picked up. As a governance model, the ALCO structure

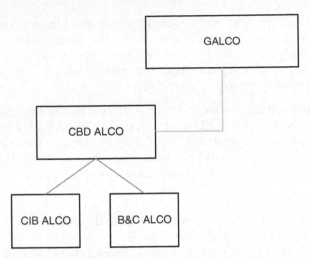

Figure 17.5 CBD ALCO governance

Table 17.5 Other arrangements

	Meeting Frequency	**Chair**	**MI Pack**
CBD ALCO	Monthly	CBD CFO (deferred it to CDB CEO)	Yes
CIB ALCO	Monthly	CIB CEO	Yes
B&C ALCO	Quarterly	B&C CFO	Yes

at this bank's CBD was distinctly *not* fit for purpose. There was another issue in that the CBD CEO rarely attended the CBD ALCO, which had two unfortunate side effects: the ALCO was viewed as being not very important (since the CEO didn't attend it) and it made risk management staff view the CIB ALCO as being the "right" one.

The CBD Treasury department recognised these issues, and frequently raised them to the CBD CFO. Despite the fact that this individual reported to the CBD CEO, for political and personality reasons he also deferred to the CIB CEO. It was a known fact that the CIB CEO preferred the status quo and wished to retain his department's ALCO (and his chairmanship of it). Hence, the Treasury department was not able to effect any rationalisation to the governance structure for political reasons.

The approach taken by the Treasury department was to wait until the Internal Audit department conducted its scheduled annual review of Treasury. In general, various internal audit reviews of operating functions rarely throw up anything material for management to consider unless there are serious flaws or issues to uncover, because the audit team have limited time, work to a template, and suffer from a lack of detailed knowledge of the department they are auditing. On this occasion, the treasurer took the opportunity to volunteer information to the auditors, specifically with respect to his concerns on the governance structure, the lack of management challenge in the CIB ALCO, and the non-attendance of key members of the committees. This is detail that it is unlikely the audit team would have uncovered if it had not been volunteered. (For example, the ALCO minutes, which the audit team did review, did not list a register of attendance).

Treasury recommendations were agreed to in full by the Internal Audit team, but the draft report sent to CBD senior management implied that these were Internal Audit recommendations. This report carried a force that the Treasury department on its own did not have, and since any final report would be escalated to the Group CFO and Group CRO, these were difficult to push back.

The result was:

- The two lower-tier ALCOs were abolished, and all relevant members attended the single unified CBD ALCO;
- Attendance was logged with an understanding that it would be monitored by Internal Audit;
- Only one ALCO MI deck was required to be produced each month, which improved efficiency and reduced workload;
- The ALCO pack itself was redesigned by Treasury into one that was more user-friendly, accessible, and succinct. This would have been a pointless exercise when three ALCO decks were being produced, because the CBD ALCO deck was not viewed as being the most important one.

The lessons learned from this experience are:

- To continuously review risk governance and operating model, to ensure it is still optimum;
- To effect improvements to risk practice, it is sometimes necessary to enlist "allies" in the effort, because what is optimum may not suit the internal politics of the organisation.

Further Reading: Choudhry (2012), Chapter 10

Case Study 6: Improving interest-rate risk in the banking book (IRRBB) hedging efficiency

European commercial banking group

Traditionally, ALM has always been associated with the banking book and conventional ("modified duration") techniques were applied when calculating interest-rate and funding risk exposure in the bank's banking book. With respect to interest-rate risk in the banking book (IRRBB), there are five primary sources of risk:

- Gap risk, the risk that revenue and earnings decline as a result of changes in interest rates, due to the difference in the maturity profile of assets, liabilities, and off-balance-sheet instruments. Note, this is in many cases "opportunity cost foregone" losses where the rates on assets and liabilities are fixed;

- Yield curve risk, the risk that non-parallel or pivotal shifts in the yield curve cause a reduction in net interest income (NII);
- Basis risk arising because assets are often priced off one interest rate, while funding is priced off another interest rate;
- Run-off risk is associated with the non-interest-bearing liabilities of banks. The level of interest rates at any one time represents an opportunity cost to depositors who have funds in such facilities. Also refers to the asset side where loans pay down quicker;
- Option risk is when banking products entitle the customer to terminate contractual arrangements ahead of the stated maturity.

Thus, IRRBB is not an optional risk-taking position but rather a by-product of repricing mismatches between lending and deposit-taking positions. So, banks are exposed to IRRBB primarily due to the following:

- Writing fixed-rate assets funded by floating-rate liabilities;
- Writing floating-rate assets funded by floating-rate liabilities referencing another index;
- To lengthen the funding profile of the bank, term funding is raised across the curve at fixed-term deposit rates that reprice only on maturity;
- Three-month repricing swaps and forward rate agreements are typically used in the risk management of term deposits and fixed-rate advances; however, short-term demand funding products reprice to different short-end base rates;
- Certain non-repricing transactional deposit accounts are non-rate sensitive;
- The bank has a mismatch in net non-rate-sensitive balances, including shareholders' funds that do not reprice for interest-rate changes.

Banks recognise this risk and hedge it away to reduce the volatility of net interest income (NII) and net interest margin; (NIM), however, this then raises the issue of how exactly the hedging mechanism should be operated. A key point is that in practical terms IRRBB hedging is undertaken on a "macro" or aggregate balance sheet basis (for example, the bank does not transact in an interest-rate swap (IRS) every time it advances a fixed-rate residential mortgage to a customer. More commonly, it will take the aggregate balance of all mortgages originated that month and enter into a pool IRS at month-end.) Commonly, this means that "hedge accounting" cannot be applied and the bank will wear mark-to-market P&L volatility on any macro hedge undertaken with derivatives.

This case study references a UK commercial bank that operated a common, conventional approach to IRRBB hedging, but one that was recognised by the Treasury department as not being optimum.

The bank in question undertook customer business that generated all of the interest-rate risks summarised above. It reported its IRRBB risk in two ways, using both the traditional modified duration ("DV01") approach and the later Value-at-Risk (VaR) methodology. Its IRRBB was reported as shown in Table 17.6 and Figure 17.6.

Table 17.6   UK commercial bank IRRBB reporting

	Rollover date or nearest interest-rate adjustment date (£mm)					
	O/n–3mo	3mo–6mo	6mo–1yr	1yr–5yr	>5yr	Non-IR sensitive
Assets	270,959	16,813	21,375	115,831	35,893	139,475
Liabilities	331,496	25,271	26,344	67,256	20,754	128,775
Repricing gap	−60,537	−8,908	−4,969	48,575	15,139	10,700
Cumulative gap	−60,537	−69,445	−74,414	−25,839	−10,700	0

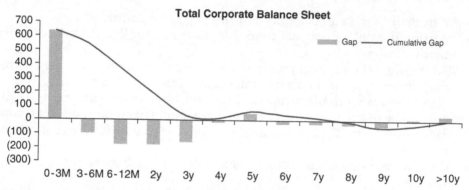

Figure 17.6   UK commercial bank IRRBB reporting

The bank operated the orthodox approach to IRRBB hedging, which one might label "ponderous". Namely, it hedged asset-side IRRBB as it appeared and liabilities-side IRRBB as these appeared. No attempt was made to consider the balance sheet as an integrated whole. Moreover, derivatives were used at all times.

The extract below from the banks interest-rate risk policy summarises the bank's hedging methodology:

Hedging can be defined as a risk management strategy used in limiting or offsetting probability of loss from fluctuations in interest rates.

From an "Interest Rate Risk" perspective, Interest Rate Swaps are the main hedging tool that a bank uses to "hedge" its balance sheet. All fixed rate assets are hedged via "Pay Fixed" & "Receive Floating" Interest Rate Swaps; all fixed rate liabilities are hedged via "Receive Fixed" & "Pay Floating" Interest Rate Swaps.

Example of business line Fixed Rate Asset hedged using internal vanilla interest rate swap (also shows internal funding ticket) [see Figure 17.7].

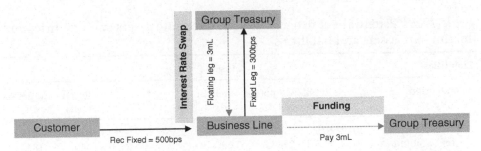

Figure 17.7   Bank IRRBB hedge structure

The approach described above, while common, is not efficient and optimum. It lacks a "strategic ALM" perspective that looks at both sides of the balance sheet, and also makes no effort at minimising the use of derivatives. The use of derivative instruments carries a cost, not least with respect to the cost of collateral, which is not always recognised or transparent.

The bank would have continued along these lines for the foreseeable future. The issue was neither raised by any of the CFO, CRO, or Treasury departments, nor by the business lines themselves. What happened that ultimately resulted in an improved hedging method was that the CFO and treasurer attended an ALM conference where one of the speakers presented on the topic of "strategic ALM". After listening to this presentation, both individuals invited the speaker to present the same lecture to their bank's ALCO.

The speaker's lecture included the following points:

The banks' existing arrangements result in Group or the "Centre" hedging both assets and liabilities individually. It also describes an internal IRS together with the funding ticket for the asset. An alternative procedure is to hedge the net exposure of both assets and liabilities, after allowing for similar, behaviour tenor matching. This benefits from natural hedges already in place and reduces reliance on derivatives. Examples include:

- Fixed rate loans versus fixed rate depos;
- Variable rate loans versus floating rate depos.

Structural balance sheet hedging should be applied on a net basis: the net A-L position.

Some assets and liabilities naturally hedge each other:

- Variable rate mortgages and NIBLs of similar behavioural tenor;
- Fixed rate mortgages and fixed rate deposits.

Hence, we hedge with external market the net un-hedged exposure. The below chart shows potential net hedged between fixed-rate assets and liabilities and floating-rate assets and liabilities, where tenors are approximately similar [see Table 17.7].

Table 17.7   Potential net hedged between fixed-rate assets and liabilities and floating-rate assets and liabilities

Liabilities			Assets			
"Convention" hedging	Retail MTA	Corporate MTA	Fixed rate		Retail loans	Corporate loans
Current accounts in credit	2012 675.3 2013 675.3 2014 675.3 2015 675.3	2140.3 2140.3 2140.3 2140.3	Loans		2012 570.5 2013 570.5 2014 570.5 2015 570.5	1875.6 1875.6 1875.6 1875.6
Fixed rate			"Convention" hedging			
Savings and deposit accounts	2012 611.2 2013 611.2 2014 611.2 2015 611.2	905.2 905.2 905.2 905.2	Credit cards/current accounts overdrawn		2012 237.5 2013 237.5 2014 237.5 2015 237.5	60.6 60.6 60.6 60.6

The recommended approach going forward is that, where possible, it may be advantageous to use cash products to hedge interest-rate exposure rather than have recourse to derivatives. For example, there may be a desire to preserve swap lines or reduce collateral funding requirements. Past examples the author has undertaken include:

- Hambros Bank: using gilts to hedge the IRS market-making book (which was net pay fixed but often on an individual swap basis);
- KBC Financial Products: using US Treasuries to hedge fixed-rate term liability issuance.

A similar approach might see banks using their liquid asset buffer to hedge fixed-rate liabilities and issuing Tier 2 or senior unsecured debt to hedge fixed-rate assets.

After hearing this lecture, the bank implemented a change in IRRBB hedging approach. This resulted in a material improvement in operational efficiency as well as lower hedge costs and reduced mark-to-market P&L volatility from hedge instruments (due to lower use of derivatives).

The lessons learned from this case study include:

- To remain in the forefront of market best practice requires continual knowledge gathered from a variety of sources;
- Continually seek to understand the unintended consequences of any operating method in place at the bank;
- Be open minded about ideas and strategies that may require you to modify what you think is already optimum.

Further Reading:

Swarup, B., *Asset Liability Management for Financial Institutions: Balancing Financial Stability with Strategic Objectives* (Key Concepts), London: Bloomsbury Information Ltd 2012

Tilman, L., *Asset, Liability Management for Financial Institutions: Maximising Shareholder Value Through Risk-conscious Investing*, London: Euromoney Books 2003

Case Study 7: Best-practice bank supervision processes through practitioner interaction

South American country bank regulatory authority

Bank regulators have the difficult and challenging task of ensuring that all the banks in their jurisdiction are accessible, long-term viable, and their business models are understood. To ensure they remain "fit for purpose" for their task, as this case study reveals, the supervisor may occasionally need to have recourse to external practitioners' training, as required. This ensures that the regulatory authority is kept abreast of developments in the market, and is better able to identify good practice and censure bad practice.

Bank supervision is generally regarded as much art as science. In the modern era, banks within a single jurisdiction are observed to exhibit widely varying operating and business models, with balance sheet size ranging from under $1 million to many hundreds of billion dollars. This makes the act of maintaining fit-for-purpose supervision a challenging one. To meet this challenge, forward-thinking supervisory authorities undertake a programme of continuous staff training, both external and in-house. This addresses some of the currency issues always associated with those undertaking oversight of an activity with which they themselves are not directly involved.

However, any form of training is only effective if it teaches current business practice. Moreover, it must reflect best practice, such that those who have undergone training are able to assess for themselves what activities they are observing represent the correct way of doing things, from the customer as well as regulator perspective. To achieve this, it is important that practitioners recognised by their peers as exponents of best-practice banking risk management art are invited by the supervisor to deliver regular training.

Objectives and scope of training

The author was invited by SBS, the regulatory authority in Lima, Peru, to deliver a week-long training course on the subject of "Bank Asset–Liability Management". The objectives of the course were stated originally as follows:

- To illustrate and explain current best practice in bank ALM;
- To understand the principal issues with respect to managing bank balance sheet risk;

- To demonstrate the impact of Basel III on bank business models;
- To provide recommendations on how best to ensure ALCO best-practice framework and governance.

The SBS and the author discussed over a series of conference calls the most effective way of delivering this course. The author is a frequent speaker at industry conferences, as well as experienced in the art of balance sheet risk management, having worked as a treasurer at different banks; this suggested the course content would be reasonably up to date. The challenges that did arise related to the best way to deliver the course. The SBS had specified a relatively large delegate number, up to 50 individuals. With this number in the room, it was decided that the course would be broken into a series of lectures, team exercises, and individual exercises.

The final agenda was split into specific technical topics, streamlined into a 5-day course as follows:

Days 1, 2, and 3
1. The concept of internal funds transfer pricing
2. Objectives of internal funding policy
3. The cost of funds
4. Setting the correct market-implied term funds transfer pricing curve
5. FTP and liquidity management
6. FTP and liabilities strategy
7. Integrated balance sheet management and strategic ALM
8. Interest-rate risk in the banking book

Days 4 and 5
1. Managing liquidity risk
2. Best-practice liquidity risk management policy: Board risk appetite statement
3. Stress testing and ILAAP results: what to look for in a good ILAAP
4. Liquidity risk management – limit setting
5. ALCO governance and process best practice
6. Basel III implementation best practice

These sections were further split into formal lectures, breakout team sessions, and individual exercises. All discussion points were then debated within the complete group. To ensure maximum understanding, SBS also engaged a professional translator to provide a continuous service during both lectures and seminar sessions.

Delegates were drawn from a number of different departments in the bank, including Supervision, Liquidity Risk, and Capital Planning.

Importance in bank supervision

A natural part of the bank supervision process is to work to identify different approaches used in bank risk management processes, and to be able to determine what is acceptable practice and what is less so. Ultimately, this is not possible to maximum effectiveness unless regulatory staff are familiar with a number of different bank business models and ways to implement ALM and risk management. A longer-term way of embedding this knowledge and expertise is to arrange for regulator's staff to arrange short-term and medium-term work placement at banks, in different departments such as Risk, Treasury, Finance, and Compliance. This is common practice at, say, the BoE.

The other effective way to embed some of this expertise and current market practice is to invite experienced practitioners, as opposed to pure academics, to lecture on current best-practice guidelines. This was the aim of the course the author conducted at SBS and its importance to the SBS supervision process was reflected in the positive feedback the author received from course delegates.

Example 17.1   UK banking licence application "challenge session" agenda

---

Example 17.1 Banking licence application agenda

We list here the typical agenda of a banking licence application submission to the UK regulatory authorities. This would form part of the challenge session conducted by the regulator.

XYZ Bank – Part I session

Identity

USP
Purpose, vision, and values
Brand strategy and positioning
SWOT

Governance

Ownership structure
Management structure and experience
Board and Board committees (skills)
SIFs (significant influence functions)/Profiles/Experience
Evolution of governance and oversight
Internal audit

Business overview – Day 1/Customer

Customer segments
Products
Pricing strategy
Channels
Market share
Risk (high level, further detail in part II)
Conduct agenda (high level, detail in part II)

Capital and liquidity (high level, detail in part II)
Resolution and recovery (high level)

Financials

Financial viability and sustainability (including key assumptions)
Profitability (including key drivers, margin assumptions)
Impairment assumptions
Cost base
Customer franchise targets
Key sensitivities/downside risks

Risk

Risk management (including strategy to identify and manage risks to the
    business)
Risk appetite
Risk structure
Risks to the plan
Risk MI and reporting
Risk policies

Future strategy

Vision/evolution
Growth
Strategic planning process

Challenge session

Why should we have confidence in the bank and its management?

XYZ Bank – Part II session

Technology platform

Capital

ICAAP process, assumptions, results
Capital structure of XYZ Bank; conclusions from the ICAAP, covering:
    Structure of capital
    Source of capital and sources of additional capital
    Control environment (including governance of capital/ICAAP; risk
        appetite)
    Pillar 1 capital calculations
    Pillar 2 assessment and quantification of risks
    Stress testing and scenario analysis
    Key areas of market risk, credit risk, operational risk, with metrics

Liquidity/funding

Overview of how Treasury operations are managed in XYZ Bank
Approach to hedging (overview)

Liquidity risk management (including risk appetite and metrics to measure and manage)

Stress testing and assumptions

ILAAP process, assumptions, results

Liquidity buffer

Control environment (including governance of liquidity/ILAAP)

Summary of contingency funding plan (CFP)

Key liquidity and funding policies

Stress testing and scenario analysis

Operating model

Overview of operating model

Overview of IT systems

Key supplier relationships

Governance

Future capacity and plans

Conduct

Conduct agenda in the bank

Customer journey

Conduct risk assessment by product

Issues to be addressed/remediated

Appendix

A

....

FINANCIAL
MARKETS
ARITHMETIC

INTEREST: PRESENT AND FUTURE VALUE

Simple interest

A loan that has one interest payment on maturity is accruing simple interest. On short-term instruments, there is usually only the one interest payment on maturity, hence simple interest is received when the instrument expires. The terminal value of an investment with simple interest is given by:

$$FV = PV(1 + r) \qquad (A.1)$$

where

    FV = Terminal value or future value;
    PV = Initial investment or present value;
     r = Interest rate.

So, for example, if PV is £100, r is 5% and the investment is 1 year. Then

$$FV = £100(1 + r) = £105$$

The market convention is to quote interest rates as *annualised* interest rates, which is the interest that is earned if the investment term is 1 year. Consider a 3-month deposit of £100 in a bank, placed at a rate of interest of 6%. In such an example, the bank deposit will earn 6% interest for a period of 90 days. As the annual interest gain would be £6, the investor will expect to receive a proportion of this:

$$£6.00 \times \frac{90}{368}$$

So, the investor will receive £1.479 interest at the end of the term. The total proceeds after the 3 months is therefore £100 plus £1.479. If we wish to calculate the terminal value of a short-term investment that is accruing simple interest we use the following expression:

$$FV = PV\left(1 + r \times \frac{Days}{Year}\right) \qquad (A.2)$$

The fraction $\frac{Days}{Year}$ refers to the numerator, which is the number of days the investment runs, divided by the denominator, which is the number of days in the year. In sterling markets, the number of days in a year is taken to be 365; however, certain other markets (including euro currency markets) have a 360-day year convention. For this reason, we simply quote the expression as "days" divided by "year" to allow for either convention.

Compound interest

Let us now consider an investment of £100 made for 3 years, again at a rate of 6%, but this time fixed for 3 years. At the end of the first year, the investor will be credited with interest of £6. Therefore, for the second year the interest rate of 6% will be accruing on a principal sum of £106, which means that at the end of Year 2 the interest credited will be £6.36. This illustrates how *compounding* works, which is the principle of earning interest on interest. What will the terminal value of our £100 3-year investment be?

In compounding, we are seeking to find a *future value* given a *present value*, a *time period*, and an *interest rate*. If £100 is invested today (at time t_0) at 6%, then 1 year later (t_1) the investor will have $£E100 \times (1 + 0 : 06) = £106$. In our example, the capital is left in for another 2 years, so at the end of Year 2 (t_2) we will have:

$$£100 \times (1 + 0.06) \times (1 + 0.06) = £100 \times (1 + 0.06)^2$$
$$= £100 \times (1.06)^2$$
$$= £112.36$$

The outcome of the process of compounding is the *future value* of the initial amount. We don't have to calculate the terminal value long hand as we can use:

$$FV = PV(1 + r)^n \qquad (A.3)$$

where

r = Periodic rate of interest (expressed as a decimal);
n = Number of periods for which the sum is invested.

In our example, the initial £100 investment after 3 years becomes $£E100 \times (1 + 0.06)3$ which is equal to £119.10.

When we compound interest, we have to assume that the reinvestment of interest payments during the investment term is at the same rate as the first year's interest. That is why we stated that the 6% rate in our example was *fixed* for 3 years. However, we can see that compounding increases our returns compared with investments that accrue only on a simple interest basis. If we had invested £100 for 3 years fixed at a rate of 6% but paying on a simple interest basis, our terminal value would be £118, which is £1.10 less than our terminal value using a compound interest basis.

Compounding more than once a year

Now let us consider a deposit of £100 for 1 year, again at our rate of 6% but with quarterly interest payments. Such a deposit would accrue interest of £6 in the normal way, but £1.50 would be credited to the account every quarter, and this would then benefit from compounding. Again, assuming that we can reinvest at the same rate of 6%, the total return at the end of the year will be:

$$100 \times ((1 + 0.015) \times (1 + 0.015) \times (1 + 0.015) \times (1 + 0.015)) = 100 \times (1 + 0.015)^4$$

which gives us 100 × 1.06136, a terminal value of £106.136. This is some 13 pence more than the terminal value using annual compounded interest. The impact of more frequent compounding is shown at Table A.1.

Table A.1   The effect of more frequent compounding

Compounding frequency	Interest rate factor
Annual	$(1 + r) = 1.050000$
Semi-annual	$\left(1 + \dfrac{r}{2}\right)^2 = 1.050625$
Quarterly	$\left(1 + \dfrac{r}{4}\right)^4 = 1.050945$
Monthly	$\left(1 + \dfrac{r}{12}\right)^{12} = 1.051162$
Daily	$\left(1 + \dfrac{r}{365}\right)^{365} = 1.051267$

In general, if compounding takes place m times per year, then at the end of n years mn interest payments will have been made and the future value of the principal is given by:

$$FV = PV\left(1 + \frac{r}{m}\right)^{mn} \tag{A.4}$$

As we showed in our example, the effect of more frequent compounding is to increase the value of total return when compared with annual compounding. The effect of more frequent compounding is shown below, where we consider annualised interest rate factors, for an annualised rate of 5%.

This shows us that the more frequent the compounding, the higher the interest rate factor. The last case also illustrates how a limit occurs when interest is compounded continuously. Equation (A.4) can be rewritten as:

$$FV = PV\left(\left(1 + \frac{r}{m}\right)^{m/r}\right)^{rn} = PV\left(\left(1 + \frac{1}{m/r}\right)^{m/r}\right)^{rn}$$

$$= PV\left(\left(1 + \frac{1}{n}\right)^{n}\right)^{rn} \tag{A.5}$$

where $n = m/r$. As compounding becomes continuous and m and hence n approach infinity, equation (A.5) approaches a value known as e, which is shown by:

$$e = \lim_{n\to\infty}\left(1 + \frac{1}{n}\right)^{n} = 2.718281\ldots$$

If we substitute this into (A.5), we get:

$$FV = PVe^{rn} \tag{A.6}$$

where we have continuous compounding. In equation (A.6), e^{rn} is known as the *exponential function* of rn; it tells us the continuously compounded interest rate factor. If $r = 5\%$ and $n = 1$ year then:

$$e^r = (2.718281)^{0.05} = 1.051271$$

This is the limit reached with continuous compounding. To illustrate continuous compounding from our initial example, the future value of £100 at the end of 3 years – when the interest rate is 6% – can be given by:

$$FV = 100e^{(0.06)\times 3} = £119.72$$

Effective interest rates

The interest rate quoted on a deposit or loan is usually the *flat* rate. However, we are often required to compare two interest rates, which apply for a similar investment period but have different interest payment frequencies – for example, a 2-year interest rate with interest paid quarterly compared with a 2-year rate with semi-annual interest payments. This is normally done by comparing equivalent *annualised* rates. The annualised rate is the interest rate with annual compounding that results in the same return at the end of the period as the rate we are comparing.

The concept of the effective interest rate allows us to state that:

$$PV \times \left(1 + \frac{r}{n}\right)^n = PV \times (1 + AER) \tag{A.7}$$

where AER is the equivalent annual rate. Therefore, if r is the interest rate quoted that pays n interest payments per year, AER is given by:

$$AER = \left(\left(1 + \frac{r}{n}\right)^n - 1\right) \tag{A.8}$$

The equivalent annual interest rate AER is known as the *effective* interest rate. We have already referred to the quoted interest rate as the "nominal" interest rate. We can rearrange equation (A.8) to give us equation (A.9) which allows us to calculate nominal rates:

$$r = ((1 + AER)^{1/n} - 1) \times n \tag{A.9}$$

We can see then that the effective rate will be greater than the flat rate if compounding takes place more than once a year. The effective rate is sometimes referred to as the *annualised percentage rate* or APR.

Interest rate conventions

The convention in both wholesale and personal (retail) markets is to quote an annual interest rate. A lender who wishes to earn interest at the rate quoted has to place her funds on deposit for 1 year. Annual rates are quoted irrespective of the maturity of a deposit, from overnight to 10 years or longer. For example, if one opens a bank account that pays interest at a rate of 3.5% but then closes it after 6 months, the actual interest earned will be equal to 1.75% of the sum deposited. The actual return on a 3-year building society bond (fixed deposit) that pays 6.75% fixed for 3 years is 21.65% after 3 years. The quoted rate is the annual 1-year equivalent. An overnight deposit in the wholesale or *inter-bank* market is still quoted as an annual rate, even though interest is earned for only one day.

The convention of quoting annualised rates is to allow deposits and loans of different maturities and different instruments to be compared on the basis of the interest rate applicable. We must also be careful when comparing interest rates for products that have different payment frequencies. As we have seen from the foregoing paragraphs, the actual interest earned will be greater for a deposit earning 6% on a semi-annual basis compared with 6% on an annual basis. The convention in the money markets is to quote the equivalent interest rate applicable when taking into account an instrument's payment frequency.

Discount factors

The calculation of present values from future values is also known as *discounting*. The principles of present and future values demonstrate the concept of the *time value* of money, which is that in an environment of positive interest rates a sum of money has greater value today than it does at some point in the future because we are able to invest the sum today and earn interest. We will only consider a sum in the future compared with a sum today if we are compensated by being paid interest at a sufficient rate. Discounting future values allows us to compare the value of a future sum with a present sum.

The rate of interest r, known as the *discount rate*, is the rate we use to *discount* a known future value in order to calculate a present value. We can rearrange equation (A.1) to give:

$$PV = FV(1 + r)^{-n}$$

The term $(1 + r)^{-n}$ is known as the n-year discount factor:

$$df_n = (1 + r)^{-n} \tag{A.10}$$

where df_n is the n-year discount factor.

The 3-year discount factor when the discount rate is 9% is:

$$df_3 = (1 + 0.09)^{-3} = 0.77218$$

We can calculate discount factors for all possible interest rates and time periods to give us a *discount function*. Fortunately, we don't need to calculate discount factors ourselves as this has been done for us. (Discount tables for a range of rates are provided in Table A.2.)

Table A.2 Discount factor table

Discount rate (%)

Years	1 0.01	2 0.02	3 0.03	4 0.04	5 0.05	6 0.06	7 0.07	8 0.08	9 0.09	10 0.1	12 0.12	15 0.15	20 0.2
1	0.990099	0.980392	0.970874	0.961538	0.952381	0.943396	0.934579	0.925926	0.917431	0.909091	0.892857	0.869565	0.833333
2	0.980296	0.961169	0.942596	0.924556	0.907029	0.889996	0.873439	0.857339	0.841680	0.826446	0.797194	0.756144	0.694444
3	0.970590	0.942322	0.915142	0.888996	0.863838	0.839619	0.816298	0.793832	0.772183	0.751315	0.711780	0.657516	0.578704
4	0.960980	0.923845	0.888487	0.854804	0.822702	0.792094	0.762895	0.735030	0.708425	0.683013	0.635518	0.571753	0.482253
5	0.951466	0.905731	0.862609	0.821927	0.783526	0.747258	0.712986	0.680583	0.649931	0.620921	0.567427	0.497177	0.401878
6	0.942045	0.887971	0.837484	0.790315	0.746215	0.704961	0.666342	0.630170	0.596267	0.564474	0.506631	0.432328	0.334898
7	0.932718	0.870560	0.813092	0.759918	0.710681	0.665057	0.622750	0.583490	0.547034	0.513158	0.452349	0.375937	0.279082
8	0.923483	0.853490	0.789409	0.730690	0.676839	0.627412	0.582009	0.540269	0.501866	0.466507	0.403883	0.326902	0.232568
9	0.914340	0.836755	0.766417	0.702587	0.644609	0.591898	0.543934	0.500249	0.460428	0.424098	0.360610	0.284262	0.193807
10	0.905287	0.820348	0.744094	0.675564	0.613913	0.558395	0.508349	0.463193	0.422411	0.385543	0.321973	0.247185	0.161506
11	0.896324	0.804263	0.722421	0.649581	0.584679	0.526788	0.475093	0.428883	0.387533	0.350494	0.287476	0.214943	0.134588
12	0.887449	0.788493	0.701380	0.624597	0.556837	0.496969	0.444012	0.397114	0.355535	0.318631	0.256675	0.186907	0.112157
13	0.878663	0.773033	0.680951	0.600574	0.530321	0.468839	0.414964	0.367698	0.326179	0.289664	0.229174	0.162528	0.093464
14	0.869963	0.757875	0.661118	0.577475	0.505068	0.442301	0.387817	0.340461	0.299246	0.263331	0.204620	0.141329	0.077887
15	0.861349	0.743015	0.641862	0.555265	0.481017	0.417265	0.362446	0.315242	0.274538	0.239392	0.182696	0.122894	0.064905
16	0.852821	0.728446	0.623167	0.533908	0.458112	0.393646	0.338735	0.291890	0.251870	0.217629	0.163122	0.106865	0.054088
17	0.844377	0.714163	0.605016	0.513373	0.436297	0.371364	0.316574	0.270269	0.231073	0.197845	0.145644	0.092926	0.045073
18	0.836017	0.700159	0.587395	0.493628	0.415521	0.350344	0.295864	0.250249	0.211994	0.179859	0.130040	0.080805	0.037561
19	0.827740	0.686431	0.570286	0.474642	0.395734	0.330513	0.276508	0.231712	0.194490	0.163508	0.116107	0.070265	0.031301
20	0.819544	0.672971	0.553676	0.456387	0.376889	0.311805	0.258419	0.214548	0.178431	0.148644	0.103667	0.061100	0.026084
21	0.811430	0.659776	0.537549	0.438834	0.358942	0.294155	0.241513	0.198656	0.163698	0.135131	0.092560	0.053131	0.021737
22	0.803396	0.646839	0.521893	0.421955	0.341850	0.277505	0.225713	0.183941	0.150182	0.122846	0.082643	0.046201	0.018114
23	0.795442	0.634156	0.506692	0.405726	0.325571	0.261797	0.210947	0.170315	0.137781	0.111678	0.073788	0.040174	0.015095
24	0.787566	0.621721	0.491934	0.390121	0.310068	0.246979	0.197147	0.157699	0.126405	0.101526	0.065882	0.034934	0.012579
25	0.779768	0.609531	0.477606	0.375117	0.295303	0.232999	0.184249	0.146018	0.115968	0.092296	0.058823	0.030378	0.010483
26	0.772048	0.597579	0.463695	0.360689	0.281241	0.219810	0.172195	0.135202	0.106393	0.083905	0.052521	0.026415	0.008735
27	0.764404	0.585862	0.450189	0.346817	0.267848	0.207368	0.160930	0.125187	0.097608	0.076278	0.046894	0.022970	0.007280
28	0.756836	0.574375	0.437077	0.333477	0.255094	0.195630	0.150402	0.115914	0.089548	0.069343	0.041869	0.019974	0.006066
29	0.749342	0.563112	0.424346	0.320651	0.242946	0.184557	0.140563	0.107328	0.082155	0.063039	0.037383	0.017369	0.005055
30	0.741923	0.552071	0.411987	0.308319	0.231377	0.174110	0.131367	0.099377	0.075371	0.057309	0.033378	0.015103	0.004213

Formula summary
Discount factor with simple interest $df = \dfrac{1}{\left(1 + r\dfrac{\text{Days}}{\text{Year}}\right)^n}$
Discount factor with compound interest $df_n = \left(\dfrac{1}{1+r}\right)^n$

Earlier we established the continuously compounded interest rate factor as e^{rn}. Therefore, using a continuously compounded interest rate we can establish the discount factor to be:

$$\left.\begin{array}{l} df = \dfrac{1}{1+(e^{r\times\text{Days/Year}}-1)} = e^{-r\times\text{Days/Year}} \\ \therefore df_n = e^{-m} \end{array}\right\} \qquad (A.11)$$

The continuously compounded discount factor is part of the formula used in option-pricing models. It is possible to calculate discount factors from the prices of government bonds. The traditional approach described in most textbooks requires that we first use the price of a bond that has only one remaining coupon, its last one, and calculate a discount factor from this bond's price. We then use this discount factor to calculate the discount factors of bonds with ever-increasing maturities, until we obtain the complete discount function.

Present values with multiple discounting

Present values for short-term investments of under 1-year maturity often involve a single interest payment. If there is more than one interest payment, then any discounting needs to take this into account. If discounting takes place m times per year, then we can use equation (A.4) to derive the present value formula:

$$PV = FV\left(1 + \frac{r}{m}\right)^{-mn} \qquad (A.12)$$

For example, what is the present value of the sum of £1,000 which is to be received in 5 years where the discount rate is 5% and there is semi-annual discounting?

Using equation (A.12) we see that:

$$PV = 1,000\left(1 + \frac{0.05}{2}\right)^{-2\times5} = £781.20$$

The effect of more frequent discounting is to lower the present value. As with continuous compounding, the limiting factor is reached by means of continuous discounting. We can use equation (A.6) to derive the present value formula for continuous discounting:

$$PV = FVe^{-m} \qquad (A.13)$$

If we consider the same example as before but now with continuous discounting, we can use this expression to calculate the present value of £1,000 to be received in 5 years' time as:

$$PV = 1,000e^{-(0.05)\times 5} = £778.80$$

MULTIPLE CASH FLOWS

Future values

Up to now, we have considered the future values of a single cash flow. Of course, the same principles of the time value of money can be applied to a bundle of cash flows. A series of cash flows can be at regular or at irregular intervals. If we wish to calculate the total future value of a set of irregular payments made in the future, we need to calculate each payment separately and then sum all the cash flows. The formula is represented as:

$$FV = \sum_{n=1}^{N} C_n(1+r)^{N-n} \qquad (A.14)$$

where C_n is the payment in year n; and the symbol $\sum$ means "the sum of". We assume that payment is made and interest credited at the end of each year.

It is much more common to come across a regular stream of future payments. Such a cash flow is known as an *annuity*. In an annuity the payments are identical and so C_n – as given in equation (A.14) – simply becomes C. We can then rearrange equation (A.14) as:

$$FV = C \sum_{n=1}^{N} (1+r)^{N-n} \qquad (A.15)$$

This equation can be simplified to give us:[1]

$$FV = C \left(\frac{(1+r)^N - 1}{r} \right) \qquad (A.16)$$

---

[1] If we multiply both sides of equation (A.15) by $1 + r$ and then subtract the result from equation (A.15) we obtain:

$$FV - (1+r)FV = C \left(\sum_{n=1}^{N} (1+r)^{N-n} - \sum_{n=1}^{N} (1+r)^{N-n+1} \right)$$

$$= -C((1+r)^N - 1)$$

This formula can be used to calculate the future value of an annuity. For example, if we consider an annuity that pays £500 each year for 10 years at a rate of 6%, its future value is given by:

$$FV = 500 \left(\frac{(1.06)^{10} - 1}{0.06} \right) = £6{,}590.40$$

The common definition of an annuity is a continuous stream of cash flows. In practice, the pension represented by an annuity is usually paid in monthly instalments, similar to an employed person's annual salary. Certain regular payments compound interest on a more frequent basis than annually, so equation (A.15) needs to be adjusted slightly. If compounding occurs m times each year, then equation (A.15) needs to be altered to equation (A.17) to allow for this:

$$FV = C \sum_{n=1}^{N} \left(1 + \frac{r}{m} \right)^{m(N-n)} \tag{A.17}$$

To make calculations simpler we can multiply both sides of equation (A.17) by $(1 + (r/m))$ and subtract the result from equation (A.17). Simplifying this will then result in:

$$FV = C \left(\frac{(1 + (r/m)^{mN} - 1)}{(1 + (r/m)^{m} - 1)} \right) \tag{A.18}$$

For example, a 10-year annuity that has annual payments of £5,000, but compounded on a quarterly basis at a rate of 5%, will have a future value of £63,073 as:

$$FV = 5{,}000 \left(\frac{(1.025)^{20} - 1}{(1.025)^{2} - 1} \right) = £63{,}073$$

Where there is continuous compounding, as before the limiting factor will result in equation (A.17) becoming:

$$FV = C \left(\frac{e^{rN} - 1}{e^{r} - 1} \right) \tag{A.19}$$

Equations (A.18) and (A.19) can be adjusted yet again to allow for frequent payments together with frequent compounding, but such a stream of cash flows is rarely encountered in practice. In the case of continuous compounding of continuous payments, the limiting factor expression is:

$$FV = C \left(\frac{e^{rN} - 1}{r} \right) \tag{A.20}$$

Present values

Using similar principles to those employed for calculating future values, we can calculate present values for a stream of multiple cash flows. The method employed is slightly different according to whether cash flows are regular or irregular.

For irregular payments, we calculate present value by applying the conventional present value formula to each separate cash flow and then summing the present values. This is represented by:

$$PV = \sum_{n=1}^{N} C_n(1+r)^{-n} \qquad (A.21)$$

where C_n is the cash flow made in Year n.

Consider a series of annual cash payments made up of £100 in the first year and then increasing by £100 each year until the fifth year. The present value of this cash flow stream is:

$$PV = 100(1.05)^{-1} + 200(1.05)^{-2} + 300(1.05)^{-3} + 400(1.05)^{-3} + 500(1.05)^{-5}$$
$$= 95.24 + 181.41 + 259.15 + 329.08 + 391.76$$
$$= £1,256.64$$

The more frequently encountered type of cash flow stream is an *annuity*, regular annual payments with annual discounting. To calculate the present value of an annuity we can use a variation of equation (A.16):

$$PV = \frac{FV}{(1+r)^N}$$

$$= C\left(\frac{(1+r)^N - 1}{r}\right)\left(\frac{1}{(1+r)^N}\right)$$

$$= C\left(\frac{1-(1+r)^{-N}}{r}\right) \qquad (A.22)$$

Consider now an annuity paying £5,000 each year for 20 years at an interest rate of 4.5%. The present value of this annuity is:

$$PV = 5,000\left(\frac{1-(1.045)^{-20}}{0.045}\right)$$

$$= 65,039,68$$

We illustrate this principle using a 20-year annuity that employs annual discounting. If a cash flow stream employs more frequent discounting, we need to adjust the formula again. If an annuity discounts its cash flows m times each year, then the present value of its cash flow stream is found using the present-value-adjusted equation – that is, equation (A.18). This becomes:

$$PV = \frac{FV}{\left(1 + \frac{r}{m}\right)^{mN}} = c\left(\frac{1 - (1 + (r/m))^{-mN}}{(1 + (r/m))^m - 1}\right) \tag{A.23}$$

If continuous discounting is employed then, this results once again in the limiting factor for continuous discounting, so we adjust equation (A.23) and the new expression is:

$$PV = C\left(\frac{1 - e^{-rN}}{e^r - 1}\right) \tag{A.24}$$

The last case to consider is that of the payments stream that has more frequent cash flows in addition to more frequent discounting. Such a payments stream will have m cash flows each year, which are also discounted m times per year. To calculate the present value of the cash flows we use:

$$PV = \frac{FV}{(1 + (r/m))^{mN}} = C\frac{1 - (1 + (r/m))^{mN}}{r} \tag{A.25}$$

The limiting factor for continuous discounting of continuous payments is:

$$PV = C\left(\frac{1 - e^{-rN}}{r}\right) \tag{A.26}$$

Payment streams that have cash flow frequencies greater than annually or semi-annually occur quite often in the markets. To illustrate how we might use equation (A.25), consider a mortgage-type loan taken out at the beginning of a period. If the borrower is able to fix the interest rate being charged to the whole life of the mortgage, she can calculate the size of monthly payments required to pay off the loan at the end of the period.

For example, consider a repayment mortgage of £76,000 taken out for 25 years at a fixed rate of interest of 6.99%. The monthly repayments that would be charged can be calculated using equation (A.25) as:

$$C_i = \frac{C}{12} = \frac{PV}{12}\left(\frac{r}{1 - (1 + (r/m))^{-12 \times N}}\right) \tag{A.27}$$

where C_i is the size of the monthly payment. Substituting the terms of the mortgage payments into the equation, we obtain:

$$C_i = \frac{76,000}{12}\left(\frac{0.0699}{1 - (1 + (0.0699/12))^{-12 \times 25}}\right) = £536.67$$

The monthly repayment is therefore £536.67 and includes interest chargeable in addition to repayment of some of the principal. (Hence the term *repayment* mortgage, as opposed to *endowment* mortgage which only pays off the monthly interest charge.) A repayment mortgage is also known as an *amortised* mortgage. An amortised loan is one where a proportion of the original loan capital is paid off each year. Loans that require the borrower to service the interest charge once a year are known as *straight* or *bullet* loans. It is for this reason that plain vanilla bonds are sometimes known as bullet bonds, since the capital element of a loan raised through a vanilla bond issue is repaid only on maturity.

Perpetual cash flows

The type of annuity that we as individuals are most familiar with is the *annuity pension*, purchased from a life assurance company using the proceeds of a pension fund at the time of retirement. Such an annuity pays a fixed annual cash amount for an undetermined period, usually until the death of the beneficiary. An annuity with no set finish date is known as a *perpetuity*. As the end date of a perpetuity is unknown we are not able to calculate its present value with certainty. However, a characteristic of the term $(1+r)^{-N}$ is that it approaches zero as N tends to infinity. This fact reduces our present value expression to:

$$PV = \frac{C}{r} \qquad (A.28)$$

We can use this formula to approximate the present value of a perpetuity.

The UK gilt market includes four gilts that have no redemption date – so-called *undated bonds*. The largest issue amongst undated gilts is the $3\frac{1}{2}\%$ war loan, a stock originally issued at the time of the 1914–1918 war. This bond pays a coupon of £$3\frac{1}{2}$ per £100 nominal of stock. Since the cash flow structure of this bond matches a perpetual, its present value – using equation (A.28) when long-dated market interest rates are at, say, 5% – would be:

$$PV = \frac{3.5}{0.05} = £70$$

The present value of the cash flow stream represented by the war loan stock when market rates are 5% would therefore be £70 per £100 nominal of stock. In fact, because this bond pays coupon on a semi-annual basis, we should adjust the calculation to account for the more frequent payment of coupons and discounting. So the present value (price) of the bond is more accurately described as:

$$PV = \frac{C/3}{r/2} = \frac{1.75}{0.025}$$

although – as we would expect – this still gives us a price of £70 per £100 nominal!

CORPORATE FINANCE PROJECT APPRAISAL

Two common techniques used by corporates and governments to evaluate whether a project is worth undertaking are *net present value* and *internal rate of return*. Both techniques evaluate the anticipated cash flows associated with a project, using the discounting and present value methods described in this chapter. Generally speaking, it is a company's *cost of capital* that is used as the discount rate in project appraisal, and most companies attempt to ascertain the true cost of their capital as accurately as possible. As most corporate financing is usually a complex mixture of debt and equity, this is sometimes problematic.

Net present value

In the case of an investment of funds made as part of a project, we would have a series of cash flows – some of which would be positive and others negative. In the early stages of a project, we would typically forecast negative cash flows as a result of investment outflows, followed by positive cash flows as the project began to show a return. Each cash flow can be present-valued in the usual way. In project appraisal we would seek to find the present value of the entire stream of cash flows; the sum of all positive and negative present values added together is the *net present value* (NPV). As the appraisal process takes place before the project is undertaken, the future cash flows that we are concerned with will be estimated forecasts and may not actually be received once the project is under way.

The net present value equation is used to show that:

$$NPV = \sum_{n=1}^{N} \frac{C_n}{(1+r)^n} \qquad (A.29)$$

where C_n is the cash flow used for the project during period N. The rate r used to discount cash flows can be the company's cost of capital or the rate of return required by the company to make the project viable.

Companies will apply NPV analysis to expected projected returns because funds invested in any undertaking have a time-related cost – the opportunity cost that is the corporate cost of capital. In effect, NPV measures the present value of the gain achieved from investing in the project (provided that it is successful!). The general rule of thumb applied is that any project with a positive NPV is worthwhile, whereas those with a negative NPV, discounted at the required rate of return or the cost of capital, should be avoided.

Example A.1

What is the NPV of the following set of expected cash flows, discounted at a rate of 15%?

Year 0	£23,000
Year 1	+£8,000
Year 2	+£8,000
Year 3	+£8,000
Year 4	+£11,000

$$NPV = 23,000 - \frac{8,000}{(1.15)} + \frac{8,000}{(1.15)^2} + \frac{8,000}{(1.15)^3} + \frac{11,000}{(1.15)^4} = £1,554$$

The internal rate of return

The internal rate of return (IRR) for an investment is the discount rate that equates the present value of expected cash flows (the NPV) to zero. Using the present value expression, we can represent it by rate r such that:

$$\sum_{n=0}^{N} \frac{C_n}{(1+r)^n} = 0 \tag{A.30}$$

where

C_n = Cash flow for the period N;
n = *Last period in which a cash flow is expected; and*
$\sum$ = *Sum of discounted cash flows at the end of periods 0 through n.*

If the initial cash flow occurs at time 0, equation (A.30) can be expressed as:

$$C_0 = \frac{C_1}{(1+r)} + \frac{C_2}{(1+r)^2} + \ldots + \frac{C_N}{(1+r)^N} \tag{A.31}$$

In corporate finance project appraisal, C_0 is a cash outflow and C_1 to C_N are cash inflows. Thus, r is the rate that discounts the stream of future cash flows (C_1 through C_n) to equal the initial outlay at time 0. We must therefore assume that the cash flows received are subsequently reinvested to realise the same rate of return as r. Solving for the internal rate of return, r, cannot be found analytically and has to be found either through numerical iteration or using a computer or programmable calculator.

To illustrate the IRR, consider the project cash flows given in Example A.1. If we wish to find the IRR long hand, then we would have to obtain the NPV using different discount rates until we found the rate that gave an NPV equal to zero. The quickest way to do this manually is to select two discount rates, one giving a negative NPV and the other a positive NPV, and then *interpolate* between them. This method of solving for IRR is known as an iterative process and involves converging on a solution through trial and error. This is in fact the only way to calculate the IRR for a set of cash flows; it matches exactly the iterative process that a computer uses (the computer is just a touch quicker!). If we have two discount rates – say, x and y – that give positive and negative NPVs, respectively, for a set of cash flows – the IRR can be estimated using:

IRR estimate $= x\% + (y\% - x\%)$

$$\times \left(\frac{\text{Positive NPV value}}{\text{Negative NPV value} - (-\text{NPV value})} \right) \tag{A.32}$$

Using a discount rate of 15% produced a positive NPV in Example A.1. Discounting the cash flows at 19% produces an NPV of ÁE395. Therefore, the estimate for IRR is:

$$15\% + 4\% \times 1{,}554/(1{,}554 - (-395)) = 18.19\%$$

The IRR is approximately 18.19%. This can be checked using a programmable calculator or spreadsheet programme; it may also be checked manually by calculating the NPV of the original cash flows using a discount rate of 18.19% – it should come to –£23,000. We obtain an IRR of 18.14% using a calculator.

The relationship between the IRR and the NPV of an investment can be summed up as follows: while the NPV is the value of projected returns from the investment using an appropriate discount rate (usually the company's cost of capital), the IRR is the discount rate which results in the NPV being zero. For this reason, it is common to hear the IRR referred to as a project's *breakeven* rate. A conventional investment is considered attractive if the IRR exceeds a company's cost of capital and the NPV is positive. In the context of bond markets, as long as the discount rate applicable does indeed remain constant for the reinvestment of all cash flows arising from a financial instrument, the IRR can then be assumed to be the *yield to maturity* for that instrument. Yield to maturity is the main measure of the rate of return achieved from holding a bond. The relationship between NPV and IRR is illustrated at Figure A.1.

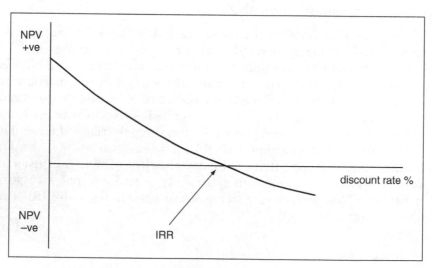

Figure A.1   Relationship between NPV and IRR

INTERPOLATION AND EXTRAPOLATION

Interest rates in the money markets are always quoted for standard maturities: for example, overnight, "tom next" (the overnight interest rate starting tomorrow, or "tomorrow to the next"), spot next (the overnight rate starting 2 days forward), 1 week, 1 month, 2 months, and so on up to 1 year. Figure A.2 shows a typical brokers' screen as seen on news services such as Reuters and Telerate.

If a bank or corporate customer wishes to deal for non-standard periods, an inter-bank desk will calculate the rate chargeable for such an "odd date" by *interpolating* between two standard period interest rates. If we assume that the rate for all dates in between two periods increases at the same pace, we can calculate the required rate using the formula for *straight line* interpolation:

$$r = r_1 + (r_2 - r_1) \times \frac{n - n_1}{n_2 - n_1}$$ (A.33)

where

r = Required odd date rate for n days;
r_1 = Quoted rate for n_1 days;
r_2 = Quoted rate for n_2 days.

Let us imagine that the 1-month (30-day) offered interest rate is 5.25% and the 2-month (60-day) offered rate is 5.75%. If a customer wishes to borrow money for a 40-day period, what rate should the bank charge? We can calculate the required 40-day rate using straight line interpolation. The increase in interest rates from 30 to 40 days is assumed to be 10/30 of the total increase in rates from 30 to 60 days. The 40-day offered rate would therefore be:

$$5.25 + (5.75 - 5.25) \times 10/30 = 5.4167\%$$

Dow Jones Markets : martin_g   Telerate 4734   Wed Dec 08 09:00:44 1999

```
08/12      8:54 GMT      [GARBAN INTERCAPITAL-EUROPE]              12/08 02:12  4734
            FRA              GBP CDS DEPO       GBP INTERBANK DEP     GBP REPO(GC)
 1X4  6.020-990  O/N         -                5  1/16-4 15/16        -              O/N
 2X5  6.110-080  T/N         -                5  3/8 -5  1/4         -              T/N
 3X6  6.230-200  1WK         -                5  1/4 -5  1/8         -              1WK
 4X7  6.330-300  1MO    5 25/32-5 23/32       5  7/8 -5 13/16        -              2WK
 5X8  6.420-390  2MO    5 15/16-5  7/8        5 31/32-5 29/32        -              3WK
 6X9  6.510-480  3MO           6-5 15/16            6-5 15/16        -              1MO
 9X12 6.760-730  4MO    6  1/32-5 31/32       6  1/32-5 31/32        -              2MO
                 5MO    6  1/16-        6      6  1/16-        6      -              3MO
 1X7  6.240-210  6MO    6  1/8 -6  1/16       6  5/32-6  3/32        -              4MO
 2X8  6.330-300  7MO    6  5/32-6  3/32       6  7/32-6  5/32        -              5MO
 3X9  6.420-390  8MO    6  7/32-6  5/32       6  9/32-6  7/32        -              6MO
 4X10 6.520-490  9MO    6  9/32-6  7/32       6  5/16-6  1/4         -              9MO
 5X11 6.610-580  10M    6 11/32-6  9/32       6  3/8 -6  5/16        -              1YR
 6X12 6.700-670  11M    6 13/32-6 11/32       6  7/16-6  3/8
                 12M    6 15/32-6 13/32       6  1/2 -6  7/16
[          FRA 695-2040, EUROSTG 695-2030, GBP REPOS 695-2255             ]
```

Figure A.2   A typical brokers' screen

Example A.3

An inter-bank desk is quoting the 7-day offered rate (the rate at which a bank will *offer* or lend money) at $5\frac{11}{16}$%, while the 14-day rate is $5\frac{13}{16}$%. What rate should he quote for the 10-day offered rate?

$$5.6875 + (5.8125 - 5.6875) \times 3/7 = 5.7411\%$$

What about the case of an interest rate for a period that lies just before or just after two known rates – but not in between them? When this happens we *extrapolate* between the two known rates, again assuming a straight line relationship between them, and for a period after (or before) the two rates.

Example A.4

The 1-month offered rate is 5.25% while the 2-month rate is 5.75% as before. What is the 64-day rate?

$$5.25 + (5.75 - 5.25) \times 34/30 = 5.8167\%$$

Appendix

B

·····································

ABBREVIATIONS AND ACRONYMS

ABCP	Asset-Backed Commercial Paper
ABS	Asset-Backed Security
AER	Annual Equivalent Rate
ALCO	Asset–Liability Committee
ALM	Asset–Liability Management
AMA	Advanced Measurement Approach
APR	Annualised Percentage Rate
ASW	Asset Swap Spread
BAU	Business As Usual
BBA	British Bankers' Association
BCBS	Basel Committee for Banking Supervision
BIA	Basic Indicator Approach
BIS	Bank for International Settlements
BoE	Bank of England
BSA	Building Societies Association
CA	Capital Allocation
CD	Certificate of Deposit
CDO	Collateralised Debt Obligation
CDS	Credit Default Swap
CP	Commercial Paper
CRD IV	Capital Requirements Directive IV
CSA	Credit Support Annexe
CVA	Credit Valuation Adjustment
DV01	Dollar Value of loss for a 1bp rise in yields
EAD	Exposure At Default
ECAI	External Credit Assessment Institution
ECB	European Central Bank
ECP	Euro Commercial Paper
EEA	European Economic Area
EURIBOR	Euro Interbank Offered Rate
FI	Fixed Income
FRA	Forward Rate Agreement
FRN	Floating Rate Note
FSA	Financial Services Authority
FtD	First-to-Default
FTP	Funds Transfer Pricing
FVA	Funding Valuation Adjustment
FX	Foreign Exchange
GC	General Collateral
GMRA	Global Master Repurchase Agreement
HQLA	High Quality Liquid Assets
IA	Initial Amount
IAA	Internal Assessment Approach
ICAAP	Internal Capital Adequacy Assessment Process

ILAAP	Individual Liquidity Adequacy Assessment Process
IM	Initial Margin
IR	Interest Rate
IRB	Internal Ratings Based
IRR	Internal Rate of Return
ISDA	International Swaps and Derivatives Association
LAB	Liquid Asset Buffer
LCR	Liquidity Coverage Ratio
LG	Letter of Guarantee
LGD	Loss Given Default
LIBID	London Interbank BID Rate
LIBOR	London Interbank Offered Rate
LIFFE	London International Financial Futures Exchange
LRF	Liquidity Risk Factor
LTD	Loan To Deposit
LTV	Loan To Value
M	Maturity
MATIF	French Futures Exchange
MPC	Monetary Policy Committee
MTN	Medium-Term Note
NED	Non-Executive Director
NIBL	Non-Interest-Bearing Liability
NII	Net Interest Income
NPL	Non-Performing Loan
NPV	Net Present Value
NSFR	Net Stable Funding Ratio
OBS	Off-Balance-Sheet
OIS	Overnight Index Swap
OTC	Over The Counter
P&L	Profit & Loss
PD	Probability of Default
PSA/ISMA	Public Securities Association/International Securities Market Association
PVBP	Present Value of a Basis Point
RBA	Ratings-Based Approach
RMBS	Residential Mortgage-Backed Security
ROA	Return On Assets
ROC	Return On Capital
ROE	Return On Equity
RPI	Retail Prices Index
RRP	Recovery and Resolution Plan
SA	Standardised Approach
SBU	Strategic Business Unit

SF	Supervisory Formula
SONIA	Sterling Overnight Interest Rate Average
SPC	Special Purpose Corporation
SPV	Special Purpose Vehicle
TLP	Term Liquidity Premium
TP	Transfer Price
TRS	Total Return Swap
USCP	US Commercial Paper
WACC	Weighted Average Cost of Capital
WACF	Weighted Average Cost of Funding

INDEX

• •

Page references followed by *f* indicate an illustrated figure and page references followed by *t* indicate a table